The Black Prairie Archives

The

Black Prairie

Archives

An Anthology

Karina Vernon, editor

WILFRID LAURIER
UNIVERSITY PRESS

LAURIER
Inspiring Lives.

Wilfrid Laurier University Press acknowledges the support of the Canada Council for the Arts for our publishing program. We acknowledge the financial support of the Government of Canada. This work was supported by the Research Support Fund.

Library and Archives Canada Cataloguing in Publication

Title: The black Prairie archives : an anthology / Karina Vernon, editor.
Names: Vernon, Karina, 1973– editor.
Description: Includes bibliographical references.
Identifiers: Canadiana (print) 20190064390 | Canadiana (ebook) 20190064404 |
    ISBN 9781771123747 (softcover) | ISBN 9781771123754 (EPUB) | ISBN
    9781771123761 (PDF)
Subjects: LCSH: Canadian literature—Black authors. | LCSH: Canadian literature—
    Prairie Provinces. | CSH: Canadian literature—Black Canadian authors.
Classification: LCC PS8235.B53 B53 2019 | DDC C810.8/08960712—dc23

Front-cover photo: *Barella & Landscape #3, Osbourne, Kansas*, from the project *Sense of Place* (2013), by Dawit L. Petros. Cover design by Martyn Schmoll. Interior design by James Leahy.

© 2020 Wilfrid Laurier University Press
Waterloo, Ontario, Canada
www.wlupress.wlu.ca

This book is printed on FSC® certified paper. It contains post-consumer fibre and other controlled sources, is processed chlorine free, and is manufactured using biogas energy.

Printed in Canada

To the memory of my mother and father,

Elvina Dyck and Walter Vernon,

and to my children,

Felix and Ursula

Contents

Acknowledgements

I could never have imagined, when I began this project as a graduate student at the University of Victoria, how large it would ultimately become; how long it would take to finish, and how much support I would need along the way.

I began this project on unceded Coast Salish territory. I finished it on traditional Huron-Wendat, Anishnaabe, and Mississauga lands. I have used more resources on these territories than any uninvited guest has a right to expect. I'm grateful for the gift of treaty citizenship. May the future, and our relations within it, be more just.

I've been honoured to have been granted access to the personal documents, family histories, and work of so many writers. To all the people who so generously entrusted me with their writing, I am grateful. I hope this book does your writing, your families, and your histories justice. I am grateful to the women—the matriarchs and knowledge-keepers of the prairies—Velma Carter, Wanda Leffler Akili, Gwen Hooks, Cheryl Foggo, Junetta Jamerson, and Crystal Mayes, among others, who have kept memory of the prairies' black histories, stories, and food cultures alive. Royalties from this book will go to setting up the Velma Carter Bursary for Black Canadians to help support high school students entering university.

I am tremendously grateful to Smaro Kamboureli, who helped to shape this project—and me—in so many ways; heartfelt thanks go to you. Thank you to Evelyn Cobley, Sheila Rabillard, and Sada Niang, whose input at the earliest stages helped me conceptualize the project. Thank you to Leslie Sanders for conversations and support around this project and far beyond; I'm grateful for your work and for mentorship. Winfried Siemerling has been a tremendously generous mentor, collaborator and friend; thank you. I'm grateful also to Laura Moss for feminist mentorship from afar.

Thank you to Siobhan McMenemy at Wilfrid Laurier University Press for her steadfast commitment to this book and for many years of support and friendship. Thank you to the whole team at WLUP, including Lisa Quinn, Robert Kohlmeier, and James Leahy.

My thanks to the many archivists, librarians, and individuals who helped track down archival documents and other information, and who brought my attention to work by black writers on the prairies, including Robert Barrow, Bertrand Bickersteth, Jim Bowman, George Elliott Clarke, Wayde Compton, Nadine Charabin, David Chariandy, Cheryl Foggo, Garry Forsyth, Addena Sumter-Freitag, April Sumter-Freitag, Junetta Jamerson, Jenny Kerber, Saje Mathieu, Suzette Mayr, Marilyn Mol, Nannette Morton, Sophie Tellier, and Lorraine York. Special thanks to the late Fred Booker and Lorena Gale for conversations about black history and families on the prairies; you are greatly missed.

Thank you to my colleagues at the University of Toronto Scarborough, and the Graduate Department of English at the University of Toronto, who make the work of teaching, learning, and administration such an immensely rewarding experience. I owe a debt of gratitude to Christine Bolus-Reichert for support during the years it took to write this book. Thank you to Suzanne Akbari, Uzoma Essonwane, Lee Maracle, and Neil ten Kortenaar for institutionally-transformative conversations. For their friendship at the university and beyond I'm grateful to Maria Assif, Katherine Blouin, Andrew Dubois, Cheryl Suzack, Marlene Goldman, Katie Larson, Nathalie Rothman, and Daniel Tysdal. Thank you to my extraordinary undergraduate and graduate students—both past and present—who give me so much to hope for in the future of Canadian literature and black Canadian studies.

Thank you to the conference organizers who invited me to speak about my research on the black prairies. They include Sarah Brophy and Nadine Atwell at McMaster University; George Elliott Clarke at the Weatherhead Centre for International Affairs (Canada Program) at Harvard University; Pilar Cuder Domínguez and Belén Martín Lucas from the universities of Huelva and Vigo in Spain; Smaro Kamboureli and Larissa Lai at the University of Toronto and the University of Calgary; Larissa Lai and Suzette Mayr at the Insurgent Architects' House for Creative Writing at the University of Calgary; Heike Paul, Katja Sarkowsky and Meike Zwingenberger at the Bavarian American Academy in Munich; and Leslie Sanders at York University. My immense gratitude to Kit Dobson, Erin Wunker, and all the participants at the Miners Bay retreat in 2014. This event made such a difference to me.

Much gratitude to Dawit Petros for permission to use the image on the cover of this book. Thank you to Erin Mouré for the beautiful translations of Francisco Fwallah and Tchitala Kamba's poems. Thank you, also, to Andrew Dubois for help transcribing some of the rap lyrics.

Gratitude to my extraordinary research assistant, Tavleen Purewal, for last-stage assistance with permissions and manuscript preparation.

I would like to acknowledge the Social Sciences and Humanities Research Council of Canada for the grant that helped support the research of this work.

For their enduring friendship that saw me through the writing of this book I'm grateful to Janet Butler-McFee, Margot Leigh Butler, Wayde Compton, Meaghan Craven, Ryan Knighton, Elaine Lam, Tracy Rawa, and Anne Stone.

I finished this book while raising of two very young children. I am grateful to all the brilliant caretakers I am fortunate to have in my life; they held my children so I could write.

I would like to thank my Alberta families, including my Morton and Emeny people, for all their support and love over the years. A special thank-you to Sylvia Dyck and Waleska Vernon—my people. I would be nowhere without you. My most heartfelt thanks go to my partner, Simon, for his wit, patience, and love, and for making a future with me.

Introduction

The Black Prairie Archives is the first of two companion volumes that bring a new regional archive of black writing to light. This volume makes the black prairie archive public for the first time; it unearths and brings critical attention to the little-known history and cultural production of late-nineteenth- and early-twentieth-century black writers on the Canadian prairies, and connects this archival literature to the work of contemporary black prairie authors. Much of the material here has never before been published. Other material, particularly by writers publishing in the 1980s and 1990s, has largely dropped out of public consciousness. The black prairie archive thus brings together—and into the present—145 years of black writing on the prairies, from 1872 to 2019.

The purpose of the anthology is fourfold: (1) to make the archive public; (2) to transform the dominant inherited imaginings of the prairies by reading the region through the aperture of the recovered black archive; (3) to establish a black prairie literary tradition; and (4) to assist readers' close engagements with the literature, thus opening up new scholarly and pedagogical possibilities.

The companion volume offers a more extended scholarly engagement with this archive. Readers may turn to the companion volume for my detailed literary-critical analyses of the literature and more theoretical meditations on the issues raised by archiving a regional black literature. In the companion volume, I employ the archive methodologically to transform how the prairies is conceived spatially, historically, culturally, and ideologically in regard to blackness; to think about the relation of blackness to Indigenous land; to theorize the radical experiments in form, language, and subjectivity that have taken place over the last 230 years of black presence on the prairies; and to conceptualize the black archive itself anew. The two volumes are designed to be used in many ways. I hope that you will read them together, though they may certainly be read individually. Readers may wish to use this first volume in the classroom to expand the archive of black Canadian cultural studies, Canadian literature and print culture, critical regional studies, and studies of the black Atlantic. Both volumes will be useful for scholars, teachers, geographers, and historians of Canada and the black diaspora.

The prairies—more than any other region in Canada—has been imagined into being through a particular archive of writing. Readers have likely imagined the prairies through the work of the so-called "prairie realist" school: writing by Frederick Phillip Grove, Sinclair Ross, W.O. Mitchell, Martha Ostenso, and Robert J. Stead, among others, shape imaginings of what the prairie, its history and its literature, is and means. In this prairie, geography—always severe, flat, and untreed—is primary, and powerfully determines prairie people's history, character, and culture (Davey; Calder). Of course, the prairies has been imagined into being by other writers too, but the "realist" tradition is the one most often taught, anthologized, and read as representative of the prairies' regional essence. Significantly, the "authentic" prairie subject that emerges from this archive is rarely gendered, never raced, and definitely not black.

But the archive upon which the meanings of prairie literature have been constructed is far from being historically, culturally, or geographically realistic. In fact, it is a sanitized and bounded archive, one that mirrors the historical construction of the region itself. Not only does this archive fetishize the prairies as a geography perpetually frozen in time, either in "the Dirty Thirties or in the romanticized golden glow of a small town sunset" (Calder 3). This archive also sanitizes the prairies of its long black history, its complex literature and culture. It excludes not only all of the writing produced by black prairie people over the last 150 years, it also excludes every literary, historical, and archival representation of the black presence on the prairies, a presence which I demonstrate goes as far back as 1780. Where, for instance, are Mrs. Bentley's black neighbours in Sinclair Ross's famous book *As for Me and My House*? Where are the black farmers and store keepers in the pages of Frederick Phillip Grove's *Settlers of the Marsh*, or, looking beyond the "realist" tradition, the black Winnipeggers in Adele Wiseman's *Crackpot*, or the black prairie poets that had *already* been grown in Robert Kroetsch's *Seed Catalogue*? More to the point, where are the black writers in all our critical assessments of prairie literature?

This recovered black prairie archive opens up the regional, national, and diasporic literary imaginations to a radically different construction of the prairies. This is not the timeless, homogeneously unraced microcosm of the Canadian regional imaginary. Whereas regional critics of the 1970s relied on this fetishized topography to stabilize and naturalize "the prairies" both as a geographic designation and as a literary-critical term, black prairie writers retain consciousness of the manifestly racial ideologies that have worked historically to produce the prairies as a social space. Thus I work with an understanding of the prairies not as a natural geographic location, but as an ideological and "ideational space," which geographer Nicholas Entrikin defines as a field "in which individual and collective identities are worked out" (1). Working with this sense of the prairies as an ideational space enables me to expand my view beyond the high-plains grasslands— the geographic terrain previous generations of regionalist critics equated with "the prairies"—toward the geographies black prairie writers are connected with, including other parts of Canada, the US, the Caribbean, Central and South America, and Africa.

Writing between 1872 and 2019, black authors reveal the key role race has played in shaping the prairies as a region, politically, culturally, and ideologically. Black prairie writers shed light on the long black presence on the prairies but also the process by which the region gained identity as a political, social, and above all, ideological formation by rejecting this presence and producing it as the outside boundary that defined the legitimate spaces of the region. Black writers produce the prairies differently, not as a vast, empty, or null space, but as place that is connected to and transformed by its relation to the black world, including the transatlantic slave trade and resulting cultures and networks of the black Atlantic. Black writers figure the prairies alternately as an inland ocean, as a crossroads, as a space that is "membrane-like alive [...] a continuous flux in common" (Bailey 134). Far from being empty, this diasporized black prairie rings with the songs, spirits, languages, and stories of Africa and its diasporas. In these black prairies we find the desert *djinn* (genies); we encounter The Red Woman, the haunting embodiment plantation injustice; we hear the Ugandan folk-tale of *Nsimb'egwire*; we hear stories and verse in Arabic, Bantu, Ebonics, Creole, Portuguese, Swahili, and many more.

Black authors write the prairies as a crucial site for radical experiments in black community and citizenship, as well as experiments in racial identification, literary genre, and voice. It is a "central space of inspiration" but also an "unwilling muse" (Bickersteth, *Afrikadey!*). The prairies is a geography intimately loved, but it is also a fraught racial relation. It is a site of dislocation, of repressed black histories, but also, it is the future. The black prairies for many of these writers comes into being on the space of the page as a network of diasporic and local influences. Above all, the black prairies is this archive, an open-ended and still-unfinished place.

Black prairie writers produce, as well, a radically different archive. Differentiating this from dominant state archives, and, indeed, what makes it "black," is not that the writers included here are racialized, or that their work is centrally concerned with the unfinished quest for black freedom. Nor is this archive black by virtue of the fact that I as editor am black. Rather, this archive is black because of the kind of reciprocal social relations that enable it to come into public being. A black archive is a network of social relations forged slowly and carefully, on the basis of trust. Negotiating permissions for this published archive has taken a great deal of time. It has meant being willing to talk at length, on the phone, in person, and over long email exchanges, about the purpose of this book, about which writers are included, and above all, about my personal history and motivations for undertaking the project. These conversations have enabled authors the opportunity to assess whether this imagined formation is one in which they wish to belong and invest their writing. Gathering and publishing a black archive has also meant opening up the editorial process to significant input from contemporary writers who have had the opportunity to challenge and change the ways that their work and biographies are framed. In other words, black archives share archival and editorial power and responsibility with authors or, in the case of writers of the past, with their living family members. Ultimately, assembling a black archive also means respecting the black Canadian language of refusal, which oftentimes takes the form of silence.[1] Not every story that I wished to include, then, is represented in the pages of this book, but black archival practices respect that the archivist is not entitled to everything, and not everything is for the public archive.

Work by black prairie writers highlights the crucial distinction between, as Katrina Leial Sellinger puts it, "an archive *of* blackness and an archive *as* blackness" (Sellinger). For instance, Claire Harris's poem "Backstage at the Glenbow Museum, Calgary," originally published in Callaloo in 1996, deals with an incident in which a single member of the black community was asked to act as an adviser for an African exhibition at the Glenbow Museum. The poet-speaker notes that although she is not an African, she feels "a kind of duty" to assume the well-nigh impossible role

---

1   For a more extended meditation on silence as archival refusal, see my essay "Invisibility Exhibit."

of Representative Black Artist and to speak for a broad and heterogenous community which the museum is failing to consult. The repetition of this line in the poem bespeaks the burden of responsibility to try to interrupt archival meaning making, which constructs blackness as an object of knowledge in the European archive rather than as an ethics of archival relation. As the poet-speaker notes, the archive *of* blackness turns black cultural production into "ideas suspended in silence/ dead." In "Backstage at the Glenbow Museum, Calgary," Harris writes:

> i float down aisles thru preserving light   temperature   humidity
> ignoring ghostly canoes launched silent into corners the parrots'
> muffled squawk and sigh   fat brown giggles clustering on window
> sills fingers like roots weaving hailing   exotic   not mine not
> mine   smoke   pots of red ochre   cedar leans cooking fires playing
> ceilings   hooked on needs i bleed on must
>   a kind of duty i suppose
>   so   break water into
>   musty silence   a dun beach behind
> which other silences should roll and tower
> should roll & tower in the usual endless peaks
>   but don't
>
>   nothing
>   nothing here
>   nothing luminous
>   here (Harris, "Backstage" 148)

Without tampering with dominant archival methods which would involve broad consultation with black community and which would thus gather the full context of the artworks in the Glenbow's holdings, the museum instead drains the vitality of African cultures, turning them into dead objects. These artworks become, in the context of the museum, "exotic   not mine." On the other hand, an archive *as* blackness is a method for archival engagement with black community that empowers community members to tell the story *they want* to be made public ("mine"). An archive *as* blackness, then, is a form of relation based on reciprocity, one which ensures that the community stands to benefit, both culturally and materially from representation in the archive.

Editing this book has taken a great deal of time, but it has always been a labour of love. I was born in Tegucigalpa, Honduras, but spent my most formative years in Calgary and Olds, Alberta, between 1981 and 1989. During that time, I thought of myself and my family as anomalies rather than what we were—members of the third wave of black migration to the Canadian prairies—a migration history that began at least as far back as 1780, and which continues, in new forms, today. I did not see black prairie or black Canadian history represented in the school curriculum, nor acknowledged nor celebrated in the prairies' official histories or public sites of memory, and so I grew up knowing nothing of the region's black history, nor its black writers. There was no sign of blackness in any of the anthologies I read that regionalized writing from the prairies, nor in any of the prairies' historical self-representations. Cheryl Foggo's important essay "My Home Is Over Jordan" suggests that encountering oneself as a historical absence in this way has been one of the hallmarks of black prairie life. She writes, "I grew up inside a history that had no official status and a community that had no geographical place. [...] Our story was casually and precariously preserved—kept alive more by word of mouth amongst ourselves than by any canonical record or acknowledgement of our presence" (151). Foggo's quotation encapsulates a collective experience of the prairies. Then, two months into my doctoral program, a seemingly chance encounter in the library profoundly altered not only the direction of my research but also of my life. Wandering among the stacks of McPherson library at the University of Victoria, I was drawn to a particular shelf of histories about the region where I had grown up. Though I had left Alberta in 1989 determined never to go back—it had been a tough place for a mixed-race teenager—I found myself now drawn to these books by an unknown but urgent intention.

One of the titles on the shelf was William Francis Butler's nineteenth-century travelogue *Wild North Land*, which documents the young British army captain's travels from Fort Garry in in what is currently called Manitoba to Fort St. John in what is currently called British Columbia. As I flipped to the middle of the book my gaze was arrested by one of the pages. In 1873, Butler recorded, matter-of-factly and without any trace of irony or surprise, witnessing a "black paddler" sailing down the waters of the Peace River. On April 20, 1873, Butler wrote: "One fine day a canoe came floating down the lonely river; it held a solitary negro—a pioneer, cook, trapper, vagrant, idler or squatter as chance suited him" (216). Reading this passage, I was stunned. The image of a black paddler inside a canoe places blackness inside the very icon of a particular kind of Canada, one that sentimentally links the nation to the wilderness and to the fantasy of white settler Indigeneity, but rarely, if ever, to blackness. In reading Butler's description I imagined the black paddler sailing into Butler's view—and thus, he sailed into my own—and finally, into the archival record. This was my first encounter with the black presence on the prairies, though clearly it was not Butler's. Like many of my contemporaries, I had until then believed that blackness on the prairies was a mid- to late-twentieth-century phenomenon, a product of my own cultural moment. Even though I had grown up within a few hours' drive of the largest all-black communities to ever exist west of Ontario, until this instant, the prairies' black history, and its literary archive existed only as an absence for me.

William Butler transcribes the black paddler's missive in its entirety. In 1873 Daniel Williams wrote:

> Kenedy I hear by
> Worne you that Com and Gett your
> persnol property if eny you
> have Got on my prmeeis In 24 hours and then keep
> away
> from me because I shal Not betrubbled Nor trod on
> only by her most Noble
> >   Majesty
> >   Governmet
> >   (Sgd) D.T. WILLIAMS

I have waited longe A-day for an ancer from that Notis you toer-Down and now It is my turn to tore down.

In this short but powerful missive, Williams's written voice rings out in uncompromising defence of both his personal sovereignty and the sovereignty of his home place. He uses his written word to declare his agency as a British subject and he admits only Queen Victoria's sovereignty over his person. The letter constitutes a powerful claim not simply to location but to black citizenship on the prairies. In fact, it contradicts Butler's own characterization of him as a trespasser, a "vagrant, idler or squatter," for Williams clearly understands himself as a politically legitimate British subject. In connecting the written word with the struggle for the political right to belong, and against the threat of further dislocation, Williams's letter anticipates the content and intent of much of the black prairie writing to come, even as it raises difficult questions about the historical entanglement of black people in Canada's settlement project. Williams's claim for citizenship, for instance, draws directly on the authority of Queen Victoria over these lands; in other words, his citizenship rights are wholly premised on a colonial formation. But, remembering that slavery was not abolished in the United States until 1865, when Daniel Williams was already located in territory that would become the Canadian prairies, claiming citizenship under the British flag remained the primary means for nineteenth-century black subjects in North America to claim anything close to political self-emancipation.

   This black prairie archive, understood as an unboundaried, non-territorial site, offers a different strategy for claiming a space for blackness on the prairies without necessarily, like Williams, staking a claim to territory against the Indigenous nations of these lands, the large Siksikawa (Blackfoot) and Nehiyawak (Plains Cree) nations, the Niitsitapi and Aamsskaapipikani, the Saulteaux and Nehiyawak, Nakoda, and Mushkegowuk nations. In other words, the archive challenges traditional colonial conceptions of the prairies as a stable and boundaried territory by "diasporizing" it. Black writers inscribe the prairies as a movable and contingent set of social relations, not a fixed territory whose boundaries might be imagined as identical with those of Alberta, Saskatchewan, and Manitoba. The archive serves as a device for remembering and perceiving, from a bibliographic point of view, the networks of exchange that have developed between black prairie people and diasporized black communities both within and beyond the prairies, but also, crucially, with Indigenous peoples, and South Asian, Chinese, and European diasporas. Thus, although I make a certain claim here for writers on the basis of their having lived at some point in the ideological space of the prairies, I recognize that many of them belong as much to "other" overlapping regional, geographic, ideological, and archival formations.

   Unearthing Williams's archival letter in the library that day I realized two key things: that a literary archive exists, but that it would take considerable effort and time to recover it. Some of the material, like Daniel Williams's letter, were buried in unexpected places: in travelogues and government documents, out-of-the-way rural historical societies, in other regions, in the US, as well as beyond public view in private, family collections. On the other hand, some of the archive's materials were hidden in plain sight—in all the usual places archival materials are to be found—in the prairies' provincial and municipal archives and museums. The black prairies' archival materials were there all along but never recognized by previous scholars either as black, as important, or as constituting an archive. Second, I realized this writing was very radical, from both a literary and historical perspective, not only because, like Dan Williams's terse ultimatum to Kennedy, it challenges the conceptions of the literary, but also because it reinserts blackness into a regional space that has been almost completely overdetermined—in both its historiographies and its literary and critical constructions—as white.

In the days following my initial discovery, I returned to the library and began poring through literary histories and regional anthologies of prairie writing. I found virtually nothing. At the moment that I discovered the black history of the prairies, then, I also discovered the erasure of it. In other words, my failure, until that moment in the library, to be aware of the black history of the prairies and its archival literature was neither accidental nor idiosyncratic. Rather, it was an ideological effect of the prairies' regional discourses, which had entirely naturalized the social and historical identity of the prairies as a non-black space, and which had even withheld the category of "black prairie" as a possible identification for me.

I am not the first scholar to be frustrated in her search for the black prairies and its literary archive. Lorris Elliott, an early scholar of black Canadian studies, wrote about the difficulty of gathering contemporary writing from the prairies (he did not then search for archival writing) for his *Bibliography of Literary Writings by Blacks in Canada* (1986). "One other problem which I had encountered early in my preparation was the belief expressed by some of my generally trustworthy colleagues that there was no significant Black population west of Toronto or east of Montreal (except for Halifax in the latter case). Since I had attended UBC, I knew that this was not true of Vancouver and Winnipeg; but I thought it to be true of the other provinces" ("Black Writing in Canada: The Problems of Anthologizing and Documenting" 725). This faulty perception that few black people live or write on the prairies still persists today.

Readers may be surprised to learn that the prairies is the *second* most densely populated black region in Canada. Alberta alone has a black population *five times* that of Nova Scotia.[2] While Halifax is widely regarded as a significantly black city, Edmonton, Calgary, Brooks, and Wood Buffalo,

2   Alberta's black population numbered 129,390 as of the 2016 Census (still the most recent census available). Nova Scotia's black population was counted at 21,915, as of 2016.

Alberta, all have larger black populations.[3] What is more, the black population of prairie cities is growing faster than in any other region apart from central Canada. Between 2001 and 2016, the black population of Alberta grew fourfold[4] as the region's oil boom economy continues to attract people from Africa, the Caribbean, and other parts of Canada. Saskatchewan and Manitoba's black populations both jumped by a significant 22.2 percent in these years.[5] By calculating the black population in each of Canada's "regions" in this way I do not intend to confirm these already ossified regionalisms, nor do I mean to play a numbers game that implies that where the black population is smaller it is somehow less important (or conversely, where it is larger it is more important). I mean only to map the extent to which dominant regional discourses manage to conceal such significant black presences.

The actual number of people on the prairies who identify as "black" is likely much higher than these Canada Census figures indicate. A full 11 percent of Canadians identified themselves as mixed-race or "white and black" on the 2016 Census, some of whom may not be counted as "black" in the national, regional, and municipal figures. What is more, a substantial number of black Canadians, especially those with long ancestral histories on the prairies, may have identified themselves as having "Canadian" origins, a new "ethnic" category introduced in the Population Census in 1996.

The problems of defining and empirically measuring the "black" population of the prairies serve as a good reminder that blackness is, as writer Wayde Compton puts it, "A folk taxonomy; a pseudoscientific demographic categorization system. Like a national border or a literary genre, race is only as real as our current social consensus" (*After Canaan* 25). Thus, the meaning of blackness has never been stable on the prairies: black people have been "Negroes" in the eighteenth, nineteenth, and early

---

3   Halifax's black communities make up 3.8 percent of the city's population, the same as the city of Winnipeg. In Brooks, Alberta, black people make up 14.3 percent of the population. In Wood Buffalo, Alberta, which includes the city of Fort McMurray, black people make up 5.8 percent of the population. In Edmonton, black people make up 5.9 percent of the population total and in Calgary 4.2 percent. All of these cities are well above the national average of 3.5 percent (Census of Canada 2016).

4   The black population in Alberta jumped from 31,395 in 2001 to 129,390 in 2016 (Census of Canada 2016).

5   The black population in Saskatchewan went from 4,165 in 2001 to 14,925 in 2016. In Manitoba, the black population grew from 12,820 in 2011 to 30,335 in 2016 (Census of Canada 2016).

twentieth centuries, "Ethiopians" in the 1920s and '30s, "Coloured" in the 1950s, "Black" in the 1960s and '70s, "African Canadians" at the turn of the twenty-first century, and "Black" again in the second decade of the new century. At times blackness has been an insidious discourse "thrust upon" (Clarke, *Odysseys* 16) writers. Yet at other times black identity has been a liberatory act of identification with revolutionary forms of blackness (Siemerling). Some black prairie writers, such as Sylvester Long Lance, never publicly acknowledged their blackness; Long claimed his Indigenous ancestry instead. Conversely, several writers, including Woody Strode and Troy B. Bailey, have Indigenous ancestry but identify primarily as black. For others, the meaning of their blackness is altered by their location on the prairies. William Beal, the only black person to arrive in a region settled by Scandinavian and German immigrants, claimed to be "among the first white men settled in the valley" (Barrow and Hambly 15). Writer Minister Faust strongly identifies as a global African or a Kenyan Canadian and never as "black." Other mixed-race writers like Marika Warner explore the possibilities and problems involved in imagining oneself as a member of a "multatto nation." There has never been one single, authentic mode of black prairie being. Still, blackness is the necessary essentialism that makes the recovery of the archive possible. I still favour the term "black" over "African Canadian" because it suggests that the nation does not function as the dominant point of reference in determining black identities, organizing group affiliations, or in preserving black archives, and so I use "black" (small "b") for writers of the present as well those of the past to name the ways black prairie people consistently challenge and ironize the related categories of race, region, and nation.

This demographic diversity of the black prairies is a result of its being a product of four periods of migration: (1) 1790–1900 (the era of the fur trade and early settlement); (2) 1905–1912 (the Oklahoma migration); (3) 1960s–present (the Points System era); (4) 2012–present (the era of neo-liberal immigration and asylum). Of course, not every writer fits neatly into these four periods; Sylvester Long and Woody Strode arrived between the second and third periods; Fil Fraser, Addena Sumter-Freitag, and Lawrence Hill arrived from other parts of Canada in the post-1960s period unconnected to the points system of transnational migration. Still, periodizing patterns of migration like this is useful as a guide to some of the broad demographic shifts on the prairies with respect to blackness—shifts that, as I demonstrate, are registered also in specific formal and thematic ways in the archive. In what follows, then, I offer a brief history of the four

Figure 1   Long Lance in Calgary circa 1920s. McDermid Studio. By permission of the Glenbow Museum and Archives

periods of migration to the prairies in order to provide the historical context necessary for further engagements with the archive.

The first period of black migration to the space that is currently imagined as the Canadian prairie began in the late 1700s and continued to 1900; this was the inaugural period of non-Indigenous exploration, trade, sojourn, and settlement. Archival documents attest to black presences in this region since at least 1779 (Porter 423). Indeed, archival documents from the fur trade period are so crowded with references to black presences that historian Kenneth W. Porter argues that "Any picture of the racial aspects of the fur trade of that period which omits the Negro [sic] is so incomplete as to give a false impression, for representatives of that race were to be found in all [...] groups connected with the trade" (423). Black and mixed-race women and men worked as enslaved, indentured, and free servants, cooks, guides, clerks, voyageurs, and Indigenous language interpreters since the North West Company, Hudson's Bay Company, and the American XY Company all regularly employed black people.

But members of this first period left behind few textual records. To date, I have not found any written material by the eighteenth- and early-nineteenth-century voyageurs and fur traders, and little from the cowboys, entrepreneurs, homesteaders, and ranchers of the early twentieth century. They belonged to an oral more than a textual culture, and their oral cultural forms—their folk spirituals, plantation songs, shouts, prayers, dances, folktales, and stories—were not adequately documented in their time. Their presences and cultural forms enter the archival record only when they become visible to their employers, and when their employers choose to write of them. Thus black presences appear, but fleetingly, in service contracts; ledgers of payment and debt; in correspondence and journal entries about the goings-on at forts and trading posts; when there are marriages, births, and deaths involving them; when there is violence and conflict; and especially when they are accused of contravening the colonial law.

Two of the black voyageurs who appear in the records most frequently in this period are the Bonga brothers, Étienne and Pierre. Both, along with their parents, Jean and Jeanne, arrived at Michilimackinac, a major trading post between Lake Huron and Lake Michigan, and gateway to the western fur trade. The Bongas were enslaved to Captain Daniel Robertson, a British commandant at Michilimackinac, who had bought Jean and Jeanne when he was stationed in Martinique. In 1787 at the end of his post at Michilimackinac, Robertson freed Jean and Jeanne. Pierre went on to marry a Chippewa woman, and together they joined Alexander Henry the Younger's Red River Brigade on trading ventures in the areas of the Red and Pembina Rivers in present-day Manitoba, Minnesota, and North Dakota from 1799 to 1814. Bonga and his wife had a daughter while in service to Henry, and Henry recorded the event in his journal on 12 March 1802 at the Hudson's Bay Company Fort on the Pembina River. "Pierre's wife was

delivered of a daughter, the first new fruit in this Fort, and a very black"
(Henry 126). Pierre appears in the archive again in 1803, when he was
left in charge of the fort at the mouth of the Pembina River (Porter 424).
On this occasion, tensions erupted, and a certain J. Duford threatened to
kill Bonga, and Bonga "did not escape without a sound beating" (qtd. in
Cochrane n.p.). Pierre appears again in the archive in 1804 as an interpreter
for the North West Company on the lower Red River. In 1819 a Bonga—
likely Pierre—was one of the principal traders among the Chippewa (Porter 424–5). Bonga's sons, George and Stephen, became well known as
"Black Indian" fur traders and translators in the Indigenous territories that
later became Minnesota.

Hudson's Bay Company Service Contracts[6] also record one Joseph Lewis
(alias Joseph Lewes or Levy Johnston), variously described as black or as
"mulatto," who was born in 1773 in Manchester, New England, and who
joined HBC to work as a steersman for a period of three years. The HBC
service contract of 1796 notes of Lewis: "his mark sober steady man excellent steersman."[7] "His mark" in this context is likely not a mark with a pen,
but a shot from a rifle. The historical record reveals that Lewis gradually
worked his way west and by 1799 he was at Greenwich House (Lac La
Biche, Alberta). Another black voyageur who worked extensively on the
part of Turtle Island that would be regionalized as the prairie was Crawford Glasgow (alias Glasco), a black man from the Montreal area (Frank
Mackey 199). In his *Journal of Occurrences in the Athabasca Department
1820 and 1821*, which documents George Simpson's journey by canoe from
Montreal, the capital of the fur trade, to Athabasca territory (present-day
northern Alberta), Simpson writes: "Crawford Glasgow, a negro serving as
middleman [paddler] and cook. He joined the HBC in 1818 and was in Athabasca from 1818 to 1821 when he left the service of the H.B.C. and went to
Montreal, August 1821" (112). The entry makes clear that although Glasgow
was not legally Simpson's slave, he was not free either. Although by March
1821 he had completed his term of service with Simpson's company and had
banked enough money to depart for Canada (Montreal), Simpson used his
accusation of "petty theft" to bind Glasgow to his service for another year:

Examined our Trader Mr Chastellain & Glasgow the cook very particularly
relative to a petty theft of Tea & Flour; they pleaded guilty which gives me a

---

6   HBCA E.4/1b,A.30/8,fo.34.
7   Hudson's Bay Company Servants' Contracts (1780–ca.1926). A.32/8 fo. 36.

firm hold of both; if the services of the former are required for another year, he must either remain on my terms or submit to a heavy fine; the latter will be a most useful Man to Mr Brown in the Mountain, for he speaks English, French &Iroquois fluently, he did intend going to Canada this season having a considerable balance in the Compys. hands, but he must prepare now for another campaign.

Although this journal entry demonstrates the value of black men to the Hudson's Bay Company, as well as the intimate relations between black and Indigenous peoples, at the same time, it highlights the terrible precarity of their positions within the Company, and thus their unfreedom as sojourners through this region.

Looking ahead to the late nineteenth century, contemporary writer and knowledge keeper Cheryl Foggo has done extensive research in the archives to document the substantial and settled early black presence in what is currently Alberta. In "My Home Is Over Jordan: Southern Alberta's Black Pioneers" Foggo uncovers dozens of names in the archive, and manages to flesh out many of their untold stories. In the African Canadian tradition of the Roll Call, Foggo names some of these presences: William Herbert Darby, who worked as a cook for the hotel in Vulcan, Alberta, circa 1900 and who had a wife and four children (Foggo 153). There was the well-known North-West Mounted Police translator Dave Mills, whose mother was Blood; Charlie Dyson who operated a blacksmith in Pincher Creek in the late 1800s; Annie Saunders, who arrived in the northwest in 1877 likely making her "one of the first people of African descent to live in Alberta" (Foggo, "Assembling Auntie"). There was George and Louie Robinson, a jockey and stable boy in High River; the cowboy Lige Abel, who worked for the Waldron ranch north of Lundbreck (154) and Green Walters, a ranching cook who, according to Ken Mather's *Frontier Cowboys and the Great Divide*, was admired for his singing (168–9). Cheryl Foggo notes that "the 1901 census counted 27 as the total number of Blacks in the entire region that would eventually become Alberta," but her own work suggests that this number is far too low as her careful and dedicated research has uncovered many more names in the archives.

As I have noted, members of this first period left behind few textual documents. They belonged to a more oral than a textual culture, and their oral cultural forms were rarely registered in the colonial archive. But in his history of frontier cowboys, Ken Mather makes a brief reference to the repertoire of gospel songs performed by one Green Walters, "a great round-up cook" who "ran a tight wagon" at the High River Horse Ranch in the 1880s (168). Green's performance was described by A.E. Cross, one of the premier cattlemen of the era, who visited the ranch in 1886. Cross writes, "Old Green was a very emotional and religious old [black] in his own particular way. Some of the boys would start him up with his camp meeting songs, the favourite one being 'Climbin' up de Golden Stairs.' He would start with a low note, gradually getting higher and higher until his emotional feeling would overcome him. With tears streaming down his cheeks he wound up exhausted" (qtd. in Mather 169). Green's performances were powerful and important enough to be entered by A.E. Cross into his historical record.

Although I include oral literature (what the Kenyan novelist Ngugi wa Thiong'o called "orature") in this archive, as well as slam poetry and rap, both oral forms meant to be embodied and performed on the stage, this is a textual, not an oral archive, and thus I deal with such material as written text, with all the limits I acknowledge this editorial decision entails. As Wendy W. Walters puts it in *Archives of the Black Atlantic*, "Our own era's fixation on the textual record as authoritative source of historical fact may cause us to miss alternative possibilities" (6), including powerful embodied performances such as Walter Green's, immaterial songs, texts and oral cultures, aspects of cultural memory that, as Diana Taylor argues, are better captured in a shift from the archive to "repertoire." As Taylor theorizes it, the repertoire "enacts embodied memory: performances, gestures, orality, movement, dance, singing—in short, all those acts usually thought of as ephemeral, nonreproducible knowledge" (20). The forthcoming companion volume to this anthology more fully accounts for these important non-textual practices than I am able to do in this brief introduction. However, the first entry in this archive holds a place for the repertoire of cultural practices such as that of Green's gospel performance, as well as all of those whose names never entered the archive but who nevertheless participated in the production and reproduction of culture, as Taylor puts it, by "'being there,' being part of the transmission" (20). The first entry in the archive that holds a place for the repertoire is a black page. This black page should be read at once as a monument to the vital presences and embodied oral practices that have taken place on the prairies since at least the 1790s that exceed the archive's limits, as well as an open door—an acknowledgement of the ever-unfinished nature of the archival project.

Even so, a few members of the first period did write. Their businesses of homesteading, ranching, and farming produced a variety of textual documents, including the agricultural diary Dan Williams kept between 1872 to 1875 in order to record the changing seasons and the growth of his crops, and Mildred Ware's letters to the brand registry office. Dan Williams's diary is spare, contracting to the few necessary nouns: "ice," "river," "snow," "geese." These short texts are terse and direct, but when read in the context of the archive and its history, they gain a powerful literary resonance. Indeed, one of the purposes of assembling the black prairie archive is to challenge Eurocentric definitions of the literary by taking such writing produced by nineteenth-century black people seriously, and by making space for it in this archive, thus helping to transform the early black prairies from absence to presence. For these reasons I also include three short letters written by Mildred Ware. Between May 1898 and June 1899 Mildred wrote repeatedly to the brand registration office to get her family's "DC" brand, used to identify range cattle and signify Ware's ownership, registered. Yet despite her previous correspondence with the office and her payment of one dollar, when the Government Printers of the Territories published its fourth edition *Brand Book* in 1898, it failed to include the Ware brand. Imagining Mildred—the first black prairie woman writer—paging through the newly published *Brand Book* in search of her own mark only to find it "not in the book" resonates with the multiple ways the black cultural presence on the prairies has gone missing in the prairies' official cultural registries.

Mildred Lewis Ware's younger sister, Alice Ethel Lewis, also contributes textual material to this archive. She left behind a short, unpublished poem composed in 1917, "In Loving Memory of Alberta," dedicated not to the province but to her sister (Alberta was born in 1891—fully fourteen years before Alberta officially became a province). The poem, written in a conventional aa bb rhyme scheme, was composed a year after her sister's death at the age of twenty-six. Though the poem is sorrowful, the formal order of the verses, including their four rhyming stanzas, reflects the poet speaker's acceptance of the loss, her belief in an ordered world, including an afterlife for the innocent with God. The original poem, along with other papers and photographs kept by John and Mildred Ware's daughter, Nettie, is being currently processed by the Glenbow Museum and Archives thanks to Cheryl Foggo's significant efforts to preserve this material.

Dr. Alfred Shadd, a member of the illustrious Shadd family—Mary Ann Shadd, the anti-slavery advocate and publisher of *The Provincial Freeman*

Figure 2   John and Mildred Ware, Millarville, Alberta. Taken at the time of their marriage, February 29, 1892.

was his aunt—is the fourth writer in the archive whom I conceptualize as belonging to this first, pre-1900, period of arrival. In 1896, Shadd, a medical doctor, newspaper editor, and farmer from Chatham, southern Ontario, arrived on his own in the North-West Territories (currently Saskatchewan). Shadd was trained as a teacher and later pursued postgraduate studies in Edinburgh and Paris, but a lack of funding forced him to return to his medical practice on the prairies. Among the stunning array of civic-building activities Shadd took on during his time in Saskatchewan was also newspaper publishing. He purchased the *Prince Albert Advocate* in 1908 and moved it to Melfort, renaming it the *Carrot River Journal*; he remained its editor until 1912. Shadd also wrote several well-crafted, articulate letters, editorials, and political speeches during his life in Saskatchewan. His prose style is highly confident—by turns elevated, direct, and playful, suggestive of a writer fully secure not only with his place in his community, but also in his language on the page.

The era I refer to as the second period of migration, between 1905 and 1912, occurred when a conjunction of political events on both sides of the forty-ninth parallel instigated a large transnational migration of black people, mainly from Oklahoma but also from Kansas, Texas, and Missouri, to Alberta, Saskatchewan, and Manitoba. The first political event was the coming into statehood of Oklahoma, which had, until 1907, been an Indian Territory and, as such, a place of greater freedom for black people. But with the coming of statehood, black people in Oklahoma were increasingly disenfranchised by Jim Crow legislation that prevented them from voting and from buying farms, and by acts of racial terror carried out by the Ku Klux Klan.[8] At the same time, the Canadian government began an extensive campaign aimed at American farmers to come north to help settle—that is to say, colonize—lands the Canadian government had recently expropriated from Indigenous nations. After his re-election in 1878, Prime Minister John A. Macdonald orchestrated a state-sanctioned famine for Indigenous communities on what is now the prairies. Robyn Maynard notes in her *Policing Black Lives* (2017) that "in one instance, in the spring of 1883, the government withheld food from nearly five thousand Indigenous people, who were then forcibly marched hundreds of kilometers to reserves in Battleford, Saskatchewan" (32). After the defeat of the 1885 Indigenous uprisings against these genocidal policies, aboriginal peoples had little choice but to cede their lands in what is today southern and central Alberta, central Saskatchewan, and northern Alberta, and to move onto reserve lands put aside by the Crown "in compensation" for relinquishing their lands. In 1896 Clifford Sifton, minister of the interior, began energetic advertising campaigns in the United States, central and Eastern Europe, and Britain to spread the word that a farmer could get a title to a quarter section of this land (160 acres) for just ten dollars if they stayed on that land and improved it by clearing, planting, and building a house. The offer was a powerful incentive to black people in Oklahoma. In many instances, black farmers were the first non-Indigenous settlers on Indigenous lands, a charged and

---

8 For instance, between 1885 and 1930, there were at least 147 lynching deaths in Oklahoma (Oklahoma Historical Society 2009); dozens more probably went unrecorded.

complex history that I explore more fully in the forthcoming companion volume.

Many of the black pioneers' narratives record their enthusiasm at the prospect of owning their own land, even if that land was to be in distant, unknown Canada. Walker Beaver remembers that "In Kansas City there was an agent telling people about Canada—the land of milk and honey— for ten dollars you could buy a hundred and sixty acres of land, a homestead. So people thought they were getting a fortune, you understand, that's why they came" (*Window of Our Memories* 59). In reality, the political and material conditions awaiting the second wave were far less idyllic. Historian and poet Gwen Hooks recalls, "My mom and dad heard that there were more opportunities for blacks in Canada and less prejudice. This proved partially true. We encountered no legalized segregation or patterns of violence in Alberta, but neither did we find a haven of tolerance, and it wasn't long before it became abundantly clear that Canada did not want black settlers" (23–4).

The first sizable group of Oklahomans arrived in Saskatchewan in October of 1909 and settled in the Eldon district, 150 railroad miles north of Saskatoon (Utendale 303). The black arrivants sought isolation from white communities, proximity to railroads, and distance from the American border (Winks 303). They spread out into Manitoba and as far east as the Thunder Bay area (303), but the majority settled in what became all-black communities: the Maidstone and Rosetown districts in west-central Saskatchewan; North Battleford, Saskatchewan; Junkins (now known as Wildwood) on the Canadian Northern Line east of Edson; Breton, southwest of Edmonton; Clyde, Campsie, near Barrhead, and Amber Valley (originally Pine Creek), located east of the town of Athabasca. Other folks went to the prairies' urban centres, Calgary, Saskatoon, Regina, Winnipeg, and notably Edmonton, which by 1911 already had 298 black residents (Daniel Hill 120). Rachel Wolters (2015) notes that the families who came sent letters back to the United States and composed newspaper articles "with useful tips about traveling and advice on where to settle" (342). Such transnational networks triggered a chain of migration. Families in Canada "eagerly anticipated the arrival of thousands more black immigrants. And the success, encouragement, and family connections of immigrants increasingly motivated more blacks to migrate from Oklahoma to Canada" (Wolters 343).

Western Canadians' reaction to the black settlers—who at their peak numbered about 1,650—was immediate. Cheryl Foggo writes that "a sampling of newspaper headlines concerning their arrival include "Negroes Not Wanted in Alberta," "Canada Will Bar the Negro Out," "We Want No Dark Spots in Albert," and "Coloured Question Up in the House" ("Over Jordan" 156). When prairie people envisioned blacks "swarm[ing] by the tens of thousands" (Winks 309), they successfully pressured the federal government to pass Order-in-Council PC1911-1324 determining that "For a period of one year from and after the date hereof the landing in Canada shall be and the same is prohibited of any immigrants belonging to the Negro race, which is deemed unsuitable to the climate and requirements of Canada."[9]

Soon after, concern about maintaining trade relations with the United States and upholding its international image led the Canadian government to repeal the Order two months after it was passed. The government instead resorted to an unofficial and covert policy of exclusion. Rachel Wolters notes that "with a large dose of irony, Canadian immigration officials took advantage of the transnational networks of information that had encouraged black migration to stop the process of immigration. They hired African Americans to lobby blacks against migrating and tapped black newspapers and churches in mounting a campaign against emigration. Moreover, as examples of Canada's own racism and restrictions on immigration emerged, such newspapers as *The Crisis* carried stories of Canada's Jim Crowism to its readership" (349). In February of 1912 the Great Northern Railway sent notices to its employees that black people would not be admitted into Canada under any circumstances and that ticket sales between Saint Paul and the border should be forbidden (Winks 312). The informal, but systematic, exclusion policy was effective. According to Wolters, "As the networks of people and information reinforced the view of Canada as an undesirable location, blacks in Oklahoma rejected migration, and the promise of a mass exodus largely disappeared" (348–9). By 1912 the second period of black migration was over, and those who remained on the prairies turned to the business of building up their farms and communities, establishing their social, spiritual, and economic institutions, and documenting their lives, histories, and unique cultures in their own ways.

This second period of immigration produced quite a lot of textual material, including the important meditations on community, socialism, and

---

9   The Order was introduced on June 2, 1911 and approved on August 12, 2011. See RG2, Privy Council Office, Series A-1-a. https://pier21.ca/research/immigration -history/order-in-council-pc-1911-1324.

black emancipation written by Reverend George Washington Slater Jr. But, by and large, the cultural production of this second period, again, was oral. Fortunately, much of the oral culture of this post-1900 period of migration was recorded and preserved thanks to the important efforts of some key historians, including Velma Carter, Leah Suzanne Carter, and Wanda Leffler Akili, who interviewed community elders and together produced the two-volume *Window of Our Memories* (1981, 1992). The Alberta Provincial Museum and Archives oral history project of the 1960s–70s recorded hundreds of hours of tape with elders of various ethnic and racialized communities in the province, including black elders. The North of the Gully History Book Committee, which recorded oral histories of pioneers in Saskatchewan, published their massive book, *North of the Gully*, with the *Maidstone Mirror*. More recently, the Black Cultural Research Society in Alberta archived their interviews with community elders on the internet. Together, these oral histories constitute a powerful, grassroots-level intervention into the historical record during a time when black prairie life had, as Foggo puts it, "no official status and no geographical place" ("My Home" 151). The archive of oral narratives produced by these various projects is substantial and exceeds the limits of this single book to publish it all. What is offered in this archive, then, is a selection of the oral literature that, to my mind, is formally and thematically representative of this genre of pioneer orature. In making selections for this archive, I also strove for as much balance as possible between men and women orators.

Orature recorded by Rosa Shannon, Jefferson Edwards, John Bell Bowden, Martha Edwards, Nettie Ware, E.A. Cobbs, Ellis Hooks, Luther Gerard, Lloyd Mayes, Goldie Gordon, and many others is formally similar; patterns can be detected in their accounts of arrival and survival on the prairies. Their first-person narratives are linear and chronological, usually beginning with the anti-black social conditions that led them (or their parents) to pick up stakes in Oklahoma, Texas, and Arkansas, and to hope greater freedom awaited them under British law in Canada. Specifically, they focus on the possibilities of freedom, equality, and independence that the 150 acres of "free" government land promised to a people leaving behind recent histories of enslavement, as well as the sharecropping arrangements of the post-emancipation period that amounted to slavery in the present. The orators were optimistic on departure, but their narratives quickly pivot to the difficult material and social conditions that met them on arrival—the stark isolation of the homesteads; the lack of community infrastructure; the lack of basic amenities; the freezing winters. Cheryl

Foggo notes that "Some pioneers lived in abandoned railway box cars, sod huts, tiny log cabins with dirt floors and tar paper roofs" ("Over Jordan" 155). On first arrival, they squatted on public land (Ellis Hooks). The oral histories are noun-heavy as they detail the things they had and the things they did not have. They speak about the new food ways they developed: they learned to hunt and forage off the land; they learned to eat moose meat, jackfish, wild blueberries, strawberries, wild chickens, squirrels, and even skunks when they had to; they learned to fish through the ice and to bake cakes without eggs. They speak of intimacies with Indigenous people. Martha Edwards gave birth to her first son with the assistance of a Métis midwife. Goldie Gordon remembers sharing meals every spring with Indigenous people coming south to look for work. Gordon's particular story includes the unacknowledged injustice of Indigenous loss of their land base at a time when black homesteaders began to prosper in their lands. Rosa Shannon concludes her orature with an proposal for a triple-faced monument to be put up in Wildwood to acknowledge the deep links between black, Indigenous, and white communities in rural, turn-of-the-century Saskatchewan.

While rural isolation is a common theme, the orators of this second period also view their circumstances in broad national and transnational terms. Rosa Shannon, Luther Gerard, and Martha Edwards speak about the isolation of the homesteads, but E.A. Cobbs also compares his history with those of other diasporas (Chinese, Muslim, West Indian), which, like black prairie people, were "allowed into the country [when] they were needed to do the dirty jobs that the white man didn't want to do." In his narrative, Cobbs views his life and those of the Alberta pioneers within a larger historical frame: the tumultuous history of the concept of "race" in the late nineteenth and early twentieth centuries. He cites the construction of the CPR railroad, the Chinese Exclusion Act, Riel's leadership, the Second World War, and Marcus Garvey's back-to-Africa movements as events that impacted the fates of black Albertans within the racial geography of North America and the prairies.

The orators relate in detail the political experiments in community and socialist economy they forged in the early twentieth century. Jefferson Edwards's orature details, step by step, how he helped to build an independent black community at Amber Valley. E.A. Cobbs notes that the black community in Edmonton, "Like any other ethnic group, we all lived in a district: 97th Street, 98th Street, 95th Street and 111th Avenue." This district is not to be mistaken for a ghetto; as he says, it was "one big loving, caring family." John Bell Bowden highlights the economic institutions they built such as the Liberty Protection Society and the United Negro Association Grocery, a grocery co-op, both of which helped support the community's economic independence. Similarly, Luther Gerard says that in Junkins, black farmers established a co-op to buy cattle. He remembers that early black prairie communities developed a trust economy outside capitalism: "There was no money paid out—they'd exchange work and the work was always done. It was a real community spirit."

The orators also speak directly of racism and their resistance to it. E.A. Cobbs remembers that black people were barred from the city pool at Borden Park in Edmonton and sat in segregated seating at the Pantages Theatre, but he notes, "This bias was good, for it caused the blacks to fight and as a result, changes were made." Ellis Hooks also recalls that black people in Keystone undertook an action against a blackface performance of *Uncle Tom's Cabin*. Not only did black prairie people not put up with racism; they did not put up with cultural *representations* of racism in their communities. Hooks says, "Anything like that that reflected on to us that much, well, we fight back, that's all."

The orators' narratives frequently conclude with poignant meditations on the future—on what needs to be done to strengthen black participation in the present location, or, as with Jefferson Edwards's and Luther Gerard's oral histories, poignant reflections on why the experiments in an all-black community did not last beyond one or two generations. Still, as John Bell Bowden puts it, "I always had a desire and a belief that there was a wonderful future in this part of the world. And I haven't regretted sticking it out."

The descendants of this second period of migration, including Gwen Hooks, Cheryl Foggo, Deanna Bowen, Miranda Martini, and the members of the Heritage Recipes Soul Food Committee, work in what I call "high-fidelity" genres like memoir (Foggo's *Pourin' Down Rain*; Gwen Hooks's *The Keystone Legacy*), video oral history (Bowen's *sum of the parts*), the recipe (*A Little Taste of Soul*), and the personal essay (Martini's "The Drinking Gourd") that continue the black prairie literary tradition of documenting, archiving, and transmitting knowledge of the unique cultures their second-wave ancestors developed on the prairies. The cultural production of the second period demonstrates how work in the cultural sphere constitutes a form of black activism: it transforms the dominant story of the prairies with respect to race and transforms the story of blackness in Canada by bringing attention to the unique and long-standing black presence on the prairies.

In addition to the large treasure trove or oral literature that constitutes the bulk of cultural production by the second period, black prairie people of this time also developed their own community news organs to help disseminate both local and transnational news relevant to them. Reverend George Washington Slater Jr., a pastor working at the Emanuel African Methodist church in Edmonton, authored a daily column, "Our Negro Citizens," that appeared in two major Edmonton newspapers—the *Edmonton Journal* (September 10, 1921 to August 12, 1924) and the *Edmonton Bulletin* (August 27, 1921 to August 21, 1922). Dan Cui and Jennifer R. Kelley have done extensive and important work on this newspaper archive, and argue that Rev. Slater uses the column to highlight issues of racism in the United States and Canada, to help consubstantiate the black community in and around Edmonton, and to mediate between the mainstream society and his own community using the paper's wide distribution to black and non-black readers (Cui and Kelley 254). In the next decades, black prairie people also established the serial publication *Jeep*, published in the 1930s in Edmonton (of which no surviving copies remain), and *The Communicant*, produced once a month by the Alberta Black Cultural Research Society between 1973 and 1980 (of which some copies may remain in restricted family archives). These publications anticipate the coming of *Caribe*, Harold Marshall's important magazine of black creative writing, published three times a year from 1979 to 1991 and once again in 1993 out of Winnipeg.

Two writers—Sylvester Long and Woody Strode—arrived on the prairies in the in-between period of 1912–1967, when few others were able to enter because the points system had not yet been instituted and the border was shut to blacks. North Carolina–born Sylvester Long Lance is an in-between figure in more ways than one; he fits neither with the second period of migration to the prairies nor the third, having arrived on his own in Calgary in 1919 after fighting with the Canadian army in the First World War. And he is an in-between figure in the sense that, as Donald B. Smith discovered (1982), his family were racially mixed, with claims to some degree of black, white, and Indigenous ancestry. In the context of Winston-Salem and the logic of the "one drop" rule (wherein a single "drop" of black ancestry going back any number of generations effectively made one legally and socially black), the Long family were classed as non-white, and hence as blacks. Though Long Lance grew up in African American religious and educational institutions, he never publicly identified as black after he left home in 1909. Whether he was or was not "black" is an impossible question to answer because, as Wayde Compton puts it, "Like a national border or a literary genre, race is only as real as our current social consensus" (25). Today Long Lance might have identified as both black and Indigenous as other writers in the archive do (Troy Bailey, Woody Strode, Frank Fontaine, and Deanna Bowen). I include Long Lance in this archive not because I make some essential claim about his identity, but because his work speaks meaningfully to the lives, histories, and literary imaginations of mixed black Indigenous people on Turtle Island and the prairies.

Woodrow "Woody" Strode, a writer and athlete best known for breaking the colour barrier in American and Canadian football, arrived in Calgary in 1948 after being recruited from Los Angeles by the Calgary Stampeders. Strode's memoir, co-written with Sam Young, *Goal Dust: The Warm and Candid Memoirs of a Pioneer Black Athlete and Actor* (1990), is a lively first-person account of the challenges and triumphs involved in desegregating American and Canadian football, and covers his life from the time Woody "discovered I was a mixed breed" to the age of seventy-six. As a sports memoir, it anticipates Georges Laraque's wonderful *The Story of the NHL's Unlikeliest Tough Guy* (2011), about his time desegregating Canadian hockey culture as an "enforcer" with the Edmonton Oilers.

The period I regard as the third phase of black migration (1953 to the present) was spurred by the gradual easing of the racial and national restrictions to immigration policy after the Second World War. In 1953, under pressure from black civil rights activists both within and outside of Canada, the federal government finally dropped references to climate from its immigration policy and in the following decades made further revisions, including the points system, which gradually allowed more black immigrants to enter. By the end of the 1960s immigration from Africa, the West Indies, Brazil, and Central and South America increased dramatically, and in 1969 black immigrants made up an unprecedented 10 percent of the total immigration to Canada in that year (Winks 444). In 1971 Census Canada counted 2,830 people in Alberta, Saskatchewan, and Manitoba whose "ethnic group" was "Negro." By 1986 that population had jumped sixfold to 13,105. Like those in the first period, these third-period arrivants came by and large individually, or in small family groups, rather than as part of a chain migration, and they went most often to the prairies' urban centres: Winnipeg, Regina, Saskatoon, Edmonton, and Calgary.

Many of the black prairie's most prolific and formally innovative writers arrived during this third period, a period that, as Fil Fraser notes in his *Alberta's Camelot*, coincided with the "Quiet Revolution" in Alberta in which the Peter Lougheed government (1971–1985) began to actively support the arts, including, especially, cultural arts from minority communities. It was a culturally fertile time to arrive. One of the best-known writers, Claire Harris, came to Calgary from Trinidad in 1966; Harris's fellow countryman, the poet Nigel Darbasie, arrived three years later and settled in Edmonton. African folklorist and children's author Tololwa Mollel came to Edmonton from Tanzania in 1966; the playwright and fiction writer Archibald Crail[10] arrived from Paarl, South Africa, in 1980 and settled in Regina. Playwright George Bwanika Seremba fled Uganda and arrived in Winnipeg in 1984. One of my motivations for publishing this anthology and connecting the work of archival writers with that of contemporary writers is to bring back into public consciousness the work of authors of the 1980s and 1990s which has lately fallen out of public view. Contemporary conversations around black Canadian writing are too presentist; they constellate around a few recently published authors, and thus neglect the important achievements of writers of earlier periods. But in many ways, Claire Harris, Nigel Darbasie, Archibald Crail, George Seremba, and Tololwa Mollel blazed the trail for contemporary writers; they were among the first to self-consciously develop a black Canadian poetics, one that, as I show in relation to work by Claire Harris, was particularly inflected by their prairie locations. Harris and Darbasie both wrote in Trinidadian Creole; George Seremba's plays immersed his audiences in the Igbo language—thus transforming the soundscape of the prairies by writing it as part of the continuum of Africa and its diasporas. These authors' strategies for "blackening," to use Paul Barrett's concept (13), the sounds of the prairie with the rhythms, languages, songs, and folklore traditions of the diaspora helped to pave the way for the next generation of writing, for instance, by Lisa Codrington, whose play *Cast Iron* is written entirely in the Bajan demotic; Kaie Kellough, whose dub-influenced poetry imagines the prairie as a dub "remix" (*Maple Leaf Rag*); Wakefield Brewster's "EbonicalPhoneticalAlphaNumerical style"; Trevor Lawrence's *Hey Lickle Bwoy* (1996), poems written in Jamaican nation language; and ultimately the regional rap of Elliott Walsh, Odario Williams, Roland Pemberton, and Frank Fontaine, among others. The first writers of this third period also introduce a variety of African oral and narrative forms into the archive.

---

10 I regret that I was not able to secure permission to include work by Archibald Crail in this volume.

Expert storyteller and story-listener Tololwa Mollel reworks African folk-lore traditions in his large oeuvre of young adult fiction and Linus Asong writes through the anti-hero tradition of African fiction. Not only were the first writers of the third period trailblazers in terms of their self-conscious diaspora poetics and narrative forms, they were among the first black writers in Canada to break into mainstream publishing and thus to reach a wide Canadian readership: both Archibald Crail and Claire Harris were nominated for Governor General's Awards in 1992 and 1993 respectively. Nigel Darbasie was widely recognized in the early and mid-1990s, including in the *Oxford Companion to Canadian Literature* (1997) (though this volume includes Darbasie, along with Austin Clarke, Neil Bisoondath, and Claire Harris, in the entry to "Caribbean-Canadian Literature in English"). Saskatchewan author Archibald Crail was involved in the conversations at the Writing Thru Race conference in Vancouver in 1994 about how to widen the horizon of freedom for black, Indigenous, and racialized writers in Canada. Students and scholars of black Canadian literature should know these writers' names.

Writers of the post-1960s period expand the imagined boundaries of the prairies with work that focuses on "elsewhere"; at the same time, this work insists that "elsewhere" is here, part of an elastic, diasporized, black prairie imagination. Work by George Seremba, Nduka Otiono, Bola Opaleke, Francisco Fwallah, Títílópé Sónúgà, Chantal Hitayezu, Tchitala Kamba, and Ahmed Ali bring the geographies, political contexts, and languages of South Africa, Uganda, Nigeria, Congo, Angola, and Somalia into the imagined space of the prairies. Readers of their work are asked to engage with the politics of apartheid in South Africa (Crail, Seremba), the troubling politics of oil in the Niger Delta (Otiono and Opaleke), the Rwandan genocide (Hitayezu), the prisons of Kinshasa (Kamba), and war in Somalia (Ali) as being fundamentally prairie concerns. Writers are also asked to engage with writing in languages other than English. George Seremba writes in Bantu and English; Francisco Fwallah writes in both English and Portuguese; Tchitala Kamba writes in French and Swahili. Readers of the archive will encounter this work in both the original language and poet Erin Mouré's original translations.

Claire Harris expresses the contours of this elastic, diasporized, black prairie geography elegantly in her 1992 collection *Drawing Down a Daughter*. Harris's poet-speaker remembers a phone call from her literary editor asking her to contribute writing not set in the Caribbean, but on the prairies. Harris writes:

> 'have you ever thought to send us some thing
> Canadian   set here' what   she   is   doing   here   is/   &
> important …
> he'll never buy it

In these lines Harris's speaker at once insists that the work she doing *is* Canadian, though she withholds this national signifier, offering instead a backslash, a space and a line break in the poem into which the geography of a so-called "elsewhere" may be imagined as part of the same: "here/ &". Throughout her ouevre, Harris works with a poetics of collage to seam together Trinidad and Calgary on the page, thus creating out of both something new: a black prairie. We see a similar black prairie geography being evoked in work by Lisa Codrington and Nehal El-Hadi. Codrington's play *Cast Iron*, whose central figure, an elderly woman named Libya who resides in an old folks' home in Winnipeg, is haunted by the figure of the Red Woman, the embodiment of the Barbadian plantation injustices she witnessed as a child. The Red Woman returns in the present to the prairie as a reminder that the transgressions of slavery, miscegenation, and past secrets cannot be left behind in Barbados, for the prairies is not a bordered, innocent, or separate space. As Libya says in the last scene of the play, "I just lef an I kep on leffin till I eventually lef an come alla de way here. I been here fuh over forty years. I ain't t'ink de Red Woman gine come alla de way up here … but she do cause I still here wit my belly startin tuh cut an no where tuh run" (40). Similarly, in Nehal El-Hadi's powerful micro-fiction "Djinn in Saskatchewan" the djinn, supernatural beings of Arab mythology, have followed the poet-speaker's family out of the desert into Saskatchewan, where they continue to sing and influence the family's lives.

The predicament in Codrington's play and El-Hadi's micro-fiction is the same one that haunts the narrator in Lawrence Hill's masterful short story, "Meet You at the Door," set in Gull Lake, Saskatchewan, in 1997. The narrator of the story, a young writer, has chosen to move to the small town to try to escape the dark, seductive voices in his mind. But as Joel becomes a CP Rail night train operator, dispatching trains through Gull Lake from Saskatchewan and Alberta, he finds himself not in an isolated prairie town, but at the very centre of a busy crossroads, not only that of the railway, but also between life and death.

Finally, Edmonton-based Minister Faust's Afritopian novels also figure prairie spaces as interconnected, diasporic zones. His novels offers readers the sounds, smells, tastes, and sights of a space he calls "Kush": "107th Ave and 107th Street, grid middle for our neighbourhood, home since I was old enough to pee. You got more Somalis, Ethiopians, Eritreans, and Sudanese here than any other place in E-Town. Some people call it the Horn. We call it Kush" (*Coyote Kings* n.p.). Faust's novel celebrates not only the built environment of shops, roads, mosques, and restaurants of Edmonton's East African neighbourhood, but also the particular social relationships that produce this urban space as Kush—a hybrid prairie-diasporic African space. Just as Minister Faust's novels represent for readers special prairie sights and tastes of Kush, so too, Addena Sumter-Freitag's one-woman play *Stay Black & Die* creates a complex aural soundscape of black Winnipeg. In her play Sumter-Freitag knits together the voices of Winnipeg's North End in the 1950s and '60s, including the multi-ethnic accents of her diverse neighbourhood, her mother's black Nova Scotian English, and the African American pop, soul, and R&B soundtrack into the soundscape of black life in Winnipeg in the mid-twentieth century.

More recently, the prairies' rappers have been working with the hip-hop tradition of representing—and thus elevating—particular regions, cities, neighbourhoods, as well as particular buildings and housing projects, in order to celebrate the black cultures produced in these particular sites and to project them onto the acoustic map of the black diaspora. Roland Pemberton represents Edmonton; Frank Fontaine reps Central Winnipeg; Nestor Wynrush lifts up the South End of Winnipeg, including especially Gaylene Place; and Odario Williams celebrates the DIY hip-hop culture of 1990s Winnipeg, including its own unique rap, graffiti, and breakdancing traditions. This work formally connects these local spaces to the ever-revolving soundtrack of the black diaspora.

Writers of the third period expand and diversify the archive also in terms of genre. One way that the writing of the third period departs from the cultural production of the second is the greater distance that exists in third-period writing between the authorial and textual "I." While writers and especially orators of the second period unite, through consistent voice, style, and perspective, the discordant and fragmentary aspects of memory and experience into a coherent narrative self, many—though not all—writers of the third period actively embrace fragmentation and disjuncture as a hallmark of the represented "I." Claire Harris's poem "Backstage at the Glenbow Museum," originally published in 1996 and not included here because of copyright restrictions, suggests that this strategy of distancing the authorial and textual selves became a useful strategy for negotiating the pressures exerted on black writers of the 1990s and early 2000s to represent or otherwise perform an authentic black identity for their audiences and for broader cultural and educational institutions. Thus, in many respects, the writing of the third period signals an important shift in the archive, from the autobiographical, ethnographic, historical, and realist modes of the second period, to less representational genres, such as poetry, including experimental poetry such as that by Ian Samuels and Troy B. Bailey; fiction (Edugyan); short fiction (Lawrence Hill); drama (Seremba, Foggo, Sumter-Freitag, Codrington, Warner, Robinson-Gudmundson); fable (Mollel); magic realism (Mayr); and Afritopian science fiction (Faust). These genres enable writers at once to register but also to transform the imagination of the prairies. Suzette Mayr's magic realism, the signature genre of her five published novels, offers her characters—often racialized and queer—the possibility of surprise metamorphoses, and allows Mayr tropes for imagining the transformation of social institutions, particularly the heteronormative family, Catholic high schools, and neo-liberal universities on the prairies. Minister Faust draws inspiration for his Afritopian fiction from ancient African civilizations in order to imagine his prairie characters as part of a larger global, and at times, cosmic, struggle for justice.

It would be wrong, however, to leave readers with the impression that after the 1960s the autobiographical and historical modes wholly disappear from the archive. In fact, there is an important emergence of the genre of the personal essay that recalls the testimonials and oral histories of the second period. The resurgence of the personal essay genre is largely due to the efforts of editors like Hazelle Palmer (Sister Vision 1997), Adebe DeRango-Adem, Andrea Thompson (Innana 2010), and Tololwa Mollel (2017), to bring out narratives of race and mixed race, identity, immigration, and belonging in Canada. Documentary filmmaker Selwyn Jacob uses the form of the personal essay to testify to the ways the hidden black history and geography of the prairies made him into a filmmaker. Essays by Chantal Hitayezu, Michelle Jean-Paul, Sheila Addiscott, and Miranda Martini are important testimonials of coming of age on the prairies in the context of anti-black racism and misogynoir. These are essays that bespeak the resistance and resilience of black women, and ultimately, the power of story to transmute experience into art.

For many writers, part of what it means to imagine and write the black prairies is to seriously grapple with the histories and legacies of settler-colonialism that forcefully assert themselves in the present. Writers in this archive wrestle with difficult questions about what it means for black people to have territorialized in Indigenous nations on Turtle Island, and about how to make things right in the present. I regard F.B. André's short story collection *What Belongs* (2007) as a key text in the archive for the way André handles questions of kinship, responsibility, and belonging. The short story "Is There Someone You Can Call?" is particularly apt; it probes the nature of rightful belonging in a settler-colonial nation. Khodi Dill's slam poem "Holes" is likewise a searing critique of neo-colonialism in Territory Six. Other writers turn attention to the related neo-colonial politics of resource extraction, especially regarding Alberta's oil sands industry. Nigel Darbasie's "New Terra," Khodi Dill's "Oil and Water," Roland Pemberton's "30 Seconds," and Nduka Otiono's "Homeland Securities" are concerned with petroculture and environmental degradation, and are suggestive of the ways that particular writers understand themselves as accomplices in the collective struggle that extends beyond the black community for climate justice and decolonization.

Migration to the prairies does not conclude with this third period, nor does its archive cease expanding and diversifying. Something intimating a fourth period can be detected in the numbers of people entering through recently established neo-liberal government programs, as well as asylum seekers arriving through so-called "illegal" or irregular land crossings. Immigrants—many of them black—arriving through the Temporary Foreign Workers Program more than doubled under former Prime Minister Stephen Harper's Conservative government—from 43,412 workers in 2005 to 104,160 in 2013, according to Immigration Refugees and Citizenship Canada. Many are arriving from refugee camps in East Africa, or from the West Indies and Central America, to work in the industrialized agricultural and meat-production zones of the prairies and to work as domestics. The program restricts the amount of time people can stay in Canada with a "four in, four out" rule, making it difficult for immigrants to obtain permanent residency or the critical mass necessary for resisting unjust labour conditions. Another stream of migrants is arriving via the Pembina-Emerson land crossing that connects North Dakota with Manitoba, a point of entry well known to black prairie people who crossed at this same location one hundred years ago when they were "deemed unsuitable to the climate and requirements of Canada" by the 1912 Order in Council. Close to one thousand asylum seekers, mainly from Somalia, Ghana, and other African nations, have risked their lives by crossing farmers' fields in winter conditions to reach this rural land crossing between 2013 and 2017.[11] The number of asylum seekers spiked dramatically in January 2017, after Donald Trump's executive orders "Protecting the Nation from Foreign Terrorist Entry into the United States" sparked fears that they would be deported from the US. Although arrivants claiming refugee status are not permitted to migrate to Canada from the US under The Safe Third Party Agreement, a loophole allows asylum seekers who cross the border to stay in Canada while their application to live in Canada is processed. But the crossing is far from safe. On December 24, 2016, two Ghanaian men successfully made it across the border by walking several miles along the Red River in sub-zero temperatures, but both men suffered severe frostbite that required amputation of their fingers. One of the men, Mohammed Kamadeenulias, explained that he is gay, and he is seeking asylum in Manitoba because in Ghana homosexuality is illegal (CTV News, January 10, 2017).

These recent migrations will again transform the prairies in significant ways in the coming decades. Communities like Brooks, Alberta, two and a half hours' drive southeast of Calgary, has already undergone such a transformation. Brooks is the site of the Lakeside Packers meat-processing plant, the largest beef processor in the country. It employs 2,500 workers who arrive through the Temporary Foreign Workers Program, mainly from Somalia but also from other East African countries. The town has quickly grown from a small village to a multi-ethnic, multilingual community of 13,000 in the span of one decade. Indeed, according to the latest (2016) census, the black residents of Brooks make up 14.3 percent of the town's population—currently the second most densely populated black urban space in Canada behind Ajax, Ontario, which has 16.7 percent. Fil Fraser notes that Brooks has changed from a white, socially conservative town to a place where hijabs are commonplace and where downtown bars feature African music. "You might hear as many as 90 languages on the street" (*How the Blacks Created Canada* 183–84). Brooks now calls itself "The City of 100 Hellos."

And the archive will again be transformed by this and future movements of immigration. I anticipate writers of the fourth and future waves will contribute to the archive more material written in Portuguese, French, Arabic, Amharic, Somali, and Swahili, and other languages. There are already four African-language radio programs in Edmonton on CJSR FM 88 that serve several East African communities ("Somalis in Edmonton," "The Africa

---

11 http://www.cbc.ca/news/canada/manitoba/refugees-manitoba-emerson-crossing -1.3926754.

Show," "The Voice of Eritrea," "Voices of Ethiopia"), and there is a new, Alberta-wide television program that is broadcasting in Somali.

There are lessons in this archive for the reader about how to approach black literatures respectfully. African Albertan writers Tololwa Mollel and Títílopé Sónúgà both emphasize the work needed on the part of the reader in the essential, but underemphasized, art of story-listening. Títílopé Sónúgà's poem "Sacrifice" suggests that in encounters with linguistic and cultural difference, listeners must learn to transform their desires for the sameness of their own voices; they must rouse their "lazy ears" lest these recovered stories continue to "h[ang] in the air." Similarly, in his work in this volume Mollel reveals that the art of story-sharing in Masaai is literally translated as "'eating words' or 'feasting on words.'" He writes, "Feasting on words involves skilful speaking as well as listening. You are only a good eater of words as you are a listener. So, you listen actively to someone talking." "You emit responsive sounds in a rhythmic pattern to acknowledge the speaker's words: Mmh, eee, hoo, mmmh, nna, aaya, hoop, eeee. You listen until the speaker finishes." "You listen," he writes, with your "whole being." I hope that the writing in this volume and the critical apparatuses I offer will continue to transform the structure of reception of black Canadian literature and that it will be received by readers in the same fullness of spirit with which it is shared.

Lastly, a note about the editorial principles that have shaped the following archive. What is gathered here is a selected, not a complete, archive of black prairie literature. There is some material I have not included because of a lack of permission or because it has vanished with time. I have chosen material on the basis of seeking as equitable a balance as possible between men and women writers, and I have focused on including work that, to my mind, best expresses the salient issues regarding the project of archiving the black prairies—material that speaks directly to questions of region, race, community, citizenship, migration, politics, territory, and archives, all of which I take up, in an expanded form, in my companion volume. Undoubtedly my selections reflect, for better or for worse, my own limited third-wave perspective on the prairies. I hope future work will expand on the perspectives I am able to offer here.

I have striven to transcribe all documents as faithfully as possible. I have not corrected spelling or grammar in order to produce Standard English; instead, I have aimed to preserve original spelling, grammar, and rhythms of speech. Where I have given titles that were not part of the original text,

I have indicated using quotation marks. I also indicate, where relevant, the archives, collections, and publications in which the original texts can be found.

I have arranged the archive chronologically by authors' birthdates, where known. Each text is prefaced by a short introductory note in non-specialized language in order to offer the reader some context, biographical information, and history on the writer's publishing career. Some of these notes are longer and more detailed than others. The reason for this unevenness is simply that the public, historical record is full for some writers and for others it is fragile and incomplete. I hope that this book will inspire more work in the field—rigorous readings, new debates, and the recovery of histories, texts, and writers not included here. But this is a task—and a collective one at that—for the future.

The Repertoire

Daniel T. Williams
(ca. 1840–1887)

There are two versions of Daniel Williams. The first imagined Williams was born into slavery in the American south and arrived in the Peace River country, currently Alberta, in 1869. He was imagined to lurk on the periphery of prairie society, squatting "illegally" on Hudson's Bay Company land, opening competing trading posts, destroying and stealing HBC property, and committing murder when the Company tried to reclaim what it thought of as its property. Williams, it is told (e.g., Peter Freuchen 1956; Nigel Hannaford 1976), was finally brought to justice after fatally shooting a police officer who entered his cabin and mistakenly killed Williams's Beaver wife, Thela, instead of him. He was tried at Fort Saskatchewan, and found guilty of murder. It is said he was executed by hanging in 1880.

But looking at the archival record, it becomes clear that this version of Williams is altogether apocryphal, a product of prairie fears of blackness and, in particular, black masculinity. A strikingly different image of Daniel Williams emerges from nineteenth-century Dominion Geological Survey records, and from archival *Edmonton Bulletin* articles published in the 1880s. In these versions, Williams is an integral member of early prairie society; he is socially connected, and he is rooted in a land he cared for deeply.

Williams was born in Canada, not the United States. He likely came from Kingston, Canada West, and he probably travelled west as a translator and cook for the famous John Palliser expedition, which surveyed the prairies from 1857 to 1860 for possible routes for the Canadian Pacific Railway. By 1872 he was well established in the Peace River district, as evidenced by the garden he wrote about. Williams was a careful and talented gardener, and he shared his work with surveyors who came by his place to gather data on soil and climate in the area. In 1876 one Dominion land surveyor, Mr. Selwyn, made note of "Nigger Dan's [*sic*] flourishing garden of vegetables and grains—he was harvesting his potatoes August 2 and his barley and oats were ripe by August 12." Williams kept a notebook in which he carefully recorded his observations about the changing seasons in the Peace

River country and regarding his garden operations. Williams shared his notebook with Dominion land surveyors, one of which published a fragment in *Province of Manitoba and North-West Territory of the Dominion of Canada: Information for Emigrants* (p. 27, 1878), published by the Department of Agriculture, Ottawa, from which the following excerpts are taken.[1] Williams's lyrical simplicity reads like a restraint poem stripped down to the necessary nouns and verbs: river, geese, ice. He sows his words on the page as carefully as seeds in earth.

On August 12, 1882, news of Dan Williams was published in the *Edmonton Bulletin*. The "Local News" article suggests Williams was a well-known local figure, enough so that his failing health was regarded as newsworthy. The article reads:

> Wheat is getting yellow.
> Eighty eight in the shade on Tuesday.
> No prospect of CPR getting to Calgary this season.
> Raspberries are plentiful and sell in town at $2 a patent pail full. [...]
> Dan Williams, of Fort Saskatchewan, who has been very ill lately, is improving slightly.

Further news of Williams is printed in the *Bulletin* on July 9, 1887, letting local readers know about his death:

> A party of nine came into the Upper Peace River last fall from Calgary by way of British Columbia. [...] The other 6 including Dan Williams, "Nigger Dan," [*sic*] went up the Finlay Branch of the Peace. They had some disagreements and Dan and another separated from the rest and came down to the mouth of the Finlay where they built a cabin in which to winter. Dan took sick in the fall and gradually wasted away until he died about the middle of February. His death was not heard of until the ice broke up and his companion came down to Christie's camp.

Williams never was hanged for murder as the legend told. Further proof is that his name does not appear in the Inventory of *Case Files of Persons Sentenced to Death in Canada, 1867–1976* (Gadoury and Lechasseur). He has likely been mixed up with one Jess[e] Williams, a black man who was hanged for murder in 1884 at the North-West Mounted Police Barracks in Calgary.

From his writing it is clear that he did have a quarrel with the Hudson's Bay Company, but there is no evidence that he ever did more than commit pen to paper in defence of land he thought was his. The ultimatum regarding this land that Dan Williams wrote to Chief Factor Kennedy in 1873 is the second-oldest surviving

---

1   Digitized and available from the University of Alberta at https://babel.hathitrust .org.

piece of writing by a black prairie person, after his "Notebook" fragment. In the short but powerful missive, Williams's written voice rings out in uncompromising defence of both his personal sovereignty and the sovereignty of his claimed home place.

❧

Notebook 1872–1875

"1872.
"Ice began to run in river November 8th.
"River closed November 28th.
"First snow October 28th.

"1873.
"April 23rd, ice moved out of river.
"Planted potatoes April 25th.
"First permanent snow November 2nd.
"River closed November 30th.

"1874.
"River broke up 19th April.
"First geese came 21st April.
"Sowed barley and oats April 22nd.
"River cleared of upper ice May 3rd."
"Planted potatoes May 5th.
"Potatoes not injured by frost until 22nd September. Then snow fell which coverd them, but soon went off. Dug over 100 bushels from one planting.
"Ice commenced to run in river October 30th.
"River closed November 23rd.
"Snowed all night November 4th.

"1875.
"Ice broke up in river April 15th.
"Warm rains from north-west; blue flies and rain, February 18th.
"Ice cleared out in front of Fort, April 16th.
"Potatoes planted 8th, 9th, and 10th May.
"Barley and oats sown May 7th.
"Snow all gone before the middle of April. This applies to both the river valley and the level country above."

❦

Letter to Hudson's Bay Company Factor, George Kennedy, April 12, 1873

Kenedy I hear by
Worne you that Com and Gett your
persnol property if eny you
have Got on my prmeeis In 24 hours and then keep
away
from me because I shal Not betrubbled Nor trod on
only by her most Noble
        Majesty
        Governmet
        (Sgd) D.T. WILLIAMS

I have waited longe A-day for an ancer from that Notis you toer-Down and now It is my turn to tore down.

Dr. Alfred Schmitz Shadd
(1870–1915)

Alfred Shadd was not only a teacher and a physician, but also a talented farmer, politician, newspaper editor, writer, and energetic civic leader. He was born in Chatham, southern Ontario, to Garrison and Harriet Poindexter Shadd, a couple known for their high-profile abolitionist work. Alfred's aunt, Mary Ann Shadd Cary, was the famed writer and educator who edited the *Provincial Freeman*, a weekly newspaper (published 1853–1857) that advocated for equality, integration, and self-education for black people in Canada and the United States, and which urged black Americans to consider Canada as a permanent home.

Although the Shadd family was well respected, they were not wealthy. Alfred Shadd began his career as a teacher and taught first at the same racially segregated school in Chatham where he had been a student (Thomson, "Alfred Schmitz Shadd"). Shadd dreamed of becoming a doctor and he studied medicine at the University of Toronto, but running short of money, he had to leave his program, and in 1896 headed west to teach in the small community of Kinistino, in the North-West Territories (now Saskatchewan). After his first year in Kinistino, Shadd returned to the University of Toronto to complete his medical degree, and in 1898 he returned to Kinistino, this time to practise medicine.

Shadd proved to be a gifted and dedicated country doctor, travelling constantly to tend to patients throughout the Carrot River valley. The tributes to Shadd published in the *Melfort Moon* after his death testify to his successes as a doctor. "No drive was too long; no night too dark; no trail too rough to deter the doctor when the call for assistance came." According to another newspaper article, he was "universally liked by all who knew him, especially those who received medical treatment from him, it being as good as medicine to hear his hearty laughter when he was cheering up a patient." A long-time resident of the area remembered, "I will never forget Dr. Shadd sitting beside my little sister keeping her swatched in cool cloths and wrapped in cotton batting and oiled silk when the measles went back in on her. She had to learn to walk all over again but he saved her. Rain or snow, road or no road didn't stop the doctor. If there was no trail for the buggy or cutter he would take to horseback (Saskatchewan African Heritage Museum).

In 1907 Shadd went to Europe to pursue postgraduate studies in Edinburgh and Paris, but once again a lack of money forced him to return to his medical practice on the prairies. On December 31, 1907, Shadd married Jeanette (Jennie) Simpson, a white woman, and they had two children, Garrison, named for Shadd's father, and Louena (or Lavina). The Shadds entertained distinguished guests in their middle-class home, including the first premier of the North-West Territories, Frederick Haultain.

Over the next decade, Shadd channelled his ambitions into a stunning array of civic building activities. His list of achievements is remarkable for any individual. Shadd purchased the *Prince Albert Advocate* in 1908 and moved it to Melfort. It was renamed the *Carrot River Journal* and the first issue came out October 8, 1908. Dr. Shadd was the publisher and editor, despite his apparent disavowal of his editorship in the October 1910 editorial, below. Shadd opened and operated a drugstore. He was instrumental in building a hospital in Melfort, and he was active on both the Melfort town council and the school board. He founded and became president of the Melfort Agricultural Society, and he belonged to the local Masonic lodge, Orange order. He reputedly called himself a "black Orangeman" (Thomson 1998).

Shadd was less successful in his political career than he was in his other endeavours. In 1901 he ran as a Conservative candidate in the territorial elections, but was unsuccessful. In the 1905 election as the Equal Rights Party candidate, he came within fifty-two votes of becoming the first black person elected to a provincial legislature in Canada. Nevertheless, Shadd's achievements are remarkable, and they are made all the more so by the fact that he accomplished it all before his early death from appendicitis at the age of forty-five.

In the following speech to the electorate of Kinistino, published in the *Melfort Journal*, readers can hear Shadd's elevated and formal tone, befitting that of a public figure. Readers can also note the way Shadd prioritized local and regional concerns above federal ones.

In his "Defamation" rant, published in the *Carrot River Journal*, which Shadd also owned and edited, readers encounter a black author ironically disavowing his own authorship. The rant should be understood in the context of Shadd's sparring relationship with the editor of the *Kinistino Representative*, whom he knew well from living in Kinistino from 1896 to 1904. Such verbal salvos were common in newspapers during this time, particularly concerning political affiliations. After all, Kinistino elected a Liberal from 1902 to 1929, whereas Shadd ran as a Conservative in 1905. The disavowal of his authorship and his pugnacious tone, then, should be understood as forms of "permitted disrespect" that testify to his security within his community. In Shadd's final editorial in the *Carrot River Journal*, on February 2, 1912, three years before his untimely death, he bids farewell to his paper readers and users. His reference to the past "three and a half years" seems to suggest it was his paper throughout.

In March of 1915, Shadd took ill and died. A Canadian black granite stone marks his burial place in Melfort, Saskatchewan.

Original copies of the *Melfort Journal* and *Carrot River Journal* (1908–1912 ed. Shadd) are housed at the Melfort and District Museum, Saskatchewan.

To the Electors of the District of Kinistino

Gentlemen, —— We have a very large district, and although I have held meetings in nearly every portion of it, still many of you may possibly not have met me or been made acquainted with my views upon the present issues. I would therefore in the first place say, I am fully convinced that in our purely local affairs it is better that we should consider the province of Saskatchewan first in the present juncture, and the Dominion as a whole second. At the General Elections for Ottawa I would certainly say, consider the Dominion first and our local interests secondary. In short, I think that as a province we will get evener [*sic*] justice when the Premier of Saskatchewan has not to think whether he will injure his party at Ottawa or not, by standing out for our full rights in questions between the local and Dominion government. I think that Mr. Haultain took that stand, knowing at the time that he would be deprived of his position as our Premier by doing so. We have not so very many men in public life who deliberately do this, and when we find them I believe we as electors should uphold their hands.

I believe also the property of railways and corporations and great land companies should be placed upon the same general footing as regards paying taxes as our farm property; and as the Dominion government failed to provide for this in framing the Autonomy Bill, in so far as the C.P.R. tax exemption is concerned, therefore, the Dominion government should increase our subsidy by the exact amount we lose by not being able to tax this property. This is only just, as we know the C.P.R. was built for Canada as a whole and not for us in particular.

We should also undertake in our own behalf the building of a line of railway to Hudson Bay at once. By the word we I mean the Western Provinces.

I don't think the Ottawa government will be in any haste to do this work, and I don't think we can wait.

I think again that if we are to become as important a province as, say, any of the eastern group of provinces, we should be handed over the control—and at once—of our public lands, and forests, as well as any minerals we may have. Without these resources we will be forever tied down to the Federal government grant or to direct taxation. Besides, without lands our borrowing power will be very little and our rate of interest correspondingly higher.

Regarding our schools, I believe the matter of their control should have been left in our own hands. Personally, I am convinced that in countries like this where men of every race and creed are coming in and making their homes, a system of national schools for all the little children alike would be the best way of forming good Canadian citizens of them all. And as we all well know, one school is certainly more apt to be efficiently conducted where settlements are sparse than two.

Apart from this, if I am returned I am prepared to give Mr. Haultain a full measure of support along all lines of general progress. And I am sure we are all agreed, both friends and opponents of his, that Mr. Haultain has in the past done his utmost to give our vast North-West Territories efficient and progressive management. As we have that experience to go by, I am convinced that the Province of Saskatchewan can do no better than return Mr. Haultain as her first elected Premier.

If you, gentlemen, think with me in these matters, I ask your support at the polls.

Believe me, your obedient servant,

A. Schmitz Shadd.

Melfort, Nov. 28

Defamation

Carrot River Journal, October 1910

In an article in the *Kinistino Representative* of Oct 13, headed "Shaddows," there are several statements to which we take objection because "they are not true," "they are defamatory," and even insulting. We wish the *Representative* to clearly understand that Dr. Shadd has no interest in the [*Carrot River*] *Journal*, "that he does not write for it," and if the Rep were to get his grey matter at work, if he has any, he would see the name of the editor and proprietor of the *Journal* at the top of the editorial column.

Having called the attention of the editor of the *Representative* to the above fact, we have not either the time or inclination to pay any attention to his braying.

❦

Sorry but Happy

Melfort Journal, February 2, 1912.

With today's Journal the present Editor is forced to bid adieu to the readers of his paper. After three or more years, we are going to lay aside the pen, for more hands to take up. We were born young, but age is making us old. And with age comes wisdom. This goddess points out that the Journal has now reached the place where a practiced newspaper man should be at the helm. She points out that while tenacity is generally a winner, there is a time when the goal is won by letting go. The goal striven after by the Journal is in sight. Younger and more practical men will be able to guide us along until we reach it.

Our successor, Mr. S.C. Lancaster, is well known to the Melfort public. He helped to get out the first issue of the paper and was with us for several months, leaving to take over the management of our esteemed contemporary. He has been in that office ever since. The lure of the first love, however, was too strong and now Mr. Lancaster returns, not as manager but as editor and proprietor. His experience in newspaper work bespeaks a bright future for him in his new venture. The Journal will now be enlarged and improved in many ways. A growing town and community requires a growing publicity medium. This has always been the policy of the newspaper and it will so continue.

The Journal during the last three and a half years has received many kindly assurances from its readers and contemporaries; also many bumps, both of which were very much appreciated. Our thanks are due our patrons and supporters, and in heartily tendering the same, we commend their continuance to Mr. Lancaster.

A Schmitz Shadd

Mildred Jane Lewis Ware
(1871–1905)

When it comes to the literary legacy of the black prairies, it is Mildred Ware, more than her famous husband, John, who left her mark. There are a number of letters written in the late nineteenth century that were sent from the Ware family ranch to the brand office that appear to be penned and signed by John Ware. But John, being born in slavery, did not learn to write.[1]

Mildred Lewis was born in Toronto in 1871 to a middle-class urban family. Her father, Daniel Vant Lewis, was a carpenter and cabinetmaker who moved with his wife Charlotte and their large family from Ontario to Alberta in 1889, when Mildred was in her late teens. After unsuccessfully trying their hand at ranching near Shepard, the family moved back to Calgary, and Daniel resumed his trade of carpentry. According to Cheryl Foggo ("My Home"), he specialized in building elaborate staircases in Calgary's upscale homes. In the affluent and educated Lewis family, Mildred learned to read and write. Before marrying Ware, Mildred was a schoolteacher, and thus it was she, rather than John, who wrote the following letters.

Mildred Lewis and John Ware were married by a pastor of the Baptist church in Calgary at the Lewis residence on Tuesday, March 1, 1892. The bride was reported to be "of a happy disposition, well cultured and accomplished" by the *Calgary Tribune*.[2] For his part, John was praised as charming and gregarious: "no man in the district has a greater number of warm friends than the groom" (qtd. in David Breen). When they married, John already had a ranch on the headwaters of the Sheep River with two hundred head of cattle. In 1902 the Wares moved to a

---

1   The Glenbow Archives contain an example (file M-1281-1) of John Ware's distinctive, shaky signature on an agreement of sale of land to John Ware by John K. Clarke (1901) that bears little resemblance to the elegant penmanship of Mildred's correspondence.

2   *Calgary Tribune* March 2, 1892. "Orange Blossoms." Glenbow Museum and Archives M-1281-1.

new ranch in the Rosebud area, but their home was destroyed when the Red Deer River flooded its banks. The family barely escaped in the night. The Wares eventually prospered, and their operation increased to one thousand head of cattle. Mildred never learned to ride a horse.

Mildred and John had six children, five of whom survived until adulthood. Mildred died at the age of thirty-seven of pneumonia. John Ware died five months later, when a horse he was riding stumbled in a badger hole and fell upon him.

While John Ware is memorialized in the name of John Ware Junior High School in southwest Calgary, the John Ware building at SAIT polytechnic, several geographical features in southern Alberta—Mount Ware, Ware Creek, and John Ware Ridge (formerly Nigger John Ridge [sic])—and the 2012 Canada Post commemorative stamp, the contributions of Mildred Ware in the running of the Ware ranch have not been as widely acknowledged. But the persistence she shows in the writing of these letters suggests that she was a significant part of the ranching operation. Indeed, she did the bookkeeping on the ranch, carried out the necessary letter correspondence, and taught her family to read and write. Mildred does not write after her letter of June 20, 1899; presumably after this she received confirmation that she had been successful in registering the 999 brand in her daughter's name. Why Mildred chose to have the brand registered in Nettie's name—then five years old—is hard to say. It could be that some part of the business was registered by the Wares in their daughter's name. But why Mildred signed her husband's and her daughter's names to her letters rather than her own is puzzling. Although Mildred appeared to be reluctant to put herself forward, the black prairie archive remembers and celebrates her as the first black woman writer on the prairies.

Recently, Mildred Ware's voice has been brought to life by author Cheryl Foggo, whose play *John Ware Reimagined* (excerpted in this volume) also constitutes a reimagining of Mildred. Foggo's description of Toronto-born Mildred's reaction to nineteenth-century prairie culture in all its roughness, the dull routine of ranch life, the wildness of her country-raised children, and her enduring love of her husband, is deeply affecting.

I have transcribed Mildred's handwritten letters exactly as I found them in the archives. While the short lines are due to the narrow letter paper on which Mildred wrote, keeping her original lineation here amplifies the possibilities for reading the texts in other ways—for instance, as found poems. Mildred's original letters are held by the Alberta provincial Brands Office. Copies are available at the Glenbow Archives (M-1283-1).

Letter May 4, 1898

Millarville May 4th 1898

Dear Sir

$1[00]

I wont to get
my brand recorded 999 on
left shoulder for horses John Ware
Sheep Creek. and I wont to get
DC on left side and hipe
for cattle treasfer from me
to Miss Nettey Ware.[3] can
Robert Ware brand † get this
brand for cattle on left
side and shipe
I am sending bil of sail to
show you that DC brand
belongs to me it is recorded
in the Old brand book
in Courtney main please
return bil of sail to me
I inclose One Dollar for treasfer

Yours truly   John Ware
                     Millarville P.O.

Letter June 6, 1898

Millarville

I am in receipt of your letter
of May 28 and beg to say
my horse brand I paid
for getting it recorded
I have nothing to show that
it is recorded 9 on the left

---

3   Amanda Janet "Nettie" Ware was John and Mildred's eldest daughter. She was born
in 1892 and would have been only five years old when the first letter was written.

shoulder I wont to now if
you will recorded it fore me
I have been useding that
brand for some time and have
all my horsese brand with
it please writ and let me no
if you recorded it and I will
fee find $1.00 enclosed for
certificate of transferred of
DC for left ribs of cattle
from me to Netty Ware

$1.00
[I?].A.P.

Please pick out one of these
brands to recorded for Robert
Ware on left ribs of cattle
please let me now soon as I
am waiting to brand and
I will send fee when hearing
from you

You trully John Ware
Millarville. P.O.
Albarta.

Letter June 20, 1899

Millarville

Dear Sir

looking Over the new
brand book I find My brand DC
is not in the book is it not recorded
I wrote and pade for to have it
treated from John Ware to Netty Ware
I wrote last June brand DC on left
side for cattle and vent DC on
left hip please send the cefficter

Nettey Ware
Millarville

Reverend George Washington Slater, Jr.
(1873–1940)

George Washington Slater Jr. was the pastor of the Emmanuel African Methodist Episcopal Church of Edmonton from 1921 to at least 1924. In Chicago, prior to his arrival in Edmonton, he became a disciple of Woodbey, the leading black socialist preacher in the first decade of the twentieth century. Slater wrote articles for the *Chicago Daily Socialist* and the *Christian Socialist*. Although they appeared only for a limited time—seven months—Slater's articles marked the first time in American history that a socialist organ carried writings by a black American on a regular basis (Foner 294). It is significant that once he arrived in Alberta, Slater actively published in the same way; he wrote for the column "Our Negro Citizens," which appeared weekly in two major daily newspapers—the *Edmonton Journal* and the *Edmonton Bulletin*—in order to advocate on behalf of the black communities of Edmonton, Athabasca, and Junkins. These publications provide an important window onto the views of one of the leading black socialist preachers in the United States and Canada during the opening decades of the twentieth century.

We know little about Rev. George W. Slater before he became a socialist. The *Chicago Daily Socialist* engaged him to write a series of articles for the paper under the general heading "Negroes Becoming Socialists," but, as noted by Philip S. Foner in his introduction to his edited collection of Slater's writings (1983), it did not bother to introduce him to its readers with any biographical sketch. Before coming to Edmonton, Slater was a minister at the Bethel African Methodist Episcopal Church in Clinton, Iowa, and educated at Wilberforce University, Ohio.

In his article "How and Why I Became a Socialist," included below, Slater reveals that during the winter of 1907–8, a period of rising unemployment and economic distress resulting from the Panic of 1907 and the ensuing economic recession, he had tried to address the sufferings of black parishioners by organizing a co-op. Manufacturers frowned upon the venture, however, and he was unable to purchase supplies. This experience opened his eyes to the futility of trying to alleviate the sufferings of poor black people under the existing capitalist system. When he heard George Washington Woodbey's analysis of how socialism could help abolish poverty, he was immediately converted and joined the Socialist Party. Once converted, Slater eagerly assumed the task of recruiting black members. This he did by means of weekly sermons in his church, Zion Tabernacle, in Chicago, by the distribution of the pamphlet *Blackmen, Strike for Liberty* (no copy of which exists), and especially through the articles published in the *Chicago Daily Socialist*.

The Socialist Party had nothing special to offer black people except the same as it would offer working-class whites—the plight of blacks under capitalism, like that of whites, would be automatically solved under socialism. But Reverend Slater's writing repeatedly emphasizes that black people would have the most to gain from a socialist victory because, as he puts it, "the coloured man is the worst off of all the working class of people" and received "less wages, less protection, less education, pays more for food, clothing, house rent, etc." ("The Cat's Out" *Chicago Daily Socialist* September 29, 1908).

In 1913 Slater was appointed secretary of the Colored Race for the Christian Socialist Fellowships, and in that capacity he published several articles in the *Christian Socialist*. In his last article for that journal, he took issue with R.R. Wright, the editor of the *Christian Recorder*, who contended that while socialism had much about it that was praiseworthy, it could not replace the social service of the church in meeting the needs of the poorer classes. Slater pointed out that "Scientific Socialism is the only systematic expression of the social message of Jesus [...] Since the doctrines of socialism were the logical fulfillment of what the prophets, Jesus and the Apostles had sought, should not Christians, the Church, and its social service element say Amen?" ("Socialism and Social Service," the *Christian Socialist*, February 1915, qtd. in Foner 296).

Slater's 1908 article "Emancipation" reveals the pessimism with which he came to regard the liberatory promise of America for poor black people. "While these younger people may sing America in these assemblies," he writes, "yet it is a more perfunctory performance—they know that they are singing a lie." Slater continues, "In fact, they recognize that they are oppressed—that they are still slaves— wage slaves." By 1921, thirteen years after his "Emancipation" article, Slater had migrated to Edmonton with his wife and had taken up his position as the pastor of the Emmanuel African Methodist Episcopal (EAME) church, one of two black churches in Edmonton at the time (the other was Baptist Shiloh church). In their scholarship on black Alberta, Dan Cui and Jennifer R. Kelly suggest Slater saw his position in the church and his role in Edmonton's black community as an aspect of his missionary work. He used his position to advocate on behalf of community members who, especially during the early 1920s, did not have social services to look after those in need. A column I located in the *Edmonton Bulletin* (February 28, 1922) confirms and extends Cui and Kelly's findings; the pastor of the Edmonton Methodist Church speaks on behalf of Rev. Slater's fight against a petition that had arisen over the sale of some land to the black church. Rev. McTavish "urged that the council would not interfere with the magnificent work that Mr. Slater had begun in the city. And not only was his influence being felt here, but as the result of personal knowledge, he found that his work was extending so far north as Athabasca and went to the community of Junkins, and he was sure that they would not want to do anything to interfere with such competent Christian leadership."

In Edmonton, Slater authored "Our Negro Citizens," a daily column that ran in two city papers, the *Edmonton Bulletin* (August 27, 1921, to August 21, 1922) and the *Edmonton Journal* (September 10, 1921, to August 12, 1924). The column consists of short descriptions of and comments about the everyday comings and goings of a nascent African Canadian community in Edmonton and environs, particularly weddings, church meetings, entertainment, fundraising, speeches, elections, and news from abroad relevant to black diasporans (Cui and Kelly 256). Striking about the column is the horizontal juxtaposition of news about local and global affairs with news about public and private spheres. All of it is prioritized equally and treated together as part and parcel of the flows of black life. The column also reveals how well-organized the community is—they are mobilized to lift one another up, celebrate one another's achievements, and share news and knowledge relevant to them. In the column I reproduce below, notice is given about a lecture by a "Hindoo Prof., DP Wadia" suggesting that the black community was not necessarily racially ghettoized but actively forging cross-diasporic networks of "Brotherhood" (to use Prof. Wadia's theme) in order to develop its political thinking about liberation and diasporic citizenship.

Slater's political ideologies—and thus his tactics for uplifting his community members—appear to have shifted after his move to Edmonton. In his speeches (which cover the period 1908–1915) published in *Black Socialist Preacher* (Foner), Slater speaks with the voice of an avowed Christian socialist. But from what I gather from the newspaper articles published in the *Edmonton Bulletin* in the early 1920s, the sermons Slater gave stopped having an explicit socialist bent. The titles of his speeches advertised in the *Edmonton Bulletin* include "When the School Bell Rings" (September 6, 1921); "What Think Ye of Christ?" (March 20, 1922), and "The Bible Way of Healing" (April 17, 1922), to name only a few, and so suggest a philosophy of racial uplift through the institutions of church and school. Also, his speeches and activism begin to explicitly connect black citizenship with property ownership. For instance, in the *Bulletin* on February 28, 1922, a conflict regarding the city sale of land to the church quotes Slater's advocacy on behalf of his church members:

> Rev Slater informed the council that the church he represented was established throughout the world and included about one million communicants. There were seventy members in Edmonton and he contended that they included the best of the colored citizens in point of view of morals, intelligence, and proprietorship. He added that they might be considered some of the best colored citizens in Western Canada. They wanted this particular location because it was central for the colored congregation.

More research needs to be done to trace how and why Rev. Slater's political ideologies shifted during his time on the prairies (did his socialism meet resistance from black prairie congregations? From non-black Canadians?) and what the implications are for our understandings of the relationship of black people to Canadian settler capitalism.

Why I Became a Socialist

Chicago Daily Socialist, September 8, 1908

Having been asked to write an article each week for the Chicago Daily Socialist pertaining to the subject of "Socialism and the Negro Race," and as I have espoused the principles of Socialism just lately, I think it will be both interesting and profitable that in my first article I should relate "how and why I became a Socialist."

Now, it is obvious to me that the reason why I had not espoused the Socialist cause heretofore was due on the one hand to ignorance of its principles, purposes, and methods, and also due to on the other hand to prejudice which had been engendered by cunning innuendoes and prevalent falsehood disseminated by its detractors. It is all so plain to me now. What a lesson I have learned. How consistent and wise it is to "prove all things" before passing judgement.

Now, for my experience which prepared me for Socialism. Last winter when my parishioners had little work and little money, and the prices of food were exorbitant, I contrived a cooperative scheme whereby I could furnish them food very near the wholesale price.

Before a salesman for a certain wholesale house in this city I laid my plans. He told me that my plans were feasible and that I could get the goods. He also said that I could save the people at least 25 or 30 percent on their gross purchases.

At once, I put up a young man to soliciting orders. After I had sent in my order I got a letter from the salesman asking me to call immediately. I complied, whereupon he said that he was sorry to inform me that the management of the firm had refused to permit him to fill my order because I was not a bone fide retail dealer, that I was not buying to sell again at a profit. He said that I must have a store and sell over a counter.

I admitted that I was not seeking a profit, but that I was endeavoring to help a large number of poor consumers, and that my plan calculated to get the goods to the people as directly as possible from the wholesale houses or the producers, thus cutting out the middleman's profit, and the added expense of rehandling. Upon these grounds I insisted that he should sell me the goods. Then I was plainly told the wholesale people had an understanding with the retail dealers that would make such a business transaction with me a direct violation of that agreement. And further, I was told that if they sold me the goods for the purpose for which I wanted hem that the retail dealers would boycott them.

To this I replied, "Is it true that there is an understanding between the wholesale and retail dealers, whereby the poor consumer is compelled to pay more than is necessary for the necessities of life?" The salesman replied by saying, "Mr. Slater, if I had my way I would sell them to you, but I am under orders."

Chagrined and indignant, I returned and told my people of the turn of affairs. But I said in my heart and also before the public that such a situation and such agreements were unjust and in the face of such hard times, positively wicked, and that I would find a way out and break up such a situation.

To carry out my determination, I began to inquire about President Roosevelt's "trust busters,"[1] as they were called; but I soon found out that the trusts were busting the busters.

---

1   A trust is the practice of creating a corporation to oversee management of the stocks of cooperating corporations in order to fix prices and drive out new competition through price wars. Theodore Roosevelt, a Progressive reformer, earned a reputation as a "trust buster" through his regulatory reforms and anti-trust prosecutions.

Several other plans were suggested to me, but I found that they were inadequate. The more I studies the more I saw the direful condition of the poor people.

About four weeks ago I saw, at the corner of Thirtieth and State streets, a colored man speaking to a very attentive audience. When I drew near I learned that it was Mr. G. Woodbey, a national Socialist organizer, whom I had chanced to meet on a north-bound Halstead streetcar one Monday morning last May, during a Socialist national presidential convention.

To Mr. Woodbey I listened very attentively. Two or three times afterwards I made it convenient to hear him. I bought several books on the subject of Socialism and read them eagerly. The more I read the more I was entranced with the purity, simplicity, and justice of the principles, purposes and methods of Socialism. I saw that tenets of Socialism were the solution of our problem; the ethics of Jesus in economic action; the solution of the poverty question with its attendant evils; the making possible of a practical brotherhood; the solution of the more serious phases of the so-called race problem.

When the facts were made plain to me I at once espoused its cause; brought it before my people, and threw open my church for a Socialist meeting every Tuesday night at 2900 Dearborn Street.

Emancipation

Chicago Daily Socialist, December 10, 1908

The word "emancipation" is from a Latin word which means to deliver out of the hand of. It was the custom that when one purchased a thing, he put his hand on it, by which act he signified the possession of the object. To take it out of or to take his hand off of by another either by force or purchase would be to emancipate the object.

New Year's day is held in sacred remembrance by the colored people throughout the United States, for on Jan. 1, 1863, Lincoln, of blessed memory, issued the Emancipation Proclamation which made them freedmen—free from chattel slavery, for they had been abject slaves, victims of a system maintained by a people who were constantly singing the "land of the free and the home of the brave."

This was a happy day to them as my parents have often told me—their ecstasy knew no bounds. They have told me of how the colored people shouted, sang, praised God, rolled and tumbled. It meant so much to them.

For a long time a note of solemn gladness and extollation of the virtues of the government was evident in their celebrations. And as long as the older people who had suffered the evils of chattel slavery, and were then enjoying such liberties—as long as this class controlled these assemblies their present burdens and oppressions seemed very light.

But this note is changed now. The celebrations are held by the younger men and women, who from training, reading and reflection have ambitions of which their fathers never dreamed. Because of which they have problems different from those of chattel slavery days; but their condition is about as burdensome to them because of their more highly cultivated tastes and broader outlook on life.

While these younger people may sing America in these assemblies, yet it is a more perfunctory performance—they know that they are singing a lie. Some eloquent man or woman may deliver a panegyric on the life of Lincoln which will bring forth hearty applause, and yet there may be even in his speech a deprecation of the dereliction of Lincoln's political descendants, and some may even dare to denounce the whole governmental regime and call the stars and stripes a "dirty rag," as has been done more than once. Whether this is well in the younger people is not the question. It is a fact and signifies a dissatisfaction and daring that must be wisely reckoned with.

Some will eulogize the brave black soldiers of the American wars, while others will say that every black man who took part in the nation's wars was a fool. For they could point to the old soldiers and their widows and orphans who are neglected, and to the further act that the very black mob who suffered from the country's protection, they and their loved ones are unprotected beneath the folds of the stars and stripes. They know that under such conditions they could not say hurrah for Old Glory without stultifying their consciences.

In fact, they recognize that they are oppressed—that they are still slaves—wage slaves—that the vast majority of them can make only a precarious living that some one else has the say-so whether they work, eat, or live; that this some one else who is not immediately responsible for their obligations has the say-so as to how much they may receive as wages, or whether they shall beg, steal or starve.

They know that there is something very wrong; but just how to remedy it they do not know. They do not know that the politicians which they are supporting are responsible for these conditions. They do not know that many of their own race politicians know the remedy, but that they fear to make it known; that these politicians are in the business for the profits only, caring nothing for their welfare.

If these assemblies could be imbued with the economic wholesomeness of the Socialist theory of giving to each man all that he produces, "enough for all men, all the time," a world-wide brotherhood, what light and hope will come to them.

From every section of the country, we are receiving news of the fact that we are reaching my people with the message. My pamphlet entitled *Blackmen, Strike for Liberty*, seems to strike the right tune. Emancipation day would be an excellent time to distribute my pamphlet among the colored people ...

Our Negro Citizens

Edmonton Bulletin, April 17, 1922

[...] Alderman Bury spoke to a splendid audience of colored men last Tuesday night at the Shiloh Baptist church on the efficiency of labor. Ref. H. Brooks, T.H. Golde, Fred Dickens and Rev. Geo W. Slater, Jr., also spoke. Rev. Slater spoke of the excellent record of colored people as workers showing that under all fair tests they have proven as efficient as any other class of workmen and that in many instances the colored worker has to his credit superiority. An orchestra composed of Messers Geo Balley, Allan Bradshaw, John Bigson, and Robt. Lipscombe, furnished very pleasing music.

Last Tuesday night at the Shiloh Baptist church was organized the Douglas Athletic club which proposes to encourage the colored men and women in all sports such as baseball, football, basketball, lawn tennis, croquette and all track work. The club is composed very largely of persons belonging and attending the two churches, Baptist and Methodist, and will be interested in encouraging the men to join the church leagues. The officers of the club are president Allan Bradshaw; vice-president Richard Slater; secretary Sam Coleman; treasurer Clifford Alexander; manager Hatcher Day; captain Eugene Dickens; honorary president Rev. H Brooks. As the boys are good sports and are out soliciting aid to help them get suits, etc. the public should help them liberally.

The last census in the U.S.A. shows that the death rate among the colored people has decreased remarkably. This shows the salutary effect of the hygienic instructions given the negro for the last two decades. The negro where he observes the laws of health, thrives wonderful in all climes. The Star Light band of the Shiloh Baptist church will give an Easter program at the church Monday night and will serve refreshments among which will be a fish-fry. You can spend a good time, as Madame Bell and her young ladies do not do things by halves.

A nice crowd attended the entertainment given by the Deborah Star club last Thursday night at the Alexander hall and were given an address by Mr. Fred Dicken, and a very beautiful song by Miss Leeta Carter. After the program, many of the people enjoyed themselves by tripping the light fantastic too.

"Another good eat," they all said. "Where?" At the parsonage of the Emmanuel A.M.E church last Monday night given by Mrs. Harrison Sneed and a committee of ladies. The good ladies were kept busy from six until nearly ten o'clock feeding the happy crowd. Don't you miss the next one.

Both services were blessed with increased attendance last Sunday at the Emmanuel A.M.E. church. The morning service was much improved by the help of the new choir. The Sunday morning the Rev. Mr. Slater will preach on the subject, "The Bible Way of Healing." At night he will preach an Easter sermon on "The Resurrection." The choir will furnish special music. Rev. Slater went to Ponoka Monday to see about an old colored lady and a little girl who are in need of care. The reverend is undertaking to make arrangements with the Town of Ponoka to have them cared for by some colored family in Edmonton.

Mr. Zack Robinson, an old citizen of the province for seventeen years, was let out of the Salvation Army headquarters Thursday night and was picked up by the city police. The Rev. Mr. Slater was called in consultation by the police and the reverend is undertaking to do something whereby this old unfortunate man may be provided for. The old gentleman is very feeble both mentally and physically and presents a pitiable problem.

The debate on the unemployment question proposed by Rev. Slater has been accepted by Rev. Geo Ritchie, pastor of the labour church and a committee representing the two churches and the unemployment association has been selected to arrange for the debate in the near future.

Mrs. Slater, wife of Rev. Geo Slater, Jr., is contemplating a business trip back to the States this spring, Mr. and Mrs. Harrison, of Calgary, spent Sunday in Edmonton and attended the Emmanuel A.M.E. church at night. Mrs. Harrison is a very intelligent woman and is a graduate of one of the largest colored universities in the States, the Wilberforce university of the A.M.E. church. They stayed with Mrs. John Sayles, having with them also the baby.

Mrs. Edna Anderson, who is taking a course in bookkeeping at the McTavish Business college, is doing excellent work. Mr. Robert Posten [?], the son of Mrs. Moorehead, stopped over in the city one day this week and made a short call on the Rev. Mr. Slater at the parsonage. Mr. Posten lives in Toronto. Mr. Hardin and Alonso Anderson are reported much improved.

Many colored citizens heard the lectures given by the Hindoo Prof. D.P. Wadia at the Memorial hall last Wednesday and Thursday nights and were will pleased especially with his lecture on brotherhood.

William Sylvester Alpheus Beal
(1874–1968)

William Beal was born in Chelsea, Massachusetts, on January 16, 1874, son of
Loretta H. Freeman, who was listed as "mulatto" in census records, and Charles
R. Beal, who was racially categorized as "multiple." The Beal family were educated and middle class; Charles was employed as a bookseller and was the sole
supporter of the family. They owned their home in what appears to have been an
all-white neighbourhood (Barrow and Hambly 17), suggesting Beal's parents were
light-skinned enough to be pheneticized (that is, read) as white.[1]

Beal spent his early years in Minneapolis, Minnesota. After a possible detour
through Montana and/or British Columbia, he arrived in the Swan Valley area of
Manitoba, between the Duck Mountains and the Porcupine Hills, in 1906 to work
as a steam engineer at a sawmill. He decided to stay, becoming the first African
American resident in an otherwise all-Euro-Canadian community, residing there
for almost sixty years. Beal was respected for his depth and breadth of interests,
including book collecting—he was known for having collected a "comprehensive
library of learning" (Barrow and Hambly 26)—as well as carpentry, electronics,
philosophy, astronomy, nutrition, religion, and dressmaking. He made electrified
fences for cattle farmers, and furniture and toys, which he gave to friends and
neighbours. He is believed to have had some medical training, as he helped local
doctors to administer vaccinations and carried his own medical bag.

In 1914 Beal tried to volunteer for the medical corps of the Canadian army, but
they wouldn't let him integrate with the white troops. Beal was asked to join the
coloured corps, so he refused to enlist (Barrow and Hambly 15).

---

1 Wayde Compton's essay "Pheneticizing versus Passing" (*After Canaan* 2010)
offers the verb "pheneticize" as an important alternative to "passing"; Compton's verb
places the responsibility for racial (mis)recognition on the viewer, rather than the one
viewed.

Figure 3   William Beal self-portrait. Glass Plate #42 by William Beal.
By permission of Robert Barrow.

Beal was involved in a wide range of civic activities reflecting his interest in education and literature. He helped form the Big Woody School District in 1912 and
was elected as its first secretary-treasurer, holding that position for thirty-seven
years. He was instrumental in the establishment of a circulating library within the
school system. In 1922 he helped to found a literary society and debating club; his
neighbours remember him as a formidable debater. He also served as the first secretary of the Big Woody Sunday School. A keen amateur photographer, a selection

of his images were featured in a 1988 biography by Robert Barrow entitled *Billy: The Life and Photographs of William S.A. Beal.*

Beal fell in love with Dora Fuson, the daughter of one of his neighbours. Dora was a talented pianist and singer, and blind since birth. She did not return his affections. A lifelong bachelor, Beal died penniless at The Pas on January 25, 1968. He was buried in The Pas Cemetery.

Beal's life was the subject of William Washington Moxam's film *Billy* (2010), which was awarded the Human Rights Commitment Award in Manitoba. Beal has also been memorialized in a plaque in the municipality of Swan Valley West. Beal's original memoir, written while he was in a senior's residence sometime in the 1950s, is housed at the Swan Valley Historical Museum, Swan River, Manitoba.

Beal's passion for glass-plate photography took off when he declined to join the coloured troops in the First World War and lasted until about 1925. His subjects were his friends and neighbours in Swan River. Although he worked in portraiture, rarely did he pose his subjects formally. Rather, Beal most often shot his subjects—relaxed in informal poses—outdoors, in every locale of the Swan River Valley, and as such they constitute a powerful documentary history of the pioneering era of west-central Manitoba. The original glass plate photographs are housed at the Ole Johnson Museum.

The following transcription of Beal's memoir has been reproduced faithfully, including non-standard spellings. Any omissions which have been corrected are indicated with square brackets.

I came up to this country during Laurer's land boom and effort was being made to settle the west by giving every man a "homestead" for $10.00, three years residence and fifteen acres cleared and broke. I did not come to this part of the country to homestead then but to follow my trade of engineer as there [were] many saw mills being operated.

The idea of taking a homestead did not occur to me at that time. It was in the fall of 1906 that one of my acquaintances asked me to spend the winter on his homestead. That was in the district that is call Lancaster now. We went out there to fix up the house and things because he had a wife to share is good fortune with him. The scrub was so dence out there that we had to climb a tree to see much of his possessions. I had originally come from the city and I thought a man must have an awfull grug against a woman to take her out in the woods like that. But it was not so bad when one got used to it. We had a few neighbours there and we had a good time of it.

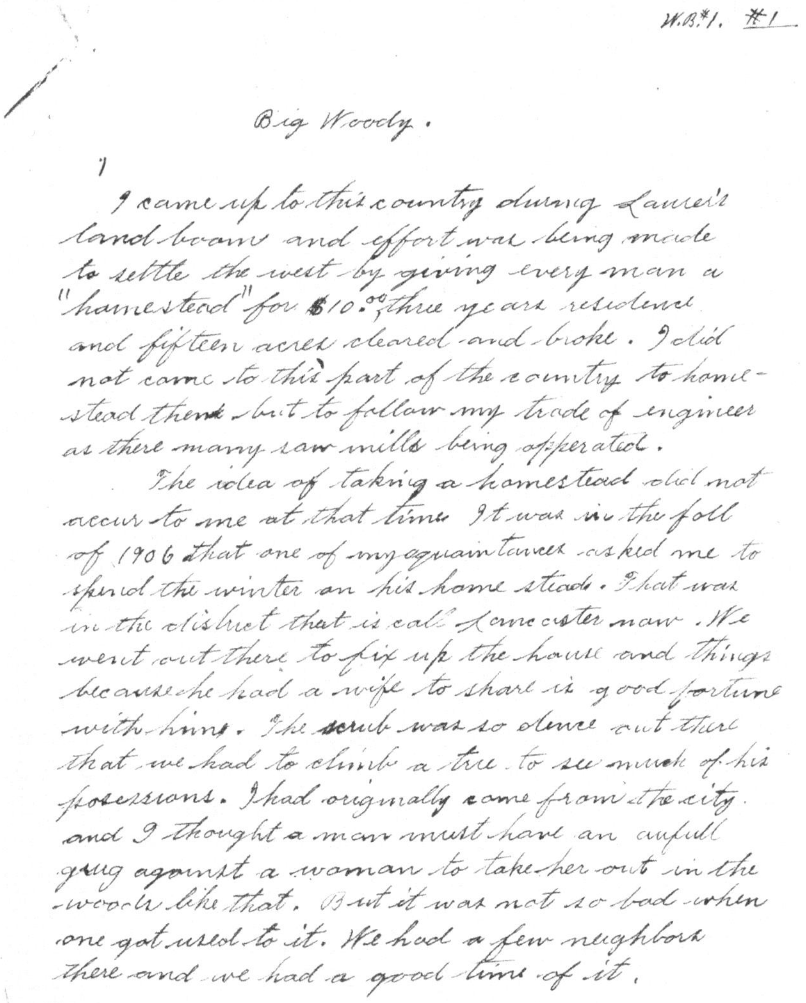

W.B.#1. #1

Big Woody.

I came up to this country during Laurier's land boom and effort was being made to settle the west by giving every man a "homestead" for $10.00 three years residence and fifteen acres cleared and broke. I did not come to this part of the country to homestead then but to follow my trade of engineer as there many saw mills being opperated.

The idea of taking a homestead did not occur to me at that time. It was in the fall of 1906 that one of my aquaintances asked me to spend the winter on his home stead. That was in the district that is call Lancaster now. We went out there to fix up the house and things because he had a wife to share is good fortune with him. The scrub was so dense out there that we had to climb a tree to see much of his posessions. I had originally come from the city. and I thought a man must have an awfull grug against a woman to take her out in the woods like that. But it was not so bad when one got used to it. We had a few neighbors there and we had a good time of it.

Figure 4   William Beal manuscript page one. By permission of Robert Barrow.

Two years after at the sawmill wher I worked most of the men were homesteaders and there was nothing but home stead talk every evening in camp. They would set around the table talked and joked each other about their braking and clearing. There was one of the mean that they used to joke a great deal and some one said to him once, "You haven't got any broke on your home stead yet, have you" and he said "Oh yes, I've got half an acre broke."

This and a book that I read that summer inspired me to try homesteading my self. So in the fall when the summer season at the mill was over, I applied at the land office in Swan River for a permit to file on a homestead. The only land then available near Swan River was ten miles north west of town some new land just opened up for settlement. It was not then even included in the municipality and I was the first one to locate there. This was in 1908. I went out to look at the land. It was very discouraging looking then, all heavy bush or rather dense trees—like a forest and I had to clear and brake fifteen acres in three years. There were no roads of course of any kind. Then too, there was the Woody River between it and town and no bridge. I had to cut a road in to haul material in to build my first shack.

The first winter passed uneventfully. It was not lonesome possibly because of the novelty of the situation. There were neighbors to the south across the river which was no barrier in the winter, when it was frozen. The wolves howled around the "shack" at night and every morning one could see fresh moose tracks in the snow. One shot moose then with impunity, for meat. The game wardens made no objections.

The settlement of this neighborhood was linked with that of the whole country for miles around. There was no distinctive district of Big Woody 'till the school was built here in 1913 and the prescribed district was called the Big Woody school district. For the first few winters, we had dances every week which took in all the people almost to Thunderhill. Every body was friendly[.] All seemed glad to make acquaintance with and welcome a new comer.

Every body had oxen in those days[.] There was no grain farming in the early days in Big Woody. Most of the people had meerely gardens, raised cattle and sheep and the women spun yarn [at] nite while the cattle roamed the whole country at will.

I spent two winters on the homestead and worked in the mill in the summer. Then, in 1911, a spring fire burned my shack and all my possessions. I had hoped when I first came here to be able to hire some breaking done but everybody was too busy with his own affairs to spare the time. The next spring, of 1912, I bought a team of oxen, built another shack and planed to stay home in the summer and work out in the winter. I scrubed land and broke. The work seemed to go extremely slow. I had my goal set on fifteen the amount necessary to get my pattent.   But fifteen acres cleared in bush

Figure 5   Portrait of Clarence Abrahamson in a field of marquis wheat, 1915. Glass Plate #3 by William Beal. By permission of Robert Barrow.

land, such as this, seemed a herculian task. We tried to make the acres as small as we could and they were called homestead acres. So when one said he had so many acres broke, they would say, "You mean homestead acres."

I had my firs garden in 1912. I was very proud of my effort with my first experience but we had a frost every month that summer and I got nothing but the potatoes. One of my oxen died and my next neighbor lost one ox too so we made a team of my remaining ox and his and worked on that way. I got my patent in five years but even then I did not have the necessary fifteen acres broke but the inspector made an allowance for that on account of the density of the scrub. Finally I rented my land on the crop share plan.

I was amazed by the eagerness of some settlers to start fires and let them run. They said, "Get the scrub cleared and get the country opened up." These fires however always [hurt] some body and besides it was burning up wood that would be usefull for fuel and for building too. Many of the first buildings were of logs. I told them, they would want this wood some day. They did not realize the advantage of having a patch of woodland on every [homestead] and would have been satisfied if they could change the whole country into bare prairie. Now we have to go ten miles or more to get our fire wood. This may have had its advantages too. The middle of my homestead appeared to be a real swamp 'till the timber was cleared off. But it dried up wonderfully afterwards. Now it is the best land on the place.

Clearing the land was a slow process, tho we depended much on fire and some lost their building mostly by somebody else's fire which was just lighted and allowed to run where it would.

It was some years befor the settlers considered raising wheat. The season seemed very short. We always had early frosts. For years our wheat was alway frosted before harvest. Most of the settlers who came to this neighborhood first had got discouraged and gone before I came here. Then I remember others who came, saw the heavy scrub and went away never to return. They thought it presented too great an effort.

Our first graded road was the so called ditch road running straight west from Swan River past the southern boundary of what is now Big Woody and on west. I think that was in about 1907 or 1908. Then by 1922 we had a road running from the ditch road north to the bridge on the river and on north of the river for about two miles. When we got the bridge and a few roads north of the river settlers came in more rapidly. By that time considerable land had been cleared and the new settlers could begin real farming and make a living. Horses were being used by this time and all the oxen had disappeared. By 1912 an ox had become quite a curiosity.

I might note a few personal incidents. One of the settlers in the early days attempted to home, less than one half mile away, lost his way in the woods and when he came out to realize where he was he was two miles away. My next neighbor who had taken the quarter section next to mine was over come by dispondency and tried to take his own life. We had an incident before there was a bridge across the river which nearly ended in a tragidy when a man and his family nearly drowned crossing the river with a horse and wagon. An other incident, in no way tragic happened when we tried to move a settler and his household effects across the river in the spring. We had only oxen and the wagon broke thru the ice. The oxen refused to pull. They would not even tighten up the traces. We had to get a neighbor with another wagon and horses and it took from ten o'clock in the morning 'till four in the afternoon befor we got out and across the river.

Figure 6   Portrait of Bob Dennison smoking a pipe, 1918. Glass Plate #11 by William Beal. By permission of Robert Barrow

Some one said back in 1906. Said, "We a just clearing this country for the second generation." The second generation is here and some are doing well. Very few of the original settlers are left. We have seen the district pass from the days of "oxen," to horses, to tractors and now to combines. What will be next?

W.m. S.A. Beal.

Rosa Shannon
(ca. 1880–1931)

There is almost no information to be uncovered about Rosa Shannon's life history in the public record. She was not enumerated in the 1919 Census, which is curious since her orature indicates that she and her family were part of the early Oklahoma migration; they were surely already in Edmonton before the border was shut to migrants in 1912. The census of 1919 does show a number of Shannons who immigrated from the United States in 1908, who were living at Section 53 Township 8 Range 5 near Junkins, Alberta, and who are counted by the census collector as "Negro." Among these are Ella and Arthur Shannon, who had a daughter named Mary, nine years old. It is possible that these are Rosa Shannon's relations, and that, for whatever reason, Rosa was not counted among them.

Despite the dearth of information on Rosa Shannon's life, it is nevertheless important to include her orature here for the way she articulates her affective attachment to the prairies of her childhood, and the way she envisions black and Indigenous histories and presences as intimately entangled. Moreover, the fire she describes that consumed her family house five weeks before Christmas recalls another, canonical, pioneer narrative, Susanna Moodie's *Roughing It in the Bush*, which describes a similar fire consuming her log home in the early part of winter 1837. But at the end of her narrative, Rosa Shannon, unlike Moodie, nevertheless declares her love of the country people who gave their lives to it at the end of her narrative.

Rosa Shannon's orature was originally published in Velma Carter and Wanda Leffler Akili's *The Window of Our Memories*.

"We gave our lives to this part of the country"

My father worked for the Government. He was a game warden and fire inspector and he worked at the camps and sawmills. He used to locate all of the lumber for these big mills. He used to go out and give an estimate of how many thousand feet of lumber they could get at a certain place. A lot of people thought he was a White man because he was very fair. He was half and half—his mother was a mulatto woman and his father was White and he was raised in Omaha, Nebraska. They went to Oklahoma before they came here.

We were in Edmonton, not prepared for travelling, and with all our household in this one sleigh. The man who brought us out was an experienced teamster and he knew how to pack a sled of household goods. We didn't have the bedsteads, just the mattresses and springs; he put them in the sleigh box and he filled it with other articles so we could ride comfortably upon them. It took us five days to come out here from Edmonton. We stopped at places that accommodated travelers going through; we would stay overnight and we would start out again the next morning. When we got to Chip Lake there was an old trap house, so we camped there until thaw up. It was just a one-room log cabin daubed with mud. It had a heater. I remember dad built a lean-to for his pack horse. It doesn't seem like anything to me now; it's been so long it seems like a dream.

We used to fish through holes we made in the lake ice. We had a pick and the boys would break the ice as much as they could and then take the axe and try cutting a hole—do what they could. You see we didn't know just how to do it. Then they would keep on working, breaking the ice until they worked down through several feet; they would throw hot bricks down until they melted a hole in the ice. When we got a hole we kept it open every day. We didn't always catch fish everyday, but we always got enough.

We stayed in this old trappers' cabin until the break up. When it came in the spring, mom, dad and the boys went up to the homestead and built a house up there. In spring we hunted for fresh meat—deer, wild pheasants, rabbits, bear, anything you wanted in the wild meat was there. Ducks and geese just swarmed the lakes—you could just go down there and rake up feathers by the bagful. This was in the summer, when they were getting ready to put on their fall feathers—getting ready for winter again. We used to hunt them but didn't have to go far because they'd fly right over our house; and we all could shoot.

After we moved up on the homestead, in the spring we had to dig wells. My dad walked out across the little cleared land that we had and he decided that down by the creek we'd dig a well; and it should be good water because the creek water was good. We dig about thirty feet and there was water, lovely water; it was real good.

Then we bought a team of oxen that weighed about twenty or thirty hundred; we used them to clear land. We'd get a chain and put it around a big bush and they'd pull it out by the root. We had what you call the squaw bush.[1] Everything had to come up by the root—cut it down and it would just sprout out the next year—then that ground would be easy to handle. The boys would just take a hand plow and plow it with a horse.

My mother would grow potatoes early in the spring, in order to get green vegetables as quick as possible for us. The early potato was a blue potato—I've seen purple potatoes, but not the blue ones like mother had. They came right up, sprouted out and started growing; and she would plant some kind of greens—I don't know what kind—but they were something that would come up quick; and then we used dandelions. We'd have a big pot of greens with salt pork—it was easy to keep salt pork. Mother would buy fifty pounds of lard in a can and would just put the pork in there and it wouldn't freeze; but if it did, we'd just thaw it and use it anyway.

We used to walk down to Entwistle—it was only about thirteen or fourteen miles from our place. Entwistle was the only place where there was a store at that time; and my brothers, myself, and my dad would walk down there if we needed anything. We just had to walk down and get it. When I was about eight years old I would go with them. It wouldn't take long to walk that far—we'd leave home early in the morning and we'd get there around noon, I guess. We'd stop and pick up a few things and get home before midnight with a pack on our backs. We kids would carry the light things and my father and the boys would have most of the load.

Our log house burned; it burned five weeks before Christmas. One morning we woke up and went to build a fire in the kitchen. My dad had neglected to take out some tar paper that was hanging down from under the shingles—just a little strip of it. Mother had told him to get up there and take that tar paper out. So this day we were in a hurry making the fire when a spark came out and caught the paper. It was about sixty degrees below zero and there was nothing we could do because our well was frozen up. We just had to take out our things and save what we could; that was what we did—took out our things and put them in the barn. We didn't have any stock anyway, but the oxen. We saved what we could and lost the rest because there were a lot of things we couldn't get out in time—like the stoves and heavy things like that.

Then we went to these bachelors who had helped us clear the land. They had built a house. "Come and live in our house," they said. There were

---

1   A shrub in the sumac family, also known as skunkbush sumac and sourberry, which has been used for its medicinal properties. It is native to the western half of Turtle Island.

just the two of them and they would batch in another little house they had built before, which was still standing there. So we lived in their house until spring.

We finally built a new house on a beautiful setting on the Foley Road. The road followed an Indian trail all the way from Edmonton to Vancouver; a lot of it is still there now. We built a beautiful log house with six rooms; it was made into an "L." The Swedish people helped my dad to build it. There were birch trees, beautiful birch trees, all over the yard. We had a beautiful yard; and then we had two big black spruce trees at the corner of the house where we had dog houses. We always had three dogs; they were smart and would take care of us and keep the bears away.

No one knows this, yes, this is why sometimes I cry in my heart; I just love it out here. I love my people but the memory of it hurts because we gave our lives to this part of the country. I would like to see something done here, put up at Wildwood to honor the old timers—the old pioneers. I thought of a drinking fountain—an old black face, red face, white face drinking fountain. The fountain could be there for that purpose and they could turn it on at certain times in the summer.

Alice Ethel Lewis
(1886–1960)

Alice Ethel Lewis was the ninth child of Daniel Vant Lewis and Charlotte (Campbell) Lewis, and a younger sibling to Mildred Jane Lewis Ware. She was born in Toronto on October 1, 1886, and died in Vulcan, Alberta, on September 25, 1960. She was a talented horsewoman, and refused to ride sidesaddle as was the protocol for women of her day. The Glenbow Archives hold pictures of her riding astride, even though she is wearing a long skirt and formal blouse. The picture confirms that she was very beautiful. Alice was also a talented carpenter like her father; a photo in the Glenbow Museum of one of her cabinets gives evidence of her skill and artistic vision.

The "Alberta" that Alice refers to in the following poem is not the province, but rather her sister, who died on December 29, 1916, at the age of twenty-six. The verses were composed on the one-year anniversary of her death, in 1917. The poem is part of Nettie Ware's files at the Glenbow Archives, and was collected as a result of writer Cheryl Foggo's detective work and years of relationship building with an elder named Mary Mallory and her son Don, who were close friends of Nettie Ware and the keepers of her archives. Foggo, worried about fire, damp, and other conditions that would harm their archives, persuaded the family to donate their papers to the Glenbow Museum. They are in the process of being scanned as part of the John Ware, Lewis Family fonds.

In Loving Memory of Alberta

You are with me, Dear Sister in thoughts today.
Although a year has slowly passed away.
From Brothers Sisters Parents and all
With sweet resignation. You answered the Call.

How we miss you. God alone can tell.
Still with you. I know. All is well.
When life's battles are won. Bye Gods Grace
Bye Your side. I hope for a place.

Your step grew feebler. Day bye Day.
Slowly You faded. Yet cheerful and gay.
Gradually weakening before we new.
Your hours on Earth were numbered and few.

With a Mothers tears upon your brow.
Goodbye, Alberta. You are dieing now.
Blessed Jesus in a fainter breath
Then silent. And cold You reposed in death.

Jefferson Davis Edwards
(1888–1979)

"No one had anything to say but me." So said Jefferson Edwards, energetic patriarch of the Amber Valley community from its formation in 1910 through to its dissolution as an all-black settlement in the 1960s. He was among the first of the Oklahoman pioneers to settle in what was formerly called Pine Creek, and it was his energy and influence that persuaded many in the Oklahoma community to follow.

Jefferson Edwards was born in Pine Bluff, Arkansas, in 1888 and grew up on a tobacco and cotton plantation owned by his father. In order to escape constant anti-black racism, the Edwards family joined the land rush to the Indian territories in Oklahoma. But the black community in Oklahoma was eventually subjected to as much segregation and racism as in Arkansas. Like his parents before him, Edwards read about the opportunities for blacks elsewhere—which for his generation was in western Canada—and in 1910, he headed north by train to Edmonton. As Edwards explained in a 1961 oral interview with Lloyd Chester Chamberlain, "I didn't really come here because it was segregation that caused me to come, but I was just looking around. I had just come out of school, and I was looking around. And when I came to Edmonton in July 1910, I liked Edmonton. I was 22."[1]

Edwards was one of the first to settle in Amber Valley, the most northerly community of black people that has ever existed. He quickly became a community leader, organizing everything from the popular three-day annual picnics, to the unbeatable Amber Valley Baseball Team (it boasted two left-handed pitchers), to lobbying the provincial government to bring roads and electricity to the community. In addition, he organized for the first high school to be built in Amber Valley; he

---

1   Oral interview with Jefferson Davis Edwards (1961). Lloyd and Eileen Chamberlain fonds, Athabasca Archives.

served on local school and hospital boards and became the vice-president of the local agricultural society and founding member of the Alberta Wheat Pool.

A clue about what motivated Edwards to be so active in his community lies in the name he gave his second son: Booker T. Edwards. Edwards patterned his community activism on the philosophies of Booker T. Washington (1856–1915), the African American educator, author, and political leader who advocated for coopera-tion with whites to raise funds and win support for schools and institutions for the betterment of black people.

Though Edwards was not a segregationist, he strikes a distinctly melancholy note at the end of his orature when he recalls the demise of Amber Valley as an all-black community after twenty-five years. Of the ten children born to Jefferson and Martha Edwards on the homestead in Amber Valley, only Kenneth, Booker, and Romeo continued to farm on the family place or on other farms nearby. Ironically, due to the success of Edwards's efforts, the majority of the pioneers' descendants, having been well educated in the institutions that Edwards himself helped build, ultimately moved away from the community. Edwards's orature underscores one of the bittersweet lessons of twentieth-century black history: the succours of commu-nity, including the sense of common history and common struggle, thrive best in a climate of anti-black racism. The "cloud" that Edwards saw as hanging over Amber Valley, then, was, really the successful integration of the second generation into the wider regional, national, and transnational world.

Edwards was presented with an Achievement Award in Humanities from the Alberta government in 1973 in honour of his contributions to sports, politics, and community life. He died in 1979 at the age of ninety.

The following orature was recorded and transcribed by Velma Carter and Wanda Leffler Akili, and is available in their *The Window of Our Memories* (1981).

"There was a cloud over Amber Valley"

I got on the train in Tulsa, Oklahoma in 1910. I waved goodbye, looked around but didn't know anyone in the car where I was sitting. The con-ductor came back and said, "there's another man going to Edmonton too—you go back with him." We went back; the man's name was Parson Harrison Sneed. I didn't know him, but we began to chat. When we got to Winnipeg we got off; I didn't know anything about a saloon, but he did. He walked along and saw one of the saloons, I guess. He said, "let's go in here." He asked for two glasses. The saloon keeper gave us two glasses with some kind of liquid in them. "Drink it down," he said. I took one mouthful spit it right over the counter. Old man Sneed laughed all the way to Edmonton.

I was going with this girl three years, off and on, in Oklahoma. In fact, I was going with two or three girls. Two of them were teachers, you know, and I could marry anyone I wanted—if I wanted to marry. So my mother said to me one day: "Which one of those girls are you going to marry?"

"I don't know, they're all nice; I don't want to marry now."

"Some of these boys are going to stick a knife in you one of these days—taking another boy's girl," my mother informed me. The girl I married, she was quiet. She never said a word about me going with anybody. I'd go with whoever I wanted and come there; she never said anything. I figured she was the best one. When I arrived in Edmonton I wrote back to her and told her I was not coming back; if she wanted to marry me, she must come to me. We were married on the 21st day of November, 1910. My wife and I have been together sixty-three years; we never had a quarrel. We lived in the same house fifty-two years and never moved. We have ten children—seven boys and three girls. The Lord has blessed us, the wife and I. As to grandchildren, oh Lord! Well I have to quit counting now, because by the time you quit counting there's another one born.

It wasn't long before we went out to Amber Valley; old man Saunders moved us out. We were out there for Christmas; we stayed with my father-in-law in a little old shack he had. He and we two were the only settlers out there then. When we went out there it was nothing but woods, just woods. All we had to live off of was rabbits and one thing or another. We spent a hard winter; in the spring there was no place to make a dollar and I wondered how I was going to get by another winter. I went to work for a man named Bill Dones, at thirty-five dollars per month; I worked for him for two months. I told the man I would give him sixty-two dollars for some cattle—he had a cow and a calf—so he just deducted the money and I had eight dollars coming. Then I had two head of cattle and the third one com-ing—the cow had a heifer calf; then I had three head cattle, but I had no hay for them. I told the man I would give him the eight dollars for him to let me cut some spots of hay down on the creek; so he let me cut the hay. A man came from Maidstone and he gave me twenty-five dollars to help him build a house. Oh that twenty-five dollars looked good. Now I was going to go to Edmonton with my father-in-law's two little ponies and his little old wagon—going to Edmonton to spend twenty-five dollars. It took me about three days.

When I got a little way from home it started to rain, and it rained, and it rained. I cut off on a road, knowing where it came out. It was night, and foggy and raining and I drove and I drove and I drove. I thought I was lost, as I should have been at old man Smith's. What am I going to do—I got no food, I got to let these horses graze. So I got out of the wagon. I can't turn the horses loose because I wouldn't be able to find them; I held one as the other ate. It was still raining; I was as wet as a rat, you know, sitting up on the wagon. The next morning I discovered that I had camped right back of Smith's garden. "Now ain't that something," I thought. Mr. Smith took me in; I got dry and I started out about noon. I drove until I came to a house. They said I could stay there. I went into the barn to put the horses up. I was wet; everything was wet—my clothes and my face and everything. I went into the house. They showed me a little room with no stove in it. I sat up all night long, until daylight, as wet as a rat. When daylight came I got out of there and drove to Edmonton.

I was quite a politician; I liked to work for the Government. I remember when the Liberal Government was in. You know how the Liberals do—they always put on something to get you to bite, you know. I wanted to vote Conservative because I knew this man in Athabasca who was running as a Liberal. They said, "You're going to get fired, you're going to get fired," because the man who was the boss of the road was a Liberal. Sure enough he did fire me. The day of the election there was only one vote for the Conservatives—that was me.

They gave me the job of enumerating all of the polls. They gave me a big territory because there wasn't anybody in there but me—they put me at the head. In 1917 I had that job; it was a big job. In 1917 they had the poll in my house. At that time all the power was in the enumerator's hand. You must have your naturalization papers in your hand when you come to vote—that was my rule for voters. I had a little office back there, so they had to come and show me their naturalization papers if their name was struck out on the wall. I would say, this man is a Liberal and don't have his naturalization papers. They had to come to me and I wouldn't let them vote if they were Liberals. We won by me cutting them out.

I have a good remembrance of the past because I was in it so long. I was on the Hospital Board for number of years. I was vice-president of the Community League; vice-president of the Agricultural Society for a number of years. I ran all the picnics from 1925 to 1940;[2] no one had any-

---

2   The annual picnics at Amber Valley were large and legendary two-day events that featured home cooking, baseball and other sports, and music. The picnics attracted a diverse array of people from far and wide, including black, white, and Indigenous neighbours (see, for example, Jennifer McKay).

thing to say but me. They turned it all over to me and I ran it. I think we did pretty well. I started working on the picnic three weeks before the day it was to open. You can do better with one guy. They would give me money, say like Athabasca, Colinton, and all the little towns. They would say, "Are you going to have a picnic this year?" We had races—horse races, riding steer—and I would have the money so nobody bothered me. I had people come from Winnipeg; people from Vancouver all came to that picnic. The M.D.A. would speak; there'd be boxing, wrestling, everything you could think of. That just kept me walking from one place to another, going from here to there. People would lay around until the next day—they wouldn't go home; they'd wait around that school house for the next day of the picnic.

In 1926 I organized the first baseball team in Pine Creek. Mr. Bowen, Mr. Mapp, Anthony Williams, Dave Saunders played on the team for a while. Later it was called Amber Valley Ball Team. We had a good team— Oswald Lipscombe, Cliff Brown, Sidney Brown, J.B. Brown and my three boys. Alonzo and Kenneth were both left handed—they were both pitchers.

I figured that our people just didn't have the money to send out kids to Athabasca school. So I went to the Divisional Board and asked them if they could give us a high school that would teach the ninth and tenth grades; because if we had to send our kids away we were not able to send them to Athabasca to go to those grades. Mr. Hodgson said, "I'll come to the house and figure out if that would last five years." He came to the house and we took a survey of how many children would be going to the school in five years, you see. "Yes" was the answer; we got the school that would teach ninth and tenth grades. Ruby taught the elementary grades and they go a man to teach the high school; otherwise Amber Valley would have just turned out eighth graders.

We used the school for everything—school, weddings, funerals, and church. Mr. Hodgson wanted to build another room on that school in the shape of an "L"; it would be big enough to have anything we wanted in it. But when Mr. Facey came in they hadn't built it, and I didn't convince him to build it. Mr. Hodgson said we would build a part on the west and we would make a folding door so we could use it for a hall, or anything we wanted to use it for. Facey wanted it on the end, so I couldn't say anything about a hall because he didn't want it—so I just gave up. Dr. Smith said Amber Valley had the best school in the province. We had the largest school; we had fifty some odd kids going to school at one time.

There was a cloud over Amber Valley; I predicted that there would be no more Amber Valley in twenty-five years—that just came out right. Well, you see the young generation they were growing up and getting educated and they were leaving; and none of us made any provision for the younger generation to stay. You couldn't live off a quarter section of land. Alright, what happened? When the young ones leave other races will come in and buy the quarter; because none of the old folk would be able to buy the land, some other race would buy it. Then there would be no more Amber Valley.

John Bell Bowden
(1888–1982)

The public record on John Bell Bowden is slim; there do not appear to be any Bowdens (not to be confused with Bowens included in this volume)[1] remaining in the Edmonton area, and so what can be known about his life beyond what he reveals in his orature is very little. Though he portered on the railroad ("I laid the business aside for about two years. I railroaded fourteen years. I didn't like it"), he died before Stanley Grizzle conducted his interviews with former porters for his 1997 book *My Name's Not George: The Story of the Brotherhood of Sleeping Car Porters*. Further genealogical research into US records may turn up living relatives who can shed more light on the contours of Bowden's life and his orature.

John Bell Bowden was the son of Nancy Nero Bowden and Lewis B. Bowden. He was born in 1888, and came to Edmonton in 1909 at the age of twenty-one. He homesteaded and cleared land in Vegreville and was a successful businessman and entrepreneur in Edmonton.

Interviewed by Velma Carter on May 8, 1973, Bowden reflects on the outmigration of the younger generations, including his own children, back to the United States. Bowden exhorts young people to remain in Canada and to be bold and make themselves a factor in public life. "The girl's gone, the boy's gone, I'm all by myself. But I *still* see a future here for the young girl and boy if they would only take it."

His detailed oral history remains available as an audio file on the Alberta's Black Pioneer Heritage website, organized in 2007 by the Black Pioneer Descendants' Society. The following is my transcription of Bowden's oral recording.

---

1   Deanna Bowen, whose work is included in this volume, is not a relation of John Bell Bowden.

❀

"Always be a factor in the community!"[2]

[…] I always had a craving to work. But not slave labour. So I decided to give up the ox team work [on his homestead in Vegreville] and come to Edmonton again. […] It was very trying times. People used to drive from Vegreville to Edmonton with a democrat, pick up groceries, but when they left Vegreville the team were nice and fat. When they got back, you could hang your hat on the horses' hips, just like hanging your hat on a rack. The black gnats and mosquitoes had ate them up. They were nothing but skin and bones, that's how bad the black flies and mosquitoes were. These black flies would bore right through your clothes, into your flesh. It was a trying time. People more in those days tried to help one another.

I used to drive a stage coach over the Low Level Bridge, bringing passengers from the north side to the south side CPR Station. There was no transportation then, see? It was quite a chore. But I always had desire and belief that there was a wonderful future in this part of the world. And I haven't regretted my sticking it out.

People didn't seem to mind doing a little "pioneering" in those days. Of course, we had a lot of drifters in and out, you know, but as far as people sticking with it, I don't know of anyone have stuck it out like I have. I am the only one that I know of that have been a permanent resident of Edmonton through those years. It's been tough.

When I first came from Vegreville I started as a delivery boy for the Gold Seal Liquor Company. Of course, through those days we'd have 60 and 65 below for a week at a stretch. I was out there hitting that cold, but stuck with it. Then I decided to cut out from that because prohibition were coming on. That was back in the teens. If a person wanted a bottle of liquor, you'd have to get a prescription from the doctor. Of course so many people would be sick and go to the doctor to get this bottle. Before prohibition they'd have bars then, you know, you could send a youngster there and the youngster go there open the door and peek in with a gallon can and the bartender would know what the youngster wanted, see? He'd go and get the pail and fill it up with beer, 25 cents a gallon. Give this youngster the pail, the youngster go down the street with the pail, taking the pail back home to mother and dad.

---

2   http://wayback.archive-it.org/2217/20101208162355/http://www.albertasource.ca/
blackpioneers/multimedia/oral/bowden.html.

Well, those times things were cheap. Living wasn't expensive then. I used to work just summertime, and didn't work in the winter. I just laid around and sucked my paw like a bear in wintertime, see? Didn't work. I didn't start to work in winter until after 1917. That's when I got married. Then I had to start to work. Couldn't loaf anymore. And of course it was quite a life. I found it quite trying. Didn't turn out just the way I planned.

[Velma Carter interjects: "But you did have two very, very sweet children!"]

That is why I have taken such an active part in church. I felt that it'd be doing my duty to raise them up to be part of the church. And that would be part of being a factor in the community. I used to offer my service to Shiloh,[3] who seemed to have been in a very tough position. I would offer my service to repair chairs, free gratis—I was in the furniture repair then—and one way that I tried to help make Shiloh's success (they'd been in very tough financial circumstances: they wouldn't have coal for the church), we had a club: Liberty Protection Society.

We were in the MacLeod Building at the time, holding all our meetings. We had a good club at the time, four- four hundred and fifty members, you know. It came up among our members that Shiloh was in very bad financial shape, so we brought it before the house. Should we clear out of the MacLeod Building and have our meetings in Shiloh church, and pay them so much a month rent? So we agreed on that. Well, we moved out of the Macleod Building—we had good quarters there—and moved into Shiloh. Our own way of operating was to put on programs, dances, and the like of that, to build up a treasure. That was our aim and object: build up a treasure to help people in the community that was in destitute and poor shape, see? Well now, some of the members in the church, they kicked on us, we wasn't having the dances in the church. Well, they had a meeting and said that we wasn't fit to be holding meetings in their church. And we should be thrown out. And they says, "Bowden isn't a fit man to be the head of no organization."

Well, I got a committee together and called on the Minister. I ask him why? What is it about my record that I'm not fit to be the head of an organization? Well, he went on to make some excuse—that I wasn't a member of the church and all of this and that. We moved out. That's another time we couldn't see eye to eye, Shiloh church.

---

3   Shiloh Baptist Church in Edmonton, on 107th Avenue at 103rd Street. One of two of the city's black churches.

Minister Smith walks up to me and says, "No, you will not fit." And then, that little breathing at me, I was going to go like two strange tomcats, and his son, he stepped in between us, and then my committee, they stepped in, and they parted us. And so, I cut out from then. No more assisting toward Shiloh church.

At the time I refused to carry on as President of the club, we had about $500 in the treasure. We would take the money out of treasure, make up hampers for people. Through those times there was no welfare. If people didn't have work they would just go hungry and suffer. So we made up hampers. For a man with two or three youngsters we'd make a hamper with a couple of slabs of bacon, apples, oranges, all different kinds of fruit, cereals. Have you seen these apple boxes? We'd fill up those apple boxes. One fellow had a car, we'd put these hampers in the car and go and deliver these hampers around. That is the way our club operated, helping people that was in destitute condition.

I tried to get some of the members to see where that we could help otherwise. People who had initiative to go out and get education, and be a factor in the community—let's sponsor that person with money, like we give these hampers out. Some of the members says, well no. If these people want help, let them come into our club. I was always a man that hate to be accused of being the bell cow—of running everything. One reason I pulled out of the Liberty Protection Society: they had an election, wanted me to run; I refused. If there was an election—city or provincial, or what not—they would form a committee to wait on that candidate and write a report. They told me, go ahead and look after that. They put it all on me. Then some of them got up in the air because I'm running everything.

[Velma Carter: "Did we ever have any black people running for offices?"]

I tried to talk that up among the younger people. To take an active part in civic and provincial elections. But it seem like the initiative wasn't there to get out. I says, Make an effort! We taxpayers, we should have men on those streetcars. We should have men on the police force.

I figure a man is like a turtle. If you never stick your neck out, you never get nowhere. That have been my motto ever since I left home very young. I stuck my neck out. Sometime it got pretty near chopped off, but I stuck it out anyway, see?

I hate to keep telling these things that I did, and like of that; I like to tell about what the other fella did, too, and what the other fella didn't do. The other fella didn't take the chances I take. Now, I think it was the last store that was operated here by the coloured people. That was UNA—United

Negro Association Grocery.[4] That was on 97th Street, right across form Alberta Flour and Feed. The coloured people would buy shares. And they owned the association, see? That went for a while. I bought shares in that.

[Velma Carter: "Did you ever get your shares out?"]

I'm coming to that!

I bought shares in that grocery store—which was always my idea: be a factor in the community!—well, it operated for a while. Every month we had to pay the wholesale for the stock that had been disposed of. The wholesaler would come and restock the place, see, what we needed. Well, the manager, he turned out to be kind of a bad manager with the wholesale house. The wholesale house come down demanding their money, and the manager couldn't produce the money. We had a meeting and he explained that the wholesale was coming down they didn't have enough money and bank to meet these expense. We says, wholesale wants to clear out, let them clear out. And the manager he says, I will replace this money. Well, we clear out the store, and he said he would replace them. He stayed around town for a while, and after a while he disappeared, and that's where my shares went!

But you see, I've always desired the black man to show that he is a factor in the community. We have got to show we have an interest in ourselves before the other fella will take an interest in us.

What have we got today in Edmonton? One thing about Edmonton, certain people have segregationist feelings. But the size this place is, we should have some kind of a business. Nothing. What's wrong? There is something wrong. I often tell my wife, I wish I was about forty years younger. We've got boys here studying to be a lawyer. You might know who I'm talking about. A lawyer! Why don't he throw his hat in there as an alderman? Why not get in there? I often think, we've been in the States. And we've seen people really doing big things, when we can do big things right here. So many girls and boys get their education and away to the States they go.

---

4   To date I have not found any histories of a United Negro Association Grocery in Alberta. It may have been associated with Marcus Garvey's United Negro Improvement Association (UNIA), which at one time operated two grocery stores—but these, as I understand it, were in New York. It is also possible that these were started by Reverend George Washington Slater, who explains in his essay "Why I Became a Socialist" (included here) that he wanted to open a food co-op in 1907–8 in Chicago, but that he was prevented from doing so by the manufacturers. It is significant that such a co-op *did* exist for a time in Alberta.

That boy of mine, he's in San Francisco, and he just thinks it's a wonderful place. When I started this business of mine I had him in view. So when I get a certain age you take it over and go on. I wanted to turn my business over to him, but he couldn't see it. He seen other boys in the army. What did he do? Got to get in the army. I couldn't keep him out of the army. I wouldn't even sign his papers to get him in the army. Someone else sign it. I says, I'm building up business here for you. At the time he quit me and went into the army, I had four men working for me. I had more work than I could do taking out basements and moving and all like of that, see. I had a good business. War come on, I couldn't even get a girl to answer the telephone. I had to answer the phone and look out for business. People says to me, "Bowden, you'll kill yourself working the way you do." I laid the business aside for about two years. I railroaded fourteen years. I didn't like it. But I couldn't operate my business by myself. The girl's gone, the boy's gone, I'm all by myself. But I *still* see a future here for the young girl and boy if they would only take it.

I can't understand why my people don't take more interest. One thing that made me feel proud here last summer: I seen one black man on the bus, driving a bus. Made me feel proud. I don't know who he is. We've got a man on the mail. Why can't we have more?

Chief Buffalo Child Long Lance
(Sylvester Long)
(1890–1932)

During his time in Calgary, Long Lance claimed to be a "full-blooded" Blackfoot Indian Chief, born in southern Alberta during the final years of the buffalo hunt. But, as historian Donald B. Smith uncovered in his biography *Long Lance, the Glorious Imposter* (1982), in fact, he was born Sylvester Long in Winston-Salem, North Carolina, in 1890 to racially mixed parents who had themselves been born in slavery.

The Long family undoubtedly had real claims to Indigenous and white ancestry, but in the context of the American south and the logic of the "one drop" rule (wherein a single "drop" of black ancestry going back any number of generations effectively made one legally and socially black), the family had trouble asserting their in-betweenness. The local whites of Winston-Salem, noting that Long Lance's father, Joe, was somewhat dark in complexion, suspected him of having black ancestry. Sylvester's mother, Sally, was phenotypically Indigenous and claimed Lumbee (then known as Croatan) ancestry. Ultimately, since the Long family could not prove they were *not* black, they were classed as non-white, and hence as blacks. Long Lance thus grew up in African American religious and educational institutions. His father worked as a school janitor in the whites' West End School but Sylvester attended the Depot Street School for Negroes and the family attended a segregated black church (Smith 32–3).

In the summer of 1904 at the age of thirteen Long left North Carolina to work for Buffalo Bill's Wild West Show. Since African Americans were barred from performing in any of the major acts in the circus, Long Lance was regularly phenetecized (or read) as Indigenous. His time with the Buffalo Bill show demonstrated to him that doors to other, more promising, worlds than that of segregated Winston-Salem might be opened.

In 1909, on the strength of the few phrases of Cherokee he picked up at the Wild West show, and with some help from his family embellishing the extent of his Indigenous ancestry, Long Lance was admitted to the famous Carlisle Indian Residential School in Pennsylvania. Ironically, in a school dedicated to assimilating Indigenous students, Long Lance learned Indigenous customs, stories, and language from other students, thereby transforming himself from a young black man to an "Indian." He went in as Sylvester Long but graduated in 1912 at the top of his class as Sylvester "Chahuska" Long Lance (Smith 50).

Long Lance went on to attend St. John's Military Academy, where he got the equivalent of a high school diploma, then won a prestigious presidential appointment to West Point. Long Lance failed the West Point examination—deliberately—so that on August 4, 1916, he could enlist in the Canadian army to fight in the First World War (the US had not yet entered the war). When the war ended Long Lance made the unusual decision of asking that his point of discharge be Alberta.

While Long Lance was occasionally "mistaken" for black on the prairie, and did encounter anti-black sentiment there, keeping his black ancestry to himself, he went very far. In the 1920s he worked as a journalist for the *Calgary Herald*. In 1922 he was adopted by the Blood Nation south of Calgary and began a freelance writing career as a "full-blooded" chief, Chief Buffalo Child Long Lance. In 1928 he published his "autobiography," *Long Lance* with the Cosmopolitan Book Company, which won acclaim as an "authentic" Blackfoot memoir about growing up on the prairies during the last days of the buffalo hunt.

Long Lance also starred in Douglas Burden's famous 1930 Hollywood feature film *The Silent Enemy*, about Indigenous life prior to contact. (The silent enemy of the film's title is hunger.) By then rumours about Long Lance's ancestry began to threaten the "authenticity" of the picture, and the film studio sent private investigators to North Carolina to investigate his origins. In 1932, amid speculation that the famous Indian writer and actor was black, Long Lance shot himself.

Though Long Lance never publicly acknowledged or confirmed his black identity, he seems compelled in much of his writing to hint at his life circumstances. He frequently writes about fraudulent identities, cultural transformation, and adoption. In the following semi-autobiographical story, "My Trail Upward," originally published in Hearst's *International Cosmopolitan* in June 1926 (Glenbow Archives M-690-14), Long Lance tells a tale of cultural assimilation—not from black to Indigenous, as in Long Lance's own life, but from Indigenous to white. It is a story that depends on troubling stereotypes about Indigenous people even as it thematizes Long Lance's journey to becoming a writer.

In the chapter "What's in an Indian Name?" the third chapter in his fictional[1] *Long Lance: The Autobiography of a Blackfoot Indian Chief* (1929), the author

---

1   For a longer meditation on the implications of reading this text as a fiction, see Vernon, "The First Black Prairie Novel."

considers Indigenous naming practices and the issue of an authentic public iden-tity. In "Wolf Brother," the twelfth chapter from the same work, we see the author's gifts for crafting a fictional narrative: Long Lance deftly develops Eagle Plume as a sympathetic figure and carefully draws the reader along by heightening tension in the story. These excerpts suggest the ways the work might be productively read not as a fraudulent memoir but as a well-crafted novel, and the first published novel in the black prairie archive.

In Long Lance's "Canoe Song," a poem housed at the Glenbow Archives (M-690-8), written in both English and what Long Lance calls "Indian," the author articulates a poignant longing for home and belonging through the voice of an Indigenous speaker, something that in the context of anti-black sentiment on the prairies in the 1920s would have been much more difficult to do as a black or mixed-race man. Finally, in the poem "Death Song of Long Lance" (Glenbow Archives M-690-7), the author finds a way of questioning the artifice of his life. The word "real" is tellingly repeated in the poem a total of eight times, and the speaker poignantly concludes that "This life I have lived […] is not real."

❀

My Trail Upward: I Took It Because I, a Blackfoot Indian, Wanted to Live Like a White Man

Missionaries on a Blackfoot Indian Reservation in southern Alberta taught me my A B C's—but an old-fashioned bar tender out in Laramie, Wyo-ming, first thrilled me with the idea that I might become educated and really make something out of my life.

This man was a Pennsylvania Dutchman and he so happened to know about Carlisle Indian School. He asked me one day when I was in the old Central Bar with a crowd of cowboys why I did not go there and become educated. He explained that it was free for Indians.

"But I can't even speak good English," I told him.

"Well," he said, "you can educate yourself for entrance to Carlisle by reading. Read, read all the time—anything and everything you come across."

I think that bit of advice changed the trend of my whole life. I was at that time sixteen years old and a full-fledged cowhand. I could break and ride bucking horses. I could barely sign my own name and spell out words. But I could ride almost anything that stood on four feet. I was proud to be a cowpuncher; that was doing pretty well at that for an ignorant, half savage young Indian buck.

A few days before I met this old bartender—I'm ashamed that I've forgotten his name—I had been fired from a ranch fifteen miles west of Laramie. At that time my temper was as wild and unbridled as a wolf's and this was the cause of the trouble.

This all happened in 1907 and I'd come down from the reservation to follow the round-ups. I had made this step on my own initiative because I was curious to know about this Pale Face who had conquered my people and compelled us to live on comparatively small reservations. Up to this time I had never done anything but follow the Indian's line of least resistance—hunt and fool around with horses. I always went on the trail alone and I thought a lot. Finally one day I made a resolution; I was going to meet the white man on his own grounds, study him and find out just what sort of fellow he was.

My first step in this great adventure was to head south and work the round-ups. I followed the round-ups all over the north-western plains and by late fall found myself on the Carr ranch west of Laramie. Carr had a nephew named Haley who was spending his college vacation on the ranch. Haley and I struck up a friendship and in the end he fixed it for me to stay on all winter—after haying and round-up should be complete.

The last round-up we made was on one of the outlying ranches, called the Ghost Ranch, so we moved our *remuda*[2] over there. On the third morning it was my turn to wrangle in the "string" horses. It was a cold, windy morning in late October and I had to roll out at four o'clock. Prowling coyotes were still yipping their dolorous chorus here and there in the gray blueness just preceding dawn.

I was riding along with my hand over my mouth chanting my medicine song so that the herd would not be frightened when I should come upon them in the darkness, when suddenly my horse stepped into a badger hole, jumped, tripped, fell and threw me to the ground which such force that I had to gasp for breath. I got up, stunned, and saw Curly tearing with kicking heels over toward the large herd of horses I had come out after. He was bucking for all he was worth, trying to kick off the saddle, which was now under his belly. Just before he reached the herd his front feet became locked in the bridle-reins, and I limped over and got him.

The wind was terrific and every time I folded the saddle-blanket and threw it over Curly's back he would buck wildly and send it speeding on

---

2 Term most frequently used in the southwest and Texas for all saddle horses on a roundup that are thrown together and constitute the remount horses for the cowboys.

the wind unfolded, flattened out and flapping like a big bat. I now remembered that the boss-hostler had warned me on the night before that Curly was an ornery horse, and that I had better watch him. It took me nearly a half hour to get the saddle on without the blanket. Curly bucked and tried to kettle me at every step of the three-mile journey back to the corral. Breakfast would be over by now, I knew; and the boys would be smoking and waiting for their "strings." I got madder and madder at each hop.

I was not fit to speak to when I finally reached the corral and found the boss-hostler waiting at the gate with several men. I drove my horses into their corral and started to turn around and go after another bunch of horses which had nighted in a different locality. But Curly absolutely refused to budge in any direction except that of the corral gate. Every time I put the spurs to him he reared as high as he could go and threatened to check back on me. The boss-hostler was cussing and I was stewing to the bursting point quietly.

Finally, when Curly jumped up on his hind feet and snorted out his resentment for about the eighth time, the naked Indian in me exploded. I jerked myself to a standing position in the stirrups and hurled my fist as hard as I could on top of his head. To my surprise, he sank to the ground on his knees, out. It was an inglorious thing for me to do and the boss-hostler rightly called me a name. I retaliated, and we were closing in to fight when some of the fellows grabbed us and held us apart.

Naturally, I was fired. And, incidentally, that was the last ranch job I ever had. I walked the sixteen miles into Laramie very downcast. Just when I had thought that I had a steady job and was making my way in the world, it all ended so quickly I hardly knew how it happened. I resolved not to cut my hair again; I would go back to the blanket.

I went into Laramie and renewed an acquaintance with Frank Stone—"the Nevada Wonder"—at that time the world's champion bucking horse rider. He had ridden the famous short-legged Steamboat to a sitting position at the Laramie Frontier Day that fall, and I had ridden a horse called Medicine Bow. He thought I could ride, and that is why he invited me to go around with him and his gang. Stone introduced me to the bartender of the Central Bar, and it was he who first put the idea of the Carlisle Indian School into my mind.

But it was only an idea tucked way in the back of my brain. At that time I thought I was through with the white man. I thought they had mistreated me because I was an Indian. And that afternoon I bought an unbroken cayuse for seven dollars, threw my tarpaulin over his back, in lieu of a saddle, and went north to the Indians, breaking him as I rode.

Shortly after this I was included among a band of Indians selected to make a tour with Colonel Cody, who was known all over the world as "Buffalo Bill." We traveled widely for a year—I do not know where we traveled, as all cities looked alike to me then, but I often see places now where I know I have been before. I was still a boy, and my bobbed hair had again gown so that I could braid it.

[...]

On the Laramie bartender's advice, and on the strength of the smattering of the "three R's" I had learned at a mission, I began forthwith to read everything I could get my hands on. I bought a dictionary to help me translate the English tongue. I never passed a word in my reading without finding out its full meaning, with its principal synonyms and antonyms. By the fall of 1909 I had prepared myself for entrance to the Carlisle Indian School.

Though I had a tremendous will to learn, my brain was as tough as raw buffalo meat when I arrived at this famous old institution. I could not make the first-year class, but the instructors, evidently sensing that I was a willing student, shoved me into the class anyway, and sat up nights teaching me on the side. Miss Adelaide B. Reichel taught me English at night, and Major Rudy would sit up until one o'clock in the morning trying to drum into my thick skull the intricacies of algebra. I was almost a hopeless case, but I had one faculty which saved me, and that was my thoroughness for learning every detail on a thing, and once learning it, never forgetting. Years later when I was attending a white school—St. John's Military School, Manlius, New York—I sat up at nights and worked the geometry and trigonometry problems for nearly every other student in my section of Hadley Hall—because I had learned every rule as I went and they had not.

I skipped the junior class at Carlisle and graduated in 1912 as the honor graduate and valedictorian—with a senior year's average of 92½ points. Having gone into athletics at Carlisle, to offset the indoor life and the mental strain of learning, I now found that it was possible to go on to higher schools on my athletic ability. I attended Conway Hall, Dickinson College, a year, and then received a scholarship to St. John's Military School, at Manlius, where I took postgraduate work and graduated in 1915 with a silver medal for class and athletic honors.

Here it was that I learned one of the most important things that have to do with white man's society—the art of conversation. It came about in a peculiar manner.

During my first year at St. John's one of the boys who was friendly with me said: "Long Lance, why are you always so silent? Why don't you talk more? You know, the cadets like you but they can't understand why you are so backwards about talking."

Of course it had never occurred to me before to "make" conversation. Among themselves, Indians speak seldom and then only when they have something important to say. They never just talk to be talking. And now I saw for the first time that there was different custom among white men.

I started at once to change all this in my own make-up. I began to make talk consciously—little talk about little things. Now—ten years later—it comes natural for me to converse, but I had to learn how to do it just as I had to learn how to read English or tie a white man's tie.

There was another important thing that I learned at St. John's. General William Verbeck had a lot to do with that—just as he had a great deal to do with instilling into me the polish and graces of modern civilization.

Since the day back in Wyoming when I had lost my temper and popped poor old Curly on the head, I had had two dangerous fights, both before I entered school. In one of them, a friend had knocked me senseless with a six-shooter to prevent me from driving a knife into a fellow being on whose chest I sat. Two weeks later a six-shooter leveled at this same fellow being was knocked out of my hand just as I was pulling the trigger. It is only necessary to say that a feud existed between us, and he had sworn to get me.

At St. John's this old temper, which I thought I had conquered, popped up again one day and I struck a fellow cadet. I was court-martialed and reduced to the ranks; and General Verbeck had me into his private office for a talk.

He pointed out to me that my uncontrolled temper was the only thing that would hold me back in life, and warned me that if I should ever let it get the better of me at West Point I would be expelled in disgrace. I was under appointment to West Point by President Wilson, but on the following March I purposely "flunked" the entrance examinations at Fort Slocum, and decided that the best place for a chap who could not keep from disgracing himself and his friends was fighting under the colours of an army that was upholding the world cause. So back west and north I came. Three weeks after I had "coughed" and said "Ah-h" for the medical officer, I was on my way to France on the Olympic, as "Sergeant B.C. Long Lance," C Company, 97th Battalion, Canadian Expeditionary Force."

What General Verbeck did not teach me about holding my temper the war did. After seeing men gutted and lacerated day in and day out intermittently for nearly three years, the vengeful ego in me disappeared. It has been supplanted by a desire to fight only for things big enough to be a principle of protection to others.

With the war over, eventually I was sent home and demobilized as a captain. And then I had to begin all over again. At twenty-five I had adopted the white man's customs, comforts and ways of thinking—and yet I had no way to earn a living commensurate with these newly acquired tastes.

Some friends suggested I go to Los Angeles where two professions might open up to me—moving picture acting or professional boxing. In France I had been Canadian light-heavy weight champion and I had been told that I could go to the very top of the heap if I continued fighting.

Almost immediately after I landed in California I was offered $500 to fight—and the heavy barred doors into the movies were open to me.

And, strangely enough, just then two more opportunities presented themselves: one a two-year army scholarship to study journalism in Canadian universities; and the other a reporter's job on the *Calgary Herald*.

That night I wired the *Herald* to hold that thirty-dollar-a-week job.

That was six years ago—and never for a day have I regretted my choice. Had I taken a different road I might have been light-heavy champion of the world—Jack Dempsey told me he would make me that in six months—and I might have been a movie star. And if I had accepted that university scholarship I might be working today on the *Calgary Herald* at thirty dollars a week.

As it is I am pretty much of a free man. I travel about a bit, lecture a bit, write a bit—and when summer comes I'm up in the Rockies. My play-work at Banff is better than being all the movie stars and prize-fight champions in the world.

Two or three times a year I go back to my Indian reservation, where I spent my boyhood and where my people still live. I was proud when they elected me a Chief. I had won my spurs fighting side by side with the white men—and my tribe had recognized this.

I'm proud to be as much like a white man as I am—but I'm proud, too, of every drop of Indian blood that runs through my veins.

I'm proud of my Indian heritage—and I'm proud, too, of the land and people of my adoption.

I have reached no dizzy heights of material success, but I have succeeded in pulling myself up by my boot straps from a primitive and backward life into this great new world of white civilization.

Anyone with determination and will can do as much.

Long Lance: The Autobiography of a Blackfoot Indian Chief

What's in an Indian Name?

In the civilization in which we live, a man may be one thing and appear to be another. But this is not possible in the social structure of the Indian, because an Indian's name tells the world what he is: a coward, a liar, a thief, or a brave.

When I was a youngster every Indian had at least three names during his lifetime. His first name, which he received at birth and retained until he was old enough to go on the war-path, was descriptive of some circumstance surrounding his birth. As an instance, we have a man among the Blackfeet whose name is Howling-in-the-Middle-of-the-Night. When he was born along the banks of the Belly River in southern Alberta, the Indian woman who was assisting his mother went out to the river to get some water with which to wash him. When she returned to the teepee she remarked: "I heard a wolf howling across the river." "Then," said the baby's mother, "I shall call my son 'Howling-in-the-Middle-of-the-Night.'"

This birth name of the youngster was supposed to be retained by him until he was old enough to earn one for himself; but always when he grew old enough to play with other children his playmates would give him a name of their own by which he would be known among them, no matter what his parents called him. And this name often was not flattering; for we Indian boys were likely to choose some characteristic defect on which to base our names for our playmates—such as Bow Legs, Crazy Dog, Running Nose, Bad Boy, or Wolf Tail. Instances are known where these boyhood nicknames have been so characteristic of the youngster that they have superseded his birth name and stuck him with him throughout his life, if he was not able to earn a better one on the war-path.

But the real name of the Indian was earned in the latter instance: when he was old enough to go out for his first fight against the enemy. His life name depended on whatever showing he should make in this first battle. When he returned from the war-path the whole tribe would gather to witness the ceremony in which he would be given his tribal name by the chief of the tribe. If he made a good showing, he would be given a good name, such as: Uses-Both-Arms, Charging Buffalo, Six Killer, Good Striker, Heavy Lance, or Many Chiefs. But if he should make a poor showing his name might be: Crazy Wolf, Man-Afraid-of-a-Horse, or Smoking-Old-Woman. Thus, an Indian's name tells his record or what kind of man he is.

But a man was given many opportunities to improve his name as time went on. If he should go into some future battle and pull off some unusual exploit against the enemy, he would be given a better name. Some of our great warriors have had as many as twelve names—all good names, and each one better than the one that preceded it. No matter how many names were successively given to him, all of his past names belonged to him just the same, and no one else could adopt them. These names were just as patently his as if they had been copyrighted; and even he, himself, could not give one of them away. Indian names were handed out by the tribe, not the family, and no man could give his name even to his own son, unless the chief and the tribe should ask him to, as a result of some noteworthy deed his son had performed. I know of only three or four instances where this has happened, and it is the rarest honor that can befall a person—the honor of assuming one's father's name. In my day every son had to earn his own name.

The foregoing is the reason why no old Indian will ever tell you his own name. If you ask him he will turn to some third person and not for him to tell you. The reason for this is that he is too modest to brag of his exploits on the war-path. His names are alike decorations in the white man's army, and the Indian has a certain reticence against advertising his bravery by pronouncing his own name in public.

There are certain "Chief Names" among the Indians which the original owners made so distinguished that the tribe never allows them to pass out. These names are perpetuated in successive generations, and after a while they become a dynastical name, such as "Ptolemy" in the Egyptian line of rulers. One of my names, Chief Buffalo Child, is a dynastical name and title among the Blood Band of Blackfeet living at Cardston, Alberta. The original Chief Buffalo Child was killed in battle, in what is now Montana, more than eighty years ago; and years ago when I became a chief of this band his name was resurrected and perpetuated in the present holder of the title—thanks to our war chiefs, Mountain Horse and Heavy Shields, and to the Blood Missionary, the Reverend Cannon S. Middleton.

I have four other names: Night Traveler, Spotted Calf, Holds Fire, and Long Lance. Of these latter four I value Spotted Calf the most, because it was given to me by my adopted mother, Spotted Calf, wife of Sounding Sky. They were parents of the famous Indian outlaw, Almighty Voice—whose lone-handed battle against the Royal Northwest Mounted Police has become a conspicuous page in nonwestern history. This wonderful woman, Spotted Calf—daughter of the renowned Chief One Arrow—who stuck to her son throughout his sensational siege and shouted advice to him throughout a rain of bullets, is still living (1928) on the One Arrow Indian Reserve at Duck Lake, Saskatchewan. I think her name ranks with those of great warriors, and that is why I value it, and her motherhood. [...]

Wolf Brother

[...] In our band at that time we had a very noted warrior and hunter named Eagle Plume. It was the custom in those days, when the men were being killed so often and the women were growing to outnumber them, for one warrior to have from three to five wives. It was the only way that we could make sure that all of our women would be taken care of when they should reach old age.

But this warrior, Eagle Plume, had only one wife. He was a tall, handsome warrior of vigorous middle age, and but for one thing he was well contented with his pretty wife. She had served him well. She was always busy preparing his meals and waiting upon him; and tanning the hides of the furry denizens of the wilderness, which were killed in large numbers by this famous hunter of the Blackfeet. But she had no children.

Indians are extremely fond of children, and to have no offspring is regarded as a calamity, a curse. Boy children were always preferred; as they could grow up to be hunters and warriors, while girl children could be of little economic use to the family or the tribe.

Eagle Plume thought of adding another wife to his camp, one who might bear him a child; but he loved his faithful young woman and he was reluctant to put this idea into execution. He was unlike many men: he could love but one woman.

However, children were wanted, and Eagle Plume's wife had spent many hours crying alone in her teepee, because the Great Spirit had not given her the power to present him with a baby with which to make their life complete. We heard our old people discuss this, and many times they would send us over to Eagle Plume's camp to play and to keep them company. They would treat us like their own children and give us attentions which we would not receive even from our own parents.

Like all great Indian hunters, Eagle Plume liked most to hunt alone. As we camped in the Northern Rockies that winter, he would go out by himself and remain for days. He would return heavily laden with the pelts of otter, mink, black wolf, marten and lynx. It was well through the winter towards spring, and the snow was still very deep, when early one morning he set out on one of his periodic hunting trips into the wild country to the north of where we were camping. That evening as he was making his way down a mountain draw to seek out a camp-site, a wolf came out of the bush and howled at him in the bitter white twilight.

It was a big wolf, not a coyote, but one of the largest specimens of the huge black timber-wolf. With the true curiosity of the wolf, it watched Eagle Plume make camp, then it went quietly away.

"Go now, my brother," said Eagle Plume. "Tomorrow I will follow you for that thick fur on your skin."

And so the next morning, running on his snow-shoes, and with a large round ball in his muzzle-loader, Eagle Plume went on the trail of the wolf.

It was easy for an Indian to follow its path, because its tracks were bigger than any wolf tracks he had ever seen. It led Eagle Plume [on] a far journey across a hanging mountain valley and on through a heavily forested range of low-lying mountains. The wolf seemed to be bent steadily on a trail that lay due north. Nothing, not even the fresh cross-trails of caribou, had swerved it from this purposeful course. It acted not like a hunted thing evading its pursuer.

Eagle Plume had traveled all day, and the late afternoon sun was making long shadows, when suddenly as he peered ahead, he saw the big wolf run out on a naked ridge that rolled up from a bushy mountain plain.

It had been snowing for some hours in a quiet, intense way; and with the descent of the sun, the wind was rising with fitful whines, making little swirling gusts of snow-drift on the white surface of the land, which foretold the approach of a mountain storm. The new snow had made the going heavy for Eagle Plume, and it must have been tiring to the wolf, too; for it was now sinking to its belly with each step.

Eagle Plume was a tireless hunter, and he knew that if the wolf kept to the open country, he, with the superiority of his snow-shoes, could wear it down. Already the big, shaggy creature was showing signs of fatigue, and the intrepid hunter was remorselessly closing up the distance that his quarry was losing.

After his first view of the wolf on the ridge, Eagle Plume lost sight of it for a while; then he saw it again, and when the sun, with its sinister attendants of two false suns, touched the rim of the mountains to the west, the wolf remained in plain view all of the time. The Blackfoot was sweeping forward on the bumpy surface of the great rolling sea of snow at a long, tireless lope, while the wolf seemed to be floundering along in distress.

The wind continued to rise, and soon the country was enveloped in a stinging, blinding chaos of drifting snow. A blizzard was coming up. And even the wolf, wild denizen of the region as he was, was now seeking harborage.

The mountain valley lay flat and expressionless under its snowy mantle. The only relief to the landscape was a pine grove which stood like an island straight ahead.

A blizzard had no terrors for a good hunter like Eagle Plume, when there was wood and shelter in sight. He knew that the wolf was making for cover, and he hurried his footsteps so that he might overtake it and make his kill before it escaped into the pines or became lost in the darkness of the raging blizzard.

But the storm gathered in strength and violence, and Eagle Plume was forced to summon all of his remaining energies to reach the shelter of the trees before darkness and death should overtake him. When, panting and exhausted, he at last made his objective, he had long since lost all sight and track of his game.

He rested briefly and then began to skirt the lea side of the pines for a suitable place to make fire and camp. As he was doing this he suddenly became aware that the wolf was watching him from a near-by snow-bank. Cautiously he turned in his tracks and leveled the long, cold barrel of his gun straight between a pair of furtive gray eyes—wild, slanted eyes, which looked calmly at him like two pieces of gray flint. He paused for a second and then pulled the trigger. There was a flash in the nipple—but no explosion. The priming had been affected by the drifting snow.

With his teeth he pulled the wooden stopper of his powder-horn and poured dry powder into the pan, keeping his eyes on the steady gaze of the wolf, which made no effort to move or escape. As he deftly reloaded and primed his gun, he spoke softly to the wolf in the manner of the Indian, saying:

"Oh, my brother, I will not keep you waiting in the cold and snow. I am preparing the messenger I will send you. Have patience for just a little while."

As he shook the dry powder onto the pan of his gun, the wolf, without any previous movement of warning, suddenly made a mighty leap—and vanished.

The swift-gathering darkness and the howling blizzard made useless any further effort to capture this remarkable pelt, and realizing for the first time the futility of his quest, Eagle Plume now laid aside his gun and unloosened an ax which hung at his belt, and made hurried preparations to shield himself from the blizzard. He cut down some dead spruce for a fire, and then made himself a shelter of mountain bushes.

During a slight pause in his labor, his ear, keenly attuned to the voices of the wilderness, caught a strange sound. When he listened intently and caught it a second time there was no mistaking what it was. It was the wail of a child.

Throwing down his ax and wrapping his blanket about his head and body, he stumbled out into the darkness and hurried blindly in the direction whence the wail had come. As he jogged along through the swirling snow, his ears alert to hold the wailing sound above that of the screeching wind, one of his snow-shoes caught in something and he fell face-forward into the snow. As he got up and reached down to pick up his blanket, his hand touched the heavy object which had tripped him. He kneeled down and looked at it—it was a woman—an Indian woman—a dead Indian woman.

Still the wailing continued. He walked around and around trying to locate it. It seemed to come from the air, not from the ground. From point to point he walked and stopped and listened. Finally he walked up to a tree, and there, hanging high out of reach of prowling animals, he found a living child in a moss bag—a baby a few months old.

Snug in its native cradle, packed with dry moss and rabbit skins, it had suffered none from the cold.

He built a great fire and made a camp, and slept that night with the foundling wrapped in his arms. In the morning he snared some rabbits, and slitting the throat of one with his hunting knife, he pressed the warm blood into the mouth of the hungry infant.

With his ax and some saplings it did not take him long to knock together a rough sleigh. And so he came back to our camp in the valley, dragging the unknown dead woman behind him; and underneath his capote he carried the child in its moss bag.

When the people of our camp came out to meet this strange company of two living and one dead, he handed the baby to his wife and said:

"Here is our child; we will no longer have need for a strange woman in our lodge."

Eagle Plume's wife cradled the child in her arms and warmed it to her bosom; and our old people said that the fires of maternity kindled in her at the touch of the infant, and that milk for its sustenance flowed in those breasts that for so long had been dry. That night as we sat around the camp fire and Eagle Plume told his story with all the graphic detail of an Indian recital, a big wolf cried its deep-throated howl form a high butte that over-looked our camp.

"*Mokuyi!*—It is he, the wolf!" cried Eagle Plume. Then raising his hand, he declared: "I shall never kill another; they are my brothers!"

And on the instant he turned to the child and christened him, *Mokuyi-Oskon*, Wolf Brother, and he was known by this name until he was eighteen.

The child grew and flourished. He became a great chief; and his name is today graven on a stone shaft which commemorates the termination of inter-tribal Indian wars in the Northwest.

Canoe Song

INDIAN[3]
Kijagamite, Kwe—Pimatake,
  Oshaie, wi Anoke.

Kijagamite, Kwe—ni wi posi
  Oshaie, ni ki posi.

Kitagamite, Kwe ni wi nissa
  Oshaie ni ki nissa

Kijagamite, wi potawe,
  Oshaie, ni potawe.

Kijagamite wi tshibakwe,
  Oshaie, ni tshibakwe.

Kijagamite, Kwe, ni wi wissin,
  Oshaie, ni ki wissin

Kijagami te Kwe, wi sakaswa,
  Oshaie, ni sakaswa.
Kajagamite Kwe, ni wi nipa,
  Oshaie, ni ki nipa.

Kijagamite, Kwa ni wi kiwe,
  Oshaie, ni ki kiwe.

---

3 According to linguist Lorna Marie Fadden (Métis), the language of this verse is neither Blackfoot nor Cree, but resembles the look and sound of languages in the Algonquian family.

ENGLISH
When the water is warm
Then is the time to swim.

I want to embark in my canoe
I am paddling my canoe

I want to hunt and kill
I have already killed.

I want to make a fire
Now the fire is made

I want to cook my meat
Now my meat is cooked.

Now I should like to eat,
I have eaten, I am full

I want to light my pipe and smoke
Now my smoke is over

Now I want to sleep

I have had my sleep.

I want to travel home.

I am now in my home.

Death Song of Long Lance

Oh, look down upon me
For thou knowest me——
the sun, the moon,
the day, the night——
Tell me if this is real,
Tell me if this is real——
this life I have lived.
Tell me if this is real,
Tell me if this is real——
this death I am dying.

Oh, Look down upon me
For thou knowest me——

the sun the moon,
the day, the night.
Tell me if this is real,
this life I have lived.
Tell me if this is real,
This death I am dying.

Now I see—I understand[4]
life is not real,
death is not real,
I shall walk on a trail of stars.
I shall walk on a——

Agh, no; agh no;
Death is not real[5]

[undated]

---

4   This line is inserted in ink in the author's hand.
5   These lines are added in pencil in the writer's hand.

Martha Edwards (née Murphy)
(1890–1977)

Martha Murphy Edwards was born in Wellston Colony Oklahoma, one of approximately sixty all-black towns founded after the American Civil War. The community was hit particularly hard by the depression of the cotton market that began in 1913 and which continued until the 1920s. Martha's father, Jordan W. Murphy, and his two sons were the first to move north to Pine Creek, Alberta (later renamed Amber Valley). Martha's sweetheart, Jefferson, followed her father north. After earning enough money by shovelling coal, digging basements, and hauling freight, Jefferson sent for Martha. The Murphys, Edwards, and Toles families formed the nucleus of Amber Valley, the most northerly community of black people that has ever existed in the world (Cheryl Foggo in Dobbins, Bailey, and Este, *We Are the Roots*). Other families soon followed.

Despite her husband Jefferson's assertion (see his entry in this volume) that she was a quiet woman, Martha Edwards proves herself a very capable orator and historian in her own right. Her honest account of homesteading in Amber Valley provides an important woman's perspective. She recalls the uncertainty and isolation involved in being the first woman to settle in Amber Valley, and having to give birth and raise children without the community of women and the church, or the basic amenities of running water, toilets, doctors, or baby beds, all of which she had grown up with as a matter of course in the United States. But in such conditions Martha forged a relationship with Indigenous people; she mentions, for instance, that it was a Métis woman who helped her give birth to her first son.

Martha and Jefferson Edwards had ten children together. She died on March 25, 1977—two years before her husband—and was buried in the Amber Valley Cemetery. Her life, along with her husband's, is memorialized in the David Adkin's film *A Farmer from Amber Valley* (White Pine Pictures 2001). Part of Martha's story is also told in *Women of Oklahoma, 1890–1920* (1997) by Linda Williams Reese.

❦

"That is what pioneers had to go through"

I didn't come with him; I came alone. I left Oklahoma around the 19th of November, or something like that, you know. No, I got here on the 19th, then we were married on the 21st of November, 1910. I felt alright sometimes, but sometimes I felt so alone, not knowing anybody; just me—a poor little girl on the train travelling all alone. I came as far as Emerson[1] and they wouldn't let me come over into Canada. I didn't know when I left home that I had to have fifty dollars above my ticket. So when I got there they kept me a week or more, until I got the fifty dollars, then they let me over into Canada. They just kept me right there at the station. They fed me; they were good to me.

The wedding was right here in Edmonton. I had some friends who came here; they were living here in Edmonton—the Dickens they called them. Mrs. Bailey was my bridesmaid; she stood up with me. Well, after we got married we stayed here in town about a week or more. Another man we knew, Mr. Saunders, that was Dave Saunders' dad, well he moved us out to Amber Valley—it was Pine Creek then. He took me to my dad's place with his wagon and team. He came in and had a load of stuff of his own—groceries and stuff like that—and he carried out our little stuff too. I rode upon the wagon with him. Jeff, he walked most of the time; then sometimes I got cold and I would walk with him. You know one thing, I just had shoes and rubbers over them; I came out here just like that.

My dad and my brothers had the first place out in Amber Valley. My dad was Mr. Murphy; he came in the spring and we came like in the fall. When we got there my dad had a poor house—you could throw a cat through the cracks. We stayed with him all winter; we had plenty of bedding and he kept plenty of fire, but it was really cold. Jeff stuffed the cracks with something. We had no bath, no toilet. Now you know what I went through. You had to go outside and you know just newly married, a girl feels ashamed. You know how that is.

We had our Christmas out there. We used a common, everyday, old iron stove; it burned wood. I made a Christmas cake; we couldn't get any eggs—made a cake without eggs. We had apple pies and the like of that for Christmas. We couldn't get a turkey but we had all kinds of prairie

---

1   Emerson, Manitoba, a rural point of entry that is being used again by present-day asylum seekers.

chickens and moose meat. Just the family had dinner together. In the spring my husband cleared a spot in the bushes big enough for the house. There was lots of fish; when we went up to the creek to fish we would get wagon-loads of jack fish. People would come in there and get wagon-loads and feed them to their pigs and chickens. There were all kinds of blueberries, strawberries, and the like.

My first child was Romeo. We had no doctor, no nothing. There was no one there but myself and a breed woman who came by to see how I was getting along. When I had the baby we finally had to send for Mrs. Robinson to help me. My mother and sister-in-law were there, so I wasn't frightened. They didn't live far from me; they could come and help me after Mrs. Robinson helped me deliver him. He was the first baby born out there. That is what pioneers had to go through.

Oh well, he had kind of a cradle made out of an apple box. You know you fix those things up for yourself. Baby clothes—well, we would go to Athabasca, I'd buy flannelette for diapers and would use flour sacks. I don't think material was as high as it is now. I remember I made him little bootees, you know, I knitted some little ones for him to run around inside the house. We'd go out sometimes in sleighs; I'd wrap the baby up. I remember one time we walked up to Mrs. Robinson's house. I couldn't carry the baby so I had Jeff carry the baby, and when we got home the baby's feet were out and cold; it's a wonder they didn't get frozen. It was quite a ways to walk.

Dr. Amanda Janet (Nettie) Ware
(1893–1989)

Janet Ware, or "Nettie" as her father nicknamed her, was the daughter of two highly esteemed figures in early black Albertan history. Her father was the famous cowboy John Ware, and her mother was the daughter of the urbane and successful Toronto transplants, the Lewises. Nettie was born on March 9, 1893, in a log cabin in Calgary, Alberta. She died on her own birthday in 1989 in Vulcan, Alberta, at the age of ninety-six.

Nettie Ware was an important community organizer and knowledge keeper of black Alberta. She helped to found the Alberta Women's Institute; she guided the Ladies Keystone Mission Circle in Vulcan; and she headed the Women's Organization of the Church of Christ for twenty-five years. Nettie Ware was awarded an Honorary Doctorate of Laws from the University of Lethbridge in 1982. When she was presented with the degree, Professor of Education Robert Anderson remarked, "Occasionally you will come to know someone whose greatness is essentially a matter of the quality of the person. Nettie Ware is such a person."[1]

The following interview with Nettie Ware regarding the life of her father was conducted by Eleanor G. Luxton of High River, Alberta, in August and September of 1956. What we have in Luxton's text is less a transcribed interview than a mediated narrative based on her conversations with Nettie. Luxton has her subject referring to herself in the third person—"Nettie" rather than "I." Similarly, she has Nettie speak of her father from an outsider's perspective as "John" or "Ware," rather than "father." Most of the memories here regard Ware's public life rather than private, family occurrences, though we get brief glimpses into Ware's private personality—for instance, his love of dogs and his fear of snakes. We get brief insights, too, into her mother's personality and circumstances. Having come to the northwest from Whitby, Ontario, near Toronto, Mildred Lewis was an urban person and never did care much for ranch life. She retained a lifelong fear of cattle and

---

1 *High River Times*, Wednesday, March 22, 1989. Glenbow Museum M1283.

never rode a horse. Finally, it is fascinating to hear of Nettie's antipathy for the racist terms by which her father was "honoured" in Alberta, and the work that Nettie did to change the name of "Nigger John Coulee" and thus honour her father's memory. The document is a treasure trove of Alberta's ranching history and the Ware family's central role in it.

The original interview, a six-page typed document, is part of the John Ware, Lewis family fonds at the Glenbow Museum and Archives, Calgary (file number M-4215-1).

John Ware

Vulcan August 1956

Fred Stimson[2] had sent Tom Lynch[3] to Idaho to buy cattle for the North West Cattle Co. There three thousand cattle and seventy-five horses were purchased and to be trailed north with Abe Cotterell as trail boss. Billy Moody came along and asked for a job in response to requests for more help. He was a good man, but he insisted that if he was hired his friend had to be also. Lynch and Billy went to the friend, and Lynch was taken aback to find he was a coloured man.

However the two were hired and trailed north with the herd. They reached the ranch headquarters September 25th, 1882. So John Ware born near Fort Worth, Texas, came to Canada—and stayed.

There is a story that he escaped from slavery by working his way West, and that he learned to ride well as a boy before that escape. His master's Overseer made the boys ride horses bareback to break them, and if they fell off they felt the blacksnake whip. This may be true, but fact and fiction seem to be inter mingled with this man's whole life. His family seem to feel

---

2   Frederick Smith Stimson, born in Compton, Lower Canada in 1842, was a farmer and rancher whose Bar U Ranch was, for seventy years, one of the leading ranch operations in Canada. Stimson incorporated the North West Cattle Company in 1881 in the Rocky Mountain foothills of Alberta. Though Stimson was an expert stockman he was not a cowboy, so he found experienced American cowboys, like John Ware, to run the day-to-day operations. Bar U sold beef to the Department of Indian Affairs, the mounted police, and, with the expansion of the railroad, to markets in British Columbia, Manitoba, and eventually England. Bar U was designated a National Historic Site in 1991.

3   Tom Lynch was a famous cattle dealer and driver who trailed thousands of cattle and horses into the northwest from Idaho to Edmonton.

this is not so—however—it might be remembered that no one really knew where Ware came from other than Texas. His family were too young to know about him when he died, and his wife predeceased him.[4] Regardless of how he learned to ride he could and did.

Ware worked for the Bar U for two years then went to the Quorn.[5] John Barter was foreman, and Ware became a top hand. He was the rep on the first large roundup for the Quorn in 1884 (the spring)[.] In the States John had worked for a large outfit that ran fifteen thousand cattle and five thousand horses, so he had plenty of experience.

John was put in charge of the horses on the Quorn and had to break the broncs. The Quorn had a lot of imported stock from the old country, and frequently they had a number of English visitors as well. These people always enjoyed Ware as much as he enjoyed hunting with them after the hounds and wolves. Ware also, often used to go on the hunts with the High River Horse Ranch when they had visitors.

John was a lover of dogs as well as of horses, and he always had a couple of collies and a hound on his own places. That he liked dogs was born out by the fact that when he was fatally injured and waiting for John Eide to come with help his dogs remained by his side.

John was foreman at the High River Horse Ranch for McPherson and Eckford.

John's great strength was one of his outstanding features. One time at the Quorn he straightened a hay hook out with his hands when the beam of a weigh scale was set at two hundred pounds. Another time he was crossing the railway and a train came. The horses became frightened and fell at the track, John jumped out and forcibly held their heads back until the train had passed.

The story of his first experience with Lynch is old, namely that Lynch gave him an old saddle and a bad bucking horse which Ware rode to a standstill. Then Ware went up to Lynch and said: "Boss, if you give me a

---

4   Mildred and John Ware died only six months apart. Mildred predeceased her husband on March 30, 1905.

5   The Quorn Ranch Company Ltd., started in 1886 by Englishman C.W. Martin, acquired land on the Sheep River west of Okotoks, and brought horses from England with the intention of breeding hunting horses for well-to-do sportsmen in Leicestershire, England. According to Kris Nielson and John Prociuk, Martin would often entertain investors at the ranch and it was not uncommon to see a western version of the popular British fox hunt take place with coyotes serving as the prey. The ranch was not a financial success; it collapsed in 1906.

little better saddle and a little wuss hoss I think I can ride him[.]" Of course he did.

1888 John took his own place on the North Fork of the Sheep Creek next to John Quirk. His brand was 9999 (Four Nine)[.] Why he chose that brand no one knew. There is a story that John was nine years of age when slavery was abolished—and he chose it as a lucky number—Needless to say there is no proof, and Bob his son does not think it is so.

In 1902 John moved to the Red Deer River north of Brooks—next door to John Eide. This location is still marked on the maps as "Ware Coulee."

His first home was on the river bank, but the next spring the river flooded and drove the family out at night, so John moved two miles south to higher ground. The old home is still in good condition.

Daniel Lewis came West from Whitby, Ontario with his family and lived in Calgary then took a homestead at Shepard in 1889 near the Bob New-bold Ranch.

Lewis was a finished cabinet maker, and many of the fine homes in Calgary showed evidence of his handicraft in book cases and stair cases.

In 1892 John married Mildred Lewis—She liked Ware but not his kind of life. She did overcome her fear of cattle enough to learn to milk one, but she was never on a horse in her life. She was a real mother and loved her home. The Wares were always hospitable, and were well thought of and liked in their community, regardless of where they were.

When they moved to the Red Deer their family consisted of Janet (Nettie), Bob, Willie and Mildred (twins). Arthur and Daniel were born at the Red Deer.

Today Nettie and Mildred live with Spencer Lewis a brother of Mildred's where he has farmed for a great many years. The girls and their uncle are held in the highest esteem by all the folks in the district, and Nettie is very active in church work and organizations.

Arthur and William served in World War One in all negro forestry battalion recruited in Calgary and Edmonton. William died in Keith San.[6] after being invalided home with T.B. after the war. Robert (Bob) has been twenty-five years with the C.P.R. on the Calgary Nelson run as porter. Arthur is with the C.P.R. run Vancouver to Winnipeg.

---

6   Keith Sanitorium, Calgary, was originally built for First World War soldiers suffering from T.B. In the mid-sixties the building functioned as a provincial residential training institute for people with mental disabilities and was known as the Baker Centre. It is now Baker Park and is located across the Bow River from Bowness Park.

Daniel died in infancy (2½ years)

1905 in early spring Mrs. Ware died of typhoid and pneumonia. That fall John and Bob (11) were culling cattle. John's horse stumbled in a badger hole, turned a somersault and pinned John under him, crushing him badly. Bob tried to get help, first the old cook, but they couldnot move the horse, so he went for John Eide. When they got there it had been too long and John died.

Ware was buried in Calgary, as was his wife, and many democrats and saddle horses with friends followed him in his last ride.[7]

John loved people, to talk, to dance and to play tricks. He was afraid of nothing but snakes, and when the boys used to tease him by dangling a snake he would go wild.

Many young men were indebted to Ware for his hints in trail work or his quick thinking in emergencies. One day Frank Bedingfeld was tending herd, Frank was only a lad then. His horse started to buck when he was drowsing in the saddle and the leg of his chaps caught on the saddle horn, leaving him dangling. John saw the trouble, dashed up and grabbed the horse by the lead, he wrestled him to a stop so the lad could get free.

John was probably the first to find oil in what is now Turner Valley. He was riding near Sheep Creek and saw what he thought was a pool of surface water and stopped to let the horse drink. The animal refused so John got off to look, and drink.

The water had a peculiar smell and taste and John threw a match in it—The whole thing burst into flames—John took to his horse and caught up with Sam Howe with whom he had been riding the range terrified that he had set the whole afire. They returned to find the pool and no fire, they sent a bottle to Dr. G.H. Mackid for analysis. In due course the report came that it was likely a seepage from a coal mine.

John made his own lariats from rawhide, he wove horse hair into saddle blankets—He could estimate the weight of animal to within a few pounds, but Mrs. Ware did all the book keeping because John never learned to read or write. But with all whom John dealt his word was good as his bond.

The tales of Ware at the stockyards are endless but one showing his courage was that when the steers would not go into the chute. John just got on the fence, walked over the cattle backs and prodded the first with a pole, much as a log man would work logs in a river.

---

7   John Ware is buried at Union Cemetary (27th Ave. and Spiller Rd. SE), in Calgary.

John loved horse play, the story of Jack Dempsey[8] and three of his friends stealing Ware's axe for a joke is well known. John told them if he did not return it he would toss them all into Sheep Creek. This was at Round Up time about 1900, so possibly the story has fact. Ware tossed the first man over the steep bank, but Dempsey was not as easy. The two tussled and rolled over the bank into the Creek, where they wrestled in the water until they were exhausted. Then Ware true to his threat came out and tossed the other two into the Creek.

John Ware was a man's man—he was known by all through the country as "the whitest Black Man that ever walked." The use of the word "Nigger" in his name was used as one of respect for him, but his family do not like it. This is instanced by the name "Ware Coulee" on the map, on then early ones it was called "Nigger John Coulee" but Nettie worked until it was changed.

Eleanor G. Luxton—High River
August and September 1956.

---

8   William Harrison "Jack" Dempsey (June 24, 1895–May 31, 1983), was an American professional boxer who competed from 1914 to 1927. The story about two fabulously strong men wrestling each other into the Sheep Creek is compelling, but likely apocryphal, given that Ware's death in 1905 came before Dempsey's rise to fame.

E.A. Cobbs
(dates unknown)

E.A. Cobbs was interviewed for the following oral history by Velma Carter in March 1986, part of a series of interviews conducted by the members of the Black Cultural Research Society between 1973 and 1986 and subsequently published in *Edmonton in Our Own Words*, edited by Linda Goyette and Carolina Jakeway Roemmich (2004).

In his narrative, Cobbs views his life and those of the Alberta pioneers within a larger historical frame: the tumultuous history of the concept of "race" in the late nineteenth and early twentieth centuries. He cites the construction of the CPR railroad, the Chinese Exclusion Act, Riel's leadership, the Second World War, and Marcus Garvey's Back-to-Africa movements as events that impacted the fates of Alberta blacks within the racial geography of North America and the prairies.

On their website, the Black Cultural Research Society note that E.A. Cobbs was the son of Jock Cobbs, but very little is known about him other than what he shares about his life story in this written/recorded narrative and what appears in other oral histories. Goyette and Roemmich note that he grew up in central Edmonton, and that his family were Doc, Harry, Hattie, and Clara.

He is mentioned briefly by Willis Richardson in Stanley G. Grizzle's oral interviews with sleeping car porters,[1] and so we know that Cobbs worked for a time as a railway porter. While Cobbs seems to have personal recollection of events from the first decade of the twentieth century, there are no Cobbs living in Alberta listed in the 1911 Census of Canada. In the 1916 Census of the Prairies, there is a "negro" family of four enumerated in the district of Edmonton West: Clarcy (56), Willie (24), Gilbert (65), and Stella Cobbs (15). What relation these folks are to E.A. Cobbs or his father Jock is not known at this time.

---

1 The interview between Stanley Grizzle and Willis Richardson is housed at the Library and Archives Canada, but it is a restricted fond and thus the interview cannot be included in this volume.

The following is my transcription of E.A. Cobbs's oral history, which provides an expanded account of what is anthologized in Linda Goyette and Carolina Jakeway Roemmich's 2004 volume. The audio file is available on the Alberta Black Pioneer Heritage website.[2]

❀

"This bias was good, for it caused the black people to fight"

As I recall, 1907, '08, '09, '10, saw the bringing in of black settlers from Oklahoma, Texas, Kansas. The Government of the day was a Conservative one, and this large country needed settlers to open it up. The railroad had been finished twenty years prior, and the CPR and Canadian Government needed to have this land settled, so homesteads—160 acres of land—was given to everyone 21 years old. For our people, this was a goldmine. So they came.

Those that arrived first—'07 and '08 arrived in Edmonton in the fall of the year, and when their horses and mules arrived by train through St. Paul it was winter. And the Government put them up in tents on the Prince of Wales Amouries' grounds.[3] Now if you care to check the weather, you will find that the winter of '07 and '08 are down as the coldest winters we have had here in Alberta.

In the spring they set out by teams: north to Athabasca; west to Junkins; south-west to Keystone; east to Maidstone, Saskatchewan. I have to remind you that the immigration laws in Canada were always lily white, and non-whites were not allowed into the country unless they were needed to do the dirty jobs that the white man didn't want to do. Point in case: to build the CPR the Government brought in thousands of Chinese "coolies," and to this day you will find no recognition of these people. Also hundreds were killed putting the road through the mountains. Those that survived were allowed to settle in BC—but no wives.[4] With the booming of the lumber mills, there was a need for labourers, and so the Hindus were brought in—but no wives.[5] As the railroads grew, we needed porters and

---

2   http://wayback.archive-it.org/2217/20101208162354/http://www.albertasource.ca/blackpioneers/multimedia/oral/index.html.

3   Located at 104th Street and 108th Avenue in Edmonton.

4   Cobbs is referring to the Chinese Head Tax (1885–1947), levied against Chinese immigrants to Canada after the completion of the railroad, which restricted the immigration of Chinese women, leading to "bachelor societies" of single Chinese men.

5   In 1908 the federal government passed an Order-in-Council that required an

waiters. So, to the West Indies, and the demand was met—but no wives.[6] This system worked like a charm. No women, no non-white children, so no "black problems." This system worked perfectly until after the Hitler war, when pressure by the Americans who were engaged in the Marshall Plan[7] to feed the world was exerted on Canada. Then immigration laws were changed and you saw black people from all over the world admitted for the first time. Now, for your information, any man who is not Anglo Saxon or European white is a black man. And that rule was enforced, rigidly.

We lived on 101st Street and 106th Avenue when I was very young, and I remember soldiers marching from the armies to the CNR Station to go overseas. I saw my first plane and balloon at that time. The war started in 1914, and several of our people felt that Canada gave them a chance for a new life, and so this country is worth fighting for. So off they went to join the army. They were told this was a white man's war and they were not wanted. This was their first taste of a racial problem. Later, within the year, conscription came into force and many of our people *had* to enlist: Fay Corothers, Boots McNeil, Lummy Bowen come to mind.

Our people that arrived were God-fearing, Bible-believing people, and were mostly Baptist. I recall Shiloh Baptist Church being in a building that was on a lane off 107th Avenue and 103rd Street. And everyone in town went. Now this would be around 1916, for I remember a Christmas concert, and I was given a piece to learn and when I saw all those faces looking up at me I froze. I started crying, and my dad had to take me up.

I remember the 'flu epidemic and people wearing masks over their faces. Many of our people died. In the 1920s racial feelings were running very high in America and pressure was put on the black people to leave. There

---

immigrant to come to Canada by "continuous passage" from the country of origin. The stipulation was aimed specifically at South Asians, and effectively banned the immigration of wives of South Asian men already in Canada. The legislation was in effect until 1951 (Ralston).

6   On this count, Cobbs's history is not accurate, but is correct in spirit. In the case of black immigration, the Canadian government permitted and even encouraged the immigration of black women from the Caribbean to come to Canada through the West Indian Domestics Scheme, initiated in 1955. The catch was that the women had to be between the ages of eighteen and thirty-five and single. No husbands or partners were permitted, and thus the formation of black families and the reproduction of black life was restricted (F. Henry 83).

7   The Marshall Plan was an American initiative to help rebuild Western European economies devastated by the Second World War.

were plans to pay these people to go back to Africa. Out of this came Marcus Garvey, the black leader, who came, I think, from the West Indies.[8] He was a born leader and started a movement called the UNIA—the Universal Negro Improvement Association. I would compare him to Louis Riel. Black people joined the movement and money came in. The plan was to buy a boat called The Black Star Line, and negotiations got underway with Liberia, and this is where these black people were going to start a new life, away from the Ku Klux Klan and all the racial hassles that were present at that time. It caught on like wildfire. And with all that money coming in, and with Garvey not having knowledge of how to set this thing up, he was surrounded by people who saw a chance to make money. So he was sold out. It collapsed, and he was made the goat. I had an auntie and uncle who sold out everything they had and went to Liberia. On their own. We never heard from them since. Maybe some day someone will write the true story of Marcus Garvey. Maybe he was a black hero, as much as Martin Luther King.

There were a fair number of black people in Edmonton at that time [the early 1920s]—the largest group west of Toronto. There were rooming houses run by Mrs. Norahan [Moorehead?], Mrs. Sales; on the south side, Mrs. Dolly Smith. There was by this time a Methodist church, and Reverend Slater was one of its pastors.[9] Henry Brooks was the Pastor of the Baptist church. Like any other ethnic group, we all lived in a district: 97th Street, 98th Street, 95th Street and 111th Avenue. We mostly went to Queen's Avenue School or McCauley, and a fight every few days.

Around 1925 several families moved out of the city: the Adams family went back to Oklahoma; the Brooks, the Bells, the Griffiths to Vancouver. Earlier the Thompsons went back to the States.

Then came the Depression, of which our people were used to, and we survived. Employment was always a problem. Only the jobs no one else wanted. There was the railroad for a few. My brother and grandfather and brother-in-law, Andy Henderson, worked in the CNR shops for years. Many worked in the coal mines and the packing plants. Several drove drays and worked on construction jobs. Several worked in poultry pools, killing and dressing poultry. [10] There was a strong Masonic Lodge, Eastern Star

---

8   Marcus Garvey was born in St. Anne's Bay, Jamaica, in 1887.

9   See this volume for Slater's writings.

10 See, for instance, orature by John Bell Bowen, and Cheryl Foggo's memoir *Pourin' Down Rain* in this volume.

Chapter. There was no encouragement to finish school, for there were no jobs open to our people. Several made a living shining shoes. And after ten years of hard times came the Hitler war, and many moved from Edmonton to Calgary, Vancouver, Winnipeg, and started to work on the railroad which paid $80 a month.

As I look back on my life in Edmonton, I see one big, loving, caring family. There were no divisions that you might expect. At Christmas time every child in Edmonton was at Shiloh Church and received a present. When I think of how those presents were secured, I have to laugh. The Women's Group would form a committee of two and the 15th of December would start out: first the manager of the Bay. A real sob story. I'm sure after twenty minutes of that he would have been willing to part with the store just to get rid of those gals. So he would come through with candy and oranges and presents, after which the old girls would call down a whole flock of blessings on the man and then they would go to Eaton's and repeat the process all over again. After that, Woodward's, James Ramsay's. And finally, up with the Jewish merchants, who usually gave money.

At the Christmas concert every black child in Edmonton would be at Shiloh Baptist Church and there would be a present for everyone. At the risk of repeating myself, it was really a large, black family, loaded with love for each other. I have often wondered where the prejudice came from. You have to realize that most of the white, Anglo-Saxon Protestants came from the British Isles, where you had no black people. The others came from the northern States, like Minnesota and the Dakotas, where there were a few black people. But it was here we were barred from the City pool at Borden Park; the old Pantages Theatre would only allow us to sit in the balcony. This bias was good, for it caused the blacks to fight and as a result, changes were made. We were encouraged to get an education, even though you couldn't see where it was going to help. You still had to buck the system.

We had students going to high school that today would be honours students: Kay Henderson, Agnes and Velma Leffler, Rhumah Utendale, just to name a few. Later, I remember Rhumah Utendale made an application to enter the Royal Ally[11] and being told that the other girls would not want

---

11 E.A. Cobbs is referring to the Royal Alexandra Hospital in inner-city Edmonton, where Rhumah Utendale hoped to train as a nurse while boarding with the other women trainees.

to live with her. When God made black people he knew, in his foreknowledge, the many problems that we would be faced with. So he gave us the ability to take the punches of race hatred and still not stay down. We are born optimists: "the sun will shine in my back door tomorrow."[12] I know. So I want to live to see it tomorrow. And that is what Martin Luther King could see in his dream.

Well, we survived the Depression. And in the 1940s the railroad got busy and so we were able to have jobs and go on learning. You see, being black has its advantages. You are forced to learn in order to survive. The only people who could hire you are the better class of white people. So as a result, you learn from them, and after a while, you know all about them and how to exist in their system. This was a God-given gift, and to this day, it works.

---

12 Lyrics to a traditional blues song.

Ellis Hooks
(1907–1979)

"Oklahoma, according to mother and dad, was not so bad, but bad enough," says Ellis Hooks. "It was being circulated there, about homesteading in Alberta, and you could own land for the price of ten dollars. That was the big drawing card. To come to a place where for ten dollars you could almost become independent. And that is the main reason they came, was on the count of equality. Which is a very important reason."

Ellis Hooks was born in the small community of Sharpes, Oklahoma, in 1907, the second of ten children of Samuel and Neoma Hooks. In Oklahoma, his father was a carpenter and a farmer of cotton, wheat, peanuts, and sorghum. Hooks was five years old when he arrived with his family in Edmonton in April 1912. Although they were latecomers in the exodus, the place where they settled in Edmonton— on 110th Street and 110th Avenue—"at that time was all bush, and all lots of the people there were immigrants. That's where we settled. We were called squatters. We were granted the privilege of squatting on this land without paying taxes or anything." The summer of 1912 the Hooks lived in a boarded-up tent; the walls were boards and the top was a tent stretched over. Hooks's father, Samuel, took up construction work, and he helped to build the High Level Bridge across the North Saskatchewan River. While in Edmonton, Ellis attended the nearby John A. McDougall School. In 1915, after three years in Edmonton, Ellis moved with his family to Keystone, Alberta, a community that at its height counted about 250 people. There, his father bought a homestead and once again returned to farming.

Hooks also pursued a trade of steam engineering in Edmonton until the Great Depression of the 1930s devastated the economy and left him out of work. In the 1930s Hooks joined the many men who rode freight trains across Canada in search of available work. Hooks found permanent work back in Alberta as a tradesman; he married and had a daughter, Lois.

The following interview with Reevan Dolgoy, a contractor with the Provincial Museum and Archives of Alberta's oral history project of the 1960s–70s, relates

120

some of Lois's school experience, and what it was like for Hooks as well as the larger black community in Keystone during the early 1960s. Reevan Dolgoy interviewed Hooks twice, on August 27, 1978, and October 3 of the same year in Hooks's home in Edmonton, and all together they recorded two full audiocassettes. While Dolgoy is not himself a member of the black community, he proves himself—for better or for worse—a highly motivated listener.

In the following transcription of the oral recordings, we hear Hooks's compelling story about a direct action undertaken by the black community of Breton in the early 1960s. The community organized themselves and rose up in effective protest against the high school's blackface production of *Uncle Tom's Cabin*. The events related by Hooks suggest that black prairie people did not tolerate racism or even cultural representations of racism in their communities. As Hooks puts it here, "Anything like that that reflected on to us that much, well, we fight back, that's all."

Ellis Hooks died in 1979 and was buried in the Edmonton Centre Cemetery.

"The way I felt, I wanted to plead guilty: I wanted the world to know"

DOLGOY: I think what we could probably get to now is what was the original purpose behind me coming over and that was—What happened during that Christmas concert? In … what was it 1960 or '61?

HOOKS: It was not a Christmas concert. It was a play that they were getting together. And it was by the high school. And it was our daughter Lois that came home one evening and told us about what they were doing.

DOLGOY: How old was she at the time?

HOOKS: Fourteen maybe. She was starting in high school. So after her telling us about this we gave it some thought and—

DOLGOY: What exactly did she tell you?

HOOKS: Well, she said that they were rehearsing this play, and she told us who was in it—a lady by the name of Mrs. Opal [?] was playing a lead part in it. And we knew what kind of people they were, the Opals.

DOLGOY: What kind of people were they?

HOOKS: Very standoffish and prejudiced they were.

DOLGOY: What was the name of the play?

HOOKS: I can't remember what it was called. But there was a main character in it there was the United minister. He was a young fella. United Church minister. And the school teacher, if I remember right, was directing the play. And there was others in it I don't remember who they were now. Knew them well but don't remember. So she told us of this so we thought it over for a few days and thought we'd better do something about it, because—

DOLGOY: What was your objection? Was it the play or the people in it?

HOOKS: No, the play. The way they were playing it.

DOLGOY: What was the story about?

HOOKS: Well, it was from the time of slavery, old Uncle Tom's Cabin.

DOLGOY: It was *Uncle Tom's Cabin*!

HOOKS: Yes. Mmm-hmm.

DOLGOY: And how were they playing it?

HOOKS: Well, the main thing we objected to was the kind of language they were using—the kind of English being used.

DOLGOY: I don't want to put words in your mouth, but was it words prejudicial to Negro people?

HOOKS: Oh yeah, sure. Of course. Very much so. And in our lives we heard too much about this kind of stuff. Some of it actually made our blood boil, that it'd been did to the Negro people.

DOLGOY: Awful words like "Niggers" and all that stuff?

HOOKS: Pardon?

DOLGOY: Was it that terrible slang words like "Niggers?"

HOOKS: Yeah, things like that.

DOLGOY: Okay.

HOOKS: We decided that we couldn't stand it to have something like that going disgracing us. So we decided to do something about it.

DOLGOY: Because you had been a very proud community, I believe?

HOOKS: Oh yes.

DOLGOY: Again, I don't want to put words in your mouth, but—

HOOKS: In our way we were!

DOLGOY: Had you ever put up with anything like that before?

HOOKS: Never. No. Oh no. Anything like that that reflected on to us that much, well, we fight back, that's all. So we decided to do something about it. So we talked it over amongst ourselves, I and my wife, and Mark, my brother, and my son in law—future son in law at that time, and my daughter. She is the one that told us all about what was going on. We wouldn't have known. And she told us that they were going to put it on at a certain time in the hall, and that they were going to travel with it around the country—different places.

DOLGOY: I just want to ask you a question now. Who the heck was playing the parts of the Negro people in this play?

HOOKS: The main one was this Mrs. Opal.

DOLGOY: But she wasn't Negro.

HOOKS: Oh no, she's a white lady.

DOLGOY: But she was going to play the part of a Negro person?

HOOKS: Yeah. Yeah. And the very main one was the church minister—

DOLGOY: Who was going to play Uncle Tom?

HOOKS: Yes. Right. This is right. We decided we couldn't stand for anything like that. So after talking it over a few days and thinking it over, I think it was my son-in-law, it was, that came up with the right idea about throwing the eggs. So, well, we didn't want to be violent, or anything of that kind, but we decided we had to break it up in a big way too. So one day I, my son-in-law, went down to the neighbours and we bought a few dozen eggs. And we had these eggs all in readiness for this night. And of course we went around and alerted what few other Negro people there was. The Fords, I think, and someone else. And had everything in readiness. Everything in readiness. And my daughter had seen them rehearse so there were some of us went inside the hall and sat and watched while some others like my son-in-law, Mark and Lois, they stayed outside. So when it came to this certain part in the play, this United Church minister he was lying down on a couch, which I can't remember just what he was saying—he was lying on the couch—and this is when they was using these different words that we didn't like. And this is the time I went outside the hall and around where they were waiting and we went to the side door where they were coming in the stage, and opened the door, and in they came. And we covered him with eggs.

DOLGOY: You egged him?

HOOKS: Yeah. There was eggs flying in every direction. You never saw anything like it. No. So this broke the whole thing up right there. There was never such a big surprise that anyone ever had, I don't think, as that was. Yeah. And of course by this time the most of them couldn't keep their head very cool so I had to step in and do what I could to get them stopped.

DOLGOY: A fight ensued?

HOOKS: Ya, a fight ensued, and we didn't want no fighting.

DOLGOY: Who did the fighting? Did some of the people from the cast fight with—

HOOKS: There was no fighting. Some of our crew *wanted* to fight but I wouldn't let them. I wouldn't let it go that far. So then after it was all over, then we heard there were charges being laid against us.

DOLGOY: Is this after you went home, you mean?

HOOKS: The next day. We heard that there was charges being laid against us.

DOLGOY: Just one thing, Ellis, before we go into the next day. Did you exchange any words with any of the people in the cast that evening or words with the people in the hall?

HOOKS: Oh yes. Some wanted to know why did we do it? People in the audience asked us why. Well, we just outright told them why we did it and we didn't ever want to hear of it again. Some said, "I don't blame you." But it was such a surprise, they were all wondering very much, it was such a surprise. Nobody had ever thought of it—they hadn't dreamed of it! Anyway, there was a neighbour of ours—white fellow—very good friend of ours, had been for years, old timer, Danny Flescher. He acted as a go-between and was very good at it, too. He got the thing all quieted down. I guess finally everybody went home. Oh—I must say that my brother in law, my sister's husband, he didn't happen to be there that night. And he heard that they was having this big meeting and there was a magistrate there at this time by the name of Walter Baines. He was at the meeting too, and my brother-in-law was there and he heard everything that they were saying, and he found out just what they were going to do. So he happened to be our authority, and he told us what they were going to do, but in the meantime, while the meeting was going on, I guess this fellow who was supposed to be a magistrate—but he was so prejudiced that he was taking part in making it worse. So I guess my brother in law couldn't stand it any longer (and he was a boxer anyway), and he's the one who knocked him down.

DOLGOY: He hit the magistrate!

HOOKS: Yes! And he laid a charge against him! Anyway, he told us all about what went on and, well, I said I think we'd better get a lawyer, maybe. At that time there was a fellow staying at my place with us by the name of Verne King—he was a nephew of Charles King—and he was quite a sharpey. And he is the fellow who knew Joe Shoctor. He said for a case of this kind you'll never get a better man. He's the man you want.[1] So after getting this information, and he told me where to find him (in the city here), he knew him well. We all decided we'd better get a lawyer. They appointed me to come up and interview Mr. Shoctor. And after coming up and going and seeing Mr. Shoctor and relating the case to

---

1   Joseph Shoctor (1922–2001) was well known in Edmonton as a lawyer, civic booster, businessman, and, fittingly, given his role in Hooks's story, the founder of Edmonton's Citadel Theatre.

him he said he'd be very glad to defend us. He said something like, he really wanted the chance to defend us. He said there's too much of this kind of thing going on. I have to think a bit ... if I remember right, Mr. Shoctor sent notice to Mr. Baines that he would be appearing at the trial. Because we'd gotten notice about the trial.

DOLGOY: You'd be charged, had you?

HOOKS: We had been charged.

DOLGOY: Who had been charged, exactly, amongst you?

HOOKS: I think the ones charged was myself, my brother Mark, my son-in-law, David Robinson, ah, Chris Ford, Larkey Ford, there was a couple of others.

DOLGOY: And what was the charge, was it assault?

HOOKS: No, not assault. Creating a disturbance. On the day of court—I hope I'm not getting ahead of myself—in the hall in Breton. He called us all into a group and he defined what he thought would be the best way of carrying it out—what he would do. He told us he was going to make a deal with Mr. Baines—and he did. He said I want to just pick out four of you to be charged. He said to plead guilty. He said you know you have to plead guilty; there's nothing you can do about this. We could carry this thing on and on if you plead not guilty. He said *they'll* feel better about it, too, if you do. If you wouldn't plead guilty, he said, then they'll keep trying to bring the thing up and never forget it. This way if you plead guilty, they'll be satisfied.

DOLGOY: Ellis, how did you feel about that at the time when he first suggested to you to plead guilty?

HOOKS: Actually, the way I felt, I *wanted* to plead guilty: I wanted the world to know. Ya. I just felt that way. Being charged didn't bother me at all, because I knew we did it, and we thought we did right, whether we did or not. So Mr. Shoctor says this is the deal I'll make. Four of you will come forward and say you plead guilty. [...] and they pleaded guilty. And after that was over then Mr. Shoctor he gave a talk to the magistrate, Walter Baines, that he never wanted to see anything like that happen again in Breton and he told the magistrate to tell the people. He did, too. And Mr. Shoctor said he'd better see that it stopped right there in Breton where it started and never go any further. That was the end of the whole thing right there. Although there was a lot of, I'd say, *hate* going on for a while. There was a few fights over it. Especially in the pub. They'd get to drinking and arguing—one for one side and one for the other side. There was a few fights before it actually died down.

DOLGOY: Where there any Negroes involved in the fights?

HOOKS: Oh yes, I was involved myself. Mostly I and my brother-in-law, mostly, involved in the fights. But after a while it all died away and it was never heard of again.

DOLGOY: The people involved in the play—whatever happened to them?

HOOKS: Well, the United Church minister after his year was up he moved away anyway; the high school teacher stayed another year and he was gone; and of course this Mrs. Opal went on as the main hater. She was a hater. She continued to live in town and she was completely prejudiced.

DOLGOY: Why? Where was she from? What made her—?

HOOKS: Nova Scotia.

DOLGOY: There was a Negro community in Nova Scotia.

HOOKS: Very big one. The largest in Canada. They immigrated from Virginia into Nova Scotia at the time of the Civil War.

DOLGOY: In your opinion, do you think she brought this prejudice with her?

HOOKS: Oh yes, very much so. She brought it right with her. She was prejudiced from the time I first knew her.

DOLGOY: I don't want to put words in your mouth but what kind of attitude did she have? Superiority attitude?

HOOKS: Superiority attitude. Snooty attitude. Real snubby.

Luther Gerard
(1914–2004)

The CNR and Grand Trunk railroads were "put in with Swedes, colored people and wheel barrows." So remembers Luther Gerard, who was a member of the community of Junkins—now called Wildwood—a black hamlet in west-central Alberta established by a group of twenty or so African Americans in 1908. Located 112 kilometres west of Edmonton, it is rural even now, but, as Gerard describes, it was highly isolated and nearly inaccessible at the time the pioneers went out to their homesteads. Being as isolated as Junkins was, the pioneers had to rely heavily on one another. Gerard's recollections are largely focused on his childhood schooldays, but he also remembers the formal and informal co-operative systems the community elders developed to help get them through hard times. Among the social and spiritual systems the community established was a cattle co-operative and the Baptist Church they founded at Junkins. Once a year, on July 1, the congregation held an annual picnic that featured dances and songs, sports, plays, and feasting.

The community Gerard vividly describes did not last more than one generation. Many of the pioneers' children left the community to find work elsewhere, most typically in Edmonton or other nearby communities. When Gerard might have left Wildwood is not presently known. After the 1916 Census the historical record remains mostly quiet regarding Luther Gerard. He died in Devon, Alberta (100 kilometres from where he was born) in 2004 at the age of eighty-nine. His orature was originally published in Carter and Akili's *The Window of Our Memories*.

"Community spirit"

Well, my parents and grandparents were sharecroppers; they worked for some big land owner, you know. He'd sublet his land out to them and they'd plant crops. They raised potatoes back in Oklahoma; they used to sell car-loads of potatoes. That's one thing my father tried to do once he got out here, but he didn't go in that big; he just sold to camps.

In 1912 there was a big migration of colored people from the States to Wildwood. They weren't the first ones; I guess the first ones came in 1910. Most of the people that migrated to Wildwood came from Oklahoma. They were quite a few colored people; some of them were Smiths, Joneses, McNeals, Jacksons, Phillips, Taylors, Paynes, Akers, Lefflers, Buckners, Rouses, Johnsons, Boones, Gerrards, Groffs, Penns, Mackies, Donohues, Bensons, Brandsfords, Tates, Philipses, Clarences, Lige Bell, Raymond Caldwell, Blairs, and Raymond Johnsons.

Our folks came in October 1912 and all the land in this area was home-steaded. You couldn't get homesteads close. The only place they could find was four miles north-east of Wildwood. Most of the people in Wildwood were colored—there were a few Germans and Scandinavians—but mostly colored people were in this area. At that time when they came they were putting the railroad through—that was the first work my dad got to do. He had a little team of mules he brought up with him and he used them to distribute ties on the railroad. This was the Canadian National Railroad; the Grand Trunk Railroad was in at that time. For some reason they had these two railroads—it was kind of a competition, I guess. That was one of the most foolish and most expensive things they could do. The railroad was put in with Swedes, colored people and wheel barrows; there might have been a little bit built with horses but most of it was built with wheelbarrows. There were no roads when they came in here, there were just trails through the bush; these trails had been cleared just so you could get through by a team and wagon—just that's all there was. And you take in the summer time—it was pretty near impossible to get with a team and wagon to town to get your groceries because there were potholes and mires that you'd get your horses down in. It took a whole day to come three or four miles with an empty wagon and team. Eventually they had to corduroy what roads they did use. They corduroyed them with poplar and spruce bedded down into the ground; at least the horses weren't mired down.

There was quite a bit of bush in this country at that time and lots of game; lots of wild game—chickens, ducks, and deer; so that way they had something to eat. But as far as the land—there wasn't an acre cleared on any land they took in Wildwood, which was then called Junkins, unless it had been burnt by a fire. But they were ambitious because the government had promised them a patent for their quarters if they got thirty acres cleared and broken, I believe it was. Most of the land was cleared by hand; they grubbed the trees out and they would use a little wooden beam breaking-plow with a team. Some people put three horses on this type of plow. I know my dad did a lot of breaking and he used three horses on this little fourteen inch, wooden beam breaking plow. That was hard work—clearing by hand—because the bush was fairly thick and there were big trees. To grub out thirty acres—that was a big, big task; they didn't do that in no one year; they may have done it in five or six years. The food ration for meat continued for a long time to be wild birds, and game such as deer, moose, and fish. They planted crops but they couldn't grow any crops as we do now—they all froze. Some people began to raise pigs and cattle but it was pretty well wild meat they ate.

It seems to me the people in Junkins formed a kind of co-op. Say ten or fifteen farmers would go together and they would sign up for Government cattle. They would get up to five hundred dollars' worth of cattle—that was around fifteen or twenty head at that time. But there was a clause in this deal saying that each one was responsible for the other one's debt until it was paid—which wasn't a very good thing. There were so many of them who didn't know much about cattle. In the winter of 1919, the spring of 1920, they had a very hard and heavy snow and a cold, cold winter; most of the people lost the bulk of their cattle. My dad paid as high as eighty dollars a ton for rotten hay that was shipped in here to save the cattle. It was very poor hay, some was not fit for anything, but it was better than licking a snowball. So my dad got shorts[1] as he was working in the bush that winter in a logging camp. He'd buy shorts and give his cattle a little, you know; he'd give each of them one-half pound of shorts. He'd cut down dry firewood and the cows at night would peel the bark off those poles—they were that hungry. But my father pretty well saved all his cattle. I believe he saved all except one two-year old heifer; and he lost two horses. The reason he lost any at all was that he had the hay, but in those days they just put it in coils; the snow got so deep that the cattle couldn't find the coils—that's right.

The house we had on the homestead was built out of logs. The cracks between the logs were chinked with muskeg. In the wintertime when those cows were so hungry they'd lick the moss right out of the cracks. This made it kind of cold, so we had to plaster it up with cow manure.

My dad was a fair manager. We moved from the homestead because we children were old enough to go to school. So he had to bring the

---

1   Shorts are a by-product left over from milling or processing grains for higher-end products.

children out to go to school because the homestead was about a mile and a half of muskeg. There was no way to come out—except you followed the river around; and half the time you couldn't get out. So at first we moved to a place a mile north of Wildwood there—for two years. The Miles' place—that's kitty cornered from Akers's there, where Jim Griffith's place used to be.

I started school about three years before Bunting came to teach in Wildwood. When I started to school we got about a month or two months of schooling a year. They couldn't keep a teacher. Bunting came here in 1923; I was nine in 1923. We'd get about one or two months of school in a year; you couldn't learn very much that way. They taught in the summer holidays then went and taught in Edmonton. They didn't care to teach in these schools in places like this, I guess. They didn't get much money. When Bunting was teaching here, he was a steady teacher. He was teaching for three hundred dollars a year, I heard, and he took half of that in vegetables. The people just didn't have the money, you know.

Catching fish was one thing I looked forward to, when I was a child going to school. We had a creek going through our school yard. In the spring the fish would come up that creek and we'd have a big sport of catching them. Most of us would snare them; we'd snare maybe a dozen or twenty fish in a day. I remember they used to come right up to the highway; they'd come to the culvert at the railroad track and come right to the highway sometimes. Some years they'd even come on the south side of the highway—come through the culvert and right over in our field, you know, where the water used to always stay in there. You could walk out there—the water was quite shallow—the fish would be right wiggling around and you could catch them in your hand.

I remember one hailstorm in 1923. It was about 2:30 p.m. and the clouds got just terribly black; the teacher got excited and she told the kids to rush home as fast as they could. She thought maybe the best thing for us was to get home instead of leaving us at school. We got out of school—just over the railroad track—and it started hailing. Hail came down like hen eggs. We had knots on our heads. Some of us were knocked out and everything else. We had to come almost half a mile; we were just played out by the time we got home. My sister, Alberta, didn't get home. She ran to a brush pile alongside the road and stayed there; but my two older brothers and myself, we made it. When we kids got home and could get our breath we saw that our sister, Alberta, was someplace along the road—we didn't know where she was. There was one of the teamsters from Hanson's; his team got away from him. He took a tub over his head to keep the hail from beating him and he went looking for my sister. He found her under a brush pile. She wasn't beat up by the hail as bad as we were. We had big knots on our hands and all over our body, and our heads were full of knots as big as goose eggs. It's a wonder the hail hadn't killed us. It knocked all the west side windows out of the houses. At that time, Fred Hanson had a sawmill south of here—about a half mile; he had men hauling lumber to the box cars in Wildwood. Everyone who was along the road with his team had a run-away that day.

Everybody was interested in the others' welfare. If a person had something to do, everybody would come to help him do it. There was no money paid out—they'd exchange work and the work was always done. It was a real community spirit. In those days there were a lot more sports and a lot more picnics and activities in the community.

I remember some of our picnics although I was quite young. One activity we had at the picnics was climbing the greasy pole. They'd get this pole and peel it, then they'd grease it. They'd place a five-dollar bill on the top of it; whoever could climb the pole would get the money. A lot of them tried it, but most of them failed. Someone would donate a pig about two months old. They'd grease the pig; they'd bring him there and turn him a loose; whoever would catch the pig would own him. That was quite a sport. No one was too anxious about getting dirty; but after a while, after quite a few had grabbed him and he slipped away—they had rubbed some grease off—others got braver. The races for the kids were a real treat for me because I was quite sports minded myself. I competed in everything I was able to, and usually I won something. If I didn't win, I'd win second or third; I was always pretty well on the winning side.

They used to have a little place—do you remember George Benson? He had a little store—a confectionary place. On Sundays when the ball games were over we had ice-cream there. My mother usually made the ice-cream we had those freezers. Everybody put up ice in those days. We'd beat this ice up and put it around the tub of the ice-cream freezer and turn the handle, and turn until the cream was frozen. We'd freeze this ice-cream nearly every Sunday; sometimes we'd have three or four freezers of ice-cream. It was pretty well all sold. It was real ice-cream because it was made out of real milk and cream. It wasn't like the ice-cream we buy nowadays.

Our first agricultural fair was held in 1936. They went around with a charter and a lot of people signed up for the fair, so we got it. We got a charter and then we started having fairs. There were no registered cattle in the country—or only a precious few, anyways—but it was for the improving of livestock. To begin with, everyone was interested in it. There were cattle of all kinds and descriptions; there were horses, pigs, and sheep. One of the biggest attractions in those days was who had the best pulling team. They used to have a pulling contest. Everybody would bring their big teams out—that was one of the biggest drawing cards. Sometimes we would win in this pulling contest, but not always.

Woody Strode
(1914–1994)

Woodrow Wilson Woolwine "Woody" Strode, born on July 25, 1914, in Los Angeles, California, was a decathlete, football player, wrestler, movie star, and writer. He is best known for breaking the colour barrier in American and Canadian football, and for his starring roles in the Hollywood films *Spartacus*, *Tarzan*, and *The Ten Commandments*.

Strode was the son of a mixed Muscogee-Blackfoot and black father and a black Cherokee mother. He attended Thomas Jefferson High School in southeast Los Angeles and college at UCLA. He was a world-class decathlete with particular strengths in shotput and high jump. Strode posed for a nude portrait, part of Hubert Stowitt's acclaimed exhibition of portraits of American athletes shown at the 1936 Berlin Olympics, although the inclusion of black and Jewish athletes caused the exhibit to be closed by the Nazis (Stowitts).

Strode began his football career playing on the 1939 UCLA Bruins football team, where he was only one of a few African American players. After serving in the United States Army Corps during the Second World War, Strode returned to football to play briefly with the Los Angeles Rams, where, as he details in his memoir, he endured his first experiences of racism. Strode repeatedly fended off verbal and physical attacks from fans and players alike. Later, Strode looked back at his days in the NFL with bitterness. "Integrating the NFL was the low point of my life," he told *Sports Illustrated* in an unpublished interview before his death. "There was nothing nice about it. If I have to integrate heaven, I don't want to go" (Wolff). Strode played ten games with the Rams in 1946 but was cut from the team the following year.

At the age of thirty-four, Strode was recruited by the Calgary Stampeders. He was part of the CFL's only undefeated team in 1948 (12-0), making the all-star team in his first year. Calgary's first championship since 1911 was marked by great celebration. As he details in his memoir, he was the infamous player who rode into Toronto's Royal York Hotel on horseback. Strode scored a touchdown in Calgary's

Grey Cup Victory, but after the 1949 season he retired from football due to a shoulder injury that caused him, for the first time in his career, to feel vulnerable. In 1986 Strode returned to Calgary to help fundraise for the Stampeders.

Strode married Luukialuana Kalaeloa (Luana Strode), also an actor, and a distant relative of Liliuokalani, the last queen of Hawaii. They had a son, Kalai, and a daughter, June. They were married until Luana's death in 1980. In 1982, Strode wed Tina Tompson, and they remained married until his death.

Strode's first exposure to the movie business was in college, when he had worked as a porter on the Warner Brothers lot, assisting stars like Bette Davis and Errol Flynn. After playing with the Calgary Stampeders, Strode entered the fields of professional wrestling and then acting. Tall, muscular, and bald, Strode had a striking screen presence. He caught the attention of famed director John Ford, who cast him in the title role in *Sergeant Rutledge* (1960), and then in a dozen more films. Between the 1960s and 1980s, Strode appeared in over eighty Hollywood movies, though he remains best known for his brief Golden Globe–nominated role in *Spartacus* (1960) as the Ethiopian gladiator Draba. With Sidney Poitier and Brock Peters, he is regarded as one of the most important black film actors of his time.

In 1990, Strode published *Goal Dust: The Warm & Candid Memoirs of a Pioneer Black Athlete and Actor*, co-written with Sam Young, from which the following excerpt is taken. It is an engaging and vivid account of his life and exploits, from birth until the age of seventy-six. His account of integrating the NFL and CFL have important contemporary resonances with the NFL kneeling protests, spearheaded by Colin Kaepernick: the words of the forty-fifth American president echo the players and fans Strode faced in the 1940s in Los Angeles and Calgary.

In 2000, the Calgary Stampeder team with which Strode played was inducted into Alberta's Sporting Hall of Fame. The induction noted that the 1948 team with their ardent fans turned "the Grey Cup into the national festival that it is today" (Alberta Sports Hall of Fame and Museum). Nearly forgotten during the war years, the Stampeders "made it into the biggest single day sporting event in Canada" and secured the Cup's ongoing place in Canadian sporting tradition.

Woody Strode died of lung cancer on New Year's Eve, 1994, at the age of eighty, in Glendora, California.

Goal Dust

I forget the exact age I found out I was a mixed breed. I thought we were all colored and everybody was similar. Nobody looked at your skin to see if you were a little bit brown or a little bit black. I looked like a Blackfoot and didn't know it. I've got the Plains Indian look from my high cheek bones. I have a picture of John Grass,[1] the Blackfoot Chief; I look just like him. But as strange as I looked, I never thought I was different from any other Negro. My daddy said I looked like an uncle who was six-feet-five and weighed 230 pounds. He worked on the wharf in New Orleans and could buck 300-pound bales of cotton. I grew to be six-feet four, 210 pounds, so I was a throwback, just on a smaller scale.

I didn't find out about my Indian blood until I got into college. I knew something had to be different because I had such a physical nature. I figured it out when the doctors started talking about me.

"You are the most physical person that has ever come through the gates of UCLA. What type of racial background do you have?"

"I don't know, I'se colored."

I went home, told my daddy what happened. He got a little indignant. He said, "You can tell them your great-grandmother was a Creek and your grandmother was a full-blood Blackfoot Indian!"

See, race was a very touchy subject for the Southerner who migrated. My daddy came to Los Angeles in 1900 to escape the racial pressure of Washington, Louisiana. I remember he had a trunk full of guns and thirty-ought-six bullets; that was based on his Southern background, fear. But he saw the white people out here were different from the white people where he came from. He wanted me to fall into their path. That's why he never talked about race.

My daddy was brick mason; his daddy taught him how to lay brick at the age of fourteen. There was no schooling then. My father got all his schooling after he moved out here to California. He got a high school education at night at Jefferson High School. But he knew construction. He helped build the City of Los Angeles. A lot of the old brick buildings downtown have my daddy's bricks in them. The faster you laid brick, the better you were. My daddy set a record, 2,500 bricks a day.

He had huge corns on his knuckles from handling all the brick and mud. If he hit you, he might as well have hit you with brass knuckles, it'd cut you. He was very strong and pretty beat up physically. He wouldn't teach

---

1   John Grass, Mathó Wathákpe or Charging Bear (1836–May 10, 1918) was a chief of the Sihasapa (Blackfeet) band of Lakota people during the 1870s through 1890s. Like Sylvester Long Lance, Grass attended the Carlisle Indian School in Carlisle, Pennsylvania (Welch and Cox).

me to lay brick. He was against me learning a trade. When I was a child he would say to me, "Daddy don't want you to do this. He wants you to go to school. He wants you to get educated."

He was smart enough to realize the importance of an education. So when I got into UCLA based on my athletic ability and became famous as an athlete, he was proud. He didn't know I was going to become a professional athlete; that was the furthest thing from his mind. But I'm glad I became an athlete; it gave me better insight and helped me integrate into society. Only the white world was involved in athletics in my generation, and I got headlined by the white press. That was unusual. You were a special Negro if they let you play.

My mother was much closer to the slave scene than my father. She was from New Orleans, Louisiana. Her mother was a slave, a servant in the master's house. The house servants were the best-looking slaves, and my mama was a beautiful woman. And she must have had some good people behind her because she went to school; she graduated from college. But even with that background, my mother was part Cherokee. That's how close the Indians and the slaves were in those days; they were both downtrodden in America. [...]

I was born in bed in a three-bedroom house near the corner of Fifty-First Street and Holmes Avenue in an area we called Furlong Tract. It was a predominantly black neighborhood, but we had some Germans, Italians, Mexicans living there. All the kids would play together in the street. We didn't have any problems like they have now. When they integrate now, they start a big fight. We fought some, but then we'd back off, shake hands, and go eat at the other guy's house.

Today, that area would be called South-Central Los Angeles. My daddy owned a half-acre of land there. He didn't build the house: it was a wood frame. And it stood twenty or thirty years before they tore it down. I lived there with my parents and my brother, Baylous Strode, Junior. He was two years older than me.

For some reason my brother inherited all my mother's side. He wasn't very physical; he was all up in his head. He was all ribs and no shoulders. He had to wear suspenders and a belt to keep his knickers up. When we'd go to the playground, he preferred to sit by himself and read a book. That made him pretty attractive to the bullies.

One day we were on the playground. Baylous was sitting in the bleachers behind the baseball diamond; I was across the field playing marbles with some friends. I looked up just in time to see some big kids throw my brother to the ground, getting ready to kick his brains out. I lost my clear blue aggie when I ran over there to help him out. There were some loose bats lying by home plate and I picked one up. I couldn't have been more than six years old and I ran over and hit this big kid right across the head with the bat. I laid him out, completely unconscious. The playground director came and carried me away, but I was exonerated because I was defending my brother. That's when Mama pulled me into church to try to teach me some rules.

My mother was like a protective old hen. That's the Louisiana attitude. She used to dress me up in Buster Brown collars with the coat, short pants, and string tie. And some big, hard, black shoes. I was a nice-looking kid anyway and after she dressed me up, I looked like a mama's boy. I used to get teased a lot for that.

If you looked too smooth, you were a marked man. But inside I had the gorilla, so I ended up fighting a lot. I could always fight well. When I got mad, I'd just black out and go. I had all my father's fire. After I got to high school he told me how glad he was my mother raised me in the church. As delicate as I looked, I had a tiger inside. That's why I excelled at football, because I had no fear. Of course we were all like that; I wasn't unusual. Everybody came off the earth and our education was kind of crude. […]

I didn't realize that going to UCLA was a rare step for a black kid. I started out there in 1934. Smokey Joe Lillard had already been to Oregon ten years before me. Iowa had Duke Slater, the first black All-American football player. He later became a judge. Fritz Pollard played for Brown; Paul Robeson played for Rutgers. And I can't leave out Ralph Bunche, who preceded Kenny Washington, Jackie Robinson, and me out at UCLA. […]

All the minorities followed UCLA because they were the first school to really give the minority athlete a chance to play. If we drew 100,000 people to the Coliseum, 40,000 of them would be black; that was just about every black person in the city of Los Angeles.

They came to see Kenny and me play. We received a lot of attention from the press that added to our exposure. It was unusual for a black athlete to get featured in the white press, but they had a special way of writing about us. I have this article written by Melvin Durslag of the *Herald-Examiner* that explains the journalistic style of that time:

THE CLIMATE OF WASHINGTON'S ERA

As a running mate of Jackie Robinson in the UCLA backfield, Kenny Washington rose to a place of prominence during a curious time in sports.

It was a period in which the black athlete was applauded, but not yet admitted to the main steam of athletics.

You didn't see Negroes playing at Notre Dame, or USC, or Standford, or Yale, or a number of other schools.

Nor did you see them in professional baseball or football.

Their place in the press was interesting, too. In the sports journalism practiced at the time, it was normal, if not fashionable, to patronize the black athlete in a way that would upset stomachs today.

Washington, for instance, was known as "Kingfish," from the Amos and Andy[2] character of the same name.

Together, he and Robinson were called the "Gold Dust Twins," a mocking appellation that might have been given a pair of black tap dancers working a nightclub in Reno.

You reflect on the routine language in the journalism of that period and you tend to wince. It wasn't uncommon to see a black runner described as a "sepia sprinter."

Nor did you blanch when you read about a "Senegambian speed merchant."

Another beauty was "dusky speedster."

Such was the climate during the time that Kenny Washington and Jackie Robinson romped up and down the lawn in college football, forming the best backfield twosome of that era.

Actually, we were called the "Goal Dust Twins." Bob Hunter of the *Los Angeles Examiner* started that, and he first used it as a reference to Kenny and me prior to Jackie Robinson joining us at UCLA. We were a running team, but when Kenny couldn't find room to maneuver he'd look for me downfield; I was his battery-mate. We didn't throw too many short passes,

---

2 *Amos 'n' Andy* was an American radio sitcom (1928–1960) adapted for television (1951–66) and set in Harlem. The character of George "Kingfish" Stevens was originally voiced by a white actor for radio; when the series moved to television the character was played by black actor Tim Moore. Kingfish was a trickster, often trying to lure Amos and Andy, both white characters, into trouble (Elizabeth McLeod).

mostly forty yards going away. And I could outrun everybody. We started hooking up on a lot of those passes and that's when Bob Hunter came up with the name.

He got the idea from a box of soap powder, Fairbank's Gold Dust, that used a picture of two coal-black kids on the cover. They were the "Gold Dust Twins." It was quite a popular advertising slogan at the time; we heard it on the radio every day. So that was just a play on words; Bob Hunter changed it to the "Goal Dust Twins" and hung that label on us. After Jackie arrived in 1939, Bob Hunter just kept it going.

Kenny and I didn't really pay any attention to it. We were always a little late because of the way we were raised. We were naïve; maybe that's why we were compatible with the white people. Hell, judging from the names we had for each other you would have thought we were the racists. This guy was a dago; that guy was a mick.

There was no enjoyment for the racists because Kenny and I had no fear of them. You call me a son of a bitch, that's fine; say the wrong thing and we are going to fight. I used to tell Kenny when we were playing for the Rams, "Thank God we thought we were equal."

We were out there knocking down people like we thought we were white. We had to have that attitude to play football in my generation; if we had felt the least bit inferior, we wouldn't have made it. We were lucky we came up on the West Coast.

I'll tell you how I was introduced to the Southern mentality. In 1936 Kenny and I were playing on the freshman team; in those days freshman couldn't play with the varsity. We started to hear some whispering among out teammates, "There are some players on the varsity saying they don't want to play with any niggers."

We came to learn that most of the talk was coming from a kid named Celestine Moses Wyrick. They called him Slats. A six-foot-four-inch, 212-pound, blond-haired, blue-eyed farm boy from Oklahoma, Slats played tackle. I played end and we figured to play next to one another on the varsity. Some of my teammates told me, "Slats ain't going to play with you, Woody. He called you a nigger, Woody."

The next year we were bound for a confrontation. We started scrimmaging and every time Spaulding put me in, Slats backed out and walked off the field. Finally, Bill Spaulding stepped in and said, "This can't go on. I'm the coach, Slats. If I put you in, you stay out there and play. Woody is a good ballplayer; he might make you an All-American."

But Slats wouldn't budge in his beliefs. He said, "I can't play next to a nigger because my folks would disown me."

Well, Spaulding was smart; he moved me onto the red team, the defensive squad. When we lined up, this put me right across the line from Slats. The whistle blew, the scrimmage started, I threw a block and Slats went down. He said, "You black son of a bitch."

The bulldog came out of me. I climbed on top of Slats and started punching. The coaches stood around and watched for a little while. Finally they said, "That's enough, Woody!" and they came and pulled me off.

Slats and I became good friends after that. He thought I was chicken. In Oklahoma, no black man would have had the nerve to stand up to him like that. He didn't know what kind of guts we had. He had no respect for Negroes, but I stood up for myself and he respected that. He had to learn.

We played Oklahoma that year. Before the game, Slats went over to talk to the Oklahoma players; he knew them all. He said, Kenny Washington and Woody Strode are my friends. They may whip you, but you'd better respect them for the good players they are!" [...]

In December, 1946, my baby boy was born. I couldn't sleep for the three weeks prior because of worrying and fretting. He kicked and thrashed so much I thought he was going to smother. Finally, when the day came, I drove Luana to the Queen of Angels Hospital in Hollywood and out he came without a hitch.

We named him Woody. He was a beautiful baby, and right from the beginning you could see lot more of the Hawaiian in him than me. His skin was a smooth cocoa brown, and he had big, luminous eyes like his mother.

We were still living in the apartment up in Hollywood, and when we brought little Woody home the Hawaiians put on a big luau for Luana and the baby in one of the vacant lots across the street. Everybody who came gave us a dollar; that's a Hawaiian custom for the firstborn. And they gave him his Hawaiian name, Kalaeloa; that means heavenly sky. Kalai is the name he goes by now. Officially his name is Woodrow Wilson Kalaeloa Strode.

Well, after I got cut from the Rams, I completely shut down. I kept myself busy cleaning and cooking, washing diapers and taking care of the baby. He and Luana were my only joy at the time. The New York Yankees of the All-American Football Conference contacted me and asked me to come back for a tryout. At first I said, "No, they don't want me to play football," and I was through integrating anything. But finally, not knowing what else to do, I decided I'd give it a try.

When I walked into Tan Topping's office—he was the general man-ager—he said, "Son, from the way they talk about you, we thought you were fifty years old!" Regardless, I didn't make their team. Once the Rams said my career was over, as far as the rest of football was concerned, that was it. "At his age, at this point in Woody Strode's career, he does not have the ability." And that ended my football career in the United States.

I took the train home from New York. On the way, I stopped in Chicago; I had some cousins living there. I got drunk for one week and licked my wounds. I was a warrior, I didn't know anything but football; now they weren't allowing me to play. I didn't know how I was going to support my wife and baby.

When I got home, Luana said, "Les Lear's been calling you from Can-ada. They want you to play football up there."

Les Lear played guard beside me on the Rams. A lot of that team had been cut one way or another, and some of them moved up to Canada to play. The Calgary Stampeders hired Les as their player-coach. He was allowed four Americans on the team; he reached for the best ones he could find.

I called, and Les said, "Woody, I got a job for you. Bring your shoes and your shoulder pads"—because he couldn't get the equipment up there—"I'll get you all the money I can." He sent me a contract offering $5,000 for the season, eighteen games, 100 dollars a week expense money, my hotel and transportation all paid for.

When I stepped off the plane in Calgary, it was like stepping back into the Old West. It was cowboy country; they were into cattle, oil, and grain. Their land was wide open. The plains between Calgary in the Alberta prov-ince and Regina in the Saskatchewan were just an extension of our great plains here in the United States.

At that time, you could get on the highway and hit a curve that would last a mile. As far as the eye could see there was nothing but acres and acres of flat land. They had Black Angus cattle up there, and I thought the Canadians were crazy, because when the temperature dropped below zero, they'd just back the cattle up against a mountain and drop hay. The cattle would all stand there bunched together. That's how they kept from freez-ing to death. And that was the healthiest meat in the world, because all the unhealthy weak livestock died.

The Canadian Indians used to bring wild game to my hotel room. I'm part Indian, but you never walk up to them and announce it. They'll see it in you. They came to all the football games, and it took them a month to ask me what kind of Indian blood I had. I told them, "American Blackfoot."

The guy who asked me had an interpreter talking for him; he replied, "We are Canadian Blackfeet." Well, that made us like brothers. And the Canadian Blackfeet were the richest Indians I ever saw; they owned oil fields and herds of Black Angus.

Now, when you visualize an American Indian, you usually see them naked except for a breechclout. The Canadian Indians wore suits they handmade out of deerskin. They wore fur-lined moccasins and feathered headdress. That was the difference between the American Indian and the Canadian; the Canadian Indian didn't get urbanized, reservationized. They were still living off the land.[3] They would hunt and fish for six months and store enough meat to last through the winter.

When the Canadian Indians harvested their grain, they'd leave a stubble one or two feet high. Across the road the white people would shave their fields clean. Well, on the Indian land you could throw a rock into the stubble and out would fly wild geese and ducks. The Indians were much closer to the land than the white men.

The Sarsi Indians were the land barons. They owned all the land from Calgary to Banff, 60 miles to the west.[4] Banff was the most spectacular place. In the springtime the lakes and streams would swell from the melting snow that covered the great Rocky Mountains. The water was sky-blue and the lakes reflected those purple, snow-covered Rockies like a mirror. The streams ran quickly and as the current flowed over the rocks, the water would back up into little white ice-cream colored puffs.

In the 1800s they built the largest, most grand resort in the world in Banff. Part of the attraction was a set of natural hot springs which were part of the national park there. After a game we'd drive up in weather thirty degrees below zero and soak out all the soreness in those hot sulfur baths.

In 1947, Canadian football players were still playing both ways, offense and defense. We practiced on a frozen hockey field. They laid the chalk

---

3   Strode's impression of Indigenous people in Canada in the late 1940s—wealthy, culturally intact, and free—belies the fact that they were subjects of the Indian Act and hence, under control of Indian Agents, limited to reserves, and subject to the genocidal abuses of the residential school system.

4   The Tsuut'ina (Sarcee) nation Indian Reserve No. 145, created by Treaty 7, borders the City of Calgary to the northeast, east and southeast, the Municipal District of Foothills No. 31 to the south and Rocky View County to the west and north. Their traditional territory was much more extensive (http://tsuutinanation.com).

marks right on top of the ice. I had to wear the old canvas pants that I hadn't worn since high school. I was playing pro football with eighteen-year-old Canadian kids, plus three other Americans: Pete Thodos, Rod Pantages, and Keith Spaith, our quarterback. Keith had tried out for the Rams but didn't make it. Les Lear brought him up to Canada, and he became a legend in their league. He married the daughter of the head of the Grain Exchange and became set for life.

We went undefeated my first year because we used the Rams' playbook. In those years, the Rams had the most innovative offense. The hardest thing about playing for the Rams was learning their system. I had never seen so many plays and had so many patterns to memorize. My Calgary teammates were just kids and ignorant about the game, so Les gave us only seven plays. Around end, off, tackle, over guard, center; he simplified it.

When we made it to the championship game, the whole town of Calgary packed up and made the trip east to Toronto. It was like traveling from Spokane, Washington to New York City. Two thousand cowboys and Indians climbed on the train with us, and everybody else followed in cars and wagons. But then, the people of Calgary wouldn't have turned out to see the Queen of England like they did to see the Stampeders play football.

See, the western territories, Regina, Winnipeg, Edmonton, and Calgary, that was dog territory. All the sophisticated, urban people lived in Montreal or Toronto; so when the town of Calgary traveled east to Montreal, that was like the American pioneer turning around and heading back to Boston. I've got this article written by Douglas MacFarlane for the *Toronto Daily News* that describes the scene.

> The Stampeders, with their ponies, their chuck-wagon, their Indian chief cheerleader, their flap-jacks and their western brand of enthusiasm, had taken over the town long before game time. All morning Saturday, the Calgarys paraded at the drop of a tuba note. They finally wound up at the city hall, fried some flaps for jacks, gave a guy by the name of Hiram [the mayor] a ride on one of their ponies, and headed for the stadium. It was quite a piece of mobile vaudeville by the time it hit Bloor St. One prairie schooner even had a little prairie schooner tagging along behind. There were wagons and trucks and cars and doggies and on them all were people peculiarly dressed in great big hats and great big boots and all of them shouting great big boasts.

We played Ottawa in the title game. Here's what happened: Ottawa had an extension play that started an end run. While the play developed, they would lateral the ball back as they approached the sideline. On the fourth lateral, they dropped the ball. I was at that spot, and I reached down and grabbed the ball. I could see the whites of the referee's eyes; he didn't blow his whistle, so I ran the ball 45 yards for the winning touchdown.

I was the hero. I left the field on my teammates' shoulders, a bottle of rye whiskey in my hand. No black athlete in the world had ever done that. I was their prized bull.

That night we partied in the Royal York Hotel, the best hotel in the city. I met an Indian friend out front, and he let me borrow his horse, a pure white multi-breed. I saddled up and walked that horse right up to the front entrance. The doorman watched me coming, frozen in his boots. My Indian friend held the door for me as I moved inside.

The lobby floor was marble cut into big squares with a black matrix. There were round marble columns that stretched fifty feet to a vaulted, cathedral-type ceiling. The night crowd was milling in tuxedos, dinner jackets and long, flowing gowns. The high-class conversation stopped when they saw me, like someone took a hammer to the alarm clock.

I walked that horse right through the crowd. I was wearing a white linen cowboy-type suit, reddish lizard-skin boots, and a navy blue silk scarf around my neck. I held the reins and my rye whisky in my left hand, my white ten-gallon hat in my right. I walked to the center of the lobby and pulled back on the reins. I kicked that horse hard and he reared up and spun around. I leaned way back in the saddle, looked up toward the ceiling and let out a war cry. The place erupted in applause and shouting. And when the police showed up, I sliced through them like cutting a cake as I charged out of there.

Lloyd Mayes
(1916–ca. 1972)

The Mayes family, along with the LaFayettes, Saunders, Shadds, and Dallards, are key families in the black pioneer history of Saskatchewan ("Heritage Individuals" sachm.org). Joseph and Mattie Mayes were leaders in their community. They immigrated from Oklahoma in April 1910 and helped to found the Shiloh Baptist Church in 1910. Mattie was the community's midwife and unofficial doctor and Joseph was the community's pastor. The church and cemetery—the only such black cemetery in Saskatchewan—were granted official Heritage Status in 2018.

Joseph and Mattie Mayes raised a large family of ten boys and three girls, including the ancestors of Lloyd Mayes. Lloyd was born to John and Viney Mayes on a homestead at 50, 23, 3W Eldon, Saskatchewan, in 1916. At the time of the 1916 Saskatchewan census, the Mayes family included eleven people: the parents, and nine sons and daughters, ranging in age from twenty-two to an infant ("Joseph Mayes" sachm.org).

The following oral history was originally published in *North of the Gully*, a community history of rural northwestern Saskatchewan, including Bear Island, Dry Gully, Eldon, Marie Hill, McLaren, Milleton, Standard Hill, and Tuidsmuir. The majority of the oral histories in this book are by Euro-Canadian and Euro-American settlers, but it also includes a few oral histories of the "Shiloh People" from the community of Maidstone, founded in 1910, and so named for the Baptist church in which they worshipped. *North of the Gully* was compiled by the North of the Gully History Book Committee and published by the *Maidstone Mirror* in 1981.

"Homebrew"

The memories of my boyhood on the farm in Saskatchewan are happy ones. I have fond recollections of wading in sloughs and prowling the woods to raid the nests of owls, hawks, crows and magpies. Each summer I would have the young of those birds for pets. The nicest bird I remember having for a pet was a blue jay.

I was a crack shot with a slingshot when I was about twelve years old. A slingshot or catapult was made of a leather pouch, two strips of rubber and forked willow branch shaped like the letter "Y." I killed rabbits, gophers and above all, ruffled grouse which my dog would chase up into a tree. We would eat the grouse. I never did worry about hunting season. I usually could hit a grouse in the head or neck on my first shot. Ammunition for a slingshot was small stones.

I would dig Seneca root in the summer (I think people made medicine out of it), and sold it at Allen's Store for about ten cents a pound. I would sometimes make a dollar or so for an evening's digging. In winter, I would trap a few weasels. Money was hard to come by back in the thirties, especially for a kid.

Growing up on a farm was not all fun as anyone who was raised on a farm could tell you. There is endless work and chores to be done. It fell my lot at a very young age to bring all the water from the well which was about a hundred yards from the house for cooking, washing, bathing, etc. Also the cutting of firewood and milking of cows, whose teats were so large my hand could not reach around them. I can still imagine I can hear my dad calling me to get up on cold winter mornings to make a fire in the stove. This was no small feat when you are about seven or eight years old and it's so cold in the house that the water has frozen in the water bucket. [...]

Christmas concerts were big in those days. The teacher would have us children practice our Christmas carols and plays for days before the concert night. Oh, the excitement it created among us kids! The tree and schoolroom with its tinsel and decorations, the packed school house with hardly standing room left. The kids were all decked out in their "Sunday best." The girls were all looking especially nice in their new dresses, and Eldon School had its share of pretty girls, like Verna Vandersterre, Esther Schwartz, Pearl Ramstead, Lily Pohl, to name a few who come to mind offhand. [...]

My uncle, Hank Mayes, liked concerts and dances because there were lots of customers for the "liquid refreshment" he pedaled. We referred to it as "homebrew." Wherever there was a gathering, my Uncle Hank was almost sure to have a few bottles stashed nearby. It was probably because of his wares that so many fights broke out at the dances. What he sold was "good stuff," according to his clientele. He used to give me one cent a bottle for all the empty beer bottles I could find for him when I was small. One of these beer bottles filled with "moonshine" or "homebrew," with cork stopper retailed for seventy-five cents. To friends or relatives, he might let a bottle go for fifty cents.

The basic ingredients for homebrew were water, wheat, sugar and yeast. All this went into a wooden barrel and was allowed to work or ferment for a certain number of days. Some folks used potatoes in place of the wheat. When the fermentation process was over, you strained the liquid from the "mash" (grain) and poured it in a vat or boiler, fitted with a top with a little round hole in it. Into this hole you inserted the end of a length of copper tubing or "quirl" as we called it. The quirl dipped or ran through a container of cold water. The boiler was placed on a stove or over a fire, and as the liquid would begin to boil the vapour or steam would rise and be forced through the quirl. As it passed through the cold water, the vapour would condense and come out of the other end of the quirl in liquid form. Where the quirl was inserted into the top of the boiler, had to be sealed around with bread dough to ensure that the vapour all went out through the quirl. This "running off" as they called it was a slow process as only a small trickle of liquid came out the end of the quirl. This liquid or homebrew was clear, like water and would burn if you lit a match to it. In the winter, manure had to be piled around the barrel while it was in the fermentation process. The manure would heat and keep the water from freezing.

I might add here that the penalty in those days to be caught with bootleg liquor was a hundred dollar fine or three months in the "school at Prince Albert," as they called it.[1] Since nobody had a hundred dollars for a fine, there was quite a number of folks who were caught and took the three-month session at "the school."

Seeing my uncle's success, my dad decided to go into the business for himself. He set himself up a still, not out in the woods like most folks, but in the little half storey we had for an upstairs. I remember my mother calling me one day and saying there was some fellows there to buy homebrew, but that Dad was away and she didn't know where he had hid the liquor. I asked her which way he had gone when he hid it. She said up in the woods, back of the barn. I trotted on up that way, saying to myself, "now where would I hide a jug of liquor if I was Dad?" Off to the side of a cut in the woods I saw a brush pile. I said to myself, "Now, there is a likely spot." I went over and looked down under the brush pile and sure enough, there was the jug. Within five minutes I was back with the jug under my arm for my mother to make the sale. When my dad came home and my mother told

---

1   Saskatchewan was not under prohibition in the 1930s, having repealed prohibition legislation in 1924, but it was nevertheless illegal for a non-government agent to make and sell alcohol (Hallowell).

him she had sold the liquor he could not understand how I had found it so easy, when he thought he had hidden it so well.

One winter day during the early part of 1937 us three kids were home by ourselves. Mother was in Edmonton staying with relatives while waiting for our brother, Richard, to be born. Dad had walked up to McLaren post office to see if there was a letter from her. All of a sudden Tunny and Neil Mayes came running through the woods and up to the house, saying that the R.C.M.P. had arrested Jeff Wright and were at Ed Mayes' place searching for homebrew, and would probably be at our place next. There was my father's still by the upstairs stovepipe. There was no time to empty that barrel, pail by pail. I was only twelve years old and I don't know where I got the strength, but I wheeled that barrel over to the top of the stairs and brought it down, one step at a time until I got it downstairs. I never spilled a drop on the floor. I wheeled it across the floor to the front door and slid it onto a little sled that we had. Tunny and Neil were laughing at me, but not offering any help. My sister, who was one year younger than I was, steadied the barrel on the sled while I pulled it up behind the barn and dumped the contents and covered it over with snow. I hid the barrel. It had only taken us about five minutes to get rid of the evidence.

A short while after my father came sauntering over the hill. We ran to meet him and told him the R.C.M.P. were in the neighbourhood. My father usually had one gait—dead slow. But when he heard that little bit of information, he broke into a run. We ran after him and told him we had already dumped the brew. He stopped running and said everything was alright then. We never did have a still in the house after that. As it turned out, the police never did make it around to our place.

In the spring of 1939, while I was still fourteen years old, I went to work out away from home for the first time. I worked for one month for Gust Behrens, for which I received the sum of twelve dollars. On thinking back now, he probably overpaid me. I took five dollars of the money and bought my first .22 rifle.

That fall when I turned fifteen I went out to work on the harvest for the first time. I went out stoking with my dad and later we worked on a threshing crew for the big wages then of three dollars per day. I liked stoking oats best of all. I did not like stoking rye or barley. Rye was very hard to make stand up and the beards would break off and work through your clothing, pricking your skin.

When I was small, Maidstone always seemed like a big town to me. However, when I came back through Maidstone on the train after moving away, and visiting such large centres as Montreal, Toronto, Vancouver and Winnipeg, I was surprised how it had shrank and how tiny it seemed.

I have such fond memories of living at Eldon, from my earliest recollection until that day in May, 1941, when we threw our meager belongings it the back of Forslund's truck and rolled away west.

Golder ("Goldie") Gordon
(ca. 1909–date unknown)

"My school days were the most important of my life. I wanted an education so badly that I read and re-read every book in the library including the *Books of Knowledge*," remembers Goldie Gordon, a member of the Shiloh community of Saskatchewan. Her schoolteachers "made a profound impression on me [...] and made me believe I was a worthwhile person." Gordon is an orator for whom little information is available, other than what she offers here. The public record reveals that she was born in Oklahoma circa 1909, crossed the border into Canada in 1912 with her family, and by the census of 1916, was living with her parents and six siblings at 50, 23, 3, Eldon, Saskatchewan.

Gordon's orature speaks compellingly not only about the poverty, hunger, and deprivation the black pioneers of Saskatchewan endured, but also how the unusually close-knit ethnically and racially mixed settler community pulled together to help feed and clothe those in need, black, white, and occasionally, Indigenous. The "tragedy" at the centre of this story is not the hard times she and her family endured; they endured them together, with music and one another's company. Such circumstances were tragic only if one had to face them alone.

Her orature was preserved in *North of the Gully* (1981), a community history of rural northwestern Saskatchewan that includes a few oral histories of the "Shiloh People" from the community of Maidstone.

"Even the bad was good, because we were together"

We were the Gordons, Rosa and James and three children, Garland, Goldie and Robert who emigrated from somewhere in the U.S.A.—possibly Oklahoma, to Canada, so that the children could have a better life than their parents had had.

Our father left us in St. Paul, Minnesota and went on to file on a homestead in Canada because Mother was about to deliver a fourth child, Ruby,

150

who was born there in December 1912. While she was still an infant, we went on to join our father in the Milleton district of Saskatchewan, where he had a sandy homestead on the edge of a nameless lake and had built a one room log house. I can vaguely remember the trip from the railroad station in Maidstone by ox team and wagon, driven by Jim Jefferson. It took two days to make the journey.

The first winter was a cold gruesome one and we might have starved to death except for the neighbours, most of whom we didn't know. The women came one day and brought us a supply of food and even some warm clothing for us kids, which caused our mother to shed the only tears I ever saw in her eyes.

Nobody had less than we did but our mother and dad taught us to read before we were school age and to sing, so we always had music to help us through the bad times.

There were many bachelors on neighbouring farms and my mother took in washing from them. She worked very hard and, as there were no doctors near, she also tended the sick and delivered most of the babies for miles around. In that way we got our first cow and almost enough food.

In 1916, my father got the job teaching at the new Eldon school and bought our first team of horses. He bought them from John Haggstrom for one hundred and seventy-five dollars, including harness. They were a large bay mare and a beautiful black and white pinto gelding.

In 1915, Claudia was born and Dad started building a larger house, still log but with a shingle roof and larger windows. There the family lived for the next twenty years.

I started school at age six with Mr. Julius Schrump as teacher in the old school with its pot-bellied stove for heat. We could not have school in the winter time, as the building was too cold. I remember twice a week, we had a hot meal prepared by the teacher and the older girls, made up of donations by different families each week. We younger girls did the washing up afterwards.

After we got the new school, we had a furnace and school was open all winter. My school days were the most important of my life. I wanted an education so badly that I read and re-read every book in the library including the *Books of Knowledge*. My teachers made a profound impression on me, especially F.K. McGill and Miss Erma Pickel. She befriended and encouraged me and made me believe I was a worthwhile person. We kept in touch by letter long after school days were over.

On Sundays, we would go by wagon and team to Shiloh Church[1] where my mother taught Sunday school and Dad took the church services.

I remember once a month, the members had a picnic dinner on the church grounds. I'll always think of those spreads and some of the few times we kids had enough to eat.

We had an aunt who was brought up by my mother and a young cousin who had rickets so badly that she spent over a year in the Lashburn Hospital under Doctor Morgan's care. I saw her walk only once, when she was four years of age. She died shortly after and was buried in Shiloh Cemetery where my aunt followed a few years later and was buried there in five feet of water, in the grave. I always thought the body would eventually petrify. She also had an infant daughter in the casket.

The winters were bitterly cold. I recall Louis Rolin would come around with a portable engine and buzz saw and cut our winter wood and chop grain for animal feed. It would sometimes take two days and the men's hands would sometimes freeze while handling the icy wood.

The winter of 1919 was particularly cold. The straw and haystacks were covered so deeply in snow that the animals couldn't feed and I can still hear the bawling of hungry cattle and every day there were more snow-covered carcasses of Mr. Hafstein's cattle.

The winter of 1918, the Spanish influenza devastated the country. My mother was called from home to home, nursing the sick until they either recovered or died. She would come home once in a while and do our laundry outside on the porch in the cold, so as not to infect the family. I particularly remember the tragedy of Eric Lundstrom's family and how the mailman, Ed Nord, died in his bachelor shack all alone.

Then there was the cold winter that my little friend, Tilmar Stone, was murdered and the R.C.M.P. from Maidstone would drive out and stop at our place for a meal and feed his team when they were searching for Mr. Stone.

Every spring the Indians would come down from the north and journey south looking for odd jobs and trapping the lakes. I especially remember George Thunderchild, whom we called "High and Low" because he seemed to have had a broken back, which left one shoulder higher than the

---

1   The Shiloh church was the hub of the black community in Maidstone, Saskatchewan. The church, constructed of hand-cut poplar logs from the North Saskatchewan River's banks in 1910, along with the adjoining cemetery, received Provincial Heritage Property Designation in 2018.

other. He could have been any age up to one hundred years and had such an enormous appetite that it became a joke to feed him.

On one occasion my mom gave him a roasted chicken, a bowl of potatoes, a loaf of bread, a pound of butter, a quart of saskatoons and a pot of coffee. He ate the whole meal, including all the butter, then he mixed the cream with the sugar in the bowl and drank that. Then he walked a mile to the Haftner brothers' place and ate three-dozen fried eggs and went on to Mrs. Thornsteinson's and ate another meal.

In the early days, threshing was done by steam engines and huge grain separators. It took about fourteen men and teams to keep the monster going and as there were only a few around, they would go from field to field threshing for everyone. I remember the Nicholson brothers did ours. It was great excitement cooking for a large threshing crew and we recognized each rig by the sound of their whistle.

I don't remember exactly when the Milleton Hall was built, but my father was given the job of custodian. It was a great thrill to go with him to clean the hall and start the fires on movie night. I saw my first picture show that way. I remember when the Milleton and Dry Gully schools would hold a joint Christmas concert. There, we would have an enormous tree, lit by real candles, with gifts for those children whose families could afford it. The Ladies' Aid always provided candy bags for all the children.

The Ladies' Aid was one of the great blessings of the times. They met, I believe, twice a month, at different members' homes. It was not just a coffee club. They really worked at sewing, knitting, etc., and gave to the needy. Our family benefitted more than once from them. I was fascinated by the weaving loom which the men built. All the old materials were cut into strips and woven into rugs which were so durable that I still have one after all these years.

At age fifteen, I had to quit school and go to work to help the family. My first job was for Mr. and Mrs. P.A. Olsen. Then I worked for P.M. Lundells, who were so kind to me and taught me so much that helped me to survive in later years.

I worked one winter for Mr. and Mrs. Chas. Haggstrom, who had a general store. We would sell men's overalls for a dollar and fifty cents and work shirts for seventy-five cents.

During the hungry thirties, no one had any cash so we made our own amusement—skating on the lake—and we formed a community club where we met each Saturday night at different homes for music and dancing. Everyone brought different things for midnight lunch. Many of those people are no longer with us but I have loving memories of them all. It was during this time that my brothers and sister-in-law formed a dance band after teaching themselves to read music. They traveled all over the country playing from eight-thirty p.m. until sometimes four a.m. They played summer and winter for about ten dollars per night when they could get it. We met some wonderful people and made friendships that lasted for a lifetime and we survived as my mother said before she died, "Even the bad was good, because we were together."

Gwendolyn Hooks
(1920–2018)

Gwendolyn Hooks was born in 1920 and grew up on a farm near Breton, Alberta. She went to elementary school at Shakespeare and Newbrook, Alberta, and attended Eastwood High in Edmonton, and the University of Alberta, where she graduated with a teacher's certificate and later a bachelor's degree in education. She taught in the county of Leduc, specializing in teaching special-needs children and becoming principal for special-needs education in 1966, a post she held for a decade. Hooks retired from teaching in 1979.

In 1997 Hooks published her 112-page memoir-cum-history of black pioneers, co-written with her husband Mark, called *The Keystone Legacy: Recollections of a Black Settler*, with Brightest Pebble Press. The book is significant for its critical reading of Canadian history and for the way it remembers the peculiar position of black settlers with respect to Indigenous people and their land. The black community Hooks writes about did not necessarily consider themselves Indigenous, despite a known degree of racial mixing. The first selection, below, "We were considered Indians," is the sixth chapter excerpted from this hybrid history/memoir. Readers may wish to consider the quick reversal in these vignettes between the acts of hunting and being hunted, and the unsettling proximity in Hooks's narrative of her discussion of wounding to her reflections on belonging to the Canadian nation.

In 1979 Hooks was elected president of her local Breton and District Historical Society. The organization earned national and international attention for its work, which included the restoration of the Keystone Cemetery, where many of the early black setters in Alberta are buried.

As Time Goes By, her self-published collection of poems, came out in 1992. The collection, written in rhyming, metred couplets, revisits pioneer history, and treats Christian topics, and themes of friendship and community building, often from a recognizably Albertan, "small-government" political stance.

For her contribution to the history of black settlers in Alberta and her promotion of education, Hooks was awarded an Honorary Degree of Doctor of Laws by Athabasca University in 2005. She died in 2018, at the age of ninety-seven.

❦

"We were considered Indians"

The first cabin Dad built was made of logs near the creek running across our quarter section. It measured about 12 by 18 feet. He built part of the cabin into the bank of the ravine, and earth was banked around the outside of it to deflect the wind, snow and cold.

The windows were at ground level. One had to descend three steps from ground level to enter. The roof was covered with the customary tar paper and slabs. Flour sack curtains divided the inside of the small cabin into four rooms. The boys occupied one small bedroom and the girls another. Mom and Dad had a bedroom, and the fourth room was the kitchen. As the family increased, Dad added more rooms.

The kitchen contained a wood-burning cook stove with a reservoir and a tall heater. We heated the house with wood—a plentiful and free source of energy. Then, of course, sitting prominently in the centre of the room was Mom's treasured oak table and chairs that she had brought from Oklahoma. Winters were bitterly cold and the snow was deep. The settlers were not used to this type of weather. I can remember my father-in-law, Willis Day saying, "We bought winter clothes before leaving Oklahoma, but they were not warm enough for the Canadian winters. It was December when we reached Winnipeg and it was so cold we had to look down to see if we had any clothes on at all."

The settlers had no winter footwear. When they went outside, they wrapped their feet in gunny sacks to keep them warm. The children did the same when they went to school in the winter.

Thick bush and tall trees surrounded our house. The entire area was covered with heavy bush except for a few cleared acres and, of course, vegetable gardens which every settler depended upon. Very little money ever passed hands. Most settlers lived off the land and bartered when a need arose.

There were about 150–200 black people living in the area. They lived a free life and didn't have to get up to go to work. They stuck together. It was impossible to live independently because it was very hard to make a living.

Loggers made between $1 and $3 a day contracting. While trying to "prove up" on their homesteads, some settlers made a bit of money hauling lumber by mule team to Leduc or Edmonton where they received $5 to $6 per load or they traded lumber for groceries, clothing, or farm equipment. Of course, in those days, the pioneers had their own chickens, pigs, and milk cows.

Money being scarce, men from Keystone usually worked in Edmonton to get money for supplies. The closest town to Keystone when the blacks first settled there was Leduc, fifty miles away. It was a four-day round trip by horse team. If the weather proved contrary, it would take a week or more to get there and back. Spring was the worst time to travel. A thick gumbo sucked up everything, making travel all but impossible. The first stop out of Keystone was Stone's Corner, just east of Warburg. Travelers usually spent the first night there.

Alfred Stone was born in Ontario and came to Alberta around 1908. He and his wife Pauline homesteaded in what is today the Warburg area. They opened a post office named Stone's Corner in the spring of 1909. Alfred served as post master and hauled mail from Telfordsville. He also operated a small sawmill and raised six children.

Settlers from Keystone on their way to Leduc would stay at Stone's Corner overnight and try to complete the journey to Leduc on the following day. They always carried their own bedding and feed for their horses. Stone was always pleased to put weary travelers in his barn loft at no charge. If for any reason the travelers couldn't reach Leduc from Stone's Corner, they would stop over at Buford, about 12 miles west of Leduc.

A trip to Leduc was always a major undertaking, but it was the closest place to store up on the necessities they could not provide for themselves such as flour, sugar, salt, clothing, etc. When the Yeoford store opened, it was much more convenient, but a trip there could still eat up a whole day. At that time you could buy butter for 10 cents a pound and eggs for 5 cents a dozen.

Most of our consumer goods were locally produced. Land was cleared for fields or gardens in areas burnt over by fires or less densely covered with bush. All of the settlers had a few cows and chickens. The women, with the help of children, tended large gardens, the produce of which supplied the community with their main source of food. The women also canned vegetables and wild berries, which grew like weeds throughout the bush.

After school, we children worked in the garden or did such chores as bringing in the night supply of wood. The older children split wood and made kindling for the next day. Weekends and holidays were spent in this fashion. Children also toiled hard in the fields, pulling roots and cutting brush with an ax. Women and children usually did these jobs because the men worked away from home to get money for other needed staples and supplies.

But they enjoyed berry picking, and there was a vast number of different types of wild berries including strawberries, blueberries, saskatoons, gooseberries, black currants, red currants, pincherries, chokecherries, three different kinds of cranberries, and others with names we didn't know. There were edible greens, mushrooms, and dandelions that made excellent wine.

After exhausting all the berries in their land, Elizabeth Hayes would ask other farmers if she and the children could pick pigeon berries on their farms. They always gave their permission with the stipulation that she not take the blueberries. She would agree, but often the sight of blueberries was too much of a temptation and she would secretly take a few and hide them under the pigeon berries.

Everyone was an expert on root cellars for storing vegetables, and each family had a unique way of constructing theirs. Our root cellar was made of logs and dug into the side of the creek bank. It faced south and was about five feet high and five feet wide. A vent protruded from the south wall. Bins were made for the vegetables—potatoes, carrots, beets, turnips, and parsnips. These were covered with straw in the winter. Because our meals were mostly home-grown, they always had the taste and texture of home-grown food—new vegetables, prairie chicken, rabbit, or tame chicken. My sister Vergie's kids remember how they used to look forward to family gatherings at Grandma's. Her meal preparation was an art form that she nurtured throughout her life. Everything was so basic, yet everything an adventure. The crowning climax of every visit for the kids was when Uncle Edward would take them down to the ravine to chop ice for homemade ice cream.

Ours was a subsistence economy; therefore, the men and some of the women in the community hunted. After all, we lived in virgin wilderness and sometimes, when our larders were low, we hunted out of season. Indians could hunt out of season; and at least in the states, we were considered Indians and the Canadian government representatives themselves referred to us as Indian on occasions. However we looked at it though, hunting out of season just wasn't right, and sometimes we got caught.

Wild animals such as deer, wild chicken, prairie chicken, rabbits, bears, groundhogs, and moose meat were plentiful. There was the ever-present porcupine, but it was unlawful to kill it because it could be used as food for travelers who were either lost or out of food in the wilderness. The existence of porcupines saved many lives because they're so easy to kill. I never ate a porcupine, but I'm told they taste something like pork.

The animals never bothered anyone unless they themselves were bothered. They would attack to defend their young. Most men went hunting, so we always had plenty of wild meat. Because of the abundance of berries, bears were a common sight.

My two older brothers actually domesticated a deer. It was just an orphan fawn when they found it. He became part of the family and followed my brothers all over the property. He used to wrestle with the kids and would come into the house looking for cake, bread, and other food. My brothers put a bell around its neck so that they could keep track of him as he grew older and wandered further afield. Then one day, he didn't come home and we never saw him again. We were a sad lot for a long time because we had all grown to love that beautiful and gentle creature. Hunters probably killed him. Being tame, he would have made an easy mark.

Occasionally we'd spot the odd pack of wolves. They never attacked anyone to my knowledge, but they could give settlers a terrible fright.

My older sister Vergie told of an incident in the early '20s. Looking out the window one day, she spotted nine wolves approaching the house. Locking the door, she warned the rest of the household of the approaching unwelcome visitors, and a frightful hush fell over the house as they peeped out of the windows and watched the wolves slink passively past the cabin and disappear into the bush.

Like any community, we had our ups and downs and our own memorable local adventures. One day my brother Richard and I were going to get milk from Walter Johnson, our neighbour. We went down the hill and across the creek where we had a garden and a large potato patch surrounded by two barb wire fences to keep the cows and horses out. Richard and I were smoking cigarettes we had stolen from Dad. It was dusk and in the distance we could hear talking and laughing. We thought it was our older sisters coming home from our brother Ellis's place.

We could not let them see us smoking or we'd be in deep trouble. Richard and I threw the cigarettes away and ran like jack rabbits across the field. I got through one fence, but forgot about the other and hit it at a dead run. A barb tore my cheek right through to my gums.

Well, we had to go home. I was bleeding like a stuck pig. My hands and mouth were full of blood. Mother was so excited she didn't even ask why we were running. She finally got the bleeding stopped and bandaged me up. I still have the scar to remind me of that little episode many years ago.

My grandmother didn't like Canada, so she went back to Oklahoma before I was born; therefore, I never knew my grandparents, aunts, uncles or cousins. My parents were too poor to go back to Oklahoma; fortunately, they stayed and raised ten children—all proud Canadians.

Fil Fraser
(1932–2017)

"No art, no life," said path-clearing broadcaster, journalist, writer, film producer, educator and human rights advocate Fil Fraser when he was awarded the Alberta Order of Excellence in 2015. "Art decorates our lives. Art makes our lives meaningful. Without the arts, life would be plain and uninspiring and unforgiving" (Alberta Order of Excellence).

Felix Blache-Fraser was born in 1932 in Saint-Léonard de Port Maurice, now part of greater Montreal, the eldest of six children. His father, Felix Blache-Fraser, arrived from Trinidad in 1920 as a scholarship student; his mother, Marguerite Wiles, was born on a Canadian ship inbound from Barbados to Montreal. Whereas the majority of Montreal's black community lived around St. Antoine Street, where men worked as railway porters, "[m]y father, for whatever reason, decided we would grow up better and stronger away from that community" (Brennan).

Fil Fraser liked to tell people his family of origin were black, rich, Protestant, and English-speaking in a Montreal community where most people were white, poor, Catholic, and French. "Nobody could attack our livelihood because my father was a real estate developer and most of the people who lived around us had brought their property from him," he said. "Most of them owed us money. Our livelihood wasn't threatened, but as kids we often fought our way home from school. It became a game. We all got to be good fighters or fast runners, or both. My emergence as a minor track star in high school was not accidental. It was motivated by fear. You only fought if you couldn't run" (Brennan).

In high school Fraser got involved in radio because, as he put it, "I liked to be heard" (Alberta Order of Excellence). He became Canada's first black broadcaster when he landed a job, at the age of nineteen, with CKFH radio in Toronto in 1951. Later, he worked at a radio station in Barrie, Ontario, where he was the sports director and play-by-play announcer, calling games for the Barrie Flyers Junior-A hockey team. In 1955, Fraser moved back to Montreal to attended McGill University, during which time he hosted an all-night show at CKVL. In 1956, he worked as a news editor at CFCF radio in Montreal, eventually becoming chief writer. At the age of twenty, Fraser changed his first name to Fil at the request of a radio program director who didn't think Felix was a suitable name for an announcer (Brennan).

Fraser moved to Regina in 1958, where he continued to work in broadcasting; he hosted the "hot stove league" between period commentaries for broadcasts of the Saskatchewan Junior Hockey League. In 1960 he founded the *Regina Weekly Mirror*, dedicated to chronicling the introduction of Medicare by the Tommy Douglas government. He was subsequently the director of education at the Saskatchewan Bureau on Alcoholism and, in 1965, moved to Edmonton to work at the Division of Alcoholism of the Alberta Department of Health, which later became AADAC.

In Regina in 1963 a real estate company refused to rent Fraser an apartment, saying the firm had a "whites only" policy. "My reaction was not one of anger, fear or shame. Rather, it was a welcome opportunity to say: 'You can't do that in this country. Any more.'" Saskatchewan had just passed a fair accommodation law and Fraser's case was the first to be tried under the new legislation. The realty company was found guilty and fined. Fraser was offered the apartment. "I declined, of course" (Brennan).

In 1965 Fraser moved to Edmonton, which he adopted thereafter as his permanent hometown. He became program director in 1969 of Alberta's Access TV Network, Canada's first on-air educational television station. In the early 1970s, he was the co-anchor of CBC Edmonton's supper hour news and public affairs program and, subsequently, hosted ITV Television's Fil Fraser Show. Later that decade, Fraser hosted "Talk Back" at CJCA, Edmonton, the most highly rated talk show on CJCA from 1974 to 1979. His warm and authentic persona encouraged guests to open up and audiences to tune in.

Fraser wrote, produced, and directed several educational films for television through his own production company. He then went on to produce films, including Alberta's first feature film, *Why Shoot the Teacher*, in 1976; it became the highest-grossing film in Canada that year. Filmed in Hannah, Alberta, it is a coming-of-age story about a young teacher in Depression-era Saskatchewan. It was followed by *Marie Anne* in 1977 and *The Hounds of Notre Dame* in 1980. In 1974, Fraser helped to organize the first Alberta Film Festival Awards. He chaired the first Commonwealth Games Film Festival in 1978 and founded the Banff International Television Festival the following year.

Fraser also published four non-fiction award-winning titles. *Alberta's Camelot: Culture and the Arts in the Lougheed Years* (2003), from which the following chapter is taken, is not only a rigorously researched social history (note that all the numbered footnotes in the text, below, are Fraser's originals) but it is also a

lively and eminently readable account of the years Peter Lougheed's Progressive
Conservatives held power in Alberta from 1971 to 1985. The book celebrates what
Fraser characterized as Alberta's own "Quiet Revolution." Whereas, as George
Bowering noted while at the University of Alberta in the late 1960s, the province
was then a "cultural desert, [...] inhabited mainly by ungrammatical pro-Socred
letter writers, stupid newspaper editors, fiery eyed fundamentalists and right-wing
politics," after Lougheed, "culture and the arts rose from the bottom rung on the
ladder of government priorities to a place much closer to the top." During this time
the province opened up to its multicultural reality, and began to celebrate and
financially support the arts. The book is written in Fraser's signature colloquial
style. He spins the social history of Alberta into a fascinating yarn with engaging
anecdotes about Alberta's quirky political figures and many social ironies.

Fraser is also the author of *Running Uphill—The Fast, Short Life of Canadian Champion Harry Jerome* (2006), a biography of the Olympic sprinter that
was filmed by the National Film Board, and *How the Blacks Created Canada*
(Lone Pine, 2009). His memoir on Canadian multiculturalism, "Black Like Me,"
appeared in the one-hundredth-anniversary issue of *Saturday Night* magazine in
January 1987.

His record of work as a human rights advocate is extensive. Between 1989
and 1992, Fraser served as chief commissioner of the Alberta Human Rights
Commission. During that time, Fraser publicly called for protection of gay people
against discrimination even though the provincial government balked at enshrining
that protection in law. He was vindicated in 2009 when Alberta's Human Rights,
Citizenship and Multiculturalism Act was amended to include sexual orientation as
a ground for complaint. In 1990, Fraser became a member of the Citizens' Forum
on Canada's Future, a federal Royal Commission also known as the Spicer Commission, established in 1990 by Prime Minister Brian Mulroney, the aim of which
was public discussion of linguistic and social divisions in Canada in the wake of the
Meech Lake Accord.

Fraser's lifetime of achievement includes a long list of awards and recognitions.
He received an Alberta Achievement Award in 1978 for excellence in filmmaking,
was honoured for public service by the Harambee Foundation of Canada in 1989,
and became a Member of the Order of Canada in 1991. He was fêted by the Black
Business and Professional Association in 1999 for excellence in the professions. In
2001, the Canadian Association of Black Journalists created the Fil Fraser Lecture
Series honouring his commitment to cultural and social diversity in Canada. In
2005, he was inducted into the Edmonton Cultural Hall of Fame and awarded the
Alberta Centennial Medal. In 2012 he received the Queen Elizabeth II Diamond

Jubilee Medal. Fraser was granted an Honorary Doctor of Literature degree from the University of Alberta in 1991.

Fil Fraser died of heart failure in Edmonton at the age of eighty-five.

"Alberta's own Quiet Revolution"

In December 1965 when I moved from Regina to Edmonton, it was almost like moving to a different country. Alberta was rich. Saskatchewan was poor. But even as a have-not province, subject to capricious weather and yoyo bounces in the price of grain, Saskatchewan was one of the most politically interesting places in North America. The province had elected the Co-operative Commonwealth Federation (CCF) party in 1944, the first socialist government on the continent. The whole country was fascinated by Premier Tommy Douglas's plan to introduce Medicare. In Saskatchewan almost everyone talked about, argued about, got involved in politics; it was, along with football and curling, their favourite sport.

Not in Alberta. It was as if the subject embarrassed people in my new province. Alberta's Social Credit was as much a prairie populist movement as the CCF, but it was at the other end of the political spectrum. The Socreds, founded by William Aberhart, burst into power in 1935. Under his leadership, and that of Ernest Manning who took over in 1943, the party won election after election by landslides. Yet it was an inside joke that you could hardly find anyone who admitted to voting Social Credit. Coffee talk seemed to be about anything but provincial politics. When the subject did come up, there were elbow-to-the-ribs nudges, winks, and behind-the-hand whispers about "funny money." One of the principal pledges of early platforms of the Socreds had been to wrest the perceived control of the economy from the (eastern) banks by creating their own currency. The Social Credit governments, like their successors the Reform and Alliance parties, saw economic issues in an "East vs. West" frame. During the 1930s, Alberta made several legislative attempts to create a form of currency. The government in Ottawa disallowed each attempt. So-called Prosperity Certificates worth one dollar when issued in 1936 have long since become collectors' items.[1] Cheque-like Citizen Royalty Dividend Certificates issued in 20-dollar denominations during the 1950s, "being dividend for 1957 in accordance with the Oil and Gas Royalties Dividend Act," have suffered the same fate.

1   A.J (Alf) Hooke, *30+5: The Incredible Years of Social Credit* (Edmonton: Institute of Applied Art, 1971), 9. Hooke was a former cabinet minister.

Orvis Kennedy, a member of the party's inner circle, summed up the Social Credit mindset in a 1951 pamphlet. Elected to the original board of the party in 1934, he was described by the *Edmonton Journal*'s Karen Sornberger as "the organizational czar of the party." In *Principles and Policies of Social Credit—A Free Individual Enterprise Movement Opposed to Socialist and all Other Forms of Statism*, Kennedy proclaimed,

> Social Creditors believe that whenever goods and services are produced there should automatically be brought into existence sufficient purchasing power or medium of exchange, to at all times deliver those goods and services to the people … It is the sovereign right of the people to demand that their government create this medium of exchange in sufficient amounts, and only in sufficient amounts, to distribute this wealth to the people, the rightful owners. Anything short of this is the betrayal of the people's rights.[2]

So, instead of discussing provincial politics, Albertans (especially those who worked for or whose jobs depended on the government) chuckled at the malapropisms of the national Social Credit leader, Robert Thompson, an American-born chiropractor who, through the 1950s and most of the 1960s, led the federal wing of the party from a base in Red Deer. He once complained from his seat in the House of Commons that, "Parliament is being turned into a political arena," and declared, "The Americans are our best friends, whether we like it or not."[3] Thompson seemed to be on a different wavelength from the provincial party upon which he was financially dependent. He resigned in 1967 when the Alberta party, whose funds were tightly controlled by Orvis Kennedy, cut him off. After Thompson, the federal party provided new grist for the banter with the equally entertaining Québec Creditiste leader Réal Caouette.

No one chuckled at the leadership of Ernest Manning. He and his government had an earned reputation for being nit-pickingly meticulous and almost insufferably honest in their management of the province's affairs. And that, not Social Credit's debatable economic theories, is what produced majorities through nine successive elections.

---

2   Orvis Kennedy, *Principles and Policies of Social Credit—A Free Individual Enterprise Movement Opposed to Socialist and all Other Forms of Statism*, 1951. [pamphlet], n.p. Available at the Legislature Library.

3   Peter C. Newman, *Home Country* (Toronto: McClelland & Stewart, 1971), 198. His statement about the Americans might not seem quite as funny today.

My move from Saskatchewan, a province of political free thinkers, to Alberta's tight-lipped, straight-laced environment required adjustment. The deep-rooted differences between the western neighbours developed early and ran deep. Saskatchewan was the province where, in 1960, Tommy Douglas, facing down the frenzied rage of the medical establishment, had introduced universal health care. The storied Roman Catholic priest Père Athol Murray, founder of Notre Dame College in Wilcox, Saskatchewan,[4] was temporarily banished from the province by the Regina archbishop during the Medicare crisis of the early 1960s. Murray's scathing attacks on socialized medicine led to accusations that his pronouncements were close to an incitement to riot. Thirty years later, in 1990 and 1991, I travelled the country as a member of the Citizen's Forum on Canada's Future, also known as the Spicer Commission, which was attempting to discover how Canadians felt about their country. It is one of our great national ironies that people invariably told me that, for them, the most important thing about being Canadian was our health-care system. Many who were prepared to fight to keep Medicare in the 1990s were the children of those who had fought bitterly against its introduction in the 1960s.

The Alberta government saw itself as anything but socialist and was, with equal irony, the place where old (left-wing) Depression war cries such as "The People versus the [eastern] Banks"[5] echoed loudly. To counter their power, the Aberhart government had created its own (near) bank, the Alberta Treasury Branches, in 1938.[6] There was shocked disbelief in his party when, after his retirement, former Premier Manning accepted membership on the board of directors of one of those "damned eastern banks." The reaction from the old guard was swift and bitter. A.J. (Alf) Hooke, one of the original Social Creditors who had come into government with Aberhart and Manning, wrote the following:

> In February 1969, the papers carried a story which I am sure surprised every Social Creditor ... the Honourable E.C. Manning, who throughout his career

---

4 Murray's story is chronicled in Jack Gorman, *Père Murray and the Hounds: The Story of Saskatchewan's Notre Dame College* (Sidney, BC: Gray's Publishing, 1977) and in my feature film *The Hounds of Notre Dame*.

5 Both CCFers and Socreds railed against the control of the eastern banks during the Depression years.

6 The legislation establishing the Treasury Branches (now known as ATB Financial) was challenged by the federal government, and the province was forced to make amendments that restricted the areas in which the "Branch" could operate.

has condemned in every way orthodox banking, has been appointed as a Director of the Board of the Canadian Imperial Bank of Commerce. I was only one of the thousands who could not believe what I read.[7]

I have always found it fascinating that the two provinces, with similar agricultural economics (until the discovery of oil at Leduc in 1947), should choose such divergent political directions. During the early 1970s, I tried hard to put together a television special that would have brought Ernest Manning and Tommy Douglas together. As a journalist, at the time co-anchoring[8] the CBC supper-hour news and public affairs program in Edmonton, I came to know Manning as well as a journalist could expect to. I knew Tommy Douglas event better, having had many conversations with him during my time in Saskatchewan.[9] I thought that an open discussion might have provided valuable insights into why men with such similar backgrounds chose such different paths; why the politics of Saskatchewan and Alberta are so diametrically opposed. The rules, as I proposed them, were that the discussion was to focus on the early days of their respective movements, and that there was to be no discussion of contemporary politics. The objective was to look back on the years when Social Credit founder and Premier William Aberhart in Alberta and CCF[10] founder J.S. Woodsworth in Saskatchewan were trying, in the midst of the Great Depression, to find ways to improve the lives of their people. Manning and Douglas were contemporaries, born four years apart. Manning was from small-town Saskatchewan, and Douglas emigrated from Scotland to Canada at the age of 15. Both became prairie preachers, powerful orators and honest, effective administrators. Each was heir to a political movement created by an idealistic, charismatic leader; each was deeply devout in his Christian beliefs. Each led successful, long-term governments; Manning from 1943 to 1968, Douglas from 1944 to 1961, when he entered federal politics. Yet these men, who had come to maturity in the same era, in the same region, who developed parallel political careers, saw the world through dramatically different lenses.

---

7 David G. Wood, *The Lougheed Legacy* (Toronto: Key Porter, 1985), 23.

8 First with Jean Patenaude, now a successful arts film producer, and with Dawn MacDonald, whose company produces religious television programs in Toronto.

9 I met him on my first day in Saskatchewan, when I found myself standing side by side with him at a urinal in Regina's Hotel Saskatchewan.

10 The Co-operative Commonwealth Foundation was the forerunner of the New Democratic Party.

Douglas was enthusiastic about the television project from the beginning and offered to turn up virtually anytime, anywhere, for the discussion. But Manning, who gave me what I thought was provisional agreement, hedged for many months about a suitable time and place. He never really said no. Years later, after I had abandoned the project, I encountered his son, Preston, on Edmonton's Jasper Avenue. He told me, lowering his voice to a near whisper, that maybe it was because his father simply couldn't stand to be in the same room with "that socialist."

By the time Manning stepped down after 25 years as premier, people in the province, especially in the cities and most especially in Edmonton, were becoming restless. It was the '60s. The western world was trying to lighten up (remember teach-ins, Rochdale, Free University North[11] and "turn on, tune in, drop out"?). But many in Alberta's old guard government still displayed a defensive, if not openly skeptical, view of culture and the arts. Some who had struggled to survive through the Depression saw them as, at best a harmless but unessential frill, less charitably as a waste of time and money, and at worst as a potential threat to their (Christian) way of life.

Canada's current poet laureate, George Bowering, while at the University of Alberta in the late 1960s, described the province as a "cultural desert, a province inhabited mainly be ungrammatical pro-Socred letter writers, stupid newspaper editors, fiery eyed fundamentalists and right-wing politics."[12] The narrow Socred view of the world also included a distinct bias against minorities. In her 2001 book, *Mavericks*, Alberta author Aritha van Herk recalled that the government exercised considerable bias against pacifist sects like Mennonites, Hutterites and Doukhabors, who were exempt from conscription, especially Hutterites, perceived as increasing their land holdings at the expense of regular farmers who were off fighting in the war. Hearings after the war reflected a pervasive hostility to Hutterites, leading Manning to implement the Communal Property Act, which stayed in force until 1972 when Peter Lougheed's government repealed the measure.

---

11 Free University North had a brief existence in Edmonton during the late '60s when people with knowledge and expertise volunteered to share their skills. The mantra was "each one teach one." Rochdale was a Toronto experiment in creating an unstructured university, where students learned what they wanted when they wanted.

12 Alan Hustak, *Peter Lougheed: A Biography* (Toronto: McClelland & Stewart, 1979), 78.

Two huge complexes most visibly symbolized the Manning government's commitment to the arts, one in Edmonton and one in Calgary. The Jubilee Auditoria were erected in 1955 to celebrate the province's 50th anniversary. The nearly identical, utilitarian buildings, each capable of seating 2750 people, were used for local symphony, opera and ballet performances. Major uses came from university convocations, high school graduation ceremonies, the Kiwanis Music Festivals and such other cultural events as the Scottish Society's "White Heather" shows. Touring extravaganzas starring popular entertainers such as Harry Belafonte, Victor Borge and the World Adventure Tour slide shows and movies filled the buildings from time to time. The Australian hypnotist/entertainer Reveen was a frequent and popular visitor. The buildings were kept absolutely free of any form of alcohol.

It was difficult to imagine the Alberta of the '60s as a place where the arts could flourish. The province's Lord's Day Act was a kind of "Thou God see'est me" checklist for what people could do, and could not do, on Sundays, and it set the behavioural tone for the rest of the week. Manning was diligent in separating the opinions and values expressed on his Sunday *Back to the Bible Hour* radio broadcasts from his role as premier. But those values permeated the way that official Alberta did its business and lived its life. You could not get a glass of wine with a meal on Sundays, even in the finest restaurants—at least not openly. Some establishments turned a blind eye when patrons brought their own bottles in brown paper bags and hid them under the table. At the drinking establishments that were allowed to exist, there were still separate entrances, one for men, one for "Ladies and Escorts." Unattached men and women were not to be trusted around the demon rum. Beer parlours were required to close between 6:00 p.m. and 7:00 p.m., to make sure that husbands who had stopped for a quick one after work went home for dinner. The only place you could see a movie on Sunday was at a drive-in, and the province's Film Censor Board was still busy excising the naughty bits from Hollywood's latest, increasingly risqué productions.

Open calls for a change from the old Social Credit ways began to surface soon after Manning's retirement. The unfortunate Harry Strom was elected to succeed him at a party convention in December 1968. A decent man, Strom tried mightily to transform the old party. He brought in young Social Credit thinkers such as Erik Schmidt, Owen Anderson and John Barr. Preston Manning got his political feet wet as a member of the group, which the *Edmonton Journal* dubbed the "whiz kids."[13] Barr and Anderson wrote *The Unfinished Revolt*, published by McClelland and Stewart in 1971. The book tried to give the party and its ideas a new lease on life. It was the first of several attempts, which continue to this day, to reinvent the party.[14]

Strom promoted some of the younger MLAs such as Bob Clark and Ray Speaker and fired Cabinet stalwarts such as the unhappy Alf Hooke, the most outspoken of the originals who had served in the Cabinet for 26 years. In his book *30+5: Those Incredible Years of Social Credit*, Hooke described his first meeting with Strom after the latter became premier. As the conversation dragged on, he gradually realized that the new leader had no intention of inviting him back into the Cabinet. "I could not do to a dog what you are doing to me," Hooke raged, but nevertheless pledged his grudging support, saying, "I am concerned with getting the government back on the Social Credit track much more than I am with personalities." "Someone has to speak out," Hooke declared in a personal note to me in 1970, "and, God willing, I intend to do so." One of the last of the "real" Social Creditors, he continued to fight for his principles until his death in 1992.

Strom was quiet and mild mannered, a strict teetotaller who affected a casual air by driving with one finger on the wheel, his right arms draped across the back of the passenger seat.[15] In his well-meaning attempts to modernize the party, he set up Canada's first provincial Department of the Environment. He brought the province into Medicare. He changed the law to allow 18-year-olds to vote. He put a plebiscite on daylight savings time, which had been defeated in the 1967 election, back on the ballot. He allowed Sunday movies for the first time, and to the horror of many Social Credit stalwarts, allowed people to order a drink with their meals in restaurants—even on Sunday. He set up a well-funded Commission on the Future of Education, chaired by Professor Walter Worth. *The Worth Report* endorsed the establishment of what was to become Athabasca University and the expansion of the Banff School of Fine Arts into a year-round institution. On March 1, 1970, the Strom government launched Canada's first over-the-air education television station, operated by the Metropolitan

---

13 Byrne, 197.

14 The Mannings, father and son, later published *Political Realignment: A Challenge to Thoughtful Canadians* (Toronto: McClelland and Stewart, 1967).

15 From an account by Jim Edwards. Southern Alberta is quite flat, and the roads may not have a bend in them for many miles.

Edmonton Educational Television Association (MEETA). The station was the pilot project for ACCESS, the provincial educational television network, which was privatised by the Klein government in 1995.

But Strom's attempts to modernize the party set the old guard on edge. He had to fight the coming election without much support from the party's aging establishment—and without much of the money that they controlled.

Early in 1971, with an election on his mind, Strom changed the name of the Department of Youth to the Department of Culture, Youth and Recreation. The department had been established by Manning in 1966 to deal with the challenges presented by youth in the 1960s and to support the province's popular, rural-based 4-H Clubs.[16]

In July 1971, with an August election looming, Strom ran the Alberta Multicultural Conference, and on July 16 published a white paper titled *A New Cultural Policy for the Province of Alberta*. But Peter Lougheed had put his response on the record two days earlier. In a July 14 news release, he committed his future government to the development of a "mosaic" approach: "We believe that the promotion of different cultures, if handled properly, would not lead to the fragmentation of our society but would provide Albertans with the opportunity of being exposed to and experiencing many cultures and traditions."[17]

In the end, Strom could not change the Manning-Kennedy image of Social Credit, now seen by voters as old and tired. He was too modern for the doctrinaire old guard and not modern enough for the new Alberta. A letter to the editor of the *Edmonton Journal* from a self-described "charter Social Creditor,"[18] chastised both Strom and Manning (who late in the campaign had offered token support for Strom) for not being "real" Social Creditors. Alf Hooke, who over a span of 14 years had been acting premier whenever Manning was away, was considerably more than upset with Strom. Hooke released his book just before the election to champion the "real" Social Credit agenda and to oppose what he saw as Strom's deviant

---

16 It is not unlikely that Lougheed influenced the departmental evolution. After becoming leader of the Conservative Party in 1965, he had made it clear that he championed a more cultural and multicultural agenda. Lougheed had recruited Edmonton businessman Horst Schmid as his advisor for the "Preservation of the Ethno-Cultural Heritage of Alberta."

17 *Edmonton Journal*, August 7, 1971.

18 Letter from Rudy Michetti to Peter Lougheed, August 28, 1971. Lougheed Papers, Alberta Provincial Museum and Archives.

approach. Bitterly, Hooke declined to run and in fact showed up at a Lougheed rally at the Edmonton Jubilee Auditorium, which had packed the hall to overcapacity with some 4000 supporters. Someone pinned a "For Pete's Sake—Vote Now" button on his lapel. Hooke said he would keep it.

Like Woodrow Lloyd who took over the Saskatchewan government after Tommy Douglas moved to the federal arena, Harry Strom had the bad fortune to come to power at the end of an era. Political sensibilities were changing everywhere. The mood was "out with the old," whatever the old was—a left-wing government in Saskatchewan, a right-wing one in Alberta. *Time Magazine*[19] noted, "Since 1969 there have been eight provincial elections, in which six incumbent governments have been thrown out.... None of the defeated governments were singularly incompetent, corrupt or uncaring." Their great sin—they "looked tired."[20]

When the change came, it was massive and unexpected. Lougheed himself was caught by surprise. At noon on election day, he told *Edmonton Journal* reporter John Hopkins, "I don't think we're going to do it."[21] But in the end, the growing stream of desire for change became a flood. Lougheed, young, energetic and telegenic, had bounded from taking over the leadership of the virtually non-existent provincial Progressive Conservative party in 1965, to becoming Leader of the Opposition with a rump of six members following the 1967 election, to winning 49 of the province's 75 seats on August 30, 1971.

"People didn't vote against Social Credit," Lougheed argued. "They hadn't done anything wrong. They voted *for* us."[22]

In an editorial titled "A Farewell Tribute" following the Social Credit's defeat, the *Calgary Herald* said the party "has maintained old-fashioned complexes in the face of altering social concepts in such spheres as liquor consumption, blue laws and censorship. It has maintained an observable sense of authoritarianism which, at times, has seemed scarcely indistinguishable from the outmoded concept of divine right."[23]

---

19 "Canada: The Realm," *Time Magazine*, September 13, 1971.
20 Ibid. Blakeney defeated Thatcher (SK); Hatfield defeated Robichaud (NB); Regan defeated Smith (NS); Bourassa defeated Jean-Jacques Bertrand (QC); Schreyer defeated Weir (MB); Lougheed defeated Strom (AB).
21 *Edmonton Journal*, August 31, 1971.
22 Ibid.
23 "A Farewell Tribute." *Calgary Herald*, September 28, 1968. History seems to repeat itself whenever any government gets too long in the tooth.

The average age of the Alberta Cabinet dropped by nine years, from 52.4 to 43.2.

The extraordinary impact of the change is difficult to appreciate without an understanding of how deeply entrenched the Social Credit party had been through more than 35 years in power. It was a true culture shock—a dramatic and unexpected change from Social Credit's doctrinaire, ideology-driven regime to Lougheed's relatively open and pragmatic approach to government. For Alberta's creative community, it presented, as Tree Frog Press publisher Allan Shuté told me in an interview, "one of those once-in-a-lifetime opportunities."

From my own perspective, the change was every bit as noteworthy, though less noticeable on the national stage, as Québec's Quiet Revolution, which fundamentally changed the way that province saw and felt about itself. In Alberta, with Peter Lougheed's active support, with Jeanne Lougheed's unwavering and enthusiastic encouragement, and with Horst Schmid's "Energizer Bunny" activism, culture and the arts rose from the bottom rung on the ladder of government priorities to a place much closer to the top.

And so the stage was set for what can only be described as a cultural revolution. The decade and a half from 1971 to 1985 saw a profuse flowering of the performing and literary arts. With recognition of the arts came official recognition of Alberta's multicultural reality. The 1971 census showed that 47.4 percent of Albertans were of neither British (46.8 percent) nor French (5.8 percent) descent. In Edmonton, in contrast to Calgary, the non-British population was considerably larger than the provincial average. Soon after the election, the premier and his wife made a point of hosting delegates in ethnic dress from a variety of cultural communities at a gala reception at Government House in Edmonton. The occasion launched the Alberta Cultural Heritage Council. The government's *Position Paper No. 7*, subtitled *New Directions Position Paper on Alberta's Cultural Heritage*, was issued in November 1972. One policy objective was "to stimulate the living arts—painting, dancing, music, handicrafts and the human drama."[24]

In telling any story about Alberta, however, it is important to recognize that there are really three major and quite distinct constituencies within the province. Edmonton, Calgary and the "rest-of-Alberta" represent three different political and cultural realities. Edmonton has, since its earliest days,

---

24 Government of Alberta, *Position Paper No. 7: New Directions Position Paper on Alberta's Cultural Heritage*, November 1972.

been more ethnically diverse, more cosmopolitan. That may have been both the cause and the result of the fact that the city is the location of both the provincial capital and its first university. Calgary, the financial capital, had a larger Anglo-Saxon base, and so many Americans lived there that it was called the largest American city outside of the US. Calgary was about cattle, oil and money. The city, as I will show, came late to the development of a full cultural life.

The rest of Alberta, like rural Canada everywhere, was losing population and economic power. Its people, older, with less formal education, are more monocultural within their communities. While there is some diversity in heritages across the province, individual communities tend to reflect, in some cases overwhelmingly, a single ethnicity—Ukrainian, German, Scandinavian or some other, usually European, culture. They, in large part, embrace ultra-conservative political and religious values. Rural Alberta was the source of Social Credit's strength from the 1930s through the 1960s and of the Reform and Alliance parties in contemporary times. An electoral system in need of repair gives them more voting power than urbanites in Edmonton and Calgary. Prior to the most recent reorganization in 2003, the smallest rural constituency, Chinook, had 15,642 voters while the largest, Edmonton Rutherford, had 38,262.[25] The new 2003 reorganization redressed some of the imbalances but still left rural Albertans with more voting power than urbanites. The new rules allow for a 25 percent variance above or below the average number of voters: 35,951.

But the demand for change by the urban majority would not be denied. Harry Strom unlocked the doors to change, but Peter Lougheed and his team swung it wide open. Alberta entered a new world. In my essay "Our Best Years," published in *Farewell to the 70s*, edited by Anna Porter and Marjorie Harris,[26] I described the decade as "our yeastiest [*sic*] years ... the world is waking to Edmonton—dare I say it?—the new Athens of North America." A bit over the top, perhaps, but indicative of the creative high so many Albertans enjoyed during that astonishing decade.

---

25 David Staples, *Edmonton Journal*, March 17, 1996.

26 Anna Porter and Marjorie Harris, eds., *Farewell to the 70s* (Toronto: Thomas Nelson, 1979), 54.

Claire Harris
(1937–2018)

Despite being celebrated by literary scholars mostly as an "Afro-Caribbean" writer, Claire Harris has said that it was her regional position in Calgary that freed her poetic voice, until then restrained by both an intensely colonial education and a tightly knit Trinidadian society. In Calgary, she could "look at society with a very clear eye. I knew I had absolutely nothing to lose. I was free to write as I wished. Thus, the advantages of liminality have allowed me to write freely about 'hush-up' and hushed up experience" (E.A. Williams 43).

Claire Harris is one the prairies' most prolific and critically acclaimed writers and a major figure in the canon of Canadian and anglophone Caribbean poetry. She is celebrated particularly for her poetics of fragmentation, collage, and her use of multiple Englishes, including Caribbean nation language. Harris's experimental and feminist poetics defied her readers' expectations about black women's experiences in diaspora: her work frequently multiplies voices and personas in order to explore the complex implications of claiming a black identity on the prairies.

Harris forcefully announced herself as a major new voice in black and prairie literature in her first collection, *Fables from the Women's Quarters* (1984), which won the prestigious Commonwealth Award for Poetry for the Americas Region. This was followed by the 1984 Writer's Guild of Alberta Poetry Award for her second collection, *Translation into Fiction*. Her first two books were quickly followed by *Travelling to Find a Remedy* (1986), *The Conception of Winter* (1989), *Drawing Down a Daughter* (1992), which was nominated for a Governor General's Award for Poetry in 1993, and *Dipped in Shadow* (1996). Her final collection, *She*, a complex novel-in-verse about mental illness, was published in 2000. Her work has been included in more than seventy anthologies and has been translated into German and Hindi.

Harris was born in Trinidad, the second of six children. Her parents were both middle-class educators: her mother was a trained teacher, and her father was a headmaster and an inspector of schools. Harris was educated at home until the age of seven and then went on to receive a British Catholic education at St. Joseph's Convent in Port of Spain, an education she has since credited, ironically, for her success: "its value to a writer working in any of the various Englishes is difficult to over-emphasize." She read Shakespeare and the Romantic poets, Blake and Chaucer. "This kind of education, since it was designed to produce a fully colonized subject, never represented any aspect of the West Indies," she said. "We were being 'rescued,' if not from 'savagery,' certainly from a perceived ignorance and crudeness. Fortunately, I was born to sufficiently skeptical parents" (E.A. Williams 42).

Harris attended University College, Dublin, in Ireland, and returned to teach at her old convent school for a year. She went to the University of the West Indies in Jamaica for a postgraduate diploma in education. In 1966 she moved permanently to Calgary, where she taught English and drama in the separate schools for twenty-eight years until her retirement in 1994. During that time, she was absorbed by the writing community in Calgary. She became poetry editor for the magazine *Dandelion*, the foremost literary magazine in Alberta for a quarter century until 1999 when it folded. In 1982, she helped to found *Blue Buffalo*, a magazine devoted exclusively to recent Alberta writing; it closed in the mid-1990s.

In the 1990s Harris's work became especially celebrated among Canadian feminist literary critics who positioned her work usually alongside that of Dionne Brand and M NourbeSe Philip—both, like Harris, Trinidadian-born authors. George Elliott Clarke has critiqued the tendency of this scholarship to eschew discussions of poetics in favour of politics—especially their treatment of "racism, sexism, imperialism, classism, and homophobia," a critical move which, Clarke says, "reduce[s] the writers to the status of sociologists" ("In Search" 164). Clarke also points out that writing of Harris, Philip, and Brand "has always been concerned with Canadian regionalism, as well as with the nation's peculiar and intractable problems related to book publication, distribution, marketing, and sales" (164). The selections below particularly highlight Harris's concerns with her regional, cultural, and material conditions, and suggest the ways these conditions shape Harris's particular prairie poetics.

The poem "Backstage at the Glenbow Museum, Calgary," originally published in *Callaloo* in 1996, deals with an incident in which the poet was asked to act as an adviser for an African exhibition at the Glenbow Museum. The poet-speaker notes that although she is not an African, she feels "a kind of duty" to assume the well-nigh impossible role of Representative Black Artist. The repetition of this line bespeaks the burden of responsibility to try to interrupt archival meaning making, which constructs blackness as an absence of culture ("nothing/ nothing luminous/ here") while simultaneously overdetermining its meaning as both animal and "exotic." In this poem, Harris can be seen using the techniques of concrete poetry: her careful lineation and generous use of white space help argue against the violence of the European archive as it seeks to contain and imprison blackness. Harris's work stretches meaning across the page, and the poem can be read productively both horizontally and vertically.

In the excerpt from Harris's now-canonical poetry collection *Drawing Down a Daughter*, we see the poet's complex construction of a black prairie place that is constituted in multiple ways: by looking through a window that, on the one hand, looks out over Calgary and that, on the other, becomes a screen for her childhood and present-day sense memories; by bringing together a field of readings—national, literary, black-feminist, African American; and, above all, by imagining, through her conversation with her imagined unborn daughter, a black future on the prairies. Harris embraces the full space of the page to create a "field" that seams together the many threads of diasporic being; this is what formally constitutes her particular prairie poetic.

Claire Harris died on February 5, 2018, in Calgary, after a lengthy illness.

❀

Drawing Down a Daughter

Dreams swarm
… wind slips into her dream   sleet and slaughter in
mountains bordering west   a snake coils on her breath
mad hands   east: black noses painted over   walls alive
with flutes   pomegranates wheat cakes wine clear water
intent on justice the land howls sandstorms   from far
monastery windows: planets   hot glimmer of skulls here
downtown Calgary dangles from a lean hungry moon/
darkness askew   motherrrr ma … she waits   the shutters
slam gunshots in empty wind   baby baby crying crying
cat in a tree   he can't not find her   he must   oh hurry   O

their bright precarious tower patched with slogans   is
balanced on the rims of earth will not suffer survival baby
we're here hand in hand   this white country light coleman
catching at night   small slitherings   ahead of them
mewling   hand in hand through cashew trees to her
river-run running fruit brush against/running   vines
bruise her stomach broken twigs milk her hair her chin

running   they scramble down the incline to river-edge and
icy revelation: his childhood   she looks where he runs
free joyous wild   her hands are sticky red   falls drown all
crying Baby i'm sorry   Bebe on the other side by the
Lopinot[1] a younger Nefertiti   bones   wild hair as if she
were lost/   now sobbing hands cross over balloon belly
suddenly empty   board-flat she searches   the man holds
her about the waist   as if she were his north   she breaks
from him   scrambles up rocks toward the ledge   baby
crying from the other's belly   river-falls pound churn in
her flat stomach   she catches at trees stones climbs on
hands and knees baby i'm coming stomach aching she
stumbles begins to roll fast to roll clutching at air   at fast
whirling earth bounces bumps stops a man in bamboo
tunnels   candy smile   gleaming shirt Burri[2] flings his
jacket over a shoulder   moves his lean easy grace past
them all fine silver buckle glimmers   the moon jiving in
his hands behind him old old woman steps   scattering
words sentences paragraphs drawing down a daughter/
she scrambles after ...

a white box without corners in a white light   a woman
trying to hold on baby bruised   crying   herself hard
strong   competent   though she has lost something   will
not find it again ...

long mournful whistle   a dawn
train scatters sleep
she is thinking 'the walls
the boulder   the child'
and does not know why
she hears her name   a sigh low
expressed into silence
then withdrawn
she looks down at her body as if surprised

---

1   A village in Trinidad.
2   Possibly Alberto Burri (1915–1995), an Italian painter and sculptor whose work
focused more on matter itself than what the work could mean.

are you there Girl
your daddy's looking to find a safe place
for your childhood   and his

she won't be able to hold out she thinks of teaching the
career she's built her writing Child if he hauls us home
your collage may never be published remembers certain
calls   'have you ever thought to send us some thing
Canadian   set here' what   she is doing here is/ &
important ...
he'll never buy it
her missionary work

such a weight about her heart

dawn slants   empty
light glues on her hands
stone in her throat
no threat of happiness

she hears her name again   calling

as she were lost

for
 her
  self
   for
    the
    child
    roped
     in
    her
womb
she
refuses

remembering anther making small in a tin tub   trying
not to splash sudden wind snuffs candles Great Aunt her
quick whisper "nothing to fear if the dead call don't
answer"

She rises

      going
        out to
          day that existed
       in/ and
     before
her body
her body
     day's
       memory
         of it   illusive
       imprint
     waiting for
her nakedness

inside her the child thrashing
daughter she needs
dreads
for who would bring a child

skin shimmering black   God's
night breath curled crisp
about her face   courage
of enslaved ancestors in her eyes
who would choose to cradle such tropic
grace on the Bow's frozen banks

and this man
fleeing racism as his body must once
have fled the coffle

high on the bluff   above a confluence of Bow and Elbow
she watches early light play against snow-clouds' grey
clotting below memorial cottonwoods Calgary stirs she
lifts to the idea of God   need
palms her   what is deep
and secret   she begins to sing
something dim   throaty   vague

as memory   lost ur
song of childbed pain
                    remembered

no dawn sun bleeds into the river
north wind rising

she observes:
a wild-wind breath
bluff her bleak-sea
room

yesterday   sink stale
she pulls the plug
watches time
swirl

eager to under/
ground ever living
to ever dying
life

then hastens to her notebooks
hand on a belly that flutters
pierced by tenderness   she is
for a moment   holy

she unlocks without a check   heart leaping   grey-green
eyes are spotlights Rosemarie laughs "you thought it was
him   sorry, only me!   how ya doing   sure you don't want
me to come back tonight"   she is laughing   "wana hike"/
her stomach achingly flat "I've got exams to mark!   sure
you don't want to go sky diving"
a whirlwind! infectious!   when her friend leaves still
clowning she is laughing   ready to write   promising 'yes/
yes... i'll if anything happens'

needs must   she writes:

a breath of wind   or hope
stirs the quiet room
sunlight invests leaves
of her nameless one
a red-edged sword thin
transparent elegance

room split open to the common
grace of Saturday morning
      leisurely pot of tea   .
      smell of newspapers
      Globe and Mail   London
      Review of Books   Our Lives   Canada's
      First Black Women's Newspaper   Utne
      the book waiting to be cracked
      Himes' *Cotton comes to Harlem*
the hour open on a long sunsplashed
corridor to evening

she rises from the couch
to feather   green
time through
her fingers   how apt
that what was weed
pestilential in Trinidad

               (where green is riotous   .
         threatens   numberless armies of thin
       spears forever poking from fecund
           earth   as if three centuries of pain
            grief   early dying
                    ensures
         an eternal
              rage   in fertility

now here is curdled
into ornament   memory scents the house

with morning gardens of Cedros[3] bee   of purple
white   pink old maids   hibiscus hedge   yellow

glories   anthuriums and bourganvilla
waist deep in snow she sees
ragged road sides explosions of tiny white
stars   orange dots   cream notes with dusky
centres   all no-name and possibility
chaos and delight

through glass walls she looks east over Calgary

now delicate haze blues the bowl where
she sits   from the rim
of this escarpment working class
houses iced with snow hike toward
the Bow   pines dusted   sparkling   cars
rush at hills   search out openings in
north sky   the whole space
occupied with the mute formidable
energy of immigrants
faint bands of blue hang above
coppery domes of the Orthodox   below
a lattice work of bridges
the city sways in gun metal
water   everything sort of glistens   sort
of doesn't   in the brisk air

she turns from the window   full
this morning's energy   its ease
the kettle boiled dry
does not alarm her

        bronze mums brilliant
premise something

_____

3 A coastal town in Trinidad, on the tip of the southwest peninsula.

Addena Sumter-Freitag
(1944–)

A playwright, performance artist, and poet, Addena Sumter-Freitag is a seventh-generation Canadian with roots in Truro, Nova Scotia, and Columbia, South Carolina. She grew up in Winnipeg's North End, lived in Yellowknife for a time, and has made her home in East Vancouver for many years.

When she first began transcribing the autobiographical stories that evolved into her award-winning play, *Stay Black & Die*, she did not consider herself to be a writer. The script was an adaptation of letters she had recorded on cassette to a childhood friend. As she revealed in an interview with Christine Lyons (2009), "years later, I saw Beverly and she pulled out this big box of letters and the tapes and everything and I thought, [...] 'Oh I gotta write this down; this is just so funny.' And, so then I started writing them. And in my head, at that point in my life, I wasn't a writer—I was a storyteller, and to me they were quite different. You know what I mean, like, the *aural, oral* was very familiar to me. The writing part was not" (n.p.).

The transcribed letters eventually became the script for *Stay Black & Die*, which toured across Canada, and won Theatre BC's National Playwriting Award and the Frankie Award for the best Fringe production at the Montreal Fringe Festival. The play was produced by Centaur Theatre in Montreal as well as the Adelaide Fringe Festival in Australia. *Stay Black & Die* was published by Commodore Books in 2009.

Sumter-Freitag's second book, a collection of poetry and creative non-fiction, *Back in the Days*, was published in 2009 by Wattle and Daub. It revisits the Winnipeg of her childhood in order to wrestle with hidden, forgotten, and repressed histories of racism, and to bring forward a vision of the self reborn.

The following selection is from *Stay Black & Die*, a multi-voiced story of Penny growing up in the 1950s and '60s in Winnipeg's multicultural North End. The story recounts Penny's coming of age as she matures into a sense of herself as a sexual woman, and as black. The play archives an aural history of Sumter-Freitag's Winnipeg, from the accents of her immigrant neighbours, to the soundtrack of 1950s and '60s pop, soul, and R&B.

183

✿

Stay Black & Die

"Get up. Get up! Get your lazy asses out of bed. You can run the streets all night and ya can't get your black asses up in the mornin'. Get up!"

Sounds of slaps. Lights snap to full. PENNY runs onstage, holding her head where her mother just slapped her. She stops, looks at the audience, and grins shyly. Her face changes. She begins to talk to the audience with delight as a mischievous smile replaces her shy one.

PENNY

That's the sound of my mother's voice, and that's the sound we'd wake up to every morning, Junior and Leslie, my two brothers, my dad and me. Well, Daddy was a porter on the railroad so most of the time he was gone and he got to escape mornings. My sister June had escaped too, by getting married, and she moved as far away as she could.

"Get your funky asses outta bed!"

And then she'd open up every door and window in the house "to let the funk out." You see, my mother believed that when you slept, your mouth gets foul, you perspire, and all that funky smell has to be aired out every morning.

There was a ritual: you were expected to jump outta bed, and throw back the covers to "air the bed out." Then you had to put some kinda clothes on, 'cause you couldn't go out of the bedroom in your pajamas, or that would mean you "had no respect for yourself walking around half naked." Then you went in the bathroom, brushed your teeth, and you washed, and she flung open the bathroom door every once in a while, and she stood there, and she eyed you to see if you were "doing it right." Then we'd have to make ourselves breakfast, wash, wipe, and put away all the dishes, then go to make the beds, 'cause they were aired out now. Then you got dressed for school. Not with the clothes you put on to go wash, 'cause now they were funky too. This was the ritual every morning, and it took so long we had to run to get to school, so we wouldn't be late.

Saturday morning was even more significant than every other morning, 'cause Saturday morning was Cleaning Day. Summer and winter, and

I'm from Winnipeg and it's thirty, or forty below zero in the winter, and it's freezing. And the wind would blow through our little house and my mother would come and stand menacingly in our bedroom doorway, expecting us to jump up and clean everything in and outta sight. She'd stand there, tall, with a defiant look on her light-skinned face. Oh! She was really, really, proud of her light skin. My mother *was* defiant! Sidney Poitier had *nothing* on my mother. She used to say *(Mimicking her mother's voice)* "I ain't afraid of nobody, and I ain't afraid of nothin'. I ain't EVEN afraid of the devil!"

You know, she threw the landlord out of the house once, for "trespassing." She actually *threw* him down the stairs, and then she kicked my baby carriage down the stairs after him. It went bouncing down the stairs, right over top of him, and right through the plate-glass door in the landing. And then she said, "He's got his fuckin' nerve comin' in MY house and askin' for his rent. It's only the first of the month. I don't owe him no rent yet. I don't owe him nothing till the day's over. I bet he didn't go askin' none of the Hunkies for their rent, and they're always skippin' out. You don't see no Darkies skippin' out on their rent!" And then she leaned over the banister and yelled down at him. "And next time, you knock before you come in MY house, sucker. You may own this shack, but I pay the rent here. Makes it MY house. And if you come in here you'd better respect me in my house." The next month, they say that the landlord didn't come near til almost the middle of the month, and then he knocked on the door, and my mother answered. *(Honeyed voice.)* "Hell-oo-oo."

(Timidly.) "Ah … Mrs. Sumter. Mrs. Sumter, I … ah … I came for my rent."

"Well come right in here, dear. I got it right here f'ya."

And then she closed the door behind him.

"You see, we're gonna get along fine now, that man and I, *because we understand each other.*"

Fast flash of the lights, then back to full wash. Knocking at the door.

(In her mother's singsong voice.) "Come i-i-i-i-n."

My mother would always answer the phone or the door in the sweetest voice, no matter what. She could be right in the middle of one of her tirades and she could be screaming, "Holy jumpin' Jesus Christ, look what you did, boy! I'll kill you!"

Stops yelling as she hears someone at the door. She leans over and puts one hand to her ear, then straightens up and calls melodically.

"Come i-i-i-i-n."

Light changes to centre spot with the scene played in centre stage.

(In a soft, articulate voice.) "Mrs. Sumter, I'm Mrs. Schmidt from down the street and I came to talk to you about your boy."

"Which boy?"

"Ah ... your boy Junior."

"What about my boy Junior?"

Well you see, Junior keeps kicking my boy Kenny. And today, well, Kenny had on his new suit, because the Safety Dog, Heenie, is coming to all the schools to do a demonstration for the patrols. Kenny's a patrol you see. Well, Junior kicked Kenny right in the—made a big hole, right in the seat of Kenny's pants, and you know, Kenny didn't do a thing to Junior!"

"Oh, is that so? Well I hear Kenny's out there every day calling 'nigger' and I told Junior, if he's big enough to call nigger, he should be big enough to take a kick in the ass!"

(Shocked.) Oh Mrs. Sumter, Kenny would never do a thing like that. He's not out there calling Junior names, he's out there calling our dog. That's *his* name."

"Well! As long as Kenny keeps callin', Junior's gonna keep kickin' his ass. So if I were you, I'd change that dog's name. Save yourself some money buyin' pants."

Lights flash to indicate a change of time. PENNY crosses to stage left.

And a few days later, my mom called all of us kids over to the window.

Stands at the window, smiling.

"Get over here you kids. I said GET. Come here! Listen. You kids hear that boy out there calling his dog?"

(Calls and whistles.) "Here boy, here boy!" *(Whistles again, frustrated.)*

"You see? *(Smiling and nodding knowingly.)* It's all a matter of understanding."

Lights fade quickly to dim then back up to full.

That 'understanding' seemed to sweep through the whole neighbour-hood. The second friend my mom made in the neighbourhood was "good old Olga," Olga Gratanowich. Olga was a big, strong Ukrainian woman who made the best pyrogies in the neighbourhood. She and my mom met because Olga's kid and my brother Les got into a squabble, and it turned into a fistfight, and Olga intervened. She had my brother on the run.

"Big Olga! Big Olga's after me, and she's gonna kill me!"

PENNY hides behind the chairs. As her mother, PENNY gets up and crosses to stage right. She reaches down and picks up an object on the way to the door.

Well! My Momma met Olga at the door. And as she passed by the cook stove, she picked up an axe.

"You step over this door, and I'm gonna cut your big fat head off. Now honey, you might of ran this neighbourhood before and got all of these people round here scared of you, but put your foot over my door, or put your hands on any of my kids, and it'll be the last time you ever raise your hand, 'cause honey, your match just moved into this neighbour-hood … Kathleen Louise Sumter!"

A few hours later, there was a knock at our door.

(Ukrainian accent.) "Meeses Somter, meeses Somter, it's me, Olga! I just made you a nice dish we call pedeheh."

Pedeheh? Ah! It was pyrogies! Gee my mom made friends fast! She made friends fastest with the other minority families in the neighbourhood. The Jewish and the French, she liked them especially. Because, she said, they were actually Black like us. *(Looks puzzled.)* There were Ukrainians, Poles, Germans, a few Chinese, and one Japanese, the Harmattas. Huh ... oh, and one of us. We were the only Black family in that part of the North End. Well, there was only about four or five Black families that lived in the North End of Winnipeg at that time, but we never saw 'em, we *never* saw 'em. They lived way across town, way across town! Near Higgins and Maple Street. My mom said they were all cousins, a million of 'em. My family loved living in the North End, because they fit in. As Mrs. Adolph said, "purr-haps dey fit in too vell."

(Merry laughter and a thick German accent.) "Oh Meezes Somter, Meezes Somter. I jost love zaat leet-el boy of yours, Lezlie. He eez zo fawny."

(Mocking tones.) Oh ya? Why is he zo funny?"

"Well too-day! I jost saw heem, and he vas sitting on za curb, and he say-ze to me, 'I am crying bee-cauze nobawdy vill play vit me.' I say-ze, Lezlie, vhy eez it zat nobawdy vill play vit you? He say-ez—*(She laughs.)*—he sayze, 'I don't know, I zink it eez bee-cauze I am German, and da Var eez on!'"

WELL! My mother went to Leslie to have a little heart to heart talk.

"Boy! What nationality are you?"

"I'm German."

"What makes you think you're German?"

"Well, Mrs. Adolph's German, Horst is German, Barry's German, and I'm German."

So! My mother waited till Sunday and she got him all dressed up, took him by the hand to the streetcar on McGregor Street, and took Leslie downtown all the way to Higgins and Maple Street, to the Coloured Baptist Church.

Lovey Eli's "Soon as I can See Jesus" plays.

Now, when she got him outside the church, she stood him on the step and gave him his warning.

"Listen boy, when you go inside that church, you hear that music, you can snap your fingers, you can tap your feet, you can sway to the music, but don't you break out and dance, 'cause them's hymns in there, and it's a sin to dance to a hymn."

Now, Les was justa grinning at the sounds of the choir coming from inside. He loved music. My mom had a big record collection of black artists, songs that we *never* heard on the radio in Winnipeg. You see, when anybody visited us from the States, or when any of the porters on the railroad 'ran' out of town and went 'across' the border to the States, they always brought back all kinds of records for themselves and their friends. We had Jazz, we had Blues, we had Gospel. Les was so excited, he just burst right through the doors and marched right up the aisle, sat down and took a look around at all the people, and he let out a bloodcurdling scream.

"Momma! Get me outta here. Oh Momma get me outta here, get me outta here! I'm scared of all these people! *(Whispers.)* They're all Black!"

My mother, she got him out of there all right. And she beat him all the way home for embarrassing her. She stood him in front of the mirror.

"Boy! I want you to take a look into that mirror and see what nationality you are. You're the same nationality as all those people! You're not German! You're Coloured, and don't you ever forget it."

Linus Tongwo Asong
(1947–2012)

Regarded as a literary giant in anglophone Cameroon, Linus T. Asong published over a dozen celebrated novels before his death in 2012. He frequently published several books per year. As he reflected in an interview with the *Cameroon Post* in 2010 (published posthumously two years later) the reason he published books in such spates "is because that is the way my Muse operates. I have always likened conceiving the idea of a book, writing and publishing it to child bearing—from conception, pregnancy and eventual birth. If a woman can only give birth to twins or triplets or even quadruplets, she has no choice but to deliver them. I have never written only one novel at any given time. They come to my mind in waves and, so, I produce them in waves" (Mbunwe).

Asong was born in the southwest region of Cameroon in 1947. In 1980 he moved to Canada to study creative writing at the University of Windsor, and from there he went on to receive an MA and a PhD in comparative literature from the University of Alberta. His dissertation examined the anti-hero in African fiction. After completing his doctorate in 1984, Asong returned to Cameroon, where he held a position as associate professor of literature and creative writing at École Normale Supérieure Bambili (University of Yaounde). He is the author of two critical monographs, *The Anti-Hero in African Fiction: An Examination of Psychological Construction and Characterization Techniques in Six Selected Novels* (1984) and *Detective Fiction and the African Scene: From the Whodunit? to the Whydunit?* (2012).

Asong's novel *Crown of Thorns* (1993) was a mainstay of the "O"-level curriculum in Cameroon, and made Asong a household name. His other publications include *Doctor Frederick Ngenito* (2006), *The Crabs of Bangui* (2010), *Chopchair* (2010), and *Osagyefo* (2008), a historical novel about the life of Kwame Nkrumah of Ghana. Of his later novels, particularly his book on Nkrumah, written while he lay dying in the hospital, Asong said, "My vision of humanity, which has always been cheerful and benign, became clouded with the fear or the likelihood of death."

No Way to Die, excerpted below, is the first of a trilogy of novels featuring the trials of anti-hero Dennis Nunqam, who, ironically, finds he cannot die, though he wishes to. The novel, in the existential tradition of African literature, is a meditation on what constitutes success and full personhood in mid-twentieth-century African society. Early in the novel Asong's central character, an artist and an office messenger, receives a letter that promises to raise him from "nothing to something," an offer that only amplifies his self-alienation. As an archetypal anti-hero, Asong's Dennis Nunqam can be read as a literary ancestor of Esi Edugyan's Samuel Tyne, the premier anti-hero of black prairie literature. Asong's *No Way to Die* was followed by *Crown of Thorns* and *Trilogy of the Dead*, all published in 1993.

Asong's novels were published in the United States and distributed world-wide by Michigan State University Press and African Books Collective in London, England, as well as online through Amazon. But since foreign publication made his books expensive and difficult to find in Africa, late in his career he began to launch his books with Langaa RPCIG, a not-for-profit publishing collective in Cameroon. As he reflected, "it is in Cameroon that my works make the greatest impact."

No Way to Die

I stood with my back to the road, in the veranda. All dust, swimming pool for the fowls. What had I not done to stop this house from leaking? Tried everything, except zinc it. Yes, except zinc. How was I to get zinc? Steal? Not me. There it stood, my home. My hands I clasped behind me. Fleshless hands! The legs of my trousers rolled up to my knees. I patched the trousers every week, but so what? Was it everything that I should take to the tailor? Look behind me and you would see exposed my calves. When you fall sick all the time, when you suffer all the time, your calves can never look fresh. Always dry, emaciated.

In front of me and half hidden in the shade of the veranda hung a broad canvas, insecurely strung from the cloth of an empty flour bag. You have to manage, man! The easel which supported the canvas I made from three sticks bound together at the top ends with a string. Easy way! The legs were opened out to stand in the form of a triangle.

Dieudonne, my small son, was squatting in the centre and holding two of the sticks in place while I painted. That's the way we always did it. On the canvas was a painting. As for me I considered it completed, whatever people may say. I had taken some few steps backward and was admiring it from the left, the right, different angles.

Footsteps behind me. I turned.

"Good even Denniz."

It was Mossah. Some people are born to die together. That I met a man in prison by accident, then we leave at the same time, get work at the same time and live in the same quarter?

"Evening Mossah," I responded.

"No work for you agen sa?" he asked. "Since tri days today, nobody to hear ya smell at de jobside?"

"Not been there," I told him. "I could not."

"You sick?"

I did not answer. Would answering keep Mossah quiet? Mossah? Unless you didn't know the man you are talking about. I went down on one knee and told Dieudonne under the canvas to pull the small stick backwards so that the picture would lie back a bit.

Manda heard Mossah talk and came out. Ask her why she came out and she would tell you she just came out to greet. Lies. She wanted to hear what we were saying to each other.

Mossah came closer to the canvas.

"What is ya man drawing like dis whish he cannot even open his mouth to talk?" he asked.

Manda was wearing a loin cloth that was folded just above her breasts and which passed under her armpits, exposing the entire upper part of her body. She took the lower front ends of the cloth in her right hand, adjusted them slightly between her legs, she bent down and spoke to the boy under the easel.

"Dieu, tell Mr. Mossah what your papa is doing." She was smiling as she spoke. I knew she just wanted to laugh at me again.

"His self," the boy said.

Manda was the first to laugh. She shook her shoulders and looked across at Mossah. She seemed to be hiding the laugh. Subdued amusement. She knew she could not get an answer from me. I had told Dieudonne what I was drawing and he did not want to make a secret of it. Things like that always made me boil with anger.

"He say what?" he asked Manda.

"Did you not hear him say his father is drawing himself?"

"Where?"

"Ask him. You see a mad man with his child and you are asking some-body else?"

Manda would never remain silent if she saw that what she would say would make people laugh at me. But I knew that when she said *mad man* she did not mean a really mad man. Just like saying somebody was doing something you did not understand. When Mossah asked again I told him. "Self portrait. It's me."

"You wan to draw dat here or how?"

"Finished. I have finished."

Mossah went over to where I was standing and looked at the canvas for awhile. I knew what he was seeing: a single dark column painted to stand against a background that began with a deep green at the bottom and ended with a blue layer to the upper section. Between the green, and cutting right across the central column which I made to look half like a man with the head slightly lowered and half like the broken pillar of a huge building, I had put a thin white line.

"But dis make no sense." Me myself did I make sense? He should have known, having been with me for that long. My end was their beginning, I thought again.

After staring at the canvas for another whole minute Mossah said, "And you buy the paint!"

Why should he be surprised? Unnecessary. I told him flat. "I make nothing Mossah, except the drawing."

Mossah was wearing a jumpa that reached over his knees and he was carrying a letter for me that was hidden inside the dress. He pulled out his hand and held the letter to me.

"Dis is for you. I saw it in your box long time. Many days."

What did I have to do with letters? I examined the painting, then picked up my brush in my right hand. I was carrying a small tin of blue paint in my left hand. He made as though something would happen if I did not take the letter. I showed the back of my right hand and he placed the envelope on it with the address side facing up.

Some things when they happened you would not really be able to explain why they happened that way. As I just threw a careless glance on the letter I felt a kind of fear so sudden that my whole body seemed to tremble. The letter fell down before I had time to look at the writing on it closely.

Manda bent down and picked it up and gave it back to me. I wonder what she thought it was. I cleaned my hands on my clothes and tried to study the stamp, wondering where it came from. I think Mossah knew what I was trying to find out because he said immediately, "Is from Menako."

Manda and I thought not only of the same thing but we asked the same question.

"From Menako?"

Then Manda asked, "Who knows us in Menako?"

"Verkomze went to Menako, Mossah?" I was sure a dirty trick was being played on me.

"So only Verkomze can fit to write you, Denniz?"

I shrugged and sighed. Mossah ought to know better than that. Had I ever received any other letter apart from queries? What else could I say?

"The only letter I receive are queries about work, and Verkmoze is the only one who queries me. You know that."

I tore the envelope and carried my eyes at once to the address of the sender.

Univ. Hospital
P.M.B. 2733.
Menako,
N.W. Province.
April 2, 1970.

The letter was written on two sheets of paper. I turned to the name of the sender on the second sheet. Not Verkomze's name. It was a rubber stamp.

Dr. Maximillian Essemo Alekwieunchaa
(M.D. Padua, Italy)

I held the letter closer to my eyes, rubbed them vigorously. I wanted to be sure that it was no dream.

"M-a-x-i-m-i-l-l-i-a-n E-s-s-e-m-o!" I said softly to myself. Even in my own ears my voice sounded as if I was just waking from a long sleep.

"D-o-c-t-or. Medical Doctor. Maximillian Essemo," I read aloud.

Manda pushed the folds of the loincloth further into her armpits and came to stand behind me, looking at the letter over my shoulder. I wanted to push her away, but something held my hands. I wanted to shout at her to go away, my tongue was tied. I whispered to her. My breathing instantly became faster and louder and I could feel bubbles of sweat rolling down my forehead. I asked for a chair but I did not wait for Manda to bring it over to me. I walked to it and threw myself on it before she touched it. I folded my arms over my bent knees and placed my head in them, face down.

The letter fell out of my trembling hands. I did not pick it up. I don't think I noticed that it had fallen. Before my closed eyes my past, that bad dream, began to rise. I saw myself on the first day at school, bare-footed, jiggers all over my toes, my small jumpa cut and stitched from my mother's old loin cloth. Otherwise I would be naked!

January 15, 1945. Government School, Bonalikondo: six mud-and-thatch huts so poorly made that they were rebuilt after every heavy rainfall, or, as people said, every two weeks. In front of the class stood a probably middle-aged man with a heavy moustache turned completely brown with snuff which he took in every fifteen minutes or so. There were so many stories about Onaba and his snuff. Under his armpit he carried his usual *casingo*, a cane which he brandished as he spoke. He introduced himself.

"Onaba is my name, teaching is my job, and this classroom is my office."

I again heard Onaba make his first announcement.

"You will begin this first day with a Sheep and Goats Test. School is no joke. That is what we do here every year ... If you pass you will sit on the 'A' side. You become the Sheep of this class. You fail, you sit on the 'B.' You become the Goats. You mistake your side, twelve strokes of this cat-of-nine-tails," he shook the cane. "'Spare the rod and spoil the child,' says the Holy Bible."

"Every week you will have a test in the assembly hall," Onaba went on. "At the end of the year we count how many times you were a Sheep or a Goat. That is how you will be promoted ..."

I saw myself being proclaimed as the first candidate in the first test. I saw myself as the leader of the thirteen Sheep, the chosen few that Onaba asked to jeer at the seventeen goats so as to make them work harder in future.

I saw myself on the day of the second test. On my side was a boy almost of my own age and height, who had started making friends with me ever since the results of the first test were announced. He wore a shirt as white as the cassock of the priest who said mass in our church every Sunday. His pair of shorts too was so clean and so well starched and ironed that he carried a bundle of newspapers which he spread on the dusty benches before sitting down. He wore a pair of black shoes and stockings which rivaled even those of the teacher by going above the calves to just behind the knees. His book remained, as I can say, blank for over fifteen minutes after we had been told to start writing.

"Are you not writing?" I was asking the boy.

I heard the boy confess.

"I don't know what to write. I know nothing. Please, help me."

I saw myself leaving my work open under my elbow for the "white boy" (as we called him thereafter) to copy from so that he could become a Sheep. If Onaba caught me I would be a dead man. That cat-of-nine-tails would finish me. *Kill me alive*, as he would say.

That Goat which I turned into a Sheep and refused to accept any money in exchange, called himself Maximilian Essemo Alekwieunchaa! And for the next hundreds of tests we took, Maximillian Essemo's place as a Sheep was guaranteed. He always made sure we sat together. And I was glad to help him pass.

Friday, December 21st, 1951, that too I saw. Why it was that every name from my school years brought back the whole past, I did not know. That day too rose before me for the—I cannot count how many times. That was the day the results of the Provincial were released. We called the graduation examination from the Primary School, Provincial. I don't know how that name came about.

Ayomaba, our beloved headmaster was talking.

Who will ever forget Ayomba's voice? Who can ever forget his name? Every word of what Ayomba said that day, that year, I still remember as accurately as he said it. There are words you hear and know you would carry with you into your grave. Ayomba's words were such words.

"Thirty candidates entered for this examination. Twenty-one passed. And the first candidate is none other than Dennis Nunqam."

Ayomba read on, until he came to the last name.

"And the last but not least to pass ... is ... Max-imil-lian E-sse-mo." Nothing added, nothing subtracted. I could hear Ayomba's farewell speech sounding and sounding again in my ears.

"You are all going out into the world that lies before you like an unpathed ocean of water. You have a future. You are the very blocks on which the future of this nation depends.... Let the sky be your limit. And wherever you go after here, whatever you become after now, always remember that you have the moral obligation as fruits of this noble institution, to leave your footprints in the sands of time.... But remember as you make this arduous journey through life that there will always be surprises. The failing list might grow longer than this. It might grow shorter. So might the passing list. For, in this world of ours no condition is permanent. Was it not written in the book of knowledge that some shall be first that were last and some last that were first? ... There lies your challenge—to retain your stain, or rise, if you have already succeeded. But never fall ..."

I opened my eyes. They ached with sadness. I looked about me. There was no letter anywhere. Surely I had just dreamt. I had not received anything from a doctor called Maximillian. Maximillian was still a Goat. My senses had played me false. Or?

"You are looking for that letter, Dennis?" Manda asked.

Curious to know what might have thrown me into such a deep thought from the letter, she had picked it up. She had just read the final word in it when I woke up from my trance.

"Which letter?" I asked, then I came back to myself and agreed. "Yes, I am looking for it. Give me."

Mossah was standing a few yards away, facing me, looking at me, wondering. I stretched out the letter, the entire upper half of my body rising and falling rapidly. I felt sick. And I had not as much as read the letter itself. I was not superstitious, but I thought that strange reaction to the few words I had read was a very bad sign. Then I read the whole of it.

My Dear Dennis,

Can you believe that I only got to know your whereabouts last month? And I returned from Italy in October 67! Three full years today. Perhaps you did not even know that I had long returned.

Ever since my days in Europe I had been thinking of you, wondering what had become of my good old friend, where you too could have gone to, what you might be doing. Sometimes I even felt the urge to write but I did not know your address and there was just no means of knowing it out there. I discovered an old picture of our junior football team of those primary school days. It was in the house of another old friend of ours, Maurice Chem. You must still remember him. He has a job now with the National Auditors Association here in Menako. Actually, he was the one who told me that he had seen you just a month ago when they came down to audit the Central Co-operatives there in Mbongo. He told me you work there.

If I should quote him rightly, he said you worked there as an office messenger. In fact, I mention this point not to embarrass you but because it leads to a suggestion I want to make. I don't know how you feel being an office messenger but I think it is not much. I am sure you must not be earning more than 20,000 francs a month. The job itself does not sound wonderful in my ears for a chap like you whose real worth I happened to have known so well. And I can almost guess that you would not insist on being there if you had a better alternative.

I want to offer you that better alternative. Quit that job and come and put up with me here. As the head of the University Teaching Hospital I have a house of over ten rooms to myself, so you will be very comfortably lodged.

Your financial problems, I assure you, will be very satisfactorily catered for because money is not one of my worries. And above all, I have contacted my fellow lecturers here and they are ready to work with me to raise you from nothing to something in this country.

Give the matter serious thought and if it sounds good (as I'm sure it should), let me know at once. We will be inspecting some of our medical students in Kolom later this month. I should be able to call at your department, on or about the 25th of this month. If you could make yourself available around closing hours on that day we could talk things further and even go and see where you live. But just in case I delay in coming, stop a blue Mercedes 280 that bears the number MSF 2314. That's my car. In the meantime, please reply to assure me that you got the letter.

Most affectionately yours,

Manda had been watching me as my eyes moved from one line to the other. My reaction which had begun with my abandoning the letter made it impossible for her to express the joy in her heart which the contents called for. She was looking at me as I was biting my lips, blinking my eyes and shaking my head the way I always did whenever I was deeply disturbed by some event. I say *whenever* as if there was a time when something had not made me angry.

I am sure Mossah too did not understand what was happening. How could he?

"Nothing bad at all, Mr. Mossah," Manda answered, angry that I did not look excited.

"It is very good news. I don't know why Dennis is looking like that when God has at last ..."

"Shut up your mouth Manda." I finally found the voice to shout. Little Dieudonne was anxious to go away. He had noticed that I was in no mood to continue painting. He came and stood between me and his mother and asked, "Papa, you no draw again?"

I denied by shaking my head. It was not unusual for people to interrupt me whenever I was painting. But I always went back to continue and either complete it or carry the work to a certain level of development. But on this particular occasion I could not get back on track. If I tried to paint, I would not know how to proceed. I had to abandon the entire exercise. After the interruption I could not continue.

A baby's voice was heard in the living room. It was my child's voice. He was crying. Mossah looked at me and my wife. I may not have been really hearing. It sounded like a voice out of the past, distant.

Manda was standing arms akimbo to my right, looking down directly at me, her surprise at my behaviour turning into shame. And perhaps she was justified in feeling so. Although she often criticised me even openly I always kept silent. Never before, not even once had I thrown a truly angry word at her and meant it, like the way I asked her to shut her mouth.

There were times when she had taunted me over matters she knew she should have ignored, but even then I had kept silent. And on the day of that letter she may not even have been guilty of any offence! Let's look at the situation objectively: we had received news which she knew or believed was going to end all the miseries in which we had lived ever since we got married. What had she done to deserve such disgrace in front of a stranger?

Stranger? Mossah was no stranger. Why did I have to be so hard on myself?

The child in the room was now screaming.

"The child cry, Denniz," Mossah repeated.

I looked at him, screwed my mouth and looked away.

"The child cry, madam Manda."

Manda to did not stir. I was never able to fathom what was going through her mind as she stood there listening, but not hearing, looking, but not seeing. It was the little boy who went in to see his brother.

"I go back home Denniz," Mossah said. The way we were behaving worried him. It would have worried anybody.

"Okay." My head was lowered as I spoke.

"You will come to job tomorrow?"

"I don't know," I said.

"Madam Manda, bye-bye."

"Mr. Mossah, I beg you please, good bye," Manda said after a whole minute, after Mossah had already left the veranda and was walking away.

She then went into the house and taking the child who was still crying into her arms returned with a stool which she placed in front of me and sat down.

"Dennis, what have I done to you?" She asked me.

I did not answer until she repeated her question.

"What was wrong with what I said?"

"Why do you think I thought there was something wrong with it?"

"Because you insulted me."

"I looked at her as if I thought I was being falsely accused. In a way it was a false accusation because it was not what I said that offended her but my reaction to the letter. I did not express the excitement that she expected. "You said I should shut up my mouth. Why?" she asked.

"I didn't know that I said so," I told her. And I was serious about that. I did not really know until I had said it to her. I tried to get her mind away from the letter.

"How could I have said so to you? Why?"

"I don't know," she said.

"I am sorry. Take the children into the house. Leave me alone," I told her.

She took the children in and after a few minutes she came back out. I had opened the letter and placed it flat on the ground in front of me. Supporting my head with my hands over my knees I was going over it, repeating the words *doctor, head of the University Teaching Hospital, Mercedes 280.*

"Who wrote to you like that Dennis?" Manda came back to the letter.

I did not answer. When she insisted I replied, "Somebody."

"A friend?"

"An enemy."

Manda smiled a bit and looked into my eyes to see if I was just being ironical as she always believed me to be. My eyes must now have become redder than before and I was chewing angrily at my lips.

"When will you reply?" She asked.

"Never," I told her.

"Dennis, please, tell me what is wrong," She pleaded.

"Who said something is wrong?"

"But look at how you are behaving …"

"If your heart tells you that something is wrong, then I cannot change it. Let whatever is wrong be wrong," I told her. Then she hit the nail on the head.

"And it is the letter that is causing it. Perhaps you did not read the letter correctly Dennis. It should not make you angry …"

I thought the error was hers not mine. I told her, "It should not make you glad, Manda, if you read it correctly. Come sit here and look at it."

I ran my finger over it until I came over the sentence in which Max said something about my job and what he earned.

"Read this, Manda," I said. "What is wrong with being a messenger? Are messengers not people? Is 20,000 francs not money? Are there no people who earn less than that? Are there no people who do not even earn anything?"

Manda did not answer. I read down until I came to where Max said he would raise me *"from nothing to something."* I thought the insult was too obvious. I asked her, "Manda am I nothing? Am I not married with two children, boys who will continue to live after we have died? Do we not eat three times a day? Do you say you read this letter?"

"I read it Dennis," she said.

"And do you say you don't know what is wrong with me?"

"I don't know Dennis," she said.

"You will never know," I told her. "When I am angry with myself, you are the first to tell me not to worry, that I should not think that I am not somebody. But when somebody else calls me *nothing*, you are the first to join to support. If people do not know how I feel about being an office messenger, tell them that I feel fine. If people tell you that I am nothing, tell them that I am something. If they want to make NOTHING INTO SOMETHING tell them that they want to make SOMETHING INTO NOTHING."

I folded the letter very carefully as though to preserve it and then began to tear it up into bits which entering the house threw into the fire that burned in the kitchen.

Nigel Darbasie
(1950–)

Acclaimed writer Nigel Darbasie was born in Trinidad in 1950 and immigrated to Edmonton in 1969. He has published two collections of poems, and has been anthologized widely in books, textbooks, and magazines. His work is largely concerned with questioning accepted narratives, probing in a voice that rings true to the ears and to the souls of West Indians and which at the same time can bespeak the complex realities of the prairies.

Darbasie's first collection of poems, *Last Crossing*, self-published by Nidar in 1988, has been read by George Elliott Clarke as belonging to the exile tradition of Caribbean-rooted writers located in Canada (*Odysseys* 331). Indeed, the poems in *Last Crossing*, from which the following three were taken, regard the prairies from a highly defamiliarized perspective and elaborate themes of estrangement and loss while at the same time celebrating the kinds of border crossings familiar to the diaspora. "Our Subdivision," below, uses the stanza form to elaborate the "immigrant/seperateness" articulated by the poet speaker. On the other hand, Darbasie's poem "Pan Man" explores the new kinds of kinships and solidarities that can and must be forged on the prairies. The poem focuses on the figure of Ravi Mohansingh, a Trinidadian in Edmonton who is harassed on the street by white men who take him for a Pakistani. The poem celebrates black and South Asian solidarities in diaspora contexts like Alberta, and exposes the ironic ways a performative gendered blackness can function as both weapon and a shield. Finally, in the future-oriented poem "New Terra," Darbasie considers the role of technology and especially story to recreate the world in the event of climate disaster. This poem belongs to the strong tradition of black prairie climate disaster literature, written from ground zero of the prairies' oil industry, and which is concerned with the effects of anthropogenic-induced climate change.

Darbasie's second collection of poems, *A Map of the Island*, was published by the University of Alberta Press in 2001 to popular and critical acclaim. It is a poetic autobiography focusing on a remembered childhood in Trinidad. In a review of the book for *Canadian Ethnic Studies Journal*, David Bateman writes, "Separately, each poem stands on its own as an elegantly written snapshot from a single life-time. The inclusion of actual photos on the back cover complete the autobiographi-cal framework and gives this text a sense of authenticity within a poetic vision that simultaneously threatens and challenges the notion of the authentic at every turn" (Bateman 208). The volume was a bestseller, with almost one thousand copies sold.

Darbasie's poems have been anthologized in *Voices: Canadian Writers of African Descent* (1992) edited by Ayanna Black; *The Road Home: New Stories from Alberta Writers* (1992) edited by Fred Stenson; the *Journal of Canadian Poetry* (2001), edited by David Stains, and *Threshold: An Anthology of Contemporary Writing From Alberta*, edited by Srdja Pavlovic (1999).

Our Subdivision

Perfunctory greetings
exchanged in winter
while shoveling snow
from driveways and sidewalks.

Summer weekend conversations
curtailed: wash our cars
mow our lawns
apply weed & feed
to grow healthy grass
and kill dandelions.

Words set down
as wood and wire fences
fixing distance
preserving our immigrant
separateness
in every season of discourse.

Pan Man

Ravi Mohansingh is a Trinidad boy
come to make good in Canada
now dat is one indian

who could beat steelpan like a lord.
One time
bout three o'clock in de morning
he was leavin a dance hall
on de east end after playin in a fete
when some bad white boys take in he ass.
Dey close in like shark
sayin how dey go sen he back to India
like a mummy
wit only he eye showin
from de bandage.

He tell dem he eh from India
but dat eh make no difference
dey callin he paki
an intend to sen he dong
de North Saskatchewan River.
What runnin in Ravi mind
is what move to make
a good few yards to he car
an dem boys tightenin up
have he in a bad way: heart beatin fas, fas
he sweatin profuse although it cold
mouth dry

he feelin sick like he want to shit.
Jes den somebody call out
"Wudds happenin, bro?"
Is Eddoes and Chanel 59
comin up de road.

Ravi smile broad
at de sight a dem two gigantic creole
movin quick an smooth under de streetlight
like two panther when dey huntin.
An dey have plenty experience too
dem boy used to ramble an ting back home
all kinda bottle an razor scar on dey body.
Since dey come Canada
dey livin respectable

wuckin as pipefitter an makin good wage.
An dem doh see no kinda trouble wit de police
not even a speeding ticket self.
But dis time anyting could happen.

Well tings turn out fuh de best.
Jes as Eddoes an Chanel 59 move in
de white boys slide out
so nuttin heavy go dong
no blood fall
only sweat
an all was Ravi own.

De nex day
Eddoes take Ravi by Deloris
de hairdresser.
She cut he hair an put in a perm
have Ravi lookin all cool an funky.
Well yuh know
de white boys stop callin he paki
dey might call he nigger
but not too loud.

New Terra

Aboard orbiting stations
children study the home planet
its swirling clouds
tinged in orange
its desiccated land forms
in relief upon turquoise seas.

From data banks they learn
about its plants and animals
many of which exist only
as computer-generated
specimens that come to life
in stories elders tell
of things that used to be.

Tololwa M. Mollel
(1952–)

Prolific and award-winning author Tololwa Mollel was born in the Ashura region of
Tanzania to Loilangisho and Sa-raa (Eleiser) Mollel. Early in his life he was sent to
live with his grandparents, who tended a coffee farm in northern Tanzania. There
he learned the art of storytelling and storylistening from his grandfather, who,
he says, was a "consummate eater of words" ("Feasting" 254). Encouraged by
his grandfather to read widely and to pursue a formal education, Mollel received
his undergraduate degree in literature and theatre from the University of Dar-es-
Salaam, Tanzania, in 1972. Between 1979 and 1986 he was a university lecturer
and an actor in a touring company in Tanzania that performed as far as Germany
and Sweden. He emigrated to Canada on a student visa and settled permanently
in Edmonton in 1989. He received his master's degree in drama from the University of Alberta in 1979, and in 2011 completed a PhD in drama.

Mollel is the author of seventeen children's books, which include *The Orphan
Boy* (Oxford University Press 1990), which won the Governor General's Award for
illustration and made both the Canadian Library Association and American Book-
sellers Association's notable book lists; *Rhinos for Lunch and Elephants for Supper*
(1991); *A Promise to the Sun: An African Story* (1992); *Kele's Secret* (1997); *My
Rows and Piles of Coins* (1999); *Big Boy* (1995), which won the Alberta's R. Ross
Annett Children's Prize; and *To Dinner, for Dinner* (2000). His books have been
published in Canada, the US, Australia, Britain, and Tanzania, and have been
translated into four southern African languages, as well as Korean, Danish, German, Serbian, and Spanish.

Mollel has been active in helping to foster the writing community in Alberta. He
served as the writer-in-residence for the Edmonton Public Library and President of
the Writers' Guild of Alberta in the late 1990s. From 2011 to 2012 he was writer-in-
residence at Athabasca University. Of his presentations and his work with schools,
libraries, and communities, Mollel says, "I aim to provide a feast of words—written and spoken—for the eye, the ear and the mind; as well as for the creative

206

imagination, and for performance" (Mollel, "Biography"). Through writing, storytelling, and drama, Mollel hopes to empower the young, and others, with the gift of story—to write, tell, share, and enjoy stories; to mentor them as he was mentored.

"Feasting on Words: How I Became a Writer for Children" was originally published in the *McGill Journal of Education* in 2001. What is offered here is Mollel's newly revised (2018) version of his story.

"Canada Dry," in which Mollel theorizes the Canadian nation as a palimpsest of stories, was originally published on the occasion of Canada's sesquicentennial in the e-published anthology he edited, *HOME: Stories Connecting Us All* (2017).

Feasting on Words

My love of books sprang out of a lack of them. I grew up in Ng'aruka in Northern Tanzania, a town so small that its school consisted of one room, Standard (Grade) One and Two only, and one teacher, who also happened to be my father. As the only one, my father came to be known as *the* Teacher—Mwalimu in Swahili. I don't remember calling him anything other than 'Mwalimu,' then or throughout his life, until he came to pass away years later. Despite being Mwalimu's son, I owned no books at all prior to starting school. No child did. We had none in our house, besides those Mwalimu brought home to mark for students, his teaching guides, the Bible and one or two hymnbooks. All those books ranked right up there with my father's shotgun, which you touched at your peril. That I couldn't touch Mwalimu's books fueled my fascination for the printed word.

How I wished I had books of my own!

My only chance of owning a book, however, lay in becoming a schoolboy. So, I ached to become one. But starting school was complicated in those days. You must be not only old enough but big enough. You had to be able to touch your left ear with the right hand over your head. Bigger than me, all my playmates started school before me. They left me outside alone and spent precious playtime in the classroom. With no toys except crude ones I could make for myself, life proved unexciting. Soon I grew so bored I took to sneaking into the classroom to be with my buddies. I found, to my joy, that my father let me stay but only if I behaved well, staying rock silent.

Inside the classroom, I watched Mwalimu write vowels on the blackboard in careful big letters. You can't form words in Swahili, the Tanzanian national language, without the vowels a e i o u, pronounced ah eh ee oh oo. These are the first letters you learned in Standard (Grade) One. I watched and listened to Mwalimu teaching the children to say the letters, and to sing in unison: ah eh ee oh oo; then to sing in syllables: bah beh bee boh boo, mah meh mee moh moo, chah cheh chee choh choo, dah deh dee ...; and finally to intone whole words: *baba* (father), mama, *dada* (sister), *kaka* (brother), *bibi* (grandmother), and so on. It was fun to watch and listen. At times I forgot I had to be quiet and I joined in.

Singing along, I marveled: "What a magical thing it is to read! How can someone give voice to a bunch of strange marks scribbled down? Is this magic? When will I muster such magic?" I couldn't wait to start school and learn that wonderful magic.

The next year I succeeded to touch my left ear with my right hand over my head. I became a bona fide schoolboy. On my first day in class, I got my very first book—brand new, glossy, with giant vowels and dozens of syllables. How special I found it! I couldn't keep my eyes or hands off it. I ran my fingers across its shiny pages. The letters, when I tried to rub them off, stayed put. "Good," I thought delighted, "they are not coming off." I put an inside spread of the book to my nose. It smelled of a far-off magical place. "Mh, that's where books must come from," I thought. Years would go by before I came to associate books with people creating them. But at the time, the mystique that books magically sprung into our midst, made me love them even more.

For Standard Three after my two years of schooling in Ng'aruka, Mwalimu sent me to my grandparents, one hundred miles away in Arusha on a coffee farm they owned. Now a famous city in Tanzania, Arusha was only a town then, but it offered several Standard One to Four primary schools—a cut above the Standard One to Two school in Ng'aruka. One primary school, called Ilboru, sat a walking distance from my grandparents' coffee farm. At Ilboru, I enrolled in Standard Three, one of two things marking a milestone for me. Meeting for the first time my paternal *akwi* (grandfather), interesting accounts of whom I had heard, proved to be the other thing. I would come to know him well and he would, possibly more than anyone else, influence me to become the person I am today.

"What will you be when you grow up?" was one of the questions Akwi shot at me when I stood before him for the first time. He did so in Swahili and not our Maasai mother tongue—for a good reason. To the question he asked, Akwi provided an answer. He told me that I should study, get a good many degrees and become, on growing up, a teacher—like my father

Mwalimu, his first-born male child. Everyone, according to Akwi, should grow up to be a teacher. He had only, alas, reached Standard Two himself. Perhaps his little schooling, coupled with Mwalimu's choice of the teaching profession, must have been what fueled Akwi's passion for education for his children and grandchildren, and his desire to have his offspring all become teachers.

Every day of my Standard Three at Ilboru, Akwi asked me as I returned from school, "So, what's new? What did you learn?" He chastised me if I had nothing much to say. "All day in school and nothing to show for it!" One day he asked me, "If all book knowledge were a shilling, how much of it do you have now?" A shilling consisted of one hundred cents. Already, even then, I had a pretty good sense of the infiniteness of knowledge. I opted for the truth. "Five cents," I told him. He yanked his pipe from his mouth. "Five cents? After all these months in school! You might as well attend my school instead—help me on the coffee farm." After that, I made sure to boast of more respectable sums of knowledge whenever he asked me the question.

Yes, at first, I did find it hard to talk with Akwi about my day at school. That was because he insisted we speak in Maasai. A grace period he had given for us to speak in Swahili as I arrived had lasted only the short time. He figured I needed to learn our mother tongue. I hardly knew any when I had first arrived at the coffee farm. I could understand it better than I could speak it. In Ng'aruka school, Mwalimu had zealously used Swahili, the government mandated language of instruction in primary education. He had abided conscientiously with that edict, meant to promote Swahili as a national language. This requirement, Mwalimu had told us over and over in class, made all the sense in a country like Tanzania with its more than 120 ethnic languages. He used Swahili, therefore, not only at school but almost all the time at home, as well. And I had arrived in Arusha almost exclusively a Swahili speaker. Aghast, Akwi made sure, in quick fashion, that this changed. After the grace period expired, he refused to speak to me in Swahili and banned anyone from talking with me in anything but our Maasai language.

Gradually, to survive, I got better at Maasai. As I grew used to telling Akwi things, it took me a while to realize that his interest in what I learned at school was genuine. It didn't take me long, though, to take advantage of his interest, to show off. Going from Standard Three to Four, I read whatever I could lay my hands on—school books, discarded magazines and newspapers, anything that I thought would interest Akwi. I enjoyed dazzling him with startling bits of knowledge, stories, anecdotes and current affairs—to all of which he listened avidly.

You couldn't have asked for a better listener.

Maasai elders are masters at listening. In an oral culture, the spoken word is of paramount importance. The Maasai call the art of conversation including story sharing—literally translated—"eating words" or "feasting on words." Feasting on words involves skillful speaking as well as listening. You are only as good an eater of words as you are a listener. So, you listen actively to someone talking. You emit responsive sounds in a rhythmic pattern to acknowledge the speaker's words: Mmh, eee, hoo, mmmh, nna, aaya, hoop, eeee. You listen until the speaker finishes, anything up to an hour later, before you speak in turn for as long as you need to.

I liked watching elders visit with Akwi. They all had different styles of eating words, especially listening. Some elders listened with eyes closed. Others doodled on the dust with a walking stick, fidgeted with a fly-whisk, or stared into a hat or an imaginary spot in space. All elders, however, including Akwi, shared a common characteristic. In listening, each took care not to trip up the speaker's words with his responsive sounds. A listener carefully responded, in a manner that didn't seem to rush the speaker. People considered it rude to do otherwise. The speaker, in turn, delivered in an unhurried style, in a rhythm that allowed the listener to respond elegantly.

So, in the fashion of the consummate eater of words that he was, Akwi listened to me with his whole being. When I said something he found truly astonishing, he stopped me. "Repeat that," he said, eyes fixed on my face. Later in the evening in her kitchen, where everyone gathered for warmth against the Arusha cold, he may say to *Koko* (Grandmother), "Listen to what your grandson told me today." And to me, "Go on, tell your grandmother what you told." Soon, prompted by Akwi, I found myself repeating things to visiting relatives, family friends and neighbors. This spurred me to read as diversely as I could. History. Greek and Norse myths. Aesop's fables. Arabian nights. Politics. For most grown-ups around me, books were an exotic experience for which they had little time, patience or inclination. But they could enjoy them, I found out, through the spoken word. My spoken word. This meant a lot to me.

Akwi himself loved dishing out words: stories about his childhood and the old days, and accounts of the Maasai way of life. He also liked to share stray tidbits about the Second World War, that he had picked up randomly. He had not been to the war himself, drafted into it like other Africans in

European-colonized countries like Tanzania, but you may think he had from the assuredness with which he spilled out those anecdotes. He embellished whatever he shared with his lively brand of storytelling. I particularly enjoyed eating words when Akwi and I worked on the coffee farm. He thrived on work and brimmed with cheer and talk while doing the endless tasks that came with owning a coffee farm. "Did I ever tell you ...?" he may start, to which unfinished question I had a ready answer. "No, you didn't." Never mind that I may have heard umpteen times whatever story he had in mind to tell me. Something else made me happy about his stories as we worked. At times, when he was really into a story, he may rummage in his pockets for his pipe, look up at the sun's position, and say, "Time for a smoke. Let's rest a little while I finish what I was saying." Not keen to become a workaholic like Akwi, despite his efforts to turn me into one, I welcomed the breaks. And therefore, the storytelling.

As for Koko, her feast of words consisted of folk tales. About monsters to keep me and my cousins awake as we waited forever for supper in her smoky, shadowy kitchen. Stories with song so we could sing along. That would stop our fights that, grumpy from hunger and a long day, we would carry out near the woodfire and a pot simmering with supper. Tales about ill-mannered, gluttonous characters like the hyena, to caution us against selfishness, greed and breaches of etiquette.

For as long as I can remember, I considered my grandparents' coffee farm to be very much home. With my growing grasp of the Maasai language over the years, I increased my contribution to a feast of words with Akwi. I indulged his love for stories from the Second World War and history; and his current affairs interest in the Middle East, Cyprus, the Cold War, Communism and the Vietnam War. It was partly my love of language that motivated me in this crusade. I found it inspiring to seek words to convey in Maasai the most un-Maasai of terms and concepts. How did one, for instance, translate 'Inter-Continental Ballistic Missile,' the kind of stuff Akwi relished, into Maasai? An interesting linguistic challenge.

For years after I had moved on to boarding Middle (Junior High) then Secondary (High) School, I would spend a good part of my holidays with my grandparents, feasting on words. Love of language. Love of words. Love of stories and of sharing them. Love of reading. All these combined to kindle in me the love of feasting on words, first as a reader, and in years to come as a budding writer. Growing up book-less in Ng'aruka and life with my grandparents had helped in various ways. Attending boarding schools would help in other, unexpected, ways.

Passing the grueling Standard Four examination at Ilboru, I moved on to Mringa, a Standard Five to Eight boarding Middle School for boys. A fail would have ended my education, or at best compelled me to repeat Standard Four and the milestone examination at the end of it. A rude introduction marked my entry into Middle School. Mringa was a nasty, brutish place of bullies, rotten food, sadistic prefects, and indifferent teachers. For a while, my love of reading sustained me. It gave me a lifeline and refuge. I was a spectacular failure academically. The only subjects I succeeded in were English and Swahili, thanks to my love of books. I gained a reputation as a reader. I loved to read aloud the books that appealed to me. I don't know how it came about, but teachers began to get me to read aloud to different classes, including Standard Eight, the top dogs in Mringa. That I, from among Standard Five boys—the lowest species in the school and therefore fodder for bullies—would read to the rough and tough Standard Eight boys meant the world to me. I felt gratified to see how my reading hushed the Standard Eight students, my tormentors among them, to silence and keen concentration.

Books, however, sustained me for no more than a year. At the beginning of Standard Six, I decided I had had enough of Mringa. I ran away from Mringa, but I didn't go home. My grandparents' coffee farm still served as home, where I had spent my school holidays in my Standard Five year at Mringa. (I would continue to consider it home during holidays throughout my Middle and Secondary school years to come.) My father, Mwalimu, was still a teacher in distant Ng'aruka, whereas only a fifty-cent bus ride and thirteen miles separated Mringa Boarding School from my grandparents' coffee farm. Home was the last place I should be, I had calculated. No way would Akwi understand, let alone go along with my decision to chuck Mringa. He would send me back promptly, if he didn't skin me alive first. I had told him before, in vain, about my problems at Mringa. Hang in there, he had replied. Be tough. Nothing in this world is easy. Look, already you've more education than my miserable Standard Two. You're in Middle School. What else do you want? You don't know how lucky you are. The school system in those days (as it may still be) was very much a pyramidal affair, with ever fewer students attaining higher educational rungs. A formidable Standard Four examination into Standard Five saw those failing dropping out of school or repeating the class (if lucky). Those students lucky to ascend to Standard Five, would face another big, even more daunting examination, at the end of Middle School in Standard Eight, to enter Standard Nine and Secondary School. And so, it went (or it goes) until the luckiest remaining few found themselves in university. So, yes, had I been years older and free of my Mringa troubles, I would have readily agreed that I was indeed lucky to have gone to Middle School. But I was who I was, an unnerved little boy who believed he had no one and nowhere to turn to.

So instead of going home, I embarked on a journey to the ends of the earth. Away from horrible Mringa, from unempathetic Akwi and all my troubles. Walking and hitch hiking, I made it to the small town of Makuyuni, about fifty miles south-east of Arusha, with one certainty. "No one will ever find me here," my ten-year old mind told me. "Not even Akwi."

Fortune favored me. A generous family, Mama and Baba Peter and their son Peter, took me in. I settled in, thinking, "Here I will live for the rest of my life." But lo and behold! After a week, Mwalimu turned up. Suddenly there before me stood my father, tall and nightmarish. Unknown to me (and how could it have been otherwise), a missing persons bulletin had been put out on the radio and in newspapers, my name and description and photo widely circulated. Also unknown to me, Mwalimu had just received a transfer from Ng'aruka, to teach in a school in Arusha. The world turned out to be a lot smaller than I had hoped. A driver with whom I had hitched a ride and who knew my father, had recognized me. Kind Mama Peter handed me over, but only after squeezing out of Mwalimu a solemn promise not to punish me when we got back home. What I had gone through, Mama Peter said, had been punishment enough. It was, perhaps, the hardest promise Mwalimu ever had to make. But make it he did. He proved no match for Mama Peter who stood her ground, holding on to me until Mwalimu had given his word that he wouldn't punish me.

Back home to my shock, Mwalimu kept his promise. And—wonder of wonders—he didn't send me back to Mringa, but to another boarding school at Longido, a place fifty or so miles north of Arusha, near the border with Kenya. The school had as its Head Teacher one of my uncles called Baba Nuru, a younger brother to Mwalimu. There I would enroll in Standard Six, the top class at the time, for Longido was still extending from the Standard One to Four school it had been. It would later come to have Standard 1 to 8 and become an Extended Primary School. We would be the first and last Standard 8 at Longido, as authorities scaled down Primary Schools in the whole of Tanzania to Standard 1 to 7, as it is to this day.

A sea of eyes greeted me as I stepped off the bus at Longido. The whole school, it seemed, had come to meet me. Word of my misadventure had preceded me. Everyone wanted to get an eyeful of this ten-year-old boy who had made it to the ends of the earth, whose name and photo had got into the newspaper and the radio. The crowd directed their grins and chuckles, gasps of disbelief and whispers, and fingers at me. I remember feeling a mix of shame and pride. Shame at what a delinquent thing I had done. Pride as I fancied myself a hero who had stepped out of an adventure story.

It could well have been at that moment that the idea to write down my adventure began. Soon after I settled into Longido, I embarked on writing the story in a hand-made little book. I didn't stick to the truth either. Why should I? It was my story and I could do with it whatever I wanted, it occurred to me. The exciting revelation spurred me on. I made the story more adventurous and heroic than it could ever have been. I divided the book into numerous chapters, for the pleasure of thinking up different chapter titles every time I revisited the story. I couldn't stay away from my little hand-made book. Every so often, I slunk off into a corner to read and feel the words anew, to revise. The story became both a toy and playground for my creative imagination, and my well-kept secret. I realized, for the first time, that the pleasure of writing lay in the benefit of hindsight that provides you with a better word, image, turn of phrase, sentence, or idea. From nowhere, hindsight sneaks a thought into your head. It does so stealthily and unexpectedly you wonder why you missed the thought in the first place.

My uncle Baba Nuru, the head teacher at Longido, proved to be another source of inspiration for my story. He taught us English and Swahili and loved literature. I remember him bursting into the classroom with any new adventure book he had discovered and figured we would like. For a few weeks after reading the story aloud, we would chatter about it, chuckle over favorite parts, assuming the characters' names and their personae. Any time we read a book he recommended and I came upon a word, description, or a turn of phrase I liked, it ended up in my story. The storybooks we read served as my writing instructor and further inspiration.

Sweating through the Standard Eight examination capped my time in Longido. The results when they came out included me among those who passed to enter Secondary School. "Lucky once again, boy. Make the most of this chance!" Akwi told me when I visited him and Koko to say goodbye before taking the train from Arusha to Dar es Salaam for my Standard Nine (Form 1) as a boarding student at Azania Secondary School.

One of my favorite haunts in Azania Secondary School turned out to be the library, a musty narrow room at the head of a steep flight of stairs. To me, no sweeter smell existed than that of the old hard bound books, mostly classics, in that room. Plays by Shakespeare and Bernard Shaw; books by Alexander Dumas, Dickens, the Brontë sisters, etc. I looked forward to Tuesday and Thursday afternoons, the only days the library opened, for two hours. One could borrow only one book at a time, so I would try to read a whole, slim book in the library itself and borrow one when I left. On Tuesdays, I borrowed a book that I could finish by Thursday. On Thursday afternoons, I would borrow a thick book that would see me through the weekend and Monday. I didn't want to be run out of reading material before Tuesday afternoon!

A second-hand bookshop not far from Azania became another of my favorite places. A stooped East Indian operated the shop. He had a quiet smile, a flowing silver beard, and a nose forever buried in a book. As soon he saw me, he beckoned me to among stacks of books, to new treasures he had acquired. He let me sit between the shelves and read. Then, painfully, I would settle on the one book I could buy with the miserly two or three shillings I had. A few times, to my delight, the old man threw in an extra book for free—a gift from one book-lover to another.

I did, besides reading, much writing around this time. After I had read an inspiring story, I may find myself creating one of my own, usually modeled on English Literature books that filled the curriculum in those days. I wrote Robin Hood stories. I wrote about knights and dragons, musketeers, and kings and princes and princesses. I once wrote more than a hundred pages of a story set on the river Thames in London! As with all other stories I attempted, I never finished it. My enthusiasm always proved greater than my tenacity. What stumped me usually was how to bring the story to a satisfying resolution. I always discovered I had not thought enough about a story before I jumped to write it. I attempted mysteries, detective and crime fiction, a cowboy novel, science fiction, and romance.

The one writing project that bore fruit was a play I wrote for a religious club to which I belonged, which had members from our boys' school, Azania. It also consisted of members from a neighboring girls' secondary school. The two schools were separated by a fence. Strict rules kept the boys and the girls from interacting, except through clubs of this nature, and at closely supervised social dances. The idea for the play, which the club members endorsed instantly and unanimously, came from me as we discussed in a meeting how to raise money for the club.

But who would write the play?

I had never written a play before. That was probably why, without hesitation, I volunteered to do so. My foolhardiness came to the rescue.

Knowing nothing about the challenge of writing a play, I plunged right in. Luckily, with a simple but catchy crime-does-not-pay theme I came up with, the play virtually wrote itself. It was a heady, exhilarating experience, which lasted exactly until we realized we had to cast the play, and someone had to direct it. Once again, my sweet ignorance about theatre making saved the day. I offered to direct it. I proved lucky, once again. I had no shortage of actors and actresses to draw on for the cast. The boys and girls in the club relished the prospect of an extended period of close interaction between them through rehearsal. As we rehearsed the play, I discovered I had to rewrite it to suit the cast I had assembled. This only added to the excitement. I took a small part so I could devote my energies to directing and revising. I felt on top of the world. My world.

Two weeks before opening night, my world crashed. The lead actor abruptly withdrew from the play. He gave no reason, apologies, or explanation. It could have been nerves. For a while, stunned, we thought the project had come to an end, still-born. For the third time, however, my foolish enthusiasm pulled us through. I decided to play the main character. Now, not only did I have to muster his lines, but I also had to coach a recruit to play my former minor role. The boy who took over that role never quite mastered it. He needed a lot of prompting, right up to opening night. I was on edge during performances, waiting to make up for his miscues in our scenes together. I remember this to have been, outside exam times, the most stressful period of my Secondary School years. Day and night the play preyed on my mind. I wrote and rewrote it mentally as I waited in vain to fall asleep. Many days I snapped awake at dawn, sweating over our fast approaching opening night.

Despite the stress or perhaps because of it, the play proved to be my most rewarding and inspiring experience at Azania. Opening night provided magic, with everyone in school hungry for the play. At the time, people rarely experienced theatrical events in schools, even in Dar es Salaam, Tanzania's cultural capital, let alone in the country at large. My play became a welcome novelty. Students packed the school auditorium, overflowing onto the stage. We had to shoo them away to make room for the performance. We performed the play at two or three other schools, to similar success, before we ran out of steam. From all the performances, we made more money than we could ever have imagined. I found the whole experience gratifying not so much because of the money, a great thing in itself of course, but more for my sense of creative accomplishment from the play. I hardly believed that actors had valued *my* words enough to memorize them, making them their own on stage. I hardly believed the audience had *paid* for and streamed in to see *my* dramatic story. I couldn't be more pleased.

Years later when I took up story-making seriously, I found the pleasure I felt then to have become mother to the pleasures of my writing stories today. I enjoy discovering a story worth sharing from my life experience or someone else's, or from folklore. I derive pleasure from unearthing the little things that make a story work. In story-making, I enjoy the thrill of a treasure hunt—following a reluctantly unfolding map from idea to a finished story. I enjoy struggling for a nifty beginning aimed at ensnaring the reader. I enjoy reflecting on what motivates and makes each character essential. I like the search for words that successfully marry action to character, setting and theme, while I listen closely to the dictates of the story. And after the characters have lived their life, I feel rewarded when I find a way to bring the story to a satisfying end.

Usually, my favorite story is any new one I happen to be working on. For me, embarking on a new story is akin to stepping onto a threshold of an adventure. I look forward to discoveries I will make. I look forward to hard questions to do with plot and character leaping out at me, and to answers that spring out when I least expect. I look forward to beautiful nuggets I can mine out of the story and my creative imagination. Nothing delights me more than suddenly alighting on a word, a phrase, a description, an image, or an ordering or paring down of words, that jolts a limp story to life. I love revision that brings clarity to an awkward sentence and tightens a slack scene or plot. Writing picture books has taught me about the microscopic aspects of writing. In a picture book story, every word is worth its weight in gold. To smelt for this gold, I revise again and again, setting the story aside between revisions to let time help me along. Then, by reading the story aloud over and over, I let my ear pick out what my eye has missed, the discordant note in the music and the rhythm of the words. I feel rewarded if that whole process enables me to present a story simply, engagingly and inspiringly and in terms relevant to children, who too should be able to feast on words, as I did and do.

Canada Dry

Growing up in Tanzania, I learned of this country through a drink—Canada Dry. Ice cold and hugely welcome on hot, dry days. I relished its sweet and potent bite, but above all its miraculous cooling effect. It became my favorite soda (pop) through the perennially scorching years in Tanzania. Canada, I thought then, must also be perennially hot and dry for its inhabitants to have named the refreshing drink (my favorite to this day) after their country.

Well, Canada is far from perennially hot, I would find out. Dry yes—in Alberta at least. It also turned out to abound with what would have been other astonishing surprises to little me in Tanzania. Surprises through Inuvik, for example, which I visited one May: its nearly twenty-four hours of daylight even at that time, long before summer; its Mackenzie river on which you could drive in winter, over an ice highway (which an all-season one has replaced)!

But the biggest surprise, even to my aging self in Canada?

Amin, an Inuvik-residing Swahili-speaking Sudanese-born cab driver!

That, besides languages from his native Sudan, Amin spoke Swahili, the lingua franca in the East African countries of Tanzania, Kenya, and Uganda, intrigued me. Though used also marginally in pockets of states neighboring those three countries, Swahili is spoken very little or not at all in Sudan, despite its shared border with Uganda. Amin told me, at the first of several restaurant meals we had together in Inuvik, that he had been a truck driver, driving all over Africa. From Cairo to Zambia, back and forth numerous times. It sounded true. Besides Arabic and a couple of Sudanese languages, he knew other African languages. That his Swahili was limited and broken intrigued me no less. I've met Somali, Congolese, Burundi, and Rwandese who spoke Swahili, but never Sudanese.

I took my encounter with Amin for granted. I didn't strive for answers to questions that began to occupy my mind. My short and busy stay in Inuvik and his demanding cab driving job and his poor English and Swahili, did not help. I contented myself with the meals I had with him, for all of which he insisted on paying. He stopped dead, every time, my attempts to chip in. It's how we do it, he said at our first lunch, which set the tone for the following ones. Back home in Sudan. The mwenyeji—'host' in Swahili—always pays, he said. He was after all, he pointed out, the host, being far more an Inuvik resident than I would ever be. I was the *mgeni*, 'newcomer,' a passing guest for a week in that Arctic outpost.

Questions about Amin belatedly bubbled in my mind.

Where and how had he learned Swahili?

What had been his experiences as a truck driver in Africa?

What was the range of his experiences in Canada?

How had he ended up in that frozen outpost of Inuvik?

Despite leaving Inuvik without full answers, my meeting with Amin got me thinking actively of Canada, this country consisting of a visible and invisible tangle of heritages unified by our desire to co-exist and to grow together. From literally every part of the world, old arrivals, and relatively recent ones like me, and those who had just come, imprint on one another our stories, some more complex than others: stories of who we are, where we come from, and of lives we're building here. In turn, we imprint and have imprinted those stories on foundational heritages, those of the First Nations prominent among them, from which Canada emerged.

This is the reality I see defining today's Canada. As a story-maker, I couldn't be happier. Such reality offers bounties of untold stories with which story-makers can work. As we celebrate it, therefore, to me Canada 150 implies a need to enable and animate untold stories such as those that possible answers to my questions about Amin could have suggested; stories that could be validated, celebrated, and disseminated in the interest of broadening our Canadian heritage.

Selwyn Jacob
(ca. 1950s–)

Award-winning filmmaker Selwyn Jacob has directed and/or produced more than fifty documentary films since beginning his career in Alberta in the early 1980s. He spent three artistically formative decades on the prairies, from 1968 to 1997; as he reveals in his personal essay "A Filmmaker's Journey," it was his close engagement with the black prairies' largely untold stories that determined the kind of hidden histories he would continue to seek out and bring to light in his films. Jacob works in the documentary genre in order to explore the experiences of black Canadians and the stories of other multicultural groups in Canada. He is best known for *The Road Taken* (1996) about the black Canadian sleeping car porters; Cheryl Foggo's *The Journey of Lesra Martin*, a 2002 documentary about a Canadian youth who helped to free Rubin "Hurricane" Carter; and *Mighty Jerome*, about the track and field star Harry Jerome (2010).

As a child growing up in Trinidad, he fell in love with television and film, but noticed that the black characters he saw on television were not people he could relate to. "They weren't role models. I had a dream as a kid to become an actor and tell stories for people that looked like they were from the Caribbean" (Samuel). Jacob came to Canada in 1968 to attend the University of Alberta, where he obtained a bachelor's degree in education in 1970. While there, he was influenced and mentored by producer, author, and broadcaster Fil Fraser (see Fraser's entry in this volume). After graduation, Jacob completed a master's degree in film studies at the University of Southern California School of Cinematic Arts, and then returned to Alberta. He spent time as a schoolteacher and principal until securing the resources to make his first film as an independent director, *We Remember Amber Valley* (1984), a documentary about the black community that existed near Lac La Biche in Alberta. He went on to direct two award-winning NFB releases, *Carol's Mirror* and *The Road Taken*, which won the Canada Award at the 1998 Gemini Awards.

Drawing a connection between his career as a teacher and the film projects he takes on, Selwyn Jacob says, "I am happy that I didn't continue my career in teaching, because a lot of what I do in film is a form of education[;] I still function as a teacher to many people. Even when it comes to subject matter, I tend to gear towards films that can still educate and tell a message outside of the classroom, and ultimately brings people out to watch" (Samuel).

In 1997 Jacob joined the National Film Board Pacific & Yukon Studio in Vancouver, and has gone on to produce close to fifty NFB films. Among his many credits are *Crazywater*, directed by the Inuvialuit filmmaker Dennis Allen; *Hue: A Matter of Colour*, a co-production with Sepia Films, directed by Vic Sarin; and the digital interactive project *Circa 1948*, by Vancouver artist Stan Douglas.

In 2017 in Edmonton, Selwyn Jacob received the Outstanding Achievement Award for his years of contribution to the media arts and body of work.

His personal essay "A Filmmaker's Journey," which relates the impact of Alberta's black community on his filmmaking style, was originally published in Tololwa Mollel's edited collection, *Home: Stories Connecting Us All*, e-published in 2017.

A Filmmaker's Journey to an Untold Story

In 1976, I obtained a teaching position with the Lac La Biche School Division in Northern Alberta. It was a decision that would forever change my outlook on being Canadian, and ultimately define the films I would direct and produce.

I had immigrated to Canada in 1968, and obtained a Bachelor of Education degree from the University of Alberta in 1970, but my goal had always been to become a filmmaker. I subsequently attended the University of Southern California from 1972–74 where I pursued a Master's Degree in Cinema. Upon my return to Edmonton in 1974, I found it virtually impossible to get any kind of film or television-related job. Capitalizing on my Bachelor of Education Degree, I became a teacher.

As a teacher, I found myself elated, frustrated, and dejected all at once. On the one hand, I was happy to be able to start paying down my student loans. On the other hand, I was disappointed in a system that denied me the opportunity to work in my preferred line of work. The fact that even at my second career choice, of teaching, I had been forced to go out of Edmonton for a job like many immigrant teachers at the time, made my disappointment only deeper.

But I kept looking on the bright side. I was hopeful I would find some filmic story that might evolve from working in that kind of, as it seemed to me at the time, isolationist environment. Two years later, by which time many people knew I was a film school graduate aspiring to be a filmmaker, a colleague urged me to consider making a film on the Black community just south of Lac la Biche, close to Athabasca Town. A Black community in this neck of the woods? The idea intrigued me. I couldn't wait to venture into the project. The following summer I was in the community of Amber Valley, to learn the history of these pioneering Black folks who had fled racial discrimination in Oklahoma, all the way to Northern Alberta, to establish an all-Black community.

With grandiose vision and a naïve sense of filmmaking, I set out to tell this epic story in all its glory. That is, until a producer from the newly-established Edmonton's National Film Board office suggested to me that maybe I should consider telling the story as a documentary. Most aspiring feature film directors, he told me, used the documentary as a stepping stone to other projects involving more dramatic storytelling. I heeded his advice.

With a small grant from Alberta Culture, I proceeded to interview some of the surviving residents of Amber Valley about their story. I asked them about the exodus from Oklahoma, their farming experience in Alberta, their integration into the larger white Athabasca community, and about their beloved baseball team.

Carrying out the project, I encountered people from all over North America, all of whom were working variously on the Amber Valley story. I met a producer from Montreal writing an opera about the Amber Valley Saga,[1] a filmmaker from Toronto who had successfully convinced the Alberta Government to fund a series of documentaries about historic Alberta communities, including Amber Valley. And I also met Charles Irby, now deceased, a history Professor from California State University, who was completing his Doctoral Dissertation entitled, *All That Blood: The Amber Valley Saga*.[2]

Eventually in 1984, with a total budget of approximately twenty thousand dollars and the help of a film co-op and volunteers, I completed my first film, *We Remember Amber Valley,* a crudely crafted documentary. It told the story of the Amber Valley community as seen through the eyes of its baseball team. Besides documenting an important episode in Alberta's

---

1   It doesn't appear that this opera has been produced.
2   Unpublished, but available in the Charles Irby Collection at UC Santa Barbara under the title *Northeast Alberta: A Marginal Agricultural Situation.*

history, the film managed to touch a sensitive chord with people of varying interests and backgrounds. I remember a gentleman commenting, when I showed it to representatives of the Alberta Government, that although he considered himself an authority on Alberta history, he had no knowledge of this group of Black migrants living in Northern Alberta. A former School Superintendent for the Athabasca School Division, called Dr. Swift, heard an interview I did on CKUA Radio about the film, and wrote a letter which said he was possibly one of only a few people who had first-hand knowledge of that community. As Superintendent he interacted with Amber Valley because not only did the community have its own school, it had its own Black School Board as well.

Twenty years later, I still get requests for this very simple but evocative documentary. And whenever I do, my mind goes back inevitably to those early days in Edmonton when I was told by some producers that nobody would be interested in a documentary on Black farmers on the prairies!

In addition to that film and others made since, I feel strongly about those Black stories, to do with belonging and identity, yet to be acknowledged and told filmically. Future generations may eventually gravitate to other stories reflecting the Black Experience, or they may choose to tell those that are simply Canadian and not rooted in any ethnicity. Either of those two options would be a positive indication that the Black Experience is being viewed through multiple lenses.

F.B. André
(1955–)

Frank Brian André was born in San Fernando, Trinidad, and immigrated to Canada as a student at the age of sixteen. On first arrival, André established himself in Ontario, but moved to Yellowknife to mine for gold, then, in 1978, to Edmonton, where he settled until 1990. Both of his children were born in Edmonton, and it is where he began to write. He currently lives in Victoria, British Columbia.

André has worked at a wide variety of jobs, including bartending, factory work, mining, catering, program administration, and he has also been a teacher and a café owner. His first collection of short stories, *The Man Who Beat the Man*, was published by NeWest Press in 2000. The stories are set in a variety of locations; "Jes Grew," about a young West Indian discovering Rastafarianism, is set in post-oil boom Red Deer, Alberta, but other stories are set in his childhood Trinidad, in Vietnam War–era Cambodia, and in present-day British Columbia. The various threads of the collection are gathered up in the poignant ethical question asked in the last story, "What are my responsibilities to my brother?" Reviews noted André's fine ear for dialogue and praised the collection's sharp focus and emotional complexity.

His second collection of short stories, *What Belongs* (Ronsdale Press 2007), is likewise centrally concerned with questions of kinship, responsibility, and belonging. "Is There Someone You Can Call?" a short story about a couple who buy a house that remains stubbornly and uncannily occupied, may be read as an allegory of the immigrant experience itself. The story, like several others in the collection, including "What the Future Holds," is set in St. Albert, a suburb of Edmonton, a location that is of enduring interest to André for its homogeneity built around shopping centres and interchangeable styles of housing. The story asks key questions about rightful belonging in a settler-colonial country. Should rightful belonging be based on first claims to a territory? How and in what ways does nature, or the other-than-human, have first rights of belonging? The hard-hitting story showcases André's signature style: verisimilitude of description and a limited omniscient narrator heighten the narrative tension and reveal, subtly and hauntingly, what is unexpected in the intimacies of ordinary human relationships.

Is There Someone You Can Call?

Today's the day. We take possession at noon. Officially.

Actually we only saw the house twice: first at the open house, and the second time was when we came out to put in our offer. We had it narrowed down. It's a little further out than ideal, but it had everything else on our wish list. We came in a little bit light on our offer expecting to be countered, but it was accepted. It just goes to show, our agent said, you never know.

It's after one o'clock, and any minute now a five-ton truck will show up with all our stuff. The problem is all the stuff from the previous owners is still here. Our new kitchen cupboards are full of their dishes. They've got the exact same set of Lagostina pots and they have the Kronvik dining room table from IKEA; we thought about buying that, but we went with the Pelto. The closets in the master bedroom are full of his suits and her dresses, like an orderly crowd waiting their turn to get out. The *en suite* bathroom is stocked with towels, toilet paper and toothpaste. There is no sign of packing up. The only room that is even remotely close to empty is a spare bedroom.

I phone my wife to bring her up to speed. "There's been some sort of a mix-up," I say.

"Are you sure you're at the right house? Did you check the address? The numbers?" she asks.

"Of course," I say. But she's already put me on hold. She's gone to double-check. I know it's the right house. I've checked the address at least half a dozen times. I've even gone all the way back out of the highway and taken the turnoff again, twice.

My wife comes back on the line, the purchase agreement and the title transfer are right in front of her. "Today is the day. Noon. We take possession."

"What about their stuff" I ask. "What's that called? What does it say about that? The chattels?"

My wife knows a lot more about legal terms than I do.

"There's nothing in here," she says, "except for the drapes. We asked for those. Are the drapes still there?"

"Everything," I say, "is still here."

"I can't do anything from here," she says. "Can't you handle this?"

"I'm sure it's just a simple screwup," I say. "Their movers must have got the date wrong. I'll put a call in to our agent. Maybe our agent can get a hold of their agent and figure this thing out? I'll call you back, okay? okay?" She's already hung up.

Their agent sounds like someone whose cheque has cleared; their problem is mine. The company my wife works for is paying for our entire move. All I had to do was show up, open the door, and the movers would do the rest. Somehow the blame for this mix-up will end up as mine for all eternity.

The kitchen leads into the garage. The double garage is what clinched it for me. It's Black & Decker all the way, and each tool has its own stenciled place along the walls. There's a Mazda minivan in one of the bays. We looked at buying one of those, but we decided to wait and put the money into buying more house. It takes a minute to find the switch that controls the garage door. It's got a neat feature: you can open one side at a time or both sides at once. I come around to the front of the house again. This time, I will turn the key, open the door, and presto! House empty! You are such a child, my wife would say if she were here. You can't just wish for things to go away.

"For a second, I thought you were Ross," the neighbour says. "I've got his leaf-blower. I didn't get a chance to return it."

The neighbour's name is Barry. He is very tall, and he's very bald. In fact Barry is too bald; he lacks the gravitas a truly bald man needs to carry off such an expanse of skin. It will take years for him to grow into that much baldness.

"It's the new, new neighbour," Barry calls to his wife.

"What does he want?" she says.

The layout of their house is the same. I hear her, but I don't see her. I'm guessing master bedroom.

"Tell her I want a cup of sugar," I say.

"He says he wants a cup of sugar," Barry plays along.

"Sugar?" His wife hesitates. "We have lots of sugar."

"I need to borrow your garage," I say.

"And he needs to borrow our garage."

Barry's wife comes to the door; her name is Cynthia. She is wearing a tracksuit and her face is flushed, as if she's been working out or something.

"Don't you think he kind of looks like Ross?" Barry asks. Cynthia agrees.

"I need to borrow your garage," I say. "Unless you know how I can reach your former neighbours in a big hurry. There's a mix-up with the movers. Nothing of theirs is packed up. And our stuff will be here any minute. I can't even use the garage. A Mazda takes up half the space, and it's like a hardware store in there."

"Ross liked his tools and his toys," Barry says. "He was a handy kind of guy."

"Do you have a number for them?" I ask.

"We have no idea how to reach them." Barry confirms this with Cynthia.

"People come and go, all the time." Barry shakes his head. "I'm not saying they had an obligation, but common courtesy. We weren't neighbours for long, but we weren't complete strangers, to leave without a word—it's too weird."

"Barry?" Cynthia says. "Barry, can I see you in the kitchen for a sec?"

I recognize Cynthia's tone. Any man who's been married for a while knows that particular tone. Cynthia tries to keep her voice down. I don't know exactly what she's saying, but I get her drift. Don't get her started, and don't get us involved. I'm at their door long enough to start to feel uncomfortable when Barry arrives, back-checking all the way.

"Maybe I'll hold on to the leaf-blower," Barry says.

I decide to walk down to the mailbox. It gives me something semi-useful to do. It's snowing. It's at the point where it's sticking to the lawns but not the road. I feel like I'm inside a diorama that's just been given a shake. It's a lightly frosted winter pastoral scene. This whole area used to be farmland: quietly rusting tractors still sit in weathered barns, and there's a stand of trees—a windbreak for the original farmhouse—that now acts like a divider between the new subdivision and the highway.

When my wife got the promotion and transfer, it was a big jump ahead for her, and not much was happening for me. I went to the university here, so I already know my way around. That's a plus. I might still know a few people. In my last year at university, the girl I was living with had a chance to go on a work-study for a year. We didn't make any promises. I don't even know if she ever made it back. I'd like to know how things turned out. I ought to look her up. Give her a call.

The mailboxes are in a cluster near the turnoff from the highway, and there's a bit of a crowd: three trucks and a couple of cars. I can make out the word SHERIFF on one of the cars, and someone is handing out orange fluorescent vests. About eight or nine guys are forming up into what looks like a posse. A banjo music soundtrack runs through my head, and I begin to make all sorts of loose jangling connections between our new house with too much furniture and missing persons.

"Deer can't read." The sheriff points in my general direction with his rifle. "They migrate along this corridor, every year."

"Looks like you're here to teach them quite a lesson," I say.

"The deer were here first," the sheriff says. "Where's the lesson in that?"

"Look at it coming down," I say. "It must be good and thick in the mountains."

The sheriff nods as the hunters begin to fan out. I collect an armload of flyers from the mailbox and sort them directly into the recycle bin. On the way back I stay on the road, trying hard not to leave any tracks.

The movers arrive. They do what movers do when faced with any problem: they have a smoke. The driver's name is Harold, and his two boys are Colby and Rob.

Colby, for reasons known only to him, counts and recounts the extra blankets that they use to cover and slide things around. Rob is looking for a mathematical solution: if X is the volume of the moving van, and Y is the available area in the garage, then … Rob is unable to subtract enough information to make a clear deduction.

"You don't have a key for the Mazda?" Harold feels around under the bumper. Believe it or not, he's come across similar situations. "These things have a way of working out," Harold assures me. Now he stands on the bumper of the Mazda, and jumps up and down. "We could tow the Mazda out," Harold suggests, "without too much trouble."

"That would work." Rob's main job is to agree with Harold. Colby does another recount of the blankets.

"What about the stuff inside?" I ask. "Is there something we are supposed to do?"

"What do you mean?" Harold asks. He's immediately suspicious.

"Could you pack it up, legally?" I ask.

Harold is not at all concerned about the legal issues surrounding the stuff inside. And he has no interest in packing anything up; his obligations end as soon as our stuff is unloaded. Harold studies the falling snow, anxious to get started. He didn't plan on this weather, and he wants to get going before dark. Rob and Colby vigorously agree.

Barry's garage yawns open, and he emerges wearing some kind of uniform. I'm guessing that he's some sort of pilot.

"Me and Ross—we talked lawns and golf. Ross was a regular guy. I know he did some work overseas, right out of university. That's where they met. Rita was the arty type. She kept busy, seemed happy. Apparently Rita just up and left him. Poor Ross." Barry shrugs as he gets into his car. That's the full extent of what he knows. Cynthia watches from her bay window. As soon as she sees me looking she turns her back.

I find a spare key for the Mazda in the kitchen. Harold and his boys unload the truck like a military operation: the only casualty suffered is a lamp that I took from my parents' home. It went with me off to college, it survived the swamp of dorm rooms and bachelor foxholes, it sat on my night table in my only other serious attempt at setting up a nest, and it went straight into storage with all the rest of my things when we started living together.

Colby broke it. Rob calls Colby a loser. Colby hangs his head in shame. Harold says there's no need for that, and that there's a procedure for accidents. There is a form to fill out. Harold insists that I place some sort of value on the lamp. It's not *the* magic lamp, I say. It's too small a thing to make any sort of fuss about. It probably would have just stayed in a box, until some garage sale in the future.

Harold and his boys turn down my offer of a drink; they are intent on beating the weather. The crescent retakes the contours of a farmer's field. The windbreak of trees near the horizon stands in close for the forest that once was. The sheriff and his men are still trolling the neighbourhood, reluctant to abandon their annual hunt. How can they see in this weather? The Mazda is already covered by a coat of heavy snow. How long before it becomes a target? If I stay outside, I'll be game soon. But I'm reluctant to re-enter the house; I have this foolish feeling—not quite like I'm intruding, but as if I'm stepping on something.

"There's been a horrible accident on the highway; a truck overturned." Cynthia comes over to inform me. She is one of those people who can make everything sound like an accusation.

"The sheriff is telling everyone not to go out. The road is going to be closed for quite a while. It's one of the charms of living out here. Barry made it through; he's ahead of the storm."

Cynthia plays the good neighbour, but curiosity is what really dragged her over.

"Come in, come in," I say. "Ignore the chaos. I found some wine. I'm assuming they won't mind. Be careful, the movers broke a lamp. I think I got it all, but watch where you step."

Cynthia can't resist taking the tour, walking through the house, and stopping in every room to take inventory.

"Is anything missing?" I ask.

"Nothing that I ever saw," Cynthia says.

Cynthia doesn't know much about Ross, but she fills me in on Rita. It turns out Rita went to the same university as I did. We overlapped. I might even know her to see her. When she was at university, Rita was seeing a guy named Edward for a while. Edward wasn't a student but he was always on campus. He was with some company that did a lot of business with the university. He was also attached to someone else. Rita didn't like the arrangement, but she had no one that she could call on for advice. Finally, she decided to take her student loan and go off to Mexico to sort things out.

When she got to Mexico, Rita sent Edward a postcard; it had a picture of a famous ruin. Rita spent a long time deciding what to put on the card, but in the end she went with her first thought.

I am here. You are not.

Mexico was not far enough away for her purposes, and Rita continued south. She would accept rides to anywhere from strangers, but she had surprisingly few adventures or mishaps. She went wherever people's lives were taking them, and most people were going nowhere special.

Rita met Ross in Belize. It was a case of mistaken identity. The driver who picked her up was sent to fetch a young woman from Canada and bring her to the compound where a group of well-intentioned young people were trying to make a difference. They had a project underway, and Ross was in charge. It was only for a brief time, but Rita had to pretend that she was this other woman—the no-show. Rita would sometimes think that she had somehow stepped into this other woman's life.

Ross and Rita returned to Canada. They looked at several houses before they bought. The house was a little further out of town than either Ross or Rita would have liked, but it had everything else you could wish for. You could see deer—right in the backyard. They decided to have a housewarming party.

Edward turned up at the party.

Rita was in the kitchen with her new neighbour, Cynthia; they had made all this Mexican food.

Here you are, Edward said.

Cynthia takes her leave. I follow her tracks across both lawns. She stops and stares into the bay window of her house for a long moment before she goes inside.

It's dark and getting darker. Just as I decide to call my wife, she phones.

"Where are you?" I ask.

"Still at work," she answers.

"There's been an accident on the highway. They've closed the road," I say.

"Good," my wife says. She's not planning on driving out in this. She'll stay and work late. She'll stay in the corporate suite; no one is using it, so why not?

"How did the move go? Is all of our stuff in the house?" she asks.

"I'm not sure," I say, "about a lot of stuff."

"I labeled all of my boxes," she says. "The movers were supposed to unload everything into the right rooms. That was our agreement. They won't get paid until it gets done right."

"There's a deer in our backyard," I say. "A big one."

"Really? What are we supposed to do about that?" she says. "Is there someone you can call?"

Cheryl Foggo
(1956–)

"I believe people around us—our fellow citizens—are affected not only by the words we say, but even by the thoughts we have," says writer, researcher, and knowledge keeper Cheryl Foggo. "The power of words is contained not just in their literal meaning, but in the weight behind them, their historical context, the vibrations they create when they're spoken and by the actions they cause us to take (or not take) when we think them. I believe that power is amplified in written language (Julie Wilson).

Cheryl Foggo was born and raised in Bowness, formerly an independent town, now a neighbourhood in west Calgary. She studied journalism at Mount Royal College, Calgary, and has gone on to publish extensively as a journalist, screenwriter, poet, playwright, writer of fiction and non-fiction, and as a young adult novelist. Her need to write, she has said, is "inborn," but her choice of subject "is influenced by my time, place and situation. That I am a woman, descended from African people who were enslaved in the Americas has politicized my life. That I came of age during the time of the civil rights movement in Canada and the U.S. politicized my outlook (Wilson).

Her superb *Pourin' Down Rain* (1990) is a coming-of-age memoir about growing up in prairie communities with small black populations, and thematizes the family, civil rights, and the learned art of black Canadian storytelling. She drew much of the material from an unpublished manuscript called "The Story of My Father's Life," written by Daisy Smith Mayes Williams, Foggo's grandfather's sister. This manuscript remains in Foggo's personal archive. *Pourin' Down Rain* was a finalist for the Alberta Culture Non-Fiction Prize in 1990. A revised and updated thirtieth-anniversary edition of *Pourin' Down Rain* is going to be released in 2020 by Brush Education and an audiobook is being released by ECW Press as part of its Bespoke series of Canadian classics.

Each of her children's novels—*One Thing That's True* (1998), *I Have Been in Danger* (2001), and her picturebook *Dear Baobab* (2011)—similarly offer positive

232

representations of black and mixed-race youth. Her children's books have been nominated, between them, for the Governor General's Award, the Silver Birch, Blue Heron, Mr. Christie's Book Award, and the Writers' Guild of Alberta R. Ross Annett Award.

Foggo has also written extensively for the stage. She adapted Chinua Achebe's novel *Things Fall Apart* for the 2010 Afrikadey! Festival and the 2010 Theatre Calgary FUSE program. Her play *The Devil We Know*, co-written with her partner Clem Martini, was produced at Ontario's Blyth Theatre Festival in 2012. *Heaven*, her play about a 1927 black schoolteacher who arrives from the east to teach in Amber Valley, was produced by Lunchbox Theatre Company in Calgary in 2001 and workshopped by Black Theatre Montreal and Playwright's Workshop Montreal. The play was a finalist in Theatre BC's National Playwriting Competition (2000), and aired on CBC Radio (2004). *Turnaround* was co-written with Clem Martini and produced by Lunchbox and Quest Theatres (1999/2000) and was a finalist for the Betty Mitchell New Play Award.

In her recent play *John Ware Reimagined* (staged in 2014 and 2017), Foggo delves into the archives to bring John and Mildred Ware to life. As she puts it in the play, "I want to be the one that finds him. Take a giant, magic eraser and swipe it over everything that's ever been said about him, cleansing the page, edging closer to what is true" (7). Her representation of John's quietude, his many hurts, and Toronto-born Mildred's homesickness for urban life looks beyond the stereotype of John as a Paul Bunyan–like giant and Mildred as dutiful wife. Her play, which frames theirs as a love story, realizes them as fully fleshed out people at last. *John Ware Reimagined* premiered with Ellipsis Tree Collective Theatre Company in Calgary in August 2014. It was restaged at the Workshop West Playwrights Theatre in 2017. Foggo's script has won the Writers' Guild of Alberta 2015 Gwen Pharis Ringwood Award for Drama. She is currently directing a documentary film about John Ware for the National Film Board.

Foggo has also written a number of screenplays, including *Playing Fair: Carol's Mirror* (NFB 1991), directed by Selwyn Jacob. She wrote and directed *The Journey of Lesra Martin* in 2002, about the young man who was the catalyst for the freeing of Rubin "Hurricane" Carter. Her television script *Love Hurts* (1998, North of 60) was a finalist for the Alberta Motion Picture Industry Awards.

Foggo has published more than forty articles or essays on black Alberta history in magazines or newspapers, including the *Globe and Mail*, *Calgary Herald*, *Alberta Views*; and the anthologies *Alberta Encore* (2010), *One Step Over the Line* (2008), *Directions—The Bicentenary of the Abolition of the British Slave Trade* (2007), *Remembering Chinook Country* (2006). She is working on a non-fiction collection of essays about southern Alberta's black history, *Hiding Place*.

Beloved in the black community for her public service and anti-racism work, Cheryl Foggo was nominated for the 2016 Obsidian Awards for Lifetime Achievement. The Obsidian Awards recognize African, Caribbean, and Afro-Canadian Culture and Excellence within Alberta.

The following vignette is taken from *Pourin' Down Rain*, a bildungsroman about the coming of age of a black prairie writer, and a memoir of five generations of her prairie family, first published in 1990. Foggo's prose, like her memory of her early childhood years, is clear as a bell, and very beautiful. The second excerpt is from her previously unpublished play "John Ware Reimagined."

Pourin' Down Rain

Upon occasion when I was growing up, we went to eat in Chinatown.

Sometimes the occasion was a visit from an out-of-town relation; sometimes the occasion was unknown to me, perhaps unknown to everyone except Aunt Edie and Uncle Andrew, who acted as co-chairs for these Chinatown excursions. All of my family—my mother, father, sister and brothers; all of our aunts and uncles, cousins and many people who I thought were my aunts and cousins and a few people who were not Black at all, but were so much a part of my world that I thought they were Black in a different way—all of us went to Chinatown.

We were stared at, of course. In 1965 it was rare to see a large group of mostly Black people in Calgary. I believed that the staring was something we had earned, an acknowledgement of our status as important and beautiful people.

The women wore hats, the men wore long coats and rubber slip-on covers for their shoes. Some faces were dark and shiny, others were light brown and waxy looking. The teenage boy cousins wore stove-pipe pants and had very lean faces, the girls wore white lipstick over textured mouths. I was in love with these people who were a magnet to the eyes of all who passed them. I loved to hear them laugh and see them point to the menu, saying, "I'd like to try some of this here," or "The onliest thing about Chinese food is you git hungry again later."

This book is for all of them—the aunts, uncles, cousins, sisters, brothers, the friends who I believed to be Black in their own way, and for those who stared at us in Chinatown and wondered what we were doing there—this is so you will know.

There was nothing amiss, nothing lacking in Bowness. In 1958, my parents bought a house there for seven thousand dollars. It had no plumbing, no basement, no porch, an unfinished yard and only five small rooms.

Our street, 70th Street, was gravel and dust. No street lamps. No trees. When the wind blew, which it did frequently, great clouds of sand would whirl up and spin across the road. My brothers and sister and I, and our friends, were delighted by these dust storms. Someone would shriek, "It's a tornado!" and we would chase the cloud, madly laughing.

Around the corner and up 46th Avenue was a cluster of businesses—the bakery, the hardware store, Gibson's Variety, a café, the library, and the Crystal Grocery, which everyone referred to as "Garry's," after the proprietor, Garry Fong.

At the other end of 70th Street was Bowcroft Elementary which my brothers attended, and the kindergarten which I attended in the basement of the United Church. Before gaining the church doors there was a long, wide, grassy field to master. Initially, the crossing of this field required a certain amount of courage-gathering. The grass was, in places, as tall as I and the boulders in the distance might have provided cover for an animal or a bully. Soon, though, bolstered by the company of my friend Ricky Hayes, the field's gently waving rainbow-coloured foxtails became a treasured part of the enjoyment in a five-year-old life.

Our street contained the closest thing to a Black community that one would find in Calgary in 1961. Ricky Hayes' parents were biracial, but he, his brother Randy and sister Debbie considered themselves Black. The Hayes', their grandparents across the alley, my family and the Saunders and Lawson families up the road comprised what I believe was the largest concentration of Black people in a single Calgary neighbourhood.

My parents had an attitude of kinship toward the other Black families on the street. The families knew one another, they knew each other's parents and grandparents, and probably because of that "knowing," they communicated to us our connection to other Black children. We played together. Without isolating ourselves from the other children in the neighbourhood and without any discussion of it, we sensed a link that transcended our environs.

Across the street from our house was another field which we had to cross to reach the railroad tracks leading to the twin bridges, the Bow River, and ultimately, to the paths that took us "up in the hills."

Most summer days were spent meandering along the tracks to the river, the usual goal being a picnic in the hills. The picnic, however, was not really the point. The point was the adventure we would sometimes encounter along the way.

On a very warm day, if there was no breeze, the heat from the iron rails and sharp smell of oil and metal bouncing up into our faces would drive us down from the tracks to walk through the high grasses. This meant slower going, but it was good to sniff the flowers instead of the heat and to dig around what someone would insist was a badger hole.

From the first time my brothers pronounced me old enough to go along with them, until I was sixteen and we moved from Bowness, the journey along the tracks to the river, across the bridges and up into the hills was real life. It was the meeting place, it was where we went to talk and light campfires, it was something we did that our parents did not do.

Across the alley from us lived two children, a brother and sister, who never joined the treks to the hills if we and the Hayes children were going. Their father forbade them from associating with us, and effectively ostracized his children from the rest of the neighbourhood by prohibiting them from joining any games where we Black children were present. When groups formed for kick-the-can or softball, we were often aware of these two children's eyes peering out from the cracks in their fence. They were there, we were aware of their presence, and in retrospect, their loneliness seems palpable.

When I was young, I was minimally aware that racism was a special problem. People who shared our neighbor's prejudices seemed so rare and to have so little effect on my life that I did not attribute their bigotry to a world condition.

My mother had implanted in the minds of my two older brothers, my younger sister and myself that we were special, not ordinary in any way. She would refer to our bigoted neighbor with utter contempt, as "the likes of him," implying that his ideas and his two unfortunate children were unworthy of our time or thoughts.

The diligence of our mother freed the minds of me and my siblings from the self-hatred that can cripple Black children born in ghettos.

Still, even a fiercely proud mother's constant reassurances cannot protect her Black child from learning, sooner or later, that skin is a badge you will always wear, a form of identification for those in the world who wish to brand you.

One afternoon upon returning from school I overheard my mother talking on the phone to Mr. Leavitt, the principle of my elementary school. He was calling to plead with her to try to persuade Floyd Hayes to discourage his children from fighting at school. Floyd was the brother of my mother's twin sister's husband and the father of the aforementioned friends, Randy, Ricky and Debbie.

"I'm afraid that I can't agree with you, Mr. Leavitt," she was saying. "I'm not going to tell them how to handle their problems. They came from a place where they can't fight. Where they come from a Black person doesn't have a chance against racists, and if Mr. Hayes has decided his children are going to fight name-calling with their fists, that's up to him."

When my mother replaced the receiver on its hook on the wall, I pestered her with questions. What did Mr. Leavitt want? Why had he called her? Were Randy and Ricky in trouble? What did she mean when she said Floyd and come from somewhere else where they couldn't fight it? Fight what?

"Jim Crow. They couldn't fight Jim Crow down there, but he's determined he's going to fight it here."

"Who is Jim Crow?"

"It's not who, it's what. It's called Jim Crow when Black people aren't allowed to ride at the front of the bus, or drink from the same fountains as Whites."

"Jim Crow?" I repeated. "Jim Crow. Where is the Jim Crow?"

"Kansas. Floyd and them were all born in Kansas."

If Floyd "and them" were all born in Kansas, that meant that my Uncle Allen, Floyd's younger brother, had been born there too, and that he had lived with this Jim Crow.

"Is Kansas in Canada?" I asked nervously.

"No, oh no," my mother said. "We don't have that kind of thing here. Kansas is in the States. Allen and Floyd and them never went to the movie houses when they were kids, not because they didn't believe in it, but because nobody was going to tell them that they had to sit up in the balcony or at the back. They came to Canada to get away from that, and they figure they're not going to tell their kids to stand by while anyone calls them 'nigger' either."

My mother was clearly quite agitated by Mr. Leavitt's call. I knew that she would repeat the entire conversation, with some embellishment, to her sisters Pearl and Edie on the telephone later that evening.

As for me, I was relieved to learn that Kansas was not in Canada. Here was yet another story, another horrific tale of life in "The States," fueling my growing belief that I was lucky to have been born in Canada.

Only short days before Mr. Leavitt's call I had learned that my grandparents, my mother's father and mother, had also once lived in America.

The discovery came to me when I asked my mother to explain why my grandpa was White, yet his brother, Uncle Buster, was Black.

My grandfather was something less than five feet, ten inches tall. He had grey eyes, he wore glasses over his long, narrow nose and he was light-skinned.

He had been called George Washington Smith at birth, but upon joining the Canadian Army in 1919 he revealed the full extent of his embarrassment of the name and lied to the commanding officer, saying that this middle initial stood for Willis. Thereafter, he was known as George Willis Smith and that is how I knew him.

I believe he possessed an average build, although it is difficult to be certain as he always dressed in loose clothing, in particular a pair of grey-beige pants and a yellow shirt.

He had a deep voice and a low, rolling, rumbling laugh. He began most sentences with the phrase, "Well, ya take." He called his five sons "Son," his four daughters, "Daughter" and he sometimes called me "Granddaughter."

He would say, "Well, ya take, granddaughter, I don't yodel when big girls (referring to my grandmother, who was singing in the kitchen) are listenin'. I only yodel for special small girls."

He was born in Chandler, Oklahoma, on October 31st, 1897. When I say that he was light-skinned, I mean that his skin colour was indistinguishable from that of any White person.

That is why, in 1963 when I was seven years old, I asked my mother how he could be White and his brother be Black.

She turned and stared at me. "Your Grandpa is not White."

"He is," I said.

I went to the china cabinet and took the photograph of my grandparents with their children taken on the occasion of their fortieth wedding anniversary. Carefully, I took it to my mother and placed it in her hands.

"Look."

My mother took the picture and brushed it gently, wiping away imaginary dust.

"He has very fair skin, honey, but he isn't a White man. What he would say if he knew his grandchildren thought so!" She was very amused and continued, "You see, just look at his hair."

I looked, but seeing nothing remarkable about his metallic-grey, brushed-back hair, did not speak.

"You're not going to find any White man on earth with hair like that," she said. "Daddy has him some bad hair."

"Bad" was how she described any head of hair, like my brother Richard's or my cousin Sharon's, that was very tight and nappy. She frequently caused me considerable grief by comparing my hair with my sister's, whose loose and supple hair qualified as "good hair."

I continued to gaze glumly at the photograph in my mother's hand. I was embarrassed at having been wrong about my grandfather. There he sat, beside my dark-skinned grandmother, to whom all along I thought he had been blissfully and interracially married.

"Grandma is Black." I finally said.

"Uhhm hmm, no one would ever mistake your grandmother for White. Daddy and Mama used to run into trouble when they went back to the States. If Daddy wears a hat, you see, he can't lay claim to his heritage. He used to wonder why nobody bothered him when he went into the White areas."

"Once, Mama and Daddy went to Oklahoma to see Mom's relatives. They'd been shopping and made plans to meet in a restaurant for lunch. Daddy got there first, took a table and told the waiter that he was waiting for his wife. He didn't take his hat off until he sat down. When Mama got there she joined Daddy at his table, but no one came to take their order. The waiter walked all around them, just like they weren't there. He acted like he was deaf when Daddy said 'Excuse me.'

"Finally a person came from the kitchen and whispered, 'I'm sorry, but we won't be able to serve you today.'

"Daddy was shocked. He was a young boy when he left the States and had forgotten what it was like there. He really got angry. He stood up and said, 'You sure were planning to serve me before I took my hat off.' He started to go toward the man, but Mama stopped him. 'No George, let's just get our things and go,' she said. 'We don't need for you to land up in jail down here.' Mama and Daddy got out of there and shook the dust of that place off of their feet. Daddy's never gone back again, never again."

Knowing my grandparents to be the gentle, lovely people that they were, I couldn't imagine what kind of madness would cause them to be treated in such a manner. I began to fear the very word whenever I heard someone refer to "The States." I vowed that, like my grandfather, I would not bother to darken America's doorstep.

It was not unusual, during the sixties, for several of my mother's siblings to be together in their parent's livingroom. Some of them lived in Winnipeg; the others would make plans to travel to that city at the same time. I feel quite certain that for most of them, the highlight of their year began and ended with the vacation that brought them together at 636 Ross Avenue.

I learned a good deal, at an early age, from those gatherings. I learned how to tell a story, the importance of the family and our history and I began to learn the way Black people, at least the kind of Black people that we are, use language.

My mother spoke to her family in a way that she never spoke to our neighbours at home. Sometimes she said, "ain't" or "don't" when she meant "doesn't," as in, "don't make no difference."

Why, I wondered, would she say "don't make no difference" when I knew quite well that at home she would say "doesn't matter?"

With the exception of Aunt Edie, who had married a man from a rural Black community and adopted some of his expressions and speech patterns, none of Mother's family used expressions like "y'all" as part of their natural speech. One would not have known it, however, from listening to them when they were together in the security of their parents' home. Their high-spirited conversation was heavily peppered with "y'alls" and "uhhm uhhm uhhms" and other colloquialisms usually associated with rural Black speech.

I began to understand, as I grew older, that they did this to entertain one another and to affirm their "Blackness." They were people with ambivalent feelings about their isolation from other Blacks. They had no desire to return to the America that their parents had fled, nor did they wish to be completely swallowed by the White society in which they all lived.

Their normal speech demonstrated to White society that Black Canadians could speak the Queen's English too.

"Talking Black" to one another, to relatives and to trusted Black friends allowed them to also *feel* Black. It was a method that they used to gain acceptance into the Black communities (small though they were) of Calgary, Vancouver, and Winnipeg when they left Regina. By manipulating their English they could demonstrate to their new Black friends that although they had been raised almost exclusively among Whites, they were still Black inside.

John Ware Reimagined

It's possible that I've read every document with John Ware's name on it. I've searched dozens of dusty old books. I've read his daughter's letters.

Did he strap himself to a wagon and pull the three people in it home when their horses were killed by lightning? Did he discover oil in Alberta?

Did a wild horse he was riding buck itself off a cliff into the river below and did he rise up out of the river, still in the saddle?

I want to be the one that finds him.

Take a giant, magic eraser and swipe it over everything that's ever been said about him, cleansing the page, edging closer to what is true.

For today, here's what I've got.

He was smart. He was funny. He hated fences.

Mildred enters.

MILDRED: I.G. Baker Mercantile and Grocery.

The tang of cloth and apples and liniment and leather. All mixed up together and handed to you on a plate, like, "Here Mildred, this is gonna be your life now."

The whole thing stank of expectations. I'd spent my life meeting people's expectations.

I was the oldest girl of ten siblings. If my brothers and sisters got to running around, it was always, "Mildred, can't you keep those children quiet?" ... (*lowers her voice*) "They're your children, not mine."

I felt like saying that, but I never did. I just went along with what was expected. I *liked* noise. The first night we spent out here? I thought my ears were broken. The street I grew up on in Toronto, King Street, was busy. The taxi's horses running back and forth, the church bells, people shouting "Mornin!" to their neighbours.

And everything was right there! If you forgot something at the dry goods you turned around and went back for it. Here, if you forgot something you just made do without. You're not going to get back in the wagon and drive 60 miles because you forgot the broom.

My great grandfather, Daniel Lewis, was free. His son Henry Lewis, my grandfather, was free. They'd been chased out of Virginia because Henry had the gall to buy my grandma's freedom and they fled to Toronto. Grandpop Henry was a carpenter but in the winter he harvested ice and sold it all over the city. I loved that ice cart. Uncle William used to lift me up, wrap me in Grandma Francis's old fur coat and let me hold the horse's reins while he carried the ice in to his customers. That's as close as I ever got to a horse in Toronto. My uncle John owned the Dominion Tobacco Works Company and had 75 men working for him. Then he became a lawyer. Uncle Henry was a member of the York Pioneers, Uncle Benjamin ran the bakery and the sausage shop ...

The Lewises owned so many homes and businesses in Toronto I started to feel like a queen, riding around in that ice cart. Look at me, I'm a Lewis.

Why? Why leave his carpentry business and our 2 story brick house on King Street and our aunts and uncles and cousins and a whole community of Coloured people who were educating their children in Latin to come out here and try to grow rocks?

I didn't understand. I went along, as expected, and here I was.

JOHN: Four times, and each one better than the time before.

Time three was like when a filly's just born and she's layin' down there in the straw and the mud, and she thinks that's all there is, but then an hour later she's runnin' and kickin' like she's never gonna stand still again—it was like everything I'd done before that was just pretend livin'.

Up here there was so much space and the big ole sky and running water so clear it hurt my eyes to look at it. I made some good friends. Oh sure, I met folks determined to trip me up. Even when I was promoted to round-up boss, there was always some dunderhead who couldn't bring himself to accept the fact of me tellin' him what t'do. One time couple'a young bucks took my hatchet without askin', and when I politely warned em it was time to bring it back they acted like I hadn't said nothin'. So I grabbed hold'a the biggest one—always best to go for the biggest one first—went to toss him in the creek, but I lost my footing and we both went in. We must'a been there 15 minutes, me dunkin' him under, then him dunkin' me under, back n'forth like that. He was as strong as me, which was kinda unusual. Finally, he says,

BUCK: Mister, it was just a joke.

JOHN: And I looked him in the eye and realized he was tellin the truth. Wasn't about him not wantin to accept the fact I was the boss. I'd almost let myself get thrown off balance by a prank.

So I quit tryin to drown him and we shook hands. "Still want my axe," I said. We helped each other up the bank and soon as I had my feet back on solid ground I approached the other fella. Threw him in the creek. Just in case.

MILDRED: It was a terrible wrench. But I had my plans. As soon as I had enough money and Jessie got old enough to help with the younger children, I was going back to Toronto to become a school teacher. I was tired of the kind of expectations that had dropped me in a wasteland where the most exciting part of every day was scraping chicken droppings off my good shoes.

And the prejudice! That was a wrench too. Not that there wasn't prejudice in the east. But you could …We had our own … spaces.

But every person I met was talking about this John Ware.

PERSON 1: Have you met John Ware Miss Lewis?

MILDRED: They'd take one look at me.

PERSON 2: Say now, there's a fella you've just got to meet Miss Lewis.

MILDRED: And then mother started talking about we should meet this John Ware. I knew what she was thinking too. People in my family didn't just marry, they "made good matches." It was the Lewis way.

I reminded mother of my plans to return to Toronto.

MRS. LEWIS: No harm in meeting the man, honey.

MILDRED: She said.

MRS. LEWIS: Might as well make the acquaintance of all the good Coloured folks we can while we're here.

MILDRED: After all the good Coloured folks we'd left behind in Toronto. I narrowed my eyes behind her back whenever she talked about him. I was determined to dislike him.

JOHN: First time I saw her up at Baker's, folks was fallin all over themselves to introduce us. But I couldn't speak! My tongue'd turned to cotton. I couldn't do a thing except nod my head up and down up and down up and down til my neck got sore. Then she spoke to me, but my ears had set to ringin so I was scared to answer, for fear she'd said "Nice weather we're havin" and I'd come back with "I like pickles."

Kicked myself all the way home—"Ware, she thinks you're the dumbest fool she's ever laid eyes on." Promised myself if I ever saw her again she was gonna know different. Well, next time I did a little better. Think I managed three whole words.

MILDRED: One day I went to I. G. Baker with mother to buy muslin to make new curtains and there he was.

John is readying himself Up Left. Mildred is re-enacting the first meeting by herself—

Big … Clean … Not rough and smelly like I'd been picturing him. He had a presence. Big hands. Big shoulders. He was really big. So, I thought to myself, well mother's right, there's no harm in saying hello. So I did, I said—

Hello.

(pause)

Um. Do you think it might rain like everyone's saying it's about to do?

And he opened his mouth, but nothing came out. He looked like he was about to faint.

He was just so … big. But when he didn't speak, didn't even respond beyond nodding his head a couple of times, I thought, well you're big but is that all? The next time I saw him was at a social at the McCutcheon's place, where he wasn't much better. Finally, when it got late and I was making to leave, he followed me out to the porch, and said (as JOHN)   "Miss Lewis, careful on that step now."

MILDRED: There was a loose board on the stair. I turned back and said, "Thank you Mr. Ware, I will."

I couldn't stop looking at him. I said to myself, Mildred, you are in trouble. And I went home and sat down in the dirt behind the henhouse and cried for 3 hours. Because what about my life? What about my plans?

JOHN: I had worked till I had enough to build my own place, get my own herd. Couldn't believe my luck, the day I settled it up at the register. My own brand. Me. Some folks say, "I never would'a dreamed this, I never would'a dreamed that." Not me. I did dream it. Every day when I was bustin' my back for somebody who thought he owned me back in time one, I dreamed it.

He takes a moment to look around, surveying his world.

And there it was. I thought it was enough. Until I saw her—

Underneath the song, Mildred exits for tea tray with 2 cups, 2 plates, 2 napkins and teapot—handed to her by other musician. Re-entering, she puts out setting, pours tea, and invites John to sit as she does. He does, removing his hat and placing it on his lap. They exchange shy glances.

MILDRED: May I offer you some cake?

JOHN: Thank you Miss Lewis.

She exits for cake plate—handed to her by musician. John stands when she does. When Mildred returns he lunges to pull out her chair and, in doing so jostles her arm, causing the plate to clatter to the floor.

They look down at the mess.

JOHN: I'm sorry.

MILDRED: Oh dear. Your coat.

She almost wipes his coat with a napkin, but thinks better of it and hands the napkin to him instead.

MILDRED: And it's such a glorious coat. Did you get it around here?

John does nothing with the napkin she's given him. She goes to pick up plate, he counters to opposite side to help—

JOHN: I'm so sorry.

MILDRED: It's all right. Why don't you sit?

JOHN: That'd probably be best.

He goes to sit. Thinks better of it and waits. She gathers the spilled items, places them on the chest. She sits and he follows suit.

JOHN: S'pose you baked that cake yourself.

MILDRED: I did.

There's more.

They lapse into silence, then speak at the same time.

MILDRED: (overlapping) I bumped into Elizabeth at I. G. Baker's.

JOHN: (overlapping) I wouldn't have stopped by if I'd known your folks were out.

Awkward pause.

JOHN: Elizabeth?

MILDRED: Elizabeth Lane.

JOHN: Oh yes. Mrs. Lane.

MILDRED: That's right.

JOHN: She's a good woman. They have a lovely family, George and Elizabeth. Quite a few children. He's a lucky man. Lots of children. Lovely children. I don't know how many.

MILDRED: Is that so?

JOHN: Yes.

JOHN: (overlapping) You were out to Baker's?

MILDRED: (overlapping) She said they're having trouble with wolves ... (trails off) eating their cattle.

She sighs.

He clutches his hat.

JOHN: I'm very sorry about the cake Miss Lewis.

MILDRED: It's fine.

JOHN: It was sent to me.

MILDRED: Pardon?

JOHN: The coat. Sometimes fellas come over here from England. They like to play at ridin' but most of em don't know what they're doin. I helped one of em out one time, well he figured I saved his life. I don't know about that, but he ...

He finally uses the napkin to brush off his coat.

He sent this to me from over there. Real nice fella. Green as a grasshopper but nice. An earl or a lord or somethin.

MILDRED: That's lovely. People ... think very highly of you.

I told her I would be seeing you soon—Elizabeth Lane—and she said to thank you for the dipping vat. I didn't know what she was talking about, but I said I would pass on the message. Half the time I don't know what people around here are talking about.

She looks at him for some kind of response, but doesn't get one.

MILDRED: She said it like I should know what it was, but I didn't. She said you've built the only dipping vat in the area. First it was the wolves, she said, and then the other trouble, but your dipping vat was the answer for that trouble. An innovator she called you ... I thought it was something for cooking, but that didn't seem to make sense. Based on what she said.

John is not listening.

MILDRED: What is it?

JOHN: I don't know. Somethin' happens when I get around you, I get nervous.

MILDRED: *Pause.*

I meant about the dipping vat. What is it?

JOHN: You wanna know bout my dippin' vat?

She smiles.

JOHN: Oh … well. It's a big ole … (*gestures with his hands*). You have to dig a deep hole first, then line the sides with tin, or you can use mortar. It's like a big tub. Then you fill it with creosote and soap and water and you drive the cattle through …

He looks up and sees Mildred listening encouragingly.

JOHN: The cattle get mites you see. Starts on the shoulders or the rump most times. The itch is terrible. You feel mighty sorry for them—they try to rub up on anything they can find and get a wild look in the eye. Well imagine how you or me would feel if we had lesions across our whole body. The cattle'll scratch till they wear their hide right down, or if they're lucky the hide'll get folded over and tough as bark, but that's no good. Big blisters crust up and pus leaks out … it looks like …

He glances up and sees an expression of revulsion on her face.

… well, it don't look too good. So. My vat, it kills the mites.

MILDRED: Very nice.

A pause ensues. Mildred stands. John stands too.

MILDRED: They knew you were coming.

JOHN: Who?

MILDRED: My folks.

JOHN: They did?

MILDRED: Yes. Remember, at the church, you told mother you'd like to come by today.

JOHN: They could have told me it wasn't a good day. I'd've understood.

MILDRED: There's nothing wrong with the day. It's a perfectly fine day.

JOHN: Well, I sure hope they won't be angry when they find I was here.

MILDRED: They won't.

He's confused.

MILDRED: They knew you were coming, so they took my brothers and sisters off to visit the neighbours.

She takes his hat from him.

MILDRED: They thought you might ... They thought we might want to be ... alone together.

JOHN: Oh.

MILDRED: I'm sorry this has made you so uncomfortable.

JOHN: Oh no. Well, yes. But I did ... do want ...

MILDRED: Want ...?

JOHN: For us to be alone together. I mean ... Miss Lewis. May I call you Mildred?

She nods.

JOHN: I been up here on my own so long now, I'd forgot I was lonely. But every minute when I'm not with you, I feel like I just hurt all over. A bad kind of hurt. Worse than anything.

(he's expecting a response but doesn't get one)

JOHN: Mildred.

MILDRED: I'm afraid.

JOHN: I know.

(substantial pause)

MILDRED: A bad kind of hurt, worse than anything.

(he nods)

MILDRED: That's terrible. I don't even want to think of you feeling that way.

JOHN: You don't?

MILDRED: No. I hate the thought of anything like that. I want to punch
            every person in the world who has ever hurt you.

            *(They look like they might kiss. He takes a tiny step toward
            her.)*

JOHN: That's good.

            (They kiss.)

MILDRED: I'm going to get us some more cake.

            Mildred exits, taking the tray with her.

            *John watches her go. He looks at the hat she's just placed in
            his hand, puts it on his head.*

JOHN: Don't know why she didn't jack-rabbit away. But she didn't.
            She stayed and when I asked her, she said she'd have me.
            That was the beginning of time four.

Lawrence Hill
(1957–)

The author of ten books of fiction and non-fiction and a member of the Order of Canada, Lawrence Hill is most often associated with the geography of southern Ontario, where he grew up, but he also has strong connections to the prairies. Hill's second job out of university was as parliamentary reporter for the *Winnipeg Free Press*, an experience that inspired the novel *Some Great Thing* (1992), whose main character is also a reporter. In 1977 Hill moved to Gull Lake, Saskatchewan, where he worked as a train operator for a number of years. Out of his experience came his fictional story "Meet You at the Door" (2011), offered here.

Lawrence Hill, a novelist, journalist, educator, and documentary writer, is one of the most public voices in Canada on issues of race, black history and culture, and social justice. He was born in the predominantly white suburb of Don Mills, Ontario (now incorporated into the city of Toronto), to American parents who arrived in Canada the day after they were married in 1953. His African American father, Daniel Grafton Hill, was the first director of the Ontario Human Rights Commission and the author of *The Freedom Seekers: Blacks in Early Canada* (1981). His white American mother, Donna M. Hill, was a human rights activist with the Toronto Labour Committee for Human Rights in the early 1950s. His brother is the musician Dan Hill and his sister Karen Hill, poet, novelist and essayist, is the author of the posthumously published novel *Café Babanussa* (2014).

After attending the University of Toronto Schools, Hill earned a BA in economics from Laval University in Quebec City and later also earned an MA in writing from Johns Hopkins University in Baltimore. He worked as a journalist, first at the *Globe and Mail* and then the *Winnipeg Free Press*, until the age of twenty-seven when he decided to quit in order to work full time as a creative writer. He moved to Spain, where he could live cheaply and devote every day to writing. The novel he produced was the coming-of-age narrative *Some Great Thing*, published by Turnstone Press in Winnipeg in 1992.

The novel's protagonist, Mahatma Grafton, is a black newspaper reporter (named for both Gandhi and Hill's father), who returns to the city of his childhood in

251

the summer of 1983 to live with his father and take up a probationary position with the *Winnipeg Free Press*. Mahatma has a serious case of what the author calls "the curse of his generation": a total lack of interest in the state of the world. He is soon drawn into the urgent issues of the city—French-language rights, corporate newspaper politics, and issues of poverty, discrimination, class, and race. Reviewers of the novel who read it only as a comedy and who critiqued the novel's approach to character, situation, theme, and plot missed the novel's real achievements. Hill satirizes Canada's conservative news industry, which mis-shapes stories in ways that sell papers rather than serve the public interest. Most significantly, Hill's Winnipeg is peopled by a wide range of complex black characters who show the city as a central hub of black diaspora: Judge Melvyn Hill is a Race Man in pursuit of racial pride and uplift; Yoyo Ali, an earnest Cameroonian newspaper correspondent, wants to see justice done. Ben Grafton, a retired railway porter with a strong civil rights legacy wishes to set his son on the right track, and his son Mahatma, an "intellectual bum," aimless and young, is wrestling with the burden of his father's famous name, the meaning of his mixed racial inheritance, and the larger question of what writing is for.

Hill's second novel, *Any Known Blood*, published in 1997, is a fictional saga about five generations of men moving back and forth between central Canada and the United States. But it was his third book, the historical fiction *The Book of Negroes* (HarperCollins Canada, 2007) that catapulted Hill into literary stardom. The novel offers Hill's fictionalized first-person account of the transatlantic slave trade told through the engaging perspective of Aminata Diallo, who is captured by slave traders in Africa and brought to America. Hill's novel is the rarest of books: it never shies away from telling brutal historical truths, including the physical, sexual, emotional, and spiritual violations involved in slavery, and yet his account is one that readers are willing to engage with. The novel has been translated into over eight languages and has sold more than 800,000 copies worldwide. It won several awards including the Rogers Writers' Trust Fiction Prize, CBC's *Canada Reads* and Radio-Canada's *Le combat des livres*, and the Commonwealth Writers Prize for Best Book. The novel has been made into a six-part miniseries written by Hill and Clement Virgo and aired on CBC TV.

Hill's electric short story "Meet You at the Door," which is set in Gull Lake, Saskatchewan, in 1977 (originally published in *The Walrus* in 2011) tells the story of a young writer, Joel Williams, trying to escape the dark, seductive voices in his head. Joel makes a radical move for a young black man, moving to the small Saskatchewan town—population 800—to live with an elderly white stranger and to work as a CP Rail night train operator, dispatching trains through Gull Lake from Saskatchewan and Alberta. Hill says that though the story is a fiction, it is the one that draws most heavily on his own personal experience.[1] In the story Joel Williams becomes a kind of Legba or intermediary figure conducting traffic at the crossroads, not only of the railway crossings but also between life and death. An abbreviated version of the story was re-published in *Ten Canadian Writers in Context* (2016), edited by Marie Carrière, C. Gillespie, and J. Purcell.

Hill's newest novel, *The Illegal*, published in 2015, focuses on an elite marathoner who lives in the fictional country of Freedom State. It is a meditation on black labour, global refugee crises, and the unfinished quest for black freedom. The novel has already been optioned for film treatment. *The Illegal* won the 2016 edition of *Canada Reads*, making Hill the first writer ever to win the competition twice.

Hill is also the author of numerous award-winning non-fiction titles and essays. He is a professor of creative writing at the University of Guelph, Ontario, and lives in Hamilton, Ontario. He is currently writing a new novel and a children's book.

Meet You at the Door

This happened back in the dinosaur days, in the town of Gull Lake, population 800. The gulls had all died, and if ever there had been a lake it had dried up. On the Saskatchewan farmlands, oil pumps bobbed up and down, up and down, looking like black grasshoppers on speed. Folks were fuming about the metric system and had a nickname for the new top-loading railway car: a Trudeau hopper. I had other preoccupations. A ghost had chased me out of university and had hounded me for a year in Greece, Italy, France, and Spain. And now I was back in Canada, to take a summer job in a place where I knew no one.

I had hitchhiked into town. I had come to work in the one-room station of the Canadian Pacific Railway. Hitchhikers held up their thumbs every which way back then and jockeyed for the best spots on highway ramps. As for me, drivers usually stared good and long and pressed the gas pedal harder. Eventually, a priest took mercy on me in Medicine Hat and drove me all the way to the Gull Lake turnoff at forty miles an hour. I walked up the gentle grade into town. On my left arm, balanced against my chest, was an L.C. Smith typewriter, heavy enough to be a weapon of war. Catapulted over a battlefield, it could have taken a man out. In my right hand was a classical guitar, purchased in Granada from the man who made it. On

---

1   Personal conversation, October 25, 2018.

my back was a knapsack, stitched with the Canadian flag, so Europeans wouldn't take me for an American. It was 1977. The summer job was part of my recovery plan.

The only advertised room for rent in Gull Lake was above the one bar in town. The Mad Dog. No way I was staying there. I knew, from my late father and from the men before him, that certain places would only bring trouble to a person like me. I passed the bar and walked into town, ringing doorbells and asking to rent a room. The first five doors did not stay open long enough for me to explain that I had a job and would pay for the full five months—in advance, if necessary.

At the sixth door, a woman answered. She looked like she had been born around the time of my great-grandmother. Everything about her was white. Hair. Socks. Nursing shoes. On her clothesline out back, flapping in the wind, hung white underwear the size of a parachute. She stood no taller than five feet. Blue eyes, clear as lake water. She stepped back when she saw me, but listened as I spoke. She said she didn't mind my working nights. She said her own son Jimmy could keep a job for about as long as she could hold a spooked horse. He was a no-account, if God's truth be told, but what could you expect from a grown man who still went by "Jimmy"? He had stayed in her basement suite for a spell. This was after his wife had thrown him out but before she had taken him back, which was about as dumb a mistake as a woman could make. She said, what can you do about foolishness but let it be? It struck me that I should nod and say nothing.

She said I was welcome to stay. Twenty-five dollar a month. She pronounced it "dollar." In the singular. The Spaniards in Andalusia had done the same thing, dropping the final *s*, perhaps to shake me off the tail of their speeding words. She asked if I wanted to see the suite. It had a bedroom, a kitchen, and a bathroom. Twenty-five dollar a month. No, I told her, I would just take it. I said, here is twenty-five dollars for the first month. You don't have to pay me yet, she said. No, ma'am, please take it. She took it. The bills disappeared into her apron pocket.

Her name was Eleanor Hadfield. She lived alone. She had been widowed long ago. Her son stopped by every Sunday for lunch after church and brought the groceries on her list. He overcharged her, she confided, but it was just a few dollar and she didn't care. She didn't get out much, but she still ruled over her kitchen, garden, and clothesline. As she spoke, Mrs. Hadfield kept checking out my hair.

Have you ever seen a mammoth pine tree in southern Spain? No branches all the way up, but at the top there is an eruption of foliage. I had an Afro like that. It was big, and it took over, and it buried me beneath it. Also, I was dark. Like the best part of a chocolate éclair. Some of my looks came from my father and his people. And some came from spending much of the past year in southern Europe. I had stayed in shared rooms, youth hostel style, sleeping inches from strangers, one looking clubbed and comatose, the next snoring like a purring brontosaurus. I had changed cities every night, on the run from that voice in my head. *Come on*, it said. *Come over here. It's not so bad. I did it. Can you provide me with one good reason to go on living? Is there one thing about the world that can justify living another day? Come over this way*, it said, *I'll meet you at the door.* The voice tracked me like a bounty hunter and charged like a bull. For a year, I had stayed on the move, but it hadn't worked. There was no dodging the voice of the dead.

From my bedroom one Sunday morning, I heard Mrs. Hadfield's son railing about me. In the small house, I heard every word. Why had she not consulted him before renting to me? What if I ransacked her house and stole her valuables? It wasn't right for her to be alone with me. Have you considered this, her son kept saying, have you even looked at him? Jimmy, she said, he's a gentleman—may not look like one, but he is. Mother, he said, nothing good can come of this. Jimmy, she said, eat your pie.

In the eyes of Eleanor Hadfield, perhaps the typewriter saved me. Soon she began to ask me to join her in the kitchen for pies, cakes, cookies, and roast beef. Most of all, she liked serving me potatoes. Fried, baked, cookie-thin and roasted, or boiled. Under gravy, over rice, in casseroles, or all alone.

One day while I was writing, she brought me a mug of tea and said, "I got more ways for potato than all the keys on your typewriter."

"I bet you do."

She ran her finger along the platen of my L.C. Smith and declared that it was as smooth and hard as her rolling pin. "What are you so busy writing?"

"Just trying to get my thoughts out."

"I hear you typing half the day," she said. "Fingers coming down like rain."

"Does the sound bother you?"

"No," she said. "I like that sound. I sleep easy with it."

I had been typing since I was thirteen. On my mother's L.C. Smith, my friend Howie and I made up our own Typing Olympics. Stopwatch in hand, he would dictate a sentence and clock me. *Have you considered, my asinine acquaintance, that it would be advisable to abdicate before accentuating the world's ailments?* He timed me, then took his turn and beat me by five seconds. On the sly, he had been typing *a*'s repeatedly. Training his left pinkie. The last time we raced each other, it got stupid. We were seventeen. Howie wanted us to give each other lines about world poverty, time the results, toss back a shot of rum, and do it again. Toss another shot. Do it again. I gave up after two shots. He kept going. Had to get his stomach pumped. At the hospital, his mom gave me a look that said, "And I trusted you." I carried that look in the back of my mind until I had something worse to think about.

Passenger trains didn't stop in Gull Lake, but freight trains had to pull off onto the side tracks to let other trains overtake or pass them on that long, single track across the Canadian prairies. The dispatcher in Calgary and conductors moving all across Saskatchewan and Alberta could not communicate directly. They had to go through me—the operator. I took orders from the dispatcher and passed them along to the trains highballing east and west through town.

I worked alone in the station, starting at 7 p.m. and often working right through until 6 a.m. I had the guitar and the typewriter for company, in the hours when I was not needed. Actual work accounted for no more than two hours each shift, but I had to be perfect for every one of those 120 minutes. It was my job to know more than any person in the world about the trains that thundered each night through Gull Lake, Saskatchewan. You had to radio for permission to leave the chair and go to the bathroom. You radioed again, once back in the chair. The dispatcher in Calgary knew how often you pissed in an eight-hour shift, and how long it took you. It was a firing offence to sleep on the job. If I slept, someone could die. And I already had one person's death on my mind. My job was to type up the dispatcher's orders, when they came—always in a rush, always at the last minute—and to pass them along to oncoming trains. I had to be able to type them up at fifty words a minute, and typos were not allowed. It was in the rule book: if you made a typo, you had to say so. Then you had to rip up your order and ask the dispatcher to give it to you all over again, while you typed. All while the train was bearing down on you at fifty miles an hour.

From my chair facing the station window, I had a clear view of the farmlands, the bobbing oil pumps, and the sky. Usually there were no clouds, and blazing stars. "We're burning up out here," the stars seemed to tell me. "Would you at least have a look?" Stars begged you to look at them for, like, five million years. And I couldn't. I had two radios to manage. On my left, the one for incoming and outbound trains. It only worked when a train was within a five-mile radius. This radio connected me to the engineer in the lead car, who usually said nothing and just drove, and to the conductor working in the caboose. It was the conductor who did all the talking—to me and, through me, to the dispatcher. In the radio to my right, I could hear the dispatcher any time, but he could only hear me when I pushed a foot pedal under my desk.

One Tuesday in June, weeks after I had settled into the job, a conductor got in my ear at 2:49 a.m. He was on a westbound train. Number 901. I knew it. It was a freight train. Usually about 100 cars. More than a mile long. Travelling at full speed, a beast like that took ten minutes to stop.

"Gullick. You there?" It was the voice of an old man. Some conductors liked to kid around on the radio. Others were all business. This one sounded as if he liked to hunt bears, drink beer, and watch strippers.

I pulled the train mike closer. "Gull Lake here."

"Are they robbing the cradle?" he said. "What are you, like, sixteen?"

You kept your mouth shut with the dispatcher, but conductors were fair game. So I said, "And are they stealing from graves these days? No live bodies left?"

His guffaw sounded like a machine gun. "Looky-looky, we have a smart one. We have one with attitude. Heaven help us. What are you, a college student?"

I just said, "Sort of."

"*Sort of.* We got a politician in Gullick. We got a right regular Pierre Trudeau." He pronounced the prime minister's name "*pee*-air." He chuckled into the radio.

Conductors and dispatchers could smell an operator's panic, right through the radios. I didn't want to sound nervous. But if I didn't take down the train's particulars, I would soon run out of time. So I just said, "I see you're facing a headwind tonight."

"Wind like this," he said, "I lose a minute an hour." I pictured him being sixty years old, which, at three times my age, seemed ancient. About five-seven. One hundred and ninety, with a pot belly and stick-thin legs. "So," he added, "got anything for me?"

He was testing me, trying to see if I would do him a favour and break the rules. He knew that operators were not allowed to reveal the dispatcher's orders over the radio. "Should know soon," I said. "Where are you?"

"Five point one miles out."

"Stand by," I said.

I didn't yet know who was dispatching that night. The dispatcher would have started his shift just minutes earlier. He would be feeling his way into the night, and calling me any moment. Each night was a puzzle, needing its own solution. Each night, the dispatcher in Calgary had to draw a map of the Canadian prairies, and send dozens of trains through it. Safely. Quickly. Cheaply. Fast trains had priority over slow ones. Except for slow trains carrying hazardous goods. And then there were passenger trains, which had priority over some freight trains but not others. It was complicated. And that was when there were no screw-ups. A train could hit a deer, or a moose, or even a bear, and not derail. The one animal that worried train engineers and conductors was a pig. If a sow got loose and found its way onto the track, there was trouble coming. A sow was heavy and thick and had a low centre of gravity. She was the mammal most likely to derail a train.

"Gull Lake," the dispatcher called, "are you there?"

I grabbed the mike and pressed the foot pedal so he could hear me. When I spoke with the pedal down, every operator between Field and Swift Current could hear me, too. Some dispatchers liked the audience. They would jack up the pressure and see how the operator took it. I kept my answer short and simple: "Gull Lake."

He let a long, slow laugh percolate down the railway line. But I knew, before the laugh, who he was. Just about every dispatcher, conductor, and operator working for the Canadian Pacific Railway in the age of the dinosaur pronounced the town "Gullick." So I knew, after just two words, who occupied the dispatcher's chair. His name was Weedman, but privately I had nicknamed him Tolstoy. He pronounced the town the way it was written. Pronounced it the same way I said it: "Gull Lake." Pausing for a nanosecond between each word.

Tolstoy was good. They said he was the most talented dispatcher in western Canada. The guy could pinpoint the location of every live train on the prairies, at every moment of the night, right down to the nearest mile. He kept an entire network of moving trains in his head, and there had not been a crash, a derailment, or a major delay on his watch. He knew how fast each train operator could type. He could squint over 300 miles of railway track and intuit, in his bones, if you had made a typo and not confessed. But he had a temper. If he was in a bad mood, he might try to make a grown man cry on the radio—while his peers listened. I'd heard him say a few nights earlier to the operator in Swift Current, Miller in case you haven't noticed I have an eastbound train highballing your way. Three miles out, Miller, and moving chemical waste. Don't make me stop that train, Miller, while you learn how to type. I got a girl in Maple Creek, just out of train operators' school, who types faster than you. Willow MacDonald. You there, Willow? Maple Creek, she said calmly, quietly. Willow, is it true that you type faster than Miller? Miller's just fine, sir, she said. Okay, Tolstoy said, enough of this. Miller, is your order paper back in your typewriter? Yes sir. Are you ready? Yes sir. Okay, here we go. And then Tolstoy ripped out a four-sentence order, knowing perfectly well that Miller would not be able to keep up and would have to confess that he had made another typo.

Tolstoy had been the lead instructor in my two-week train operators' course in Calgary. He was six-three, had a goatee, and was as thin as a fence post. He was twenty-eight, which seemed ancient. Tolstoy had dropped out of philosophy at university, but he knew his trains. His most memorable contribution during training had been a two-hour talk he titled "How Not to Piss Me Off." He didn't speak much to me during the course, but took a good, long look at me on the first day. Before the day ended, he said, "Where are you from, man?" He didn't use "man" with anybody else in the course. But nobody else in the course looked like me. I told him Toronto and left it at that. He asked where I was studying, and I said UBC. "You're from Toronto, and you study in Vancouver, and now you're taking a train operators' course in Calgary?" It didn't seem wise to tell him about Spain. Or France. Or the rest of Europe. So I just smiled. The course lasted eight hours a day, five days a week, two weeks straight, at no pay. That's how it worked, in the dinosaur days. No pay for training, and you brought your own lunch. At the end of the course came a test with three parts. You had to memorize the location and spelling of every train station between Field, British Columbia, and Swift Current, Saskatchewan. Wetaskiwin. Pemukan. Glamis. Tompkins. And on they went. Easier than Spanish verbs. You had to memorize the train operators' manual. There were fifty rules. And you had to be able to type fifty words a minute. They dictated 500 words to you, and you had to finish them in ten minutes. You were allowed five typos. But you were penalized twelve seconds for each one. The typing test was to blame for the average failure rate: 75 percent. But I found that part easy.

At the end of the test, Tolstoy checked the results. Out of fifteen students, two of us passed. The other was Willow MacDonald, my age, who came from Maple Creek. Tolstoy shook our hands. Quick, he said to me, where is Gull Lake? It's in Saskatchewan, I said, between Maple Creek and Swift Current. Good thing you memorized the railway map, buddy boy, he said. Get yourself to Gull Lake tomorrow. You'll be on the night shift, and you start Monday.

"Hello, white boy," Tolstoy said to me through the radio. "I could spot your voice 300 miles off."

"Calgary to Gull Lake, 286 miles," I said.

Tolstoy had never called me "white boy" during training, never to my face. For that, he waited until he had me on the line, where our conversations would be commented on by the other operators. He waited to trot out "white boy" until I had a train bearing down on me. I didn't care what he called me. I had coped with worse.

On Christmas Day of my second year at university, my best friend's mother called and begged me to come over. She wouldn't say why. Stepping into their home felt like sliding into a casket. I sat so terrified of their pain that I didn't know how to touch my own. They poured endless mugs of tea, in the hope that I could tell them something about their son—chess player, world traveller, hobby Marxist. They didn't know, and I didn't tell them, that their son was a long-time book klepto. Howie Rosenbaum had read more books than you could shake a stick at, but he had not bought even one of them. By the age of thirteen, he kept a list, penciled on foolscap, of donors and donations. Coles Books in the Don Mills Plaza had donated *Crime and Punishment* to Howie's private collection. *The Wretched of the Earth* had come courtesy of Third World Books on Bathurst Street. I asked why he didn't just ride his bike over to the Don Mills library. Then he wouldn't have to steal, I said. He grinned and made me stand, pulled the blanket off the plastic fruit crate I'd been sitting on, and unveiled a collection of library books. Never borrowed, and never returned. In my dreams, I became accountable for everything Howie had stolen. Even his own life. It was my responsibility to explain it, to make up for it. In my dreams, he would accuse me of living a phony life. I would reply weakly that he had given up too soon. Come over here, he said, and I'll prove it. Come this way. *I'll meet you at the door.*

"Any word from 901?" Tolstoy said.

"He's just in radio radius."

"Impatient?"

"Headwind."

"Location?"

I glanced at my watch. "One minute ago, he was five miles east of Gull Lake." That meant I had four minutes to take down Tolstoy's order, arrange the original and the carbon copy, clip one each onto wooden hoops, and get myself out the door and onto the platform.

"Where'd you learn to type so fast?" Tolstoy asked.

"My mother taught me on her L.C. Smith."

"That takes the cake. White boy's mother taught him to type? Who *does* that?"

That hit a nerve. My mother was white. But, white or black, you didn't make fun of somebody's mother. Not where I came from.

"I'm going to be a writer, Tolstoy," I said. It slipped out. Before I knew it.

"What was that?"

"I am going to be a writer."

"Did you call me something?"

It was ridiculous, this rule of having to take all manner of trash talk from the dispatcher but not being allowed to talk back. "Tolstoy was a fine writer. But don't take *War and Peace* to work—you might fall asleep on the job."

He laughed. "You have some nerve, white boy. Is Johnson conducting the 901?"

"I'll find out."

I pushed away the dispatcher's mike and pulled the conductor's radio closer.

"Dispatcher wants to know if it's Johnson conducting."

"Yep. And let me guess who's in the chair in Calgary," the conductor said. "It's Weedman, right?"

"Yup," I said. But I never thought of the dispatcher as Weedman, even though it worked with his goatee. If Tolstoy had any sense, he would go back to school before he flamed out. They said five years was the longest any dispatcher had lasted. Nervous breakdowns. Ulcers. What thinking person would take a job that was known to drive delicate souls to suicide?

The conductor said, "Pass on a message to Weedman. I had been stuck in the Peg so long that I thought I'd been sent to jail. That's right. But I'd break out of Stony Mountain Penitentiary faster than this train was crossing the prairies. No more fooling around! Tell Weedman I want to highball right through Gullick and Maple Creek."

"Got it," I said.

I could hear the conductor laughing on the radio. He was laughing for my benefit, and for that of the engineer up front in the first car of the train.

I told Tolstoy that Johnson was conducting the 901.

Tolstoy said, "Stand by for orders, white boy."

The conductor said, "Did you tell Weedman what I said?"

"I communicated your whereabouts," I said.

"Communicated your whereabouts," the conductor said, mimicking my voice.

The dispatcher got me again. "Gull Lake, are you ready?"

I rolled the order paper with the carbon copy into the typewriter. "Ready."

Tolstoy fired off a message I had learned to decode and type, at top speed and with no mistakes, in training. He said it once. I heard it and kept listening while blasting away on the typewriter keys so the carbon copy would look clear. In a nutshell, this is what he told me:

"Westbound 901, take siding no. 2 at Maple Creek July 23 at three hours aught aught minutes and allow Westbound no. 463 to pass at three hours aught eight minutes. At three hours twelve minutes, continue westbound, maximum thirty miles per hour, direction Calgary. Prepare for more orders at Medicine Hat."

I finished a breath after his last word and read it back to him. There was a mistake in the word "Medicine." I had typed it "Mecicine." But now it was too late. I had no time to start all over again. I banked on the theory that the engineer and the conductor wouldn't notice it or report it, so I told Tolstoy that the sheet was clean and I had made no mistakes.

"You're good, white boy."

Thirty seconds later, the conductor buzzed me on the radio. "Gullick, whaddya got for me?"

If I revealed the orders and the dispatcher got wind of it, I would be sacked for violating rule no. 21, which Tolstoy had summarized in training as *Don't tell the conductor a single thing on the radio, because if he gets it wrong you could be looking at two things: a train derailment and life-long unemployment.* But if I didn't give the conductor something, he might report my typo. So I said, "Prepare for a long order." Then I pressed down the foot pedal to the dispatcher, so he could hear the conductor hollering at me through his radio.

"Tell that college dropout dispatcher I'm going to rip his head off and pitch it to the seagulls," the conductor said.

"901, where are you now?" I said, still with my foot down for the dispatcher's benefit.

"Two point four miles east of you," the conductor said.

Now Tolstoy was at me again. "Was that Johnson yapping at you?"

"He's piling up one or two adjectives," I said.

Tolstoy laughed for the benefit of all the operators listening in on our conversation. "Tell him to fire up his coffee pot," Tolstoy said.

Turning my mouth to the connection to the conductor, I said, "The dispatcher says to enjoy the coffee in Maple Creek."

"There is no coffee in Maple Creek," the conductor said. "Tell that goa-teed golden boy—" He kept ranting while I prepared the hoops. I kept the pedal down on the dispatcher's line so Tolstoy could hear Johnson ranting.

And then I cut off the dispatcher and said to Johnson, "901, I will be hooping you up."

I could hear Tolstoy laughing, but had to interrupt him, putting my foot down on the pedal again.

"Permission to hoop up train," I asked.

"Get out there, white boy," he said. "Steady against the wind. And watch out. Reports of a Trudeau hopper with a loose wire. Stay back, but try to give me the exact location of that hopper."

I ran outside with the two hoops that allowed, in the age of dinosaurs, for formal communication between the train and the dispatcher. Each hoop was shaped like a number nine. A loop and a long neck. The big one had a loop about eighteen inches in diameter and a neck about four feet long. The short one had the same loop, but a neck of just a foot or so. At the intersection of the loop and the neck was a metal clip. Into the clip of each hoop, I attached the message from Tolstoy in Calgary. Using the hoops, I would have to pass up the fresh copy of the train order to the engineer leaning out the front car of the train. Then I would have to step back and wait for the train to thunder by, stepping back up to the edge of the platform in time to hoop up the conductor in the caboose at the back of the train.

Outside, the sky was lit with stars, and the wind pushed hard from the west. I stood by the edge of the track and saw the train's headlight, like a burning star itself, growing brighter. The train whistle wailed like a broken man. Distorted, dopplerized, it came at me like a parent, mightily aggrieved and forever offended. The rails shook by my feet.

After Howie hanged himself from the branch of a tree in High Park, his mother glued herself to me, desperate for explanations I couldn't offer. But Howie also stuck to me. He didn't care where I slept, or how much I paid for a cot in a youth hostel. The dead had an unfair advantage. They could hector you all they wanted through the deepest, darkest Saskatchewan nights, where there was no movement but oil pumps bobbing in agreement. When the dead spoke, it was always a monologue. There was no changing anyone's mind.

I held my ground against the rumbling rails and the judgmental train wail and the wind that swirled under the belly of the train. As the locomotive drew 200 yards, then 100 yards, then just fifty yards away, I hoisted the long hoop high some twelve feet overhead, angling it ever so slightly toward the path of the train so the circle in the number nine became a hole through which the engineer could punch his arm. The train barrelled forward. I saw the engineer lean out the window, bending his arm into the shape of an *L*. I released the hoop at the instant the engineer put his fist through the hoop, caught it, and lifted it up and away from me. He plucked out my message and threw down the hoop.

I stepped back to avoid the swirling wire, wherever it was. I counted back from the lead locomotive. Car one. Car two. Car three. Starting at car eighteen, a string of Trudeau hoppers. They irritated some farmers, because you could only load grain in them, and only from the top. Car twenty-five was a black Trudeau hopper, dragging a loose wire and intent on laceration. I danced back and jumped. The wire swirled and hissed underneath me. I thought of my mother, and how she would have freaked out if she knew I was being paid seven dollars an hour to dance out of reach of slashing wires. And I thought of Eleanor Hadfield, sleeping in the night. The day before, she had come down to my room, sat down on my bed, and placed her hand on my shoulder. I jumped as if I'd been shocked by the paddles of a defibrillator. I opened my eyes. She invited me upstairs. It was one in the afternoon, she said, and I had been screaming. Something about my shoe caught in the railway tracks with a train coming on. Come upstairs, she said, for potato with more character than the prime minister of Canada. I followed her, and slid into a chair at her table. The potatoes were steaming and ready, on a china plate. Eleanor Hadfield had tugged them straight from her garden. They were scrubbed, halved, and boiled to perfection: just a hint of resistance against the tines of my fork. I smothered them in butter and fresh parsley, salted them to taste, took the first bite, and thought, *I have never eaten a potato before*.

The train stretched more than a mile long. It had slowed to thirty miles an hour. I got ready, stepping closer. I could see the last Trudeau hopper, and then the caboose. The conductor was leaning out, taking a good look at me. I was all lit up on the station platform. He was calculating the height at which I held the hoop. He was 200 yards away. One hundred. Fifty. Johnson was closer to the ground than the engineer, and easier to hoop up. No need to reach high in the wind. The conductor was up just a foot above me, so it was practically an intimate encounter. As he bore down on me and stuck out his arm for the catch, I heard him call out, "By Christ, it's a nigger." And then his mouth fell. He knew I had heard him.

Johnson caught the hoop. The wind blew his hat off. The 901 drew away, and I hunted for the two hoops among the grass and stones. I also found the conductor's cap. I made my way back to the station and told Tolstoy in Calgary that I had hooped up both ends of the train, and that the loose wire was twenty-five cars back from the locomotive. But I did not tell Tolstoy that the conductor had radioed me, from his position a mile west of Gull Lake, while he was still inside radio radius.

"Gullick," the conductor said, "what's your name, anyways?"

"Williams."

"Got a first name?"

"Joel."

"Well, Joel, don't mind an ignorant old man, and don't take offence. I'm not prejudiced. I just never saw the likes of you before in Gullick. You hoop up like a pro. Don't be mad."

"No sweat," I told Johnson. It all came down to dignity. And the easiest way to retain my dignity was to act like it didn't mean a thing.

"You've got a loose wire twenty-five cars back from the front," I told Johnson.

"Did it hit you? You okay?"

"It's swirling around. But I'm okay."

"I'll check it out at Maple Creek," he said, pronouncing it "Crick." And then he continued, "After all, we don't want to be taking out our college students, irregardless of race."

I didn't call him on the word "irregardless." I just said, "I found your cap."

"Hang onto it for me. And son, I won't tell Weedman about how you spell 'Medicine.'"

"Thanks," I said.

"You a university kid?" he asked.

"Yup," I said.

"Where you going?"

"UBC," I told him, "if I make it back there."

"What on God's green earth is UBC?"

"The University of British Columbia."

"Are your parents proud?"

I didn't tell him I had lost my daddy months before my best friend went and ruined Christmas Day for the rest of my life. I said my mom wanted to see me back in school.

"Then do it," he said. "Train jobs are going the way of the dodo bird."

"Right."

"I'll make a deal with you. In September, on one of my overnights in Vancouver, I'll come out to UBC and make sure you started up again."

"It's way out on a peninsula. Point Grey."

"Son, I know every city in Canada that has a train station in it. I get a day or two off, and I go walking. What's the name of the building you study in, out there at UBC on Point Grey?"

"Buchanan."

"I'll bring you a back-to-school gift, high noon on the first Saturday after Labour Day, and I'll meet you at the door."

There was some kind of gravel in his voice that felt good to hear. He sounded like an old fart of a grandfather in that moment. Something in his voice made me feel I'd soon be getting through the nights again. Dream-free. Or free, at least, of one particular dream.

"Okay," I said. "Thanks. What's your name, anyway?"

"Ed Johnson," he said.

"Well, hello Ed."

"Hello, Joel."

"Knock 'em dead out there and come back to CP Rail and become vice-president or something, you hear me? You can do better than me. I'm just a dumb-ass who says stupid things to the first black kid I've ever seen at three o'clock in the morning in Gullick. I only noticed you were black from a distance, 'cause of your hair. Man alive, that is one head of hair you got."

So he wanted to banter before disappearing into the night. I obliged, and told him his head looked like a baby's ass and that it was time to lay down some sod.

He came back one last time. "If I was your daddy, I'd whip your ass and cut your hair."

I was going to offer to set him up with Bert, my Jamaican barber in Toronto, who was trained in the art of waxing bowling balls. But Johnson was gone, out of radio radius. I didn't know if he would make good on his promise to visit me at UBC, but he would come back through Gull Lake a week later, on the Eastbound 902 out of Calgary. So I planned a little surprise for Johnson. I would go to the city on my weekend off. It helped, even that summer, to stay on the move. The voice was coming at me less and less, but my legs twitched and shook in bed. I figured it was Howie, out walking with my legs when I had no need of them. In the city, I would go shopping. I planned to buy a gift and rig it to the bottom of the hooping stick. On his next trip through Gull Lake, Conductor Ed Johnson was going to catch the hoop and pull out his message and find his cap tied near the bottom of the stick. Under his cap, he would find some black thing hanging like a trapped raccoon. He would be startled and take a second look and find himself the owner of a massive Afro wig. That would give him something to talk about, next time he came into radio radius in the age of the dinosaur.

Margaret Robinson-Gudmundson
(1957–)

Margaret Robinson-Gudmundson was born and raised in Winnipeg. Her Jamaican mother was recruited as a nurse during the polio epidemic and immigrated to Winnipeg in 1955. Her father, a Winnipeg General Hospital administrator, also Jamaican, arrived in Winnipeg the following year.

Robinson-Gudmundson earned a political science BA (Honours) from the University of Winnipeg in 1992, and for a time made her living in the music scene. A classically trained pianist, she played jazz piano and was the leader of her own full-time jazz band, Maggi May & Co, from 1999 to 2003. The band had a regular gig playing at Winnipeg's Windsor Hotel. She left the music scene to earn a Master's of Public Administration from the University of Manitoba in 1996. She is currently the club coordinator at the University Women's Club at the University of Winnipeg.

Robinson-Gudmundson married into a Saskatchewan farm family; her father-in-law, Fred Gudmundson, was, with Cy Gonic, founder and editor of the leftist *Canadian Dimensions* magazine (published out of Winnipeg since 1963) and was her writing mentor until his death in 2002.

Her play *Severance*, based in part on a trip she took in 1982 to "the homeland" to heal from an unhappy marriage, won second prize in the Caribe playwriting contest in 1989. The play elaborates a conviction Robinson-Gudmundson holds about the fundamental limits of Canada as a space for black people, as compared with a country like Jamaica, where black people are a majority population. As she says, "I've done not bad for myself, I own rental property, I have an interesting job, and I won't starve when I retire. Still, I am convinced I would have done better if I had been born away."[1] She is currently expanding the play into a full-length novel.

---

1 Personal correspondence, November 8, 2015.

The Severance

Characters:
Wendy: Canadian—mid-twenties, wearing chic American summer clothes and hairstyle.

Andrea: Jamaican, cousin of Wendy, mid-twenties, wearing conservative American blue jeans, bright cotton blouse and Afro hairstyle. Brush in hand. Painting.

Setting: Jamaica 1980s. Artists' studio. Several paintings on walls and easels. Andrea putting finishing touches on portrait of her Canadian cousin who is modeling for her.

WENDY: (*Sitting as still as possible*) Spend a lot of time here, Andrea?

ANDREA: (*Concentrating on applying paint to portrait*) Not as much as I'd like. I come in at least once a week and paint—maybe five hours. The others are here more often.

WENDY: How many of you share this place?

ANDREA: (*Concentrating more noticeably on each stroke of the brush*) There's four of us. That way, we each get a wall. We share the cost of a model from time to time, which works out pretty well. Other than that we don't see much of each other.

There is silence for a few moments while Wendy watches the artist. A smile slowly crosses Wendy's lips. Andrea looks up from her work as Wendy begins to chuckle.

ANDREA: What's so funny?

WENDY: You look so serious.

ANDREA: (*Smiling back. Looking back and forth from her model to the canvas*) I'm doing your eyes. There's something missing in the expression. (*Becomes serious. Concentrates closely again and resumes painting*).

WENDY: (*Sighs softly. Getting impatient. Opens her mouth as if to speak, then stops short. Remains in quiet thought for a moment then speaks*) I'm sorry I missed you last time you were here.

ANDREA: (*Looks at Wendy and smiles*) I'm sorry I missed you too. I was writing my final exams at McGill, if I recall. *(Makes a sour face and resumes painting)* When was it? 1980?

WENDY: I think so. (*Becomes pensive)* That was a strange period of my life. Come to think of it, it's probably better that we didn't cross paths just then. You would have thought I was crazy.

ANDREA: (*Objecting*) Oh, I don't know. I heard I missed some great moments. You singing at the Intercontinental with the Butler Jazz Quartet. Uncle Charles still plays the recordings you left with him, every time he has guests. He boasts about his niece, the famous recording artist from Canada.

WENDY: (*Embarrassed, puts a hand to her brow momentarily*). My parents made far too much of that. It seemed like they had to give the impression I was on the verge of a brilliant career, or else I'd pale in comparison with all my cousins who were getting grand degrees in Florida, Montreal and London.

ANDREA: (*Stops painting and looks at Wendy in disbelief*). How can you say that? Those songs on that tape are fantastic accomplishments. I was jealous when I first heard them. I'm embarrassed to admit it.

WENDY: And I was jealous of you.

ANDREA: (*Shaking her head*) And now you've given it all up to go to university. Does that mean you now expect me to become a recording artist like you? (*Resumes painting*).

WENDY: (*Laughing*) I'm **not** a great recording artist, I assure you. The government-owned Canadian Broadcasting Corporation offered a cash prize to the young person who could write the most insipid pieces of music in Canadian history. I swallowed my pride and my creativity, and won. CBC studios recorded the songs, then I took the money and spent it all on drugs. And that, my dear cousin, is the honest truth.

(*Andrea stops painting and stares at her cousin*)

WENDY: Don't give me the old look-of-surprise (*Smiles knowingly*). You're a world traveler. You're a creative type yourself. I read your radical letters to the *Daily Star*. My dad is on the mailing list, you know. And I've heard about that left-wing magazine you edit. Don't tell me you don't know how creative types can self-destruct.

ANDREA: (*Puts her hands up*). All right. All right. (*Resumes painting*) I just wasn't aware you were so heavily into the counter culture.

WENDY: Let's just say it is not like a bottle of Appleton rum was the only souvenir I took home the last time I left here.

ANDREA (*Shaking her head*). You must have been crazy.

WENDY: I told you would have thought so.

ANDREA: (*Chuckling*). I really envy you, you know.

WENDY: For what? Living dangerously.

ANDREA: For using your creativity instead of ignoring it. That's practically unheard of in this family, you know? (*Stops painting and gestures with hands for emphasis*). Everybody is so damned obsessed with following the beaten path, and you are the only one out of all these cousins who couldn't have cared less. That's what I admire most about you. My painting and my work with the magazine … they're just hobbies. But I never thought about actually attempting it. The family would have frowned on it. God forbid. (*Resumes painting*). Still I had the distinction of being considered the family radical for a little while. Then word came of what you were doing in music and I lost that. My hobbies started to look like child's play. I was terribly jealous. Now here you sit being so humble about it.

WENDY: You have to understand Andrea. I'm hardly going to get puffed up about four, artificial, meaningless songs being sugar-coated and promoted, while ten others, straight from my soul, collect dust on sheets of paper.

ANDREA: (*Looks at her cousin*) That must be awful.

WENDY: It's a thing of the past. Anyway, when it was happening I was too inebriated to notice.

(*Silence for a moment before Andrea resumes painting.*)

WENDY: You know what I envy most about you?

ANDREA: Don't tell me. Never-ending summers?

WENDY: (*Smiles*) Besides that. (*Becomes serious*). I envy your closeness to the family. There were times in my life when I was so lonely I would have given anything for a baby sister or even a big brother to beat me to a pulp. It only recently occurred to me that being an only child wouldn't have been half as bad if I'd grown up here.

ANDREA: I can see how twenty-four cousins would help.

WENDY: And I would have killed for a beaten path to follow. Just once. By the time I was sixteen I'd broken enough ground to fill in the whole Caribbean Basin.

ANDREA: What about your dad and mom? They must have had some tried and true advice to offer.

WENDY: I think my mom, for one, was overwhelmed by my ... (*Searching for the right word*). I don't think I was the type of child she expected, or was familiar with. I was this neurotic, depressed teenager who rebelled almost to the point of no return by the age of fourteen. She treated me like a bit of a landmine which was not to be disturbed. As for my dad, even though he and mom were successful, he was still a stranger in a strange land. I guess for a lack of something more concrete to say, the most I ever got from him was: "You have to do better. You have to work harder," and a kick in the rear when I didn't. And besides, to be quite honest, nobody I knew where I grew up ever listened to their parents.

ANDREA: Did you encounter a lot of racism where you grew up?

WENDY: After we moved from a sort of multiracial, working class neighbourhood to a new housing development there was a lot to it. For mom and dad it was important to move into the Canadian home-owning middle class. For me it was the beginning of a nightmare. I was left with no friends for two years.

ANDREA: (*Stops painting to look at her cousin*) No friends?

WENDY: Hard to imagine, isn't it? For one thing, for years we were the only non-white family around. On top of that, I doubt if any of those kids had ever seen a black before they saw me.

ANDREA: That is hard to imagine.

WENDY: Don't get me wrong. It wasn't as if every kid around me openly abused me. There were only a handful, really, who did the classic routine: the spitting and the chasing. It was very persistent though. Then there were the others who'd do the name calling now and then. All the boys did, now that I think about it.

ANDREA: Some kind of rite of passage for the white Canadian male?

WENDY: (*Laughs*) That's about it. The girls were totally passive, as I recall. They either just stood and watched, or ignored the whole thing. If I'd had just one friend, just one, who said: "Hey, you're not ugly." Or, "Here, let me help you wipe the spit off your face," maybe things wouldn't have gotten under my skin the way they did.

ANDREA: (*Resumes painting*) Poor Wendy. I wish I had been there for you.

WENDY: I wish that I had been here.

ANDREA: (*Nodding*) You would have been a lot better.

WENDY: Even on the beaten path.

ANDREA: Absolutely. (*They laugh*) I know when I was studying in Montreal, I heard that racism was a problem. That, for instance, a black girl walking down the street was automatically considered to be a prostitute, and so on. I never actually saw any of it. There were many black, particularly Caribbean students, and we stuck together. Because, I guess, we had things in common. I suppose the group sort of insulated us from prejudice. But then, university life is a lot different from the real world, isn't it? I mean you don't apply for jobs in packs, do you?

WENDY: (*Fleeting smile*) Not the last time I checked. I never had that group security when we moved. It was offered much later in my teens but I could never bring myself to really latch on to it. To top it off, I was truly friends with only one black person my own age. We'd known each other since we were babies. But he lived across town and went to a different school. He wasn't exactly in a position to be of much help. What was he going to do, anyway? Beat up the whole school? Besides, it was a very long bus ride.

ANDREA: (*Chuckling*) At least you seem to have a sense of humour over it.

WENDY: I don't really (*Sighing*) It's just a kind of denial. I did a lot of denying things. It got to the point where I looked in the mirror and didn't see a black person anymore. I actually started imagining myself as white. And when I did, I didn't have a care in the world. I was invincible. It's funny. It was around that time that I finally started to make friends.

ANDREA: (*Stops painting to look at Wendy*) Coincidence?

WENDY: (*Shrugs*) I remember when the boys started getting interested in girls ... you know ... sex. Yelling "nigger" at me suddenly became passé. They started coming up to me, really intimate, you know, and saying stuff like (*Mimicking*), "That Ole Black Magic."

ANDREA: (*Making a sour face*) Talk about innuendo.

WENDY: Yeah. Well you have to remember by that time anything was better than the N-word. But like one minute I'm treated like a leper and the next I'm voted the most likely to be the neighbourhood slut. Is it any wonder I can't have a decent relationship with a man?

ANDREA: (*Cynically*) You don't have to live in Canada to feel that way.

WENDY: (*Sarcastically*) Well, that's good news.

(*They laugh. Then they are silent for a long moment. Wendy stares off into space and Andrea watches her closely before she resumes her painting.*)

WENDY: For some reason the experience I had the last time I was here just came to mind.

ANDREA: What was that?

WENDY: I was with the guy who runs that lovely restaurant at the Blue Lagoon, or Blue Pond, or something like that. He's missing part of one arm. (*Gestures from her elbow down*).

ANDREA: Oh, you mean Corey at the Blue Hole, over in Portland. I know him.

WENDY: Uncle Dale took us there. I remember Corey was very friendly and outgoing. Very physical. Always hugging or patting someone on the back or shaking hands.

ANDREA: He's a very nice person. Quite popular. (*Dabs paint on the portrait for the last time. Puts down her brush and turns to Wendy*).

WENDY: I hate to admit it, but that missing part of his arm drove me crazy at first. I was so squeamish, I didn't even want to look at him. I kept thinking about this good looking human being so disfigured and crippled. I kept wondering how it had happened and imagined seeing his severed arm lying in some place decaying and useless. (*Shudders*) Then I saw him dancing calypso with this woman. He was good. Expressive and graceful. What got me was that while he was dancing it was as though the part of his arm wasn't really missing. It was as though he was feeling it and using it too. I could almost hear his invisible fingers snapping and see the arm gesturing.

ANDREA: The phantom.

WENDY. Right. I found myself waiting for it to grab the woman and dip her. (*Shakes her head*).

ANDREA: You mean trip? (*Gestures with leg kicking and arm flailing*).

WENDY: Yeah (*Chuckles*) For the life of me, Andrea, I can't figure out the connection between the amputee and the conversation we've just had.

ANDREA: (*Turns portrait to her cousin*)

WENDY: (*Gasps softly. Puts her hands to her mouth.*)

George Bwanika Seremba
(1958–)

A playwright as well as a stage, film, and television actor, George Bwanika was born in the southern Ugandan province of Buganda, in the city of Kampala. Seremba describes his childhood as "traumatic, since we witnessed such violent events so young. My fondest memories were listening to my mother tell stories" (Koehler). Even after Uganda's independence from British colonial rule in 1962, Seremba says, "it was a world of edicts and pronouncements, impossible for an innocent childhood. I remember how we sang and danced in the streets when Amin took power in 1971. We thought that this gentle giant would be a good leader. After that began the nightmare."

Following Uganda's independence, Milton Obote gained power for a second time after overthrowing Idi Amin in 1979. His second period of rule was marked by repression and deaths of many civilians; Obote's list of enemies included activist students like Bwanika. As a drama major at Makarere, he organized protests against Obote. "It was guerrilla theater. The stage was where I developed my sense of individuality and of how art had the power to make a difference. […] I was listened to because I was an actor and known as willing to face up to evil" (Koehler).

Government spies noticed, and Bwanika was abducted. He was taken in a Jeep by a firing squad to the jungle. He made a final statement and he was shot seven times. One of the bullets hit Bwanika's left leg and sent him rolling into a marsh. The rain started falling, and that, he writes in his play *Come Good Rain*, is what saved his life.

Seremba escaped to neighbouring Kenya in 1980, where he lived in exile for three years. Then, in 1984, he fled to Winnipeg, where he began to write and act professionally under the new name Seremba. In 1992 he moved to Dublin, Ireland, where he earned a PhD in theatre studies from Trinity College.

Seremba is the author of three full-length plays— *The Grave Will Decide*, *Come Good Rain* (Blizzard Publishing 1993), which won the Dora Mavor Moore Award for most outstanding new play in Toronto, and *Napoleon of the Nile*—as well as of poems and radio plays. An accomplished actor, he has performed in feature films including *The Escapist* (2008), *Sanity Clause* (1990), *The Midday Sun* (1989), and *Dream Weaver* (2003), for which critics gave Seremba's performance "special mention, not just for his fine acting but for radiating humanity" (Kaplan).

Seremba is best known for his autobiographical play about the harrowing events that led to his exile from Uganda, *Come Good Rain*. In the Playwright's Note, Seremba reveals that the central image of the play began taking shape in his mind even as he boarded the plane to flee Uganda. The image comes "from a story my mother told me as a child," he writes. "The tale of a little girl who was abandoned by her stepmother to rot and die in the wilderness. Her only offense: beauty and virtue" (11). With the story of Nsimb'egwire now in his mind, Seremba began working on the play a month after he arrived in Toronto. Seremba knew his story needed to be told as a play: "I'd always loved the theatre, its immediacy and impact, its collective nature" (11). Seremba began by writing the climax, then worked backwards. He wrote, he says, to "tell my story, my country's story, tragic and triumphant as the little girl in the myth" (11). A month after he began writing, Seremba had completed the first draft of his two-act play. What is excerpted below is the first part of Act One in which Seremba retells the story of Nsimb'egwire and Act Two in which Seremba relays the climax of his story.

In the original production, Seremba played himself and thirty other characters. Integrating Ugandan song and folklore as well as live percussion, he depicts his deep love for his country of birth, but also the horror of the political climate of the 1970s and his own near escape from execution. During performances of the play in Ottawa in 1993, Obote supporters stood up and "made a ruckus." Nevertheless, Seremba took the play on the road throughout the United States, and it was staged again in Toronto by the Black Theatre Workshop and in Montreal at the Eti! East Africa Speaks! Festival, both in 2008. "This is a play of witness and memory," he said. "And just like any survivor of the Holocaust, I never want to forget these scars I carry" (Koehler).

Come Good Rain

Act One

(The stage is dark. A flute plays a haunting melody that will become a recurring theme throughout the play. A solitary figure makes his way through the auditorium. He's holding a candle and singing a song—or is it an invocation? Once on stage, almost ritualistically, he finds a convenient spot. He tells the story with the infectiousness of a seasoned raconteur.)

GEORGE *(Singing.)*

Abe mbuutu
N'abe ngalabi
Banange munkubire ngenda
Mbaire yagenda nga alidda
Aligenda okudda
Nga luwedde okwaba
Mbaire yagenda nga alidda
Aligenda okudda
Nga luwedde ngenze.

["My friends play me the ceremonial drums
Come bid me goodbye
My father Mbaire went as though he would return
By the time he does
it will be too late.
My father Mbaire went as though he would return
By the time he does
I will be long gone."]

This is a story that the old people tell. Once upon a time, a long time ago, there lived a man called Mbaire. Mbaire had a wife and two daughters. One was from an earlier marriage. Her name was Nsimb'egwire. Mbaire was also a good hunter his expeditions sometimes took him away for many a day and many a night.

Nsimb'egwire was a humble teen. She was the talk and bride of the village, not only because of her breath-takingly good looks, but also due to her remarkably good manners. This did not sit well with her stepmother. Her own daughter did not have much to cheer by way of any of these attributes.

It so happened once that Mbaire set off for another one of his expeditions. Both girls were promptly summoned by the wife. The next day was market day. There would be a lot of people to and from the *nalubabwe* (*"market-place"*). She shaved Nsimb'egwire's head with a vengeance, then smeared her with soot and ashes and made sure her own daughter was clean and smart. That done, the girls were paraded by the roadside.

Unfortunately for her mother, even long before the sun set at the end of the day, each and every passerby she asked who of the two was more beautiful pointed at Nsimb'egwire in spite of all the soot and ash.

She couldn't take it any more! So she dragged the girl off into the wilderness. There she found a secluded spot, deep in the jungle, where even the herdsmen seldom ventured with their cattle. Behind the amour of thick foliage and branches, she found a spot in the heart of an old passion tree. There she dug a shallow grave in which half the girl's body was buried under the sticky earth. Secure in the knowledge that the only likely company would be dreaded tropical snakes and animals, and that there would be no chance of human encounter, she abandoned her under the cover of darkness.

Condemned alive to solitary death, Nsimb'egwire waged a stubborn struggle to come out of her grave. For days and nights, come rain or steaming heat, she continued to struggle. But her energy was dissipating. Hunger and thirst made matters even worse. Now more than ever she wished her father would come home—death would obviously rear its ugly head. Sooner or later it would certainly knock on her door!

And yet she sang.

(He sings.)

Ani oyo
Ani oyo
Ani oyo ayita ku mutunda
Ku mutunda kuliko Nsimb'egwire
Nsimb'egwire muwala wa Mbaire
Mbaire yagenda nga anadda
Aligenda okudda nga luwedde okwaba
Mbaire yagenda nga alidda
Aligenda okudda
Nga luwedde ngenze…

["Who is that?
Who is that?
You who happen to pass by the Passion tree
Let it be known that it harbours Nsimb'egwire.
Nsimb'egwire is Mbaire's daughter.
Mbaire left as though he would return in good time
But by the time he returns it will be too late.
By the time he returns
I will be long gone."]

(Lights come on. George blows out his candle. He gets on his feet and plunges into his sea of memories with childish excitement and innocence.)

Act Two

FIRST SOLDIER: *(Thick north Ugandan accent.)* Sasa we lia kama mbugi.

(George bleats like a goat.)

Stop. Now you laugh.

(George laughs wildly.)

Stop. Now you cry like a cow.

(George ends up bellowing like a bull.)

Stop. Now bark like a dog.

(George barks.)

Now cry … stop.

(George continues moaning.)

Stop!!

GEORGE: *(To audience.)* I stopped. So too did my hopes of striking a human chord.

With me spread-eagled on the floor of one of the military vehicles, we made our way through the speedbumps and potholes that filled the streets. I was a doormat to their thick boots.

(He tries to absorb the hits in a spread-eagled stance. A position he takes and discards as occasion demands it.)

Sometimes the butts of their guns would have a little dialogue with my ribs. The first soldier who was the leader issued orders quietly and his pistol kept my wrists busy.

A blinding flood of lights hit my face. This was Nile Mansions; the five-star hotel where the top brass lived and worked, indulged themselves and felt more secure than living among the real people.

FIRST SOLDIER: Toa viatu. *["Take your shoes off."]*

GEORGE: *(Takes his shoes off.)* The walk into the building was an interesting display; you should have seen it, a soldier at the back and one at the front as well. All around us imaginary foes that kept them busy.

FIRST and SECOND SOLDIERS: He wants to somersault. He wants to somersault. He wants ...

GEORGE: Me in the middle. Encaged in the now familiar and spectacular island of steel and human hands. Definitely more protected than any Life President.

SECOND SOLDIER: Have you been to Israel?

GEORGE: The voice sounded almost friendly.

SECOND SOLDIER: Have you been to Israel?

GEORGE: *(Not answering the soldier.)* I couldn't help but smile looking at him ... were they more afraid than I? One doesn't have to go to Tel Aviv to fight this rag tag bunch. Still, I would neither confirm nor deny.

We finish the final flight of stairs, pass through a door into what looks like the outer chamber of a bigger office. Less than a year ago someone was killed in this building, I recall. A teenage girl. Her father, a Cabinet Minister, was at work down the street. They said it was a stray bullet that did it. There tends to be a lot of those when certain governments are changing ... in Africa.

The office is full of gadgets. A uniformed figure sits behind a huge desk.

FIRST SOLDIER: *(Clicks his heels. Executes a quick salute.)* We have brought him. The man who had come to cause chaos at Makerere.

GEORGE: *(To audience.)* I had finally met the boss. No less a man than Brigadier David Oyite Ojok.[1] His name alone made the blood of many a Ugandan freeze.

"Sir ..." I struggled through bleeding lips ... His eyes were so small they looked like little slits ... so red, more red than they used to look on television. He looked tired. Ruthlessly cold. Insensitive.

(To Brigadier Ojok.) Sir ... some of my friends and relatives fought alongside you in the struggle against Amin.

---

1   David Oyite Ojok (1940 –1983) was a Ugandan military commander. He was a member of a powerful sub-committee of the Uganda National Liberation Front (UNLF), which ruled the country after Idi Amin's overthrow.

(No response.)

FIRST SOLDIER: Do you deny that you escaped from prison?

GEORGE: Sir, I have never been to prison. Which prison?

FIRST SOLDIER: You were supposed to be in prison anyway. We have it in your file.

GEORGE: *(To audience.)* The boss gestured to him to move this "walking blasphemy" out of his office. I was shoved onto a small balcony.

FIRST SOLDIER: Talk! Talk! Talk, you bloody bandit! Do you deny that we have seen you in Nairobi? Do you deny that we have seen you in Nairobi with certain exiles? Talk. Talk. Name them.

GEORGE: *(To audience.)* I knew which name they wanted most. Robert Serumaga;[2] the playwright, buried in a foreign land. Cause of death: dubious. Even in his death I couldn't betray him. All I could say was " *(Mutters.)* … let his soul rest in peace."

I could have dropped a few names of prominent exiles who were still alive. Even silent response earned me another blow, the pain was more and more distant. I reduced my body to an empty husk. Now I was a little bird preceding a little branch witnessing perhaps what mankind enjoys most.

(After a few more blows, he resolves to say something.)

(Facing the soldiers.) Thank you … Thank you … Thank you.

FIRST SOLDIER: *(Disturbed.)* Why are you thanking us? Why are you …?

GEORGE: Because you know what you are doing.

(There is a beat. Soldier laughs menacingly.)

(To audience.) His friend had returned with an ashtray full of burning cigarette butts.

FIRST SOLDIER: Bend forward. Put your chin under your knees.

---

2   Robert Serumaga (1939–1980) was a Ugandan playwright, director, and novelist known especially for his works representing the absurdity of human existence within repressive political regimes. He left Uganda in 1977 and became involved in the liberation army that ousted Amin in 1979. Serumaga died in mysterious circumstances in Nairobi in 1980, reportedly of a brain hemorrhage.

GEORGE: They were stuffed in to my shirt. All over my back. I remembered a story about a Greek Cypriot mercenary on the eve of his execution somewhere in Africa. His sister who'd visited him in prison couldn't bear to say goodbye. She broke down and wept. All he would say was: "Never let them see you cry, remember you are a Greek." A youthful officer approached the scene.

OFFICER: What has he done?

(Silence.)

GEORGE: *(Turns to him.)* Sir, among other things they are accusing me of having escaped from lawful custody ... But I have never been to jail.

OFFICER: *(Cautious reprimand.)* You should not take such drastic steps if you don't have enough evidence.

FIRST SOLDIER: Chacha hi mkubwa nasema nini? [*"What the hell is this boss saying?"*]

GEORGE: *(To audience.)* It was as though this was the stupidest statement they'd ever heard. They were enraged. They dragged me back to the inner chamber. Promptly explained everything in their mother tongue. The "almighty" Ojok issued some rapid orders and took a good long look at me.

Back at the waiting vehicle the soldier with the friendly tone leaned over to brief the one in the driver's seat.

SECOND SOLDIER: He says kill!

GEORGE: Lord, now lettest thou thy servant depart in peace.

(George assumes the spread-eagled position once again.)

(To soldiers.) Gentlemen, since I do not have that much time left, can you please allow me a final look at the moon and stars? *(Sits. Begs for a little more.)* And please don't hit me as hard. All you'll do is deprive me of the pain at the end. If you don't mind, I'll say my last prayers.

(Head tilted skyward, arms together, he begins secret prayers.)

Two things, good Lord ... One, these men have humiliated me a great deal, when the moment comes let me not go like a coward. If nobody else sees my body at least let my mother see it, so she does not spend the rest of her life thinking I'll one day show up. Do shorten the family's grief, Lord, and give them as long and as safe a life as possible.

FIRST SOLDIER: Lie down.

GEORGE: I could tell we had reached the major roadblock at Ntinda.[3]

SECOND SOLDIER: *(At the checkpoint.)* We are members of the G Branch. We are on a mission and we shall be back soon. Thank you.

GEORGE: *(To audience.)* And so we went through Banda, Kireka, Bweyo-gerere and finally stopped in the middle of the road. This was the famous Namanve Forest,[4] the place where lots of Ugandans had met their deaths. The place where Nalongo's daughter went shopping.

The soldier with the friendly tone pulled me side. He was a bit of a giant and reminded me of the noble savage in Swift's voyage to Brobdignag.

SECOND SOLDIER: You refused to talk so now ... you will talk when it is too ...

GEORGE: When the bullets begin to flower.

SECOND SOLDIER: Take off your watch. What about the money ... Is this all you have?

GEORGE: I wish you had told me before ... I would have given you more but I left it at John's place, tucked in my little diary.

SECOND SOLDIER: Where?

GEORGE: In a corner below the bench I was on.

SECOND SOLDIER: You have a diary ... Anyway, we have to go back and pick up two students who were seen in your company.

GEORGE: *(To himself.)* Thank God they weren't with me at John's. Thank God the soldiers are going back there though, now at least people will know and spread the news of my tragedy.

(To audience.) For a moment I thought about Dora Block, the elderly Israeli woman who was dragged from Mulago Hospital as soon as the Israelis rescued the hostages at Entebbe. What were her last thoughts? Her remains were finally discovered not too far from here. "Do not let them see your tears ... remember you are a Greek."

---

3   A location in northeastern Kampala, the capital city of Uganda.

4   Namvane Forest Reserve is located approximately 15 kilometres, by road, east of downtown Kampala. Most of the reserve has been demolished to pave way for Kampala Business and Industrial Park.

It was getting dark. The front door opened for the mean little boss who'd called the shots all the way from Makerere. He stuck his pistol in my lower ribs.

FIRST SOLDIER: Escort me.

GEORGE: Excuse me, could you please not shoot me through the back? I would prefer to look at you while you shoot. *(Takes a few short backwards steps.)* Is this okay?

(Internal.) Goodbye Mum, I owe you an apology for overstaying this night on the campus. Goodbye Dad … Goodbye my lovely sisters, Abby, little Tony, every single one of you. Remember he loved you all and loved this country.

(To soldiers.) Please give me a minute or two to say my last words. Now that you have come to power through the ballot box and not the barrel of a gun, even if I had committed a treasonable offence you should at least have taken me to prison or a court of law. I know it's too late for me to live but whoever will continue to live in your country will find it hard to forgive, let alone forget. I am ready.

(To audience.) So were they, except for the "noble savage."

SECOND SOLDIER: No I'm not shooting, but you can use my gun.

GEORGE: *(Internal.)* Oh, Robert Serumaga, what would you have done …? Give me strength to go through this.

(A gun goes off.)

(To audience.) The first bullet had hit the right leg. I was down on my knees … I actually squatted. Before I knew it the left arm was grazed.

(Another shot is heard.)

The body now contorted as another got a bit of skin just above the fore-head. But this time the body moved back and forth, never still and unwilling to give them a clean shot at the chest or the stomach.

(Yet another shot is let go.)

There was a brief lull. Someone picked up "my friend's" gun. It was a rocket propelled grenade. There was a grin on his face as he put the gun over his shoulder. I stared at him in disbelief. Oh God, there goes the rest of the body.

(The deafening sound of a small rocket-propelled grenade is heard.)

A big bolt-like cluster of sharp little machetes had drilled through my thigh ... I was on my back, the feet were burning, there were a few flames and a pungent smell. I rolled backwards. I could see a little thicket and some undergrowth to my immediate left, a bit of a ditch as well.

(The familiar and by now comparatively tame sound of another bullet is heard.)

A solid bullet went through my left ankle as I rolled over.

(An instantaneous barrage of bullets is heard.)

The AK 47s were now on rapid fire. There was lead all round me ... sort of like popcorn. The AK 47s were quite clearly on rapid fire.

(Another stomach-churning barrage.)

I had landed in a shallow stream or marsh. I could smell the clay. Except for the head I had practically sunk. There was still one crucial bullet. The one I couldn't see. The one that would end it all. The one that would enter through the back of my head.

(Shooting ends as suddenly as it had begun.)

It is quiet. Frighteningly quiet!

(Very quietly. Internal.) Be still, George, still as a stone. What are they up to? ... God, let it not be that they are planning to cut the head off the corpse to show their boss! Or simply dump it in the lake or the Nile: the "Poet's Corner" or Idi Amin's Uganda. After the longest five minutes of my life, they turned and drove towards Kampala ... God save my two friends ...

Grant me enough strength to come out of the marsh and save my body so my mother can see it. It's dark. The abduction was around nine. The latest it can be is eleven-thirty. By dawn I will finally leave the world.

(To audience.) I turned towards the east; a few meters in that direction was the foundation stone for a monument that was never built, "To the Memory of all that had died in Idi Amin's Uganda."

(He summons incredible energy and drags himself out of the marsh.)

I stumbled eastwards. Got to the road. Turned toward the highway. *(Pause. His inner voice takes over.)* Zig zag on the edge of the tarmac, George.

Avoid leaving a blood trail.

(Points to the other side after a few more steps.)

(To himself.) That's the spot where the shooting was. The sky is getting even darker. Around me is a misty grey colour. The pain throbs like unrelenting high-pitched drums. Tears are welling in my eyes. The earth feels like a rag slowly pulled away under my elephantine feet. *(Pause. To audience.)* Still I "walked," supporting myself by leaning against a tree or holding onto a branch.

My entire family, relatives, friends, place too, were rolling over the screen of my mind. All the faces looked shocked. Lord let this Government not last, at least not kill too many people.

(Soft throbbing drums.)

The images kept rolling. My entire life … its landmarks from primary school … the best years. Short, intense …

(Internal.) God if there is a way of coming back to this earth … make me a little bird, a spirit of the woods and custodian of Namanve Forest. I will always come back to my nest at sunset and sometimes disrupt the foul murders … enable the victims to escape.

You my ancestors, all of you from Kabaka Kalema whose remains lie in Mende, Kakungulu and Mugujula the two valiant warriors. My grandparents back in Masaka. My grandmother, Bulaliya Nakiwala, you who always danced agile as a duiker without touching a drink in your entire life. Yekoniya Zirabamuzale, you who lost your sight and never your wisdom and legendary charity. My stillborn brothers, you who never left the void, please pave my way and ease my transition.

(To himself.) I see distant flares cut through the dark hide of night … *(Thunder is heard.)* and feel a few drizzles drop on my body. It's raining.

(Internal.) This is a good resting place. The Ministry of Works Labour Camp is close, someone will see the body and "radio Katwe," the grapevine telegraph will do the rest. I also have an uncle not too far from here, if he is home he will save the body and deliver the news.

(To audience.) The right arm is already swollen by more than half its size.

(He removes his shirt and folds it into a pillow.)

The trees and the undergrowth swirl at an incredible pace. Their shapes begin to change, taking on the threatening ones of the gnomic creatures and spirits that inhabit my folklore.

I have made my peace and put my borrowed time to good use. I'm a bird flapping my wings and gazing at the husk that was my body. Maybe I'll be like Christopher Okigbo, the Nigerian poet.

They say he was sent back to earth after his death. Condemned to sing his lines eternally, at a village well. To this day when the little children are sent to the well, they sometimes hear a pair of little birds singing:

So let us sing tongue tied[5]
without name or audience
and make harmony
among the branches.

I don't recall anything else.

(The drums stop. More thunder and lightning. A tropical downpour is heard. It stops. Dawn: birds and other forest sounds. A determined tropical sun makes its way through the foliage. George opens his eyes. Slight pause.)

(To himself.) Am I in Heaven or Hell? *(Another pause.)* It must have taken about five long frightening minutes to come to terms with the discovery that I was still alive. That was far more shocking than the previous night's events. There was a long pregnant moment of silence. As if body and spirit were getting in sync. *(Pause. Very muffled agony.)* The pain is enormous. The earth is wet and soggy. I can hear occasional trucks in the distance … Obote has finally returned to power.

You know how much I love life, Lord. Why tantalize me with another glimpse of it? *(Pause.)* If I had my way, my request would be to live long enough to tell this tale. But even if you allowed me to live long enough just to see my mother, I wouldn't complain. But home is Jinja and Jinja is almost fifty miles away. And between here and Kampala the military roadblocks are manned by Obote's henchmen who will ask me to identify myself and explain my wounds.

---

5 Lines from Christopher Okigbo's poem "Limits III: Banks of Reed" published in his collection *Labyrinths; With Path of Thunder* (1971).

Will the forest be my perpetual prison? Perhaps all I can do is sing like Nsimb'egwire, the little girl in the proverb.

(Flute.)

Yes I feel a certain kinship with her. Understand her in a way I have never done. Her voice clear as a bell:

(A female voice is heard singing the solitary lyrics.)

FEMALE VOICE: *(Singing.)*

Ani oyo
Ani oyo ayita
Ku mutunda …

GEORGE: *(Picks up story from where it stopped.)* She was not ready to quit yet. Unknown to her neither was her father who had recently returned from the hunting expedition. Something told him not to believe anything her stepmother said. So he put a search party together.

One day they heard a familiar voice.

(Singing continues.)

FEMALE VOICE: *(Singing.)*

Ku mutunda
Kuliko Nsimb'egwire
Nsimb'—Egwire
muwala wa Mbaire…

GEORGE: She'd finally been found. They unearthed her, half rotten and famished, and headed home. As for me Obote has finally returned to—

(Interrupting himself.) Who's that? A little boy. Must be about twelve.

(He beckons to the boy.)

Tontya. Who sent you?

BOY: They sent me to check and see whether the village lost one of our own. Whenever we hear the bullets at night we come to check in the morning.

GEORGE: Go check across the road. My two friends might be there … No. Thank God. Then please, go back and tell them I'm the only one.

(To audience.) Soon they arrived. Headed by an elder, a chief of some sort.

(To the villagers.) No, they took all my papers ... but believe me, there is nothing sinister about this. Thank you. Thank you also very much for the risk you're taking. The little boy should go ahead as a scout. At a sign from him simply dump my body by the side; should worst come to worst ... well at least you will have done your best.

(The villagers load their "delicate cargo" onto their backs. They walk for a while, unload without any incident.)

(To audience.) As soon as we got to the village, I was placed on the floor of a tiny concrete grey store. We were right next to the highway and more and more people were milling around. No one had ever come out of the Namanve alive. Then said the chief ...

CHIEF: What would you like us to do?

GEORGE: I have an uncle around here. His name is George Kakaire.

(To audience.) We wasted no time after his arrival. Kampala was so near and yet so far. Our best bet was Jinja. The roadblocks were fewer and except for the one at the Owen Falls Dam practically all of them were entirely manned by Tanzanian troops.

The first roadblock was Mukono. We stopped. We soon got to Lugazi. Mabira Forest. Bulumagi, and finally reached the roadblock at the Nile, the one stop we feared most. Will our story work? *(Slight pause.)* "He had an accident between here and the last roadblock. We've been referred to such and such hospital."

SOLDIERS: Pole sana! Mumuharakishe. *["How sad! Rush him."]*

GEORGE: *(To audience.)* It worked. We had crossed the Mighty Nile. The next stop was home.

Mother had just come out of the bathtub when Uncle George walked in. Before he said anything she asked:

MOTHER: What brings you here so early ... is he dead?

UNCLE: Not yet. No. Dress up. He's in the van. We have to get him to hospital.

GEORGE: *(To audience.)* At first my sister Mary and my mother just looked at me through the window. With tears streaming down my mother's face they edged closer. The blanket was lifted. There was a little relief. At least the chest and stomach seemed intact.

At the hospital, it was as if all our friends had conspired to be on duty at the same time.

(Looking at the X-rays.)

FRIEND: You're lucky. Doesn't seem to be any bone injuries. Two bullets have to be dislodged. One from the right thigh, the other from the right arm.

GEORGE: *(To audience.)* All along there were no questions asked. Down in my warm and cozy bed I looked at the ceiling, highly impressed ... tried to sum it all up for myself. There was a knock at the door. Dr. Walugembe walked in.

WALUGEMBE: *(Very calmly.)* The surgeon in charge is already pacing up and down ... asking leading questions. I'm not saying it is true, but given his political stripes there is no guarantee that if he got wind of your story, he may not leave you on the table.

GEORGE: *(To audience.)* He didn't have to say any more. Outside a different car was waiting and ready to go. Destination: twenty-eight miles away, in the famous town of Iganga.

My sister Mary got to work.

MARY: See this?

GEORGE: *(To audience.)* It was the bullet in the right thigh.

MARY: You have to tell the Doctor it's come out. Lest they start drilling and fishing for it where it's not. It's also left another wound. Remind them about it.

GEORGE: *(To audience.)* There was something else on my mind this afternoon. Anybody with bullet wounds had to have a certificate of some sort from the police before getting any treatment. Dr. Walugembe would vouch for us. For my part all I had to do was remember a story we had gone through in the car. Inside the operating theatre the story is subjected to a severe test.

(To doctor.) My name is Paulo Nyende, Doctor. I was over-speeding along the Jinja-Kamuli Highway ... It all happened too quickly and it's entirely

my fault. Before I knew it, I was passing a roadblock manned by our esteemed army. Realizing my mistake I'm sure they never shot to kill. If you ask me, they were extremely kind in the execution of their duty ... to say the least.

DOCTOR: How can you say you hadn't anticipated the roadblock?

GEORGE: I don't live here. In fact I am a student at the University of Nairobi.

DOCTOR: *(Literally pouncing on him.)* You can't say Kamuli in one breath and then Nairobi in the other.

GEORGE: *(To the doctors.)* With due respect to all of you. There is a difference between the Hippocratic oath and the Spanish Inquisition. My pain is unbearable. With the last ounce of my physical and psychic energy, I put it to you sirs, with all my heart, that I made a mistake. It's none but me to blame. Please don't turn this operating table into an abattoir. If I have committed any crimes against the state ... believe me, I will be more than happy to face a firing squad. I'll answer any other questions after the surgery.

DOCTOR: Count one, two, three.

GEORGE: *(To audience.)* Late in the afternoon, the next day, I opened my eyes for the first time. What's this? There is a drip hanging over my head. Here behind a partial screen in an open hospital ward ... Why does it look so familiar? Their positions as well: Mary, Mother, my grandmother ...

But oh ... the pain is a lot worse, unparalleled by anything I've gone through before the operation.

They have begun to arrive. Soon this corner of the ward will be full to the brim with relatives, friends, just like my grandmother's house at Rubaga. One of the first ones to arrive is my Auntie Gladys.

AUNTIE: You look too anemic, my son.

MOTHER: For some reason they refused to give him even a single drop of blood.

AUNTIE: *(Angry and sad.)* I'm not surprised.

(Methodically, she circles around pointing to the wounds.)

Look. Look. Look at this ...

(Pulls Mother aside.)

Can I tell you something my dear sister ... of all the years of training and practice both at Mulago and the hospitals in London ... I have never seen the like! Did you have a good look at those sutures? God, I hate it when people put my Christianity to the test. They stitched our son up like a gunny bag. Only post mortem surgeons do that. It's for dead bodies.

GEORGE: *(To audience.)* Uncle Paulo Kasekende was the next one to arrive. Right next to him was my great uncle, good old Brother Stephen. Now in his sixties. Still far from frail.

I had no doubt he would gladly have traded places with me or any other victim in the family.

He reminded me of Mark Antony on seeing Caesar's body.

BROTHER STEPHEN: *(Vents his spleen. Quoting Shakespeare. Flourish of trumpets is heard.)*

"Oh judgment, though art fled to brutish beasts,[6]

And men have lost their reason ...

You blocks, you stones, you worse than senseless things!

(Removes his glasses. Pulls out a handkerchief.)

"Oh you hard hearts, you cruel men ...

These dogs. These shameless, Godless ... beasts."

Forgive me. *(Pause.)* You know Brother Andrew ... Yes, the Canadian. He goes to Nairobi from time to time. He's promised to help. Once your condition improves, he'll have to get you across the border. God willing.

GEORGE: *(To audience.)* Three weeks later we celebrated a rather sunken eyed but warm Christmas. We had moved to an anonymous little house next to the District Prison in Igana. Auntie Gladys headed the underground medical team that included my cousin Betty and a male nurse. Except for the right arm, all other wounds were healing fast.

Now I could sit and stand. But I couldn't stand the bedpan any longer! *(Tries walking.)* By hook or crook I had to get to the toilet.

---

6 *Julius Caesar*, act 3, scene 2.

(He toddles his way across the stage.)

I stood under the mid-afternoon Boxing Day sun, pleased as punch.

Half-way between the toilet and stairs, I stopped. First I heard the sudden curious sound, then right in front of me a military jeep. They've finally caught up with me ... They will take my body but not my spirit. The door opens. Brother Stephen steps out.

BROTHER STEPHEN: Sorry for the lack of warning. These are Tanzanian officers. I talked to the commander himself and he graciously offered to help. Go in and say goodbye. We'll say a little prayer. Then we'll leave as soon as your grandmother is ready to board.

GEORGE: *(To audience.)* Soon, I was having my last look at the mighty Nile. Then came Mukono, Namanve, Bweyogerere. I thought about all those people that rescued me. Uncle George, the pilot, the gentleman who offered his car and drove us on the morning after. Forgive me, I would like to pay tribute to the so called African extended family. Then and in the days that followed the stream of relatives that poured in to reaffirm their love, support, best wishes, uplifted my spirits, hope, faith, and accelerated the healing process ... their presence alone gave me something to live for. They will always be etched into my memory.

We finally arrived in Kampala. I even had a glimpse of the famous Nile Mansions from my front seat. After the roundabout at Kibuye, we stop to let Grandma off.

For a person in her late sixties, she's tall and erect. The lines on her face more pronounced than ever before. But no amount of oppression will remove the inner dignity and proverbial wisdom of Semei Kakungulu's daughter and granddaughter of a noble King of Buganda.

GRANDMOTHER: You come from a line of brave and courageous people. I need not say much. You've seen it all. You know! Just one favour: When we die, even when you hear we are all dead and gone ... I beseech you, never come back to the land of your ancestors. Let us pray for one another.

GEORGE: *(To audience.)* We embraced again. Scared of attracting too much attention at this busy intersection, I get back into the vehicle nursing a lump in my throat. We drove towards Kisubi.

Photographs are taken. A new identity card is issued and stamped. For the first time I use the name Seremba, a name I had never used before officially.

I'm also listed as a postulant, a Brother in the making so to speak. The card also calls for a brand new story: I had gone to visit some friends at the senior seminary in Masaka Diocese … all of a sudden the car swerved off the road … you should see the condition it's in! But God is great. If all goes well I could be back in two weeks … just as soon as a few more experts examine me. God knows I love Uganda.

Brother Andrew and Brother Aidan were both flying on the twenty-eighth. My name had been attached to the travel Permit Clearance form, signed and stamped by no less a man than the Honourable Minister for Internal Affairs.

The next afternoon Dad came to say hello and goodbye. We shook hands. Embraced. Shook hands again. I knew at least in his eyes I was a hero.

That evening Auntie Gladys arrived. Offered me a sling.

AUNTIE: You have now become a seasoned patient … from time to time you may have to dress the wounds yourself. I hope they get to look at that arm again. Son, always remember to thank God and the rain. Without that and your will, this would have been a different story. So remember to get down on those knees. Don't forget to say: "Come good rain. For none but I will bear my cross."

GEORGE: *(To audience.)* As we drove to the airport the next morning it was my mother's turn to bid me goodbye.

MOTHER: God alone knows how many of us you'll ever meet if things change. You know the rest as you have yourself witnessed. I beseech you though, do us one favour. Please do not write that story. Wait.

GEORGE: *(To audience.)* It is Sunday, December 28th. Obote the second was sworn in last night. There is not much staff at the airport because of the big victory celebration the night before. Brother Stephen leaves us at the check-in counter and goes to the waving bay where Mary, Mum and the rest are.

Brother Andrew has already started chatting with some acquaintances. They let Brother Aidan pass. After a few casual explanations I pass through too. With Brother Aidan at the front and Andrew at the back we proceed to board.

(Panting and nervous, he stumbles across the tarmac.)

Halfway up the stairs I take one last look.

(Inside the plane, a flight attendant's voice comes on.)

FLIGHT ATTENDANT: Mabibi na mabwana, tuna wakaribisha ndani ya Kenya Airways … *["Ladies and Gentlemen, we welcome you on board Kenya Airways …"]*

GEORGE: *(To audience.)* We were up in the clouds.

(Closes his eyes. Internal.) Thank you Lord. Goodbye Uganda.

(To audience.) Soon we would be getting into Kenyan airspace. Lake Victoria would be behind us, over the Rift Valley … Finally we'd landed at Jomo Kenyatta International Airport.

It was my turn to go through Customs and Immigration.

OFFICER: Wapi kitambulisho?

GEORGE: *(To audience.)* I can't believe it! I check through all my pockets. Hand luggage. No sign of my identity card. Check again. Nothing!

OFFICER: You'll have to board the next flight back to Entebbe.

GEORGE: It must have dropped on my seat or the toilet.

OFFICER: This is a country not a toilet. That plane is leaving for Mombasa. You'll have to go back to Entebbe.

GEORGE: Not with all these wounds … Look sir … Besides niko mwalimu *["I am a teacher"]* … here in your country. *(Beat.)* Yes. Kilungu Day High School, in Ukamban, they call it Kwa Mwanza.

OFFICER: You're lucky. That's my home area. No Immigration Officer is allowed to do this. But because you teach our children I'll let you go but next time … next …

GEORGE: *(To audience.)* Next time. Hmmm … when would that be?

With my arm firmly in the sling, I limp through a corridor and behind a door for my first pee on Kenyan soil. *(Brief pause.)* Here is to freedom. That evening we knock on the door of the Rubadiri's at Hurlingham. *(To them.)* Lazarus has come to see you.

(To audience.) The whole family gathers. All sure glad to see me. David too was short of words.

DAVID: My son, you are larger than life. Do you feel sorry for yourself, my son?

GEORGE: No.

DAVID: Here. This is more important than the medicines.

(George relights the candle with which he first entered.)

GEORGE: *(To audience.)* He opened a bottle of brandy. He places something on the turntable. A Welsh voice booms its way through the African night.

VOICE: "Do not go gentle into that good night,

Old age should burn and rave at close of day;

Rage, rage against the dying of the light."

GEORGE: *(To audience.)* If there was rain that night, I didn't hear it. Two little birds stood guard outside my window. Their sweet song cut my dream short; I remember seeing a step-mother hastily pack and desert her home after an abominable act, to live like a pariah for the rest of her life. Then I saw a beautiful young figure. Her song sounded familiar:

(He sings.)

Abe mbuutu[7]
N'abe ngalabi
Banange munkubire ngenda
Mbaire yagenda naa alidda…

(George picks up his candle and returns to the place on stage where he first began. There is a slow fade to black. He blows out his candle and exits. The End.)

---

7 Lines from the song of Nsimb'egwire.

Valerie Mason-John
(1962–)

Valerie Mason-John, also known by her Buddhist name Vimalasara ("she whose essence is stainless and pure") and her spoken-word name, Queenie, became a creative writer when she gave up on journalism. She had written for the *Guardian*, the *Voice*, and the *Pink Paper*, and had done freelance work for the BBC, Channel 4, and the Arts Council. But, she says, "It was impossible to tell true stories, the media didn't want the truth, and it was these stories I wanted to tell" (Mason-John, "Uncensoring"). Seeking ways to tell stories about taboo desire, repressed racial histories, and oppressive national myths, she studied clowning, took a course at the Desmond Jones School of Mime and Physical Theatre, and started writing plays. "I realised I could say anything I wanted in theatre, without it being censored before my audience got to see it" (Parker 1).

Mason-John identifies as a trans-racially raised queer dyke of African descent ("Uncensoring" 397). She was placed into care as a young child by her single African mother, who had recently moved to Essex, England, from Sierra Leone. She experienced homelessness at the age of fourteen and incarceration at the age of fifteen. At the age of nineteen she attended Leeds University and encountered a lesbian feminist separatist community which she credits for saving her life. "It was the beginning of a healing journey within a community where I could talk about the abuse in my life without being judged" ("Being Fair"). In the 1980s she was involved in the move to ban trans-racial adoption in England.

In 1998, she wrote and produced her first play, *Sin Dykes*; as the title suggests, the play celebrates identities and desires previously regarded as sinful or taboo. In 1997 she performed her one-woman show *Sweep It under the Carpet*, which she revised and published as *Brown Girl in the Ring*, about miscegenation in royal European families. It focuses on the discovery that Queen Sophia Charlotte, wife of King George III and great-, great-grandmother to Queen Victoria, had African ancestry. Although based on historical facts, Mason-John reflects, "I could never have got away with telling this story as a journalist" (Parker 2).

Her other plays include *The Adventures of Snow Black and Rose Red*, a family pantomime, and *You Get Me*, which premiered in 2006. As an editor, she has published *Talking Black: African and Asian Lesbians Speak Out*, published in 1994, and *Lesbians Talk: Making Black Waves* with Ann Khambatta, published in 1993. Since relocating to Edmonton, she co-edited the first national anthology of African Canadian poetry, *The Great Black North* (Frontenac House), which includes an introduction by George Elliott Clarke; it won two Alberta book honours: the Education Book Award and the Robert Kroetsch Poetry Book Award.

Her first novel, *Borrowed Body* (2005 Serpent's Tail, and republished in 2007 as *The Banana Kid* by BAAF), tells the story of Pauline, a young black girl of Nigerian descent, growing up in white foster homes and orphanages, then reclaimed by her mother. It won the 2006 MIND Book of the Year Award. Her self-help book, *Detox Your Heart* (2006), entails a mindfulness program to heal personal histories of trauma, addiction, and abuse.

In 2008 she moved to Edmonton, a city that is changing the direction of her creative focus as well as her poetic method. Her current writing focuses on queer black histories in Canada, as the following two poems demonstrate. The first poem, "Self Portrait Two" (originally published in thegaydomcom in 2014, and subsequently revised in 2019 for publication here), celebrates queer identity even as it acknowledges the ongoing risk of doing so. As the formal couplet structure of this poem suggests, queerness remains a dialogue and negotiation with a dominant other. In the second poem, "Yellowknifed," published originally in her edited collection *The Great Black North* (2013), Mason-John delves into the Canadian historical record for histories of black and queer women. She locates her historical ancestor—but in the criminal record. The poem is based on the first same-sex lesbian assault criminal case to be tried in a Canadian court. As her notes to the poem explain, "In 1955 a white woman "Laura" (pseudonym used to protect her identity) took Willimae Moore, an African American woman, to court for gross indecency, in Yellowknife, Northwest Territories. Ms Moore was found guilty. She and her white Canadian lover, Beatrice Gonzales, were hounded out of the town. Even though she subsequently appealed the decision, her name was tarnished forever" (97).

Asked in an interview where she considers home to be, she reveals, "It's always changing, especially now that I've moved to Canada. Diaspora is at the centre of my life, which means there are many homes. England is home because that's where my history is. Africa, or Sierra Leone, is also home because that's where I originate from. I have the foster family, the children's home family [...] And now the Buddhist family. So, home means many different things. Really, home for me is here in my body" (Parker 23).

Self Portrait Two

My queerness is part of my identity
The love of my chosen families

My queerness is one of nature's resplendence
The flowering of my ancestry

My queerness is being out of the closet
The karma of my queer bashers

My queerness is the emancipation of all beings
A fact of life

Queer, Bull Dagger,
Nancy Boy Zami,
Adofuro, Yan Daudu,
Ikihindu
Our Pride before
Colonizers came

Gender fluid, Non
Binary, Genderqueer,
Gender Variant,
Intersex, Agender,
Bigender,
Transgender, pan
gender, third gender,
gender neutral Two-
Spirit, Mx, Ze, Hir is
what we reclaim

My queerness is your fear
My courage

Your exclusion
My embrace

Your shame
My pride

Your fantasy
My reality

Your perception
My revelation

Now say my Name.

Yellowknifed

When it was a mere 20 below, i'd think,
"Boy this is a great day, I can push back
my parka hood." I was used to New York winters,
this was nothing. 1953, Yellowknife,
in love with Beatrice Gonzales.
Followed her home to her native Canada.

Found work in a government office typing pool.
Some of us slept on the floor
when it was too cold to go home.
We'd fall asleep exchanging stories of our past.
Some women made it clear to me
my type of life was quite foreign.
They had absolutely no interest in me.

I made it clear that I was not desperate.
That would be foolish.
Beatrice was a professional woman
of good standing, Vice Principal.
I was content with my comfortable life.

Now, you see, had I been a man, I could have got away
with touching a woman's cleavage, lifting
her petticoat up, even rubbing against her genitals.
If the woman tried to press charges,
she would be told she had encouraged it.

Asked what she was doing alone in a room,
with a man who wasn't her husband?
Told she must have made advances.

An attempted kiss would have been considered
Trifling. Nothing to write home about.

Headlines read: "First Same-Sex Lesbian Case."
Branded a freak of nature.
The public need to be protected.
Yellow Knives were out to get me.
Gross indecency was my crime.
Nobody asked me any questions.
Guilty on a white woman's evidence alone.

In court Laura claimed that she looked up at me
from her desk. I was supposed
to have looked strangely at her,
a rather concentrated look.
She claimed to look down. She said
I grabbed hold of her, tried to kiss her.
As she pushed me away,
I was to have said "You're very cruel," and she
began to cry.

Of course I looked at her, even undressed her with my eyes,
And she undressed me too.
"Exotic" she whispered,
in the next breath spat out: "You beast."
She locked eyes with me,
Our lips brushed and she cried,
"No stop! I can't. I'm not strange like you."

I was the first woman arrested and tried
In a Canadian court, gross indecency
Against another woman. I was
Yellowknifed.
I was Black.
Guilt?

Nduka Otiono
(1964–)

"By the time I arrived in Edmonton in the middle of the first decade of the new millennium, the city was witnessing an influx of diverse newcomers trooping to Alberta during the economic boom driven by the rich oil sands," says Nduka Otiono. "In many ways, Alberta's petroculture and the tension between oil exploration and environmental rights remind me of my ancestral home in the troubled Niger Delta."[1] Born in Kano, Nigeria, Nduka Otiono is an assistant professor at the Institute of African Studies, Carleton University. He was educated at the University of Ibadan and the University of Alberta, where he obtained his PhD in English and won numerous awards including the Izaak Walton Killam Memorial Scholarship, and was nominated for the Governor General's Gold Medal for academic distinction. During his time at the University of Alberta, Otiono used to enjoy the views from his favorite campus pub, Room at the Top: "I fell in love with RATT essentially because it was my aperture to the topography of Edmonton—the winding river, ravines, green zones that herald the downtown area, the creeks."[2]

Otiono went on to a postdoctoral fellowship at Brown University where he was also appointed a visiting assistant professor, and won a Banting Postdoctoral Fellowship to Carleton University. He is a two-time recipient of the Carnegie African Diaspora Fellowship (2015 and 2016), winner of a 2017 Carleton University Faculty of Arts and Social Science Early Career Research Excellence Award, and winner of a 2016 Capital Educators' award for excellence in teaching.

Prior to turning to a career in academia upon relocating to Canada in 2006, Otiono was a journalist and cultural activist in Nigeria and had published hundreds of stories on arts, culture, and political economy. He served as general secretary of the Association of Nigerian Authors (ANA); member of the National Committee for UNESCO's Intangible Cultural Heritage; and founding member of the Board of

---

1 Personal correspondence, August 2018.
2 Ibid.

the Nigeria Liquefied Natural Gas (NLNG)–sponsored $100,000 Nigerian Prize for Literature. A fellow of the William Joiner Centre for War and Social Consequences, University of Massachusetts, Boston, Otiono is the author of *The Night Hides with a Knife* (short stories), which won the ANA/Spectrum Prize; *Voices in the Rainbow* (poems), a finalist for the ANA/Cadbury Poetry Prize; *Love in a Time of Nightmares* (poems) for which he was awarded the James Patrick Folinsbee Memorial Scholarship in Creative Writing. He is the co-editor of *We-Men: An Anthology of Men Writing on Women* (1998), and *Camouflage: Best of Contemporary Writing from Nigeria* (2006).

Otiono's early years were marked by Nigeria's civil war and the challenges of internal migration with family from northern Nigeria to his hometown in midwestern Nigeria. The passion to write originated from an early exposure to oral narratives and English literature. His decision to focus on an interdisciplinary doctoral research on street stories and popular media at the University of Alberta was a progression of his early childhood experiences and work as a journalist. Alberta enchanted Otiono, who found its prairies ecoregion inspiring and suitable to his poetic sensibilities, much so that his collection of poems, *Love in a Time of Nightmares* grew out of his five-year sojourn in Edmonton.

The poem "Homeland Securities" looks to the tensions in the Niger Delta over oil exploration from the vantage point of Alberta's own petroculture, and the tension between profit and the environment. In "Archive Fever" and "University of Work" Otiono reflects on his graduate education, giving Jacques Derrida's notion of "archive fever" a satirical, post-colonial twist. The tradition he wrestles with in the archives is white, European, and American—not even Canadian—but as he notes in "University of Work," "I love my books [...] Inside them I'll live and die." Some of the Edmonton poems have been anthologized in *The Story That Brought Me Here: To Alberta from Everywhere* (2008) edited by Linda Goyette.

Homeland Securities

Security is morals' chiefest enemy.
—William Shakespeare

today a grey weather camouflages time
and i track the uneasy mangrove swamps
from the Garden City[3] where poisoned

---

3   Garden City is the nickname of Port Harcourt, the largest city of rivers State, Nigeria. It lies along the Bonny River and is located in the Niger Delta.

flowers transfigure into bullets and blood
to Buguma,[4] frightened by the frothing
waters as the speedboat churns its way and
the innocent water laughs with shy waves
oblivious of the fate that's befallen her.

i witness new pollutants thicken the sea
as a boil ripening, sack the fishermen
with their worn-out nets and perfume
the hooded creeks reeking of gunpowder
crystalline salt and suppliant hostages.
aerial roots of halophytic plants plead
for protection from the rippling, septic sea
as muse-ings over homeland securities
overwhelm me, lost in my mourning sickness.

it's dawn in the creeks and the fear of embittered
militants is the beginning of safety.
youths *immunized* against bullets by Egbesu,[5]
faces laced with ancient magical symbols,
chant subversive litanies and contest the feds'
control of Nature's honeyed gifts to them.
tenants in their homeland, you will not dare
stare at the amulets tied around their necks,
here's the new faces of homeland securities, rag-tag
citizens of a country sewn with fabrics borrowed
from ethnic nationalities like a coat of many colours.

---

4   A smaller town in Rivers State, southeast of Port Harcourt, also on the Bonny
River.
5   Egbesu is the Ijaw diety of warfare in the Niger Delta region. Since the 1990s, the
militant wing of the Ijaw Youth Council, known as Egbesu Boys, have been fighting against authorities in response to environmental and other problems caused by oil
exploitation and lack of investment of oil revenue in the local economy. Many young
men have joined the Egbesu boys, undergoing initiation rites, and wearing amulets
that impart the supernatural powers of Egbesu that members believe make them bulletproof (Andersson).

the boat cruises with my sailing thoughts as an odd
poem yearns to be written on the tablet of the mind.
i think of Odi[6] where there are no road signs
but ruthless graffiti in charcoal, chalk or etched with
some pin-point item by an insane army: "Weep not Odi,"
"The God almighty is the destroyer of any manmade god."
And laugh not or do so at your own peril: for you
will learn the meaning of homeland securities
under a leaking green-white-green[7]
          umbrella
                    in the gathering storm.

it's dawn in the creeks and news of another kidnap
floats through the cobwebbed airwaves as I track
the mangrove swamps from Garden City to Buguma.
"In the Niger Delta," says the newscaster,
"there's no security, only gangs, guns and oil."

Archive Fever

(for Jeannine Green and David Gay)

Chaucer didn't look happy when we visited.
He sat on a horse hemmed in between
Musty Ellesmere's covers, a tired pilgrim
Who had lost his honour.
He didn't know where he was either—
Inside the special collections section
Of Rutherford Library, calm as a cemetery.

---

6   Odi is a town in Bayelsa state, Nigeria. It was the site of a massacre against Ijaw
people, carried out on November 20, 1999, by the Nigerian military acting on the
orders of then-president Chief Olusegun Obasanjo. 2,500 Ijaw people were killed in
the attack, which was carried out by the government amid disputes over oil resources
control and environmental protection.
7   The flag of Nigeria has three vertical bands of green, white, green.

But he kept sparkling company, fellow
Tablebearers from the United Kingdom,
All part of a colonial bequest.
There was John Bunyan, lost in his pilgrim's progress.
Milton was there too, rediscovering his paradise lost.
Jane Austen glowed with feminist pride and prejudice,
Not persuaded by Emma and concerns for memory and
Time, nor by the temperaments of sense and sensibility.
She didn't seem to care about Cupid any more
And the nightmares that wrap love.
Oh, and there was William Wordsworth, romanticist
Trying to recollect emotions in tranquility.
"This is from Jonathan Wordsworth, the
literary executioner of Wordsworth's estate,"
says the librarian, passionate guardian of the archive.
Her eyes are apertures to the writer's lives.
Forever smiling, she maps the treasured walls
Between the pages like reels rolling.
Enter Shakespeare, so content with his stature
As a playwright he doesn't mind being called W.S.
So great he left poetry and name to honour Wordsworth.
King of the stage, he's magnificent in a fourth edition folio.
And the visitor's eyes widened with great expectations,
Smothered by a smoldering reputation
Shouldered by time, art, and fame.
Finally, there was Charles Dickens, vagrant of the city,
Master of romantic side of familiar things, staggering
with nineteen pamphlets of David Copperfield,
but with our mutual friend, Oliver Twist, nowhere in sight.
"Dickens was so fussy about his illustrations," says
the librarian, as if in an old curiosity shop.
In two months it will be Christmas, but there
was no time to contemplate a Christmas carol
as we left our enchanting new buddy,
bodies tempered by a new archive fever.
And someone remained to chat with Chaucer,
To confirm if his name really meant "shoemaker."

❦

University of Work

He crouches like the hunchback
In Arabian Night's entertainment
Each time he hauls onto his rear
His multicoloured rucksack
Filled with assignments
And heavy books
Full of arcane knowledge
And inanities of lonely authors.

Then he thinks of Rutherford[8]
Lost in tomes and stacked in bookcases
And remembers that wall gecko again
Hunting book worms
In the Presidential library at Aso Rock[9]—
These are times he sings:
"I love my books; I won't lie,
Inside them I'll live and die."

If he means it, I won't know,
But I'll never forget the times
He's whispered like a lunatic
Calling U of A "University of Work"
And blaming nature for his woes
Like the artist stuck in the attic
While hurricane Katrina
Swelled with livid waves.

---

8   Alexander Cameron Rutherford (b. Ontario, 1857–1941) was a lawyer and politician who served as the first premier of Alberta from 1905 to 1910. He went on to become chancellor of the University of Alberta, a university he helped to found. The University of Alberta's Rutherford library is named in his honour.

9   Aso Rock is a large outcropping of granite rock on the outskirts of the city of Abuja, the capital of Nigeria. The Nigerian Presidential Complex, including the presidential library, Nigerian National Assembly, and Supreme Court are located around it.

Back in his room on Monday nights,
He'll tarry in front of his broken mirror
Staring at his hair greying like old Papa's
And his hairline receding strand by strand.
Then he'll curse the poet who sang:
"I'll follow knowledge like a sinking star
Beyond the utmost bounds of human thought ..."[10]

For each grey hair,
He remembers a book
Buried in his memory
Like coins in the vault of a bank,
Or details in books of history—
These are times he would sing:
"I love my books; I won't lie,
Inside them I'll live and die."

---

10 Alfred Lord Tennyson's "Ulysses."

Sheila Addiscott
(1964–)

Sheila Addiscott is a journalist and editor living in Calgary, Alberta. She identifies as mixed-race, having an Irish mother and a Mauritian father. She immigrated from London, England, to Calgary in 1974 and grew up in the Forest Lawn neighbourhood in the southeast quadrant of the city. She reflects, "Forest Lawn was an affordable neighbourhood that attracted immigrant families, but at that time they came mostly from predominately white countries from Europe. My brother and I, our brown skin, in a way made us a different kind of pioneer."[1] She recalls that she was often the first person of colour that Calgarians would meet and speak to. At the time, she says she "was a shy, awkward teenage girl, struggling to fit in and to acknowledge and accept her own skin colour. I was on their side; I didn't like me either."

Addiscott spent fourteen years living in the UK, and lived also for a time on Vancouver Island, British Columbia, but ultimately returned to Calgary, where she is interim director of Kerby News. Addiscott reflects that in the decades that have passed, "much has changed; Calgary and I have both grown up. There were only 6 or 7 people in my graduating class that were not white. Looking around Calgary today, that is very hard to believe. There are mixed race couples and children everywhere, including my own and I am finally comfortable in my own skin."[2]

In her personal essay "Coloured," Addiscott confides to the reader her thoughts, desires, and memories of racial abuse experienced in Calgary. Although factual, the personal essay feels like a short story with a narrative arc. It relays how the shifting demographics on the prairies also shifted Addiscott's own sense of self and belonging. It was originally published in *Other Tongues: Mixed-Race Women Speak Out*, edited by Adebe DeRango-Adem and Andrea Thompson (2010). In addition to her published journalism, Addiscott is the author of an unpublished

---

1 Personal correspondence, December 10, 2018.
2 Ibid.

children's novel, *The Qualicum Witches*, about four sisters who immigrate to Canada and slowly discover that they have special magic drawn from nature. She is currently in search of a publisher.

Coloured

When I was nine my parents decided to immigrate to Canada. My step-father's brother was a doctor in Alberta and he sponsored us to come over. We arrived in Canada at night in August, 1974. My stepfather, who had arrived before us, picked us up and drove us to a rectangular two-story building that had two balconies on the front. An outside light illuminated the green front lawn. I now had a lawn. It took a month of school to dispel the illusion.

We had moved into the basement suite of a four-plex. I didn't care, we had grass and, after living in a London tower block, I loved it. The novelty of my English accent quickly wore off on the other kids at school, especially when they found out where we lived. Most of their families owned their own homes and were living on a poor street in a poor area. Like most immigrants we owned next to nothing.

It's not that there weren't friends or acts of kindness by many people, it is just that as human beings we are more easily shaped by our negative experiences. Our survival instinct means that we are influenced more easily by the bad things that happen to us than by all the good things put together.

When do we first realize that skin has a colour? It happened to me when I was four years old playing on the swings with my brother. It was summer and the city playground was busy. Moms sat talking on benches, it's easy to make friends, to strike up a conversation with strangers when you have children in common. It was hot and I was thirsty so I ran up to my mother who was sitting and chatting to one of these playground acquaintances.

"Mom, I'm thirsty," I said. She gave me that look.

"Sorry. Please may I have a drink?"

Manners were important. You got into big trouble for not remembering your manners, especially in front of strangers. The woman got up and looked me up and down, appalled, and almost spat the words: "She's colored" at my mother and then walked away. It was an era when white women like my mother were just not expected to have brown skinned children. I did not know my father, and it was the first time I realized my mother and I were different. When I went to school I got called nigger, coloured, and half-breed. By the time I was seven, every wish on my birthday cake candles or falling star, was for white skin and pale-coloured eyes. It seemed to me an unfair act of fate that I didn't look like my mother who is translucent pale Irish white with green eyes and red hair. I don't look a thing like her, except for her freckles. Both my brother and I have bands of them across our noses and cheeks, incongruous on our brown skin. We got lucky, my mother is so covered in freckles that I used to tease her that she had brown skin with white spots.

My mother's words to describe my brother and me were "half-caste" and "coloured." She tried to comfort me by telling me that I was half white and that made me as white as the next person. She never tried to comfort me with the fact that I was nearly black. She had the prejudices of her time and yet she stepped away from them to love my father. I grew up angry at my mother for choosing my father. There were so many white men, why did she have to choose him? She was living in London, England in an age where people still put signs on doors that said "No Blacks, No Irish." I was both.

History looks back at the "permissive" sixties, but forgets that it wasn't so permissive between the races. She loved my father so much she would have done anything for him, and she did. She had two children out of wedlock, a second sin. My father was a nurse from Mauritius, a small country in the middle of the Indian Ocean that most people have never heard of. He had dark brown skin, brown eyes and his thick, curly black hair was just like mine. He was the oldest of seven children and he shouldered the responsibility of setting a good example for his siblings, of taking care of his relatives, and adhering to their strict Hindu customs.

My mother was born and raised in a small village in County Claire, Ireland. She saw enough Catholic hypocrisy and alcoholism to swear her off Irish men, alcohol and religion for the rest of her life. Perhaps she rebelled in her own way by falling in love with my father. He left her when she was eight months pregnant with my brother and I was thirteen months old. I never met him. When he left, he destroyed their letters and pictures, all evidence they had ever been together. I have one picture of my father taken with a group of other staff members at the hospital where he worked. I look like him, my brother looks a lot like him, but both of our skins are a milked down version of his darker brown skin.

My mother married my stepfather when I was six. For years she wouldn't say why, though when pushed she would say it was a love match. I thought it was a colour match. I believed she felt that after my father left, my step-father's brown skin would hide her mistake of not being married to our father and validate our existence in the eyes of the world. Because from the day they got married she told me that we were now half Pakistani and half Irish, and that is what she told the world. It was the first time that lie was told, but not the last. Years later I was finally brave enough to ask her about it, and the truth was so much better and so much worse. My mother did marry my stepfather because he was the right colour, but not for the reasons I had thought all those years. It was because she wanted to keep us safe, as she was scared that a white man would be cruel to us because we were brown. I never doubted my mother's love for us growing up, and this admission humbled me. What a huge sacrifice she made for us.

I may not have looked white, but I wasn't black enough to be black either. I went to a Catholic convent day school in London until I was nine. Half of the students were black, the rest white. The only two exceptions to this were my brother and me, who were mixed race. My father's Muslim culture was more alien to me still than anything I had experienced so far. I felt more at home with the black and white kids in my school who at least spoke with the same East London cockney accent that I did, than with the various Pakistani "cousins" that came to the house. My stepfather's presence in my life made me feel even more alienated from the world, another sign that I didn't belong anywhere.

My being mixed race was more revolting to some than if I had been all black. As a young girl I sat across from an educated white man in Alberta, while he told me what my parents did was wrong and that I was a freak of nature. Like a donkey and a horse mating. I should be a "sterile" mule. Other people also told me that the races shouldn't intermarry because their children look wrong. The thing about being of mixed race is that there are plenty of ways for people to hate you. Most people can't tell what mix you are, all they notice is the colour of your skin. So if they happen to hate Mexicans, First Nations, Pakistanis, or any race that has brown skin, there is a good chance their prejudice will extend to include you.

My mother worked hard and kept her head down. She believed that as long as we didn't get above ourselves, we would be fine. She was of a generation that deferred to educated people, doctors, teachers, and policemen. She knew she wasn't as good as them, the problem was that she also deferred to everybody else. She would walk away from rudeness and prejudice, and her advice to us was the same. Don't talk back, ignore them, and walk away.

I walked home from school with my head down; I spoke as little as possible. But inside I was filled with anger because I just wanted to be ordinary. I wanted to belong, to fit in somewhere. Coming to Alberta had just added other layers of difference. I was now a foreigner and immigrant as well as mixed race. No one spoke like I did. I could not swim, ice skate, or ski. In an inner city London school that doesn't matter, nobody else can either. In Calgary, to me, all the kids seemed rich and able and white. I was the only brown child in my grade five class and suddenly there were no black kids. I saw my first black children, two boys, in junior school. That was the prairies.

Some of the kids didn't even learn racism until they met me. I was the first brown person that they'd met and it didn't matter to them that I was half anything, only that I wasn't all white. Mostly I was called paki, sometimes nigger, with the added new insult of being told to go home, back to where I belong. I had no idea where that was. There was little physical violence; bullies didn't need it. We were already intimidated. My mother said sticks and stones will break my bones but names will never hurt me. She was so wrong. It was the taunts, the name-calling that did the real damage.

I remember the day I raised my head and realized that times were changing. I was fifteen, all legs and long curly black hair. A boy who had called me names when we were children whistled at me from across the street. He knew who I was and he catcalled me not paki or nigger, but "Hawaiian princess." It didn't make me feel better about myself, it just added another layer. Now I also learned bitterness.

I couldn't wait to leave the strict Muslim household of my stepfather and I moved out on my sixteenth birthday, the first day I was legally allowed to leave my parents. My stepfather didn't talk to me for the next three years.

Over the years we had been in Canada, ethnic minorities had immigrated to Calgary by the thousands, and people intermarried; I was a visible minority no more. By the time I graduated high school, nobody was calling me names anymore. As I went on to work and university, it has seemed to me that the only one who knows that I am mixed race, that my skin is different anymore, that it isn't white or black, is me.

Western Canada grew up and so did I. There wasn't a single watershed moment, no sudden light bulb of understanding. The anger and resentment that had been so much of my life growing up and had shaped me simply dissipated over the years. I grew up and travelled, got married and had children. Surprisingly to me, my husband is white. He has blond hair and pale blue eyes. We have six children, and only one of them has my brown skin, my oldest. When she was three years old I told her that she was mixed race, that she had brown skin. A leftover from my own childhood, it was important to me that I was the one to tell her that skin has a colour so that she would feel proud and not shame.

I have experienced only one act of racism in Canada in recent years, and it wasn't even addressed to me, it was to my husband. He was at a business meeting and an older man came up to him and said, "I hear you have six kids, that's great, we need big families."

"Thank you," he replied.

"It's good that you're keeping the Aryan gene going," the man said.

My husband was taken aback for a moment, then said: "My wife is black. I look forward to more mixed families so people don't have the excuse to discriminate based on race or colour." And he walked away. I was so surprised to encounter such outspoken racism again. It has become so rare in my life that he seemed like a dinosaur out of time, out of place.

I recently went to Vancouver on a school trip to soak up the Olympic experience with daughter number three. There were people of all nationalities walking in the streets, and I noticed a lot of mixed-race children. Hopefully the identity that they feel the most is Canadian and skin colour isn't a part of it.

Do I feel Canadian? I grew up eating white bread, wearing clothes from Sears and watching the same movies and TV shows as the kids I went to school with. My mother still tries to convince me I am as Irish as my red-haired, green-eyed cousins. She taught me to be Irish but I have never felt it. I know nothing about being Mauritian either. I am something new. Canada has given me a place where I can belong, where the definition of "Canadian" includes people like me.

I grew up feeling like I didn't belong anywhere, but when I became an adult I realized an important truth. It isn't that I don't belong anywhere, but perhaps quite the opposite. I belong everywhere. Rather than being scared or intimidated anymore, I feel comfortable sitting with all people no matter their skin colour or culture. Being mixed race, has instead, given me a passport to move comfortably among different kinds of people, and find that I have something in common with many of them.

When I was a child I used to be terrified of South Africa. I saw the signs on the television news, "Blacks," "Whites," and "Coloureds." I worried so much that their ways would spread and the rest of the world would have signs like that too, that I wouldn't be able to be with my mom. So much in the world has changed from my childhood. From Nelson Mandela and the end of apartheid to Barack Obama becoming President of the United States. I am not American, yet I cried when he was inaugurated. A mixed-race person proved to me how much the world is changing. I hear people say that because Barack Obama is mixed race he can represent both white and black perspectives. It is our actions, what we do, what he can do, that will count.

Being mixed race still shapes me. I will always feel labelled. However, I am comfortable in my own skin and the ghosts of my childhood are just that, ghosts. When people ask my ethnic background I describe myself as mixed race, because I am comfortable with that tag. I don't want to be called half-caste and definitely not half-breed and with all respect to the NAACP, don't call me coloured.

Suzette Mayr
(1967–)

Asked in a recent interview what view she prefers when she writes—mountain, European plaza, blank wall, or the sea—Mayr chooses the one she sees as the closest to the prairie. "The sea is flat and plain and is all about possibility because pretty much anything can come charging at you over that horizon. I'm from the prairies. The drive between Calgary and Winnipeg is the best. Flatness is where it's at" (*CBC Books* 2017). Mayr's statement about the ways the prairie landscape holds in tension the ordinary and the possibility for surprise is also an apt summation of her own narrative style. Mayr's magical realism, the signature genre of her five published novels, offers her characters—often racialized and queer—both ordinariness and the possibility of surprise transformation. The effect is a style of characterization that is often funny, poignant, and deeply humanizing.

A poet, novelist, and professor of creative writing, Suzette Mayr was born and raised in Calgary. Her mother immigrated from Nassau, Bahamas, in the mid-1960s; her father is likewise an immigrant from Germany. Her interest in magical realism developed at an early age. She grew up in a household with books, and was encouraged by her parents to read widely. "We knew about Greek myths the way other children know about fairy tales. I was always fascinated by the transformation stories and the interspecies stories" (*Why We Write* 169). When she started writing in the late 1980s and early 1990s, the works of Toni Morrison, Gabriel Garcia Marquez, and Isabel Allende were an influence. "[T]he possibility magic realism presented for me as a writer to write about my own reality as a queer, biracial person in ways that were unique and made sense to me [...] Saying the unsayable is what I endeavor to do, and the weird and fantastic are the languages that work for this" (Grubisic).

Although she entered the University of Calgary planning to pursue a science degree, a creative writing course with Chris Wiseman changed her focus to English and inspired her to pursue a career as a writer. She graduated with an honours bachelor's degree in English in 1990, and she went on to earn a master's degree in creative writing from the University of Alberta in 1993.

Her first three collections of poetry, *Zebra Talk* (disOrietation Chapbooks, 1991), *Chimaera Lips* (University of Calgary Master's thesis 1992), and *Tale* (an illustrated story co-written with Geoffrey Hunter and Robin Arsenaeult, 2001) explore the in-between spaces of human and animal, male and female, as well as racial identifications and queer desire.

Her 1995 novel, *Moon Honey*, a funny and satirical tale about mixed race, physical transformation, and the limits of heterosexual marriage, brought Mayr popular and critical attention; it was nominated for the Georges Bugnet Award for Best Novel and the Henry Kreisel Award for Best First Book.

Mayr followed up her first novel with an unexpected second book about elderly German-Canadian characters, their sexual desires, and zest for adventure. *The Widows* (NeWest Press 1998) pushes back against expectations that black writers should write only (or even mostly) about black characters. *The Widows* was nominated for the Commonwealth Prize for Best Book in the Canada-Caribbean Region, and has been translated into German.

With her third novel, *Venous Hum* (Arsenal Pulp 2004), Mayr delved into the genre of horror to further explore the politics of place and race. As with her magic realism, Mayr in this novel uses horror as a mode of satire. "Scariness does not come from a big monster that lumbers into the room and kills you," she says. "Scariness comes from something which is slightly off. I think that's what horror is all about—taking the normal and cranking it a bit to the left. I think satire is sort of the same thing" ("Why Suzette Mayr" 2018). The novel represents vampires, cannibals, and the undead to intensify her critique of Canadians' fear of racial contamination. It was nominated for the ReLit Award.

Mayr's critically acclaimed fourth novel, *Monoceros* (Coach House Books 2011) garnered, as she says, "a lot more attention than I was used to." It is a tragicomic treatment of the after-effects of the suicide of a seventeen-year-old boy in the context of a repressive Catholic high school. It is a beautiful, deeply affecting, and unexpectedly joyful novel about high school bullying, institutionalized homophobia, and the possibilities of personal and communal transcendence. Mayr's eclectic cast of characters includes unicorns, Wonder Woman, and drag queens. It won both the 2012 ReLit Award and the City of Calgary W.O. Mitchell Award, was longlisted for the 2011 Scotiabank Giller Prize, and was also included on the *Globe and Mail*'s 100 Best Books of 2011. A new Canadian musical based on the book is currently being developed by the Musical Stage Company.

Mayr's fifth novel, *Dr. Edith Vane and the Hares of Crawley Hall* (Coach House Books 2017), in the genre of the campus novel, is a humorous and cathartic satire of campus life. The novel's central character is a stressed-out English professor whose work, which focuses on the life of a black prairie pioneer, takes decades to come to fruition, and so puts her job at risk. Mayr's novel is frequently laugh-out-loud funny but holds serious lessons about the risks involved in producing knowledge within the structures of institutions that continue to be animated by their anti-black, homophobic, and patriarchal histories, and which are ever more invested in instrumentalizing knowledge for profit.

In addition to her creative work, Mayr has co-edited, with Julia Gaunce, the *Broadview Anthology of Short Fiction* (2004). She is an associate professor at the University of Calgary, where she teaches creative writing and contemporary litera-ture. Mayr lives in Calgary with her partner Tonya Callaghan.

Monoceros

Monday

The End

Because *u r a fag* is scrawled in black Jiffy marker across his locker.

Because after school last Thursday, the girlfriend of the guy he loves hurled frozen dog shit at him, and her friends frisbeed his skateboard into the river. Even though he stomped and cracked through the ice shelving the banks, waded in to rescue it—after the shouting and shoving, they're stronger than they look, all those girls with their cello- and violin-playing fingers, yanking him back by handfuls of coat, handfuls of hair, hooking with their elbows and digging with their fingernails as he scrambled after his skateboard—the banks too slippery and shattered with ice, the current too swift, the water too cold and deep and brown. Freezing river water up to his chest, the water and ice shards wicking into his armpits, scratching his heart. His black coat wet and sucking him down into the current. His skateboard buried in the river.

Because the Tuesday before that horrible Thursday, the guy he loves gave him a kiss so electric electrons shot into his penis, his toes, it was like he dis-covered Planet X, and he ejaculated into his pants, luckily they were black, luckily it was dark outside, luckily when he got home his mother was squeal-ing into the phone about how she wanted to replace the new stone kitchen counter with a new, stonier kitchen counter, and his father's face flickered blue before the TV, mouth open and tongue like a leftover slice of roast beef drying out with snoring, his arm triangled behind his head.

Because in a text the girlfriend of the guy he loves said, *we're going 2 kill you.* Because she knew he lived at 2279 Moth Hill Crescent SW; knew that when he wasn't in school he was playing *World of Warcraft* or the faggy JRPG *Divinity XII* with his imaginary, online, why-not-just-buy-a-blow-up-doll loser friends; knew Monday nights he watched his favourite TV show, *Sector Six;* knew that every Tuesday, Thursday and Saturday, like a wobbly-assed soccer mom trapped in a dead marriage, he ordered a large iced cappuccino from the drive-thru at the Tim Horton's on 12th Avenue; knew that anytime he could, weekends and weekdays, nighttime and daytime, he'd yank it in his cubby-hole bedroom, splattering himself like the *devient* he was because he was a loser with no friends *n thts Y u deserve 2 di u FKng fag cocksucka fuckface royal sht eater.* In the text, she has almost all of his days right, except for two things she'll never know: 1. he's not watching *Sector Six*—they're all reruns in February, and 2. one or two pockets of time he's on secret dates hooking up with her boyfriend when she and her foot soldiers have their junior serial-killer cadet training classes. Lucky him. And the spelling is *deviAnt*, not *deviEnt.* Though it still means he's a dead boy.

Because that last glorious Tuesday, Ginger, the guy he loves, met him at their special place in the cemetery, halfway between their houses. Their breaths misted in the cold air, little white ghosts dissipating in the light of the tall lamps that lined the graveyard, the ache evaporating when they finally touched, their lips colliding, eating, so much time had drained away since they last met. The dead boy pulled away, burrowed into the front of his shirt and brought out a heart-shaped locket in a pool of gold chain, the dead boy smiling so hard his face nearly cracked heart-like in two, the metal heart a hot star in his icy hand.

—I'm wearing it this time, said the dead boy. —See? I haven't lost it.

—You lose it and my granny's ghost will haunt you forever, said Ginger, and he laid a hand overtop the locket, over the dead boy's hand, pushing against the dead boy's chest. Kissed him again, bit the dead boy's bottom lip. Ginger wearing layers, a blue sweater on top of a striped T-shirt on top of a long-sleeved white shirt; all the layers still showing off his flat, gorgeous abs, the smooth mounds of his pecs. The soon-to-be-dead boy, smiling, clicked open the heart, snap.

—When will you give me your picture for it? asked the dead boy.

—You crazy? asked Ginger, his eyes darting over the graves, his mouth blowing on his cold hands, on the dead boy's. —What if you lose it? Anyways, you don't need a picture, we can see each other in the halls. But see the rose engraved on the front? It's red. Red means love.

—No it's not, said the dead boy. —The heart's the same gold metal as the chain. It's red because you say it's red? Are you on crack? The dead boy laughed, his voice erupting in the marble and granite forest.

—Yeah, it's red. I am telling you it's red.

—So love is red, said the dead boy. —Then why can't you red me at school?

—That's stupid, said Ginger.

Layers peeled and discarded, Ginger's and the dead boy's lips and tongues and bodies fitting puzzle piece into puzzle piece, skins moulted in the dead grass, the gold locket pressing skin into skin.

The dead boy and Ginger fumbled their clothes back on in the dark, chilled their bodies dizzy as newborn kittens, Ginger hurrying into his jacket, the dead boy pulling on Ginger's sweater, then his own long coat, the smell of Ginger knitted to his skin.

Now Monday. Because today, nearly a week since that starlit Tuesday, the dead boy doesn't want to leave his house because Ginger will still be cold to him like he always is in the days right after hooking up in the cemetery, because he doesn't want to leave his house in case today is the day the girlfriend and her hive finally kill him. His mother gnaws at him with her mandibles to hurry up, —The sun doesn't beam out of your bum even though *you* seem to think so, she says, and she gulps a spoonful of bran flakes.

He hates the way his mother says *bum* like he's a kid, like he doesn't know what you can use it for. He crunches his cereal, one sugary shamrock, one star, one diamond, one Lucky Charm at a time, and listens to his parents drink their orange juice, their swallows loud and revolting, watches his mother X-ray the Monday morning paper, sometimes her lips moving, the heart-shaped locket swinging on the outside of his three T-shirts and a blue argyle sweater, where she can see it, where his father sloshing his coffee into a travel mug can see it. He watches his parents not watch him, drive away in their separate, oversize pollution machines. His father slinging a briefcase stitched together from an endangered species, his mother meandering out to buy hunks of dead animal for supper before barricading herself with paint, paintbrushes and canvases big as sails, small as stamps, in her studio in her fashionable yoga pants, made by tiny brown children for less than a nickel a day.

Because the Friday right after the horrific Thursday, he fought to see the principal to tell him about his skateboard thrown in the river. The dead boy had to scramble up the fortress wall of secretaries and vice-principals. The principal straightened his tie, rolled forward his chair, jingled the keys in his pocket, said, —If they purloined your skateboard when you were all off school property, there's nothing I can do. That would be more of a matter for the police. The principal clearing his throat emphatically to indicate the matter was Closed.

Because the dead boy ran into his English teacher at the Pita Pit after talking to the principal, in her black clothes punctuated with her own white, chalky handprints, her face splotchy white and pink. The only teacher who ever says anything like, —That attitude smells worse than poo, when someone says *The Glass Menagerie*'s a gay play. He told her about the principal, and she said, —He really said that to you? You've got to get out of this deadbeat school.

Her eyelids and pinked lips twitched.

Because the dead boy and Ginger wrestled into scorching sex in the dead grass, hot enough to start a grass fire, their bodies flaring in the dark, in the middle of a February chinook, the smell of chinook wind and Ginger in his nose, Bed Head shampoo, blue wool sweater the dead boy pulled up over Ginger's head, Ginger's sweaty silky ribcage, flowery fabric softener from all six of their shirts, Ginger's tongue pushing bright as a meteor into the dead boy's, Ginger's nipples, the warm salt of him, behind a tombstone that said, *Lél Somogyi Gone But Never Forgotten 1987–2004*. Ginger's torso naked and slick, dead grass and twigs sticking to his skin. After-ward, the dead boy accidentally on purpose pulling over his head Ginger's blue sweater in the dark, and Ginger was so sweaty and hot he forgot the sweater, tugging on his other shirts and his jacket in a rush because he was late for home. The next morning in the hallway, Ginger's fingers sticking in his girlfriend's tangled hair, stroking, while they prodded their way through the waves of students pushing, bumping, and clanging lockers around them, the dead boy wading toward them as though by pure cosmic coincidence, Ginger hovering over a tangle in his girlfriend's hair, and not catching the dead boy's eye, not for a second even though they had agreed last week that occasional eye contact was not completely verboten, they could kiss and fuck with their eyes, no one could tell if they just fucked with their eyes. Ginger's irises radiating aurora borealis from Hershey Kiss brown into caterpillar green, a hazel colour meant for kissing. Their bodies' protons and electrons zinging across the shortening space between them; Ginger staring at the top of his girlfriend's head. The dead boy and Ginger, each of them a sun, each of them a planet in orbital thrall to a sun, the dead boy hugging himself, suddenly cold, in Ginger's blue knit sweater. The body slam of Ginger twisting away from the dead boy, not a single eyekiss, like the dead boy was already dead. Though not a surprise: Ginger frozen subzero like he always was in the days following a cemetery date.

Because on Friday, Valentine's Day, an envelope with the dead boy's name on it was slipped into his locker, just a corner of it peeping out from the metal crack between the locker's metal frame and the locker door, and when he pulled it out and ripped it open starting at the crumpled corner, he found a card—a painting of a bowl of fruit, circled by a ballpoint-pen heart. Inside, scrawled in more ballpoint, *Happy Valentine's Day Faggot. Love, G.* Calling him *faggot* was Ginger's idea of a joke. An exhausted, pathetic joke.

Because Ginger's girlfriend hissed at him, she is such a dyke-in-training and she doesn't even know it, so he hissed back and he was doomed. Once, a long time ago, he overheard her playing a waltz on the piano in the band room. He had to fight not to cry, the song tugged at him so.

Because he scraped himself down the crowded walls of the cafeteria, past a jughead accompanied by a jughead parasite who said, —Out of my way, homo, as they chewed their way into the middle of the cafeteria lineup.

Because on his walk to school this morning—he's a dead man—a cat pads across the dead boy's path with a grey and yellow bird in its mouth, stepping into human boot steps pressed into the ice and snow, neat, like a dog carrying a newspaper.

Because today, tromping his way to school through mushy cigarette butts, a lost comb in the muck, waiting at this intersection as the cars slop by exhaling exhaust that burns his eyes, his phone chirps, Ginger: *i cant hang out wit u any more this time its 4 real ... I want my locket back*

Ginger will never change.

Because the crosswalk light shines its red eye, refuses to blink into green, cars spitting gravelly snow, one slap to his face after another on this Monday that refuses to start and refuses to end, he has to stand and stand, waiting for the light beside the brick wall spray-painted *Ava is a muff muncher.* Ginger wants the locket back, the only thing Ginger's ever given him, the only thing that keeps the dead boy going through all the days of Ginger pretending he doesn't exist. Monday. He can't bear it. He turns and tromps back home, ignoring cars, his frozen rubber soles scuffing iced concrete. The wind slathering cold, his exposed throat, the locket a hunk of metal pounding against his sternum, the chain winding winding round his neck.

Because he can't bear it.

He can't bear any of it. It will never get better.

Because he wants to be in charge of his own ending.

✹

Dr. Edith Vane and the Hares of Crawley Hall

Her heart flutters, like the pages of a discarded paperback. It took her nine-teen years to write *Taber Corn Follies: The Western Canadian Life Story of Beulah Crump-Withers*, soon to be published by University of Okotoks Press, a William Kurelek prairie painting reproduction on the cover. Twelve years as a PhD student, seven as a professor, and just in time for this year's Academic Achievement Overview. This giant diamond that will sit in the platinum, Times New Roman setting of her AAO. The pages being folded and glued likely at this very second on a massive printing press. She can't wait for the buzz of the intercom in her condominium lobby, the mail carrier in his or her smart uniform asking her to sign for the cardboard package, her slicing open the package to copies of her very own book with her very own name on it, the pages smelling of coastal forest and binding glue, the covers shiny and perfect, then moistened with her tears of elation and success. Her discovery and revival of the lost work of Beulah Crump-With-ers, former sporting girl, then housewife, prairie poet, maven memoirist, and all-round African-Canadian *literary genius*, finally complete.

She hugs the new clothes to her chest. *Beulah.*

The cardigan will drape long, like a cape with sleeves. An *author's* cardigan.

Edith wonders if maybe she could somehow reboot her washing machine by unplugging it, then plugging it back in? If she runs a cycle without detergent or clothes, just hot water, maybe the machine will resurrect and return to her? She strokes the new clothes in her arms, their uncomplicated cleanness. It's too bad she can't phone Coral for washing machine repair advice. Coral would know.

The professor from Drama and Philosophy left the store almost forty-eight minutes ago, and Edith has no idea what she bought, but she esti-mates that all the other female professors who have published books wear long cardigans like this, or unstructured blazers that drop past the hips, or skirts that fall below the knee. Patterned blouses. She has never man-aged to dress au courant. She imagines she would be happier in the 1920s housewife clothes Beulah wore. Dresses recycled from sturdy, sprightly patterned flour sacks. A single, Sunday-best dress for special occasions. Her outfits always morph into ill-fitting costumes once she rolls her car up to the university campus, sits through meetings, pontificates in classrooms. But this year will be different. This year she will look like everyone else. With a book, she will *be* like everyone else. And finally Beulah will get her due and eventually settle into her place in the Canadian literary canon. This year will be perfect.

She tugs a credit card from her wallet, deposits the ironed folds on the counter, their buttons ticking on the glass. Her watch bangs the glass too: 3:03 p.m. This afternoon is drifting away from her.

A pair of fake pearl earrings, each pearl the size of a knuckle, perches on an oily faux-satin ball under the glass of the counter.

—I'll need those too, she says. She taps her credit card on the glass. — And this scarf. Please.

She twitches a scarf from a stand on the counter, it waterfalls into her hands. She smiles at the clerk. The clerk shows Edith her teeth.

She could perhaps wear the scarf, an airy tulle thing with harlequin diamonds, around her neck. The pattern moves her, the cloudiness. But she never wears scarves. At best she might twirl around with it exactly once in her bedroom, pretending she's Josephine Baker. But then it will likely just go in a drawer. Or she'll tie it around the handle of the small suitcase she takes to conferences.

She needs the proper clothes to start the academic new year right. Her new psychologist told her to try it. —They don't call it *retail therapy* for nothing, said Vivianne. —Back to school shopping isn't just beneficial for children, she said, her voice rich and nutritious as an avocado on the other end of the line.

Edith has never met Vivianne in person, but she imagines her as an older black woman, with elaborate gray braids, round and wise as a fir tree. An older version of Beulah, but contemporary. Silver drop earrings. Or old Roman coins. A stuffed owl on a perch in the background.

Edith will continue filling out her Academic Achievement Overview and finish her third course outline tonight. Also write the first draft of an abstract for a conference she should attend next year.

Next Edith will buy shoes from Hangaku even though they don't look that comfortable, verging on too architectural for human feet. All the fashionable female professors wear Hangakus. The distinctive hourglass-shaped heels. Edith learned about them last year when she finally broke down and asked a history professor in line at the IT help desk what they were. She scribbled the name down on the edge of a student's essay, ripped the corner off the paper, and stuck it with a magnet to the fridge.

—Clothing is how you want the world to see you, said Vivianne. —See *me*, your clothes say. Look at who *I* am.

Edith will tighten up her marshmallow body, too; she's signed up for a Wednesday night Ballet for Beginners class at a ballet studio near her house, and she will do some kind of exercise at least once a week. Vivianne suggested she try a scheduled, regular fitness class to encourage her to balance her work and life. When Edith told Vivianne she enrolled in a hatha yoga class some years ago, bought a mat and everything, but thought it made her too twitchy and worried about inadvertently farting, Vivianne told her to try a class that didn't seem like exercise and didn't happen in a gym. Like ballet class with the Inivea City Ballet Company. Or scuba diving.

Edith said, —I like watching ballet. I like to swim.

Vivianne said, —Excellent! So swim your heart out. The negative ions in the water will stimulate your happiness centre. The University of Inivea has an Olympic-calibre swimming pool, so you could slip in a swim before or after your day.

—But there's never any time.

Vivianne cleared her throat, turned pages. No doubt in a notebook she uses to write down assessments of her patients. No doubt Vivianne's fingers starred with silver rings and turquoise rectangles. A hippie earth goddess with multiple PhDs who begins each morning with a hundred fervent sun salutations.

—There's time for anything if you *make* time, said Vivianne. —Time is an illusion. Think about the metaphors. Time spent, lost, wasted, behind the times, passing, keeping time. Time being made. What's something you like to make, Edith?

—I like to ... when I was a teenager I used to like making ... matrimonial squares.

—Make your time the way you would make matrimonial squares. Time is your tool. Delicious.

—Time is my tool, Edith repeated. —Delicious.

—Time doesn't own you. You own time.

—I own time.

—Yes!

—Yes.

—Make the time. Eat the time.

—Make the time. Eat the time … like matrimonial squares.

—You own yourself.

—I own myself.

Once upon a time, Edith's PhD supervisor, Lesley Hughes, said, *I own you.* But that was a long time ago. And of course Lesley lied. Edith blots out the thought.

Vivianne always told Edith to forget about Lesley. Edith would fret about Lesley becoming an Endowed Chair at the university, worrying about how she would cope with being in the same room, the same building, as Lesley, day after day.

—That's a history best left interred, Vivianne's voice would cluck from the phone.—Move on with your life. Let Lesley move on with hers. You are a *Philosophiae Doctor.* You have tenure. You are not her puppet. She is not your puppet master. Bulldoze away that room. There. We've bulldozed it.

In her brand-new Hangakus with their hourglass heels, Edith stilt-walks past the Victorian lotion and the caramel corn shops without stopping, wobbles past the escalator leading up to the rows and boring rows of white and stainless steel refrigerators, dishwashers, washing machines and dryers, her hands swinging a cloth bag with its P.T. Madden logo, another bag with the Hangaku brand swirl holding her old loafers, her wrists smelling like imaginary gardens. She bought a bottle of the perfume that smells like vanilla pudding too, so her neck smells new. She attempts to stride, swinging her bags, like a proud professor, about to swing into a new academic year. Bold, brilliant, and fresh as a girl in a tampon commercial.

The shoes still stiff, she admits, the odd heels like walking with spurs. But all shoes need some breaking in, right?

She piles her bags into the Taurus.

Riding a wave of self-congratulation, she tops up the gas tank at the Novacrest station at the east end of the mall parking lot, the clicks of the litre indicator matching the clicks of happy retail-therapy self-righteousness. Her credit card bloats just a little bit.

She revs around the concrete silos of the shopping centre parking lot to the ramp leading onto the highway, her right Hangaku heel digging in, her car bullying its way into belligerent traffic. She motors past the campus, past Crawley Hall, barely registering its brutalist gloom. She drives five more minutes, then clicks to turn left toward the thicket of brand-new condominiums where she lives.

On her quilted bedspread at home, the P.T. Madden bag crinkles as she slides out the clothes in their tissue paper envelopes. She unfolds the first envelope. She holds the navy-blue flowers up to the fading afternoon light through the window.

Sweet william. Or … lobelias.

She peels off the P.T. Madden sticker on the second envelope. Black sweet williams or lobelias.

The third envelope. Olive-green lobelias or sweet williams.

She slides her hands into the armholes of the navy-blue blouse. Buttons it closed one by one from her throat to her lower belly. The mirrored closet door reflects the petals back at her. She smooths her hands down the sides. Strange little florets. No one will pierce this armour.

Not Lesley, her old supervisor.

Not even Coral. Her former, now returning, colleague. Her sometime ex-inamorata. Her *friend*.

Whom Vivianne told her to stay away from. —Sometimes, Vivianne told her, her earrings tinkling, —sometimes too much passion is not good for a person. Occasionally, said Vivianne, —in certain circumstances, a person's unchecked imagination, her misdirected intelligence as it were, can lead her on a journey into an unhealthy place.

—But then maybe I should try to help her?

—Or you could just stay away from her, said Vivianne, sounding like she was smacking her lips. —Not let her speculations and imaginings splash onto you and distract you, jeopardize your reputation as a scholar heading into mid-career under a newer, more energized headship. This next round of your Academic Achievement Overview. You're not … ah … the most prolific academic, Edith.

Edith's right eyelid had twitched so hard she'd clapped her hand to her eye. The eyelid bucked twice again under her fingers. Vivianne paused.

—You have a book coming out soon, and kudos for that. But you can't afford distractions. So that means you have to excel at many things, which you certainly do, I assure you. You just have to excel at a few other things too.

Edith could hear Vivianne's likely Madeira Wine lipstick smile on the other end of the phone. Why was Vivianne being so cruel?

—But if you watch your p's and q's, maintain your work-life balance, stay out of the company of troublemakers like Coral, well, that definitely helps in the long run. Avoid negativity. Correction: *flee* negativity. I've witnessed the positive effects with other clients from the university.

—You really think so?

—I *know* so. Say this with me: *I am the architect of my life. I build its foundation and select its furniture.*

Edith had closed her eyes. She would do this right. She would make Vivianne proud of her.

—I am the architect of my own life, Edith said. —I build its foundations and select its fixtures.

—Furniture, said Vivianne.

—Furniture, repeated Edith.

—You, said Vivianne, —you, Edith, are the architect of *your* life. You don't have to invite anyone into your house if you don't want her there.

—You're right. Thanks, Vivianne.

—Your welcome, Edith. We're at the end of our time now. Goodbye.

The phone clicked before Edith had a chance to say goodbye. Her appointments with Vivianne always end like this. The only disappointing thing about Vivianne.

She sits alone in her shiny condo. New clothes, new shoes, new smell, new tank of gas, but barricaded on every side by paper stacks, reports and reviews and letters she doesn't want to write but should. Must.

She empties crusted clothes from inside the washing machine. Slams the door closed. Unplugs the washing machine cord, then plugs it back in. She programs an extrahot extralong cycle on the control panel.

Water rushes into the empty machine, and Edith shoots her fist into the air in triumph.

She rustles back into sitting behind her desk. Clicks on the Academic Achievement Overview webpage button.

Oops! This page does not exist, the computer barfs.

Her email pings. An email from Coral. She remembers how bumpily they kissed that one time, their lips refusing to match.

Edith needs to find a new friend.

She unbuttons the top button of her new blouse.

The very next morning, the sun still stretching itself awake, Edith pulls her car into the parking lot by Crawley Hall, refusing to let the frowny building guilt her for working from home yesterday. She'd like to park by the Kinesiology building, but her expensive university parking pass applies only to her assigned space next to Crawley Hall. Unless she wants to pay the parking fee at the Kinesiology parking lot. Ten dollars and fifty-five cents when she's already paid for a pass! Forget it. She would rather take the seven-minute shortcut through Crawley Hall to get to the pool.

She'll scoot through Crawley Hall and be side-stroking through invigorating waters in no time. She shuts her eyes and, clutching her duffle bag of swim gear, dashes through the tight hallways, dives past empty classrooms with gaping, vacant student desks, turns corner after corner in the mini-labyrinth, doors groaning as she tugs them open, hissing as they ooze closed behind her. Left, left, right, then left, then left again, then a short flight of stairs, then a final right, then straight through. No direct routes in this building ever, but she's memorized them all. She avoids the main lobby, determined that the building will not entice her up to her office, to the piles of unopened envelopes and the unread stacks of journals she left on her desk two days ago, and the phony satisfaction that comes with shuffling though paper in her office so early in the morning. She's not teaching yet; she doesn't *have* to be here.

She wipes her nose with a disintegrating Kleenex as she run-walks, her nose suddenly dripping for no reason. She dumps the tissue in one of the overflowing garbage bins lined up in an already tight hallway and climbs the last short set of stairs to a tiny landing.

But this door's stuck or locked, even though it has no keyhole. She tugs and heaves, pushes, and tugs again at the door, slaps it, huffs. Like the door resents her wanting to exercise and improve her life. She has psychic *furnishings* to buy for her psychic *foundation*. She contemplates the door, trying to ignore the odour emanating from the walls, the ceiling: dust, mould, or fossilized compost in a recycling bin. She sneezes. Pulls out a nearly fresh Kleenex from her bag. Maybe a mouse got trapped in a nearby vent and expired. She wonders if she should call Security to unlock the door. If she circles back out the building and takes the long way, she'll miss the first ten minutes of lane swimming. If she phones Security, she'll also miss the first ten minutes of lane swimming. She can't let Vivianne down this way, this very first real day of being the architect of her life. She kicks the door with her runner.

Edith jumps when the door thuds open. Shoot! Maybe she broke the door. She hesitates in the doorway. The ceiling lights appear spotty with dust, as though they haven't been cleaned in years, the insides of the light panels clotted with grime.

And in front of her a matchbook-sized landing, and yet *another* set of stairs, this time three steps leading down. She doesn't recognize the landing. Or remember these stairs.

She's travelled through every part of Crawley Hall since she started her job seven years ago, but this hallway looks unfamiliar, the stairs redundant—what kind of pointless architecture is this?

Three steps leading up to a doorway with a tiny nothing of a landing, just to go three steps down again? She's sure this design must violate some kind of building code. The lights grim, the corridor even narrower, if possible. Maybe it's the eerily early hour? No matter, she's late for swimming and as she steps through the doorway, the door bangs closed *hard* into her shoulder.

She yelps in alarm, in pain. She rubs her shoulder as she steps carefully down the stairs. At the bottom, empty study carrels line the walls to the right and left of her, a single chair neatly tucked into each cubicle. She registers a flicker of movement at the end of the line of carrels, hears skittering, the far-off scrape of a chair. Probably students necking in the dark. But so early in the morning? Probably the same dorkmeisters who jammed the door closed so they could have their sex; she knows how sex ruins logic.

She starts to swing her bag to work the ache out of her shoulder as she walks, but swings too high once and almost slips, catches herself before she falls on the sparkly clean floor. The janitorial staff always polishes Crawley Hall's floors until they glisten at the beginning of every school year. They must have already started for the fall semester. Last time she checked, the floor in her office still held last year's scuffs and leftover grit from the snow, now evaporated. No one's emptied her office garbage can all summer, not since the spring Liberal Arts budget cut announcement, and her wastebasket brims with used bubble envelopes, old Cup-a-Soup containers, cellophane wrappers from journals and cardboard coffee cups. But soon her wastebasket will be fresh and empty, perhaps it already is. The overcast light notwithstanding, this hallway gleams.

Silence has dropped like snowfall. She hears none of the white noise that insinuates itself everywhere else in the building: air vents, buzzy fluorescent lights, the distant ding of an elevator, the hum of a photocopy machine. Her sneaker squeaks violate the silence, as though she's accidentally trespassed into a medieval chapel. Or a dungeon. The shiny silence makes her want to tiptoe. She peers every so often under the cubicles to see if she can unearth the student lovers.

Nothing but skinny metal chair legs. No sound but the *memory* of sound.

She jogs toward the dawning sunlight slanting through the window in the exit door. It says *Push*.

But the door pushes back. Locked.

Through the wire-meshed glass in the door, a jackrabbit on the lawn pulls at grass tufts with its teeth. Crawley Hall's dawn shadow lies thick on the quad. The Kinesiology building twinkles only a hundred metres away.

She piles herself into the door, pushes and grunts, her bag clumping to the floor. She refuses to acknowledge this door's refusal.

She spins and rams her back into the door, but this door is so locked it's really just a wall. She wipes her nose on the back of her hand. Rests her back on the door.

The hallway unspools ahead of her; her earlier rubber-soled footsteps are matte splotches dotting the floor's oily and unrelenting cleanness.

She slings her bag over her shoulder and walks slowly back down the hallway, her sneaker soles squelching.

Her sneakers stop squeaking in the gloomy light. She stops. Hairs prickle awake on the back of her neck, her shoulders, her forearms.

Where is she?

The tidy carrels with their neat, tucked chairs are no longer neat. The chairs scatter themselves in her way, every one pulled askew and turned around willy-nilly from their cubicles.

Who moved the chairs? Without making a single sound?

She just wants to go for a damn *swim*. Why is exercising always so damn *complicated*? Now she has to deal with supernatural bullshit too? She's always suspected something was off about this building. Coral used to say so too.

Time to leave, shortcut or no.

She wades between the parallel lines of study cubicles and their disordered chairs. She pushes and scrapes the flimsy chairs out of her way, rams herself through them. She refuses to register misplaced clusters of shadow under the cubicles, shadows that weren't there earlier, shadows too small and numerous to be a single pair of mischievous or desperate lovers. A shining red eye—she swears it's an eye—mirrors at her from a shadow under a cubicle.

She barrels toward the very first door—the door with the needless steps leading up only to stairs down the other side. But the steps on this side of the door, those steps that have been there in the first place, have disappeared. The floor all the way to the door gleams clear and flat and wide and shining.

She pushes away a cold drip of fear.

Fed up, she violently shoves herself into the door, ready for it to stick. The door whooshes open and she stumbles forward, panicked that she'll tumble down the other set of stairs and snap her skull in half, shatter her knees. She stretches out her hands, lands on her palms—her hands and feet staggered on the steps—her bag thumping as it rolls down the steps. Excellent save. Her knees intact.

She stays crouched, panting, then gathers up her bag in her arms.

She scurries away toward a side door she knows leads to some outdoor nowhereseville, but that hopefully will take her *out*. She turns a perfectly oiled handle, and the door bursts open.

A jackrabbit abruptly leaps away.

She gasps in the fresh air.

A rush of dusty, dead-mousy air billows around her, announcing her to the outside world.

The door lolls open behind her.

The door yawns, moist air from inside the building soughing out the doorway. An inappropriately human sound.

She sways a little, her wrists still shocked, her shoulder bruised and aching, a new crick in the small of her back. Her synapses frizzled.

She has a feral desire to flee—hightail it for her Taurus, hurtle home, and collapse into bed wrapped inside two comforters. But she hasn't swum for three years. Vivianne told her to choose her furnishings. She will not let anyone or anything else, some grumpy sticky-doored building with a half-assed paranormal hallway, choose her furnishings.

Illogical. Irritating. Time-consuming. Her time *consumed*. A small black marble sticks to her left palm. A jackrabbit turd. She flicks at it until it unsticks, bounces, thocks into the grass. She looks back at the Crawley Hall door swinging listlessly, like a tooth, in the dim, grim doorway. She needs to call Vivianne.

No. She needs to make Vivianne proud.

She plods heavily, warily, the long way around Crawley Hall's giant, protruding concreteness, past normal pine trees, along normal sidewalks past the library, past the students' union building to the Novacrest School of Kinesiology building. The electronic front doors slide open and wait for her, like gentle, non-racist butlers. She enters the glamorous, state-of-the-art building, its brand-new open-concept loveliness, and pool-chlorine and squash ball smell enfold and embrace her.

Dawn Carter
(1968–)

A performance poet and writing instructor in Edmonton, Dawn Carter calls herself a "BBC"—a British Barbadian Canadian. She was born in Yorkshire, England, but overt discrimination against black immigrants convinced her parents of the need to emigrate. In 1972 she and her family landed in Ponoka, Alberta, where a small contingent of Barbadian immigrants had settled after securing jobs in the large Alberta Hospital.

Growing up in Ponoka, Carter remembers "quotidian, private battles with racism."[1] "Getting dressed for school felt like I was girding myself for another attack; who was going to say something cruel, who was going to threaten me, how could I survive yet another day? Naturally, I questioned my identity from several fronts; as a black person; a girl growing into a woman." Her early writing questioned her identity, but later, she reflects, "I embraced my black womanhood and my sexuality, and rejected patriarchal religious values. I explored my female pain, sorrows, and anger, fired by rage and spiked with humour." Her current work is confessional and provocative, playing with and disrupting inherited ideas about black female sexuality, as well as the power dynamics involved in interracial dating. At the beginning of her career she was dubbed "the angry sex poet," a designation, she says, she accepted for a time. But today, she believes the moniker reveals that her audience, mainly white and male, "has misinterpreted and misunderstood me."

Now in mid-career, Carter says, "I feel that finally I can write from a place of joy, peace, and pride; I feel an unshakable confidence and a broader sense of what my writing mission is. I've reconciled with the small towns I've lived in; they are more inclusive than they were when I lived there as a girl. I relish bike rides on back roads and walks through fields in winter and that's ok!"

---

1 Personal communication, May–July 2016. All author quotations are from this correspondence.

This sense of personal security is palpable in Carter's poetic expression, which is unabashedly erotic and playful in its direct address to the object/subject of desire. Carter performed these poems as part of the Raving Poets nights in Edmonton, an open-mic night with improvised musical accompaniment that ran from 2000 to 2010. The following poems have never before appeared in print, but an earlier version of them was published on the Raving Poets website (now defunct).

Carter has published work in the anthology *But Where Are You Really From? Stories of Identity and Assimilation in Canada* (Sister Vision, 1997). She also has work in *Other Voices* (2002), in *Contemporary Verse 2: Sexing the Poem: A Celebration of Desire* (2003), and she has, with Adriana Davies and Delvina Greig, recorded a CD entitled *The Lover's Journey.*

Restoration

let me restore you
buffing chrome fibreglass steel
licking off the dust that clings to your topcoat

my tongue slipping
sliding
around the edges of your rims

I am upward inside outbound

down down down
blind spot

grease nipples
male/female
getting down to our own universal joint

when I cling to you
I seep under rivets and quarter panels
corroding and corrupting
a catalytic ecstatic conversion

I want to rock on your leaf springs
like a four-wheel in back country

a deer in the headlights
only I catch you in mine
I want to climb your chassis
like a virgin jungle gym
in a brand-new playground

bounce in your leather bound back seats
like I'm in a jolly jumper for big girls

you are downward outside inbound
up up up
drivin' stick
but whose hands are really behind the wheel?

A Monumental Love

I want to slip you
the tongue
at the peace memorial in Hiroshima
crush you
against the walls on Robben Island
grab your bare ass
where Golgotha once stood
and
ravish you
ragged in rwanda

for I believe our love
is more powerful
than the hate that existed
in such places

that our love could heal hate
and teach the lessons
these silent monuments could not

Get into My Car

get into my car
oh ethnic booty
come on
come on
get into my car

get into my car
my sarong song
picture you in a thong
makin' my ding-a-ling
long

come ride in my sedan
got your name written all over it
and your name is jungle love
written all over my vinyl back seats
I'll show you
that a white man's spunk
got spunk
slam dunk
fill you with my funk

when you whisper your English
I twist it into patois kreyol
a thousand diasporic dialects I do not understand
really don't want to understand

bend your words
to fit my ear
like I want to bend you
your tongue ticking mine

no, I don't hear you saying
no
I'm from here
from here

here could be planet earth
and guess what
I'm from here too
who knew we had so much in common?

drum a beat deep into my bones
as you baptize me
in virgin's blood
voodoo stylin'
electrifying

when no means
yes
yes
yes

Minister Faust
(1969–)

"If readers don't perceive my politics, they aren't paying much attention," says the Kenyan Canadian writer Minister Faust (Shawl). Minister Faust's politics are not just thematic, but part and parcel of the genre in which he works, which he calls "Afritopianism," the Africentric science fiction and fantasy that he writes. He draws "inspiration from a large number of ancient African civilizations and focuses on a future in which people struggle for justice" (Shawl).

Minister Faust is the literary *nom de plume* of this celebrated Edmonton-based science fiction and fantasy author, playwright, teacher, activist, journalist, and one-time political candidate. Faust's work is concerned with the ruptures of diaspora, war, violence, and popular global-African culture, particularly as they shape masculinity. He returns repeatedly to ancient African history and myths in order to mythologize the East African enclave in Edmonton and to offer it edifying new myths rooted in Afro-centrist and black power literatures. His work was recognized as being of key importance to the city when he served as writer-in-residence at the University of Alberta in Edmonton in 2014–15.

One of Minister Faust's first works was the science-fiction play *The Undiscovered Country* for Montreal's Creations Etc. in 1987. His debut novel, *The Coyote Kings of the Space Age Bachelor Pad* (2004), written in his signature amped-up, comic, and pop culture-infused prose, received major international release by Random House. It was a finalist for the Phillip K. Dick award, the Locus Best First Novel Award, and the Compton-Crook Award. A buddy novel set in Edmonton in 1995, it follows two main characters, a Sudanese Canadian former honours English student working as a dishwasher, and a Trinidadian Canadian working as a video store clerk, as they get swept up in a quest for a mysterious ancient relic. The novel mythologizes the Somali, Ethiopian, Eritrean, and Sudanese district of central of Edmonton as a new "Kush," named for the ancient Nubian Kingdom in East Africa 1070 BC–350 AD.

His second novel, *From the Notebooks of Dr. Brain* (2007), a fictional self-help book for superheroes, parodies mainstream characters from DC and Marvel comics while earnestly exploring the problem of individual responsibility in the context of social injustice. It won the Carl Brandon Society Kindred Award and was the runner-up for the Phillip K. Dick Prize.

In 2011 Faust published his third novel, *The Alchemists of Kush* (republished 2017 Resurrection House), which focuses on two Sudanese "lost boys," Raphael ("Rap") and Jamal ("Jackie Chan"). After joyriding a stolen car and almost getting killed, the boys are taken under the wing of a mentor, who ushers them into a world of powerful knowledge. The book is a meditation on myth, and how a community can be created by the stories it tells itself. Faust is also the author of the War and Mir series, which consists of two novels, *War & Mir, Volume I: Ascension* (2011), and *War & Mir, Volume II: The Darkold* (2014), with a third novel currently being written.

Minister Faust produced and hosted an Afrocentric radio show (1991–2012) at Edmonton's CJSR 88.5 FM. Originally called *The Terrordome: Black Radio in the Hour of Chaos* and later *The Terrordome: The Afrika All World News Service*, the show featured interviews with many prominent personalities including Chuck D, Angela Davis, Nalo Hopkinson, Tariq Ali, Noam Chomsky, Vandana Shiva, and Ralph Nader.

❦

The Coyote Kings of the Space Age Bachelor Pad

Passing through the Belly of the Whale

Maybe me and Ye were fated to live together, ever since we met in high school. We were like anode and cathode, and we've been a reaction of one sort or another ever since.

Sometimes we talk a lot on the way home, shooting the skeet, hyucking it up. Other times, like tonight, I'm in one of these funks and Ye figures it's easier just to let me be. Two guys been together this long (not like *that*), it's easy. You know the echo of each other's heartbeats. You know the creak of each other's hinges.

This damn walk home, however many nights a week since life turned to manure, this is salvation here on nightdark streets. So quiet out, city lights sentinels and a chorus of stars above, yelling their whispers at us, talking up dreams we forgot we had. Me and Ye, and the long walk, slapping souls on E-Town concrete.

(And it's E-*Town*, by the way. Super deejay Grandmaster and General Overseer T.E.D.D.Y. *created* that phrase.[1] Not E-*ville* like some of these cooler-than-thou/alt-hip/fake indie shitbacks are trying to promote. Yeah. "Evil" is cool. Should go Vader on these punks. See how well they can type their arty-cles and wipe their arty asses with one hand.)

We cross the North Saskatchewan River via the High Level Bridge,[2] one of the few remaining black metal girder bridges left, like the spine of some midnight cosmosaur. We walk it, walk the decommissioned train tracks on top of it, ghost lights flickering off and on beneath our feet as the occasional car drives below, the last nerve cell messages from a time before time.

Can I read that primeval code? Or that prime evil code? How many sins from the past are we made to suffer for?

Aw, forget it, and don't go calling me self-important, self-indulgent, or self-whatever. Twenty-five, alive, but washing dishes …? Brain rot transmitted through yellow gloves, wrinkled fingers, and an aching back? I'm al*lowed*. I'll indulge myself if I kot-tam feel like it.

You know, in the summer, they turn on taps on the east side of this crazy bridge, and suddenly E-Town has an artificial waterfall. I remember when the city first installed it, damn near everybody turned out for the show.

Now nobody cares.

You make some magic, and freaks don't care. If a magician pulls a rabbit out of a hat, and nobody's watching, does it still eat carrots? (Not the hat. You know what I'm saying, freak.)

We're over the bridge, past the west side of downtown up 109th street, past Ibex Ethiopian Restaurant and through an underpass everyone calls The Rat Hole. Not my dad, though—he always calls it the Belly of the Whale. Which is more lyrical, eh?

When we were kids, Dad'd drive us through it, this long skinny tunnel, and he'd tell us stories Mum'd later tell us to forget in case we got nightmares, all about being swallowed by Monstro the Whale, or how Jonah the foolish prophet ended up as fish bait.

Mum was good at that, undermining Dad's magic. But *she* showed *him*, when she did her own disappearing act.

---

1   Possibly a reference to the late radio DJ Teddy Pemberton, known as "the man who brought hip-hop to Edmonton" on his show on CJSR FM.

2   Completed in 1913, the High Level Bridge was built, at least in part, by a previous generation of black arrivals. See Ellis Hooks's orature in this volume.

Speaking of Jonah, you know, back when I was doing my English degree, I remember a real conservative Calvinist professor in King James Bible class (it was an English course, understand), who nevertheless always gave us solid academic explanations of biblical amazements.

He said the ancient Hebrews were never intended to take the Jonah story seriously. Said it was satire, and the ancient Jews all recognized it, how some fools are so damn full of themselves and their own pain that they won't listen to God, and even if God drops a freaking whale on em, they still maybe don't wake up and climb outta their own peat bog of misery and self-pity.

Reminds me of so many freaks I've known over the years, beach fleas who can't read the neon billboards a million miles tall: STAND UP AND STOP CRYING, TURD-BOY.

Outta the Belly of the Whale. Me and Ye are careful coming out, eyes and fists ready. It's creepy down there, cold even in the summer. If you aren't careful, you could easily get jumped, cuz anybody on the lookout could signal guys on either side to come after you, and there's only two traffic lanes, so if you hadda leap into the road to avoid some freaking tigers, you'd get completely skwushed under a cab.

I guess we could just walk another way, but we take the Belly every single night we walk home.

E-Town doesn't have much graffiti, but, like, half of it is down there in the Belly. Somebody scrawled *Indian Police* on the north entrance. I never did figure that one out.

My dad told me that in Egypt, at the Step Pyramid, which was the first pyramid, on the inside wall of the outer complex, is graffiti, as in *So-and-so wuz here*, but in hieroglyphics. Like they had tourists three thousand years ago, when this pyramid was already almost two thousand years old. I mean, that is simultaneously amazing and depressing. Monuments defaced by fossils.

Now we're up on 107th Ave and 107th Street, grid middle for our neighbourhood, home since I was old enough to pee. You got more Somalis, Ethiopians, Eritreans, and Sudanese here than any other place in E-Town. Some people call it the Horn. We call it Kush.

In the skin-baking heat of a July day you got merchants and bazaars and the gut-puckeringly delicious aromas of roasting lamb, and squadrons of flies near the grills and men in white desert robes with kaffiyehs and women in silk scarves and sashes and dresses more colorful than sunset over canola and the music of a dozen different languages and a hundred different dialects and people going to mosque with the echo of the *mued-dhin* calling them to prayer and the laughing-sparkle of kids romping and running after the Dickie Dee teenager pedaling his ice-cream bicycle cart of frozen-milk-fat-sugar-temptation.

But it's night now, and all the stores are shut, and there are no kids, and when you see somebody, you don'wanna meet their eyes. The Addis Ababa Obelisk is lit up, a massive stone finger pointing up to Andromeda and the Crab Nebula and black holes and quasars and every place other than here, a buried titan's last message to fools like me:

Leave Tatooine.

But there's no Academy, and no Alderaan. And no Ben.

We're here, at last.

The Coyote Cave. [...]

Thursday Mourning

Hamza's not up. My turn to make breakfast.

Hamza and I have radically different kitchen styles. I would describe him as a culinary free radical, whereas I'm more like a carbon isotope, proceeding in its transformation (not decay) with dependable precision.

The H-man's "method" involves getting out *all:*

a. fresh ingredients,
b. leftovers,
c. spices,
d. crockery, and
e. electrical appliances.

In short, all organic and nonorganic matter in the kitchen, to begin his restauranteurial regimen. (Sidebar: *Restaurant* comes from the Italian, meaning "restore"—which helps illuminate the vital role of chefs and cooks as alchemists, or, as I prefer, scientists.)

Hamza and I agree on the power of food, but it's *method* where we don't meet monocle to monocle. His mm-good Merlinry occasionally produces gastromiracles, but almost never can he *replicate* his results, which is the tragedy.

I, on the other hand, employ precision methodology. Even when experimenting, I carefully mentally catalog ingredient vitality, the doses and synergistic potencies of various spices, energy levels, reaction times, gustatory activation levels, the psychological complements of serving dish and table-cloth colours, and so forth and so on.

Sure, Hamza's manic kitchenary flailing is entertaining in an *I Love Lucy*-esque sort of way and occasionally produces deliciosity, but my dignified, controlled approach is key to dietary stability, both in import and export biological functions.

This morning I'm making pancakes.

Hamza still isn't up. That jimp. It was *his* turn to clean up the kitchen and before I can even begin, I have to transform chaos to cosmos in this joint. This is the *eighty-fourth* time he's failed to fulfill his cleaning contract since I moved in. And that was only 1,421 days ago!

Cleaning is quick when you're as efficient as I am, but the problem here is the principle of the matter. I'll take my reparations in ice-cream sandwiches for Hambone's numberous infractions, but I shouldn't *have* to.

YEHAT'S PLANETQUAKES

241 mL *whole wheat or quadrotriticale flour*
253 mL *pure wheat bran*
18 mL *cumin*
16 mL *baking powder*
2 *ripe bananas or* 4 *sweet Chinese small bananas, mashed*
1 *ripe mango, minced*
2 *brown egg whites (oh, the seeming contradiction ... egg* clears, *then, in the non-Scientology sense)*
259 mL *goat milk, 1 degree Celsius*

Mix and cook as standard—beware burning due to thickness of cakes. Serve hot with creamy feta, dark honey, or red mung bean paste.

Hamza's still not up and usually the smell of breakfast has him trotting in here and nibbling and sampling.

His door's closed.

I overcome the urge to knock. I'm afraid I already know what's going on.

I open the door as silently as I can. He's there, in the chair, eyes closed, slumped over, drool crusted white at his mouth edges. The Box is on the shelf, but not where it was the day before, and I know, because I check every day and even place a hair there to see if he's opened the stupid thing.

And damnit, he's been into it again. If only his brain were a long string of code, I could go in and cut and paste. I could digitally divide and heal. But that stinking jimp refuses to be free.

I close the door as silently as snow falls.

❦

The Alchemists of Kush

2.

[…] Evening. Mum wasn't in yet, as usual. In front of their glacial-speed computer, sipping Lipton's Chicken Cup of Soup broth just so he didn't starve.

An email popped up. Which was weird, since he never got email from anyone. But the school insisted everyone have an email account linked to their and their parents' home accounts.

It was that fool JC with a link to Somal-E-Town.com, a video story posted form the CBC news site, with still photos and footage doubling up on the reporter's narration:

Part Good Samaritan, part Bruce Lee, Mr. Yimunhotep Ani is a Kush-area store-owner who intervened on Saturday's multiple homicide while it was unfolding next door to his own store, as this stunning security footage leaked to YouTube demonstrates.

Freaking a*maz*ing! Rap'd been face-down—there he was, that was him, nothing to ID him, thank god—so he never actually saw what'd happened.

This old man, Yim-something-something, smashed through the two killers like an axe through dry branches.

Rap jabbed the spacebar, rewound, watched it again. And again. And again.

According to the video file clock, the whole combat lasted less than two seconds.

Clicking, frame by frame:

Killers in long coats standing over victims.

Black blur slipping from the back.

Hand chop into neck of Killer #2.

Rushing leg takes out #1's feet.

#1 spinning in mid-air, as if his hips were on an axle.

#1 on floor, blur moving toward Killer #2 turning around.

#2 hefting shot gun.

Blur's left hand intercepting barrel, gripping, yanking forward.

Rotating trunk, right hand spearing into #2's throat.

Right hand raking #2's eyes and face, right foot puncturing #2's groin.

#2 on the floor.

Blur slowing into a man, stomping #1's knees.

Then #2's.

Finally Rap let the rest of the video roll:

Crippling the two assailants, Ani saved the lives of two unidentified teenage boys who escaped immediately after.

But when police arrived, instead of thanking Ani, they arrested him. And, says Mr. Ani, they brutalized him.

Although police initially denied any wrong-doing, the leaked security footage has gone viral, becoming an internet sensation, and racking over a hundred thousand hits in two days.

The resulting public outcry has forced police to change their story, release Ani and issue an apology.

Meanwhile the reluctant internet icon has issued no statement of his own but is now widely known as "Blackbelt Jones," the "Bulletproof Monk" and "Morpheus."

Thousands of adoring comments from a range including pro-gun groups and inner-city renewal activists have claimed Ani as a hero.

In regard to a civil suit against the police and the City, Ani's lawyer, Bamba Diabate, says, "all options are on the table." Ben Coxworth, CBC News, Edmonton.

Was this guy for real? Had Rap actually been inside the same room as this superhero?

Hoped when he finally went to apologize to him, the man would shake his hand and not rip it off.

3.

The next day Rap and JC were busing it up 127th Street, a traffic-clogged lane of stout, drab businesses that city planners must've forgotten during extended lunch breaks, or maybe designed while sniping at each other. [...]

4.

They rode in silence, got off on 132nd Avenue and took a transfer over to 113th and the single minaret that stood in front of the CIC.

Building's front had onion-peak arches built over the doors, and a white exterior going into perpetual dirtiness. Above was a dome with a crescent-and-star glinting the high sunlight of a late afternoon in June.

The parking lot was jammed with cars, and so were the streets. People streamed toward the CIC, Somali men wither in blazers or flowing white *jalabeeyahs* or sometimes both, men with short hair and men wearing embroidered fezzes, and *muhajabaat* in long iridescent skirts and black blouses floating down the sidewalk like a rainbow of swans.

Cop cars, four of them, up and down the block and a few jive plain-clothes White men with short mustaches joining the marchers who looked like the only time they'd ever seen the inside of a mosque was from surveil-lance photos.

Rap and Jackie Chan slipped inside a throng of mourners, hoping like hell the cops wouldn't see them or connect them to the security camera footage on YouTube—maybe there'd been more that hadn't made it onto the news that showed their faces. Who'd posted it, anyway? Was that Morpheus guy still in jail?

Burn was bad as ever, sizzling his legs and arms and forehead. He thought he was going to pass out on the way inside, but JC caught him.

"You okay?"

"Yeah," he said. "Just tripped. Thanks."

5.

Found two empty chairs together near the back of the auditorium. Jackie Chan went to make *wudu*.

When he came back his face was still wet from washing.

Rap didn't practice his mother's family's Islam or his father's Christianity. So he didn't make *wudu* or genuflect or look in vain for holy water or anything else.

What he did do was sit raging to himself how JC could walk around the CIC with Somalis by the boatload nodding to him like he was a cousin, but him, looking Dinka right down to the facial scarification, might's well've been invisible.

To these people his mother's side was invisible or didn't count, and it didn't matter that he could speak Somali or that he almost got murdered on the same floor as the two Somalis who got shot did.

And that's who this funeral was for. The service for the two murdered Sudanese was going on at the same time somewhere else, which he knew because his mother, in her morning briefing to him, said that's where she was going to be.

She still had no idea about his connection, and so he didn't say word-one about heading to any funeral.

"Our commoonity has suffered another loss," said Mr. Bashir.

Fifty-ish, a community organizer. Chubby-cheeked and happy-faced. Bashir man looked sadder than his facial anatomy should've made possible.

Every second he spoke, the room got muggier and hotter. Bashir shifted back and forth from Somali into English for the benefit of reporters who came for the blood and didn't care about Black people unless they were shooting, crying, rapping, singing, running or throwing a ball.

"How many uff our young people haff we lost in the laast few years?"

Shouts and wails.

"Yes, you're right—nutt only young people. Our braather driving cab, Mr. Yussef, who wuss left to die inside his own traank?"

Murmuring engorging into shouting, a grass fire turning inferno.

Mr. Bashir waved it down with his hands and a few *insha'Allahs.*

"The young men at the, the ... Foolton Place party? Grumbles from somewhere up front. "Yes, that too—the drive-by shooting at the lounge. How many more haff there been? And, and how many more will there be?

"Some uff our young men, they haff lost. Lost their baliefs. Lost their sense of right and wrong. Lost their hope that they can *do* something or *be* something ... something more than a confficted prisoner or a, a jaankie. That they could be fathers. With careers ..."

Mr. Bashir eulogized the dead Somalis. Hassan the store owner. Hard working businessman. Loved to discuss the news. Committed soccer player. Had a twenty-three year-old wife. Two sons, one three, other only three months. Both orphaned by a shotgun shell that permanently interrupted their father's attention.

6.

Then it finally came to talk about eighteen-year old Dawud Abdi.

Mr. Bashir must've microscoped that boy's life to find something, anything to say that wouldn't shame his ghost: about his loving parents, great smile, sense of humour, his dream of owning a restaurant or a record store or his own music label.

Didn't mention that the streets knew him as Nuke, a long-time car-thief guaranteed to die by steel one way or another.

And didn't tell the mourners any time that afternoon that drug-related assaults were plaguing the Somali community so much that a whole lotta people didn't even bother reporting them to the police.

But quadruple-homicides, yeah, those still filtered through to the cops, and to the news.

Mr. Bashir's speech ended with thanks to the people who'd come up from Calgary and all the way from Vancouver, Winnipeg, T.O. and even the States. Rap wasn't surprised—Somali families (other than his) were always big and tight enough to form their own FIFA divisions.

And then there was an appeal from another speaker to join some local Somali group with the name "Brotherhood" in it, and someone else asking on the imam's behalf for everyone to come for prayer at the front.

Rap moved aside for Jackie Chan, stayed by himself.

7.

After prayer, with the congregation breaking up, Jackie Chan scrambled back form the lobby, shoving folded-over newspapers at him.

"That guy who rescued us?" whispered JC. "Paper says the police only let him go after his lawyer got involved. Betcha Mr. Lawyer-Man's the dude who YouTubed that *kung fu* tape."

Screen-caps from the tape blared up on the page.

Rap shook his head. "What if the cops've got our faces off that tape?"

"Cops can't tell us apart, man," said JC, actually smiling. "Otherwise they woulda grabbed us on the way inside here."

"Unless they didn't want to cause a riot and're waiting until we leave. To follow us home—"

"Kinda paranoid, fuh real."

"Don't 'paranoid' me! I would'n even be *in* this mess except for you!"

Jackie Chan looked down, chewed his lip. "Thought you'd be happy. Cuz the guy's out."

Rap hit JC's shoulder. "That him?"

JC looked over. Shuffling out with the rest of the mourners was a moustachless man with a goatee, a black-and-gold skullcap and BandAids marring his neck and face.

The boys tried getting to him, but the crowd crushed them back while they wedged their way with *excuse me*s and *sorry*s.

They almost caught him near the door, until several old men in white *jalabeeyahs* stopped in front of them as if the doorway were the most natural place in the world to have a conversation.

Over the shoulder of an old man with a beard red from henna, the boys saw their savior descend the stairs and disappear.

By the time they cleared the blocking-line of seniors, Morpheus was gone.

And Rap didn't feel like tearing all over the place looking for him to thank him and beg forgiveness for abandoning him, just in case the cops *could* tell Sudanese apart from Somalis. He had more to lose than JC did.

"Now what?" said Jackie Chan.

"I don't know," said Rap. "Wait. What's his name again?" He scanned the paper. "Yimunhotep Ani ... and get this, you know why he was even there that night? He owns the store next door, the one—"

"The one with the 'opening soon' sign?"

"Yeah!"

"Okay!" said Jackie Chan. "Let's go!"

Even though he'd just been chasing the man, hearing JC's words dropped Rap's stomach like he'd stepped into an open elevator shaft.

8.

An hour's bus ride later and the sun still hot and high in the June sky, the boys were back in Kush, walking along 111th Avenue over to 96th Street.

Passing pawn shops, a Burger Baron, Norwood School, the rainbow-flagged Pride Centre, a car wash with a dozen bays, a run-down body shop.

From the south bank of 111th they saw the yellow police tape on Bootays, a ribbon wrapped around the worst birthday present the community'd gotten in years.

Dodging cabs, cars and buses, they landed in front of the Hyper-Market and its *OPENING SOON* sign.

"Well?" asked JC. "Aren't we going in?"

Rap glared at him. "Don't rush me. Wanna think what I'm gonna say first."

JC pushed on the glass door, but it was locked. He knocked loud and long.

Finally the forty-something man in the goatee and black-and-gold skullcap came to the door.

"Hello?"

Up close they saw what the Band-Aids had failed to cover: bruises, scrapes and the gut-puckering purple-brown ghost from a fading black eye.

"Uh ... we're ... we're the, uh," fumbled Rap.

The man stepped forward into the doorway, blocking it.

"Kot-*tam*!" He snapped. "You're those two kids!"

"Yeah," said JC. "Look, our bad, the other night—f'real. But man, the way you absolutely Bruce Lee'd them boys. You went Abu Ghraib on they asses! Think you could teach us that shit?"

"Jamal!" snapped Rap. This wasn't in the plan. And jazzing about a mass murder that almost included all of them, as if it were a movie trailer or something—was he nuts?

"You got a hell of a nerve," growled the man.

Rap glared at JC.

"Look, look, look, man," spluttered JC, "I know, I know we shoulda—"

"*Man*?" he spat. "I took a beating and an arrest from the cops and stayed in jail overnight because I stepped in to save your lives! And you two little shits ran off and didn't say word-*one* which coulda saved me from all that.

"And now you show up here expecting me to train you like I owe you something ... and you call me *'man'*?"

Rap: "Sir. Sir, we're—we're sorry. But honest, we were just terrified!"

"*You* were terrified? How do you think I felt when the police had their guns out and were kicking the shit outta me?"

Jackie Chan: "We thought we were gonna die—"

"I thought *I* was gonna die! Thanks to you! Now get the hell outta here!"

Shoved himself back inside, leaned on the glass door's metal frame till the hydraulic hissed shut. Then he latched all three clanking latches and stormed off to the back room.

Music blasted to life: extremely loud jazz. Battering cymbals and sobbing saxophones, like someone using a wrench to beat a robot to death.

Standing on the street, Jackie Chan had already given up. "Dude *hates* us, man."

9.

The next day during a lull in their English class's review of *To Kill a Mockingbird*, Rap argued in whispers to convince JC (who'd begun sitting next to him) to go back to the man's store.

"After your brilliant, 'Train us in your Snake-and-Crane style, dude,' now we owe the man *two* apologies. And this time, let me do the talking?"

"Aiight," conceded JC. "My bad, my bad ..."

"Oh, god," said the man at 4:33 pm on Thursday afternoon, the day after the funeral. "You two *again?*"

"Look, Mr. Ani," said Rap, "I know we screwed up. And my friend here shouln't've come around asking for any favours. But seriously—"

"We just wanna say thank you," said JC, oblivious to Rap's immediate glare. "And, like, we'll work here."

Rap: "What?"

"You expect me to *hire* you?" he laughed. Angrily.

"He means—"

"—we'll volunteer, y'know?" said JC. Sounded thrilled with his own improv. "You can work us like slaves!"

"*Slaves,*" sneered the man. "Do you even hear yourself"?

Rap: "We owe you or lives, Mr. Ani. At least let us try to pay you back a little."

"Like I'm gonna let two carjackers into my business!"

"We ain't carjackers—we just car thieves!"

"Jackie Chan, would you let me—! We're not car thieves. He's a joy-rider. His friend, the one who died, was the thief. And this idiot, look, I just know him from school. He offered me a ride and didn't bother telling me the car was stolen—"

"That's true!" enthused Jackie Chan, as if he were helping.

"So you're saying," said the man, as if he were laying out the plot of a particularly bad movie, "that I should let a joy-rider ... and a kid who climbs into cars with sketchy almost-strangers ... inside my business, handle my cash, learn the intimate details of how I make a living, and have access to all my equipment and merchandise? Have I, have I got that right?"

JC: "Well, when yall put it like that—"

"Okay," said Rap, his shoulders falling, "I get it. But."

The man shook his head. "Stand there." He pointed at a tile on the sidewalk. "No. Not there. *There.*" They moved over two steps. "*There!*"

They moved back one step.

He retreated into his store.

Through the window they saw him sitting at his computer, typing for a furious sixty seconds hard enough to break most keyboards.

Stood up, gathered something out of the printer, marched back to the door.

"Here!"

They each took a sheet. Rap scanned it quickly:

World's Great Men of Colour by J.A. Rogers
The Autobiography of Malcolm X
Always Outnumbered, Always Outgunned by Walter Mosely
Allah is Not Obliged by Ahmoudou Kourouma
Life from Death Row by Mukia Abu Jamal
An Autobiography by Angela Davis
Brown Girl in the Ring by Nalo Hopkinson
Black Girl Talk by the Black Girls
Thomas Sankara Speaks
Black Spark, White Fire by Richard Poe

Rap looked up at him with eyes that must've said, *What*.

"Read," he sighed. "All you hafta do is read *one* of them. And you," he said, glaring at Jackie Chan, "read a different one. Then teach em to each other so between the two of you, you know two books. Do that, and then come talk to me.

"And if you don't," he said, his lower lip a receding drawbridge, his hand forming a fist whose fingers actually cracked as they closed, "don't ever come back here again. And I freaking mean it!"

10.

The door jangled as the man leaned on the door to shut it.

Click.

Jackie Chan: "Damn, bwoi, we just got *served*."

"No, we just got *owned*."

"That guy for real? Expects us to read a book just so we have permission to say sorry?"

"Look, JC, he saved our lives. What, we gonna just drip away? I mean, obviously it matters to this guy that we do this. You can't even read one lousy book? What's it gonna hurt? What're you afraid of?"

"What're you, Oprah? Analysin me an shit?"

"Naw, I'm Dr. Phil. 'Joy-riding. How's that working for ya?' How much worse could one book be than almost getting killed for kicks?"

"Where we even gonna *get* all these? Ten books or whatever? That'd cost like fifty bucks!"

"You don't havta get em all. Just one. And ever hear of a library?"

"*Library*?" The word blasted out of JC's mouth like Rap'd just said they should get advanced plastic surgery to turn themselves into fully operational Transformers.

"Yeah. The library."

"Man, what's he care what books we're reading? Got enough reading to do for school, an I ain't even doin that *To Cook a Mockingbird* an whatever."

"Well, look at this list. Look at these titles. You ever have a teacher get you to read books with these kinda names? There's even a Muslim one here."

JC glanced at the list, then eyed him.

"Well I'ont even have a library card anymore. I owed like two hunnid dollars for some CDs my lil brother destroyed."

Rap tried shaking the disgust out of his head. Couldn't even *imagine* not having an active card—the library was his best and only source for DVDs, and he couldn't afford renting them at five bucks a piece.

If he ran up a bill like JC's he'd never get to watch anything. And his mother'd lecture him about irresponsibility and money-wasting until two weeks after he died of old age.

Rap: "You done making excuses?"

"Nope."

"Then *I'll* take em out."

"F'real?"

"Yeah."

"Well, get me suh'm unner a hunnid pages, aiight? I got things t'do."

"No you don't."

"Dude, figure of speech. *Damn.*"

"And you're coming with me."

Jackie Chan put his palms up, shoulders high, horrified. "Man!"

Rap walked away. JC drooped his head and followed him like they were hoofing it to the electric chair.

But that would've been too short a walk. Instead they soled it ten blocks south to downtown to the biggest library in the city where, without realizing it, they were about to begin their revolution.

Deanna Bowen
(1969–)

"It's been a long, long journey of unpacking Blackness in Canada, the problem being that it's such a complex, ultimately violent story that I'm talking about," says Deanna Bowen, who was born in Oakland, California, and raised in Vancouver. "So how do you frame it properly?" (B. Chan). A multidisciplinary artist investigating the hauntings of racial trauma, slavery, migration, and the legacy of the KKK in Canada and the US, Deanna Bowen works by multiplying the frames that can effectively remember and tell difficult black histories. Working with film, video installations, performance, drawing, sculpture, photography, and an intensive archival research method, Bowen explores personal and public histories of trauma, especially as it has shaped her own family lineage. She is a descendant of the Alabama- and Kentucky-born black prairie settles of Amber Valley and Campsie, Alberta, and she is recently uncovering a family lineage that is Afro-Creek. These ancestral legacies are the key site of investigation of Bowen's artistic practice. Her work has been widely shown throughout Canada, the United States, and Europe.

Bowen received a diploma in fine arts in 1992 from Langara College in Vancouver and a diploma in sculpture from Emily Carr College of Art and Design in 1994. After a year of study at Simon Fraser University, Bowen moved to Toronto, where she worked in art organizations such as the Liaison of Independent Filmmakers of Toronto, the journal *Canadian Woman Studies*, and InterAccess Electronic Media Arts Centre. During this time Bowen honed her skills in video and film production. She went on to attend University of Toronto's master in visual studies program from 2006 to 2008.

In *sum of the parts that can be named*, a video oral history she produced and performed in 2010, Bowen continues to explore the nature of intergenerational trauma by performing to camera a visceral oral history of slavery and migration. Drawing both on ancestral memory and archival documents, this history explores both the power and limits of black memory in the contexts of slavery and displacement. *sum of the parts* was screened at the Kassel Documentary Film & Video

354

Festival (2011) and the Oberhausen Film Festival (2012), and in 2012 curator
Srimoyee Mitra selected it for inclusion in *Project 35_Vol. 2.* The version that
appears here has been updated (2018) to reflect Bowen's recent research into her
Afro-Creek ancestry.

Bowen's exhibit *Paul Good Papers*, presented in Toronto's Gallery 44 in 2012
and York University in 2013, investigated the presence of the KKK in Canada. The
exhibit included a re-enacted CBC interview with Klansmen and reproductions
of KKK posters and robes, as well as hundreds of pages of the 1911 Anti-Creek
Negro Petition, which sought to prevent black migrants from entering the Canadian
prairies. This work challenges audiences to grapple with the anti-black histories
of the prairies, and to rewrite the myth of Canada as a promised land for black
freedom seekers.

More recently, Bowen's exhibit ~~Hunting the Nigs in Philadelphia~~: *Or An Alter-
nate Chronology of Events Leading Up to and One Year Beyond the Columbia
Avenue Uprisings, August 28–30 1964* was shown in the Institute of Contemporary
Art at University of Pennsylvania's group exhibition *Traces in the Dark* in 2015.
This emerges from Bowen's research on Canadian and US Ku Klux Klan activi-
ties. Bowen argues that iconic images of civil rights protests ironically occlude the
Klan's activities, a history she wishes to bring more fully to light.

Bowen's body of work has been recognized with the 2014 William H. Johnson
Prize and the prestigious Guggenheim Fellowship in 2016. She was an invited pre-
senter in the Creative Time Summit at La Biennale di Venezia—56th International
Art Exhibition in 2015; and her writings and art works have appeared in numerous
publications, including *Towards an African-Canadian Art History: Art, Memory and
Resistance; North: New African Canadian Writing—West Coast Line*; and *Má-Ka:
Diasporic Juks: Contemporary Writing by Queers of African Descent.*

sum of the parts that can be named

First *known* generation: my great, great, great, grandparents.

Details are few. I barely have dates …

I don't know their names.
I don't know their parents' names.
I don't know if they had siblings.
I don't know when they died.

I do know that my great, great, great, grandfather was born somewhere in Africa and my great, great, great, grandmother was born in the State of Georgia. I believe that both were born around 1815—about 196 years after the first Africans were brought to Virginia and about 21 years after Eli Whitney patents his cotton gin.

My great, great, great, grandparents were brought sixty miles south of Montgomery, Alabama to Butler County and had at least 3 boys: Dick, Reese and Jack between 1835 and 1840. Records indicate the likelihood that other siblings exist.

Growing up, my grandmother told me that a white family by the name of Thigpen owned us. I haven't found relatives by that name, but have found family by the names of Peagler, Powell, Gregory, and Bowen.

I believe we got our name from descendants of Charles Bowen of Jones County, Georgia.

I suspect that the Bowens follow Revolutionary War soldier John Carter and his family to Butler County just shortly after Bowen's daughter Martha marries John Carter's middle son Jarrett in 1818. Martha and Jarrett died in 1843 and 1845. My grandmother's stories and those of the Bowen & Carter families' overlap when Martha and Jarrett's daughter Martha marries Elijah T. Thigpen in Butler County, December 20, 1855.

To give you a better sense of the situation ... In 1850, there were 3,204,313 registered slaves and 434,495 free blacks in all of the United States.

In the State of Alabama, there were 342,844 slaves of which *black belt*[1] counties like Butler averaged about 7000.

At this same time, there were four free blacks in Butler County.

A decade later, in 1860 the number would rise to 44.

---

1   A term for the large agricultural regions of the southern US, particularly Alabama, where plantation agriculture was intensively developed and, thus, where there is a high population of African Americans.

Second generation: my great, great grandparents.

Details are more abundant here ... though most of what I have are names and dates.

Presumed to be the oldest, Dick Bowen was born around 1835; a year after Great Britain would abolish the slave trade.

I believe he lived and died in Butler County.

Little is known of presumed third child Jack Bowen. His name was found in a family bible owned by descendant Doris Peagler.

Jack was born enslaved around 1840 and died 'free' before 1910. I believe he was survived by his wife Jane.

Jack and Jane had four children: Lula, Frank, and twins Martha and Mary.

Twin daughter Mary weds Joe George, and together they have ten children. Their ninth child Eva has two known daughters: Doris Peagler and Sarah Powell born in Butler County in the early 1940s.

Doris and Sarah's family has lived and worked on what used to be John Carter's youngest son Alfred's land for several generations; first as slaves and then as sharecroppers.

The Carter family lost the land in the Civil War. Since then, the acreage has been owned by the family of slave holding planter, Harry Poole—deceased 1997, of Pine Flat, Butler County.

Sarah and her husband live in the Greenville area. In 1969—the year I was born—their 8th child Eric would be the first family member born off the Carter/Poole plantation—some 106 years after Abraham Lincoln wrote the Emancipation Proclamation.

Dick and Jack's brother Reese—my great, great grandfather—was born about the same time that runaway slave and novelist Harriet Jacobs would go into hiding in 1835. He lived most of his life with his wife Sytha in Butler Springs until her death. At the age of 76, great grandpa Reese moves to Greenville and marries second wife Callie Goldsmith in 1911. I have no additional information about Reese beyond this date. I assume that he dies in Greenville sometime before 1925.

His first wife Sytha—my great, great, grandmother—was born in Alabama in 1852 the same year that *Uncle Tom's Cabin* was published. She married Reese in 1863 at the age of 11 and had nine children. She died in Butler Springs sometime between 1900 and 1910.

Born into slavery, it's hard to say what my great, great grandmother would have known about the world taking shape around her. In her lifetime, Fredrick Douglass would write *My Bondage and My Freedom*, the US Supreme Court would hand down the Dred Scott decision,[2] blacks from California would settle in British Columbia,[3] abolitionist John Brown would be hung for leading an attack at Harpers Ferry,[4] and the Civil War would begin in 1861.

Reese and Sytha's first son Gus would be born in Butler Springs in 1864. In 1865, the war ended, slavery was banned, and Lincoln was assassinated.

In 1867, the BNA Act passed and John A. Macdonald became Canada's first prime minister. Reese and Sytha's daughter Mittie would be born around 1869. In that year, Louis Riel would lead the Red River Rebellion and Manitoba would become Canada's fifth province.

In 1870, daughter Minta would be born. In 1871, British Columbia joined the Confederation. Daughter Alice was born in 1872, son Johnie in 1874, and in 1875, Reese and Sytha's sixth child Missie would be born.

Mark Twain would write *The Adventures of Tom Sawyer* in 1876, and the Exodusters[5] would begin their migration from Kansas in 1878.

In 1879 son Edd would be born.

---

2 *Dred Scott v. Sandford* (1857) was the US Supreme Court decision that the American Constitution did not include citizenship for black people, whether enslaved or free.
3 In 1858, 600 black people migrated en masse from San Francisco to the colonies that would become British Columbia (Compton, *Bluesprint*).
4 In 1858 abolitionist John Brown led an attack on Harpers Ferry in Virginia in an effort to initiate an armed slave revolt.
5 Name given to the first general migration of African Americans after the Civil War.

In 1882, Texas cowboy John Ware—Alberta's first black cowboy—would move to Alberta, and in 1883 Reese and Sytha's youngest son, Augustus would be born.

The last spike was driven for the CPR and Louis Riel was hanged for high treason in 1885. In 1887, the Dawes Act[6] was invoked and in 1889, Vincent Van Gogh would paint his famous *Starry Night*.

Details about the lives of Reese and Sytha's children are scarce.

Minta (Bowen) Lucas was a divorced mother of 5 children and caretaker of widowed father Reese, by 1910.

Reese and Sytha's son Edd and his wife Lizzie Lucas migrate to Freestone, Texas around 1905. Together they have four children: Thelma, Fred, Hubbard and Edd Jr.

Edd Jr. marries Bessie Lee Carroll. Together they have 6 children including son Kennard Bowen. Kennard weds Mary Louise Turner in 1966 and has two children: Camelia Bridget and Kennard Jr.—who would then go on to have Jonathan and Ashley with his wife Sheree Hunter.

Third Generation: My great grandparents.

My great grandfather is Reese and Sytha's fifth child.
Early census records list him as Johnie but I know him as Willis Bowen Sr.

I know little of his life in Butler County except that he was born in 1874 and married wife Genie in his father's house in 1893. Some have said that he left Butler County because he had killed—or nearly killed—a man after an argument at a dance sometime around 1901.

Great grandma Genie was half black and half Cherokee.[7] She was born in Wilcox County, Alabama in 1875.

---

6 Provided authority to break up reservations by granting land allotments to individual Native Americans.

7 Since writing this piece in 2010, Deanna Bowen has learned, through patient archival work and relationship building, that her family is Afro-Creek, not Cherokee, as she originally believed.

Her maiden name was thought to have been Thigpen, but discovery of her marriage license shows that her family name was actually Gregory.

I have no details about her parents, nor do I have any clues about how they came together. The family myth is that great grandma was the daughter of a chief … which might be true … Though, the most likely scenario is that great grandma's father had enslaved her mother, as the Cherokee nation is known to have kept black slaves then.

Together, my great grandparents Willis and Genie had thirteen children. Siblings Mary, Ivy, Willa, Reese, and Boadie were born between 1894 and 1900.

The family settled 650 miles west in Freestone, Texas with great grandpa's brother Edd and his family around 1901.

There, they had daughter Magdaline and son Geoffrey between 1902 and 1903, though Magdaline would become ill and would not survive the year.

The family kept moving to what was then Indian Territory—now Oklahoma. Not yet a state, and free of Jim Crow laws, the territory was a haven for blacks who hoped to create and govern their own lives. In 1904, the family settled around Clearview—a black town seventy miles south of Tulsa, Oklahoma.

Son John Henry was born there in 1905—just a year after Saskatchewan and Alberta became provinces of Canada.

Willis and Genie's 9th and 10th children Obadiah and Elrene were born in Clearview as well, around 1907 and 1909.

The family thrived in Oklahoma; the children got good educations and the family owned their own land. In-laws Albert and Mary Gregory and cousin Columbus Bowen, his wife Martha and their 8 children were doing well there too.

But the climate changed when Indian Territory became the state of Oklahoma in 1907. Segregation laws were put in place soon after statehood and relations between blacks and whites eroded. Around the same time, the

Canadian government had been encouraging settlement of the West with the promise of free or cheap land. Scouts from Clearview were sent to Canada as Oklahoma repealed voting rights and segregated the schools. An exodus from Clearview began soon after.

Some families joined a movement to return to Africa. Others opted to settle 120 miles north of Edmonton, Alberta in Athabasca Landing around 1909.

My great grandpa Willis left for Canada from Guthrie, Oklahoma with our family, a few bachelors, and four other families—40 people in total—in a chartered railcar in the summer of 1910.

The government had not anticipated the rush of black immigrants and quickly adapted entry restrictions in an effort to keep them from coming in. In 1911, a white mob would rape a black woman and lynch her and her son as they awaited his trial for a shooting some thirty miles from Clearview, in nearby Paden.[8]

At this same time, Prime Minister Wilfrid Laurier drafted a regulation that banned blacks from coming into Canada. Less than a year later, the order in council would be repealed because Laurier's government was defeated in the general election.

The trip from Alabama to Canada was especially hard on Great grandma Genie. She had suffered a stroke before leaving Oklahoma at the age of thirty-four and had never fully recovered.

One of each family member in the chartered railcar was turned away for health reasons after inspection in White Rock, BC. Immigration rejected the Bowen family because middle boy John Henry had a broken leg. The family had no choice but to wait for the leg to heal in Bellingham. When it did, Great grandpa Willis decided to take John Henry across separately through a different entry point. The rest of the family crossed at White Rock and continued on to Vancouver without issue.

---

8   Laura Nelson and her son L.D. were lynched on May 25, 1911, near Okemah, Oklahoma. After being sexually assaulted, Laura was hanged, along with her son, from a railway bridge over the North Canadian River.

In July 1912, Willis and Genie's 11th child Edward Hubert Bowen would be born in Vancouver.

The First World War had just begun.

Raised on the farm, great grandma Genie had no interest in the city. She hated Vancouver because it always rained and she didn't trust a place that had an ocean on one side and mountains on the other. She blamed the loss of her 12th child on Canadian doctors, believing that the child could have been saved if the family was around black people. So, the family moved to Amber Valley, Alberta—a black settlement near Athabasca Landing—not long after.

Eldest daughter Mary was stricken with meningitis along the way, so the family stayed at a public stopping house. Mary recovered, but the family contracted body lice and their belongings burned to the ground in Athabasca.

Great grandpa Willis was given $125 dollars in compensation for thousands of dollars of household belongings because he could not prove its value.

With virtually nothing, the family lived in an abandoned house until Great grandpa Willis built his own—six miles from the post office, three miles from the country store, and a combined four thousand one hundred miles from Butler County.

In 1915, Willis and Genie's twelfth child Purvis Kitchener (a.k.a. P.K.) was born in Donatville, Alberta. Great grandpa Willis was hauling freight to Fort McMurray when his thirteenth and final child—my grandmother—Jean was born, February 27, 1919: 3 months before the General Strike shut down Winnipeg and 2 years before hundreds of blacks would be killed in the race riots in Tulsa.

The Bowen children were an integral part of the Amber Valley community in the early years. The older children began to marry within the community while the younger attended school. Their ailing mother Genie Gregory Bowen died (some say crazy) on April 27, 1932 in Amber Valley. She was 57 years old.

Six years after her passing, youngest daughter Jean married Albert Sterling Risby of neighboring black settlement Campsie—on June 15, 1938.

Great grandpa Willis continued to work the farm and was the first postmaster of Amber Valley through 1942. He returned to the States once, in 1943, when he tried to convince brother Edd to come to Canada.

Edd decided to stay in Freestone Texas with his family, who continue to live on the land to the present day. The brothers stayed in contact by writing each other regularly until it was no longer possible to do so. Their grandchildren Kennard and Norma Jean wrote on their behalf until their deaths in the 1970s.

Mama and Daddy—that's what I call my grandmother Jean and grandfather Albert—spent the early part of their lives together in Amber Valley. Jean and Albert's first three daughters: Eldith, Leora—my mother, and Ardith were born on the farm as the Second World War played out. Seven children followed between the years 1946 and 1957, including: Wayne, Donna, Verna, Ross, Carmen, Barbara, and Danny. Mama and Daddy thought that their kids would get a better education in the city, so they sent the older ones to Vancouver to live with Great Grandma Rose Risby in the early 1950's.

Great Grandma Rose took ill around the same time, so the rest of the family moved from the farm to live together in Vancouver's East end. Daddy worked as a porter for the CN then and Mama worked for her nephew at Vancouver's only black nightclub, the Harlem Nocturne, on Hastings Street.

In 1955, my mother Leora was 13 years old and had started grade seven at an integrated school when the Montgomery Bus Boycott began in Alabama. She graduated from high school in 1961 and though Vancouver was as hostile as the States for blacks, she was working for the City of Vancouver when the March on Washington[9] took place in 1963. She was working

---

9   The March on Washington for Jobs and Freedom saw about a quarter-million people gather near the Lincoln Memorial to demand civil rights for African Americans. It was the event at which Martin Luther King Jr. delivered his famous "I Have a Dream" speech.

at the University of Washington in Seattle when the Marches on Selma began in '65 and was back in Vancouver in 1968 when Martin Luther King was shot. My mother met my father Lamarre Zack Smalley in Seattle at the Checkmate on 23rd not long after King's assassination.

About a year later, I would be born in Oakland, California—six months after Apollo 11 landed on the moon. My parents married in April 1972 and were separated by 1973 when my father's unresolved first marriage was brought to light.

In that same year, Shirley Chisholm would announce her candidacy for the Democratic nomination for president of the United States and the Watergate Scandal would break. A year later, Pierre Trudeau would be re-elected as Prime Minister of Canada, and less than a year after that, my great grandfather Willis Bowen Sr. would die in Amber Valley, Alberta, October 21, 1975.

He was 101 years old. I was six.

My mother lived between Seattle and Vancouver throughout much of the 70s and 80s.

Mama and Daddy raised me in the times when I didn't live with her. When my mom did live in Vancouver, we'd go to Seattle on weekends to visit her sister Eldith and her kids. I remember watching *Roots* there in 1977 with all of them.

When I lived with Mama and Daddy I went to bible camp in Newbrook, Alberta and Friday night teen meetings at Great Aunt Lena's church in Vancouver on East 22nd. I sang hymns with Daddy in church and grew up around a lot of old people I didn't understand. As a result, my childhood is marked by the passing of Mama and Daddy's church, many friends, brothers, sisters, cousins, nephews, and nieces.

Between the years 1970 and 1991 my grandmother's siblings Reese, Boadie, John Henry, P.K., Willa, and Edward would pass, as would my grandfather's siblings Frank and Herman.

I remember when, in 1979, my grandparent's fourth daughter Donna died on Hastings Street. I remember when their son Carmen followed in 1982 … when eldest son Wayne died in 1990. Jean and Albert's youngest daughter, and my favorite aunt Barbara passed more recently in 2003.

There were seventy-five 7th generation and ten 8th generation descendants born to the Bowen family by the time I finished high school in 1987. As of today, I know of 652 Bowen family members in total.

Mama and Daddy moved back to Alberta and started preaching again when Daddy was given his own church in Edmonton in the late 1980s.

I changed my last name to Bowen to honor my grandmother in 1991 and graduated from Art College in Vancouver in 1992.

Jean Bowen Risby died of a heart attack in Edmonton in 1993. Reverend Albert Sterling Risby died in Vancouver six months later.

My name is Deanna Jean Bowen. I moved to Toronto shortly after their deaths, and have lived here since August 1994.

This project began in 1996. What happened between then and now is another story.

Bertrand Bickersteth
(1969–)

Bertrand Bickersteth, poet, spoken-word artist, playwright, and scholar of black Alberta, refers to Alberta as his "central space of inspiration," but also his "unwilling muse" (Afrikadey!) —unwilling because it is always reluctant to reveal its black past and present.

Bickersteth was born in Sierra Leone and raised in Olds, Alberta. He holds a BA in English literature from the University of British Columbia and an MA in comparative literature (African/Arabic) from University College London. He taught as an assistant professor at Grand Valley State University for a decade, but ultimately returned to his "unwilling muse," Alberta, in 2009. He currently lives in Calgary and teaches writing and communication at Olds College. His research focuses on black identity in Alberta and in western Canada. He has published scholarship on Wayde Compton (2015), and has published poetry in *Kola, The Antigonish Review, Freefall*, and in the anthology *The Great Black North.* He is a contributor to *Abronet Magazine*, an African periodical published in Calgary in both English and Amharic. He is also the founder and director of DiversityWorks Organizational Consulting, a firm that provides consulting on matters of diversity. Bickersteth's first play, *The Wandering Tribe of Black-White Men*, was mounted by Centre Stage Theatre in Calgary for Black History Month in 2011.

Bickersteth's poetry indicates the full range of affective and formal responses that arise out of a deep and meaningful—though not necessarily easy—relation to place. In "Accidental Agriculture" (originally published in *The Fieldstone Review* 2016–17) the poet-speaker reflects on how a "blunt encounter," not just with school kids racializing him but also with the white gaze, planted in him the seed of difference that would eventually allow him to grow into a poet. It is a poem that can be read along with Robert Kroetsch's *Seed Catalogue* and Kaie Kellough's "Boyhood Dub II," both of which consider how you nurture a black prairie poet who "suddenly sees everything" "through black eyes."

In "What We Used to Call It," originally published in the the *Antigonish Review* (2018), the poet-speaker travels through southern Alberta searching for traces of black history that might lead to a sense of identity and connection. But when the speaker calls to mind the racial epithet used as the toponym given to a creek "in honour" of the black cowboy John Ware, he is brought into a discomfiting, ironic relation to place and history. The speaker can't forget "what we used to call it." Still, the poet's long lines, wispy as the clouds above a chinook sky, suggest how a connection to southern Alberta shapes a black prairie aesthetic.

In Bickersteth's poem "We, Too" (originally published in the anthology *Great Black North*, 2013) he constructs a celebratory collective sense of black identity and a unified, epiphanic voice constellated around second-wave history. The evocative "The Invisible Man on the Prairies" (*Kola* 2013) addresses the continual negation of black history on the prairies ("No one sees this, no") that threatens to render the poet-speaker's own presence spectral.

His long poem, "Wakanda, Oklahoma," was longlisted for the 2018 CBC Poetry Prize. The poem was inspired by Bickersteth's work in the archives reading the advertisments aimed at a black Oklahoman readership that enticed black families to settle on the Canadian prairies at the start of the twentieth century. The poems put flesh on the bare bones of those historical advertisements by imagining the complex lives of the black farmers "seizing slavery's seeds" (CBC Poetry Longlist 2018).

❦

Accidental Agriculture

The bruising beginning
face rubbed in
central Alberta's finest
Orthic Dark Brown Chernozem
where wheat flourishes
and barley wails
After the fight
we congregate in the principal's office:
punishments
meted out to him
the aggressor
who impugned my face against the ground
because its darkness inspired
a simile

part-time prairie poet that he was
And punishments
meted out to me
the victim so called
Well, why did you fight back?
Why do you people
always fight?
Now I have to punish you
too
The principal glared at me
his eyes a shock
of literal blue
Outside
on my way home
I pondered the view
from the top of a rare hill
a field spilled
with dandelions splayed out below
This accidental agriculture
will be swallowed
by an instantaneous city with
its blindness
its inevitability
I saw the whole against the horizon
A nine-year-old
a timeless landscape
a flatness ensuing
My tender head still throbbing
from the blunt encounter
I reached with a quiet fist
to rub at the soreness swelling
around my eyes
Well
why *did* you fight back?
When the black child is six years old
in Harlem
he suddenly sees everything he has been before
and all that is to come laid out before him and
how
it has been laid out before him and this

muses James Baldwin
is the fundamental difference between
any child growing anywhere
in Alberta
and every child that must see things
through black eyes

What We Used to Call It

and that's not all, have you seen this one, this place this prairie
space, look at its wide open spaces

its Chinook arched above unclaimed coulees its
snow covered skin ice white riddled carapace dotted dirt yellow its singular snow owls sentinels on unexpected telephone poles

and that there is Nigger John's Creek
but we don't call it that anymore and this

here is the end of the Bar U Trail and this and
(and) this here is the shadow of the Stoney mountains cutting
across unforgiving winter ground and this here is the ground itself now
dead to the

drip of wheat sounding in its summer soul and the braids of oil coursing
through its

golden veins and this vein yeah and (and and) that's not all *that* there is
where I
would belong if I only knew

what that there is called.

I know what we used to call it.

❦

We, Too

We, too, sing Alberta, from the first jail in Calgary[1] and the wronged belonging of this familiar place.

We, too, sing of Cyclone the Big Black Buck,[2] too, sing for Cyclone, sing like Cyclone the Big Black Buck,
>   the eternal Northern Star of the greatest outdoor
>   show on earth.
>   We, too, wail in these Northlands this side of la rivière
>   de la paix
Oui, tu peux chanter, te *faut* chanter ici aussi.

This *faux* was not our fault, this dislocated Harlem farming, just north of Athabasca: You
>   called/We responded
>   All right, all right, now we are OK here, too (and KS, MS, MO
and, OH, even IL, here, too).

And we, too, sing Alberta
the Babylon psalm rounded up along

the erupted rockies, one renamed ridge, and
the evaporating elevated grain

the faded stain of segregated schools
the suppressed success of our homes

steaded in the prairie bush
the land, its hues

the language we hews
the semple blues of Hughes

---

1   A reference to Jesse Williams, the first person hanged in the Northwest Territories in 1884.
2   John Ware, who reputedly invented the sport of steer wrestling which features as an attraction at the "the greatest outdoor show on earth," the Calgary Stampede.

with the grinning dues of Ware
granted by MacEwan, our prairie uncle.[3]

Too, the bellows in the bowels of the overground
railroad, we sing, portered and pulled, man,[4]

prairied by night
moonstruck by the days

The Invisible Man on the Prairies

Featuring Ralph Ellison

No one sees this, no
But he is a part of this
Landscape too.
Right here. Here, right
in front of your long nose.
Not impressed?
It's no trick.
Hold out your hand and
Move it back
and forth
in history.
He is still going to be there
and here.
What a sight not to behold!
His OK

---

3   Grant MacEwan (August 12, 1902–June 15, 2000) was an author, historian, mayor
of Calgary, and the ninth lieutenant-governor of Alberta. His *John Ware's Cow Country* (1973, 3rd ed., 1995) helped to mythologize John Ware, even as it produced him as
a racial caricature.
4   A reference to the black Pullman car porters. The railways were one of the few
Canadian industries to hire black men in the early twentieth century. But the job
came with discrimination and poor wages. From the First World War until the 1950s,
railways did not hire or promote black men to the post of engineer, conductor, or any
other job on the train. For a full history, see Stanley G. Grizzle.

your AB
See?

Anything and everything
was to be found in the chaos
of Oklahoma; thus
the concept of the Renaissance
Man has lurked long within

the shadow of my past.

See?
The shadow in the act
that is what you
feel hauting your hand
(you can pull it back now).
Impressed?
(You will be.)

More than just looked over
he is inverted presence
that unexpectedly
shapes
the landscape you
walk on

unrevealed
invisible
unwholed

Watch your step!

Troy B. Bailey
(ca. 1960s–)

Author of the long poem cycle *The Pierre Bonga Loops* (2010), which explores, in part, a history of black-Indigenous intimacies in the northern part of Turtle Island, Troy B. Bailey claims his own history of black-Indigenous *métissage*. His people have "a long self-awareness of being a mixed-race people in Canada going back to the 1700's. This lineage includes some of the first known mixing with Indigenous peoples."[1] His Nova Scotian father was mixed Africadian Black and Mi'kmaq (his father's grandmother was Mi'kmaq), though his relatives encouraged Troy to hide his Indigeneity. "Canada in the 1960's," he says, "had clearly separate racial lines and 'the natives had it worse than the Blacks,'" according to his family oral history. Bailey claims the term "Afro-Métis" as specific to the self-identity of cultures in the Afro-Euro-Indigenous diaspora on the eastern seaboard of North America going back to at least 1604.[2]

Bailey writes from the perspective of this *métissage*. His writing style, he says, is informed by personal and collective experiences of Afro-Métis, as well as "by my English, Scottish, Irish, Mi'kmaq, Nova Scotia Black blood-memories of the Atlantic African Diaspora." He weaves this perspective together with histories of little-known figures forgotten by the chroniclers of history, such as Pierre Bonga and his children, some of the first-known Afro-Métis born in the Red River Region in the 1790s to early 1800s.

Bailey was born and raised in northern Manitoba, in the small community of Thompson, where his father worked underground as a nickel miner while his mother worked as a post office clerk. His early childhood years in Thompson were idyllic, as this was the time when the Inco mine made the community prosperous, and his family reaped the rewards of a booming economy. Bailey began to

---

1 Personal communication, January 2, 2019.
2 See, for instance, Jack D. Forbes.

understand himself as "mixed blood" only when the family moved to Winnipeg, just before the Inco mine had a downturn and his father began working for CP Rail. "At that time the series *Roots* by Alex Haley had come on T.V. Our family would sit together and watch *Roots* every week. I think like most people I was quite shocked about what had gone on in slavery in the U.S. About that time, my father also brought home a series of books on Black history he got from a co-worker at CP Rail."

The Pierre Bonga Loops, Bailey's first published volume (2010), is a documentary poem that uncovers the historical and archival black presence in the Canadian west. It is also about fathers and sons, now and then, as well as about the poet's relationship with the archive. Using images and text from documentary sources including the Hudson's Bay Company Archives, as well as furnishing his own personal experiences as a long-distance solo and expedition paddler, Bailey produces an experimental textual pastiche of a figure he calls "one of the unacknowledged founding fathers of the Prairies."

Bailey holds a BA in creative communications from the University of Winnipeg. He lives in Treaty 1 Territory, the traditional lands of the Anishinaabeg, Cree, Oji-Cree, Dakota, and Dené Peoples, and the Manitoba Métis.

The Pierre Bonga Loops

He Left This Note:

<u>1780</u>   <u>NEGROES</u>

'From Mr Samuel Hearne Chief at Churchill to Mr Humphrey Marten Chief at York Fort
Dated September 2 nd 1780

> … Mr Holt arrived here yesterday, for the Contents of his Cargo please to accept my thanks I could not have wished Sir you had sent me an Account of the things sent by Mr Holt, otherwise I shall not know what is chargeable in our Accounts, as yet I have only seen two Hogs and four Negroes …'

(H.B.C. Arch. B.239/b/40, fo. 27d.)

1780 NEGROES
'From Mr Humphrey Marten Chief of York Fort to Mr Samuel Hearne
Chief at Churchill
dated Sept. 12 th 1780'

'… When Mr John Turner saild. for Churchill he had an account of
things consigned to that place. Mr George Holt had also an Acct. if
it as not deliver'd blame cannot rest with us. The Hogs were bred at
York fort, those Persons you are pleased to stile Negroes at Prince
Wales Fort, I need not inform you Sir that one is the Grandson of Mr
Ferdinand Jacobs, that the other three are the Father, the Aunt and the
Cousin of that child …'

H.B.C. Arch. B.239/b/40, fo. 28

Encore, Une Autre Fois

I don't think Samuel Hearne went across
The Copper Tundra to find the Western Ocean
With some Negroes
And Hog meat.

But Mr. Hearne;
Does "Stile" mean an instrument for writing, a passage, or maybe a vertical bar?

Is it their Manner or Characteristic, or does Mr. Humphrey say?

Perhaps, Mr. Hearne,
"They,
The Negroes,"
Sketched in ledgers,
Insist on writing themselves as
"Persons!" of account

Refer again to: "Pleased to call them that; Negroes …"

You should know better, Mr Hearne.

If only you could muster Ferdinand Jacobs, John Turner, and George Holt,

you could establish a strand of associates in this story of an African-Cana-
dian Voyageur—

May 20

A command of paddlers loaded with trade goods left Montreal today
under the command of Alexander Henry the Younger with the intention
of reaching Lake Athabasca by snowfall. The fledgling North-West
Company hopes to compete with the established Hudson Bay Company
and also be the first outfit to reach the Pacific Ocean in order to claim the
land for the King of England and by extension the Dominion of Canada.
The men who carry the expedition are as follows:

Describe these men. {   }

Electroshock

Grand Michelle,[3] the *Voyageur*

Who paddled for ages
The *Canot du Maître*[4]
Ten to twelve meters long
With eight to twelve men,

And the children sometimes—,

Accepted four tons

Who paddled the *Canot du Nord*,[5] advancing to the Athabasca,
In sickness and in health, till death did its part,

---

3   An African voyageur.

4   *Canot du maître* was the large and sturdy canoe used in the route between Montreal and Lake Superior. It could transport up to 90 *pièces* of 40 kilos or 90 pounds
each as well as a crew of eight to twelve voyageurs, their equipment as well as a few
passengers.

5   The *Canot du Nord* was the smaller and flimsier canoe used in the interior for voy-
ages starting on Lake Superior. This boat was paddled by four to six voyageurs and
could carry thirty-five bales, for a total capacity of 1,700 kilos or 4,000 pounds.

Seven or eight meters long
carried 1½ tons

Who paddled
The *Canot du Nord*,
With four to six, with the things that England liked most,
Only portaged by 2
Voyageurs.

The bowsman *Avant*, the first to hit the rocks,
Gouvernail the paddler
Who steers from the back, the last to crack
Bonga at the bow—
out by a riverbank—

In Rapids

Two times Two times tow—

A Negro voyageur Convulsed,
Split Into Pieces

In torrents
7 or 8 meters long

Corbeau

Corbeau, you trickster, you change at first to black then colourless, you
want to send me to the tomb.
They call you raven not because of black feathers, but for you,
underneath, you came from some wound,
some womb, once killed and plucked, your blue skin dies of fright,
coverd in eyes.

Well I stray over the north Atlantic sea,

                                        Separated from my

body

To invigilate over slave captors,

Oh my, I came through the middle passage
While you
Sat in the pine trees hung from a wing, an indiscernible message;

Corbeau, you true Caliban, you turn white into black under the sun
Squishing Cree terms into the night tarnish, squeezing polish,

In the metaphor of a bright sky, or in the pitch
Unconnected,
Wondering what to do here
... why you want to oversleep inside my pure mink mantle of ink

{... *perchance here you need greets my infinitive* ...}

Wakefield Brewster
(1972–)

Wakefield Brewster is often taken by his audiences to be a rapper. But as he says, "Those who believe that I'm up on stage rapping simply aren't listening carefully. I'm influenced by rap and hip-hop, I have an undeniable flow, but it's poetry" (L. Taylor).

Since 2000, Wakefield Brewster has been recognized as one of the most popular and prolific performance poets in Canada. Brewster is a Toronto Slam Poetry Champion, and three-time Calgary Poetry Slam Champion and Team Captain (2006, 2008, 2009). He was born and raised in Toronto to parents hailing from Barbados and has resided in Calgary since 2006. Brewster says one of his "greatest and most reputable claims to fame is that you will consistently find him performing poetry in places where you wouldn't expect poetry to be heard." Besides in classrooms, featured readings, workshops, and lectures, you will find him performing at retired teachers' conventions, pharmaceutical conventions, and political fundraisers, as well as mentoring struggling young men.

Brewster wears many professional and personal hats, including founder of the reading series Poésie à la Pâtisserie and the Pitbull Poetry Reading Series. He works as a poetry coach and mentor, poet and teacher-in-residence, literacy advocate, vocal coach, classical pianist, percussionist, father, youth mentor, massage therapist, healing arts advocate, and canine massage therapist. He is 1st Dan, Black Belt in World Tae Kwon Do Federation.

Brewster has recorded two CDs of poetry, *Wakefield Brewster da Lyrical Pitbull* (Kill Whitey Records, 2007) and *East2West* (Kill Whitey Records, 2008). His writing has been anthologized in *T-Dot Griots* (2004), *The Great Black North* (Frontenac 2013), and *The Calgary Project: A City Map in Verse and Visual* (Frontenac 2014).

The following poem, "i can," is about the poet's confrontations with intolerant educational institutions from grade school through university, due, he says, "to Mental Illness, undiagnosed until my 30's; I was simply labelled as a failure, a nobody, a nothing, overlooked, underestimated, misunderstood, the whole nine." However, discovering poetry and his own talent for performance, "I went from stupid to stupendous—straight."[1] The poem "mediumz" is Brewster's "Black history piece, a shout out at those in the Black community who believe they have the right to deem who is and who is not Black enough." Brewster's poem is written in his "EbonicalPoneticalAlphaNumerical style" in order to direct readers how to hear black slang and the particular voice of the poem. The poem's intelligent wordplay, fast metre, and rapid-fire rhyme structure make it clear why Brewster has been crowned slam champion four times to date. Both poems are previously unpublished.

i can

after a decade of delivery on the m.i.c.
unbelievably
people still asking me

what can you DO with poetry?

that question used to make me angry
it used to make me hot
now i tell 'em take a seat
and ask 'em how much time dey got

for you see
with poetry

i can
duly dance down dem same halls of learning where i once had the yearning
to be a well accomplished human with a 4.0
but my G.P.A. was sadly way far below
i never got the knack of the educational flow
they made me sit still
so
i
stood
still

---

1   Personal communication, September 15, 2018.

i can
comfortably confidently cruise into classrooms where i was coerced to
create
a cornered captured mental state so i could clearly create a way to hate my
own mind

by my educators
they were edu-haters
they formed a form to form my formative years
tainted with intolerance and a tidal wave of tears
that sailed all of my dreams away from me
for they likened my self-image with one of stupidity
it was all that i heard
and all that i could see

i can
now be free
where i was once imprisoned by a mental prism
my errant splayed thoughts were like hot coloured rocks
endless ammunition for the slings of possibility
but impossibly
all of my targets alluded me
for i was living in the kingdom of 'couldn't be me'

i couldn't see the lock
so i didn't need the key
and when they finally let me go
they said you don't know
poetry

i can
versify being victimized into a valiant victory
verify that when you vilify you eventually gotta deal with me
the transformation was tremendous
i took the word stupid and i made it stupendous
i be-gan to man hand-le the land 'o language dat languished in apathetic
and anonymous anguish
i did decide to dissect and divide
indefinitely indubitably what diction was doing to me

stab a psyche with a simile and sometimes slip left of centre see
so to step off into a skill-iloquoy
ail the english alphabet with an oral
aural atrocity

i can
wear the face of mental agility
dispel the myth of dental fragility
and proudly embrace my so called disability
ADD
ADHD
OCD
PTSD

now i've made an acro-nympho-maniac outta me
and never once before have i so ever loved

m.
e.

i can
turn my inventive imagination into a physical infatuation
not like sugar
not the hard refined
not like sweetener
not the artificial kind
don't need heroin
cuz i'm a hero in
my own mind
spent some time with my mentality
and what i did find
is

i can
learn

and poetry taught me
when the truth is unfurled
i'm the only one man

who can change my world

so i can do

anything

what can i DO with poetry?

i ask YOU

why don't you tell me?

mediumz

i swallow sum blackboard paint
so i can paint da word
ain't a word
spittin ink or chalk i still talk
a facts machine paradox proper truth stopper
can't stop me or mock me
europea-emcees can't top me
when a nigga gets a hold of technology
it's microphone wreckology
dealin' wit yo lame footin' cyan step-upatallogy
i offer no apology
for bovine or swine domesticated equine 4 mankind
my own mind
up an' mixed artistic wit linguistic
an' i slung a hot rock
like basquiat
when he brought
da black thought
bleedin' paint upon paper
he changed and den deranged
da sight ov man de earth raper
he closed de eye caper
an' sum yearz later since my brothas life broke
i realize i am a smudge
a perfect brush stroke

wit
pretty colourz
pretty colourz

i am orange an' yellow an' red
i surprized myself when poetically bled
myself
i was tongue twisted up like a dread
wit thoughtz dat rotz stckin' up in my head
thrust back to life like lazarus
strife had me strike me a hazardous
poze
wide open wit wrists and neck expozed
liquid life tricklin' eclectic flowz

from my veinz
pure fiyah
voodoo rainz
funeral pyre

my heated aspiration to be an element or at least an elemental
not simply instrumental
but a song
and a symphony
wit self pity sympathy
i'm conducting doze in da first row who think dey know
i make em all play second fiddle
if they doan jump out da middle
and flee like dey wuz escaping da passage
piss shit an' vomit on da slavery comet
founded inspiration in black and broken bonez
da songz ov da landz dat we called our homez

and we can all hear it
drawn to its timbre like whipz to crackz
lix to bax
feet to axe
funny how we stood taller when we lost our toez
an' held our headz high in a regal manner

defying da yokez
learning da language to create great stainz
kingz an' queenz now bound in chainz
and walking like godz
unlike the ghosts ov our gracious hosts
now passed on 2 da land ov duppiez
weighted down by da shacklez ov brutality dat dey constructed
in da hall ov shame each 1 haz been inducted

back to da books
back to da beginning
back to da future wut we were an' wut we are
back in da black hidin' in da back row
back in da black like deze catz doan know
black like my namesake
black like death row
black like rum cake
black like afro
black like my tae kwon do brothas afro dojo

cuz you can't make wake a blank slate
cuz on da willing you c'yan reap a rape
i take yo' shots like i be in da russian system
off da shoulder wrist strike
to da throat I'm a diss em

and i'mma talk louder
and i'mma walk prouder
diss hour'z mine cuz i'm leadin' by design
i leave ya wit da fever an' your lip catch a slap
from de onoshobishobi ingelosi of rap

diss here iz de evolution
amoeba 2 man
gruntz 2 griots
slavery 2 bravery
cryptic like messagez written on rice
rolled up in blunt paperz
burned like our foremotherz at the stake

hung like our forefatherz dancing from treez
a painful slow waltz dun in black an' broken kneez

pleaze pleaze pleaze

help me find da method
i talk so much dat my teeth itch
an' my hair hurtz
lyrical spurtz
i try and i try and i try
you say you want a sensitive man
an' den you hate me when i cry
i gotta internalize
an' re-energize
an' represent
cuz you know my wordz quick clever can never be spent

in diss industry
no poemcee mediocrity can mess wit me
peace peace leaf to kool keith
he'z a poet i'z a poet

black is poetry

c?

Odario Williams (Mood Ruff)
(1972–)

Mood Ruff, a hip-hop group formed in 1994 in Winnipeg, was one of the most prolific and critically acclaimed acts in the '90s Canadian hip-hop underground. Founding members Odario (Odario Garfield Williams) and Spitz (Eli Epp) met at Kelvin High School in Winnipeg. They were joined by Odario Williams's younger brother Kevin, who goes by the name of ICQR, and eventually, Breakz. After releasing a few singles and five albums, Mood Ruff disbanded in 2006, after over a decade of activity that put Winnipeg on the map of the global hip-hop scene.

Odario Garfield Williams was born in a small village in Guyana and raised in Winnipeg. He attended the University of Manitoba, where he studied creative writing, theatre, and film. Eli Epp (also known as DJ Dow Jones) was born to a Canadian military family. During his childhood, he and his three younger brothers moved to a different city every four years. In the early 1990s the two founding members started recording their first demos on a karaoke machine in Spitz's basement. Their influences draw from the golden age of hip hop—artists like A Tribe Called Quest, KRS-One, and Public Enemy (for whom they once opened). The group was also influenced by other genres, including 1980s pop and rock; Odario has said that Joni Mitchell is one of his favourite Canadian artists.

Mood Ruff first started playing their music live in 1994 to small audiences in clubs around Toronto. In 1997 the group founded a music festival called Peg City Holla, which helped to energize Winnipeg as a hotbed of hip-hop creativity and self-expression. Winnipeg hip hop began to be known for its DIY spirit—for doing things their own way and for not following the lead of hip hop in other urban centres. As Odario puts it, "Winnipeg despises trends" (Larkins).

Mood Ruff soon gained an underground fan base throughout Canada. In 1997 they started their own record label, Slo Coach Records, and released their albums through this label. When they began making professional music videos they gained the attention of mainstream radio and television stations, including MuchMusic's *Rap City*. Their first hit was a single called "No Hooks" which received heavy rotation on MuchMusic. Their first album, *Night.Life.Types*, was released in 1999 on their own Slo Coach Recordings. This album was followed closely by *Politic Different* (Slo Coach, 2000). Both albums received positive reviews and sold well. Their third album, *Antarctica (Cold, Cold World)*, was released in 2002. This album featured ICQRI, the group's first DJ and the newest member of Mood Ruff. The album again received positive reviews, but was unable to achieve any large commercial success.

Their fourth and last album, *I Do My Own Stunts*, was released in 2005. For this album, Mood Ruff introduced another new member, Breakz. *I Do My Own Stunts* continued the streak of critically acclaimed albums, and it also contained their first commercially successful single, "Rocketship." The group broke up following *I Do My Own Stunts*. Odario is currently fronting the group Grand Analog (2006–present). He is currently host of the CBC Radio 3 program *Afterdark*. Eli Epp remains active on the Winnipeg hip-hop circuit.

The track "Front from the Past Pt. II" is taken from the album, *night.life.types*. On this track Mood Ruff raps in the hip-hop boasting tradition that emerged out of the old-school rap battles. Odario and Sptiz boast about defeating their competition with their skilful rhymes, but also about surprising their competition with their regional origins: "Expression on your face when you realize who done it / Two cats from Winnipeg achieving everything you wanted." Mood Ruff's track diasporizes the US boasting tradition by infusing it with the sounds of Odario's Guyanese nation language.

"Front from the Past Pt. III" is from the album *Politic Different*. On this track Mood Ruff make a connection between the art of hip-hop freestyling and broader cultural and political struggles for freedom. This hip hop is literate, intelligent, and fluid. Readers are encouraged to go to YouTube to listen to the audio recording of "Front from the Past Pt. III" to hear Odario's freestyling rhymes set over hypnotic drum and base and scratching contributed by DJ Brace.

Front from the Past, Pt. II

[Odario]
My man Walter P
Yeah man, heh heh
See a tings a gwan going brethren
Yah man, tings a get bad
Word
Hit me dem have ta realize, a serious tings a gwan

Yo, stop fantasizing 'em, big up themselves
Correction ya know
Check it out
Buss a now man
Check it out
Buss it, come again (echoed)
Yeah man

CHORUS: [Odario]
Look with real eyes and you will see the real lies
Then you will realize that you guys
Are living in disguise, for real
But so am I, together we need to make a compromise
Dry the tears and stop the cries
Quit living behind what we hiding
Set ourselves free like, exhibition rides
Exhibition rides

[Spitz] Feeling you dog
[Odario] Exhibition rides

[Spitz]
Sinister plots as we administer shots
Through your cerebral cortex, watch as enemies rot
Essentially they not, destined to be on top
You do so much as blinking I'mma steal stop
Feel the knot, in your stomach as you plummet from a summit
Expression on your face when you realize who done it
Two cats from Winnipeg achieving everything you wanted
With deadly rhymes skill and we're not ashamed to flaunt it
Next isht we on it, bad isht you got it
Odario grip the steel and finish what I started

CHORUS

[Odario]
These MCs think they so big they want hypnotize
Looking for love, and talking about all eyes on me
Want to be big willie MCs

Doing nothing with themselves, but fantasize
Doing nothing with themselves, but fantasize
Can't you see, the deal is a fantasy
He's dealing with his mind
That you could live here
And that's my word

CHORUS

Set yourself free

Front from the Past, Pt. III from *Politic Difference* (2000)

[Odario talking]
I think it's about the music, and how you use it, feel it, and not abuse it, you know?
Uh, it's about vinyl, keeping it alive, putting your love on wax.
It's about non-fiction livin', beyond any confinement, you know? It's about freestyling, the new movement, new ideas, accumulated years.
Yeah …

[Odario Rapping]
I'm not one to seek the existential style of existence
Just expand mental powers with ideas
Urges so loose, and splurges in unidentifiable areas
Straight note chasin'
Creative creation of art, placed and laced in city parts
Directly sparked from the heart of the hiphopper
The night life types
He walks in dark spots, the sleepwalker
Dream weaver[1] sick with anguish and fever
I can't stand it
He never planned it
A self-made insomniac, up late just to finish his rap
Now branded by the culture
We choose not to understand it
Just feel it (×2)

---

1 Possible allusion to early Canadian rap group the Dream Warriors.

[Scratching and background voice]
So
So ... Damn ... Fresh
Fresh Fresh

[Odario Rapping]
Forever
Revolution
Forever Revolution
Track pants and Krylon[2]
We find answers to live and die on
We keep movin' till we sick of ourselves
And do windmills from hollowbacks[3]
End-to-end burners with German fat caps[4]
Practice the crab until the physical formation of my hand curls from endless tension
I look and see guys and girls dancing
Aging, but not romancin' the culture that made them
What does it all mean?
[echo] What does it all mean?

[Scratching and background voice]
So
Say What?
[Odario] Culture
So ... Damn ... Fresh
[Odario] Culture created
[Odario] Culture
Culture created music less sacred
We try to take it back to the birth
And hear it fax from the earth
And spirit from those that were first
Releasing the verse, unrehearsed pieces of mind decreasin'

---

2 Krylon is a brand of spray paint used by graffiti artists.

3 Windmills, hollowbacks, and the crab are breakdancing moves.

4 End-to-end burners are long, horizontal pieces of graffiti art, like on a train car. German fat caps are caps for spray paint cans that produce a very wide line, good for filling in large areas.

Media voices, hurtling internally from disintegrated choices
I see movements of red, yellow, and green[5] rust into a dull flaky gray
Nah, you can't see me
Or even hear me
Or even care
I speak in blacks and blues
Mood Ruff
Hip Hop
Headline News

[Scratching and background voice]
So
So ... Damn ... Fresh
Damn Fresh
[Odario talking]
Alright, that's it.
[ruffling of papers, cough, door opens and closes].

---

5   Pan-African colours.

Bola Opaleke
(1973–)

Winnipeg-based poet Bola Opaleke is a Best of The Net, Pushcart Prize, and CBC Poetry Prize–nominated writer. He immigrated from Nigeria in 2011 and became a Canadian citizen in 2016. He holds a degree in city planning from Obafemi Awolowo University, Ile-Ife, Nigeria, and a diploma in addiction and community service. He currently works as a youth care practitioner in Winnipeg.

Born in Ede, Oyo State (now Osun state), Nigeria, and raised in Lagos during the oil boom of the 1970s and the military juntas of 1966–79 and 1983–99, Opaleke recalls his childhood as a time "where almost everyone had forgotten such a thing as Democracy existed." He reflects: "I grew up in the collective regimented life of a people who go to bed and rise at dawn with infused fear of the 'boots and the gun.'" The violence of Nigeria's military regimes, he says, "lurks in my dreams even after the military left the corridors of power in 1979, and again in 1999." Opaleke found solace during these turbulent childhood years in books and by writing. His father, who trained himself to become a schoolteacher and then a qualified professional accountant, encouraged him to read widely. "So, even when there was no money for groceries, he would squeeze out money to buy me books."[1]

Starting from the age of eleven, Opaleke began writing poetry. His first poetry collection, *A Note from Hell*, self-published in 2012 by an American publisher, consists mainly of poems written during these teenage years, including poems written as early as twelve. Widely published in literary journals, his poems have appeared or are forthcoming in *Frontier Poetry*, *The Puritan*, the *Literary Review of Canada*, *Dissident Voice*, *Poetry Quarterly*, *Canadian Literature*, *Pastiche Magazine*, and many others.

His long poem "The Autobiography of Water" was shortlisted for the 2018 CBC Poetry Prize. He has a micro chapbook forthcoming from Pen and Anvil Press titled *Our Bodies and the Sea*. He is currently at work on a collection of poems.

---

1 Personal communication, November 9, 2018.

❧

The Autobiography of Water

& this is how the story goes—

our ancestors dissolved & become lilies
& become water in the belly of the sea.
we squandered every comma in our sentences
to make room for children to be squeezed
into that family photo hung on the wall of its flowing

i.

as the family portrait changes
slowly   like a civilized truth
    like a hand buried under
the skin of lady Justice decaying
into worms to eat its eyes
& then its ears as its blood

ferments. as the light
at the bottom of the ocean dims

ii.

the river on the eastern side
of our country (folded
into a burning cigarette stick)
touches our lips by mistake
    it apologized & returned
to being solid tears

iii.

    unflowing like the furious Atlantic
beckoning to us   oblivious
of our return journey from searching
for folks locked behind its very doors.
we hid our tears & caressed the orchids
on its belly the way the eyes caress
a wound the body despised

iv.

painfully. before death arrived
    we met a god that is not Catholic
he says he's from a country
not known to the atlas on our palms.
he would eat our confessions   later
like the same god   drawn
on our kindergarten workbook   .
— wearing white beards.

v.

weren't we told a song does not
have to walk when it can fly? to us
    only a requiem & dirges
have wings like vulture's
    only they can hover over our grief
like a shark over its meat.

vi.

this ferocious crocodile inside
the black gold inside the Delta mangroves
turned to an epidemic   chased us up north
to the lonely villages—to Chibok & Dapchi
    where young girls that embraced
morning sunshine at night deliquesced
into dusty lamentation   into regrets
too heavy on our aching shoulders.

vii.

like them   we   too   have no tongues
of our own. when they brought us
white dolls   asked that we point
where the pain forces itself in
we said these dolls looked
nothing like us & we knew not
where to point   knew not
what pain means to an ordinary toy.

viii.

though   our toy-skeleton has its own
language   it speaks in metaphors hidden
underneath the red tongue
of our black skin

ix.

   of our black bodies. we knew
we have always been an open field
   we knew different scouts stake
different flags on us
like a conquered territory

x.

rudely governed. on the mouth
of the Niger river
   on the brink of our night
of disappearance
   the ghost of Democracy
re-appeared to us wearing
colorful shroud   its melting bones
made of in-audible whispers

xi.

of echoes. lost   like a prom night
that doesn't last   the flowers
that started growing atop
our breasts soon withered
in the name of resistance
   we tied the hands of words
that once fondled our nascent nipples
to the back   chained them
to the dingy corners
of our strangled voices.

xii.

& that is the history of water.
from generation to generation

small wars waged against us
become big battles
    they claim our bodies first
then our mind. they bound us
to a spot like a tree. & though
    we roam everywhere
    still   like the sun
that gives no heed to a broken foot

xiii.

we become
the snapshots of the Congo River—
a widowed blood that died & becomes water—
buoyant but lifeless but helpless
    flowing to who knows where.

Chantal Hitayezu

"I need my grandfather's poem. I am an exile like him," writes community organizer Chantal Hitayezu in her personal essay "My Grandfather's Poem, My Grandmother's Dance." Hitayezu[1] comes from a line of writers and artists; her grandfather wrote a form of poetry called *Ibyivugo* in Rwanda—a long poem about the struggles of his life in exile in Burundi. Alas, much of her grandfather's poetry was lost during the Rwandan genocide. In exile now herself in Edmonton, Hitayezu remembers and relates her grandfather's poetry, her grandmother's famous traditional dances, and in so doing she confirms the artist in herself.

Chantal Hitayezu is the director of African Arts Sound & Events, an organization that manages events in the African community in Edmonton. In 2013 she was nominated for the Afro-Canadian Heroes Community Award for her work with this organization. As well, Hitayezu assists newcomers to Alberta through her work with the Multicultural Health Brokers Co-Operative. She is a member of the 1994 Genocide Memory Keepers Association, and she performs with a traditional drumming group in Edmonton.

"My Grandfather's Poem, My Grandmother's Dance" was originally published in *The Story That Brought Me Here: To Alberta from Everywhere*, edited by Linda Goyette (2011).

❦

My Grandfather's Poem, My Grandmother's Dance

I grew up in Burundi, in the capital city, Bujumbura. My parents and grandparents had come to Burundi from Rwanda as refugees in the 1950s. The troubles in Rwanda did not begin with the genocide in 1994. It started

---

1 Birthdate withheld at the request of the author.

before. My grandparents and parents had to leave all of their belongings, and risk everything, to travel to Burundi to save their lives.

At that time, life was very hard for them. They had nothing when they arrived in their new country, and they were very sad. My grandparents were artists. They had to reorganize their lives in a way so that they wouldn't feel this sadness every day for the rest of their lives. They searched for happiness through their art.

My grandfather, Mazina Denis, or Diyoniziyo, was a writer. He had once been a judge in Rwanda, and a vice chief, but he had escaped to Burundi with nothing but his life and his family. In his new home, when I was visiting him as a child, he would get out of bed at two or three in the morning to write, and he would wake up us children to go and get him something. He wrote a form of poetry that Rwandans call *Ibyivugo*, a long poem about the struggles of life and heroism. He chose to write about his experiences as a refugee in this way. He described how he left his country and how he loved his country. He wrote about the large house he had built for his family in Rwanda and how he missed it. This house had seventeen rooms, and tourists would come to look at it and admire it; unfortunately, it was destroyed during the genocide of 1994.

I grew up with my parents and five brothers and three sisters in the same city in Burundi where my grandparents lived. We lived in a different house, but we would go to visit them at Christmas, at the New Year, and other times. We all gathered together, about sixty cousins, uncles and aunts, on these occasions. Today the members of this big family live in countries all over the world: Canada, Cameroon, Italy, South Africa, Belgium, Zambia, France, Congo, Holland, the United Kingdom, Tanzania, Uganda, and Kenya—one cousin is even in Tahiti. But back then we gathered in my grandparents' small house, the meeting place for all of us. Of course, we weren't all there at the same time.

Often, we heard my grandfather's long poem.

When I was young, I listened to this poem from the beginning to the end many times. Perhaps, fifty times altogether. It was a long poem. It might take my grandfather fifteen minutes to recite it. In our language, Kinyarwanda, this poem was called *Icyivugo cya Mazina cyo Guhunga*, which means in English, *A Poem of Mazina from Exile*. This poem explains how he and his friends escaped the Hutus who forced them to flee their country. Some of these people ended up in the bush and were killed by animals. In the poem, my grandfather would talk about the pain that brought him to Burundi, but also about his happiness to live with his beautiful second wife, my grandmother. He wrote about how he met her and how much he loved her. He wrote that he was fortunate to have his wife, his children, and his grandchildren around him in a new land.

The first time I heard the poem I was about fifteen. I didn't understand it, but the words sounded very beautiful to me. I loved the way he talked about his feelings, his actions, and how brave he was.

People would sit outside my parents' house, under the eucalyptus trees, the papaya trees, the green trees, to listen to him when he visited us. He said he remembered the first time he saw white people when he was a child in Rwanda. He called them "the big babies" because their skin was so light like an infant.

He was very tall and strong and a little strict with us, but we loved him. He was also a guitarist, with the *inanga*, a traditional instrument. Even as an older man, he would ride a bicycle. He refused to take a ride in a car. He preferred to walk instead, in traditional clothes, a proud, old man. He would tell us: "I've had a dream that I am going to die soon." When he was 105, he was hit by a truck. So everyone said: "Now, he is going to die." But he didn't! As an old man he continued to write, to paint, and to make carvings as gifts for people he liked—but his writing was the most important to him.

"Everything I write in my notebooks you will have when I die," he told us. He said his poems and stories would make us proud of him after he left the world. He locked his many notebooks in a suitcase. He hoped to carry it back to his country because he wanted to be buried in Rwanda.

Unfortunately, that didn't happen. My grandfather died in Burundi at a very old age in 1988. We were told he was 118 years old.

There is a sad reason why his writing of a lifetime was not passed on to us, or published. Something terrible happened. At the time of his funeral, someone who was working inside his house found the box, the suitcase, where he kept his notebooks, with his important life poem, and many other poems. This person was curious because the suitcase was locked. He thought there was money inside it. He took the suitcase away, and then he just disappeared.

My grandmother, and all of us, were sad because we knew that the writing was the possession that my grandfather valued the most.

Somehow at least his long poem survived. My uncle, Hassan Harbi, who is also a writer, found the suitcase at last. My grandfather's voice is still with us, too. I have two cousins, Ephrem and Georges Sebatigita, who have a tape recording of my grandfather reciting his poem. The tape is in Burundi. My dream is that I will put my hand on this tape, or the note-books, and write down every word, and find a way to publish it here.

I moved to Canada with my husband in 1991. Why did I come here? Even in Burundi, a person does not always feel safe. The hatred that caused a genocide in Rwanda spilled in other countries. People kill each other. I was a young woman, a peaceful person, with a baby. I did not want to raise my children in a society where they were not safe.

Now I want to tell you about the courage of my widowed grandmother and her sisters when they were very old.

My two grandmothers, I call them—that would be my grandmother Mukazi Pascasie and her sister, Nyirankoko Costasie—had been famous in Rwanda as dancers and singers when they were young women. They were like twins. They composed songs, and they taught children how to do the traditional dances in a special school they organized. They had even danced for the King in Rwanda when they were younger.

By the time I was a little girl, my grandmother and her sister were older women, but they still looked strong and beautiful. They were very active. I knew they were famous because so many people would come to see them. The two sisters held women's gatherings, and in 1988, they started a small humanitarian organization of eleven Rwandan women called Benimpuhwe, a word that means compassion, to help the Rwandan exiles who were com-ing to Burundi more and more.

Women would come to their house to sing, to recite poems, to tell sto-ries and jokes to one another. My grandmother was well-organized with these activities, and so generous. Once she gave away all of her clothes to someone who needed them. Many years later, here in Edmonton, I went to my son's school and found pictures of Rwanda in a display window, and one picture was of my grandmother. That amazed me. Perhaps her picture arrived here before I did.

I was here in Canada in 1994 when the genocide happened in Rwanda. The massacre left 800,000 men, women, and children dead, probably many thousands more. All of the killing happened in just one hundred days, from April 6 until the middle of July. A great-grandfather of mine, Kayijuka, had known that this massacre would happen. He had predicted Rwanda would face a terrible genocide but that refugees would return to Rwanda after many years in exile. He knew what was coming. Like many, many people with family roots in Rwanda, I lost cousins and friends in the genocide.

I have only returned once from Canada to see my family in Africa, in 1995, but we did not enjoy the visit too much because it was such a sad time for us all.

Do you know what happened after the genocide?

My grandmother and her sister decided to leave Burundi and go back to Rwanda together with the Benimpuhwe women. They were very brave. They said they would never live anywhere else again, they would die there, too, in their true country. My cousins in Europe said: "Come to us." But they would not go.

Like many people, they were hungry to go home to Rwanda. It was hard for them to start life in a country with so much grief and suffering around them. They didn't know whether the dangerous times would come back. But these two grandmothers and the other women collected money and started a village in the countryside—Rilima in the Gashora district—to make a home for the people who had lost their families to the massacres, and lost their homes, too. They made small farms and handicrafts centres, and their group built 180 houses with the help of international organizations. Today, more than 1,600 people live in Rilima. That's where they stayed, too. My grandmother's sister, Nyirankoko, died there on April 18, 2008. She was ninety-four.

I am going to see my grandmother in Rwanda in December. We will have a big celebration for her 100th birthday. She uses crutches now and can no longer dance, but she is still beautiful. She teaches traditional singing to people who come to see her, and she makes baskets and necklaces and other handicrafts. Her songs and dances survived the genocide, and a new generation of Rwandans is learning them.

She says, "I don't want to die until I see Chantal again." She has only seen one of my three children.

When I came to Canada I realized how much I missed my grandparents. I said to myself: I need my grandfather's poem. I am an exile like him. When I lived near him, I thought: The poem is here. It will always be here. But then it was taken away from us.

When you move away, you lose so much, but not everything.

I brought my memories to Canada. I missed watching Rwandan dances, but my grandmother had taught them to me, so I know them. I brought my thoughts about my grandfather's poem. I had grown up in an artistic environment so I couldn't live without these things.

My husband and I moved to Montreal at first because we spoke French, as well as our own language. When my sisters-in-law moved to Edmonton with their families, I didn't want my children to be lonely without their cousins, so we moved here in 2000. It was a struggle to speak English all the time, although I had known some English before I came.

To feel better, and more at home, I tried to get involved in art and performance as soon as I came here. I joined a global choir and traditional drumming groups. I am also involved in different kinds of fundraising for African students here, because so many of them are suffering from homesickness and loneliness.

I want Canadians to understand the genocide that happened in my country. I want them to welcome Rwandans and other African refugees and feel the pain of these people, the pain that still exists in their souls. Many Canadians don't understand the life of Rwandan refugees here. The genocide is still traumatizing for these people. They were not used to this kind of violence. They remember their childhood years when their neighbours loved one another and shared their homes with strangers before the hard times came. Many people who come here to Edmonton from another country are isolated because of the bad memories and fears that still haunt them. They need our support.

My dream is to open a cultural centre in Edmonton to teach traditional dancing, songs, and drumming, and to bring Rwanda's highly developed drama to this city. We Rwandans are now around two thousand people in Alberta. We are everywhere.

Art can heal people. Music and dance and poems can take away suffering. This is the healing my grandparents experienced when they escaped from Rwanda to Burundi. They realized they were happy when they were expressing their artistic feelings. They gave me this spirit, too: the love of the drum, the dance, the song, and the poem. They gave me strength of my family. I want to bring their happiness to Edmonton.

Ian Samuels
(1975–)

Avant-garde poet Ian Samuels was born in Manitoba and grew up in Calgary. His father arrived in Winnipeg from South Africa in 1969, and the family moved to Calgary in 1981, the city in which Samuels continues to live and work today.

Samuels pursued an MA in creative writing at the University of Calgary, where he was mentored by Nicole Markotić and Fred Wah, and he continues to be active in the writing community in Calgary. He is a former editor of the experimental writing journal *filling station* and currently works at WordFest: Banff-Calgary International Writers Festival. His first publication was a short run of fifty copies of *Fuga: Being a Selection of the Historical Document on the Nature of Slaves* (sixteen leaves of prose), published by Derek Beaulieu's micro press, housepress (which published from 1997 to 2004) in 1998. The material in *Fuga* eventually went into his first collection of poetry, *Cabra* (Red Deer Press, 2000), a long exploration of the mythical imagination of Brazil, a country to which Samuels has never travelled. *Cabra* focuses on slavery, race, dispossession, and ultimately the poetic space created by the ruptures of the middle passage and diaspora.

Samuels's work has not been given as much critical attention as it deserves, perhaps because it tends to be fragmentary and discontinuous, and resists cohering into stable, reader-friendly meanings. Samuels names as influences poets like American Lyn Hejinian often associated with the L=A=N=G=U=A=G=E tradition, which has roots in the anti-capitalist, sometimes Marxist critiques of bourgeois values, including those that assume literature is meant to be easily consumed. But Samuels's work also challenges and expands the L=A=N=G=U=A=G=E tradition, which has been critiqued for arguing that poets should be against "self-expression" and "post-identity," tenets that maintain rather than destabilize the whiteness of the tradition. Blackness, as represented in Samuels's two poetry collections, *Cabra* (Red Deer Press 2000) and *The Ubiquitous Big* (Coach House 2004) is an ironic text—a pastiche of myth, popular culture, ambient conversation, and found text. Black subjectivity is a product of the "ubiquitous" discourses of postmodernity, as well as productive of it. Samuels's poetry is dense, heady, and impressively self-assured.

Samuels's writing has appeared in *W*, edited by the Kootenay School of Writing Collective, and in a number of collections published by Beaulieu's housepress, including *I do not know this story / boneyard: a suite* (1998); *Sidereal: a shining luminary calendar for 1999* (ed. Ruth Grenville); endNote #1 (ed. Derek Beaulieu, rrickey, and tmuir) and endNote #3/4 (ed. Ruth Grenville). Most recently, his writing is considered in *Writing in Our Time: Canada's Radical Poetries in English*, edited by Pauline Butling and Susan Rudy (2006). He has spent the last decade considering how his poetic fits into the emerging contours of the twenty-first century, considerations which may yet result in another book.

Meat country

The sausage king lounged in a villa, blew smoke
rings in the shape of Martha Raye's last dream of
Broadway and slipped a waltz under an arch of
bologna through a two-inch layer of fat on the
cobbles shining a cheap pickup line at the
moon.

Somewhere under the town, all the vanished
children gathered over the ancient bones of
dynamited coolies communion style under a
cleaver-wielding stone image of Our Lady of the
Primal Rib, proving this was meat country
pillaged straight from an emperor's gut.

Bullish

Product placement behind the explosion of
signs directed at a civilization's march into a
random recall of the blood-speckled past,
flanked by faithful shepherding tanks into
unyielding dreams of blasted corpses powdered
under the treads of freedom.

Corporal

The prisoner choked down a chunk of liver and begged for conquest, swaying one step at a time away from the whip toward a mind's-eye utopia of sealskin tires and teardrop-flavoured Jacobin edicts mixing with salt and a journey home to scar over the traces of the first time—to achieve a blur of red into azure and the open road at last.

Hajj

The Word fell in front of a firing squad.

The Word touched the walls of its prison sentence of savannah strewn with T-34 husks, their barrels trained on a forgotten enemy and playing ghost harmonies with the dust storms.

The Word got up and limped east to where a cool new river trickled down, glacial tears from a White Mountain already locked in dreams of Funicello frolics.

The Word stumbled over a corpse face down and dressed to kill in pearls and ermine on a slow journey from a nameless cocktail party of pounding mortars.

Gumption

Captain Industry stripteased a hillside under an infinite cloud Canadarmed in EH-SL on CNN in a single morning's hard-earned mutation.

His house stayed on its back for nine days until its hermetic-chambered mummies packed their bags and climbed into a main-street coin-toss career, hoping eventually to become a prime-time episodic family.

Extinction

The Negro invasion headline's trumpet note hangs on C minor.

It kicks until a harmony inhales the dustbowl pollution and the moneyed blood of a generation of planters runs back to Atlantic where television screens croon 'Being the Beguine' in ghost signals to five centuries of fish carcass and drowned songlines point to the Door of No Return or Refund policy.

Symmetry

Most bandits came through the pandemic with a talisman of virgin violation and secured the order of things in a desert made for sacrifices, for the forced removal of every unwanted pound with a fullproof flesh-eating strep diet (no more fads guaranteed just ask our satisfied ...)

They rebuilt culture's perpetual myth mechanism with driver's side airbags and remote keyless entry to the automated murder sweepstakes, a chance to dream Africa as continental playground for the dictator bloating on hijacked riches to pass the savings on to you.

Westphasic

The Word listened for a hint of The Magnificent Seven still trapped somewhere in the guts of a robot factory whose cool hands shaped long grass blades with tenderness and churned electric signal code into miles of cool prairie under a cumulus Arch of Triumph.

The Word confronted a siren god with sinews of red and blue light, hands curled around intimate crack of club against bone on a lonely stretch of road.

Kaie Kellough
(1975–)

Living in Calgary, Vancouver, and Montreal—cities where black diasporas have localized in particular regional ways—has been fortuitous for Kaie Kellough; it has encouraged him, he says, to "become more responsive to [...] local experience." Living and working in such cities "can release us from narrow constructions of authenticity. This can allow us to create more freely, to select freely from Black history, and to mix and match elements that seem unlikely: mixing the social protest poem with constraint-based writing, for instance" ("Honouring Black History Month"). Thus, as a poet, editor, and "sound-systemizer," Kaie Kellough draws influence freely from both the literary and extra-literary. "I look to music, linguistics, visual arts, urban planning, recycling, journalism, internet searches, advertising, graphic design [and] everyday speech." In terms of literary influence, he names poets from across the diaspora, including Wayde Compton, Dionne Brand, Lillian Allen, Kamau Brathwaite, Derek Walcott, and Jean Binta Breeze, to name only a few.

Kaie Kellough was born in Vancouver and raised in Calgary, and he has been based in Montreal since 1998. His first book, *Lettricity*, was published by cumulus press in 2004. He was writer-in-residence for the 2005 Toronto International Dub Poetry Festival. *Maple Leaf Rag*, his second collection of poetry, was published by Arbeiter Ring in 2010. These are synesthetic poems that work with jazz syncopation, dub-influenced rhyme, as well as concrete visual elements in order to inscribe Canada as a kind of remixed "Babylon." As he puts it, "the aim was to lift a concept out of its cultural niche and 'remix' it in my own secular, Canadian way." *Maple Leaf Rag* is the collection from which the following three poems were drawn.

Beyond the page, Kellough is also involved in making experimental music. His first full-length jazz-influenced CD, *Vox: Versus* (Wow 2011), is based around duets, and features collaborations between poet (the "vox" of the title) and instrumentalist. The tracks include collaborations with trap kit, upright bass, a DJ's sound collages, piano, trumpet, and another voice. A second full-length CD, *Creole*

Continuum (Howl 2014), explores the expression that can be made with the "creole" sounds that emerge when languages mix.

Kellough's first novel, *Accordéon*, a deconstructed narrative focusing on the 2012 Quebec student protests, was published by Arbeiter Ring in 2017. Woven throughout the narrative is The Flying Canoe, an image with origins in Quebec folklore, which, in Kellough's hands, becomes a radical trope for relation—the boat's dimensions are capacious enough for all of the city's dispossessed. The novel's unnamed narrator speaks for all the dispossessed and oppressed in modern day Montreal. *Accordéon* was a finalist for the 2017 Amazon.ca First Novel Award.

Kellough's third book of poetry, *Magnetic Equator*, was published in 2019 with Penguin Random House Canada. Its poems migrate between South and North America and return to a deep engagement with the prairies of the 1980s.

boy hood dub II

self portrait. st gerard's elementary school, calgary.

i remember the school soccer field
sun scorched grass
trampled to tufts, rocks, dust

member a legged blur
corduroy, patched jean
boys' shrill speed

shrieking after the black
n' bruised ball. i render a pink freckle
flecked face flexed

reendure
a screamed *nigger*. baited
i member re

flex. flinging four
knuckles at braced
teeth. i merember

blood, a silver ember
drip from wire snarled

torn lisps

membrr rip
roaring
as big boys' blows blitzed

my afro coco—

k.o.
       k.o.
k.o.   k.o.
       k.o.
k.o.
       k.o.
k.o.   k.o.

k.o.

       k.o.
k.o.   k.o.

       k.o.
k.o.
       k.o.
k.o.   k.o.

       k.o.
k.o.

       k.o.

k.o.   k.o.

       k.o.

k.o.

nut

my uncracked cranium.
welcome. hail.

later, bruises risen to mock my crown, i waited
(vexation unabated)

in the pink-jowled principal's office
for his vice voice to shlurr my sentence

watched the light spit
& polish his bald spot. glared into its gleam

& dreamed no day—

o. no day

  -ay

  -ay

o. no. day-

dreamed bob marley's wail
could ail centuries. still time. split skulls. cleave cultures. freeze earth's
slow mo rotation.
i alone, intent, mobile, could rhyme

a soccer ball around my frozen

schoolyard foes'
foiled heils. could ram
that bichromatic pneumatic sphere

a comet streaking thru the atmosphere
burning thru their unfair fear, & i

dribbling, fancy-footing, could veer
blood through life

could weave
wavelengths from strife

could trump
& triumph from beneath

ugly

cloud stucco ed
prairie sky

❀

night gallery

reggae nights at the night gallery, calgary, circa 1995.

no lovers' rock nor slackness talk
gunman cock nor backward walk
alternative nor classic rock
strictly roots
rule nonstop

monday night we
move up to di
night gallery fi

dig a roots reality
dee
perriddim. ital rockers. bass kulcha. black

waxen wheel
of fro-tune. wheelin us
fro-ward ever. reggae

shakin di system. stakin
sound claim to dis

port. dis
place. this

home of the rage. calgary. oh

no lovers' rock nor slackness talk
backward walk nor gunman cock
          alternative nor classic rock
strictly roots
               ride di clock

          mighty selecter
          shepherd an ebon
          wanderer's return

          to his lock. rewind i
          mind i, black star line i
          align—and cock

          the diamond akai
          needle in its spiral
          groove. one

          drop. spin a new cycle. spin
          a sub-dub bass undulation
          to undergird

          our onward trod

no lovers' rock nor slackness talk
gunman cock nor backward walk
          alternative nor classic schlock
strictly roots
               rock nonstop

          dance ram.

          skankin. chantin. top
          volume. synchro

          nicitously rankin. represantin. blackmancipation
          from babylon dam

          notion: red black green. afri-
          demption. een? soundin

          an reboundin from dis
          transatlantic transplantation

grounding to the bass reverber. irator. dub
        murmurer. repatriator. no

        lovers' balk nor gunman talk
slackness cock nor backward walk
        alternative nor hockey jock
strictly roots
        rule di rock.

❦

vox versus

i was there. —walt whitman

i.

you can't say
to blacks today:

"if history were real estate
you wouldn't own one
stolen Canadian acre."

we who slaved with the *panis*[1]
bit frost in preston[2]
broke and seeded frozen scotian ground

you can't say
to blacks today: "the nation's heart
don't be or box beneath your sternum." we

---

1   Indigenous slaves in New France. In 1709 the *Ordinance Rendered on the Subject of the Negroes and the Indians called Panis* legitimized slavery in New France. As Bonita Lawrence notes, "The ordinance stipulated that both Indigenous and Black slaves brought to the colony would be considered the possession of those who purchased them" (B. Lawrence).
2   Preston is an area in central Nova Scotia populated primarily by black Nova Scotians.

seamed by faults: the coquihalla,[3] the 401[4]
who feel a notion's muscled pulse
in black asphalt, a *canadiana suite*
a diasporan iration

can't be cautioned: "be
have or be deported." whose caustic
grandfathers portered? whose maroon an
cestors, x

pelled from xamaica's blue mountains
to scova notia, were spelled back back
to ac
ir
far
back back back
to the black
man
lan'?

you can't blam
blacks today: "you sow violence and woe
in t-dot-o"

smith & wesson aint' head
quartered on vaughn & oak
wood, no.
the metro po-po ain't
no *kardinal official* in blue you

can't castigate
blacks today
when pale prairie

studs get mailed
back from iraq in black
caskets wrapped in flags

---

3   A north-south highway in southern British Columbia.
4   A highway running between Windsor in Ontario to the border of Quebec.

and newsprint flak. you can't balk
when perckerwoods endear
one another as nigger, headphones

married to the boom-bap, seeding rap
in both errs—

or when cornrows kink
your daughters' heirs

we are, have been, will be—

h   -   e   -   a   -   r

Georges Edy Laraque
(1976–)

"How you start out does not determine where you end up," concludes Georges Laraque's autobiography, *The Story of the NHL's Unlikeliest Tough Guy*, published by Penguin Canada in 2012, the year after he retired from professional hockey. "Looking back, what still surprises me is how impossible it would have been to guess how things would turn out for me for those who knew me only as a little kid in Sorel-Tracey" (339).

Georges Laraque is best known as a power forward or "enforcer" during his career in the NHL. His nickname was "Big Georges"; his 6'3" frame, quick temper, and habit of fighting made him both a feared and respected player. His willingness to speak his mind to the press made him a hockey celebrity. He was unanimously awarded the "Best Fighter" award from *The Hockey News* in 2003 and "Number One Enforcer" by *Sports Illustrated* in 2008.

Laraque was born in Montreal to middle-class Haitian immigrant parents who had arrived in the city in 1975. His mother, Evelyne, was a nurse, and his father, Edy, an engineer. Georges and his younger siblings, Daphny and Jules-Edy, spoke French and Creole with their parents at home; he learned French at school and English on the road. When he was five years old, the family moved to the small Quebec town of Sorel. He writes on his official website, "this was a really tough time for us. Back then, there was a lot of racism and all of us learned at a pretty young age to stick up for ourselves. And as you can imagine, playing hockey was not something easy for me, I got called every name you can imagine" ("Growing Up"). Yet, as he chronicles in his memoir, excerpted below, this message—that a black player does not belong in Canadian hockey—is what made him so determined to succeed.

In fact, Laraque was not the first black professional ice hockey player. He followed in the footsteps of Willie O'Ree (b. 1935 in Fredericton, New Brunswick), who became the first black NHL player—the "Jackie Robinson of hockey"—as a winger for the Boston Bruins, and Mike Marson (drafted by the Washington

418

Capitals in 1974). Still, the hockey culture Laraque encountered in the late 1980s and early 1990s when he and contemporaries like Jarome Iginla (b. 1977, St. Albert, Alberta) and goalie Grant Fuhr (b. 1962, Spruce Grove, Alberta) entered professional hockey was far from welcoming of black players.

Laraque played for a variety of teams at the Junior level, and stood out for both his high scoring and his penchant for fighting: in 173 games he scored 107 points and served 661 penalty minutes. He went on to spend two seasons with the American Hockey League's Hamilton Bulldogs. His career in professional hockey lasted thirteen years. In 1995 he signed a three-year contract with the Edmonton Oilers for $1.2 million plus a quarter million signing bonus, a sum that "changed my family's perception of me." He writes, "On paper I was now a hockey millionaire. Members from my wider family were now trying to get closer to me. Acquaintances tried to become my best friends. I wasn't the same Georges Laraque anymore." After six seasons with the Oilers he signed with the Phoenix Coyotes as a free agent. He was traded to the Pittsburg Penguins in 2007 and signed with Montreal as a free agent in 2010. After thirteen seasons of intensely rough play, he suffered a herniated spinal disc and retired at the age of thirty-three. As he explains in his autobiography, it was more than the injury that made him retire; "Fighting got harder when I had kids. […] It was tough doing something for a living I didn't want my kids to see" (241).

In 2009, after being deeply affected by the animal rights documentary *Earthlings*, Laraque abruptly transformed his diet and reoriented his life. "And with that tendency of mine to always go to extremes," he writes in his autobiography, "I decided right away to become a vegan." He is an investor in two raw vegan restaurants called Crudessence and is part owner of the Delicieux Café Veg Fusion restaurant. In 2010, Laraque joined the Green Party of Canada and that year was named one of the party's deputy leaders, but in 2013 he resigned both as deputy leader and as a candidate in the riding of Bourassa, Quebec.

Since his retirement, Laraque has been active in media and film. He hosts *The Team 1260*, an afternoon radio sports program in Alberta, and is a commentator for TVA Sports. In 2011 he took part in the CBC's Canada Reads literary competition; he championed Angie Abdou's *The Bone Cage*. Laraque appeared in the 2011 film *Goon* as an enforcer for the fictional team the Albany Patriots. In the off season, Laraque resides in Edmonton.

His autobiography, written in the direct and engaging style characteristic of sports reporting, belies the memoir's philosophical and political bent. Though it centres on his thirteen seasons playing professional hockey and his humanitarian and environmental efforts since retirement, it squarely situates its subject as part of the long and unfinished history of civil rights activism. In addition to his work as an animal rights activist, Laraque has been working with World Vision, International Child Care, and the Canada-Tibet Committee. Laraque has become widely beloved for his humanitarian efforts. In 2018 the Montreal Pride festival asked him to enter a drag show competition, though he does not identify as 2SLGBTQ+. Georges Laraque won the $1,000 prize with his performance of Whitney Houston's "I Will Always Love You," and promptly donated the money back to the festival. As Laraque said, "It's one thing to say you are supportive, but I've always liked to do it in action" (Maimann).

❦

The Story of the NHL's Unlikeliest Tough Guy

February 1, 1999. Edmonton. Skyreach Centre is crackling with anticipation.

I'm lined up for the faceoff along the boards.

I'm shoulder to shoulder with Tony Twist. He is a beast of a man. Two hundred and forty-five pounds of intimidation and aggression. His job is to scare grown men.

And I'm just a rookie.

The puck drops, and the play moves away from us.

There we stand, nose to nose, our gloves dangling. All eyes are on us now.

In a moment I will drop my gloves and do battle with one of the toughest guys in the NHL.

Why?

That is a question that will take a whole book to answer.

The short answer is that I had dreamed my whole life of making it to the NHL. But that doesn't explain much. That's a dream I shared with millions of other kids.

The longer answer is that dreams are complicated things, and maybe I dreamed mine a little differently from the way my friends and teammates dreamed theirs. Maybe I was a little more competitive. Maybe my dreams had a slightly sharper focus.

And maybe that's because someone called me a nigger.

I heard that word a lot … I heard people shouting it at me. Even when it was whispered, it would create a deafening noise deep inside.

And always, that word was preceded by another word. *Fucking* was the most common among them. Sometimes, people would put it in a degrading short sentence. Above all, it was never pronounced entirely. With contempt, people would modify its last syllable, pronouncing it "nigga."

I've thought about that word a lot. It's not the word itself that needles me—it's what people mean when they use it. Today I've come to understand all the intrinsic beauty and strength of that word. The writings of the founders of Negritude, the literary and ideological movement that preached solidarity in a common black identity in the 1930s, have enlightened me as to what truly constitutes the essence of the word Negro. Those extraordinary writers bravely refused the inferior condition into which slavery and colonialism had put them and all black people. Negro means black, and there is nothing insulting about that.

Léopold Sédar Senghor, for instance, who in 1960 would become the first president of a liberated Senegal, wrote an article in 1936 in which he said, "The concept of Négritude includes all the black world cultural values, whether they are expressed in everyday life, in institutions or in works of art created by black people. It is a reality: a knot of realities."

Then came the ceaseless battles led by Malcolm X, Martin Luther King, Rosa Parks, and dozens of other great individuals. History may have forgotten most of their names, but their actions were crucial in black history.

Thanks to them, I know for certain that all men are created equal. Thanks to them, I know for certain that all the cruel and racist words that buzzed around my mind during my youth were only meant to soil a beautiful word, a word full of history.

That's what's perverse about the corrosive words I faced when I was young—they weren't just about me. They were about something bigger than me.

But here's the thing—and I've thought about this a lot: if I hadn't heard that word so often when I was young, I wouldn't have been there that night, a scared kid squaring off with a guy whose reputation was enough to intimidate just about every professional hockey player in the world. If I hadn't faced the threats I had growing up, I might not have had the courage to try to make a living facing other people's fears. And if I hadn't been confronted by challenge after challenge as a kid, I know I wouldn't have had the willpower to do what it takes to make it to the world's best hockey league.

So that's why I was about to tangle with Twist in front of 18,000 people that night. Not because he had insulted me, or because I was angry. I wasn't angry at all. I had achieved what I had set out to accomplish. I was where I had dreamed of being since I first fell in love with hockey—under the bright lights of an NHL rink. As a kid, I dreamed of scoring goals to lift my team. I dreamed of being a leader in the dressing room. I dreamed of making big plays to change the game. Even if my dreams didn't take exactly the shape I wished for so passionately as a kid, I would one day do all those things. And though the most cherished moments of my career were still in front of me that night, the fact that Tony Twist was glaring at me was proof of my success.

Even before our gloves came off, I had won the biggest fight of my life. [...]

For as long as I can remember, I've known I would become a professional athlete. I was taller, stronger, and faster than all the other kids my age. I was good at all sports, from judo to football, from soccer to hockey. Even track and field smiled on me. The question was never whether I would excel at a sport. The only question was which one.

Soccer had always been my favourite, and it still is today. Football was a natural choice, considering the way I was built. Yet hockey was the discipline I devoted most of my energy and time to. I remember those hostile hockey arenas as if it was yesterday. Players, referees, parents, coaches— virtually everyone made me feel as though I didn't belong.

No one ever believed in my dream of getting to the NHL one day. Not because of a lack of talent. No, because of the colour of my skin, a colour that would never be suitable to the whiteness of the ice. How did the ostracized child that I was back in the 1980s who often wasn't even invited to play in the intercity leagues, manage to never stop pursuing his goal, to never duck his head? I must add that I've always been a very sensitive person, which means that every insult, every act of racism I was the victim of hurt me deep inside. But my pride was stronger. I didn't want anyone to see or even think that the xenophobic comments and attitudes were doing any harm to me. I would keep my anger and sadness inside until, late at night alone in my room, I would cry my eyes out.

But pride wasn't enough. Neither was my strong temper, nor the very strict education I received at home. The courage to follow my dream was the result of what would seem an innocuous event to anyone else but me.

One day I picked up a book from my sister's bookshelf. It was part of a series published by Grolier that had been given to her as a gift, called "Un bon example." The objective of that series was to introduce children to men and women who had changed history in a positive way. The range of personalities it covered was large, from athletes like Maurice Richard to inventors like Thomas Edison, and from scientists like Marie Curie to philosophers like Albert Schweitzer.

The book from that series that piqued my curiosity was about the legendary baseball player Jackie Robinson. I devoured every page of it, learning in detail how a small boy from Georgia managed to become the first black man in history ever to play in major league baseball. Coming from a part of the United States where racism was a way of life, Robinson had the nerve to rush headlong into the fray, to fight prejudice, to ceaselessly push back every limit in order to become a better player. On April 15, 1947, when he ran onto Ebbets Field a Brooklyn Dodger, he also entered history. And nowadays, who can imagine major league baseball without any coloured players?

Historians have written about that Jackie Robinson debut, saying it paved the way for the civil rights revolution that would eventually abolish any form of legal segregation in the United States. And not only was Robinson one of the greatest baseball players of all time, elected to the Team of the Century in 1999, but he also involved himself in black people's causes for years after his career ended.

When I closed that book, the eight-year-old boy I was knew he wouldn't ever be the same. I had found a role model; I had found the way I would forever approach life.

From that day on, I started praying to God every night, begging him to give me the strength to achieve my goal. Being an NHL player had become the goal of my life. I had the deep impression that it was where I belonged, that it was where I'd be able to play my role.

By the time I turned seventeen, it had become obvious to everyone that I'd be a professional athlete. Just one question remained: would it be hockey or would it be football?

At the time, I was playing for the St. Leonard Cougars football team in the north of Montreal. I remember the coach, Danny Maciocia telling me, "You won't go anywhere in hockey, Georges. No black players in the NHL. And I don't expect to see one in the near future. You should stay with me and become a professional football player. That's where your future lies. And it'll be bright one, trust me."

He couldn't have known that his words only made me want more than ever to make my mark on the ice. I smiled at him and said, "I'm sorry, Danny, but I'll stick to hockey. I belong there. There are lots of black players in football. If I succeed in that field, I'll just be another black guy playing football. Hockey is different."

A few years later, Danny became the head coach of the Edmonton Eskimos. I was playing for the Oilers at the time, and one morning I went to see him at the Commonwealth Stadium. As soon as he saw me, he smiled and said, "You succeeded, you stubborn, you!" Against all odds, I *had* succeeded. My real mission had now begun.

The end of summer 1998 was approaching really fast and so was that crucial training camp I dreaded so much. But this time I felt better than ever, mentally speaking, and my physical condition was top-notch. During the camp, I gave it my all. Still, I was again among the last of the cuts. It didn't get me as mad as the year before, though, because Ron Low had reassured me right before I went back to Hamilton. He took me aside and told me that I'd made great progress and that my stay with the [Hamilton] Bulldogs would definitely be temporary. I knew I could trust him, and so I went down to the AHL[1] with a positive attitude.

Low kept his word, and on December 28, 1998, after having played twenty-five games with the Bulldogs, I got a call from the Oilers. The team was about to leave for a five-game road trip against a few pretty tough teams. The thing would be exhausting, the coach warned me. I would be playing with Boyd Devereaux and Mats Lindgren on the fourth line.

During that trip I played only a few minutes a game, but the coach as well as the press agreed that I was playing my part perfectly. I stayed with the team and my reputation started to grow, slowly but surely, throughout the league. My opponents figured out pretty quickly that I could fight, but what really made them keep their heads up was the toughness of my bodychecks. There weren't many players on any team that could be expected to fight me, but anyone at all could get hit if they held on to the puck too long. Not that I ever went out to hurt anyone, but in short order I added Vladimir Tsyplakov of the Kings, Jan Vopat of the Predators, and Darren van Impe of the Bruins to the "injured reserve" list.

Game after game, the press along with the fans began praising the way I was playing. The team was playing better hockey, and more than one person came to the conclusion that my presence in the lineup had something to do with that. I could also feel my power of intimidation growing during that time. The icing on the cake came when I finally scored my first NHL goal against the Phoenix Coyotes on January 7, 1999.

---

1   The Hamilton Bulldogs were the American Hockey League affiliate of the NHL's Edmonton Oilers and the Montreal Canadiens from 1996 to 2002. After the 2002–3 season, the Oilers officially relocated their franchise to Toronto and became the Toronto Roadrunners.

Tough guys have to work twice as hard as other players, and goal scoring is no different. I actually had to score twice before I was credited with my first goal in the league. For my first goal, which no one knew I'd scored—except me—I was crashing the net when a Dean McAmmmond shot went in off my shin pad.

Not exactly a highlight-reel goal, but I wanted it. The refs gave it to McAmmond.

I was on fire, though. Later in the game I went hard to the net just as McAmmond was loading up to shoot. This time I got my stick on it and deflected it past Coyotes goalie Jimmie Waite. No one was going to take that goal away from me.

I kept the puck, of course. And how many players can say they have the puck used to score their first *and* second goals?

It wasn't that goal, however that really established my reputation. Or a hit either. More than anything, it started with something I said. Some people called it a "youthful mistake" at the time. I'm sure some people still think that now. But opening my mouth when there was a bunch of microphones in front of me began the process of turning me into something of a celebrity.

We were facing the Sabres on February 26. That meant I'd be lining up against Rob Ray, the Sabres tough guy. Ray was a first-class fighter, a bone fide NHL heavyweight with a league-wide reputation. Since I was trying to build up my reputation in the league, I gathered my courage and asked him if he wanted to fight. He answered with a no. He wanted only to play his game that night.

That's how it works with tough guys. They respect each other enough that even if one of them invites another one to fight, the bout won't necessarily take place. The one who's invited simply has to say he doesn't feel like it and that he just wants to play his game. If he doesn't mess with the best players of the opposite team, he won't be worried for the rest of the game. If a guy like "Rayzor" didn't feel like fighting me right then, frankly I was more than happy to let it go.

All throughout the game, Ray stayed on a thin line. He played a rough, tough game, but he didn't do anything so out of line that he had to be put in his place. By the time only a few minutes were left in the game, I was beginning to feel relieved that I wouldn't have to fight that huge, powerful player.

That's when Ray jumped Bill Guerin, one of our top skill guys. Maybe he wanted to send a message, since we were winning the game handily.

There was certainly all kinds of bad blood between the teams and no short-age of penalties. Doug Weight tried to come to Guerin's rescue, but Weight, another skill guy, was no match for a player like Ray. Ray quickly had my two teammates on their heels.

On the bench, I was mad with rage. I totally forgot my fright and had only one desire: to make Ray pay the price for what he'd just done. But the referees got in the way of my revenge—they sent Ray to the locker room with a game misconduct.

Right after the game I was so angry I could barely see clearly. Journal-ists saw that and came up to me to ask what I thought of Ray's behaviour. I didn't even pause to think before answering. You have to remember here that I was a very young player with little or no understanding of how the media machine worked. So when I started talking, all my anger came right out. I said he was a coward, a man with no sense of honour. Moreover, I promised the entire universe that I was going to make him pay for what he'd done and that I certainly wasn't going to ask for his permission next time to punch him in the head.

Recklessness can sometimes put you into trouble. I had no idea whatso-ever how those challenges would spread around the hockey world. I was just answering a question as honestly as I could. I simply couldn't imagine that my words would be repeated, ad nauseam, in every single media in Edmonton *and* in Buffalo.

The fans couldn't have been more pleased with what I'd said, and my teammates certainly had no objection. The only person who didn't like it was the head guy of the Oilers' media relations department. And God knows he was right, but at the time I couldn't understand why. He took me aside in the locker room and said, "Georges, I never want to hear such words coming out of your mouth, ever!"

I looked at him, a bit surprised that he wasn't glad I'd gone out to defend my teammates. "I just want that swine to pay for what he's done." He took my hand and told me the following: "You want to break his neck, that's your business, but if you say so publicly and you hurt him badly one day, he'll have everything in hand to sue you—and his lawyers won't have any trouble proving it was no accident but that it was in fact premeditated. If you bear someone a grudge, if you feel like sorting him out, do it, but for God's sake, don't brag about it in front of the whole world."

Suddenly I had one more thing to worry about.

When I woke after an agitated night, I had come back to my senses. I read every newspaper I could get my hands on and realized my blunder.

Emotions and anger had blinded me the evening before. In the following days journalists went to see Rob Ray, asking him to respond to my words. Ray is a funny guy, and he had the perfect response to put me in my place: "Georges who?"

We were going up against the Sabres again only a few days later, on March 3. I was still angry, but now I was furious with myself, not Ray. Why couldn't I have kept my mouth shut? Why did I have to provoke one of the most intimidating fighters in the whole league?

Some newspapers started printing countdowns in their pages. Only three days left, two days, one day ...

No one was talking about the actual game.

In the meantime, journalists gave Ray every opportunity to mock me. Asked for his thoughts on my promise to get justice, Ray answered with a confident grin: "What's he going to do? Beat me up?" That made the journalists laugh out loud.

All this back and forth was making me more and more nervous. Reading it, I had the sensation that a boxing match was being promoted, not a hockey game. Or maybe they were talking about my impending death.

The night before the game, I couldn't sleep. I was swimming in sweat. The only thing I was hoping was that a tragedy would happen to me. I even wished I would die. I told myself I was going to pretend to be sick, and I even came up with the perfect ailment: I would be stricken by violent gastroenteritis.

Just to rub more salt in the wound, I had watched and watched again clips of Ray's fights. The guy was a fighting machine, crafty, poised, relentless—not to mention strong. Watching him punch one NHL tough guy after another to the ice, only one conclusion seemed plausible: this guy was going to kill me in the most gruesome way.

The third of March arrived all too soon. The game was in Buffalo, in front of Ray's adoring fans. I perfectly remember not eating a single thing for more than ten hours before the game. I was standing outside the hotel we were staying at, waiting for my teammates to join me. I was looking at all those taxis coming and going and I sincerely thought of throwing myself under one of them, figuring that death by taxi was at least preferable to a public mauling at the hands of Rob Ray.

The whole team left the hotel in the direction of the HSBC Arena, the Sabres temple where my doom awaited. We had our morning training and workout, a pretty light one that day. Right after it, journalists came up to me, looking for one more juicy quote before the brawl.

For obvious reasons I couldn't back off the very day of the game, no matter how I felt. I had set myself on this course, and I had to stick with it. What had been said had been said. I had to live up to it. I tried to temper things a bit, but journalists knew just what to ask in order to make my answers as provocative as possible. So I said yes, I was ready for him.

And yes, I was still angry about what he'd done to Guerin and Weight a week ago.

And yes, I would accept the challenge if he was still up for it.

Back to the hotel for a little pre-game nap, I still couldn't find sleep. When the time came for me to dress in my hotel room, to get ready for the real thing, my shirt and pants stuck to my skin, soaking wet with sweat. The next three hours were to be the longest of my entire life.

I kept thinking about the fights I'd seen involving Rob Ray. Trying to give myself an ounce of confidence, I started remembering some of the fights that had gone well for me in the NHL prior to that day. The only problem was that they were all fought against middleweight guys. I'd never met up with a super heavyweight like Ray before. I truly was scared to death.

The game finally started. Sitting on the bench, I was shaking, sweating like a fountain. And the more I tried to hide my terror, the more it affected me. Right from the outset, Ron Low started teasing me with huge smiles on his face. I'm positive he knew what state of mind I was in, how I was feeling inside. After all, he wasn't born yesterday.

I wanted to die.

The coach grinned at me again, and asked if I was ready. Still faking confidence, I heard myself answer, "Whenever you want!"

Now was the time. My heart was racing. I had the distinct impression that it was going to make my chest explode … and strangely, I really wanted that to happen before Ray had the time to make my face explode.

Ray jumped on the ice, Low slapped my back, and over the boards I went. My mind was a total blank. I had only one goal. I rushed up to him without even taking the time to figure out where the puck was. I didn't care, and I doubt that he did either. He saw me coming, of course. He dropped his gloves so quickly that it was clear he was ready for it. After days of anticipation, I could finally stop thinking. The media, the fans, the worry—none of that mattered once each of us had a fistful of the other's sweater. My punching arm started firing away like a furious machine.

He never got to hit me once.

After so much hype, it was over pretty quickly and very decisively. How I managed to claim that undisputed victory, I really have no clue. I can talk about it today only because I was able to watch replays of it. At the time my mind wasn't nearly as fast as my hands. I do remember, however, how relieved I felt after the fight. All that stress I'd experienced in the week before the game just vanished when the fight was over. Sitting in the penalty box, I felt like I was made of jelly.

The very same evening, all the sports reports on North American television opened up with the news. Sports pages in the newspapers did the same the morning after. There wasn't a single hockey analyst who could have predicted what happened. They were amazed to see that an inexperienced, twenty-two-year-old player had not only challenged one of the top fighters in the NHL, but had kept his promise to knock him down. Nobody could remember having seen Rob Ray treated that way.

In less than thirty seconds, on March 3, 1999, I had built myself a solid reputation throughout the league. Nothing would be the same anymore, either for me or for the Oilers.

In the coming games I lined up against some of the most fearsome fighters in the NHL. I'm talking about Donald Brashear, Tony Twist, Stu Grimson, Krzysztof Oliwa—all heavyweight legends. I was still just a kid, but I managed to take care of myself among those giants. But more important, on March 3, 1999, the whole league learned one thing: you don't mess with the Oilers anymore.

Esi Edugyan
(1978–)

"As the daughter of Ghanaian immigrants, raised in a household where Twi, Fante and Asante were as likely to be heard as English or French, my life has been an uneasy one in relation to the ground under my feet. Home, for me, was not a birthright, but an invention" (5). So writes Esi Edugyan in her 2013 Henry Kreisel Memorial Lecture, *Dreaming of Elsewhere: Observations on Home.* Such a sensitive understanding of the double-sided nature of home for black people in diaspora—whether on the prairies, Barbados, or in Europe—is what she explores so powerfully in her three nationally and internationally celebrated novels. Her first novel, *The Second Life of Samuel Tyne*, was met with great critical acclaim. Her second novel, *Half Blood Blues*, won the prestigious Giller Prize, and her third novel, *Washington Black*, won the 2018 Scotiabank Giller Prize and was longlisted for the Man Booker Prize, making her a bona fide literary celebrity.

Esi Edugyan was born in Calgary in 1978 to Ghanaian emigrant parents. In Calgary her father worked as an economic forecaster and her mother as a nurse. She stayed in the city until she left for a creative writing program at the University of Victoria at the age of seventeen. She credits supportive English teachers at Central Memorial High School for sparking an interest in writing. Her first novel, *The Second Life of Samuel Tyne*, was published in 2004 by Knopf Canada's New Face of Fiction program. Like her second novel, it focuses on reclaiming a history that has been denied and buried—in this case, the history of early-twentieth-century black migration on the Canadian prairies. As Edugyan revealed in an interview after the novel's publication, "The discovery of Amber Valley's existence (and other Albertan settlements like it, such as Campsie, Wildwood, Breton) was the novel's main spur. I have no historical ties to Amber Valley. The appeal for me was this: Having grown up in 1970–80s Alberta, in which there seemed to be very few black people, I was fascinated to discover the existence of these black settlements" (*Tyee* 2005).

In the following selection from *The Second Life of Samuel Tyne*, we see Edugyan staging the novel's central thought experiment: what happens when a family from Ghana moves into a town founded historically by a previous period of black settlement? The novel's curious central character, Samuel Tyne, emerges out of the African anti-hero narrative tradition; for instance, Linus T. Asong's character Dennis Nunqam can be read as a literary ancestor. When readers first meet Edugyan's Samuel, he is an unhappy man has who lost his way, but he is quickly delivered a chance for reinvention and life: he inherits a house from his mentor (whom he calls "Uncle"). However, the house is not in Calgary, but in a village called Aster on the Athabasca River. Though he cannot return to Ghana, Samuel sees in this house an opportunity for a surrogate kind of return to black community, a "second chance" at life.

The scene below sounds a warning against the potential dangers of such historical and archival return—Samuel's wife Maude tells her twin daughters to take a quick look around the old, uncanny house they've inherited, but warns them not to get "comfortable." And yet the children decide they want to stay. Edugyan's novel goes on to negotiate with the historical archive as an important site of black memory for current and future waves of black immigrants to the prairies.

Despite the critical success of *The Second Life*, Edugyan's second novel failed to find a publisher. At the time, she contemplated abandoning writing altogether. "I thought I could have gone off and studied law or anything else with very tangible, forward-moving results." But a writing residency in Stuttgart, Germany inspired her to look into another buried history, that of the Afro-Germans that so often goes missing when narratives of Nazi Germany are told. The novel focuses specifically on the children of African immigrants born to German mothers, the "Mischlings" or half-breeds whom the Nazis dubbed "Rhineland Bastards" in the period after the First World War.

The resulting novel, *Half-Blood Blues*, published in 2011 by Serpent's Tail, was highly acclaimed for the sophistication of its narrative structure, the use of black vernacular, and the originality of its story. It won the Scotiabank Giller Prize, and was nominated for a slew of other awards, including the 2011 Man Booker Prize, the 2012 Orange Prize for Fiction, the 2011 Governor General's Award and the 2011 Rogers Writers' Trust Fiction Prize. The novel was also selected for inclusion in the 2014 edition of CBC Radio's *Canada Reads* and was defended by runner Donovan Bailey.

The story is told through the perspective of jazz bassist Sidney "Sid" Griffiths in 1939 Berlin and 1940 Paris as he and his bandmates attempt to flee the "Boots," the Nazi threat looming over Europe and Edugyan's black, mixed-race, and undocumented characters. Canada does not exist far from this landscape; it is not only represented by the character Delilah, from Montreal, with whom Sid falls in love, but is also detectible in the pervasive authorial concern with hidden black histories and isolation. As she has recently revealed, growing up "in the 1980s, Alberta was not a racially diverse place. In Canada today, around 3% of the population is black, and that percentage was even tinier in the 80s. I did feel very conspicuous everywhere I went. And that could be hard. There were a lot of little incidents. Maybe this is why I'm always looking at stories of people who aren't necessarily part of the social fabric. They're this one outlier, or they're at a strange moment in history. It's almost like I'm looking for the most marginalised within the marginalised, and this is what's attractive to me, maybe because it comes out of my childhood (Edugyan and Locke 2018).

Like her previous two novels, Edugyan's third published novel, *Washington Black* (Knopf 2018), focuses on historical silences; this one about black participation in nineteenth-century science. The novel begins in the 1830s on a sugar plantation in Barbados, but twelve pages into the narrative the eponymous eleven-year-old enslaved George Washington Black is chosen by naturalist, explorer, inventor, and abolitionist Christopher Wilde to be his manservant. The ambitious and imaginative narrative then follows the characters to the Arctic, Nova Scotia, London, Amsterdam, and Morocco, in pursuit of science, art, and the full meanings of freedom.

Edugyan lives in Victoria, British Columbia, and is working on another novel.

The Second Life of Samuel Tyne

No one could refute that Stone Road was one of Aster's stranger beauties. And though the river it bordered was murky, an oily strip that boiled out its mulch every autumn, there was a dry order to its rocks that implied that water never touched them. Myth told of the town's birth as the first black hamlet in Alberta, one not so welcome in those days. As more blacks migrated from Oklahoma to set up lives on the prairie, the locals, folk who had themselves migrated little earlier, took action. Everything from petitions to newspapers to name-calling was used to cure the province of its newcomers. To keep the general peace, the government decreed that no other foreigners of this class would be allowed into the country. These words, intended to hush the public, sounded like perverse cowardice. Certainly, no more would enter, they would see to that, but what to do with the ones who'd already claimed land? Not a single local paper didn't fatten with advice on how to cope with the strange pilgrims, this epidemic of filth and sloth that would soften Alberta's morals.

Public prediction rang true. During the next few months the surrounding homesteads lost their morals to the cold pleasure of sabotage. Never had they felt so futile as when the blacks accepted these offences as just another facet of Canadian life, no more trying than dry fields or mean spruce roots. In what seems like purely historical myth, they were said to have set up a Watch; eight-nine families met once a week and, after a brief vote, decided to pitch up their fear in the form of a wall. Discretion, they believed was vital to such a plan, and so they used only those materials that would give the wall a modest look: pallid rock, cement caulking. As if, should what they built be pale enough, their neighbours might fail to notice any difference at all. If the benefits were to be shared, so was the effort. Each man took his hand in the construction, and before long every layer read like a patch in a stone quilt, with a detailed square from each family. No one knows the details of what came next, whether a war of sorts was started, or if the backbreaking nature of the work itself was enough to tame the project, but the wall remained ten inches high for several decades. The passing of years saw it kicked down, eroded by constant rain. Now it rises scarcely two inches, a skirt of parched rock at the river's edge. So the myth goes. Truth is, no one knows how Stone Road came to be. Too mathematically perfect to seem natural, its mystery is the theme of an annual town contest.

"A shadow! A shadow!"

People fell from their homes, not from the belief that there was a shadow on earth worth the intrigue, but because Galla Jefferson was a quiet, nervous girl who'd spoken less than ten words all summer. And here she was, screaming in the streets about a shadow. Women left their kitchens, babies began crying; even those few shiftless men always between business rose gamblingly from their hammocks, knowing once their feet hit grass they'd be back at a job, their wives slicing the tie-strings from the trees for good this time. These men tailed the crowd as though they might go unnoticed. And much of the same must have been happening on the other side, in the skirts, because high noon saw a mass of people lining each side of Stone Road, struck and amazed at the five-foot shadow tracing the proper side with no seen object to put it there. People took it for a sign, though by now no one knows how differently both sides would take it. The shadow faded in the night, and with it most of the townsfolk's memory of the event, so that waking on a new day, Aster proper had founded a race of lost prophets. Such people claimed to remember the event. No one believed them.

Aster was so isolated and secretive, Albertans worried about an uprising. Within Aster, though, isolation meant community. Whole families congregated on their stoops, sipping orange juice from Mason jars and calling across to their neighbours the paraphrase of some curiously deft comment just spoken by the man of the house.

But among all this, one building retained its silence. That worn, splintered house was rumored to have hissed with all of Aster's secrets in its heyday. It cut a splendid figure against the town's purple dusk, and many believed that the weathervane, for all its ostentation and screeching (which woke even the deepest sleeper on windy nights), was used as a landmark to guide its residents home. For, since Aster's beginnings, the home had borne the misfortune of a boarding house. Not that it had officially been one; simply, one of the town widows had opened her home to those ready to pay two dollars in exchange for a month of shelter and meals that, even sweet, stung with cayenne. Her contemporaries didn't know what to make of her, and neither does history.

It's been said that she housed mostly men, weary travelers in need of a night of peace. But was it a brothel or simply a sanctuary? No one ever knew. Only that after the May rains came, she appealed to the town council to sell her their surplus cement wholesale, so that she could wall off more rooms and boost her profits. After three years in which the matter was passed from one hesitant official to the next, she was finally given the cement for free on the anniversary of her husband's death. Two teenage boys volunteered their help, and despite her praise for their altruism, they were amply paid by their own parents. Next spring the house was finished, though not without complications. Two hormonal boys and a construction guidebook aren't a likely mate for precision, and the extra walls looked like rows of cauliflower. Time has drawn all colour from the details, but it's been said that the walls didn't last long, that the hasty layers, knuckling from under each other like nursing kittens, left only piles of rubble and a keen view of your neighbour's room. The house was sold not long after, its ruins passed from hand to hand until, generations later, it was cheaply sold to one Jacob Tyne.

By then the Second World War had changed the nature of the town, so that very few blacks remained. This didn't bother Jacob. As soon as the purchase went through, he gutted the rooms and rebuilt proper walls. Even old age didn't slow him. Half-blind, he masked his lack of sight by aiming shy left of where he meant to go. His intuition was so exacting that even at his death no one was the wiser. Jacob was a man of little tolerance and his face wore the brunt of his nature. Roman-nosed and thin-lipped in a way unusual for those of his tribe, he cut a strict figure in Aster, where his repute grew as a man of morals, one to turn to when in need of advice. Myth has him sitting on a chair in his backyard, advising his few friends on the know-how of life; and having come from nothing, he'd deem he'd seen the worst of it. His brother's house in Gold Coast had grown poor after his sudden death, and Jacob was said to have renounced his chieftaincy to care for his prodigy nephew. He'd toiled the fields, his small reward his sister-in-law's hot meals between shifts. If these words didn't move his listeners, he'd go on to explain how he'd also put Samuel though high school in Legon, had seen him through his studies on scholarship at Oxford and his now lively career as an economic forecaster. His belief in his nephew was so strong he'd toiled his back out for it. His eyes, too, he wrote in his journals. The fields brought out the worst of a man's fastidiousness, and searching out the most futile buds in a dark cracking with mosquitos, Jacob had strained his sight to his one-eyed blindness. He regretted nothing, though, given how far these efforts had taken Samuel.

But Samuel didn't know he was still spoken of, and miles away felt pained that Jacob had so easily disposed of him. Even a decade and a half later, as he loaded his reluctant family into the car to claim the Aster house, his feelings of abandonment had not healed.

Rain made the weather yet another worry Samuel had to bear on moving day. The cramped Calgary house, which until then had been his kingdom, was now so clogged with boxes it was close as a cage. In the final days before the drive, the house was piled with frowzy stacks; once you'd crossed a room, you never knew what treasures you'd find in your hair. Often dust, the brine of old lamp oil, once, in the collar of Samuel's shirt, a crustened moth. He took them for what they literally were, signs of decay, and from these signs he drew his sense of luck.

Despite the usual irritations of a move, Samuel felt blessed in how smoothly his life was now going. He had quit his job free of the imagined horrors that had kept him from doing it all these years. He was a free man, and his freedom proved he was, after a decade of doubt, a man of action. And Maud, usually so obstinate, had simply watched him do it. Not a word had been said since Yvette had let it slip, and though Maud made her anger clear by overdoing her gestures, he took the lack of a lecture as a sign of her reluctant consent. Even the twins had stopped giving him those off-putting grim looks. So life continued: he ate, he slept, he soldered, while his life began to rise in sloppy piles around him.

After leaving a duplicate key with the Bjornsons (Mrs. Tyne, insisting the arrangement was temporary, demanded Samuel keep up the rent),

Samuel checked the hitching on the trailer and, satisfied, climbed into the car with his family. He had not forgotten the Bjornson's warnings about an arsonist in Aster, but it was a chance he was willing to take in that tranquil town.

"My whole family was born by firelight," he said. "There is no reason to fear it now."

He also suppressed his guilt for not holding the Forty Days Ceremony. It seemed to him that in these last forty days he'd thought less about Jacob than about the house. Jacob's life, his character, his passions, had been abstract to Samuel even when the men were supposedly close, so that to talk about them now would be an empty gesture. Also, who was there to gather in Jacob's home to remember him? A recluse these fifteen years, Jacob had given up the privilege of being remembered. And Samuel was not going to make himself uneasy by dragging past traditions into his life when the man he would do it for had willingly, in all but ink, tried to forget him.

Mrs. Tyne turned her stern look straight ahead. Samuel almost laughed. His wife's anger might have made him second-guess himself in the past; not so now. […]

The car rocked over gravel, and one could see they'd reached some place so private that all roads leading in broke off. The gravel cracked like static underneath them, then suddenly became clean road. They rode down a heavily treed street on which well-dressed people milled about at the pace of a Sunday afternoon. Almost everyone was white, with the occasional dark face among them. A stocky man shook a carpet in the street, and a woman in checked pants skipped out of the path of dust he created. Samuel slowed down as the carful took in the scene. After a minute he asked Mrs. Tyne for a map, which she searched for while reading the storefronts aloud: Woolworth's, Eaton's, Hudson's Bay. Even the twins seemed impressed. Goodwill filled the car, and they were even on the verge of speaking to each other, when suddenly the road turned bad again. Mrs. Tyne directed her husband through pretty, but empty streets, toward a river gilded in oil. Vast and flat, the Athabasca's green, fluent waters smelled weakly of algae. Samuel slowed before moving on. Then the foliage thickened again, as if they'd driven back to the bush. The car stubbed its wheels against stubborn tree roots.

And just as the woods deepened, they began to clear, the backlit leaves parting with a slow sort of awe. The streets now became strips of hard, unpaved ground, with pale wood sidewalks on which men in worn clothing strolled, pinching the smokes from their mouths.

Despite a sharp overhead sun, the dusty trees created the feeling of dusk. And yet they were sickly and anemic trees, their trunks thin as a schoolgirls' legs. Only the tops bore leaves; their sheer multitude made them imposing. Heavy boots beat the footways, and the roads echoed with the hollow sound of so much walking. Women in simple beige dresses walked the streets like prisoners on day-leave.

"We tore through some hole in time right back into the thirties," said Maude, giving Samuel a look, for if her sense of direction was keen (as it was sure to be), they'd now driven to the heart of Aster proper. She led them through a few more streets, some filled with catcalling men, others with decaying handmade storefronts, none of which changed her opinion of the place. She directed them past all this to another grove, into which the car pitched with a dark gurgle. Samuel motored it from the rut, and the car stumbled over holes and stumps, greenery that breathed its bitter stench. Chloe leaned across Yvette and closed her window. And even through the closed pane, even through the anguished rattle of the car, a high-pitched whine rang out like the coarsest voice in the choir.

"What's that?" said Chloe, putting her fingers in her ears. "Sounds like a whole field of dying cats."

It was not the first time the sound of the weathervane had been mistaken for something else. Driving up they made out its shape against the sky.

The house distinguished itself in the distance. The carload was speechless. But what could be said of such a house? Brown and ivory, it sat fat and pacified among the overgrown foliage. Thick, thorned vines veined its face. It had the white front stoop so classic of Aster culture, but flanked by colonial pillars, as if built by a Confederate. It was beautiful in a brooding sort of way. The railings, gnawed loose from the porch, drifted in towards each other like saloon doors. Every nook looked green with mildew and weeds. Nearby shrubbery shuddered with the panic of small animals. The ground shifted when the car drove over it.

Samuel parked on the house's east side, and with trembling hands thumbed through the papers in his wallet to find the tiny envelope with the key the neighbor had given him that first evening. It had been dark then, and he'd parked off the property and fumbled his way through the dark to test the key in the lock. It had opened easily. He'd been too tense to move beyond the foyer, fearing the sadness he'd been trying to stave off all day. Now, as he found the key, his fear worsened. They all climbed from the car, Maud with a meaningful slam of her door, and strode over the shifting, rank land towards their new home.

Nestor Wynrush (Elliott Walsh)
(1978–)

Elliott Walsh, a Winnipeg-born and -raised hip-hop artist, named the first track on his second album, "Winnipeg South Blues," both to echo the name of the city's minor hockey team and thus to sum up his family's experience in the city. "I always felt my family were on thin ice or trying to navigate the slippery ice when all we had were running shoes. We were cricket & football (soccer) people; hockey was foreign. It represented everything that was in this new world our families had come to. It also symbolized the line of difference between our first generation and our immigrating parents."[1]

Walsh was raised by his single Trinidadian Canadian mother whom he writes about frequently and tenderly in his work. The family relocated briefly to Mississauga, but he moved back to his birth city of Winnipeg in the late 1990s, where he found the support of a thriving hip-hop community, a scene he contributes to today by mentoring youth in the literary and technical arts of hip hop and by hosting his popular radio program on 101.5 UMFM in Winnipeg.

Walsh's musical style is influenced by hip hop, soul, blues, and calypso, but he doesn't see these musical styles as foreign to the prairies; he calls his sound "traditional prairie, regional-referencing music." His first album, the ten-track *Guy, I'm from Here*, released on Your Brothers Records in 2003, features moody beats from Gumshoe Strut and heart-on-your-sleeve lyrics about immigration, new hopes, and the tug of war for self-identity. The songs are all named after the people who have been an influence in Walsh's life, including Canadian professional basketball player Denham Brown and Lincoln Alexander, the first black member of parliament in the Canadian House of Commons.

When his first album was released Walsh went by the name Satchel Paige, a reference to Leroy Robert "Satchel" Paige (1906–1982), the American Negro Leagues baseball player who is widely regarded as the best pitcher in baseball

---

1 Personal communication, December 2010.

history. Legal issues arose over the name, and Walsh became Wynrush, a reference to the SS *Empire Windrush* that brought the first generation of Caribbean immigrants to England and the name of a Lord Kitchener calypso tune.

His second album, *Trinnipeg!78*, from which the following lyrics were taken, was released on the Saskatoon-based Clotheshorse Records (2009). It was called "one of the most thought-provoking local releases of the year" as well as "one of the best albums [of] 2009" by the *Winnipeg Free Press* (Augustine). The album pulls together melancholic beats from veteran Canadian producers mcenroe, soso, Odario Williams, Kutdown, Lonnie Ce. and Murdock, and overlays Wynrush's vulnerable, heartfelt vocals, which speak of hardship, hope, family, friendship, culture, and loss. The album, Wynrush says, "could also have been called Immigration Blues." It is peppered with references to athletes like Conredge Halloway, "the Artful Dodger" (Toronto Argonauts / Ottawa quarterback of the '70s and '80s), and Edmonton quarterback Warren Moon. Walsh notes that these figures "were big inspirations for me. My uncles would sit drinking Club beer watchin' CFL football in the 80s. For some reason the NFL didn't want these guys. Their treatment was a symptom of the stereotypes that Black males had to fight; not being able to be good leaders, lacking discipline nor showing elevated levels of intelligence in the eyes of many in society at the time. They were underdogs, in an underdogs' league. I could identify. Many fathers played the role of an 'artful dodger.' My father was no exception."

Walsh was born without bones in his lower legs and uses two prosthetics to walk, a fact of his life that he alludes to in the title of his third album, *Roxbury & Wooden Legs*, which is scheduled for release in 2019.

Winnipeg South Blues[2]

This is Fort Garry, South End Winnipeg business
Exile blues, here we go

The family broke
Before it was built
Broke was the word
Financially on stilts
Love was the word

---

2   The Winnipeg Blues were a local minor league hockey team that played in Winnipeg's south end until 2010.

That choked at the throat
A child, commitment
The future was wrote (dig it)
Live from 26 Gaylene Place[3]
The anger, arguments
Late paid rent
Lights out
Cable gone
U know the song?
Pink slip handed
Manhood robbed
Dreams fall apart
Phone's disconnected
Family with a virus
Totally infected
Superwoman breaks
She can't take the heartache
Sincerity is faked
A dividin' earthquake
It gets
stranger n stranger
dads sleeping with strangers
Now, Junior
Just wants his dad back
But dad can't even bear
to make eye contact
a braid unlinks
with every blink of the eye
N Shirley standin' there
sayin' why why
Did she leave the warmth
of those West Indian skies
Oh my

My mama raised me
cause my pops was gone

---

3 Gaylene Place (with Harambee Co-op) is an area of low-income housing in the
Fort Garry section of Winnipeg's traditionally better-off Southside. Many emcees and
DJs who have contributed to the local scene have come from these complexes.

This is a song
Tell ya now where I'm from
I'm from Winnipeg
Winnipeg, Baby
Winnipeg, Baby

It's that overcast pain
Winnipeg, snow rain
War of the hearts
Can bring Fort Garry to flames
A Sade Saturday
Beautiful hurt
Hateful words
How hate will stir
When doubts occur
Hands from his sideburns
Run through his beard
Beers pouring out
As they voicing his fears
men, claim kids
That ain't theirs
Court cases come
Judge tells 'em
It ain't theirs
eyes to the train tracks
feelings in the dump
eyes to the skyline
this ain't what he wants
Stove stain green
curry spillin over
A roller & roti
beside burnt goat meat
He an artful dodger
Conredge Holloway
A part time lodger
Mom wants him to stay away
bucket in his hands
Son, I'm back from my holidays
Fuck this man

Junior smiles in the hallway
Legoland's fallin' apart
Dad ain't playing his part
Too busy chasing
Cynthia Dale's Tale
Olivia Novaks[4]
Mom's too Black
She beyond the line
of the brown paper sack
My Mama
she got so much soul
My Mama
She got so much soul
So much soul
So much soul

My mama raised me
cause my pops was gone
This is a song
Tell ya now where I'm from
I'm from Winnipeg
Winnipeg, Baby
Winnipeg, Baby

[*Song transitions to conversational chatter*]

[*Laughter*]

"Do you worry about the kids in the future not holding on to, say, what our folks came here with?"

"Like our traditions and culture? I'm sure that'll stay alive. Ya, I care. I for sure care. I have my niece and nephew at my house, and they're talking 'bomba-claat, and I was like, 'What?' What does that mean? I don't even know what that means, I just said it! 'Pussy claat, come out to the bomba-claat.' I don't know what I said! [*Laughter*] You can pass stuff down."

---

4   Olivia Novak was a character on the Canadian '80s drama *Street Legal*. She was played by Cynthia Dale.

"Do you worry about the duppy[5] at all, though?"

"I don't want to hear any duppy stories! No, no, no, no. [*Laughter*]. They're afraid about the bun and cheese, but they'll eat some dumplings."

Old Mine Town

WE'RE COMING UP COMING UP
COMING UP FROM THE SOUTH
WE'RE COMING UP COMING UP
FROM THE OLD MINE TOWN

ZIGGA ZAY ZIGGA ZAY ZIGGA ZAY ZAY ZAY

[*Verse 1: Odario*]
I say what man … I say yo man
let patience and focus align with the plan
we're doing what we can, coming from islands
on my land we settle for a little sustenance
coming from the trends of sex and violence
and complications of a shady government
now open up your hand, they're looking for coin man
you'll need a couple grand if they're going to let you in
my mama said pack your bags 'cause we're be heading up north
opportunity and such, community core
they get ice from the sky, commercial farms
maple syrup in the trees never seen before never heard before
inform the older folks, we'll be sending them boxes on Atlantic coast
with scriptures and pictures and packets of goods
get an edumacation, bring it back to the hood

WE'RE COMING UP COMING UP
COMING UP FROM THE SOUTH
WE'RE COMING UP COMING UP
FROM THE OLD MINE TOWN

ZIGGA ZAY ZIGGA ZAY ZIGGA ZAY ZAY ZAY

---

5   In Caribbean folklore, a duppy is an evil ghost or spirit.

[*Verse 2: Nestor Wynrush*]
U say man? u say what man?
I need a jacket for the snow n the rain?
With just a rain coat she came off the plane
So col' She cha-cha-chatter up she name
From the ole mine town She meet ole man winter
Rollin' she roti No hamburger for dinner
Jus' Trynna Hol' on Jus Trynna Hol' on
It's more than this verse It's more than this song
It's tamarind balls Parang, deckin' the halls
Hatin' delays on long distance calls
Blood lines become strained
I'm kola champagne at Blue Bomber games
Sun'll be shinin' Still it be freezin'
Blast this place n it's change of seasons
no change of reasons fa crossin the ocean
isolated they call me Billy Ocean

WE'RE COMING UP COMING UP
COMING UP FROM THE SOUTH
WE'RE COMING UP COMING UP
FROM THE OLD MINE TOWN

ZIGGA ZAY ZIGGA ZAY ZIGGA ZAY ZAY ZAY

Nehal El-Hadi
(1979–)

"We have relationships with the places we live in," writes poet, short story writer, journalist, scholar, and geographer Nehal El-Hadi. "I'm not from Toronto. I'm not from anywhere, really." By including place names in her work, "I claim both known and unknown geographies. That way, I get to say, no, I'm really from here, look, I wrote about it. I know these places, even when I don't" ("Author Note").

Nehal El-Hadi defines herself as "Sudanese, ethnically African, culturally and linguistically Arab, and visibly black. I feel and think first in Arabic and write in English." She was born in Khartoum, grew up in London, England, and Muscat, the capital city of Oman. In 1998 her family immigrated to Canada, landing in the Thorncliffe Park area of Toronto, but the following year the family relocated to Moose Jaw, Saskatchewan. After completing high school, she moved to Regina to attend the University of Regina, where she earned a bachelor of journalism in 2003. She left the city in 2003 to pursue a master's degree in environmental studies and environmental communication (2005) at York University and then a PhD in geography at the University of Toronto in 2018. She has been affiliated with the University of Toronto, Scarborough, as a lecturer in the Department of Human Geography, City Studies program.

Although El-Hadi has not lived on the prairies since 2003, she returns to Saskatchewan at least once a year to visit her parents, who remain in Moose Jaw. She reflects, "Although I only lived in Moose Jaw and Regina for short periods of time, it's a landscape that gets in your bones. I've seen the sky do things I never knew a sky could do; the prairies loom huge in my becoming-Canadian personal narrative. I lived, studied and worked there during years that were very formative for a number of reasons."[6]

El-Hadi's creative work has been published in *Puritan Magazine*, *The Great Black North*, edited by Valerie Mason-John and Kevan Cameron (2013), *Min Fami:*

---

6 Personal communication, October–November 2017.

Arab Feminist Reflections on Identity, Space and Resistance edited by Ghadeer Malek and Ghaida Moussa (Innana 2014), and *The Unpublished City, Volume II*, edited by Phoebe Wang, Canisia Lubrin, and Dionne Brand (Book*hug 2018). She is the author of the chapbook *city/heart* and is currently working on her first collection of poetry.

Her 500-word micro fiction "Djinn in Saskatchewan" focuses on the djinn (also known in Arabic as *Jann* and anglicized as *genies*), the supernatural beings of Arab mythology who have followed the poet-speaker's family out of the desert into Saskatchewan, where they continue to influence and torment them. The story elaborates the etymological meanings of djinn (which include the Arabic *jann*, meaning "concealed," *majnūn*, "possessed" or "insane" and Jannah, "garden") in the new prairie location. The piece was selected for *Room Magazine*'s Winter 2017–18 Short Forms Contest List but has never before been published.

Her short story, "La Puerta," originally published in *Puritan Magazine* in 2016, is an uncanny exploration of the human/non-human boundary. Readers may wish to consider what particular histories haunt Zola, and why she might choose to fashion a non-human being to act as a repository for these overwhelming emotions. Readers may also consider the significance of the name Zola gives the automaton—La Puerta—in the context of black Atlantic and prairie history.

Djinn in Saskatchewan

We should have left them behind. These djinn of the desert do not belong in this country of winters and subjugation. But we brought them with us, along with our hopes and aspirations, and like our dreams, they transmuted into grotesque manifestations of our survival, perversions.

In my parents' home in Moose Jaw, they huddle at the end of the large garden, whispering among themselves as they pace through the trees, fruitless. My mother doesn't see the djinn, but I do, their tall figures a constant in my life. They drove me away from my parents' house, sent me east to Toronto, somewhere loud and noisy and chaotic, where the sky wasn't so empty.

I think my father sees them too, but he never lets on, dismisses what I have to say as fancy that needs to be reined in before it becomes delusion.

Walking on Yonge Street on a smoggy Sunday afternoon, homesickness makes me call, and I hear the djinn raucous in the background, wailing in laughter or tears. This unexpected reminder of their presence the sound of metal on metal.

"What's wrong?" I ask my mother, my voice leaking panic.

"Nothing's wrong. Are *you* okay?" she teases. "You sound horrible. Did you just wake up?" Then suspicion. "Are you *high*?"

The din pitches up. "No, no," I stammer. "Can't you hear them?"

"Hear what? Are you sure you're sober? Maybe you should come home."

"Whatever. Where's my father?"

"In the garden. I'll get him to call you when he gets in."

"Can you get him now, please? I have to ask him something."

She sighs, puts the phone down too quickly, loud clash into my ear. She opens the back door, yells out to my father. I start to doubt my own sobriety but the noise in the background is still real.

A click as my father picks up another line. He pauses and then yells hello into the phone, a habit ingrained into him by decades as an émigré. My sisters and I can't get him to stop, and I automatically lower the volume on my phone.

"I … just wanted to say hi." Then all the words jump out together. "Are you ok? Is Maman okay?"

He chuckles. "We're all okay. How about *you*?"

"I'm fine. Baba, tell me, can you hear them?"

Silence. And then he says something in a voice so low, I turn up the volume.

"I'm not quite sure what's happening," he says. "But it's a celebration."

There's an unusual tone to my father's voice, and it takes me a few seconds to figure out what it is.

"Baba, are you laughing?"

"They're going back! I don't know when or how, but you understand that we move together! We're going home!"

A streetcar is screeching past me on Queen Street, and through the sound of metal on metal, I am aware that I would not be returning with them.

Under a sky suffocated with high rises, I know a new envy.

La Puerta

It had been a tough year—that winter, I'd lost my father suddenly to a heart attack, and then Grandmamma had passed away two days after that. A few weeks later, as we went through our father's possessions, my sister casually mentioned that our old babysitter had passed away. I wasn't even in touch with her, but my response to her death dwarfed the grieving for my more intimate relatives. My sorrow at the loss of a woman who was now a stranger contained the under-expressed sadness of the other two deaths. I wailed for a woman whose last name I didn't know, wasn't sure if I ever did. Spent hours on YouTube playing on repeat high-pitched, nasally versions of the French nursery rhymes she used to sing to me, until *Alouette* soundtracked my dreams.

It was summertime, hotter and muggier, the air yellow and difficult. The garbage strike in the city had added the perfect backdrop—a stench to the discomfort I felt. My employment insurance had run out, and nobody was hiring, a recession. I was overqualified for service jobs and unqualified for temping. I killed time until my inevitable eviction, dodging Matthias, my ESL landlord who was a retired contractor. I hadn't found a job, and got by on the money I made covering shifts for friends who bartended or waitressed.

I walked home late one night from a shift in Chinatown, and was cutting through Kensington Market when I noticed a figure slumped against the door of a closed store. In the shadows, I wasn't sure what I saw, my mind registering a human shape with unexpected and frightening proportions. I crossed the street, a small woman out late, alone at night, clutching my cellphone in my pocket. As I passed the figure, I recognized it. During the day, an incongruent mechanical figure sat outside the Persian carpet place, catching the attentions of passersby. The figure's arm moved in a goodbye motion, and the mask that sat on its face was hideous. I had associated Persian carpets with refined tastes, but the character used to promote the store looked like a deformed twin of the Billy-puppet in *Saw*, misshapen cheeks and a chin that protruded uncomfortably. It had been painted at one time, but now the thing looked like it was afflicted with the mechanical equivalent of necrosis, whatever was used for hair now a matted nest of foulness.

Curious, I let go of my fear and disgust and went back to look at it. I had never noticed it outside when the shop was closed, but I imagined that had I been the owner of the store, having it stolen would be a relief. Seeing it immobile and half-hidden in the shadows had freaked me out, and something about it was disgusting and sinister. I fantasized that the carpet-seller had once been a magnificent mechanical specimen, one that matched the caliber of the complex hand-woven Persian carpets sold, but years of Canadian winters and recessions had distorted him into something grotesque. Standing there on Baldwin Street, I cried until the sun came up for his sadness and mine, body-shaking sobs interrupted by unwashed hippies who treated me like I was crashing. And I was.

The anguish was unbearable, and I needed somewhere to hold my feelings. Something like that ugly old thing, something cold and metal, robotic and mechanical, an embodied repository for those feelings that kept pushing me under.

"It's just your first Saturn return, Zola," explained my friend Sarah, who had an administrative job with summers off at the local school board. I was haunted and broken, but her explanation didn't provide any reprieve from the heaviness at all.

Sarah had invited me to my local bar, and had brought along Rohan, a painter we had met at a friend's opening days before. Rohan asked me for my contact information, I agreed to give it to him and then deliberately left the gallery before I did. I knew a set up when I saw one, but I was too desperate to be mad at Sarah. In the bar, I told them both about my plan to build an automaton to hold my feelings, but I hadn't gotten any further than my desire to do so.

"I'll help you," Rohan said. "At the end of the month, I'll drive you around Parkdale and Queen West and we can see what people have thrown out before moving day."

Sarah mumbled something into her drink, and I knew that she had passed judgment, but whether on Rohan or my plans, I wasn't sure. "Pardon?" I asked.

"You shouldn't humour her," Sarah pivoted her chair around to face me. "Listen, my therapist is really awesome, I'll give you her number."

"Unemployment doesn't come with benefits, remember?"

"She does sliding scale. Counseling makes way more sense than trying to build a droid."

"I haven't made rent in two months. And it's an automaton. They're easier to build."

"Ro, you're not seriously planning to support her in this, are you now." A command, no question.

"Well yeah, of course I will," Rohan reached for my hand underneath the table. I twitched away at the unexpected contact, then reconsidered and felt for his hand. Rohan was a painter who had been described in a local weekly as "an art brat grown up," a brilliant painter, all deep and high in his work as well as his person. I found an escape in him, some way to move through the depression that didn't leave me at the change of the season.

Since the night with Sarah at the bar, Rohan and I hadn't been apart any longer than the amount of time it took to have a shower, do laundry, and hit the liquor store for some more wine. Up all night, we searched online, and drew plans for my automaton. Once, when he left my house to meet his sister for brunch, I gathered all our notes and sketches and put them in a bucket of water.

"Why would you do that?" Rohan asked.

"I don't know. It doesn't feel right," I shrugged.

"What doesn't feel right?"

"It feels too planned. I need something more spontaneous, more organic."

"You're making a robot, not a wildflower garden."

"Our plans, they're too complicated. They're too—" I wasn't sure how he would react.

"They're too you." I couldn't stop. "They're too final-year art school project."

Things weren't getting easier, hayfever aggravated with cheap red wine. The last day of the month came around and Matthias served me with a 30-day eviction notice.

"I'm sorry, Zola, but you don't pay your rent. I don't know what to do for you. Maybe you should call your parents," Matthias said as he handed me the letter.

Standing at my front door, I burst into tears.

He turned bright red. "I'm very sorry. Pay me what you can. I won't go to court."

"Thank you. It's okay, I expected this." A part of me did feel guilty for the stress I was putting him through.

It was also the last day of the month. I hadn't spoken to Rohan in two weeks, but I texted him at midnight.

"Everyone's throwing everything out. Are we doing this tonight?"

"Zo! I'll be there in thirty."

Rohan didn't show up for almost three hours, even though he only lived in the Junction, a twelve-minute drive away from my house. I lived further east of him, in a featureless pocket of west central Toronto, on a street with an industrial past that had been erased before the developers could capitalize on it.

"Famous writer lived over there, around the corner," gestured Matthias when he first showed me the apartment on the main floor of a plain house with a pastel green door. He couldn't remember who the writer was or anything about them. After I moved in, the first time I went to the corner store, the lady who owned it welcomed me to the neighbourhood.

"That was Margaret Atwood's house over there on Marchmount."

Ro picked me up in his old Chevy Beauville and we headed to Parkdale. There, thrown out on the street we found almost every item on the Ikea top 20 list. We loaded his van with anything we thought we could use, plus three identical birch Billy bookcases picked up at three different apartment complexes we thought we could sell online. Scavenging for parts was made easier by the ongoing garbage strike.

"I'm glad you reached out," Ro said when we got back to my place. "I brought wine." A cheap, Argentinian red. "I'd been thinking about you. I've been working on this show, I think you'd find it interesting."

"Yeah? Well, I guess you can come in."

Instead, we took everything around to the back deck. I brought out mugs, and poured the wine while he rolled a joint.

"It's about nostalgia. Did you ever watch *Hedwig and the Angry Inch*? Well, there's this one song in it, where Hedwig's singing about how lovers share the same body and then Zeus or someone got pissed off and separated all the lovers with lightning bolts. And that's why everyone's searching for their one true love."

"Yeah, we talked about this. *I* showed you that video. It's called 'The Origin of Love.'" I was annoyed.

"Well, yeah, anyway. This show tells the story of two lovers who reunite and, inspired by the Hedwig story, decide to surgically attach themselves to each other, except no one will do it for them so instead they build a giant robot body where each one of them controls one half."

The first night we met, we spent hours online as I showed him video after image of everything I knew about automata and robots. Rohan listened carefully to me, and I was flattered by what I thought was his attentiveness to me. But this taking of the information I gave him was a kind of theft. "Like the mechanical Turk? It's not really a robot then, more like a fancy suit."

"It'll be my first show that isn't all paintings. Since we've been talking, I've been building these mechanical sculptures."

"Cool." I didn't really have a response to Rohan, and now he was annoyed.

"I thought you'd be more excited," he pouted. "It's right up your alley."

"That's great, you can help me better with my automaton now."

We went through what we had collected, and started building. That night, we put together a humanoid figure. Several of its parts were discernible as Ikea products, trivia of mass production. The head was a slightly rusted stainless steel bucket, Höstö, limbs a hotchpotch of table legs, the torso the brown-black of a Malm panel.

"It matches your skin," Rohan said.

That night, we named her La Puerta—the door—after the bottle of wine Rohan had brought.

Rohan had to spend the night because he couldn't drive as stoned as he was. When he went inside the house to pass out, I lit another joint, and started talking to the pile of junk that we had connected with twine, hot glue, and bright pink leopard printed duct tape that I had picked up on a whim from Dollarama. Rohan had rigged together a simple pulley and attached her head to it. As I spoke to La Puerta, I reached around the back and carefully tugged on the twine, made her nod as I spoke.

I told La Puerta her origin story, how I had decided, and then Rohan and I had brought her into the world. I told her about how although it wasn't where she was right now, she was a total Parkdale baby, all the parts she comprised found in between King and Queen Streets, Dufferin and Jameson. I imagined that she looked weirdly cold, and I left her to get shawls for us. I chose a plain grey one for her, orange for myself. I talked more and more, going back in time to the choice to make her, through my depression, to the death of my father, grandmother, and babysitter. The entire time I spoke, La Puerta nodded, and she didn't stop nodding because while we were scavenging, we had found a perpetual motion office toy that we had connected to the pulley system that moved her bucket head.

I told La Puerta about my joblessness and eviction, and she kept nodding. I grew angrier, told her about my relationship with Rohan. My tone changed and my language too, from the gentle, soft, almost-cooed phrases I had spoken at her inception, to jagged, blunt harsh words, and her head bobbed to the rhythm of my words. I hadn't wanted her to be so pathetically acquiescent.

Rohan woke up and saw that I hadn't come back indoors. He found me sobbing, large silent body shakes, my neck creases wet with tears.

"I don't want her. All she does is nod."

"Shhh, you need to go to bed," he snubbed out the cigarette that I had been holding.

That first night began a week of getting drunk and stoned and speaking to La Puerta on my back deck, hours at the confessional of her junk heap. I disdained her nodding and found release in the sadness that turned into aggravated anger which then loosed itself in undisciplined tears. I felt her become more substantial the more I spoke, the energy of my emotions making her stronger. I'd added a dollar-store masquerade ball mask, a wide-brimmed hat, beaded South African necklace, pleather driving gloves. She was ugly and I could see myself falling in love with her ugliness.

I didn't go into work that week. My mobile phone had been disconnected because I hadn't paid my bills since all the deaths happened. When Sarah came to my house and rang the doorbell, I pretended I wasn't home. I waited for three hours after she left, and then I crossed the street to use the wireless network that belonged to the Davenport Public Library, and sent her a fake-cheery email to let her know that everything was absolutely fine, I was just taking some time to re-align and re-set, I'll call you when I'm back, love Zola.

I ignored all the texts that downloaded at once from Rohan. I pretended I wasn't home the first time he stopped by, too, and then actually wasn't home the second time he stopped by a week after he had helped me build La Puerta because I had gone to get cigarettes and that was when he took her. In her place, Rohan had left a flyer for his show's opening in three days.

"What the fuck?!" I messaged him from the front steps of the library. I chain-smoked while I waited for him. He didn't respond and I ran back across the street to get change to use the payphone outside the library, which smelled like no one had cleaned it since cellphones had taken over. I contemplated going back home for some disinfectant, but wanting to get La Puerta back was more urgent, I had told her too much. Rohan answered on the first ring.

"What the fuck?" I repeated.

"You didn't get back to me. Didn't you get my messages?" he replied.

"My phone's been cut off. You don't get to walk into my house and take my stuff," I tried not to scream.

"I didn't walk into your house, I took the robot from the deck."

"Her name's La Puerta."

"Yeah. Uh, look I'm really sorry. Can you come to my show? Please, please come to my show. I told Lisa–Lisa, she's the curator–about it, and she thought it, sorry La Puerta, would be great as the focal piece. You must come. I'm setting it up at the gallery now. I left you a flyer." Rohan stumbled over his words.

I forgot that I was on a payphone, and in my attempt to stomp off I was jerked back hard by the receiver's cord. My head started to hurt, and I wondered if the symptoms of whiplash could manifest instantaneously.

"I don't know. Listen, just bring her back," I said. I waited for him to tell me why he couldn't.

"I can't do that. It's …"

"She."

"—She's the centre of my show. Everything else derives from her. I can't take her out now. I'll give it back as soon as it's done, I promise." His voice stopped pleading. "It's just as much mine, you know. I helped you build it, drove you around to get all the stuff."

I pushed down the phone cradle, disconnecting. I looked at the receiver I held in my hand, wondered why it had to feel so heavy, before I put it back.

I didn't talk to anyone for the next three days, and when I walked into the Queen West gallery for Rohan's show, I was overwhelmed by the number of people in there. It was so loud and everyone seemed to be yelling at everyone else to make themselves heard. I felt panicky and nauseated.

"Zo!" Rohan called me from behind.

I turned around, fake-smiled so hard the corners of my eyes hurt. "Congratulations! This is awesome."

"You think so?"

"Well, I haven't seen anything yet, but I meant all the people," I replied, still smiling.

Rohan leant in, pushed himself against me, body too close. I shrunk but he didn't notice.

"It's good to see you. I was so worried you wouldn't come," he whispered in my ear.

"Can I see La Puerta?" I asked. "I don't think I can make my way through this crowd."

"Of course, sure," Rohan took my hand, pushed people away as he smiled, nodded, promised to talk later but first he had to show someone something.

She was sitting still in the centre of the large room, a low-slung velvet rope keeping the masses from touching her. Seeing La Puerta on display under bright gallery spotlights was discomfiting for me, it wasn't what I had made her for. I had a strange feeling that La Puerta was enjoying herself and I resented her, and then I chided myself for thinking that a collection of objects would feel anything, let alone something as complex and human as vanity. I moved around to face her and she nodded. I flinched, La Puerta's head had been holding still. There was no breeze, no contact, nothing that could have started her movement. La Puerta kept nodding.

I looked away, and noticed the object label, which read "The Portal/ Gateway to a Better Person."

I saw a red dot on the lower-right corner.

I tensed up and my voice went low, lower.

"I didn't hear you, what did you say?"

"She's sold. You can't do that, no one can have her," I started to cry.

Rohan inhaled deeply. "No way! I had Lisa price it really high so that no one would buy it. It's listed for thirty-six thousand. There's no way anyone would pay that much for it, that's crazy!"

"No," I said. "She is absolutely not for sale."

"Let me talk to Lisa. The gallery takes half, which means that I would get eighteen thousand for her, and half of that is yours! Nine thousand dollars! Not bad for some Parkdale garbage!"

Rohan started jumping up and down in excitement.

I had nineteen days left on my eviction notice. Less than three weeks to pay Matthias in full or become homeless. Nine thousand dollars would fix that.

"Okay, I'll wait here."

Rohan moved into the crowd of people. I stared at La Puerta, who had stopped nodding. I felt her disappointment. I lowered my eyes, fixed them on a pair of worn red heels positioned as her feet.

Rohan came back, noticeably deflated.

"What happened?"

"Oh, Lisa put the sticker there because I had told her that the piece wasn't for sale. We were going to list it for a ridiculously high price so that no one would buy it, but she thought it made more sense to just say that it was sold," Rohan said.

"Oh."

La Puerta started nodding. I shivered as I looked at her, and her nodding felt slower more sinister. Just you wait, she seemed to say. I turned to Rohan.

"When will you bring her home?"

"I promise, as soon as we tear down the show. It's running for one week, and there's another one right after it, so you can have her back by then."

I didn't respond to him, just turned and walked away.

The next day, I called my mother and asked to borrow three thousand dollars to pay my rent. I took thirty one-hundred dollar bills, and three buses to Matthias' house in Woodbridge. When I got there, he invited me in and told me things he had never told me before about his deceased wife and estranged daughter. Matthias told me he understood my pain and wanted to help me, and I understood that he was seeking atonement for his broken relationship with his daughter.

I picked up any cash-in-hand shifts that I could while I applied for social assistance. With my mobile phone still disconnected, sitting on the Davenport library steps was a late-night ritual where I downloaded emails and messages, which became fewer and fewer until there were only two or three at a time. Rohan had messaged or emailed every day, asking if he could come over, asking if I would call him, inviting me out for drinks. I deleted each message after I read it, I only wanted La Puerta from him.

On the last night of Rohan's show, I sent him a message, letting him know that I wouldn't be at home the next day and if he could please just leave La Puerta on the deck where he had found her. When Rohan came in the evening, I had been lying on my bed for hours, careful not to move too much, not wanting him to know that I was home. I heard Rohan's voice and another man's voice that I didn't recognise. I heard Rohan moving parts of her around and I wondered how much disconnecting and reattaching he had needed to make to move her. She had seemed improved, upgraded at his show's opening. Rohan sat on my front steps for half an hour before I heard him leave. I waited in bed for another hour to make sure that he had gone before I moved again.

I opened the door to the back deck and La Puerta was in the same place he had taken her from, her black-brown torso wrapped in the same grey shawl even if now red shoes were placed underneath her in the same way they had been at the gallery. I picked up the shoes and dropped them in the city-issued curbside bin that was kept beside the deck. Rohan had also left behind a bottle of red wine, the same wine we drank when we made La Puerta, the one that she was named after. I opened the bottle and didn't bother with a glass.

I started talking to La Puerta, tried to pick up where we left off. I reached behind her head, and plucked at the twine. She nodded once and stopped. Puzzled, I tried it again. Again, La Puerta's bucket head moved up and down, once. I turned her around, looked at the pulley system, thinking something must have shifted when Rohan took her away. Everything seemed as it was, even when I disconnected the perpetual motion toy and tested it. I reattached it, pulled at the twine. One nod, this time with a firm and definitive stop. La Puerta wasn't going to nod anymore, not for me.

I finished the bottle of wine and stumbled across the street to the payphone.

Rohan answered immediately. "I've been waiting for you to call me."

"You need to come over now," I said, holding onto the side of the phone-booth for support. I hung up.

When Rohan arrived, I was unsuccessfully trying to set fire to La Puerta. I was crying but I wasn't sure if it was the alcohol or the acrid smoke that smouldered into my eyes. Rohan stood away from me, not sure what to say or do. Take me to the lake, I asked without looking at him.

"Sure, if that's what you want," he replied.

It took both of us to carry La Puerta to his van. I sat in the back with her, thought about how to make a ritual out of her ending, offer her up to Lake Ontario. That time of night, Sunnyside Beach was empty and we carried La Puerta up to the water's edge. I stood there silently, tried to figure out where the horizon was. I wanted Rohan to leave us, but his presence felt necessary. Together, we dismantled La Puerta, Rohan handing me each piece as I threw it into the water and then watched it wash up on the shore a few feet away. All that was left of La Puerta was the large board that had been her base.

"Can I keep this part?" Rohan asked.

"All of her has to go in, it's part of the ceremony, but you can pick it up when it washes back." I was making it all up as I was going along, but death has rites and they must be observed. It took both of us together to swing the board out far enough. When it washed back on shore, Rohan decided that he didn't want it anymore because it was covered in something slimy.

"I wonder if they'll get us for littering?" Rohan asked.

We moved further back and sat on a bench, waiting until the sky started to warm up in pre-dawn. We could see the parts of La Puerta moving back and forth with the waves. I asked Rohan to drop me off and the sun rose as we drove north. In front of my house, he asked if he should park.

"No," but I wanted him to.

Francisco Alexander Fwallah
(ca. 1980–)

"My eyes weep under the sky of forced exile—far away from the land that had nurtured my people through centuries," writes Angolan Albertan writer Francisco Alexander Fwallah in *My Love Letter to Africa*. Fwallah was born in Quinguagua, a village in the rural Uíge province of northern Angola. He fled to Edmonton in 1999 to escape the country's brutal twenty-seven-year-long civil war which began in 1975, immediately after Angola gained independence from Portugal. The struggle between pro- and anti-communist forces in Angola set the stage for a proxy war between the United States and the USSR, and the war continued until 2002. Half a million soldiers and civilians were killed during that time. Though the fighting officially ended in 2002, Angola remains in economic and social turmoil with a massive refugee crisis and millions of landmines impeding farming today.

Fwallah became a poet in his exile. As his speaker writes in his English-language collection, *A New Journey*, "I write to escape the poverty / And the injury / Of unrealized dreams. / I write to breathe. / I write for my sorrow / And rage / I write to wipe away my tears." He works in both Portuguese and English and is the author of three books of poetry—*A New Journey* (2008); *Quinguangua—Kikolo Meus Pensamentos* (2010); *Outros Pensamentos* (2012)—and one book of essays, *My Love Letter to Africa* (2013). His poetry is spare, immediate, impressionistic, and deeply introspective; it often packs the dense emotional resonance of haiku. The poems thematize love, sorrow, despair, and the process of writing itself. The following poems are taken from his collection *Outros Pensamentos* and translated from the original Portuguese by poet Erin Mouré.

Fwallah is active in the Portuguese and African communities in Edmonton. He was a subject of the documentary film *Portuguese Cultures in Edmonton* (2015) directed by Julio Munhos; he has participated in Celebrate African Arts: African Poetry and Arts Day in Edmonton, and has published work in the anthology *Home: Stories Connecting Us All* (2017), edited by Tololwa Mollel.

Na Corrente do rio

Sou
Teu
Irmão
Encontrie paz
Na corrente do rio
Refugiei-me
Na poesia.
Palavras
Cruzadas
Preocupadas
Com o meu bem estar,
Sou
Teu
Irmão
Refugiei-me
Na
Poesia
Acarinhando
O esplendor
Da vida
Com bastante amor
Sou teu
Irmão.

In the River Flow

I'm
Your
Brother
I found peace
In the river flow
Took refuge
In poetry.
Words
Down and Across
Intent
On my well-being,
I'm
Your
Brother
I took refuge
In
Poetry
Cherishing
The splendour
Of life
With enough love
I'm your
Brother.

Aquilo que Mereces

Seja o que for
Teus olhos
evocam
Nitidez
absoluta
Algo emotivo
História
dolorosa.
Seja o que for
Vou dar-te
aquilo
Que mereces

What You Deserve

Come what may
Your eyes
evoke
absolute
clarity
A heart-rending
History
of pain.
Come what may
I'll give you
what
you deserve

Amor abençoado	Blessed love
Amor abençoado	Blessed love
Teus olhos	Your eyes
evocam	evoke
Nitidez	absolute
absoluta	clarity
Vou a luta	I'll put up a fight
Amar-te	To love you
Noite	Night
E	And
Dia	Day

Michelle Jean-Paul
(1980–)

Michelle Jean-Paul is a mixed-race Haitian Mennonite educator and administrator in Winnipeg whose pedagogy focuses on issues of identity and equity. She graduated from the inaugural class of UWinnipeg's integrated educational program (Arts/Education) in 2003 then began work in Winnipeg School Division as a classroom teacher and vice-principal. She has since joined Seven Oaks School Division and completed her master of education degree, and is currently the principal of École Belmont in Winnipeg.

During research for her master's thesis, "Canary Songs: A Study of the Relationship of Black Youth to Winnipeg Schools," a study which examines the narratives of black youth and their parents about their experiences in Winnipeg high schools, Jean-Paul founded the Educators of Colour Network, a grassroots organization that supports diversity in education by providing free professional development sessions.

Her confessional personal essay "Learning to Love Me," originally published by Adebe DeRango-Adem and Andrea Thompson in their *Other Tongues: Mixed Race Women Speak Out* (2010), lays bare the psychic risks involved in coming of age in particular white-dominant spaces in Winnipeg. Yet this should not be read as a narrative belonging to the tragic-mulatto tradition. The tragedy is not racial mixing, but rather the injustice of misogynoir, or gendered racism, that is frequently directed at young girls and women and from which there is little reprieve in the dominant culture. Narratives such as "Learning to Love Me" will be deeply meaningful to present and future generations of youth who will recognize not only that they are not alone, but that they are part of a sisterhood of black prairie girls who are stronger than those who would hurt and hinder them.

❦

Learning to Love Me

As a brown-skinned girl, I have received many messages over the course of my life, some covertly and others very directly, that I am undesirable. As a child, my world was presented to me through two very different lenses. One was the reality of a Black, Catholic, francophone Haitian man and the other was that of a White, Mennonite, German speaking woman. Neither of my parents' realities reflected my own and as a result, these two distinct lenses resulted in my developing a divided view of the world and of me. I was fortunate to have four sisters but we were each so embroiled in our own struggles with identity that we weren't much support to one another.

For the longest time, I struggled with the idea that I am two different people. It began with my mixed-race identity, but over the years, I have come to realize that there are two very distinct parts to my personality. For a long time, I thought that this almost schizophrenic quality to my character was a good thing, but as of late I have come to understand how detrimental my divided perspective of myself has been. I don't believe that any one quality is tied to my Blackness or my Whiteness but I do believe that the dichotomy presented by my racial identity is the reason for my inner conflict.

I grew up in a white world with few positive examples of Black women in my environment. But even if there had been, in my teenage years I was very attached to the notion that I was neither Black nor white, but some-where in between. I felt isolated and believed that no one could understand my realities. I know that my parents did their best in raising us. I can only imagine how difficult it was for my white mother to raise brown daughters. She struggled to care for our hair. Her frustration became mine; I hated my nappy afro. As a child, it didn't seem to matter if my sisters and I were wearing earrings, pink dresses and standing in the women's restroom, some ignorant person always wondered if we were boys. This taught me that my life was a deficit. It taught me that I was not perceived as an attrac-tive woman. My hair became a symbol of my undesirability. I often wished to have long, straight hair like that of my friends. I also wished that I had a mother who could braid my hair. I admired the little black girls I would see on occasion whose plaited hair was like a work of art. Once my father's family moved to Winnipeg from Haiti, I would look forward to the rare opportunities to get my hair braided. While I would still get teased by my classmates about my cornrows, they made me feel beautiful and feminine.

As a young brown-skinned girl, I believed the negative messages that were being sent my way. I believed that I was not as smart, as beautiful, as deserving as my white friends. I was so wrapped up in myself that I could not understand that the people I was letting hurt me were just acting out of their own insecurity. Somewhere along the way, in spite of all my struggles with my identity, this insecure girl grew into a vibrant, powerful woman. One who works hard and always pushes herself to be better. But the 12-year-old version of me never went away. I manage to hide her yet every once and again, she appears. Her appearance always brings self-doubt along with it. She doesn't feel deserving of the accomplishments or accolades that come along with the adult version of me. Slowly, I am unpacking the layers and making peace with the 12-year-old version of me. This reflection is only a small part of that process. I now realize that much of her self-doubt arises from her perception of her physical self, namely, her attractiveness.

I find that many of the insecurities that I have carried into my adult life are related to my race and specifically to my hair. I can't recall ever agonizing over my caramel coloured skin. For whatever reason, I could accept that difference as it was who I was but I always felt that I would be more desirable if I could just get a handle on my hair. In my teens, Black women began to appear in the mainstream media with more frequency but even they had long, beautiful, flowing hair. I thought that a relaxer would solve my hair dilemma but quickly learned that even though my hair was straight, it still would not move like my friends' hair. I ended up wearing it pinned up for the next eight years of my life. Around the same time that I began relaxing my hair, I began to develop a real interest in boys and hoped to have my first real boyfriend. Boys would talk to me, flirt with me, and tell me that they liked me, but they always ended up dating my friends. This continued into high school. Guys would call me, write me notes, and confess their feelings, but again, they always ended up dating my white friends. Although it was never stated explicitly, the message became very clear to me on a subconscious level. As a brown-skinned girl, boys would lead you on when no one else was watching but, at the end of the day, they would always walk away with a white girl on their arm. Carmel skin and nappy hair were not attractive. In university, I began to feel that Black men weren't interested in brown-skinned girls either. I grew extremely self-conscious about my hair when pondering the possibility of dating a black man. I worried that his mother or his sisters would mock the fact that I didn't know how to handle my hair. In my heart, I felt that no man would find me beautiful because beauty equaled whiteness. I had several experiences with men that reinforced that idea to me. The most poignant was when a boy who I had been friends with since high school, and had shared a secret romance with, told me after he had loosened his lips with alcohol that he was still surprised at how attracted he was to me. He went on to explain that he didn't find Black women attractive with their wide noses, large foreheads, and weird hair. He had finally named the issue that I had pondered for years. And almost a decade later, I am still carrying the heartache that came with his confession.

Growing up as a brown-skinned girl, I always wished that I belonged to one world or the other. I often wished that I was Blacker so that I would have full membership into a world that I felt society associated me with, but I did not entirely belong to. At some point along my journey, I realized that I could not control my physical appearance so I worked tirelessly to control the things that I could. I shied away from activities that I did not excel in because it was important to me to be perceived as one of the best in the things I participated in. And even when others expressed delight in my abilities, I still felt as though I had to be better than I was.

I have learned a lot from the 12-year-old version of me. For the longest time, I hated her because she represented my weakness and I try to present myself as unflappable. I tried to understand her so that I could conquer her but all I was doing was pushing her further down inside of my soul. I am learning to love her. I am learning to feel grace for the girl who doesn't feel deserving of the love she desires so she accepts love as and when it is given to her. That part of me is broken and sad and lonely. That vulnerability also made me into the powerful beautiful woman that I am today. By getting in touch with that side of me, I am understanding that I do not need to define myself as part Haitian, part Mennonite; part English speaker, part French; part Black, part white. The conflicting sides of my personality are just the evidence of my humanity. I can be the sinner and the saint, plain and exotic, powerful and pathetic. All of these qualities and all of my experiences are part of my authentic self. This is a lesson that I will continue to learn over again throughout my lifetime and it is an essential one. It informs the lens through which I see the world and through which I will engage with my environment. I will always carry within me the young, brown-skinned girl who felt as though she was undesirable. And I will be better because of her.

Marika Warner
(1981–)

Marika Warner is a writer, actor, dancer, and theatre creator from Winnipeg who is now based in Toronto. She was born to a Trinidadian/Bajan mother and Polish/German father. Her maternal family underwent what Warner calls "three generations of migration" to Canada: her great-grandfather made a failed attempt to settle in Canada at the turn of the century. He was cheated out of money hard earned with indentured labour. "He got here but was scammed with this phony business deal … and had to go back" to Trinidad. "Then my grandfather came and worked on the railroads." He was active in union organizing as a member of the Brotherhood of Sleeping Car Porters but eventually returned to the Caribbean islands. Her mother immigrated to Canada as a child and eventually found a home on the Prairies (Keung).

In 2008 Warner interned with Jumblies Theatre in Toronto and was later involved with the company as artistic facilitator. She was co-artistic director of the Movement Project, a multi-arts company which she co-founded in 2007. She was a member of b current theatre company's raiz'n ensemble, and also performed with Les Coquettes Nouveau and Stand Up Dance. She was also an associate director of Nightwood Theatre's Busting Out girls' program. Her work includes *Wise.Woman* (b current), *Forbidden Science* (HBO), *Breakout* (CBC), *How We Forgot Here* (The Movement Project), *King Kaboom* (TVO), and *Private Eyes* (Global). Marika Warner completed a residency with Mammalian Diving Reflex, where she explored new projects with and about sexy teenagers, skinny women, and prayer. Her short play *Lockout* was also produced by Sarasvati Productions in Winnipeg.

Her full-length play *Mulatto Nation*, which was originally developed with the assistance of Nightwood Theatre's Write from the Hip Program, has had a workshop production in Toronto and was produced in Montreal in 2011 by Black Theatre Workshop and subsequently published in its entirety (57 pages) in *Kola* (Fall 2011). It is a provocative exploration of the current troubling climate of race relations in

466

Canada and the United States, which has given rise to both the #BlackLivesMatter movements as well as the desire to position mixed-race people as a unique and distinct ethnic population.

Mulatto Nation takes place in the alternative future where "mixed is the new white." Maizey, a mixed-race young woman, is taken in by miscegenation-enforcement officers and detained for not accepting the new order. Maizey rails against those in the "Mulatto Nation" who wish to claim her by arguing that regarding mixed people as a distinct category weakens racial solidarity around ongoing issues of black rights. At the same time, the play questions Maizey's problematic investment in discourses of racial purity. It is a complex and provocative investigation of the afterlives of slavery in the everyday experiences of racialized and mixed people in contemporary Canada.

Mulatto Nation

Scene 2

It is the near future, summer, early on a weekday evening. D and Maizey are seated across from each other in a stark interrogation room inside the Mulatto Nation Headquarters (MNHQ). A long-handled mirror sits on the table. D holds a pencil and clip board. He makes notes as he talks to Maizey).

D: Okay, Maizey. Complete the following sentence—I call myself black because …

MAIZEY: Because I am. I look almost exactly like my mother; no one has ever questioned our race.

D: Got it? Next. I started feeling the need to stand out when …

MAIZEY: What do you mean by "stand out"?

D: Okay, how about this—I want to differ myself because:

MAIZEY: Differ myself from what? You're not making sense.

D: Well, differ yourself from me, for starters. Why do you set yourself apart?

MAIZEY: Why would I water myself down?

D: Well, for example, do you think that being "black" will get you a better job than a mulatto?

Maizey gives D an icy stare.

D: We'll move on. These are hard questions.

Scene 3

(The Mulatto Nation Station announcer pops up periodically, like targeted marketing on YouTube or Gmail.)

ANNOUNCER: … The near future has arrived. We are living in a truly blended society, where mocha-lattes outnumber regular coffees, and grandparents eagerly welcome their little bundles of interracial love, wondering if they'll look more like Paula Abdul or Nicole Richie. Hair troubles are a thing of the past; white, black, and brown mamas alike buy "Mixed Chicks Leave-In Conditioner" for their wavy-haired offspring, whose wild curls blow freely in the winds of change.

What was once tragic is now magic, and life seems to be easier for those carrying the genes of both the slave and the colonizer. But as in photography, some wish for the good old days—when everything was black and white …

Scene 4

(Interrogation continues with D and Maizey.)

D: Date of birth?

MAIZEY: Why?

D: So we can do up your astrological chart. It may be relevant.

MAIZEY: I'm an Aries.

D: I see. March or April?

MAIZEY: March 23rd.

D: Mulatto History Month.

MAIZEY: Seriously—a whole month? Shouldn't it be—

D: Place of birth?

MAIZEY: I was born here.

D: Okay. Did you mother stay at home, or …

MAIZEY: No.

(Brief pause)

D: Public or private school?

MAIZEY: Public.

D: Catholic?

MAIZEY: Uh, no.

D: Were you involved in any extracurricular activities as a child?

MAIZEY: Mmm—No. The usual.

D: —

MAIZEY: Basketball, cross-country … I was in a choir …

D: Can you tap dance?

MAIZEY: No.

D: Highest level of education?

MAIZEY: That's a long story.

D: High school?

(Brief pause)

MAIZEY: Yes. Some college.

D: Sexually active?

(Brief pause)

MAIZEY: Yes …

D: Okay, uh, number of pregnancies?

MAIZEY: What?

D: *(looks directly at Maizey)* Pregnancies?

Scene 5

Maizey walks her bike down a city sidewalk in her bike courier gear. The street is in the downtown of a bright, vibrant, diverse city. She speaks to her dispatcher via headset.

MAIZEY: I'm off the clock, Chief—sorry.

Yeah. Talk to you in the a.m., alright?

No. I start at six. Sharp.

Okay. Have a good night.

She finds a bike rack and removes her ear bud and two-way radio before locking up her bike. Whee! Quittin' time. Her phone rings, just as she turns it on. It is Miranda. This is a fast-paced but not rushed, playful conversation between two friends who have the ability to finish each other's sentences.

MAIZEY: 'Sup, girl.

MIRANDA: Hey babe, you're on Wha's gwan?

MAIZEY: Mmm, not much, might grab a drink here …

MIRANDA: With dude?

MAIZEY: Nooo.

MIRANDA: Who with?

MAIZEY: Just—me.

MIRANDA: Well, then come to this thing with me.

MAIZEY: —What thing?

MIRANDA: There's a Miscegenation Pride Parade today.

MAIZEY: A what?

MIRANDA: It's a march. People are going. I wanna check it out, come.

MAIZEY: Miscegenation Pride Parade. That's a mess. What—

MIRANDA: Why you so … Just come.

MAIZEY: … Do I have to?

MIRANDA: Do you love me?

MAIZEY: —Yes.

MIRANDA: So? It's gonna be fun! The organizers are really—

MAIZEY: Okay. I'll come.

MIRANDA: Of course you will. Thanks. It starts from city hall, so—

MAIZEY: Alright, I can be there in like five. We're getting drinks after …
Bye.

Scene 6

(Back at Mulatto Nation Headquarters, the interrogation continues).

D: Pregnancies. Live births. No? No dependants?

MAIZEY: No dependants.

D is about to speak again when Maizey interrupts.

MAIZEY: You know what, why don't I just go over to the police station? At least they're not going to ask me about my personal life.

D: But, if you're as black as you say they may beat you for no reason.

MAIZEY: I may beat you.

Pause.

D: I see I've hit a nerve. Can we continue?

Scene 7

Back on the street, Maizey hangs up her phone and begins walking down the sidewalk in the direction of the march. A crowd is heard chanting: "Make mulattoes, not war!" Soon, Maizey is surrounded by a large, spirited march. Music plays, people smile and groove, and the rhythm of a New Orleans-style marching band can be heard.

Maizey takes in the crowd. It is made up of people of all races and people of no race; mainly groups of teenagers, pairs of friends, and inter-racial couples in their 20's and 30's, many with mixed-race babies and small children.

Scene 8

Back at Mulatto Nation Headquarters, the interrogation continues.

D: Okay, Maizey—can you tell me a bit about what it was like growing up in your home?

MAIZEY: Like? What? It was fine.

D: —

MAIZEY: My mom has five kids.

D: Five.

MAIZEY: Yeah. Five. Me first.

D: Did you all—share a father?

MAIZEY: I didn't need a father.

D: No, then?

MAIZEY: —

D: So—a happy childhood.

MAIZEY: It was fine.

D: Fine. Do you like music?

MAIZEY: Yeah.

D: Alright.

Shuffling of pages to a new section of the questionnaire.

D: Who was Sammy Davis Jr.?

MAIZEY: Uh—well, he played—he was in ...

D: Next. Preferred music genre?

MAIZEY: I guess pop, punk, you care why?

D: Personal top ten guitar heroes?

MAIZEY: Okay, Robert Johnson, Hendrix, uh, Kirk Hammer—whoa. What's in this for you?

D: It's just an intake survey.

MAIZEY: Intake?

Scene 9

Out on the street, Miscegenation Pride Parade participants march past energetically, having fun. Maizey is approached by a young woman in a t-shirt that says "Mulattos Unite! Take Back the White" (Cassie). Cassie also wears a two-way radio with an ear bud.

CASSIE: Hey sister! Welcome to Mullatopia! Care to join the march?

MAIZEY: Uh—I'm meeting a friend.

CASSIE: Oh yeah? At the march?

MAIZEY: —

CASSIE: I'll walk with you—If I may.

Maizey hesitates before stepping onto the street to walk with Cassie.

CASSIE: (*Cassie extends a hand*). What's your name?

MAIZEY: Maizey.

CASSIE: Pretty. Where does it come from?

MAIZEY: Thanks. Nowhere.

CASSIE: Okay.

Pause.

CASSIE: Beautiful day. We really got lucky. And I'm not just talking genetically! Jokes aside, I'm really happy with the turnout. And no five-O anywhere. I mean I know it's not a black people thing, but, you know, we thought they might send half the force.

Shift.

CASSIE: So, what's your mix?

MAIZEY: Uh, tonic?

CASSIE: …?

MAIZEY: I'm not mixed; I'm just light-skinned.

Slight pause.

CASSIE: Oh—you came to support. Okay.

MAIZEY: Yeah. I'm here to meet my friend. She's not mixed, either—

CASSIE: —Just light-skinned.

MAIZEY: —

CASSIE: Hey sis: there's no such thing as a light-skinned black—only a self-hating mulatto. Give it up. Just because the original mixture happened a long time ago, and possibly through rape, doesn't mean it didn't happen. You're clinging to your so-called racial purity, mamacita. Let it go. Here; read this.

Cassie pulls out a pamphlet and extends it towards Maizey. Maizey eyes the pamphlet.

CASSIE: Mule? Yeah. What's a mule?

MAIZEY: Mulatto Nation. Eulch—why do you call yourselves that? Don't even get me started. That word is so ... don't you know it's derived from ...

MAIZEY: —

CASSIE: Half-donkey, half-stallion. I find that flattering. If I can be a strong, tough work animal, and a beautiful show pony, all at the same time—hey! That's alright with me.

MAIZEY: Impressive. You compare yourself to a farm animal.

CASSIE: Not just any farm animal. The only one with more intelligence than either of its parent species. So really, Maizey ...

Pause.

CASSIE: What's your mix? Come on—what are the ingredients in that sassy cocktail, hm? What kind of tropical fruit got blended up with the premium vanilla ice cream in your badass smoothie?

MAIZEY: I'm not a milkshake. And I don't want to be part of this. Like I said, I'm—

CASSIE: "Black." (*Yawns*) Are you?

Cassie lightly handles Maizey's black t-shirt as she speaks, tugging slightly on the sleeve or collar with her index finger and thumb, noting the contrast between the fabric and Maizey's skin.

CASSIE: Have some pride, Maizey. It's okay to be what you really are. More than okay: mixed is the new white. I want you to think about joining the Mulatto Nation. We're growing; we're going places. No pressure. Take my card.

Cassie whips out and presents a business card, which Maizey takes and holds in her hand.

MAIZEY: Again, I'm not "mulatto." This conversation is over.

(As she speaks, Cassie holds her forearm to Maizey's, comparing skin tones.)

CASSIE: Okay. You're telling me there's no white in you? Not even ... one little eighth? Really? ... You're in the one hundredth percentile of blackness.

Maizey pulls away.

MAIZEY: I'm black. How can you say I'm not?

CASSIE: Well—I know how to spot a muli. *(Cassie touches Maizey's hair, body and face lightly as she goes through this list.)* For starters, you have all the standard characteristics of the average mulatto, though really there's no such thing as an average mulatto: the loose afro; the complex eyes; Germanic features, with a touch of the continent; nice guns; the sexy caramel skin; extreme defensiveness—

MAIZEY: I'm not defending myself, I'm telling you who I am. You're being extremely offensive.

CASSIE: Settle down. It's okay; enormous chip on the shoulder is also part of our phenotype.

CASSIE: *(Snaps her head to observe another group of marchers).* Whoa. Did you hear that?

She turns to watch the scene unfold on the street and immediately begins using her two-way radio; Maizey also turns to watch.

"Ho-latto"? Who says that?!

Cassie speaks into her radio.

CASSIE: Yeah, we've got a bit of a situation at the rear of the march; one of the Jewlattos is making slurs towards what appears to be a group of Gelattos ... yeah, looks pretty aggressive, I'm gonna need *all* the marshals at the back ASAP, okay?

Word. Roger that. Over.

Cassie disengages her ear bud and turns back to Maizey.

CASSIE: We do have factions. It's not encouraged, but unfortunately it happens. Hey, I've really got to take care of this situation; we can't have violence going down at a public event, you know? There's already enough rumours flying. Like the whole body odor thing.

MAIZEY: Isn't that true?

CASSIE: I'm genuinely happy to meet you. Please stay in touch. There's an after party tonight—I can get you in, let me know. We've got a Velvet Revolver cover band. It should be hilarious.

MAIZEY: ... Velvet Revolver?

CASSIE: Yeah. Slash is mixed.

Cassie walks purposefully towards the scene of the altercation, speaking into her radio.

Back at Mulatto Nation Headquarters, the interrogation continues.

Scene 10

MAIZEY: INTAKE?

D: Yes, it's designed.

MAIZEY: What gives you any indication.

D: It's all right, Maizey. Settle down. What's in it for us is a more in-depth understanding of the tastes and values of young mulattoes.

MAIZEY: Not mulatto!

D: In this geographical region. We need to know how to reach you, what excites you, your ideals ...

MAIZEY: ——

In the pause, D stands, approaches Maizey, pokes his pencil into her hair, and lets go of the pencil. He then picks it up and scribbles on his clipboard.

MAIZEY: What are you doing?

D: Pencil test. We have to do it to everyone.

Silence.

D: I'm sorry. I like your hair. It's ... cute. If you don't want to finish the survey now, that's fine.

Short pause, during which D flips his papers to a new section.

D: Our research department in conducting a study in economics, to determine certain undefined variables. The next series of questions are part of the investigation. One. How much do you tip?

MAIZEY: —

D: Tip. Gratuitize. Waiters, bartenders, estheticians, cab drivers ... Okay, allow me to re-phrase. If the bill for dinner is twenty dollars, do you tip a) ninety cents, b) a dollar fifty, or c) a dollar ninety-five?

MAIZEY: Those are all bad tips.

D: Yes, but, well, it's widely acknowledged that ... black people are lousy tippers—statistically, substandard. So, if the average black person tips, say, three fifths of what the average white person tips, does the average mulatto then tip half of the black tip; tip half of the white tip; or split the difference between the black tip and the white tip? Can you see ... Fine. Why don't we just ... talk?

Horrible silence.

D: Why do you insist on calling yourself black?

MAIZEY: What else ... why do *you* insist on calling yourself mixed?

D: Black is not necessary. It's definitely not factual. Am I wrong?

MAIZEY: Yes. I am black. I was raised by a black woman in a black family. Almost all of my friends are black; I am not usually put in a position where I have to defend who I am, you know?

D: Maizey, you've mentioned a lot of other people—black people—who are part of your life. But you haven't actually spoken about *yourself* yet. Why can't a mulatto woman like you—a mulatta, if you'll allow me—be surrounded by black friends and family, the way you are? Would that create a *problem*? Would you encounter undue stress, unwanted expectations?

MAIZEY: That's not the point. Black. End of story!

D: Just try it on. You might like it. I hate to be the one, but black doesn't look so good on you.

MAIZEY: What? And "mulatto" would? That word is ridiculous, no doubt made up by white people.

D: So if black people had created terminology by which to refer to their mixed-race relatives, you would embrace it?

MAIZEY: That didn't happen for a reason.

D: Hm. "High yella"?

MAIZEY: That wasn't an insult.

D: Oh yeah? I'd like to see you convince a mulatto of that in the Southern states just after abolition. Any name used to draw lines is utterly degrading. Aren't we all a little mixed?

MAIZEY: No. Some people are a lot mixed up. And not everyone wants to be mixed.

D: No? When presented with a choice, most people of our complexion choose to be with us. Maizey. It's a good place to be.

MAIZEY: No. I already have a place to watch the world from; I'm not moving for you. Besides your whole thing is a cop-out—black people trying to get away from being black. Why would I hide? I'm proud.

D: If you'd acknowledge your truth, you'd have a lot more to be proud of. You don't take pride in your white heritage? Your ... father, correct?

MAIZEY: No! Capitalism, slavery, genocide, sitcoms ... That's your fucking white history.

D: Hm ...

D furiously takes notes.

MAIZEY: Gonna use that in your next pamphlet?

D: No. It sounds like something a guilty white person would say.

MAIZEY: —

D: Was your father a guilty man?

MAIZEY: How do you know about my father?

D: Point! We've conducted fairly extensive research to determine if there are particular traits shared by mulattoes with black mothers as opposed to mulattoes with white mothers. The findings are remarkable; I was making an educated guess. You seem to fall into the WCWF-type.

MAIZEY: WCWTF!

D: Working Class White Father. One of the most rare types. Differentiable from, say, a Bougie White Father—BWF-type by a number of reliable indicators.

MAIZEY: Whoa whoa whoa whoa whoa. You are so full of shit. You can't make up stuff like that! You can't just jump—

D: Have you met a mixed girl with a wealthy black dad?

MAIZEY: —

D: Was she a lot like you?… I didn't think so.

Things seem to slow down slightly.

D: The way you're identifying yourself doesn't help black people, Maizey. You need to take a long look in the mirror. You need to look her in the eye, and tell her that you love her. Give her a name. Hannah, Claire. Talk to her.

D lifts the handled mirror off of the table and holds it up to Maizey's face. She pushes the mirror down.

MAIZEY: I see a black girl.

D: I see a mixed girl. No—I see a black girl and a white girl so at odds with each other, they're not even on speaking terms, stare that poor, self-hating white girl inside of you dead in—

MAIZEY: This is insane. And actually racist. So, every black person who isn't the appropriate shade of midnight has to call themselves "mixed." There'll be no "black" people left.

D: Interesting, isn't it? Maizey, who benefits if self-identified "black" people make up a larger percentage of the census population?

MAIZEY: Black people. Obviously.

D: Really.

MAIZEY: Yes. You don't get it. White people don't know how to deal with us. We're their worst nightmare.

D: You think that they know how to deal with me, with *us?* If you ask me, white people seem to have figured out exactly how to deal with black people. That didn't take them very long. It's when things get more complicated that they get confused. It's not black and white, Maizey. There's … *much* more. And as hard as you try to see things that way, you *can't* make it so. You can't polarize your world. We've evolved from there. You seem to want to be left behind.

Pause.

MAIZEY: I don't know … Can I go now?

D appraises.

D: Are you still black?

Maizey looks at the back of her hand, then to D with a fuck-you smile.

MAIZEY: Yeah.

Lisa Codrington

"I think for me it's important to make sure that the stories that I perhaps didn't necessarily see on stage when I was younger, to put them on stage. I think it is part of my duty..." So says Barbadian Manitoban actor and writer Lisa Codrington ("2008 Theatre Co-Award Winner"). Born and raised in Winnipeg, she notes, "...when I was growing up I didn't really see black people on stage, and if I did, they were singing or dancing or serving—or *American*. There was no sense of Canadian black people...so I think that is something that is important for me to do, that I really want to do, to explore that voice...I don't want to speak for a group of people, but I do want to explore the voices and the people that perhaps I didn't get to see on stage but I think should be on stage" ("2008 Theatre Co-Award Winner").

Lisa Codrington holds a BA in criminology from the University of Manitoba and a BFA in acting from Ryerson University. She currently lives in Toronto, where she has been playwright-in-residence at Theatre Direct Canada and co-director of Youth Initiatives at Nightwood Theatre.

Her one-woman memory play, *Cast Iron*, produced by Nightwood and Obsidian, opened at the Tarragon Extraspace in 2005. She says that when she started working on the play while at Ryerson she did not know how to write but she did know how to act; thus, she wrote the play while standing on her feet, as she figured out what the characters needed to say. Writing in the Bajan dialect, a language "that deserves to be heard," Codrington says she realized how ingrained the voice is, and how much she knew about it, and how expressive and rich she found it to be. But the Bajan dialect initially alienated one Toronto critic, who wrote, "I get the impression that the main impulse behind the writing is not sharing and disseminating the story but placing a territorial flag on it that discourages others from appropriating, understanding or even sympathizing with it" (Al-Solaylee). Ultimately, the play won both popular and critical acclaim. It was nominated for the 2006 Governor General's Award for Drama, and has been published in *Canadian Theatre Review* and in the anthology *Beyond the Pale: Dramatic Writing from First Nations Writers and*

481

Writers of Colour (2004). It was published in its entirety by Playwrights Canada Press in 2006. Codrington also won the K.M. Hunter Award for Theatre in 2008.

In the following selection from *Cast Iron*, the figure of the Red Woman can be read as the haunting embodiment of plantation injustices. She returns to the prairies in the present as a reminder of the transgressions of slavery, miscegenation, and past secrets that can never be fully forgotten. As Libya says in the last scene, "I just lef an I kep on leffin till I eventually lef an come alla de way here. I been here fuh over forty years. I ain't t'ink de Red Woman gine come alla de way up here … but she do cause I still here wit my belly startin tuh cut an no where tuh run" (40).

Codrington is also the author of *Skylar*, a radio drama which aired on CBC Radio's Sunday Showcase, and *Vegas*, a monologue presented in Theatre Direct Canada's production *The Demonstration*. As an actor, she has appeared in plays for Mirvish Productions, Prairie Theatre Exchange, the Winnipeg and Toronto Fringe Festivals, the Hysteria Festival, and Toronto's SummerWorks Theatre Festival.

Her most recent plays are *Up the Garden Path* and *The Adventures of the Black Girl in Her Search for God*. *Up the Garden Path* was produced by Obsidian at Theatre Passe Muraille in March 2016, and won the Carol Bolt Award, an annual Canadian literary award presented by the Playwrights Guild. Set in the late 1960s, it tells the story of a young seamstress from Barbados who disguises herself as her brother to work on a winery in the Niagara region. The script was published by Playwrights Canada Press in 2017.

Cast Iron

"The Red Woman"

Scene 1

LIBYA's room.

Late evening.

LIBYA age 75.

LIBYA's small room at the Red River Health Centre and Personal Care Home in the north end of Winnipeg, Manitoba. It is a dark and windy winter evening (about a quarter to eight). The moonlight streaming through the small window in LIBYA's room is just enough to illumi-nate her. She paces and quietly rants in protest of the

*nurses, doctors, visitors, residents and intercom pages
making noise in the hallway outside her room. Frustrated,
LIBYA stares out the window. The hallway sounds begin
to fade and the clanking sound of the heater in her room
becomes audible as the wind shakes the trees outside. The
sound builds and morphs into sugar cane swept aside by
a machete. LIBYA stands silent until she is ambushed by a
sharp cutting pain in her belly. This is the first time LYBIA
has felt the call of the Red Woman in over forty years.*

LIBYA

Oh Lawrd! (*to the Red Woman*) Ha! You t'ink you gine catch me,
but you can'. Just wait ... just you wait nuh. Yuh ain' even cut
muh! Dis here is a piece of gas ... it gine ease off soul. (*LIBYA
rubs her belly.*) Den I gine come fuh yuh! (*The rustling in the
cane disappears and the lights in LIBYA's room snap up.*)

Scene 2

*LIBYA's room
Late evening.
LIBYA age 75.*

LIBYA

(*out to the audience*) Hallow? Hallow? What yuh want? GET de
HELL outta my room fore I lick yuh upside de head wit mu cast
iron! Who de BLAST you t'ink you is, and what de hell kinda
monkey manners yuh is use tuh enter de place? Yuh CAN' just
WALK into a person ROOM! Yuh supposed tuh KNOCK, and
den WAIT fuh dem tuh SAY, "WHO DAT?" Doan mine if de
door OPEN, nor if de ROOF blow off, yuh must STILL say who
you is fore yuh is enter a person room ... SO GET DE HELL
OUT!

LIBYA approaches.

Who?
Triston? Who de hell is Triston?

Youse, who?

Stan where you is!

Triston-James? I ain' know nobody name Triston-James.

Gracie?

My sister Gracie dead! How de hell you is she, she ... she—
SHE SON ... From Barbados? Oh, Winston-James Blackwell—
Yes, yes I am Libya Geraldine Atwell. I KNOW who I is. You ole
auntie mine ain' gone yet soul—

(LIBYA retreats.) Stan where yuh is! I rader you not get suh
close. Alla wunna out der always bringin de flu in here ... killin
alla we. Mine you if yuh kill half a we wit de flu, dat might open
up some beds. Lawrd knows dem always carryin on about, "not
enough beds." So maybe I will shake you han. Den dey can cover
muh up ... wheel muh out ... an lef me in de hallway till dey get
space in de morgue.

But later ... fuh now stan where you is.

I ain' know de body was you yuh. I ain' remember de last time I
see you ... it been dunkey years, but I get de face recognize now.
You got you muder big mout an you fader Black face. Shut off de
light an you disappear ... Except fuh you big eyes.

Yuh lucky I ain' lic out you big eyes fuh blastin true my door like
so. Yuh is have tuh protect yuh self in dis place cause yuh ain'
know who gine come true de door. But I guess dis mussy be how
alla wunna is enter a room in Barbados dese days. Glad I lef den,
I ain' able wit dat soul.

Pause. LIBYA stares at WINSTON-JAMES.

I wouldn't sit der if I was yuh. Dat chair is dirty boy ... yuh is
liable tuh get TB. Alla de people in dis blasted place is got TB.
Coughin an spreadin dey germs. Like dis room here is need a
whole bottle a bleach t'row pun de florin tuh kill de smell a de
last soul who die here. I here t'ree momfs now, an I still see he
hair and smell he stink all over de blasted place. De only t'ing
dat is clean is de bed, cause I is soak muh sheet wit water every

night suh as tuh get new one put on in de morning. Blasted
housekeeping in dis place ain' ever hear of a mop an pail. All
dem do is sweep an dust. Dustin what? Do you see any fine china
in here? It a room wita rust up ole bed, an a hardback chair dat is
pain yuh boxie baaaad mannnn …

LIBYA stares at WINSTON-JAMES then sucks her teeth.

Suh what, we is gine stan up like dis de whole time you here?
Wha'yuh come here fuh? A piece a talk? You an me ain' nuh
friends. I ain' see you in over forty years, what de hell we gine
talk bout? De people here in Canada is de same as dem back
home. Alla de Black people you see here dat get dey stay is
runnin all about de place buildin up a bundle a big house in de
outskirts, workin t'ree jobs tuh pay fuh it, an prayin in church
every Sunday tuh win de Lotto six-forty-nine. Dat ain' fuh me
boy cause in de end we is all gonna end up in de same place.
(*quietly*) A brown skin one dat usta turn she nose up at me on de
bus, WHO I KNOW had a bundle a big house, is now lyin up
in a room smaller dan dis. But even dough she got tubes down
she t'roat an life-water hook up in she arm, she still turnin her
nose up at me. Black people is de worst people in de world soul.
Gawd mek a mistake when he mek we. But all you all back home
in Barbados is de same. Alla wuna t'ink everybody dat gone
overseas got somet'ing but we ain' got nutin'. Dat why I never
guh back home. You t'ink I want tuh listen tuh alla wunna askin
why I ain' bring dis, an why I ain' send dat. I guess I could guh
back now cause everybody I know der dead.
My reckless fader dead …
My half n half gra'muder dead …
My licorice muder dead …
You Black face fader dead—

Pause.

You muder?
How you mean, 'what about you muder?'
Look, you muder, my sister Gracie … my half sister as de
Canadians is say, dead every sense. *We family die off fast soul.*

De Lawrd ain' interested in kepin none a we around long, cept
fuh me an I ain' interested in talkin about she. Beside I ain' like
tuh talk ill a de dead and I ain' got nut'ing good to say bout dat
long-legged loud-mout Black bitch Gracie!

> *LIBYA gets a cutting pain in her belly but hides it as the
> wind outside builds.*

Look, I sorry you come all dis way … cause I doan have anyt'ing
good tuh say tuh you … and I ain' want tuh spen what little life
I got lef listenin tuh a big man like you run yuh mout bout what
happen tuh you over de last forty yers, nor guh on bout how you
wish you had know you muder an—

> *LIBYA gets another cutting pain in her belly but continues
> to hide it as the wind gains strength and the heater kicks in.*

Look, yuh too late.
I have *held my tongue* fuh so long.
I mean, where was you before? Where was you when Mr. and
Mrs. Wasserstine t'row me outta dey house an intuh dis nursing
home? I work fuh dem fuh over t'irty years. I cook an clean fuh
two generations of dey family but dem still turn muh out …
telling me I need tuh be in here cause a my diabetus—
Diabetus my ass! Dem done wit me, but now you callin on me.
Yuh empty an yuh come tuh Libya so she can fill yuh up. But not
wit food, not in dis day an age but wit answers. But my days in
domestic done. I ain' got nuh damn t'ing tuh tell you suh lef dis
place! Guh long and get outta my chair cause I ain' invite you tuh
sit down an I sure as shite ain' invite you tuh come alla de way
from Barbados tuh Winnipeg in de middle a winter.
It too cole here tuh be playin de fool soul.

> *LIBYA gets another cutting pain that she cannot hide. The
> wind explodes into a rumble and the sound of sugar cane
> swept aside by a machete grows. LIBYA attempts to ignore
> the pain and talk to WINSTON-JAMES but by the end of
> the next short speech she can't help but speak to the Red
> Woman.*

Look,

Dat ain' you name pun de door ...

Nor none a you t'ings in de drawer.

Dis here is my place.

Libya Atwell room t'ree-fifty-two: diabetic, mince meal, cause I got no teef tuh CHEW.

I got glaucoma dat is increase de pressure in my right an lef eye,

An tugeder it gine blow me up an mek me lie down an DIE.

But fuh now I still know dat I is GOT enough SIGHT,

Tuh FINE you an PELT you wit ALLA my MIGHT!

> *LIBYA is hit with a final sharp cutting pain. She rubs her belly as she warns the Red Woman.*

I gine tek my cast iron an mash up you face bad man! You may have catch everybody else but I get dis far, an yuh lie if you t'ink I gine let you catch me—

(to WINSTON-JAMES) Who? Who de hell you t'ink I takin to? You!

Wait. Wait. Wait.

Nurse? What'yuh callin out for nurse fuh? LOOK, I ain' need no damn nurse tuh mek me feel better. If I ever fine myself feelin better it is because I dead soul, suh just wait. A woman is have tuh talk tuh she pain if dat is all she got ... suh wait.

> *Silence.*

I mean, I taught you come here fuh a piece a talk.

I taught you want tuh hear story bout you muder.

Come den an sit yuh Black ass down. *(LIBYA laughs and sucks her teeth.)*

LAWRD, you is wait just like Gracie! You muder torment an exile me from de first day I meet she till de day she die. *(as GRACIE) Look, I ain' want yuh tuh play my game. Especially since you gone an uproot a piece a sugar cane you was only supposed tuh name.*

Scene 3

Inside Winston Sugar Cane Plantation.
Midday in the hot sun.
LIBYA age 8.
GRACIE age 11.
Sugar cane rustles in the wind as GRACIE exiles LIBYA
from the cane.

GRACIE

(to LIBYA) Ain' you know we gra'ma is de gra'daughter a
Charles Winston who usta own alla dis sugar cane plantation.
She muder was Charles Winston White daughter, and she fader a
Black cane cutter an I doan t'ink none a dem would like tuh see
what you gone an do in dis here sugar can, fuh trut. Lef de cane
Libya.

LIBYA

(to WINSTON-JAMES) Gracie was raise by we gra'muder in
a broken down squatter dat cross de road from Winston Sugar
Cane Plantation. I was raise by my fader on Shipley Sugar Cane
Plantation side. I was eight when I first met Gracie. She was
eleven and had a big soft soursop head, a loud stout smellin
push up mout an long tin sugar cane legs *(LIBYA impersonates
GRACIE.)* Every Saturday my fader drop me at my gra'muder
house. De man need someone tuh watch over me while he bettin
at de track. *(as SANTIFORD) Everyt'ing on Number 35 Black
Thunder.*

Scene 4

The road that separates Winston Sugar Cane Plantation
from LIBYA's grandmother's house.
Early morning, the sun is rising.
LIBYA age 8.
The faint sound of dogs, chickens and goats can be heard
as SANTIFORD drops LIBYA off at her grandmother's
house for the first time.

SANTIFORD

>*(to LIBYA)* Libya, what happen when a White plantation owner
>daughter get mix up wit a poor Black cane cutter an he "sword"?
>Your gra'muder, a half n' half picknee who is run she mout worse
>dan a madmun. *(laugh)* You muder was de same way suh I lef
>she, den Gawd tek she ... BUT DAT AIN' TUH SAY dat I ain'
>want yuh tuh know you gra'muder ... nor you sister ... suh guh
>long. You ain' see Gracie der stanin up waitin fuh you tuh come
>an play?

LIBYA

>*(to WINSTON-JAMES)* All Gracie is have tuh do is WAIT. Like
>you, stanin up der waitin tuh hear bout you muder, an all pun a
>sudden I talkin bout she. Gracie would wait, an alla de chil'ren
>pun Winston Plantation side would pour like grain a rice out of
>a bag dat brek open, cryin out *(as the children)* Graaaacieeee,
>Naaaame some sugar caaaane aftuh we! Stupid ass chil'ren
>skinning dey teet an stannin up stiff like dey tryin tuh avoid de
>lash in class. An yuh muder der like a headmaster, givin lecture
>for she let any a we play—

Scene 5

>*Just outside Winston Sugar Cane Plantation.*
>*Midday in the hot sun.*
>*LIBYA age 8.*
>*GRACIE age 11.*
>*GRACIE is preparing her friends to play in the cane field.*

GRACIE

>*(to the audience)* Name Every Piece a Sugar Cane in Winston
>Plantation, *(Gracie points to herself.)* MY plantation. My
>mummy say, "everyt'ing including sugar cane is need a name,
>or else it get tek up by de devil an die in shame." SO, let we go
>name some sugar cane ... *(takes a breath in)* OH, but mine dis
>here, it a dangerous game runnin true Winston Plantation sugar
>cane. People is get cut up running true de cane ... well all except
>dose dat is related by name *(GRACIE points to herself.)* Gracie
>Winston. *(GRACIE takes a breath in.)* SO, dat why alla wunna

can only come in dis cane, if I give a piece of it you name, *(waits)* cause I own it. My family is de only one tuh avoid de RED WOMAN sword, an if yuh all follow me, DAT will be you reward. *(GRACIE takes in a breath.)* BUT, if I fine any one a yuh all suckin on de stalk or stealin from de crop, I will call fuh de RED WOMAN tuh chase you till yuh drop, an after alla wunna stop, I ain' afraid tuh get she tuh cut off yuh top. *(GRACIE takes in a breath.)* SO, Tracy an Clotell Morgan next tuh you … muh little sistuh Lib-ya hidin behine you … an ohhh yesss, my BIG BLACK BOY *(waits)* yes James dat is you! Alla you please come run behine me, an hole tight a de cane I give yuh tuh name. *(GRACIE takes in a breath.)* OH but watch fuh de RED WOMAN dat stomp true dis cane, an shout, "IT GONNA RAIN" if she catch sight a we game. Alla wunna come we is gonna mek some fun!

LIBYA

(to WINSTON-JAMES) Fun what? You muder pullin me by de arm MEKIN me run true Winston Sugar Cane Plantation fearin fuh de Red Woman? You mussy hear bout de Red Woman growin up on Winston Plantation side … especially after wha'happen tuh you muder.

Scene 6

Inside Winston Sugar Cane Plantation.
Midday in the shaded cane field.
LIBYA age 8.
GRACIE age 11.
GRACIE explains the myth of the Red Woman as she leads
LIBYA and her friends deep into the cane field.

GRACIE

(to LIBYA and the audience)
Old Charles Winston who first own dis cane,
Get he meat from de butcher who live down de lane.
But dis one time …
De butcher ha fine …
Dat she ain' have nuh meat fuh Charles Winston tuh eat.

So she kill some lout mout chil'ren in de cane,
An wrap dem up like meat, (as if dey de same).
But when she business get back pun it feet,
An she bring Charles Winston sweet pig meat tuh eat,
He say, "Grrrahhh! Dis ain' as sweet as de meat I get las week!"
So she run true de cane and start cuttin again.
An when she han start tuh turn red,

> *GRACIE looks down at her hands and then shows them to*
> *LIBYA.*

An alla de people children end up dead,
People change and call she de RED WOMAN instead.
De ole people is say she die …
But we gra'ma say, "It is ah bundle ah lie,"
So if yuh hear de RED WOMAN t'rashin true de cane—
Whooosh wooosh woosh!
Stop where yuh is an shout, "IT GONNA RAIN!"

LIBYA

(to WINSTON-JAMES) Gracie's game lead me right down de paf
tuh de Red Woman.

GRACIE

(to LIBYA) Libya you will go … oh no I am goin dat way … oh
an dat way is fuh Tracy an Clotell. NO, not dat way girl, dat way
fuh my boy James. Libya you will go … dis way.

> *GRACIE points down an ominous looking path that leads*
> *deeper into the sugar cane.*

LIBYA

(to WINSTON-JAMES) She mek me she own sister, run de way
wit de most spread out … swibble up … trample up, hungry
lookin piece a sugar cane growin.

GRACIE

(to LIBYA) GO!

LIBYA

> *(LIBYA moves down the path looking for an adequate piece of cane to name. Suddenly she feels the presence of the Red Woman and she mouths, then whispers "it gonna rain.")* It gonna rain. It gonna rain. *(LIBYA is hit with a quick cutting pain in her belly, like the jab of a sword. Unscathed, she begins to yell out, "it gonna rain.")* It gonna rain! IT GONNA RAIN! *(to WINSTON-JAMES)* I ain' even have tuh turn round tuh know it was de Red Woman. I just tek up de firs hungry piece a cane I see an run strait back de way I came. IT GONNA RAIN, IT GONNA RAIN! My eye catch Gracie and I grabble she up too. IT GONNA RAIN, IT GONNA RAIN!

Scene 7

> *Outside Winston Sugar Cane Plantation.*
> *Midday, in the hot sun.*
> *LIBYA age 8.*
> *GRACIE age 11.*
> *GRACIE lectures LIBYA in front of her friends.*

GRACIE

> *(to LIBYA)* Lib-ya, *(GRACIE waits.)* why yuh gone an shout out, "it gonna rain?"
> I ain' see nuh RED Woman in dis here cane.

> *GRACIE takes a breath in, then waits a moment.*

> Look, I ain' want yuh tuh play my game.
> Especially since you gone leffin me mash up an maim,
> Cause you t'rashin true de cane,
> Uprootin a piece you was only supposed tuh name,
> While alla de resta we tryin tuh play my game.
> Lef de cane Lib-ya cause YOU is de only RED WOMAN here.

> *Shouting and taunting LIBYA*

RED WOMAN, RED WOMAN, WRAP YUH DAMN MEAT

WIT YUH BLOOD RED HANDS, AN YUH BUTCHERIN
SHEET! RED WOMAN, RED WOMAN, WANNA TEK
WE LIFE, WIT YUH BLOOD RED HANDS, AN YUH
BUTCHERING KNIFE!

LIBYA

(to WINSTON-JAMES) Gracie an she friends shout suh hard I
ain' get a chance tuh tell she dat, DE RED WOMAN WILL CUT
OFF YOU PIG EARS ... AN RIP OUT YOU LOUD MOUT ...
TEAR OFF YOU BLACK FACE AN CUT YUH IN YOU BIG
TEEF! Too bad cause she do. Gracie ain' believe me an hear yuh
shout, she get cut up by de Red Woman.
Dat it it ... end of story.

The sounds of the nursing home begin to fade back in.

Yuh can stop waitin now. I have t'ings tuh do. *(pause)* Just cause
I in a nursing home doan mean dat I ain' have t'ings tuh do.
(LIBYA begins to do leg exercises.) De doctor always t'reatnin
tuh cut off my legs if dem is get cole an stiff, so I is have tuh kep
de blood circulatin. I am de last diabetic in dis place still able
tuh walk soul. Alla de rest a dese stupid ass people in here let
gan'green eat up dey foot. But I ain' like dese White people soul,
I can' afford tuh go an buy false foot, an I ain' want tuh be tie up
in nuh wheelchair. Beside who gine push me bout? You an you
big eyes? No tanks!
I barely convince de nurse tuh let me do exercise in my room.
She rader me walk wit she up an down dat blasted hallway. But I
am already on my way tuh deaf an ain' need tuh race de rest a de
dyin tuh be de first tuh my grave. Stupid ass nurses tryin tuh mek
it like a game sayin, de first tuh be done getting a prize. Fuget dat
boy, I have diabetus an de last t'ing I want is tuh fine out de prize
a bundle a tubes tie round my mout, shove up my ass an squeeze
out my nose. I ain' want tuh get catch like you muder suh I have
tuh kep fit, cause, DE RED WOMAN WILL CUT OFF YOU
PIG EARS ... AN RIP OUT YOU LOUD MOUT ... TEAR
OFF YOU BLACK FACE AN CUFF YUH IN YOU BIG TEEF!
*(LIBYA gets hit with a cutting pain in her belly that transforms
into two hard lashes from her father.)* AYE! AYE!

Khodi Dill
(1983–)

Born in Nassau, Bahamas, and raised in Saskatoon, Saskatchewan, Khodi Dill is a teacher, hip-hop artist, rapper, and spoken-word poet. His lyrics are marked by a concern for social justice and what he calls his "lit hop style," a hybridizing of traditional literature with hip-hop poetics. He was the 2010 Saskatoon Slam Champion, and, with his team, he placed second at the Canadian Festival of Spoken Word in 2012.

In 2005, Dill received his bachelor's degree in education from the University of Regina. Dill has also taught anti-oppressive education at the University of Saskatchewan, where he completed his master's degree. His thesis, "The Safest Place: Anti-Oppression in Spoken Word Poetry" (2013), focused on how spoken-word artists use the genre to promote social justice in Canada. What is "slammed" in his spoken-word performances are the systems of colonial and racial oppression that manifest in the present, and which are belied by Canada's official discourses of tolerance and multiculturalism.

Dill's poem "Grey," performed at the 2011 Vancouver Poetry Slam Festival, addresses and complicates the inherited meanings of his own mixed racial inheritance. As the feminist, anti-racist online resource *(web) site of praxis* notes, Dill identifies everyday issues that exist only for those who experience them through narrative sarcasm (*praxis*). Dill's use of "stereotyping could be named problematic," but his "'politically incorrect' words are drawn and borrowed from experiences of everyday or 'invisible' systems of racism to question them."

In an article titled "Khodi Dill Sums It Up Nicely," Métis writer, scholar, and public intellectual âpihtawikosisân (Chelsea Vowel) writes that Dill's poem "Holes," about the housing crisis on the isolated Attawapiskat First Nation in northern Ontario, performs important ally work, for it addresses the "basic lack of knowledge" that many Canadians have around "First Nations health-care, education, housing, taxation, self-government, settlement claims and so on." She suggests that such spoken-word performances can be useful pedagogical tools to help "untangle the web of

494

confusion" and "incorrect claims made about aboriginal people so that underlying prejudice can be addressed." Dill performed the poem at the 2010 Ottawa Festival; published here is his newly revised version of the poem.

Similarly, "Oil and Water," a poem Dill delivered at the Vancouver Poetry Slam on February 24, 2014, is a searing critique of the environmental devastation wreaked by the tar sands extraction in northeastern Alberta. Dill identifies in the extractive resource industry the conjoined forces of patriarchy, colonialism, and capitalism, and he condemns both the elected politicians and the public who, in their ongoing inaction, become complicit in the acceleration of the global environmental crisis.

"Grey," "Holes," and "Oil and Water" are previously unpublished, but Dill's spoken-word performances of them are available online on YouTube. Readers are encouraged to watch these video recordings; Dill's passionate delivery, combined with audience interaction, make for electrifying performances.

Khodi Dill's debut hip-hop mixtape, *New Technology*, was released on August 11, 2014, and is available on iTunes. His incisive lyrics, delivered over strong, driving beats, are compassionate and humble, again focusing on issues of social justice to challenge traditional ideas, promote social change, and entertain. As he raps on the track "Lay Low; Stay Workin'," "You can never go wrong when you've spoken the truth / My heart is so large that it's broken in two."

Grey

I am made from black and white
So my "essence" is grey—how flattering.
Though all things considered there is at least a smattering
Of blonde hair and blue eyes
Though by a look you'd never guess
Cause I am brown skinned and therefore my essence is less.
They call me "mulatto," from mule.
Well that's at least half-crass:
It makes one parent a thoroughbred and the other, an ass.
So I'm hoping these words become a thing of yesterday
But they mixed brown and white ice-cream and called it "MooLatte."[1]

---

1 Dairy Queen attracted controversy when it started marketing its light chocolate–coloured frozen desert as a "MooLatte" in 2004 because the name, deliberately or not, sounds like "mulatto."

When I was twelve I won a contest at a Christian Youth Centre.
Turns out the winner got a free CD. I was thrilled.
The pastor took me into the back room and he took one look at me and he
    said,
"You look like you like rap music."
I swallowed hard and thought to myself, "You're lucky you're right."

See, they try to pinhole my future. I'm tryin' to make plans
That don't involve b-ball, beat-box or break dance.
I'm tired of Sandra Bullock movies with clichés of white saviors,
Saving poor black kids from poor, black behaviors.
It reminds me of back when they used blackface
Thought the straight-haired blacks musta been a new race.
You'd think that new producers would be more creative
But the Twilight movies had a white play a Native.

When I was in Grade 4 the class bully called me and my best friend niggers.
It was sad but strange because my best friend was middle eastern.
But anyway we told the teacher and she made everything better, God bless
    her,
She slapped the bully on the wrist and said, "The word is *Negro*."
My middle eastern friend thought he was black for three years.

If we're building a nation then pain is in the mortar.
I'm watching grasses get greener even south of the border.
They got a black man in office. The paradox means we're equal
But my life hasn't changed so I'm waiting for the sequel.
I don't want to be the same, I'm just tryin' to be a peer
But whether black, brown, Muslim, disabled or queer
Although we are citizens we're still second class, still
Outside the circle, still others in the mass.

They say Jim Crow is dead, and that we're free from separation.
But if you come to Saskatoon and you want to find the First Nations
Just look on the West Side.
See, when they wrote segregation out of policy they left it in economy
And wrote it into geography.
It's whites to the east and browns to the west like a line in the sand,
Take your race to the left.

I never cease to be amazed how soon we forget
That racism's still alive; we haven't beat it yet.
I'm still watched at the store, still my freedom's rescinding
Still the police call me "bro," condescending.
I pray that this poem could have a good ending
But as it turns out we're broken, not blending and breaking not mending.
I'm still a little less than kin, although my heart is more than kind.
And now that I'm finally proud to be black the world is colourblind.

Holes

So Mike Holmes[2] is rebuilding First Nations housing.
He's making a pledge to make it right.
Ain't that your job, Mr. Harper?
Now, please excuse my spite, but do the rules not apply
To the "red-skinned" masses 'cause they tote eagle feathers
And smoke sweet grasses?
It took you two days to hit flooded white communities.
And been two years since Nicky lost his immunity
To the mould in the basement where it grows cause it's dim
'Cause each year in his basement you could go for a swim.
And his mama stopped trying; she just lets it in
And embraces her boy in the dry spot.

Mr. Harper, this is real.
This is real;
I didn't write it. I'm just telling the story
Of the very undelighted and the very blindsided
By this tragedy; it's tragic
But go unprovided for
It's the last thing they was hoping for
If it was you I wouldn't ask what you was dopin' for.
Maybe now you understand what I'm mopin' for.
And if you're not gonna help just say so

---

2   Mike Holmes, a celebrity Canadian contractor known for tackling substandard
housing construction on his television show *Holmes on Homes*, partnered with the
Assembly of First Nations in 2011.

Because right now they don't know what they're copin' for.
And why bother?
Your inaction speaks louder than your residential school apology.[3]
See Mama is weepy and the kids are sleepy, but awake
cause their house is so damn creaky that it's almost creepy.
You promised 'em a house but they'd rather a teepee
Maybe then they'd stay dry, and out of the cold—
At least then the roof would only have one hole.
Mr. Harper, when the holes in your promise become the holes in the dyke
It's *your* job to plug them, thanks anyways, Mike.

I mean, somebody tell me: how is it that our First Nations people
Live like second class citizens in Third World conditions
In the UN's fourth-best country in the world to live?
Somebody ask that question on W5
'Cause out in Treaty Number 6[4] they just trying to survive.
Hungry for seventh heaven but they already eight a belly full of lies
Little Nicky almost died many times.
Who said only a cat has nine lives?
So he breathes but he cries, no surprise, dry his eyes.
That's *ten* reasons why we should try.

You said that these rights would last just as long as the river.
If not, it turns out *you* are the "Indian giver."
But whatever you decide behind closed doors, just remember:
If you take their rights then they ought to have yours.
Oh, you forgot that your rights were Treaty rights too?

---

3   On June 11, 2008, Prime Minister Stephen Harper made a Statement of Apology to former students of Indian residential schools on behalf of the government of Canada. Standing in the House of Commons, the prime minister acknowledged that, "The treatment of children in Indian residential schools is a sad chapter in our history. Today, we recognize that this policy of assimilation was wrong, has caused great harm, and has no place in our country."

4   Treaty 6, signed between the Crown and Plain and Wood Cree Indians and other First Nations at Fort Carlton, Fort Pitt, and Battle River in 1876, is arguably the most controversial treaty. First, it allowed an Indian agent to keep a medicine chest in his home, a move some later interpreted as a promise by the government to provide free health care. It also passed the Indian Act, which effectively made all Indigenous people wards of the state.

You forgot that Native peoples weren't lesser than you?
Forgot that this land is still on loan and you default
But reserve the right to cast the first stone?
Excuse my tone.

Mr. Harper, you can take my house but not my home
And my pride is still alive.
We traded land for rights and if you want to trade it back
Start with Sussex Drive.

Oil and Water

Is there not only so much weight
That these flat prairie mountains can take?
Until the breakdown of fate
Until black waterfalls
Until that water falls to a depth that it can't be reached
Until it's all so dirty that it can't be cleaned
Until bitumen cocktails will get us all drunk
Until penguins and orcas must swim in the gunk.

This is nature's ghetto
It's only middle-aged waste land
This is what happens when you come and you take land
Because when you take enough
You become taken by it.

Have you heard?
The animals have all taken quiet—
Muzzled by money and a future so near
That it's already bursting with economic fears.
If these numbers are not imaginary, then I don't know what is.
Is it the world that we dream and that we picture for our kids?

Is that less real than this infinite growth in this finite atmosphere with infi-
    nite smoke?
Do we wait until choking?
Do we wait until asthma?

Do we wait until cancer's transfusions of plasma?
Do we wait until mortality? Do we wait until lupus?
Do we wait for empty MPs to constantly dupe us?

The writing's on the wall, in street journals and art
The only thing left pumping on this earth is her heart.
We need a revival, we need defibrillation
We need atheists and believers—this is the tribulation.
The great furnace is burning;
The sky is going black
And the pit of the abyss—well it's a fort called Mac.

We must kneel to our young and away from forefathers;
We must look up to our children and learn our own smallness
This is lawless, not flawless and our timing is crucial
Drills spin faster than clocks while we wait for a future
That's already here. All from keepin' quiet and covering our ears.

That's our signal for the machines to charge on
And ought to be our signal that the world is far gone.
I mean, if the planet goes dry, where will we live?
If life is give and take
Then when do we give?

Ahmed Ali (Knowmadic)
(1984–)

The seventh Poet Laureate of Edmonton (2017–2019), Ahmed Ali is a spoken-word poet, writer, actor, comedian, speaker, and youth worker who was born in Mogadishu, Somalia, to pastoral nomad parents. In 1989, with help from their local community, Ali, his three older brothers, and his mother emigrated to Italy to escape the civil war. After several years and many attempts at seeking sponsorship, Ahmed's father secured a sponsorship from an organization in Canada. His family arrived in Edmonton in the winter of 1992.

When he was sixteen, his parents decided to go back to Somalia, but they went without Ali, leaving him to attend school and to work at Tim Horton's to cover rent. While his parents were away he became involved in crime. He was arrested and expelled from school for fighting a student who was racist. Ahmed's older brothers gathered enough money to fly him to Somalia and visit their parents. Seeing the difficult conditions of life, he awakened to the opportunities that he had in Canada. He returned to Canada a changed person, focusing on drama classes and theatre lessons.

In 2009 he co-founded Edmonton's only spoken-word collective, Breath In Poetry, which teaches poetry classes and performs outreach in the community. In 2011, Ali became the first Somali spoken-word champion at the Canadian Festival of Spoken Word. In 2012, he was given the RISE award for community involvement in the arts and culture, and, a year later, was appointed artist-in-residence at the Langston Hughes Performing Arts Institute in Seattle, Washington.

Ali was named a "Difference Maker" by the *Edmonton Journal* in 2013 for his contribution to poetry in Edmonton. In 2014, the Alberta Council for Global Cooperation recognized the young poet as Alberta's Top 30 under 30 for his work with Islamic Families and Social Services Association, Big Brothers Big Sisters, Mennonite Center for New Comers, and Ghandi Peace Conference and Edmonton Public Schools. Becoming Poet Laureate of Edmonton, Ali says "is a testament that art is boundless and that it does not recognize borders. It also affirms my belief that our experiences are a collection of poems that are written into history" (Griwkowski). In 2017 Ali also ran for school board trustee in Edmonton's Ward A; while he was the top fundraising public candidate, he came second in the race. Ali is currently working on a collection of poetry.

"Child Soldier" is a strong example of the genre of slam poetry written to be performed on stage; the poem is meant to be heard and seen, and uses repetition, rhyme, alliteration, wordplay, and slang to amplify the impact of the performance. This poem is a narrative account of a single dramatic moment in the poet's life. The poem was originally published in the anthology *The Great Black North* (2013).

Child Soldier

Before I could reach to pick up the soccer ball that had rolled under
the pick-up, I found myself peering
into the darkness of an AK barrel of a Somali kid I didn't know.
Forget what I was looking for. Last thing I wish
to see is my soulless bloody body from a spirit's perspective that is
no more. Little could I think, but I
must admit that I never thought that I would be belittled by a little
kid who knows little of what I did … to
him. I began to shiver as my sweat gathered mass like an avalanche,
time stood still, my body began to
chill and then began to tremble. My mind wandered searching for
and chasing dreams I let go years
before while it tries hard to assemble what values that I currently
resemble. Death excuses life and
welcomes regret and remorse as darkness begins to take its course.
But of course, like everyone about
to die I never loved long enough, deep enough, appreciated what I
had and stuff. But the African in me is
saying life is hard why complain be tough. So I gather my
composure and get a little closer. He might be
a kid but its for sure he's not a poser. My mouth gathers spit my
throat can't swallow, while I stare at
his eyes that are deep and hollow that made their home a mind that
is weak and shallow, with a record
of lives taken so I know I'm not mistaken to assume that if he kills
me, he will feel no sorrow. The tip of

the AK rests on my forehead, as he screams you're dead. I used logic but he wasn't buying it because his
mind was too poor to afford it. Being it the reason why he had a gun to make history and not a pen
to record it. Minutes have passed but I haven't passed I'm always first for everything so I know I won't last.

Now I'm thinking, because it's all starting to sink in. You're already dead Ahmed, hit him with your right on
his chin and then follow through with its twin. Why today, why a kid of 14, why the first time back in
Somalia when I'm only 18. So many thoughts that they eventually become gridlock bumper to bumper in
my head like an American highway. Got me to thinking that if I had it my way, he would be pointing a
microphone in my face asking me what I thought about current issues in Somalia that day. Just a poor
skinny little kid with rags staring at me with bags under his eyes that sag, meanwhile unlike his
personality his brand new polished AK shines. I never thought light would hit me from the reflection of a
gun pointed by a kid who could have been my relatives' son. When I had given up and fear became
anger and frustration and I no longer had the patience I heard a voice say ... "give him his ball we are
moving to the next location." He replied, "I was just playing around with him I never had the temptation."
I got the ball back but I'm still searching for an explanation.

Tchitala Nyota Kamba
(ca. 1984)

In his evocative postface to Tchitala Kamba's debut collection of poetry, Pierre-Yves Mocquais,[1] writes, "Here is the emigrant self far from self and yet so close, and the other distant and yet present, known. Here, too, our own self that departs, that stays behind but is no longer there, and the other who departs so as to better remain. Self and other return, meet again, recognize each other along the migratory paths of the planet. Infinite quest for self! Her poetry is an eternal quest for meaning, for words, for life itself, for our own life."

Tchitala Nyota Kamba[2] was born and raised in the Congo. She graduated from the Royal Conservatory of Music of Brussels, Belgium, the first African woman to do so, and holds a PhD in French literature from the Université de Montréal. In 1983 she began her theatrical career as a spokesperson for the culture of Africa, and in Calgary she continues this work under the umbrella of Apapi Film & Theatre, an association for the promotion of Afro-Caribbean arts. She taught French at the University of Calgary and the Alliance Française. Her first collection of poems, *L'exilée de Makelele*, appeared in 2007 from Éditions de Plaines (Winnipeg), and she also has work in *Coming Here, Being Here: A Canadian Migration Anthology*, edited by Donald F. Mulcahy (Guernica, 2016).

Kamba dedicates her first volume of poems "to all immigrants and refugees, to political officials, researchers and NGOs that plan services to care for the mental health of immigrants and refugees." Her poems elaborating the dreams that beckon Congolese into becoming undocumented migrants have a powerful immediacy that arises from her use of narrative poetic forms, a striking use of repetition and rhetorical questions, and the inclusion of untranslated Swahili that registers difference on the page. The author explains her focus on the undocumented this way: "Migrations

---

1 Pierre-Yves Mocquais is professor emeritus of French literature at the University of Calgary, and dean, Campus Saint-Jean, University of Alberta.
2 Date of birth unknown.

exist since men first appeared on the planet. For all sorts of reasons, human beings have always sought 'happiness,' even very far from their first homes." Yet the loss of social reference points often takes a large psychosocial toll on migrants and refugees. "Having realized this," Kamba writes, "I felt the need to render homage to immigrants and refugees in my first collection of poems, 'The Exile from Make-lele.' I'm preparing further reflections for my next publication. Its title already speaks loudly: 'Exile and the Mental Health of Those Who Come from Elsewhere.'"

Récit d'un voyageur: Rêve ou utopie

Je ne savais pas qu'en lui brûlait l'envie de partir.
Voilà qu'un matin de bonne heure,
il liquide son stock de chikwangue et de makanzenza,
afin de pouvoir réaliser son rêve le plus cher,
partir, partir clandestinement vers d'autres cieux.
Oui, plein d'enthousiasme, il ne rêvait que de ça,
partir, partir au loin pour s'instruire
et revenir la tête pleine de savoir
et les poches remplies de devises étrangères.

Nakozonga éééé.
Nakozonga éééé.
Naza na nga nalikambo na moto téééé.
Nakozonga mboka, nakozonga mboka aaaa!
Nakeyi ééé, nakeyi; mobembo ézali liwa téééééa.

Je ne savais pas qu'en lui brûlait l'envie de partir.
Voilà que, l'argent récolté dans la poche,
il prend sa valise, son passeport périmé
et se dirige vers le port de Moanda
où il paye le passeur
pour un long voyage: rêve ou utopie?
Le passeur le cache au fond de la soute à marchandise
d'un vieux bateau rouillé sans souffle qui méritait
depuis fort longtemps d'être relégué à la ferraille.
Mais notre rêveur avait-il vraiment le choix?

Nakozonga éééé.
Nakozonga éééé.
Naza na nga nalikambo na moto téééé.
Nakozonga mboka, nakozonga mboka aaaa!
Nakeyi ééé, nakeyi; mobembo ézali liwa téééééa.

Je ne savais pas qu'en lui brûlait l'envie de partir.
Voilà que, le passeur lâche les amarres,
ayant à bord notre passager clandestin
qui a pour seuls compagnons des souris et des cancrelats.
La vieille ferraille se traîne vers le large du fleuve Congo,
bravant crocodiles et hippopotames pour un long voyage périlleux.
De Moanda à Poto-Poto, puis toute la côte ouest de l'Afrique,
luttant contre vents et marrée,
son hôte, confiant, invoque ses dieux à longueur de journée.
Il égrène son chapelet et récite toutes les prières
que l'on dit dans ce genre d'aventure.

Nakozonga éééé.
Nakozonga éééé.
Naza na nga nalikambo na moto téééé.
Nakozonga mboka, nakozonga mboka aaaa!
Nakeyi ééé, nakeyi; mobembo ézali liwa téééééa.

Je ne savais pas qu'en lui brûlait l'envie de partir.
Voilà que, la vieille épave allant clandestinement
de port en port, traîne toujours à son bord son hôte secret.
Au fil du temps, sa santé accablée
par la malaria et la faim persistante.
Il était devenu méconnaissable avec une peau pâle,
gercée par les intempéries des océans.

Nakozonga éééé.
Nakozonga éééé.
Naza na nga nalikambo na moto téééé.
Nakozonga mboka, nakozonga mboka aaaa!
Nakeyi ééé, nakeyi; mobembo ézali liwa téééééa.

Je ne savais pas qu'en lui brûlait l'envie de partir.
Voilà que, après trois semaines
à bord de ce bateau improvisé,
le passeur le fait monter
dans une pirogue de fortune
en compagnie d'autres clandestins,
embarqués de port en port.
Tous se nourrissaient du même espoir:
partir, partir vers les horizons lointains,
pour une vie meilleure.

Nakozonga éééé.
Nakozonga éééé.
Naza na nga nalikambo na moto téééé.
Nakozonga mboka, nakozonga mboka aaaa!
Nakeyi ééé, nakeyi; mobembo ézali liwa téééééa.

Je ne savais pas qu'en lui brûlait l'envie de partir.
Voilà que les voici enfin,
à quelques kilomètres de leur destination.
Une lueur d'espoir éclate
dans leurs yeux hagards.
Un sourire se dessine
sur leurs lèvres fendillées et sanguinolentes.
Soudain, surpris par une grosse vague,
ils sont projetés dans la mer
et entrainés au large sans réaction.
Et pourtant, c'était à quelques kilomètres
du grand port tant rêvé.
Efforts vains, malédiction ou cauchemar?

Nakozonga éééé.
Nakozonga éééé.
Naza na nga nalikambo na moto téééé.
Nakozonga mboka, nakozonga mboka aaaa!
Nakeyi ééé, nakeyi; mobembo ézali liwa téééééa.

Je ne savais pas qu'en lui brûlait l'envie de partir.
Voilà que les espoirs s'effondrent.

Tous les corps vont à jamais disparaître
dans les abysses de la mer de Gibraltar.
Mais moi, je ne savais pas qu'en lui brûlait l'envie de partir.
Je ne savais pas, je ne savais pas
qu'en lui et en eux tous brûlaient l'envie de partir.

Nakozonga éééé.
Nakozonga éééé.
Naza na nga nalikambo na moto téééé.
Nakozonga mboka, nakozonga mboka aaaa!
Nakeyi ééé, nakeyi; mobembo ézali liwa tééééa.

Tale of a Traveller: Dream or Utopia
(translated by Erin Mouré)

I never knew he burned with the desire to leave.
So that one morning early,
he sold off his stocks of chikwangue[3] and makanzenza,[4]
in search of his cherished dream,
to go, to go in secret toward other skies.
Yes, so enthused he was, he dreamed no dream but this,
to go, to go off yonder, to learn
and return with a head full of wisdom
and pocketfuls of foreign cash.

Nakozonga éééé.
Nakozonga éééé.
Naza na nga nalikambo na moto téééé.
Nakozonga mboka, nakozonga mboka aaaa!
Nakeyi ééé, nakeyi; mobembo ézali liwa tééééa.

I never knew he burned with the desire to leave.
So that, his savings clutched in his pocket,
he takes his bag and expired passport
and heads to the port in Moanda

---

3   Manioc cake.
4   Salt fish.

where he pays off the smuggler
for the trek ahead: dream or utopia?
The smuggler packs him low into the hold
of an old and rusted wheezing boat that should
have hit the scrap-heap long ago.
But did our dreamer really have a choice?

Nakozonga éééé.
Nakozonga éééé.
Naza na nga nalikambo na moto téééé.
Nakozonga mboka, nakozonga mboka aaaa!
Nakeyi ééé, nakeyi; mobembo ézali liwa tééééa.

I never knew he burned with the desire to leave.
So that the unflagged ship weighs anchor
with our stowaway aboard
sharing space with mice and cockroaches.
The rust-bucket lists in the deep Congo River,
braving crocs and hippos in its perilous long journey.
From Moanda to Poto-Poto, then all up the west coast of Africa,
battling winds and tides,
our stowaway, trusting, invokes his gods all day.
He rubs his rosary beads and recites every prayer
on which this kind of adventure depends.

Nakozonga éééé.
Nakozonga éééé.
Naza na nga nalikambo na moto téééé.
Nakozonga mboka, nakozonga mboka aaaa!
Nakeyi ééé, nakeyi; mobembo ézali liwa tééééa.

I never knew he burned with the desire to leave.
So that the old wreck in stealth
bobbed from port to port, still with its secret guest.
Over weeks, his health is crushed
by malaria and gnawing hunger.
Unrecognizable now, his skin so pallid,
pitted by ocean storms.

Nakozonga éééé.
Nakozonga éééé.
Naza na nga nalikambo na moto téééé.
Nakozonga mboka, nakozonga mboka aaaa!
Nakeyi ééé, nakeyi; mobembo ézali liwa téééééa.

I never knew he burned with the desire to leave.
So that after three weeks
aboard this rusty hulk
the smuggler urged him out
and into a makeshift skiff
crowded with other undocumented folk
taken on in every port.
All were fed by the same hope:
to go, to go off yonder
seeking a better life.

Nakozonga éééé.
Nakozonga éééé.
Naza na nga nalikambo na moto téééé.
Nakozonga mboka, nakozonga mboka aaaa!
Nakeyi ééé, nakeyi; mobembo ézali liwa téééééa.

I never knew he burned with the desire to leave.
So that finally fate finds them
a few kilometres from their goal.
A shard of hope glints in
their haggard eyes.
Smiles begin to widen
across split and blood-crusted lips.
Suddenly a huge breaker hits.
They're flung from skiff to sea
and dragged into the deeps with no time to react.
Scant kilometres
from the great port they'd dreamed of.
Efforts in vain, curse or nightmare?

Nakozonga éééé.
Nakozonga éééé.

Naza na nga nalikambo na moto téééé.
Nakozonga mboka, nakozonga mboka aaaa!
Nakeyi ééé, nakeyi; mobembo ézali liwa tééééa.

I never knew he burned with the desire to leave.
So that is how all hopes crumble.
All their bodies, gone forever
in the abyss of the Strait of Gibraltar.
Yet I never knew he burned with the desire to leave.
I never knew, I never knew
that he and so many burned with the desire to leave.

Nakozonga éééé.
Nakozonga éééé.
Naza na nga nalikambo na moto téééé.
Nakozonga mboka, nakozonga mboka aaaa!
Nakeyi ééé, nakeyi; mobembo ézali liwa tééééa.

Makala!

Célèbre prison de Kinshasa,
au parfum nauséabond.
Prison semblable à celles d'Alcatraz,
du Goulag et de Guantanamo.
L'ONU est enfin là,
avec son arsenal pour de juger.

Ta célébrité légendaire et ta petitesse d'esprit
ont conduit les fils du Congo au désastre.
Visionnaires congolais,
innocentes victimes de la dictature,
pour avoir dit non au monstre hideux sur le trône,
et crier justice à la face du monde.

Peuple meurtri et enchaîné depuis de décennies,
tes moeurs bafouées,
tes femmes et enfants violés,
mutilés à la vue de tous.

Pères et époux cloitrés à Makala
pour avoir dit non à l'oppresseur,
comment vous oublier en ce jour du 30 juin?
Brisez ces murs de Makala
volez aux quatre horizons
et respirez le vent de liberté.

Le peuple congolais saigne et s'interroge,
les pommettes crevassées
par des vallées de larmes.
Ventre creux sous l'oeil impuissant
de l'Internet et des humanistes
des quatre coins du monde!
Les minerais indescriptibles de tes ancêtres
font de tes enfants des esclaves éternels.

Innocentes victimes torturées et noyées
au beau milieu de la nuit dans la fleuve Congo,
sous l'oeil de géants caïmans,
votre précieux sang, répandu à travers le fleuve,
les monts et les forêts vous vengeront.
Votre précieux sang peint les corridors de Makala.
Vos cris ont transpercé les entrailles du monde.
Vos cris ont atteint le sommet du mont Kilimandjaro.
Vous êtes des martyres inconnus
aux noms indescriptibles qu'on ne peut compter.
Votre disparition ne restera pas impunie
car vous êtes morts pour la délivrance du Congo,
du grand Congo de nos aïeux,
notre Congo, mon Congo!

Les oubliés et les survivants de Makala
brisez ces murs et clamez votre innocence
car l'ONU est enfin là,
avec son tribunal pour vous rendre justice,
en ce jour du 30 juin.
Dites-moi, comment vous oublierai-je?

✤

Makala![5] (translated by Erin Mouré)

Famed prison of Kinshasa,
nauseating stench.
Prison infamous as Alcatraz,
the Gulags and Guantanamo.
The UN is finally here
with its arsenal to pass judgement.

Your notoriety and pettiness of spirit
have led Congo's children to disaster.
Congolese visionaries,
innocent victims of the dictatorship
for saying *No* to the hideous enthroned monster,
for demanding justice to the world's face.

A people murdered and enchained for decades,
their traditions flouted,
their women and children violated,
mutilated before the eyes of all.
Fathers and husbands shut up in Makala prison
for saying *No* to the oppressor,
how can we forget you on this day of 30th June?
Break through the walls of Makala,
fly to the four horizons
and breathe the wind of liberty.

The Congolese people bleed and question,
cheeks crevassed
by valleys of tears.
Sunken belly under the powerless gaze
of the Internet and of humanists
all over the world!
The ineffable ores of your ancestors
make eternal slaves of your children.

---

5   Makala means "noise" in Swahili.

Innocent victims tortured and drowned
at night in the Congo River,
as giant caymans look on.
Your precious blood, smeared in rivers,
on mountains and in forests will avenge you.
Your precious blood paints the hallways of Makala.
Your cries have pierced the viscera of the world.
Your cries have reached the summit of Kilimanjaro.
You martyrs with names beyond description,
whose number can't be counted.
Your vanishing will not go unpunished
for you died for the deliverance of the Congo,
the great Congo of our ancestors,
our Congo, my Congo!

Oh you forgotten ones, oh you survivors of Makala Prison
break down its walls and proclaim your innocence
for the UN is finally here
with its courts to bring you justice,
on this day, the 30th of June.
Tell me, how could I ever forget you?

Je suis d'ici, je suis d'ailleurs

Clandestin sans papiers ainsi me surnomme
ma nouvelle terre d'accueil.
Emprisonné sans raison dans mon pays natal,
torturé parce que ma peau n'est pas comme la leur.
Partir ou rester, tel fut mon dilemme.
Mais partir où et pourquoi?
Je suis d'ici, je suis d'ailleurs.
Ma culture est d'ici et d'ailleurs.
Elle est ma source d'inspiration et ma force.

Être sans papiers, c'est être un sous homme.
C'est recommencer à zéro dans la clandestinité,
être cloîtré dans un appartement insalubre
où les gens passent sans y jeter un regard,

tellement l'insalubrité et l'odeur nauséabonde laissent
à désirer, ne convenant qu'aux sans-papiers.
Mes nouveaux amis: les maringouins, les cancrelats
et les bibittes m'adoptent sans me poser
les questions sur mes origines.

Être sans papiers, c'est vivre au jour le jour
sans être sûr du lendemain.
C'est être au bas de l'échelle.
Aucun droit aux soins médicaux,
aucun droit à l'instruction,
aucun droit à la promenade publique,
aucune adresse permanente,
aucun droit à travailler légalement
sauf au noir, en se faisant exploiter par le boss.

Être sans papiers, c'est vivre dans l'indifférence absolue,
même brûlant de fièvre … Chut! Silence!
Aucune responsabilité véritable,
hypocrisie extrême, vie précaire,
Esclavage moderne bien entretenu dans les manufacturiers
en remplacement de champs de cotons d'autrefois!
Cela se passe encore de nos jours
dans un pays soi-disant civilisé.

Être sans papiers, c'est vivre dans la clandestinité,
dans la peur d'être dénoncé à l'immigration,
dans la peur d'être déporté,
dans la crainte de mourir en sol étranger sans identité véritable,
dans la crainte de voir sa dépouille rapatriée,
un jour, vers une terre inconnue,
dans la peur de se retrouver clandestin,
de nouveau, même dans la mort.
Le problème est réel.

Être sans papiers. Quelle affaire!
Que dire à mes enfants natifs d'ici
mais qui ne sont pas d'ici, ils sont d'ailleurs.
Que faire de ces grands diplômes non reconnus

parce qu'ils sont d'ailleurs.
Être accepté dans sa nouvelle terre d'asile
avec ses droits et ses devoirs, c'est le plus grand bonheur
auquel toute personne aspire,
même venant d'ailleurs.

Clandestin sans papiers ainsi me surnomme
ma nouvelle terre d'accueil.
Emprisonné sans raison dans mon pays natal,
torturé parce que ma peau n'est pas comme la leur.
Partir ou rester, tel fut mon dilemme.
Mais partir où et pourquoi?
Je suis d'ici, je suis d'ailleurs.
Ma culture est d'ici et d'ailleurs.
Elle est ma source d'inspiration et ma force.

✿

I'm from Here; I'm from Over There
(translated by Erin Mouré)

Undocumented illegal immigrant is my name
in my new homeland.
Imprisoned for no reason in the country of my birth,
tortured because my skin's unlike theirs.
Go or stay, that was my dilemma.
But go where and why?
I'm from here; I'm from over there.
My culture is from here and from over there.
It is my source of inspiration and my strength.

To be without papers is to be sub-human.
It's to start all over crouched in hiding,
cloistered in a filthy apartment
past which people walk without even looking up,
revolted by the grime and stench
that's good only for those without papers.
My new friends: the mosquitoes, cockroaches,
and bugs adopt me without interrogating me
on my origins.

To be without papers means living day to day
with tomorrow always uncertain.
It's clinging to the bottom rung.
No right to see the doctor,
no right to schooling,
no right to stroll outside in public,
no fixed address,
no right to work legally,
just under the table, exploited by the boss.

To be without papers means facing blank indifference,
even if wracked with fever ... Shhhh! Quiet there!
No one admits responsibility,
hypocrisy in the extreme, life of precarity:
modern slavery still goes on in factories
that replace yesterday's fields of cotton!
It's happening even today
in a country that calls itself civilized.

To be without papers is to live in the shadows,
in fear of being denounced to Immigration,
in fear of being deported,
of dying on foreign soil with no real identity,
scared that even your corpse will be repatriated
when the day comes, to who knows what land,
scared of being treated as illegal all over
again, even in death.
The problem is real.

To be without papers. It's sheer torment!
What to tell my children born here
who are not from here; they're from over there.
What to do with these grand diplomas, dismissed
because they're from over there.
Acceptance here in the land of asylum,
with its rights and responsibilities, is the greatest happiness
any human can aspire to,
even if they're from over there.

Undocumented illegal immigrant is my name
in my new homeland.
Imprisoned for no reason in the country of my birth,
tortured because my skin's unlike theirs.
Go or stay, that was my dilemma.
But go where and why?
I'm from here; I'm from over there.
My culture is from here and from over there.
It is my source of inspiration and my strength.

Títílopé Sónúgà
(1985–)

A prominent poet and spoken-word artist, as well a civil engineer, Títílopé Sónúgà was born and raised in Lagos, Nigeria, and immigrated to Edmonton at the age of thirteen. She came to prominence in Nigeria in 2015 when she became the first poet to perform at a presidential inauguration (that of Muhammadu Buhari). Her performance of her poem "We Are Ready" grabbed headlines ("The Inauguration Poem That Blew Us All Away," Fuad Iawal). As she explains, "spoken word poetry is a fairly new artform in Nigeria. While there exists a rich oral tradition, the spoken word style is growing" (Wordup 411). Before this performance, Sónúgà had been performing in spoken-word circuits in Edmonton and had founded a poetry slam series called Rouge Poetry.

In 2011 Sónúgà won the 2011 Canadian Authors Association Emerging Writer Award for her collection of poems *Down to Earth* (Okada Books, 2011). Sónúgà's spoken-word album, *Mother Tongue* (CD Baby) was released in 2013 followed by a second collection of poetry, *Abscess*, in 2014. She was a speaker at Tedx Edmonton ("Speaking into the Void") in 2014. In 2012 she won the *Edmonton Journal*'s 2012 Maya Angelou Poetry Contest. Her latest collection of poetry, *This Is How We Disappear*, was published by the Canadian press Write Bloody North in 2019.

In 2015 Sónúgà completed a large-scale stage production of her poems at the Agip Recital Hall in Lagos called *Becoming*. She describes it as "a series of poems I had been writing about the journey into womanhood." Her follow-up show, *Open*, ran in June and July of 2017, and she is currently taking it on tour. Sónúgà also continues to work as an actor on the Nigerian television series *Gidi Up*, which airs across Africa.

Sónúgà is active in the cultural scenes of both Edmonton and Lagos. She is the founder of both Breath In Poetry Collective and Rouge Poetry, and she worked, until 2016, as an ambassador for Intel's She Will Connect Program in Nigeria. The program is dedicated to empowering women and girls toward greater opportunity, technological literacy, and knowledge of commerce.

In the following poem, "Grandpa Igobi," which originally appeared in her self-published collection *Down to Earth* in 2011, Títílopé Sónúgà sings a song of praise to her ancestor, and in so doing, she claims the role of *griot*, since all of her grandfather's poetic traditions live in her. In the tender poem "Sacrifice," a poem in the same collection, the poet-speaker recalls watching her mother become racialized ("just another black face") in encounters with speakers with "lazy ears." Sónúgà first performed this poem at the Edmonton Poetry Festival in front of an audience that included her parents. She reveals, "my dad is a very strict and stoic guy, but as soon as I started doing this poem, he started to cry in front of a room full of people, which he would never usually do. I think at that moment I knew this spoken word thing has the power to do something to you" (I. Thompson).

Grandpa Igbobi

I wanted to write you a poem
Etch you bold and timeless
Wanted to sing your praise
Find words to describe you flawless
Dug deep in the recess of memory
To piece together
Smell, touch, sound

I wanted to write you a poem
Something to look back on
In remembrance
Speak of your success
Give you one last dance
Show your legacy in your
Children, grandchildren,
Great grandchildren

I wanted to write you a poem
Fluid and beautiful
Tell of your kindness
Show your strength
Explain your quiet nature
Describe you
Smile, suit, mahogany cane

I just couldn't find the words
Didn't know the things to say
To describe you
Truly and completely
I just couldn't find the words
To paint you vibrant and wonderful

But your poetry
Is in
Yewande, Eniola, Funke,
Adeola, Abiola, Abimola,
Funlola, Adebiyi, Somide,
Morenike, Ibilola, Afolake,
Ayodele, Olukemi, Ibilola Coker
Taiwo, Kehinde, Dupe,
Tunde, Oluwaseun, Ayoola,
Morgan, Korede, Blake.

In me

Sacrifice

You were the artists of our lives
Began to mold us
From the moment
our eyes felt first light
You
Would model
the men
that we would chose
The women
that we would grow up to be
Yours
Was no easy task

You wanted us to learn
That for every action
A re-action

Replaced "I love you's"
With something more valuable
Than four letters
could possibly contain
We felt your love in
Sacrifice

In turn
you demanded of us
more than we felt capable of
Taught us life
in mathematics
How to add up
our blessings
that even though
as four
we were even
we were still
indivisible
that when
you subtract
money and status
all you'll find
is character

And
When the time came
to choose between
The life you had
dreamt for yourselves
And the one
you wanted us to have

You
Packed up 11 suitcases
full of hope
Towards the life
you knew was necessary

It wasn't until the true tests came
That we realized the strength
you had given us
From the years
when you told us that
Tears
Don't provide answers
And all problems have solutions

So
it angered me
To see them
Frown slightly when
You
In an attempt to be fully understood
Pursed lips to speak words
That hung in the air
A little too long
Fluttered and fell before lazy ears
Already turned away

you became
just another
black face
with a name too
complicated to say
Ademolu
Temilolu
Morenike
Ibilola
Olukemi
Titilope

I will sing your story now
voices will hush
to hear how you
saw us
beautiful before we
recognized
ourselves

I will hold on
tightly to the memory
us before
we began to
navigating the space
between our traditions
and this new
existence

You
Leaders amongst
your peers
respected by many
deserve better
than to have
children
half the age of
your children
calling you by
first name

You
deserve better
than to
start from scratch
10 steps behind
to provide for
a family of 6
in a system
that had already
counted you out

But you
recognized the
future in our eyes
Fought
hard to keep us
whole in tradition
reclaimed our tongues

to speak the language
of our mothers
etched the stories
of our fathers
on our hearts
so we could
hold a piece of
home there
So
I will
tell them now
how four little girls
would've never
had this chance
without you
and
to make you proud
was our only choice
and we do it
because we could
never let your sacrifice
go unacknowledged

Roland (Rollie) Pemberton
(Cadence Weapon)
(1986–)

"I feel that regions are very important in music," says Roland Pemberton, who served as Edmonton's Poet Laureate from 2009 to 2011. "It interests me when I hear landmarks in a song. Like in New York you'll get a rapper who'll be like 'Brooklyn in The House!' But I want to know more!"

Pemberton, who is also known publicly by his stage name Cadence Weapon, was born and raised in Edmonton. His father was Brooklyn-born Teddy Pemberton (the late, great hip-hop DJ on CJSR-FM), and his grandfather was Rollie Miles, a football player for the Edmonton Eskimos. He began rapping at thirteen. "It was around me all the time when I was growing up, my dad was a DJ and he would play all sorts of stuff around the house, hip hop, electro, funk and my mum would play piano. And I suppose I just randomly got into rapping. I remember rapping in math class, I failed maths, but I suppose I did OK in other things" ("Cadence Weapon Interview").

"Musically there were a lot of hardcore, straight edge bands (in Edmonton), and a tiny rap scene that no one really shone out of or got any exposure from. But the music scene that I really associated with were the electro-rock bands, groups like Shout Out Out Out and The Abominable Snowman. They were bands that I really got on with and Nik Kozub, who's in Shout Out Out Out, mixed my album."

Before he had released his first album Pemberton became famous as a hip-hop reviewer at the online venue *Pitchfork*, as well as for *Stylus* and *Wired*. He launched his own mp3 blog, RazorBladeRunner, and began remixing artists as a producer. In 2005 Pemberton compiled his remixes and released his "Cadence Weapon is the Black Hand" mixtape. Canadian label Upper Class Recordings signed him on the spot. His first album, *Breaking Kayfabe* was released in 2005 to great critical acclaim, including a Polaris Prize nomination. The following lyrics from "Oliver Square" and "30 Seconds" are taken from this first album.

Pemberton subsequently signed with the American record label ANTI-, releasing the albums *Afterparty Babies* in 2008 and *Hope in Dirt City* in 2012. All three albums have been nominated for a Polaris Prize, which awards $30,000 to the winning artist. His first book of poetry, *Magnetic Days*, was published by Metatron in 2014. His poem "How Black" from this collection is reprinted below.

The following rap lyrics from "Oliver Square," full of 2004-era references to the people and places of Edmonton, is the rapper's ode to his city (Blinov). It chronicles the Edmonton neighbourhood named after Frank Oliver, federal minister of the interior in the early twentieth century. Oliver was known for his anti-black and anti-Indigenous sentiments. In 2017 Pemberton reflected, "I'm still trying to figure out how to do the song without hyping the guy [...] At the time I wrote it, I had no idea, of course, but now I need to address this. I'm currently thinking of a new way to do it without actually mentioning his name" (*Edmonton Journal* August 30, 2017).

Oliver Square

Yo, it's corrupt where I'm from,[1] Edmonton, tough
The streets could speak about the heads with drugs, rough
City life will leave you red with blood
Punched holes in the wall, and they fed the thugs lunch
After they rocked the party in the literal sense
Sedimentary propensity, they hit the kid in the lips
Shit, you could be on Whyte Ave having the time of your life
Then you get your arm broken by a random cab driver
Ask Katie, the nightlife is mad crazy
When a drunk tries to steal your car, he was tryna play me
But I didn't let him, we peeled off quick
then we parked at IGA to break the seals of the lid
Don't generalize, you must think and wonder
Why I drink 40s and memorize BusLink numbers
Well, I don't have a license, but I'm tryna to gain prominence
'Cause I'm living in a house with a fridge full of condiments

[Chorus] × 4
See me on the bill, better follow me there
I solemnly swear, I'll make it back to Oliver Square[2]

---

1   A reference to Jay Z's "Where I'm From."
2   One of the ubiquitous strip malls in Edmonton. Oliver Square is on 104 Ave, in northwest Edmonton.

So I'm drunk at the Funky Pickle,[3] nothing difficult
Came out with just napkins, it was something pitiful
Currently unemployed but I depend on my friends
To contend with my impending impulse to spend
So I let Jan cover my pitchers at the Strat[4]
Until I get a little bit of richer from this rap
But I digress to these cherries in the rearview
RCMP, check for drunks on a steer through
I take the 7 off 82nd to get to Jasper
So I can hit New City[5] with the electro clashers
And Dub Thursdays, at Savoy, I spit wordplay
To chicks I want suited like their birthday in the worst way
See me at Victory,[6] don't ask to see the skill
Sick of fanboys, more obnoxious than Peter Hill[7]
More robotic than Bill Smith, I come with the ill shit
Still good, more dangerous than Millwoods.[8]

[Chorus] × 4
See me on the bill, better follow me there
I solemnly swear, I'll make it back to Oliver Square

You need to listen like records, y'all oughta get dismissed,
On the wake up, I tend to politic with Kris[9]
Don't stick your nose up just cause the sick flow's up
Like if you go to a show, to might see Nik Kosub[10]
Like if I'm on the mic, you better get froze up
Cause I cut aluminium like a bus station smoker

---

3   A gourmet single-slice pizza restaurant.
4   Old Strathcona Hotel and Bar on 82nd Avenue remains a steadfast anchor against
gentrification on Whyte Avenue; it has a reputation as a dive bar.
5   New City Likwid Lounge at 10081 Jasper Avenue.
6   The Victory Lounge still exits, but it is now called Brixx Bar and Grill.
7   An enduring public-access television figure.
8   A racially diverse area of Edmonton, often stigmatized.
9   An inside reference to the Edmonton music industry. Kris Burwash from Listen
Records.
10 Nik Kozub recorded and mixed *Breaking Kayfabe*, and was a mentor to Pemberton as an artist.

Anyway, we tend to Black Dog it[11] on Tuesdays
Any crew with useless talk, don't give a fuck what you say
Better lay low if connected to lame prose
I might hit you with a Stella bottle at Halo[12]
Ugly chicks at the Armory,[13] talk sweet, how coy
Girl, I don't wanna be seen in you like Cowboys[14]
And I don't rap for free, not one dirty line
Even if she'll go downtown like the 135
Lampin' real pretty, don't care what rappin' can get me
I'm just lettin' y'all know, I'm from Champion City[15]

[Chorus] × 4
See me on the bill, better follow me there
I solemnly swear, I'll make it back to Oliver Square

From Millwoods to the West End
Ask any one of my best friends

You know what it is

30 Seconds

So tell me, why has the climate flipped?
The truth is black and white like Nanaimo chips
Or the No Logo logo, used to buy hardcore for dolo
Now I'm trying to put holes in their barcodes like promos
Shit, I even know why we spend
Companies concentrate on our camp like IBM
Ever seen a CEO smile? They get focused as hell

---

11 The Black Dog Freehouse pub is a Whyte Avenue institution.
12 A bland hotel bar on Jasper Avenue.
13 A nightclub, now closed, that was on 85th Avenue and 103rd Street.
14 Cowboys Dance Hall on Stony Plain Road, also closed.
15 The city's official slogan. It came about after a tornado killed twenty-seven people in Edmonton in 1987. Mayor Laurence Decore saw the community's response to the tornado as evidence that the city was a "city of Champions." The slogan has since been removed from the entrance to Edmonton in 2015.

Coal burners after oil murders, ghosts in the Shell
Hello, what's yellow and red and Bush's fellow in bed?
You better get the point like stilettos to head
Dead, right, they map out a path that'd kill a tourist
There's smoke on the water, straight outta Philip Morris
Look at Wal-Mart, they thug down the nicest
Gun through their sweatshops and run down the prices
As far as wrong plans go
They're a bigger public enemy than Flavor Flav working for Monsanto

[Chorus] × 2
Don't spend a dime until they get the price filed
Even I'm selling a lifestyle
Testing the cost, from freshest temp to veteran boss
30 seconds gets my message across

I am a man at odds with companies far from even-handed
But I've even handed out cash for their jeans and hats
It's seeming that I contradict quite slightly
Conflicted, wearing orange, blue and white Nikes
But does it really make a difference since everyone's interest is green paper
Many companies thrive off cheap labour
Like I told this punk to watch his feet, he said "fuck off"
Told him Nike owns Converse, you aren't safe with Chucks on
Now it seems what you wear is a cotton ideology
Or a homespun philosophy for grown-up autonomy
But you are not alone like a festival lineup
Your closet, to find the tree that they want you to climb up
I'm not hung up on thrift stores, but I feel a little better
Spending cheddar on a used button-up or sweater
I won't say stop buying 'cause it isn't realistic
But cop because you want it, make your own damn decisions

[Chorus] × 2
Don't spend a dime until they get the price filed
Even I'm selling a lifestyle
Testing the cost, from freshest temp to veteran boss
30 seconds gets my message across

First, you are being watched and no, I'm not fucking paranoid
A pair of boys with pens are getting locked to your latitude
An attitude to get is real smart with your aptitude
Before you let 'em in, quite proper to batter you
Your game's not all fixed, because your name's on a list
You're an actor in a play and they're not changing the script
It's amazing dissent, grassy knoll, magic bullet
Had to pull from a tape loop, don't get juiced like a grapefruit
Product placement in your moving pictures, hatred in your schooling
    system
Forsake your patron saint, 'cause the president will use religion
For his own devices, vice grip, grip tape, tape roll
Roll up, up start, start this, this play is a display
Of politrickery, Kerry, wouldn't call it victory
Whether red or blue, they're giving you wood like hickory
This is the gravest record of vast instruction
Signing off, Cadence Weapon of mass destruction

[Chorus] × 2
Don't spend a dime until they get the price filed
Even I'm selling a lifestyle
Testing the cost, from freshest temp to veteran boss
30 seconds gets my message across

How Black?

She said I was the whitest black person she'd ever met and
she laughed when she said it

A kind of nervous jagged laughter the rest of the room tried
to gloss over
Like a white glove over a black hand

I wanted to show her a colour wheel
Point at it
Point at myself
And then say, "Where am I on here?"

How black did I need to be?
How black would I need to be to avoid hearing things like that?
And if I wasn't black enough
How black was too black?

My shade deepens and dilates
Shifting shape with the size and timbre of the room
My nebulous form frightens some and pacifies others
Making for a self-relationship fraught with confusion

If I'm not black enough, then I must be some colour
Could I be grey?

"Which of your parents was white?

That's what they actually say

There must be something else in my broth of being
Something in the mix to make up a strange thing like me

Am I too black to be walking behind her in the evening?
Can I black my way through the barber shop?

Am I black enough to darken her bedsheets with my
shadow at night?

She later apologized to me
Under the strobing beams
Of the black-owned danceclub
In front of the white DJs
Playing black music to other white people

But I still won't call her White Girl
Because living with absence of colour might be just as tough
As it is coping with the whole blinding spectrum

The gradients of Civil War black and Kenyan black and
Alberta black

And French Canadian white and Scandinavian white and
Confederate white
Do not have to matter tonight

Because I am not black, you are not white
I am me and you are you

Frank Fontaine (Young Kidd)
(1988–)

Winnipeg-born and -raised rapper Frank Fontaine is considered by many to be "Winnipeg's breakout star" (Martin Patriquin). Fontaine, whose rap name is Young Kidd, is of both Indigenous and Jamaican descent. He began rapping in 2004 while attending Technical Vocational High. He makes music now, he says, "for people who grew up in my neighbourhood and went through the same things that I went through." "My goal is to keep it positive for everyone. I want to influence the younger generation to turn to music instead of crime" (*The Uniter* 2009).

Fontaine began performing in 2005, and released six mixed-tapes between 2006 and 2011. His first full-length album, *I Go Hard*, released in 2009 by Winnipeg's CTL records, pays tribute to his community, central Winnipeg. "I'm talking about the area in the middle of the city, the core area around the Salter Bridge [the Slaw Rebchuk Bridge]. Growing up there you see a lot of things" (*The Uniter*). The tracks on *I Go Hard* address the tensions between Winnipeg law enforcement and the black and Indigenous communities, which are tangibly felt in the presence of prejudice and judicial apathy.

In 2010 Fontaine released his second full-length album, *10x10* (CTL Records) which was nominated in two categories, including Album of the Year, at the Aboriginal Peoples' Choice Music Awards. In 2011 Fontaine released his third full-length album, *Criminals Turned Legit*. The album displays his characteristic style and swagger. In "You Ain't Got to Ask," Fontaine raps, "Everyone knows that I'm king of the town / You aint gotta ask / I'm breaking it down."

In 2015 Fontaine released an introspective hip-hop song charting the course of his recent years. "In My Dreams" spins a tale about family, incarceration, love and loss, and his determination to get right. "When you locked up, all you got is time," he speaks at the track's close. "It's just a matter of what you do with that time."

"Wonderful Winnipeg," from the album *10x10*, samples the 1967 civic pride recording by the *Swinging Strings*, written for the 1967 Pan American Games. In the original song, a Sinatra-esque voice croons "hail my town, hail my home / the

world that moves round and round / where I belong and joys renown in Winnipeg."
Fontaine "blackens" the sample by speeding it up and putting it over a driving
beat, thus ironizing the naive, uncomplicated sense of belonging the original song
expounds, at the same time as Fontaine exploits its message of pride to speak to
his loyalty to his black and Indigenous urban communities.

In "Hometown," the ninth single on the album *10x10*, Fontaine references the
African American inner-city origins of rap as a genre to bring to light the not-dissim-
ilar conditions of black and Indigenous kids in inner-city Winnipeg. In giving voice
to local realities in the language and forms of rap, Fontaine projects urban black
and Indigenous Winnipeg onto the acoustic map of the black diaspora. I encourage
readers to visit YouTube to watch the affecting video, directed by Wab Kinew, to
hear Fontaine's evocative and moving track.

The lyrics to "Wonderful Winnipeg" and "Hometown" have never before been
published. The following are my own transcriptions of Fontaine's lyrics.

Wonderful Winnipeg

"Winnipeg, Winnipeg, wonderful Winnipeg"

I love, I love

Winnipeg, stand up
It's your boy YK
I do this for y'all
I'm representing for my city, see me ridin'
I'm buzzin in the streets, you see my grindin'
Everybody show me love
My hood it be full of thugs
We all about our money
Everybody sellin' ssshhhhhhh
Cold winters, hot summers
Boy my money long
All black, mobbed out
We look like the Corleones
West side, north side, south side, to east side
They rockin' with me
I'm a show you how the G's ride

The cat scan told me I had money on my mind
The same place that I was raised,
Boy, I'll probably die.
Where the girls fine and the d-boys fly
To Sunday night cruise homey's pullin' out they rides

And I'm tatted up
Haters getting mad at us
Cuz I'm ten times ten, homey add it up
My city, my home, my town
I'm the youngest in charge,
Boy you know I get down—I rep.

Chorus: I love "Wonderful Winnipeg, Winnipeg"

You know I'm about to put my city on the map
I'm repping for the hood and all the homies in the trap
Where we get fly, what you know about dat?
Then we hit the club guaranteed to blow a stack.
I love my city, the winter's so chilly
I go hard population just under a milly
Where we get high, we call that "get silly"
And everybody know your boy because I'm illy.

I'm from the C-side, I'm bout my money, man
And never forget where I'm from that's why they love me, man.
In the middle of July make the block feel like Mexico
I ain't one to play games this aint X and O's
My city got my back I'm the next to blow
I'm from the city where the hustlers allergic to broke
My city, my home, my town
I'm the youngest in charge
Boy, you know how I get down—I rep

Chorus: I love "Wonderful Winnipeg, Winnipeg"

My city show me love, they know I keep it real
Boy I'm posting on the block like Shaquille O'Neal
And I do my own thing, I ain't worry 'bout a deal

If we was down south, boy, they say I keep it real
Summer it be hot and the shorties top knotch
So I'm smokin' on that bubble—just watch
Watch me while I do my thing, ain't no body in my lane
I go hard, all you others rappers sound the same. Ha ha!
Every hood you know they bumpin my ssshhhh
So all you haters should get off of my ssshhhh
We got the best dro
Winnipeg, we get dough
We be ridin' round the town let the kush smoke

I'm a soldier boy, ya I done told ya boy
I'm looking over my city just like the Golden Boy.[1]
My city, my home my town
I'm the youngest in charge
Boy, you know how I get down—I rep.

I love "Winnipeg ... wonderful Winnipeg"

Hometown

Chorus:
From my hometown
From my hometown
Oooh the people I've named
Ah the wonders of my world
Ah the wonders of my world
Ah the wonders of this world
I wonder now

This is my city, my home, my town
Walking down the same streets as I did when I was just a child
I'm a young nigger in the hood runnin' wild
Not caring bout a thing now I'm seeing clearer now
And u you see most these girls in my hood getting knocked up

---

1   The Golden Boy is a twenty-four-carat gold statue perched atop the dome of the Manitoba Legislative Assembly in Winnipeg.

85% of my hood done been locked up
Fresh memories
God will you help me please?
I done seen too much wrong the hood count on me
I'm reminisce when I was just a kid
Running from the cops so I don't catch a bit
The hood lookin' the same, but shit, a lot changed
Days used to be sunny but it seems all we get is rain
I'm tryin to shine the light
I'm givin' hope to ghettoes
You know my timing's right
It'll hold you down forever

'Peg city, you know where a nigger from
And I'm getting love

Chorus:
From my hometown
Oooh the people I've named
Ah the wonders of my world
Ah the wonders of my world
Ah the wonders of this world
I wonder now

The hood crazy
Things will never be the same
Money on my mind
You know a nigger still stuck in the game
But I've overcome obstacles, it's obvious
That I done seen some shit in my time without binoculars
Little kids running the block with no one watching them
No father figures around so ain't no stoppin' them
So they turn to the streets to find a better way
Dropped out of school young, now they on the corner selling cane
That's the life of a young nigger from my side
Selling chickens for money but no Popeye's
Certain things make me take a stroll down memory lane
Like when I post up on the block but so much shit has changed
I started rapping hoping I could see a better day

I thought that if I do it, homey, that the weather change
And I made my mark:
Now this city show me love
Tell me where we from

Chorus
From my hometown
The people aren't made
Oh the wonders of my world
Oh the wonders of this world
I wonder now

Miranda Martini
(1990–)

Miranda Martini says that having grown up a child of many continents in a city obsessed by a monolithic lone-cowboy narrative, she is acutely aware of the complicated joy of having multiple identities—the identities we're born with and the ones we choose, day after day. An essayist, writer, and musician, Martini explores the issues of mixed-race and literary inheritance for black prairie people. She is a fifth-generation black Canadian: her mother is the black prairies' eminent historian and writer Cheryl Foggo, and her father is acclaimed playwright Clem Martini. She was born and raised in Calgary.

Martini studied English literature and creative writing at the University of British Columbia, and recently completed a master's degree in songwriting at Bath Spa University. Her writing has appeared in a variety of Canadian publications, including *Alberta Views Magazine*, *Reader's Digest*, *Discorder Magazine*, and *Other Tongues: Mixed Race Women Speak Out* (2010), which is where the following piece of creative non-fiction was originally published. Her music was a finalist in the 2010 Calgary Folk Music Festival and Ship and Anchor Songwriting Contest. Recently she contributed her live original music to Cheryl Foggo's *John Ware Reimagined*. Her recently released album, *Calendar*, is available online on Soundcloud.

Her story "The Drinking Gourd" testifies to the incredible strength of memory of black storytelling that can reach back five generations and more to remember an enslaved ancestor on a plantation in Texas and bring knowledge of him across borders of time, space, and nation into the present moment. Martini's is an important reflection about the stories we tell and don't tell; about which stories we feel permitted to keep, and which stories we continue to need. Ultimately, "The Drinking Gourd" reveals how it is stories that, time and again, show us the way back home.

❦

The Drinking Gourd: Three Tales

When the sun comes back, and the first Quail calls,
Follow the drinking gourd;
For the old man is waiting for to carry you to freedom
If you follow the drinking gourd.

Rufus

My journey could begin in several places: it could begin with the 1910 exodus of between one and two thousand Blacks, who escaped the Jim Crow South by emigrating to the Canaan Land, Heaven, also known as Canada; it could begin 48 years before, with 6-year-old Rufus, my great-great-grandfather, being kidnapped along with his two brothers from their Arkansas home and taken to Texas by slave traders. The story goes back farther still than that, but I suppose the real beginning—and ending—is with me, nine or ten years old, and my grade five class' First Nations study project.

At the end of the unit on First Nations art and culture, we were asked to write our own First Nations legends. I wrote about how the night sky is a beautiful woman who wears a cloak of many colours when she goes out walking, and how it shifts in purple and orange and becomes the Northern Lights. I loved the sky stories best, because they belonged to everyone. You don't see much of the Northern Lights in Alberta, I'll grant you, but everybody in the world looks at the stars. In those days, I was beginning to consider myself something of an aficionado of world mythology. The Greek and Roman myths were my particular interest, but I was also being exposed to the Norse, Egyptian, and West African traditions. I think I lived more deeply searching the sky for the story maps laid out there than I did here on earth.

Our next assignment was to share a legend that came from our parents. My parents both grew up in Bowness, a district of Calgary nestled against the Bow River that used to be its own town. Now, there are so many suburbs stacked like shingles way out in the Foothills, Bowness is almost considered "city centre." But in my parents' minds it's still dusty and rural, with the river valley and train tracks for its playground.

My father's stories all began the same way: "I grew up in a grey house with a blue roof, and I had three brothers—Nic, Liv, and Ben. And we had three pets—Sirius the dog, who was black as night; Nosey the bunny, who was white as snow; and Smokey the cat, who was grey as a puff of smoke." The stories were word-perfect each time, and soothing as a litany. My mother's stories were different. They tended to be longer than they at first appeared, because time and an interweaving cast of characters attached them to one another. You pulled one end of the scarf from my mother's pocket, and out came yards and yards of story.

She was the third-oldest child in the family but the oldest girl, which meant the *de facto* caregiver and second in command to her mother, my Nana. She was—is—also the primary storyteller. It was my mother who first instilled me with the knowledge that I was half-Black, and that my ancestors had emigrated from the States in 1910 to found communities in the "Last, Best West," the prairies of Alberta, Saskatchewan, and Manitoba.

I knew I was half-Black years before I was even aware of differences in skin colour. My mother, never one to miss an opportunity to tell stories, is the pre-eminent historian of Alberta's Black pioneer community. My knowledge of the 1910 exodus goes back further than I can remember. I also knew my father's parents were German and Franco-Italian. It didn't seem all that complicated growing up. My maternal cousins, most of them half-Black as well, varied in colour from "darkish-white" (a phrase I coined to describe my own shade at around the age of three) to the creamy coffee brown of my mother, aunt and uncles.

The concept proved difficult to translate to others. When we were little girls, my best friend overheard one of her parents refer to me as half-Black. She spent the next several months wondering which half of me they were referring to. When no one was looking, she would examine my arms, legs, neck and face for some sign of my blackness. She eventually gave up looking and assumed it was the part of me that was covered by clothes.

It was my half-Black-ness that led to the difficulty with the project. I could write only one myth, which meant I would have to choose between a story from my mother and one from my father. My father, as I've mentioned, told mainly boyhood stories, detailing the adventures of his pets and his brothers as they hiked through the Rocky Mountains. If I chose one of his, it would definitely be the one about the time Smokey gave birth to a litter of kittens on my dad's chest. If I elected to tell one of Mom's stories, it would have to be that of my great-great-grandfather Rufus, but where to begin?

In 1862, when he was six years old, Rufus and his two brothers were taken from their home in Arkansas to work on plantations in Texas. Rufus was unaware that as he was entering captivity, the Civil War was raging around him. The family Rufus worked for saw no need to tell him when the end of the war finally came. He had been a slave for four years when he overheard that the law had set him free. Shortly after making this discovery, he hid in the field until he was sure all of the inhabitants of the house were out of doors working; snuck into the house to steal onions and a few scraps from the kitchen; and made a dash for it.

Too old and feeble to chase a healthy, work-hardened ten-year-old, the master sent Red, the snarling family dog, after the boy. The master had forgotten that Rufus had raised Red from a pup, and the two friends made their escape together. When he was 18, Rufus returned to Arkansas and found his mother and aunt still living there. He found his younger brother Billy by chance many, many years later, at a travelling circus show.

Isn't that perfect? Couldn't it be a page out of the *1001 Arabian Nights*? I'm not sure why I decided in the end to tell the delightful but less emotionally resonant story of Smokey and her kittens. My best guess is that I was afraid Rufus' story was too complicated, that it had too many layers and would take too long to adapt for a grade five-level laminated picture book. Part of me wonders, though, if I shied away from it because I felt it wasn't mine to claim; that Rufus, wanderer, adventurer, was too far away from my world, which was small, and sheltered, and darkish-white.

By grade five I was already awakening to a new fact: my mother told one story and my skin told another.

John

My education from that point on was, consciously or unconsciously, bent towards finding a point of entrance into my self. The next foray into my mixed race identity was a grade seven culture studies project, for which I presented on African American culture, starting with food. I made cornbread, and wrote a paper about how the slaves in the U.S. took the worst cuts of meat (the only cuts they were allowed) and used them to make button bones, the pungent and sticky dish of tiny, meaty back rib tails. The cornbread smelled at home in my kitchen when I baked it, and the button bones were already a part of me—they had been taken straight from the best meals of my childhood. Button bones meant family, noisy joviality, a hot cramped kitchen. Button bones can now be purchased at Safeway. They're no longer dirt-cheap because, well, it's pork, and because white people eventually caught onto the decadent nature of ribs slow-cooked in barbeque sauce and brown sugar. I recently gave up pork, after an ill-timed screening of the film *Babe* and the discovery that an adult pig can play Pong. Still, from a distance I see a little bit of myself in those foods.

For the next unit—language—I researched urban 'ebonics.' I was fascinated to learn that entire English sentences can be translated into ebonics and be almost unrecognizable. "For example," I wrote, "Instead of 'I'm going home,' say 'I'm coppin' my trill to my pile of stone.'"

What am I doing? I thought, even after Ms. Elliot gave me an A+. It felt a little like bringing a cool uncle to school on Parents Day. I don't know if what I was talking about was real to someone else, but it certainly wasn't me I saw in there. Even though I was 12 years old and not yet well-versed in the ethical issues associated with white scholars going into Black ghettos to "document" their lifestyles, I instinctively felt that the assignment was cheap, exploitive. I needed a new story.

So, I tried again. In grade eight I went back further, to cowboys and ranch-hands, some of them freed slaves who found their way to Canada from the South. I gave a presentation on John Ware, the cowboy, the great Albertan legend—one of the only true legends to come out of Alberta. It's believed that he was a slave in South Carolina; after the Civil War, he ended up working on a Texas ranch and came to Alberta on a cattle drive in 1883. Once he was introduced to the Big Sky Country—the clear blue eye that hangs above the Rocky Mountains and the golden sea of prairie grass rippling over the hills—he started to wonder if a Black cowboy might do better to settle here than in Texas.

He stayed, and the rest is breathless movie poster fuel: He was never tossed from a horse! He could lift an 18-month-old steer clear over his head! Like Davy Crockett or Robin Hood, he has taken on the character of the land to become something more emblematic than human. The myth-starved little girl I still was responded to the larger-than-life stories that were tied to his legacy.

I say he fell in love with the land; he stuck mainly to the vast rural expanses and rarely travelled into the city. Non-natives don't realize just how big a country Canada is. The travel time between urban centres is generally one of about three hours minimum. In John's time, it was more like two days, if you were in a hurry. In the countryside, John was free to roam about and feel the pull of the Big Sky all around him. When yours is the only face for miles, it's easier to believe that you're your own property.

When John was forced to do business in Calgary, the weight of being a person in the world, a Black man at the turn of the century, came rushing back to drag his solid form to the earth. He was one of the city's most lauded men; his funeral was the best attended in the young city's history, but to his death he was known "affectionately" as Nigger John.

"Did his Black friends call him that?" I asked my mother when I came across this tidbit. I was at the dining room table researching my report while she was cooking dinner.

"Oh no. Of course not." She made a characteristic face, pursing her lips and looking into the middle distance. I immediately felt it had been a stupid question. After all, those were different times. No doubt his white friends assumed he didn't mind, or else they thought so little of it that they imagined he never thought of it either. It was just his name: Nigger John. They couldn't know that he heard what every other Black man hears: Worthless John. Brainless John. Third-Class Citizen John.

I think that was the moment John Ware's legendary life lost its glamour for me. The truth is, no hero's legacy is entirely without taint. Secret prejudices and rancid thoughts have the power to infect even the most hallowed memories.

Holden, an old boyfriend of one of my cousins, was around my family a lot a couple of years back. His desperate desire to be Black himself caused him to spend as much time around my family as possible. One of the first times he was at my parents' house, he noticed a picture taken of my sister and I one Halloween. My sister, a genie, was smiling her serene smile, her cheeks perfect pink apples in a golden face. I was a princess for the third year running, and my golden hair made an angelic frame for my round blue eyes and little pink lips. (It would be 11 years before I started dyeing my hair a deep, dark brown.) The natural light of the picture caught everything just right. We looked like a couple of dolls in our plastic costume jewelry, holding onto each other and grinning. "That's got to be the whitest thing I've ever seen," Holden laughed, snorting. The picture still sits in the same place on the side table in my parents' living room. I always loved that picture, and I burned with anger at Holden for making me feel a little ashamed of it.

I would have loved to claim John Ware for my mythology, my extended family, but Nigger John kept getting in my way, forcing my own shameful thoughts upon me. What no one knows: I secretly crave to be Nigger to someone; to have the foul word thrown at me, or anything that would ignite a righteous fire in me, that would let the Black part out, give it reason for being. I hate the desire—I cringe to feel its presence in me—but it's there for all that. I imagine vivid scenes in which I'm coolly chewing out some faceless, ignorant bigot for a comment that slipped out in my presence.

Playing the race card, I believe it's called. "I don't know if you realize that *I'm* Black. My family's been in Canada for five generations. We are not from 'an island,' English is our first language, and I'd appreciate it if in future you wouldn't use words like that around me." Then I throw down my share of the cheque and saunter out the door, blind to the amazed glances of the other patrons.

Outside of my elaborate fantasies, I'm hardly that hostile. I rarely have reason to be. The most I have to deal with is the occasional Holden, or else having to explain to my incredulous Australian roommate that *mulatto* means mule: half-donkey, half-horse. I don't deal with "racism" as it appears in Public Service Announcements and anti-racism posters. Instead, I defend and re-defend my territory in the fracturing world of racial categorization to people who are just as Franco-Italian and German and English as me.

I'm not great at dealing with these situations. When my roommate, a cheerful redhead, saw the discomfort telling on my face, she quickly defused her comments, laughing and hugging me. "Don't be offended," she said. "I'm just jealous I don't have your beautiful tan."

My skin. The emblem of either my whiteness or my Blackness—or perhaps more accurately, my Otherness. In the eyes of an observer, I take on whatever Other they want me to be: Latina, Filipino, Italian. My mother and I went into a church in downtown Calgary the other day to get directions. The man who greeted us at the door asked if we were Portuguese. Normally I'd put up my defenses at such a question, but I got the sense that the man wasn't about to ask us what island we were from. When we told him we were Canadian, he didn't look embarrassed; only a little sad.

"No? You look like you Portuguese, or Latina, you and your daughter. Pretty girl." He sighed and smiled, and led Mom to a phone book. After we had thanked him and left, Mom told me that he was a recent immigrant from Portugal and had very few contacts here. Perhaps he was hoping that we'd be able to hook him into some sort of community. I felt bad to have disappointed him. In a lot of ways it would be easier for me—and other people—if I "passed," if I pretended to be Latina or Italian or Portuguese. Some community where my deceptive, chimerical skin would be an unquestioned VIP pass.

But I can't pass, because at the end of the day, in the immortal words of Popeye, I am what I am. And what I am, I realized in grade eight, doesn't allow me to share hardships or skin colour with my ancestors, for good or ill. I decided that John Ware's story wasn't mine after all. It was close to me, but it wasn't inside of me. He was like the evening star: the more earnestly I reached out for him, tried to be a part of him, the farther he seemed to retreat from me into his distant realm of make-believe, of steer riding and steer lifting and never being tossed from a horse. His story wasn't the home I'd been expecting.

Better to let the dead rest.

The Gourd

My mother read the original draft of this piece and said I had gotten only one thing wrong, when I said I didn't share my skin with my ancestors. "Haven't you seen pictures of Grandpa? He was exactly the same colour as you."

How could I have forgotten about my great-grandfather? George Smith had nappy hair from Africa, the "bad" hair, as Nana calls it, but he was extremely light-skinned and endured glares and looks of pity or confusion when he was seen sitting with Coloureds in restaurants.

This reminder, plus a quick refresher in my American history lessons, brought a hundred other similar examples crowding into my mind. Rosa Parks, herself light-skinned, wrote in her memoirs about how her grandfather's straight hair and light complexion allowed him to pass for white. He used this to defy Jim Crow etiquette, shaking hands with white men and neglecting to address white acquaintances as "Mister" or "Miss." The Incongruous, figures in the early Civil Rights push, also famously used their ambiguous nationality to do dangerous work for the movement. Rufus, the escaped slave, was of mixed race, another *mulatto*, but this didn't protect him from being enslaved for four years.

Of course, I'm not the same person I might have been if I had been born one or two generations ago. Is anyone? There's no Civil Rights movement for me to join these days, and I don't share skin or experience with my ancestors, but their memories are mine by right. Three generations after Alberta's first Black communities moved to urban centres, and the wild pioneer story came to an end, I can only identify my family with the voices that whisper their stories to me. I listen intently and scribble things down when I can, but I'm not a perfect scribe. I'm too much of a dreamer; I'll always want to mix my history with myth and high adventure to make it more palatable.

But sometimes history needs no embellishment. When slaves sought the freedom of Canada, they sang a song called "Follow the Drinking

Gourd"—ostensibly a Spiritual, in fact a detailed map of the Underground Railroad. The refrain instructed them to travel in the direction of the North Star, the bright one at the tip of the Drinking Gourd. There is a reason humans have always looked at the stars. For the escaping slaves, they made a bridge to home, one that went on forever and ever into a rarely-illumined dark. I take great comfort knowing that for all of the great chasms between us, we—John Ware, my mother, my great-great-grandfather, and approximately two thousand African American emigrants—we are all looking up, together, at the same map to freedom. This is the beauty of the stars: they are, in a sense, everyone's home.

Works Cited

Alberta Order of Excellence. "Fil Fraser." 2015. https://www.lieutenantgovernor
.ab.ca/aoe/arts/fil-fraser/index.html.

Alberta Sports Hall of Fame and Museum. 2013. https://ashfm.ca/
hall-of-fame-honoured-members/browse/teams/calgary-stampeders-1948.

Al-Solaylee, Kamal. "Throwing Her Weight Around." *Globe and Mail*, February
18, 2005.

Ali, Ahmed (Knowmadic). "Child Soldier." *Great Black North*. Ed. Valerie Mason
John and Kevan Anthony Cameron. Calgary: Frontenac, 2013. 218–19.

Andersson, Hilary. "Fighting the Oil Firms." *BBC News*, November 6, 1998.

André, F.B. *The Man Who Beat the Man*. Vancouver: NeWest Press, 2000.

———. *What Belongs: Stories*. Vancouver: Ronsdale Press, 2007.

Âpihtawikosisân (Chelsea Vowel). "Khodi Dill Sums It Up Nicely." November
28, 2011. http://apihtawikosisan.com/2011/11/khodi-dill-sums-it-up-nicely/.

Asong, Linus T. "The Anti-Hero in African Fiction: An Examination of Psychological Construction and Characterization Techniques in Six Selected Novels." PhD diss. University of Alberta, 1984.

———. *Chopchair*. Cameroon: Langaa, 2010.

———. *The Crabs of Bangui*. Cameroon: Langaa, 2010.

———. *The Crown of Thorns*. Cameroon: Langaa, 2009.

———. *Detective Fiction and the African Scene: From the Whodunit? to the
Whydunit?* Oxford: African Books Collective, 2012.

———. *Doctor Frederick Ngenito*. Cameroon: Langaa, 2006.

———. *A Legend of the Dead*. Cameroon: Langaa, 2009.

———. *No Way to Die*. Cameroon: Langaa, 2009.

———. *Osagyef.* Cameroon: Langaa, 2008.

Augustine, Anthony. "Hip Hop: Nestor Wynrush." *Winnipeg Free Press*, May 23,
2009. https://www.winnipegfreepress.com/arts-and-life/entertainment/music/
hip-hop-45910647.html.

Bailey, Troy Burle. *The Pierre Bonga Loops*. Vancouver: Commodore Books, 2010.

Barr, John, and Owen Anderson, eds. *The Unfinished Revolt: Some Views on Western Independence*. Toronto: McClelland and Stewart, 1971.

Barrett, Paul. *Blackening Canada: Diaspora, Race, Multiculturalism*. Toronto: U of Toronto P, 2015.

Barrow, Robert, and Leigh Hambly. *Billy: The Life and Photographs of William S.A. Beal*. Winnipeg: Vig Corps Press, 1988.

Bateman, David. "A Map of the Island." *Canadian Ethnic Studies Journal* 35.1 (2003): 208.

Beal, William. "Big Woody." William Beal Papers. Ole Johnson Museum, Swan River, Manitoba.

Beaver, Walker. *Window of Our Memories*, vol. 1. Ed. Carter and Akili. St. Albert: Black Research Society of Alberta, 1981.

Begamudré, Ven, and Judith Krause. *Out of Place: Stories and Poems*. Regina: Coteau, 1991.

Bickersteth, Bertrand. "Accidental Agriculture." *Field Stone Review* (2016–17). http://www.thefieldstonereview.ca/poetry10.html.

———. "Artists." *Afrikadey!* Accessed July 21, 2016 (expired web link).

———. "CBC Poetry Longlist." November 3, 2018. https://www.cbc.ca/books/literaryprizes/wakanda-oklahoma-by-bertrand-bickersteth-1.4876309.

———. "I Look at My Hand." *The Great Black North: Contemporary African Canadian Poetry*. Ed. Valerie Mason-John and Kevan Anthony Cameron. Calgary: Frontenac, 2013. 68.

———. "The Invisible Man on the Prairie." *Kola* 25.2 (Fall 2013): 20–22.

———. "We, Too." *The Great Black North: Contemporary African Canadian Poetry*. Ed. Valerie Mason-John and Kevan Anthony Cameron. Calgary: Frontenac, 2013, 69.

———. "What We Used to Call It." *Antigonish Review* 193 (Spring 2018).

Black, Ayanna, ed. *Voices: Canadian Writers of African Descent*. Toronto: HarperCollins, 1992.

Black Pioneer Descendants Society. *Black Pioneer Centennial: A Little Taste of Soul*. Edmonton: Black Pioneer Descendants Society, 2005.

Blinov, Paul. "Ten Years Later: Tracing a Decade of City Changes through Cadence Weapon's 'Oliver Square.'" *Vue Weekly*, November 18, 2015. https://www.vueweekly.com/ten-years-later-tracing-a-decade-of-city-changes-through-cadence-weapons-oliver-square/.

Bowen, Deanna. "sum of the parts: what can be named." *Deanna Bowen*, 2009. www.deannabowen.ca/sum-of-the-parts-what-can-be-named/.

Breen, David H. "John Ware." *Dictionary of Canadian Biography*, vol. 13: *1901–1910*. biographi.ca. U of Toronto / U Laval, 1994–2019.

Brennan, Brian. "Remembering Fil Fraser, 1932–2017." http://brianbrennan.ca/remembering-fil-fraser-1932-2017/.

Brewster, Wakefield. *East2West.* Kill Whitey Records, 2008.

———. *Wakefield Brewster da Lyrical Pitbull.* Kill Whitey Records, 2007.

Broadway, Michael. "Meatpacking, Refugees and the Transformation of Brooks, Alberta." Unpublished paper. No date. Studylib.net, studylib.net/doc/7377383/meatpacking--refugees-and-the-transformation-of-brooks--alberta.

Butler, William Francis. *The Wild North Land: Being the Story of a Winter Journey, with Dogs, across Northern North America.* London: Sampson Low, 1896.

Calder, Alison. "Reassessing Prairie Realism." *A Sense of Place: Re-Evaluating Regionalism in Canadian and American Writing.* Ed. Christian Riegel and Herb Wyile. Edmonton: U of Alberta P, 1997. 51–60.

———. Rev. of *The Literary History of Alberta, Volume Two. Canadian Literature* 170.1 (2001): 240–1.

Calgary Herald. "Farewell Tribute." September 28, 1968.

Calgary Tribune. "Orange Blossoms." March 2, 1892.

Camper, Carol, ed. *Miscegenation Blues: Voices of Mixed Race Women.* Toronto: Sister Vision, 1994.

Canada. Department of Agriculture. *Province of Manitoba and North West Territory of the Dominion of Canada Information for Emigrants.* Ottawa, 1878.

Canada. Governor General and Queen's Privy Council. Order-in-Council PC1911-1324. https://pier21.ca/research/immigration-history/order-in-council-pc-1911-1324, 1911.

Canada. Statistics Canada. Fourth Census of Canada, 1901. Vol. 1, "Population." publications.gc.ca, 2010.

———. Statistics Canada. Fifth Census of Canada, 1911. Vol. 1, "Population." publications.gc.ca, 2010.

———. Statistics Canada. Sixth Census of Canada, 1921. Vol. 1, "Population." publications.gc.ca, 2010.

———. Dominion Bureau of Statistics. Ninth Census of Canada, 1951. Vol. 1, "Population: General Characteristics." 2010. publications.gc.ca.

———. Statistics Canada. 1971 Census of Canada. Vol. 1, "Population." publications.gc.ca, 2010.

———. Statistics Canada. "National Household Survey (NHS) Profile, 2011." Statistics Canada, August 5, 2013, statcan.gc.ca.

———. "Census Profile, 2016 Census Canada." Census Profile 2016, Government of Canada, Statistics Canada, April 24, 2018, www.12.statcan.gc.ca.

Carrière, Marie, Curtis Gillespie, and Jason Purcell, eds. *Ten Canadian Writers in Context*. U of Alberta P, 2016.

Carter, Velma, and Wanda Leffler Akili. *The Window of Our Memories*. St. Albert: Black Cultural Research Society of Alberta, 1981.

Carter, Velma, and Leah Suzanne Carter. *The Window of Our Memories*, vol. 2: *The New Generation*. St. Albert: Black Cultural Research Society of Alberta, 1990.

Chan, Byron. "In the Studio with Deanna Bowen." *Canadian Art.* https://www.chanbyron.com/Canadian-Art.

Clarke, George Elliott. *Directions Home: Approaches to African-Canadian Literature*. Toronto: U of Toronto P, 2012.

———, ed. *Fire on the Water: An Anthology of Black Nova Scotian Writing*. 2 vols. Lawrencetown Beach, NS: Pottersfield, 1991–2.

———. "Harris, Philip and Brand: Three Authors in Search of Literate Criticism." *Odysseys Home: Mapping African-Canadian Literature*. U of Toronto P, 2002.

———. "Honouring African-Canadian Geography: Mapping the Black Presence in Atlantic Canada." *Border/lines* 45 (1997): 35–39.

———. Introduction. *Eyeing the North Star: Directions in African Canadian Literature*. Ed. George Elliott Clarke. Toronto: McClelland and Stewart, 1997. xi–xxviii.

———. "No Respect." Rev. of *Rude: Contemporary Black Canadian Cultural Criticism*. *Canadian Literature* 74 (2002): 187–89.

Cobbs, E.A. *Oral History*. Alberta Black Pioneer Heritage. Albertasource. 2007. http://wayback.archiveit.org/2217/20101208162354/http://www.albertasource.ca/blackpioneers/multimedia/oral/index.html.

Cochrane, Timothy. *Gichi Bitobig, Grand Marais: Early Accounts of the Anishinaabeg and the North Shore Fur Trade*. U of Minnesota P, 2018.

Codrington, Lisa. *Cast Iron*. Toronto: Playwrights Canada Press, 2006.

———. "Lisa Codrington: 2008 Theatre Co-Award Winner." K.M Hunter Charitable Foundation Video. 2008. http://www.kmhunterfoundation.ca/artist_videos/2008/lisa_codrington_2008.html.

Compton, Wayde. *After Canaan: Essays in Race, Writing and Region*. Vancouver: Arsenal Pulp, 2010.

———, ed. *Bluesprint: Black British Columbian Literature and Orature*. Vancouver: Arsenal Pulp, 2001.

Crail, Archibald. *Archie Crail's Exile*. Winnipeg: Blizzard Publishing, 1989.

———. *The Bonus Deal*. Regina: Coteau, 1992.

Cross, A.E. "Bovis." "Reminiscences of Round-Up of 1887." *Farm and Ranch Review*, August 5, 1919.

Cui, Dan, and Jennifer R. Kelly. "'Our Negro Citizens': An Example of Everyday Citizenship Practices." *The West and Beyond: New Perspectives on an Imagined Region*. Ed. Alvin Finkel, Sarah Carter, and Peter Fortna. Athabasca, AB: U of Athabasca P, 2010. 253–77.

Darbasie, Nigel. *Last Crossing: Poems*. Edmonton: Nidar Communications, 1988.

———. *A Map of the Island: Poems*. Edmonton: U of Alberta P, 2001.

Davey, Frank. "Toward the Ends of Regionalism." *A Sense of Place: Re-Evaluating Regionalism in Canadian and American Writing*. Ed. Christian Riegel and Herb Wyile. Edmonton: U of Alberta P, 1997. 1–17.

DeRango-Adem, Adebe, and Andrea Thompson. *Other Tongues: Mixed-Race Women Speak Out*. Toronto: Innana, 2010.

Dill, Khodi. "Grey." Vancouver Poetry Slam. youtube.com. 2011.

———. "Holes." CFSW Ottawa Festival. youtube.com. October 21, 2010.

———. "Oil and Water." Vancouver Poetry Slam. youtube.com. March 9, 2014.

———. (web)site of praxis: anti-racist feminist resources. "Creative Resources: Slam Poetry by Khodi Dill." March 8, 2012. http://antiracisms.blogspot.com.

Dobbins, Deborah, Jenna Bailey, and David Este. *We are The Roots: Black Settlers and Their Experiences of Discrimination on the Canadian Prairies*. Bailey and Soda Films. 2018. Video.

Dowden, Richard. "Breathing Lines of Fire: Thirteen Years Ago, George Seremba Was Dragged in Front of a Ugandan Firing Squad and Shot. Amazingly He Survived. He Is Now Reliving the Experience on Stage." *The Independent*. October 17, 1994.

Edmonton Bulletin. "Local." 12 August 1882, 3.

———. "Local." 9 July 1887, 1.

———. "Our Negro Citizens." September 6, 1921.

———. "Our Negro Citizens." February 28, 1922.

———. "Our Negro Citizens." March 20, 1922.

———. "Our Negro Citizens." April 17, 1922.

Edmonton Journal. "New Alberta-Wide Somali TV Show to Connect with Community, Says Host." March 1, 2015. edmontonjournal.com.

Edugyan, Esi. "Attica Locke and Esi Edugyan, in conversation: 'There is so much of our existence that has not been heard.'" *Guardian*, 3 August 2018. https://www.theguardian.com/books/2018/aug/03/attica-locke-esi-edugyan-interview.

———. *Dreaming of Elsewhere: Observations on Home*. Edmonton: U of Alberta P, 2014.

———. *Half Blood Blues*. Toronto: Thomas Allen, 2011.

———. *The Second Life of Samuel Tyne*. Toronto: Alfred Knopf, 2004.

——— *Washington Black: A Novel*. Toronto: HarperCollins Patrick Crean Editions, 2018.

Edugyan, Esi, Wayde Compton, and Karina Vernon. "Black Writers in Search of Place. *The Tyee*. February 28, 2005. thetyee.com.

Edwards, Jefferson Davis. Oral interview (1961). Lloyd and Eileen Chamberlain fonds 1955–2009. CA ATH ath-2013, Athabasca Archives.

El-Hadi, Nehal. "Author Note: Nehal El-Hadi." *The Town Crier*, September 21, 2016. http://towncrier.puritan-magazine.com/author-notes/nehal-el-hadi/.

———. "La Puerta." *Puritan Magazine*, issue 34 (Summer 2016). http://puritan-magazine.com/la-puerta-nehal-el-hadi/.

Elliott, Lorris, ed. *Bibliography of Literary Writings by Blacks in Canada*. Toronto: Williams-Wallace, 1986.

———. "Black Writing in Canada: The Problems of Anthologizing and Documenting." *Canadian Review of Comparative Literature/Revue Canadienne de Littérature Comparée* 16 (1989): 721–27.

———. *Literary Writing by Blacks in Canada: A Preliminary Survey*. Ottawa: Department of the Secretary of State, 1988.

———, ed. *Other Voices: Writings by Blacks in Canada*. Toronto: Williams-Wallace, 1985.

Entrikin, Nicholas. *The Betweenness of Place: Towards a Geography of Modernity*. Baltimore: Johns Hopkins UP, 1991.

Faust, Minister. *The Alchemists of Kush*. Edmonton: Narmer's Pallette Books, 2011.

———. *Coyote Kings of the Space-Age Bachelor Pad*. Edmonton: Narmer's Pallette Books, 2004.

———. *From the Notebooks of Dr. Brain*. New York: Ballantine, 2007.

———. *War & Mir*, vol. 1: *Ascension*. Edmonton: Narmer's Palette, 2011.

———. *War & Mir*, vol. 2: *The Darkold*. Edmonton: Narmer's Palette, 2014.

Foggo, Cheryl. "Assembling Auntie: Illuminating a Long-Forgotten Pioneer." *Alberta Views*. January 1, 2009. albertaviews.ca.

———. *Carol's Mirror*. National Film Board of Canada. 1991.

———. *Dear Baobab*. Toronto: Second Story Press, 2011.

———. *I Have Been in Danger*. Regina: Coteau Books, 2001.

———. "My Home Is over Jordan." *Remembering Chinook Country*. Chinook Country Historical Society. Calgary: Detselig, 2005. 151–70.

———. *One Thing That's True*. Toronto: Kids Can Press, 1998.

———. *Pourin' Down Rain*. Calgary: Detselig, 1990.

———. *The Road Taken*. National Film Board of Canada, 1996.

Foner, Philip S., ed. *Black Socialist Preacher: The Teachings of Reverend George Washington Woodbey and His Disciple, Reverend G.W. Slater, Jr.* San Francisco: Synthesis Publications, 1983.

Fontaine, Frank (Young Kidd). *10x10*. Winnipeg: CTL Records, 2010.

———. *Criminals Turned Legit*. Winnipeg: CTL Records, 2011.

———. *I Go Hard*. Winnipeg: CTL Records, 2009.

———. "Interview." *The Uniter* 63.30 (August 13, 2009).

———. "Wonderful Winnipeg." *Wonderful Winnipeg Mixtape*. Coast to Coast Mixtape Promotions, 2011.

Forbes, Jack D. *Africans and Native Americans: The Language of Race and the Evolution of Red-Black Peoples*. 2nd ed. Champaign: U of Illinois P, 1993.

Fraser, Fil. *Alberta's Camelot: Culture and the Arts in the Lougheed Years*. Edmonton: Lone Pine, 2003.

———, producer. *The Hounds of Notre Dame*. Dir. Zale Dalen. Pan Canadian Film, 1980.

———. *How the Blacks Created Canada*. Edmonton: Dragon Hill, 2009.

———. "Our Best Years." *Farewell to the 70s*. Ed. Anna Porter and Marjorie Harris. Toronto: Thomas Nelson, 1979.

Freuchen, Peter. *The Legend of Daniel Williams*. New York: J. Messner, 1956.

Fwallah, Francisco Alexander. *My Love Letter to Africa*. Edmonton: Pagemaster, 2013.

———. *A New Journey*. Edmonton: Pagemaster, 2008.

———. *Outros Pensamentos*. Edmonton: Pagemaster, 2012.

———. *Quinguangua—Kikolo Meus Pensamentos*. Edmonton: Pagemaster, 2010.

Gadoury, Lorraine, and Antonio Lechasseur. *Persons Sentenced to Death in Canada, 1867–1976: An Inventory of Case Files*. Fonds of the Department of Justice Government Archives Division, National Archives of Canada, 1994.

Gilroy, Paul. *The Black Atlantic: Modernity and Double Consciousness*. Cambridge, MA: Harvard UP, 1993.

Gorman, Jack. *Père Murray and the Hounds: The Story of Saskatchewan's Notre Dame College*. Sidney, BC: Gray's Publishing, 1977.

Government of Alberta, *Position Paper No. 7: New Directions Position Paper on Alberta's Cultural Heritage*. November 1972.

Griwkowski, Fish. "Ahmed (Knowmadic) Ali Is Edmonton's Newest Poet Laureate." *Edmonton Journal*, 27 June 2017. https://edmontonjournal.com/entertainment/local-arts/ahmed-knowmadic-ali-is-edmontons-newest-poet-laureate.

Grizzle, Stanley G. *My Name's Not George: The Story of the Brotherhood of Sleeping Car Porters: Personal Reminiscences of Stanley G. Grizzle.* Toronto: Umbrella Press, 1998.

Goyette, Linda, and Carolina Jakeway Roemmich, eds. *Edmonton in Our Own Words.* Edmonton: U of Alberta P, 2004.

Grove, Frederick Philip. *Settlers of the Marsh.* Toronto: McClelland and Stewart, 1966.

Grubisic, Brett Josef. "An Interview with Suzette Mayr." *Plenitude Magazine,* June 28, 2017. http://plenitudemagazine.ca/an-interview-with-suzette-mayr/.

Hallowell, Gerald. "Prohibition in Canada." *Canadian Encyclopedia.* August 12, 2013. https://www.thecanadianencyclopedia.ca/en/article/prohibition.

Hannaford, Nigel. "The Death of Nigger Dan." *Canada West Magazine* (Summer 1976): 13–15.

Harris, Claire. "Backstage at the Glenbow Museum, Calgary." *Concert of Voices—Second Edition: An Anthology of World Writing in English.* Ed. Victor J. Ramraj. Peterborough, ON: Broadview Press, 2009.

———. *Drawing Down a Daughter.* Fredericton, NB: Goose Lane Editions, 1993.

———. *Fables from the Women's Quarters.* Toronto: Williams-Wallace, 1984.

———. *She.* Fredericton: Goose Lane Editions, 2000.

Henry, Frances. "The West Indian Domestic Scheme in Canada." *Social and Economic Studies* 17.1 (March 1968): 83–91.

Hill, Daniel Grafton. *The Freedom Seekers: Blacks in Early Canada.* Agincourt, Ontario: Book Society of Canada, 1981.

Hill, Karen. *Café Babanussa.* Toronto: HarperCollins, 2014.

Hill, Lawrence. *Any Known Blood.* Toronto: HarperCollins Canada, 1997.

———. *The Book of Negroes.* Toronto: HarperCollins Canada, 2007.

———. *The Illegal.* Toronto: HarperCollins Canada, 2015.

———. "Meet You at the Door." *Walrus,* January 12, 2011. thewalrus.ca.

———. *Some Great Thing.* Winnipeg: Turnstone Press, 1992.

Hitayezu, Chantal. "My Grandfather's Poem, My Grandmother's Dance." *The Story That Brought Me Here: To Alberta from Everywhere.* Ed. Linda Goyette. Edmonton: Brindle and Glass, 2011. 160–66.

Hooke, A.J (Alf). *30+5: The Incredible Years of Social Credit.* Edmonton: Institute of Applied Art, 1971.

Hooks, Ellis. Audiocasette. August 27, 1978. Provincial Archives of Alberta. Accession # 78.65/28.

———. Audiocasette. October 3 1978. Provincial Archives of Alberta. Accession # 78.65/32.

Hooks, Gwen. *The Keystone Legacy: Recollections of a Black Settler*. Edmonton: Bright Pebble Press, 1997.

Hopkins, John. *Edmonton Journal*, August 31, 1971.

Hustak, Alan. *Peter Lougheed: A Biography*. Toronto: McClelland and Stewart, 1979.

Iawal, Fuad. "The Inauguration Poem That Blew Us All Away." *Pulse Nigeria*, May 30, 2015. https://www.pulse.ng/we-are-ready-the-inauguration-poem -that-blew-us-all-away/740zmyz.

Irby, Charles C. *Northeast Alberta: A Marginal Agricultural Situation*. 1978. Simon Fraser University, PhD dissertation. Charles Irby Collection 1790– 1988. UC Santa Barbara Special Collections. Box 12, Folder 7. https://oac .cdlib.org/findaid/ark:/13030/tf8t1nb692/dsc/.

Jacob, Selwyn, dir. *Carol's Mirror*. National Film Board of Canada. 1991.

———. A Filmmakers Journey to an Untold Story. *Home: Stories Connecting Us All*. Ed. Tololwa Mollel. 2017. http://emcn.ab.ca/corporate/media_assets/ Stories-Master.pdf.

———, producer. *The Journey of Lesra Martin*. Cheryl Foggo, director and writer. National Film Board of Canada, 2002.

———, producer. *Mighty Jerome*. National Film Board of Canada, 2010.

———, dir. *The Road Taken*. National Film Board Canada, 1996.

———, *We Remember Amber Valley*. Alberta Heritage Foundation. Filmwest, 1984.

Jean-Paul, Michelle. "Learning to Love Me." *Other Tongues: Mixed Race Women Speak Out*, Ed.. Adebe DeRango Adem and Andrea Thompson. Toronto: Innana, 2010. 126–28.

Kamba, Tchitala Nyota. *L'exilée de Makelele*. Winnipeg: Éditions de Plaines, 2007.

Kaplan, Jon. "Dreams Weaver." *Now*. April 17, 2003. https://nowtoronto.com/ stage/theatre/dreams-weaver/.

Kellough, Kaie. *Accordéon*. Winnipeg: Arbeiter Ring, 2016.

———. *Creole Continuum*. Howl Arts Collective. Montreal: Treatment Room, 2014. CD.

———. "Honouring Black History Month: An Interview with Black Poet Kaie Kellough." *Black Coffee Poet*. 2 February, 2011. https://blackcoffeepoet .com/2011/02/02/honouring-black-history-month-an-interview-with-black -poet-kaie-kellough/.

———. "Howl!" howlarts.net/kaie. N.d.

———. *Lettricity*. Montreal: Cumulus Press, 2004.

———. *Maple Leaf Rag*. Winnipeg: Arbeiter Ring, 2010.

————. *Vox: Versus.* Bongo Beat, 2011.

Kennedy, Orvis. *Principles and Policies of Social Credit—A Free Individual Enterprise Movement Opposed to Socialist and All Other Forms of Statism.* Toronto: Social Credit Association of Canada, 1951.

Keung, Nicholas. "Stories a Moving History." *Toronto Star*, 14 August, 2008. https://www.thestar.com/entertainment/2008/08/14/stories_a_moving_history.html.

Koehler, Robert. "The Politics of 'Good Rain.'" *Los Angeles Times*. September 30, 1993. http://articles.latimes.com/1993-09-30/entertainment/ca-40641_1_george-seremba.

Kreisel, Henry. "The Prairie: A State of Mind." *Transactions of the Royal Society of Canada*, 4th ser., June 6, 1968. 171–80.

Kroetsch, Robert. *Seed Catalogue: Poems.* Winnipeg: Turnstone Press, 1977.

————, ed. *Sundogs: Stories from Saskatchewan.* Moose Jaw: Thunder Creek Publishing Co-operative, 1980.

Lai, Larissa. "Other Democracies: Writing thru Race at the 20 Year Crossroad." 2015. http://smarokamboureli.ca/wp-content/uploads/2015/01/Lai_Essay.pdf.

Laraque, Georges. "Growing Up." https://georgeslaraque.com/gl-youth.php.

————. *The Story of the NHL's Unlikeliest Tough Guy.* Toronto: Penguin, 2011.

Larkins, David. "20 Questions with Odario G. Williams." *Winnipeg Sun*, March 22, 2014. https://winnipegsun.com/2014/03/22/20-questions-with-odario-g-williams/wcm/5344da7f-0416-476c-bdc7-c011bece2bc7.

Lawrence, Bonita. "Enslavement of Indigenous People in Canada." *The Canadian Encyclopedia*. November 22, 2016. https://www.thecanadianencyclopedia.ca/en/article/slavery-of-indigenous-people-in-canada.

Lawrence, Trevor. *Hey Lickle Bwoy: A Collection of Poems.* Rosenort, MB: PrairieView, 1996.

Lewis, Alice Ethel. "In Loving Memory of Alberta." John Ware, Lewis family fonds. M-9677-26. Glenbow Museum and Archives.

Long-Lance, Chief Buffalo Child (Sylvester Long). *The Autobiography of a Blackfoot Indian Chief.* London: Faber and Faber, 1956.

Lougheed, Peter. "News Release." *Edmonton Journal*, August 7, 1971.

Lyons, Christine. "When 'your ears are tingling from the inside out': Addena Sumter-Freitag on Storytelling and Recording Life, from Stage to Page." *Canadian Literature*. February 1, 2009. https://canlit.ca/when-your-ears-are-tingling-from-the-inside-out-addena-sumter-freitag-on-storytelling-and-recording-life-from-stage-to-page-february-2009/.

MacEwan, Grant. *John Ware's Cow Country.* Saskatoon: Western Producer Prairie Books, 1976.

Maimann, Kevin. "Former Edmonton Oilers Enforcer Georges Laraque Wins Drag Competition." *Toronto Star*, August 13, 2018. https://www.thestar.com/edmonton/2018/08/13/former-edmonton-oilers-enforcer-georges-laraque-wins-drag-competition.html.

Manning, Earnest. *Political Realignment: A Challenge to Thoughtful Canadians.* Toronto: McClleland and Stewart, 1967.

Martini, Miranda. "The Drinking Gourd." *Other Tongues: Mixed-Race Women Speak Out.* Ed. Adebe DeRango-Adem and Andrea Thompson. Toronto: Innana, 2010. 104–10.

Mason-John, Valerie. "Being Fair: 'We must be the change we want to see in the world.'" *Equity Matters*. May 28, 2010. https://www.ideas-idees.ca/blog/being-fair-we-must-be-change-we-want-see-world.

———. *Borrowed Body*. London: Serpent's Tail, 2005.

———. *Brown Girl in the Ring*. London: Get a Grip Publishers, 1999.

———. *Detox Your Heart*. Somervile, MA: Wisdom Publications, 2005.

———, ed. *Talking Black: African and Asian Lesbians Speak Out*. London: Cassel, 1994.

———. "Uncensoring My Writing" *Alternatives within the Mainstream: British Black and Asian Theatres*. Ed. Dimple Godiwala. Newcastle: Cambridge Scholars Press, 2006. 397–401.

Mason-John, Valerie, and Kevan Anthony Cameron, eds. *The Great Black North: Contemporary African Canadian Poetry*. Calgary: Frontenac, 2013.

Mason-John, Valerie, and Ann Khambatta. *Lesbians Talk: Making Black Waves*. London: Scarlett Press, 1993.

Mather, Ken. *Frontier Cowboys and the Great Divide: Early Ranching in BC and Alberta*. Victoria, BC: Heritage House, 2013.

Mathieu, Sarah-Jane. *North of the Colour Line: Migration and Black Resistance in Canada: 1870–1955*. Chapel Hill: U of North Carolina P, 2010.

Maynard, Robyn. *Policing Black Lives: State Violence in Canada from Slavery to the Present*. Nova Scotia: Fernwood, 2017.

Mayr, Suzette. "Chimaera Lips." Master of English thesis, University of Calgary, 1992.

———. *Dr. Edith Vane and the Hares of Crawley Hall*. Toronto: Coach House, 2017.

———. *Monoceros: A Novel*. Toronto: Coach House, 2011.

———. *Moon Honey*. Edmonton: NeWest Press, 1995.

———. "Suzette Mayr." *Why We Write*. Ed. H. Nigel Thomas. Toronto: TSAR, 2006. 164–77.

———. *Venous Hum*. Vancouver: Arsenal Pulp Press, 2004.

―――. "What Poet and Novelist Suzette Mayr Hates (and Loves) about Writing." *CBC Books*, October 17, 2017. https://www.cbc.ca/books/what-poet -and-novelist-suzette-mayr-hates-and-loves-about-writing-1.4107979.

―――. "Why Suzette Mayr Set Out to Write a Horror Novel." CBC Radio, "The Next Chapter," July 9, 2018. https://www.cbc.ca/radio/thenextchapter /full-episode-july-9-2018-1.4353127/why-suzette-mayr-set-out-to-write-a -horror-novel-1.4353230.

―――. *The Widows*. Edmonton: NeWest Press, 1998.

―――. *Zebra Talk*. Calgary: disOrientation Chapbooks, 1991.

Mayr, Suzette, and Julia Gaunce, eds. *Broadview Anthology of Short Fiction*. Peterborough, ON: Broadview Press, 2004.

Mayr, Suzette, Geoffrey Hunter, and Robin Arseneault. *Tale*. Calgary: Stride Gallery, 2001.

Mbunwe, Chris. "Interview with Linus T. Asong." In Francis Wache, "Linus T. Asong, No Way to Die Author, Dies." *Cameroon Post*. July 22, 2012. https:// cameroonpostline.com/linus-t-asong-no-way-to-die-author-dies/.

McKay, Jennifer. "Redefining History: The Memory of Amber Valley Lives On." N.d. www.academia.edu.

McLeod, Elizabeth. *The Original Amos 'n' Andy: Freeman Gosden, Charles Correll and the 1928–1943 Radio Serial*. Jefferson, NC: McFarland, 2005.

Michetti, Rudy. Letter to Peter Lougheed, August 28, 1971. Lougheed Papers, Alberta Provincial Museum and Archives.

Mitchell. W.O. *Who Has Seen the Wind*. Toronto: Macmillan, 1972.

Mollel, Tololwa. *Big Boy*. New York: Clarion Books, 1995.

―――. "Biography." 2019. tololwamollel.com.

―――. "Feasting on Words: How I Became a Writer for Children." *McGill Journal of Education* 36.3 (2001): 251–60.

―――, ed. *Home: Stories Connecting Us All*. Edmonton Mennonite Centre for Newcomers. 2017. http://emcn.ab.ca/corporate/media_assets/Stories-Master .pdf.

―――. *Kele's Secret*. Don Mills, ON: Stoddart, 1997.

―――. *My Rows and Piles of Coins*. New York: Clarion Books, 1999.

―――. *The Orphan Boy*. Toronto: Oxford UP, 1990.

―――. *A Promise to the Sun: An African Story*. Toronto: Little Brown, 1992.

―――. *Rhinos for Lunch and Elephants for Supper*. Toronto: Oxford UP, 1991.

―――. *To Dinner, for Dinner*. New York: Holiday House, 2000.

Moodie, Susanna. *Roughing It in the Bush: Or, Life in Canada*, vol. 2. London: Richard Bentley, 1852.

Mood Ruff. *Antarctica (Cold, Cold World)*. Slo Coach Recordings, 2002.

———. *I Do My Own Stunts*. Slo Coach Recordings, 2005.

———. *Night.Life.Types*. Slo Coach Recordings, 1999.

———. *Politic Different*. Slo Coach Recordings, 2000.

Moxam, William Washington, and Ernesto Griffith. *Billy*. 2010. Film.

Nakache, D. "The Canadian Temporary Foreign Worker Program: Regulations, Practices and Protection Gaps." Ed. Luin Goldring and Patricia Landolt. *The Research Alliance on Precarious Status Workshop: Producing and Negotiating Precarious Migratory Status in Canada*. Toronto: U of Toronto P, 1992. 213–30.

Newman, Peter C. *Home Country*. Toronto: McClelland and Stewart, 1971.

Newswire.ca. "Building Homes and Building Skills." 21 July 2010. https://www.afn.ca/uploads/files/usb/15_-_atikameksheng_-_holmes_2.pdf.

North of the Gully History Book Committee. *North of the Gully*. Maidstone, SK: Maidstone Mirror, 1981.

North-South Institute. "Migrant Workers in Canada: A Review of the Canadian Seasonal Agricultural Workers Program: Policy Brief." http://www.nsi-ins.ca/english/pdf/MigrantWorkers_Eng_Web. Ottawa, 2006.

Okigbo, Christopher. *Labyrinths; With Path of Thunder*. London: Heinemann, 1971.

Ostenso, Martha. *Wild Geese*. Toronto: McClelland and Stewart, 1961.

Otiono, Nduka. *The Night Hides with a Knife*. Nigeria: New Horn, 1995.

———. *Love in a Time of Nightmares*. Baltimore: Publish America, 2008.

———. *Voices in the Rainbow*. Toronto: Oracle Books, 1997.

Otiono, Nduka, and Odoh Diego Okenyodo, eds. *Camouflage: Best of Contemporary Writing from Nigeria*. Nigeria: Treasure Books, 2006.

Otiono, Nduka, and E.C. Osondu, eds. *We-Men: An Anthology of Men Writing on Women*. Nigeria: New Horn, 1998.

Palmer, Hazelle, ed. *'... but where are you really from?' Stories of Identity and Assimilation in Canada*. Toronto: Sister Vision, 1997.

Parker, Emma. "'Odd Girl Out': An Interview with Valerie Mason-John, aka Queenie." 2011. https://lra.le.ac.uk/bitstream/2381/9791/1/%5B08%5D%20Mason-John%20Interview%20TP%20March%202011.pdf.

Patriquin, Martin. "Straight Outta Winnipeg: A Primer." *Maclean's*, December 6, 2010.

Pavlovic, Srdja, ed. *Threshold: An Anthology of Contemporary Writing from Alberta*. Edmonton: U of Alberta P, 1999.

Pemberton, Roland (Cadence Weapon). "30 Seconds." *Breaking Kayfabe*. Upper Class Recordings, 2005.

———. "Cadence Weapon Interview." *UKHH.com*. (expired link).

————. "Dirt in Hope City." *Hope in Dirt City*. ANTI-, 2012.

————. *Magnetic Days*. Metatron, 2014.

————. "Oliver Square." *Breaking Kayfabe*, Upper Class Recordings, 2005.

Porter, Kenneth W. "Negroes in the Fur Trade." *Minnesota History* (December 1934): 421–33.

Prociuk, John and Chris Nielson. *Illustrated History of Cattle Feeding in Alberta*. Calgary: Alberta Cattle Feeders' Association, 1998.

Ralston, Helen. "Canadian Immigration Policy in the Twentieth Century: Its Impact on South Asian Women." *Canadian Woman Studies* 19.3 (1999): 33–37.

Reese, Linda Williams. *Women of Oklahoma, 1890–1920*. Norman: U of Oklahoma P, 1997.

Ricou, Laurie. *Vertical Man / Horizontal World: Man and Landscape in Canadian Prairie Fiction*. Vancouver: U of British Columbia P, 1973.

Riegel, Christian and Herb Wyile, eds. *A Sense of Place: Re-Evaluating Regionalism in Canadian and American Writing*. Edmonton: U of Alberta Press, 1997.

Robinson-Gudmundson, Margaret. "The Severance." *Caribe*, August 1990.

Ross, Sinclair. *As for Me and My House*. Toronto: McClelland and Stewart, 1970.

Rozum, Molly P. "Indelible Grasslands: Place, Memory, and the 'Life Review.'" *Toward Defining the Prairies: Region, Culture and History*. Ed. Robert A. Wardhaugh. Winnipeg: U of Manitoba P, 2001. 119–36.

Samuel, Danica. "Selwyn Jacob: An Educator through Film." January 29, 2015. byblacks.com.

Samuels, Ian. *Cabra*. Calgary: Red Deer Press, 2000.

————. *Fuga: Being a Selection of the Historical Document on the Nature of Slaves*. Calgary: House Press, 1998.

————. *The Ubiquitous Big*. Toronto: Coach House Books, 2004.

Sanders, Leslie. "Review of Revival: An Anthology of Black Writing." *New Dawn: Journal of Black Canadian Studies* 1.1 (2006). http://aries.oise.utoronto.ca/dawn/journal/.

Saskatchewan African Canadian Heritage Museum (sachm.org). 2019. "Alfred Shadd." http://sachm.org/biography/alfred-shadd/.

————. "Heritage Individuals and Families." 2019. http://sachm.org/virtual-museum/.

————. "Joseph Mayes." 2019. http://sachm.org/biography/joseph-mayes/.

Scheier, Libby. "Writing Authentic Voices: The Writers' Union and Anti-Racism." *Fuse Magazine* 14 (1990): 14–15.

Sears, Djanet. *Testifyin': Contemporary African Canadian Drama*. Toronto: Playwrights Canada Press, 2000–2001.

Sellinger, Katrina. Panel discussion. "Permission, Refusal and Responsibility in Black Archives," 20 November, 2019. McMaster University, Hamilton, ON.

Seremba, George. *Come Good Rain.* Winnipeg: Blizzard Publishing, 1993.

———. *The Grave Will Decide.* [unpublished?]

———. *Napoleon of the Nile.* [unpublished?]

Shadd, Alfred Schmitz. "Defamation." *Carrot River Journal,* October 1910.

———. "Sorry but Happy." *Melfort Journal,* February 2, 1912.

———. "To the Electorate of the District of Kinistino." *Melfort Moon* (Melfort, Saskatchewan), 28 November 1905.

Shawl, Nisi. "Interview with Minister Faust: Writing Is Not a Performance Art." *Science Fiction and Fantasy Writers of America.* December 5, 2010. https://www.sfwa.org/2010/12/interview-minister-faustwriting-is-not-a -performance-art/.

Shepherd, Bruce R. *Deemed Unsuitable: Blacks from Oklahoma Move to the Canadian Prairies in Search of Equality in the Early 20th Century Only to Find Racism in Their New Home.* Toronto: Umbrella Press, 1997.

Siemerling, Winfried. *The Black Atlantic Reconsidered: Black Canadian Writing, Cultural History, and the Presence of the Past.* McGill-Queen's UP, 2015.

———. "May I See Some Identification? Race, Borders, and Identities in Any Known Blood." *Canadian Literature* 182 (2004): 30–50.

Simpson, George, and E. E. Rich. *Journal of Occurrences in the Athabasca Department.* Toronto: Champlain Society, 1938.

Smith, Donald B. *Chief Buffalo Child Long Lance: The Glorious Imposter.* Calgary: Red Deer P, 1999.

Stowe, Harriet Beecher. *Uncle Tom's Cabin: or, Life among the Lowly.* London: Frederick Warne, 1873 and 1879.

Sónúgà, Títílopé. *Abscess.* Oxford: Gecko Publishing, 2014.

———. *Down to Earth.* Nigeria: Okada Books 2011. https://okadabooks.com/ book/about/down_to_earth/25.

———. "Grandpa Igbobi." N.d. poemhunter.com.

———. *Mother Tongue.* CD. https://store.cdbaby.com/cd/titilopesonuga.

Staples, David. *Edmonton Journal,* March 17, 1996.

Stead, Robert J. *Grain.* Toronto: McClelland and Stewart, 1963.

Stenson, Fred, ed. *The Road Home: New Stories from Alberta Writers.* Edmonton: Reidmore, 1992.

Stowitts, Hubert Julian. *American Champions: Fifty Portraits of American Athletes.* Berlin[?]: [Publisher not identified], September 1936.

Strode, Woody, and Sam Young. *Goal Dust: The Warm and Candid Memoirs of a Pioneer Black Athlete and Actor.* Toronto: Madison Books, 1993.

Strom, Harry E. *A New Cultural Policy for the Province of Alberta.* Edmonton: Queen's Printer, 1971.

Sumter-Freitag, Addena. *Back in the Days.* Vancouver: Wattle and Daub, 2009.

———. *Stay Black & Die.* Vancouver: Commodore Books, 2007.

Taylor, Diana. *The Archive and the Repertoire: Performing Cultural Memory in the Americas.* Durham, NC: Duke UP, 2003.

Taylor, Lonnie. "Introducing Wakefield Brewster." *Huffpost*, September 29, 2012. https://www.huffingtonpost.ca/lonnie-taylor/introducing-wakefield-bre_b_1837524.html.

Thomas, H. Nigel. *Why We Write: Conversations with African Canadian Poets and Novelists: Interviews.* Toronto: TSAR Canada, 2006.

Thomson Colin A. "Alfred Schmitz Shadd." *Dictionary of Canadian Bibliography*, vol. 14 (1911–1920). biographi.ca. U of Toronto / U Laval, 1998–2019.

———. *Blacks in Deep Snow: Black Pioneers in Canada.* Don Mills, ON: J.M. Dent, 1979.

Thompson, Isha. "Titilope Sonuga, Poet." *Ish.* May 1, 2013. https://www.isha thompson.com/blog/2013/6/30/titilope-sonuga-poet.

Time Magazine, September 13, 1971.

Time Magazine, September 18, 1972.

Utendale, Kent. "Race Relations in Canada's Midwest: A Study of The Immigration, Integration and Assimilation of Black Minority Groups." Diss. Pacific Western U, 1985.

Van Herk, Aritha. *Mavericks: An Incorrigible History of Alberta.* Toronto: Viking, 2001.

Vernon, Karina. "The First Black Prairie Novel: Chief Buffalo Child Long Lance's Autobiography and the Repression of Prairie Blackness." *Journal of Canadian Studies* 45.2 (Spring 2011): 31–57.

———. "Invisibility Exhibit: The Limits of Library and Archive Canada's 'Multicultural Mandate.'" *Basements and Attics, Closets and Cyberspace: Explorations in Canadian Women's Archives.* Ed. Linda Morra and Jessica Schagerl. Waterloo, ON: Wilfrid Laurier UP, 2012.

Walcott, Rinaldo. *Black Like Who? Writing Black Canada.* Toronto: Insomniac, 1997.

———. "Introduction to the Second Edition." *Black Like Who? Writing Black Canada.* 2nd ed. Toronto: Insomniac, 2003. 11–24.

———. "Mary Ann Shadd Cary and the (Im)Possibility of Black/Canadian Studies." *Atlantis: A Women's Studies Journal* 24 (2000): 137–46.

———, ed. *Rude: Contemporary Black Canadian Cultural Criticism.* Toronto: Insomniac, 2000.

Walsh, Elliott (Nestor Wynrush). *Guy, I'm from Here.* Your Brothers Records, 2003.

———. *Trinnipeg 78!* Clotheshorse Records, 2009.

Walters, Wendy W. *Archives of the Black Atlantic: Reading between Literature and History.* New York: Routledge, 2013.

Wardhaugh, Robert A. *Toward Defining the Prairies: Region, Culture and History.* Winnipeg: U of Manitoba P, 2001.

Ware, Mildred. Letters. John Ware, Lewis Family Fonds. M-1283-1. Glenbow Museum and Archives.

Warner, Marika. *Mulatto Nation. Kola* 23.2 (2011). 57 pp.

Welch Alfred Burton, and Everett R. Cox. *Chief John Grass.* Fort Berthold Library, 2006.

Williams, Dan. "Agricultural Notes." *Report of the Select Committee of the Senate Appointed to Enquire into the Resources of the Great Mackenzie Basin. Session 1888. Printed by Order of Parliament.* Ottawa: Brown Chamberlin, Queen's Printer and Controller of Stationery, 1888.

Williams, Emily Allen. "An Interview with Claire Harris." *Wasafiri* 16.32 (2000): 41–44.

Wilson, Julie. "In Conversation with Cheryl Foggo on the Personal, Political and Creating Space for Characters of Colour in Children's Literature." *49th Shelf,* October 11, 2011. 49thshelf.com.

Winks, Robin W. *The Blacks in Canada: A History.* Montreal/Kingston: McGill-Queen's UP, 1997.

Wiseman, Adele. *Crackpot: A Novel.* Toronto: McClelland and Stewart, 1974.

Wolff, Alexander. The NFL's Jackie Robinson." *Vault,* October 12, 2009. https://www.si.com/vault/2009/10/12/105865272/the-nfls-jackie-robinson.

Wolters, Rachel. "As Migrants and as Immigrants: African Americans Search for Land and Liberty in the Great Plains, 1890–1912." *Great Plains Quarterly* 35.4 (Fall 2015): 333–55.

Wood, David G. *The Lougheed Legacy.* Toronto: Key Porter, 1985.

Wordup 411. "Titilope Sonuga: Beautiful, Confident and Poetic." December 9, 2013. https://wordup411ng.com/titilope-sonuga-confident-beautiful-and-poetic/.

Wynrush, Nestor. *Trinipeg!78.* Clothes Horse Records, 2009.

Copyright Acknowledgements

The editor has made every reasonable effort to secure permissions. If any errors should be noticed, please contact Karina Vernon care of Wilfrid Laurier University Press. Corrections will follow in subsequent editions.

Thank you to the following for their permission to reprint:

The photograph "prairie.2005" by Dawit Petros. Reprinted by permission of the artist.

"Letter May 4th 1898," "Letter June 6th, 1898," "Letter June 20th 1899" by Mildred Lewis Ware. Reprinted with the permission of the Glenbow Museum and Archives.

"Big Woody" and "3 Glass-Plate Photographs" by William Sylvester Alpheus Beal. Reprinted with the permission of Robert Barrow.

"We gave our lives to this part of the country" by Rosa Shannon. Published in *Window of Our Memories* by Velma Carter and Wanda Leffler Akili, Black Cultural Research Society, 1981. Reprinted with the permission of LeVero Carter.

"In Loving Memory of Alberta" by Alice Ethel Lewis is reprinted with the permission of the Glenbow Museum and Archives.

Photograph of Alice Ethel Lewis is reprinted with the permission of the Glenbow Museum and Archives.

"There was a cloud over Amber Valley" by Jefferson Davis Edwards. Published in *Window of Our Memories* by Velma Carter and Wanda Leffler Akili, Black Cultural Research Society, 1981. Reprinted with the permission of LeVero Carter.

Excerpt from *The Keystone Legacy: Recollections of a Black Settler* published by Gwendolyn Hooks. Published by Brightest Pebble Press, 1997. Reprinted by permission of Brightest Pebble Press.

Excerpt from *Alberta's Camelot: Culture and the Arts in the Lougheed Years* by Fil Fraser. Published by Lone Pine Publishing, 2003. Reprinted with permission of Lone Pine Publishing.

Excerpt from *Drawing Down a Daughter* by Claire Harris. Goose Lane Editions, 1992. Original publication © 1982, 2007 by the Estate of Claire Harris. Reprinted with permission of Goose Lane Editions.

Excerpt from *Stay Black & Die* by Addena Sumter-Freitag. Published by Commodore Books, 2007. Reprinted by permission of the author.

"Our Subdivision," "Pan Man," and "New Terra" by Nigel Darbasie. Published in *Last Crossing* by Nigel Darbasie, Nidar, 1988. Reprinted by permission of the author.

"Feasting on Words" by Tololwa Mollel. *McGill Journal of Education* 36.3 (2001). Reprinted by permission of the author.

"Canada Dry" by Tololwa Mollel. Published in *Home: Stories Connecting Us All*, 2017. Reprinted by permission of the author.

"A Filmmaker's Journey to an Untold Story" by Selwyn Jacob. Published in *Home: Stories Connecting Us All*, 2017. Reprinted by permission of the author.

"Is There Someone You Can Call?" by F.B. André. Published in *What Belongs* by F.B. André. Ronsdale Press, 2007. Reprinted by permission of the author.

Excerpt from *Pourin' Down Rain* by Cheryl Foggo. Published by Detselig Enterprises Ltd., 1990. Reprinted by permission of the author.

Excerpt from *John Ware Reimagined* by Cheryl Foggo. Reprinted by permission of the author.

"Meet You at the Door" by Lawrence Hill. Published by *The Walrus*, 2011. Reprinted by permission of the author.

"The Severance" by Margaret Robinson-Gudmundson. Published in *Caribe*, 1989. Reprinted by permission of the author.

"Self Portrait Two" and "Yellowknifed" by Valerie Mason-John.

Reprinted by permission of the author.

"Homeland Securities," "Archive Fever," and "University of Work" by Nduka Otiono. Published in *Love in a Time of Nightmares*. Published by Publish America, 2008. Reprinted by permission of the author.

"Coloured" by Sheila Addiscott. Published in *Other Tongues: Mixed Race Women Speak Out*, edited by Adebe DeRango Adem and Andrea Thompson. Published by Innana, 2010. Reprinted by permission of the author.

Excerpt from *Monoceros* by Suzette Mayr. Published by Coach House Books, 2011. Reprinted by permission of Coach House Books.

Excerpt from *Dr. Edith Vane and the Hares of Crawley Hall* by Suzette Mayr. Published by Coach House Books, 2017. Reprinted by permission of Coach House Books.

"Restoration," "A Monumental Love," and "Get into My Car" by Dawn Carter. Reprinted by permission of the author.

Excerpt from *The Coyote Kings of the Space-Age Bachelor Pad* by Minister Faust. Published by Random House, 2004. Reprinted by permission of the author.

Excerpt from *The Alchemists of Kush* by Minister Faust. Published by Resurrection House, 2017. Reprinted by permission of the author.

"sum of the parts that can be named" by Deanna Bowen. Reprinted by permission of the author.

Excerpt from *The Pierre Bonga Loops* by Troy Burle Bailey. Published by Commodore Books, 2007. Reprinted by permission of the author.

"Accidental Agriculture" by Bertrand Bickersteth, published in *The Field Stone Review* (2016–17). "What We Used to Call It" by Bertrand Bickersteth, published in *Antigonish Review* (issue #193). "We, Too" by Bertrand Bickersteth, published in *The Great Black North*, edited by Kevan Cameron and Valerie Mason John, Frontenac House 2013. All reprinted with permission of the author.

"i can" and "mediumz" by Wakefield Brewster. Reprinted by permission of the author.

"The Autobiography of Water" by Bola Opaleke. Reprinted by permission of the author.

Excerpt from *Mulatto Nation* by Marika Warner. Developed with the assistance of Nightwood Theatre's Write from The Hip Program. Published in *Kola* 23.2 (Fall 2011). Reprinted by permission of the author.

Excerpt from *Cast Iron* by Lisa Codrington. Copyright © 2002 by Lisa Codrington. Reprinted by permission of Playwrights Canada Press.

"Holes," "Grey," and "Oil and Water" by Khodi Dill. Reprinted by permission of the author.

"Récit d'un voyageur: Rêve ou utopie," "Makala!," and "Je suis d'ici, je suis d'ailleurs" by Tchitala Nyota Kamba. *L'exilée de Makelele* by Tchitala Nyota Kamba. Published by Éditions des Plaines, 2007. Published by permission of Tchitala Nyota Kamba and Éditions des Plaines.

"Grandpa Igbobi" by Títílopé Sónúgà. PoemHunter.com, 2017. Reprinted by permission of the author.

"Sacrifice" by Títílopé Sónúgà. *Mother Tongue,* 2013. Reprinted by permission of the author.

"Oliver Square" and "30 Seconds" by Roland Pemberton. *Breaking Kayfabe*, Upper Class Recordings, 2005. Lyrics reprinted by permission of Roland Pemberton.

"How Black" by Roland Pemberton. *Magnetic Days*, Metatron, 2014. Reprinted by permission of Roland Pemberton.

"Wonderful Winnipeg" and "Hometown" by Frank Fontaine. *10x10*, CTL Records, 2010. Lyrics reprinted by permission of Frank Fontaine.

"The Drinking Gourd: Three Tales" by Miranda Martini. Published in *Other Tongues: Mixed Race Women Speak Out*, edited by Adebe DeRango Adem and Andrea Thompson. Innana 2010. Reprinted by permission of the author.

Index of Authors and Titles

The Black Prairie Archives: An Anthology recovers a new regional archive of black prairie literature, and includes writing that ranges from work by nineteenth-century black fur traders and pioneers, all of it published here for the first time, to contemporary writing of the twenty-first century. This anthology establishes a new black prairie literary tradition and transforms inherited understandings of what prairie literature looks and sounds like. It collects varied and unique work by writers who were both conscious and unconscious of themselves as black writers or as prairie people. Their letters, recipes, oral literature, autobiographies, rap, and poetry provide vivid glimpses into the reality of their lived experiences and give meaning to them.

Included are introductory notes for each writer in non-specialist language, as well as notes to assist readers in their engagement with the literature. This archive and its supporting text offer new scholarly and pedagogical possibilities by expanding the nation's and the region's archives. They enrich our understanding of black Canada by bringing to light the prairies' black histories, cultures, and presences.

Karina Vernon is an associate professor of English at the University of Toronto, where her teaching and research focus on black Canadian literature, archives, and decolonization.

ISBN 978-1-77112-374-7

90000

9 781771 123747

**WILFRID LAURIER
UNIVERSITY PRESS**
www.wlupress.wlu.ca